Interdisciplinary Handbook of Adult Lifespan Learning

Interdisciplinary Handbook of Adult Lifespan Learning

Edited by JAN D. SINNOTT

Greenwood Press
Westport, Connecticut • London

Library of Congress Cataloging-in-Publication Data

Interdisciplinary handbook of adult lifespan learning / edited by Jan
   D. Sinnott.
      p.   cm.
   Includes bibliographical references and indexes.
   ISBN 0–313–28205–6 (alk. paper)
    1. Adult learning—Handbooks, manuals, etc. 2. Adult education—
  Handbooks, manuals, etc. I. Sinnott, Jan D.
  LC5225.L42I58   1994
  374—dc20   93–7711

British Library Cataloguing in Publication Data is available.

Library of Congress Catalog Card Number: 93–7711
ISBN: 0–313–28205–6

First published in 1994

Greenwood Press, 88 Post Road West, Westport, CT 06881
An imprint of Greenwood Publishing Group, Inc.

Printed in the United States of America

The paper used in this book complies with the
Permanent Paper Standard issued by the National
Information Standards Organization (Z39.48–1984).

10 9 8 7 6 5 4 3 2 1

To Lynn
and Kiersten, Gavyn, James, Gwenn

Contents

Preface

We are now experiencing a period in history that seems to demand rapid change and the learning of new ways of being and acting. On every front, individuals of many nations are faced with large tasks, with demands to restructure their nations, alliances, and personal relationships. What does it mean to be human in communities that change so rapidly? How can one learn to survive and thrive in an environment that, as a child, one couldn't even imagine? We need to keep learning as adults. We need to learn rapidly.

In the recent past relatively few studies were made of how adults learn or of where they learn because change was less rapid and much less *adult* learning was needed for adaptation. The scientific study of adult lifespan learning got off to a slow start in many fields, even in education and psychology, because there was greater stability in the parts of the developed world where such studies were likely to be done. Of course, with increasing numbers of older adults surviving into true old age, investigators began to turn their attention to the potentially negative effects of illness and aging on learning. But the collective belief of the scholarly community was that most interesting questions about human learning could be answered by studying children. Most efforts were devoted to just that kind of study.

We have also come a long way in creating models of human change and psychological processes. Like our colleagues in the natural sciences, in our new social and behavioral models we include many factors and complex ways to analyze process and dynamics. As experienced scientists we have gradually noticed that available models or world views drive the kind of questions an investigator asks.

The book you are about to read is titled *Interdisciplinary Handbook of Adult Lifespan Learning* for the reasons just suggested. It is *interdisciplinary* because the sophisticated current questions about the subject refuse to stay in one field alone. They demand we consider psychology, education, biology, sociology, political science, religion, and the natural sciences to arrive at meaningful answers. Consequently, scholars in all those fields are active in the study of lifespan learning. The book is about *adult lifespan* learning (rather than about the learning children do) because the needs, intentions, learning contexts, and demands for learning are significantly different in the middle and end of the lifespan. In fact, more learning may go on during the middle or end of the lifespan than has gone on earlier. The book is focused on lifespan *learning* (rather than lifespan decline) because early work already emphasized decline, because decline has always been measured from the wrong (incomplete) standard (that of young and inexperienced persons), and because most learning abilities do not decline but increase from the 20s to the 70s.

PLAN OF THE BOOK

The handbook is divided into four sections. In the first, we see theories and models for adult lifespan learning. These theories and models are meant to offer new ways of looking at this particular field. Cognitive theory and child and youth education are not reviewed here, because of space considerations. The second section contains work on learning in *contexts*, specific contexts in which adults find they need to learn. The learning of adults in more standard ''school/ university'' contexts is also reviewed. The third section contains chapters related to the effects of aging, sometimes coupled with severe injury or illness, on learning at that point in life. In this section we review the more-abundant laboratory work in learning, and here several chapters do overlap with child/youth learning studies. Finally, the fourth section offers a crystal ball to the reader, to allow him or her to speculate on what will become of adult learning and the activities flourishing around it within the next century.

OVERVIEW OF THE CHAPTERS

The chapters offer a wealth of ideas about lifespan learning, ideas that have not been available in one place before. This information should aid the reader in contrasting ideas and making syntheses across fields.

The first set of chapters describes models and theories. John Cavanaugh and Lisa McGuire begin that discussion in chapter 1 by applying the new field of chaos theory to adult lifespan learning. Chaos theory is a theory about dynamic systems. Chaos is understood to be a situation in which an underlying deterministic system appears unpredictable or predictable, depending on the point at which it is examined. Chaos theory seems to provide a brilliant and parsimonious explanation for much that seems disorderly in adult lifespan learning.

In chapter 2 Lynn Johnson views the profound effects that modern changes in communication technologies have on information transmission and therefore on adult learning. Information is presented to adult learners in many forms, such as television and computer networking, that influence the content and utilization of the information. Even the "facts" about whether events are "really" taking place in the current moment are altered by the technology. Technologies also change the relation of learners to each other and to teachers.

In chapter 3, Deirdre Kramer and Weizhen Bacelar ask what characteristics would be required for a student to flourish in an educational environment (like that of the university) oriented toward connections among disciplines and responsible yet individuated citizenship. They conclude that wisdom may foster and be fostered by general education. Following this, Diane Lee in chapter 4 describes models of collaboration among teachers and among scientists. Collaboration can foster both connection and individual free thought or can favor one or the other. As adult learning frequently means that individuals collaborate, we need to see which models lead to the various learning outcomes for adults.

Acknowledging that adult learning occurs in a social context, John Meacham and Cynthia Boyd discuss in chapter 5 how individuals learn to expand their "circle of caring" from local to global as they develop from adolescence through adulthood and aging. This learning seems to involve the reconstruction of the individual's sense of identity. Models of the circle of caring have a direct relation to the content and the process of adult learning.

Sharan Merriam's chapter looks at the relation between learning and life experience that underlies models of adult learning. The purposes of this chapter are to explore how learning and life experience are connected in adulthood and to review what is known about the nature of learning from life experience.

In chapters 7 and 8, Jan Sinnott examines the utility of "new science" models for teaching adults, focusing in the latter chapter on the new postformal cognitive developmental model. These models frame the knowing of reality in dialogue terms; teacher and learner co-create the reality they discuss and share. The new cooperative biology, chaos theory, systems theory, and postformal Piagetian thought are examined as ways to inform our questions about adult learning and its connection with life experience over time.

The last chapter in the first section, by Patricia Weibust and Eugene Thomas, uses models of spirituality to address the content and process of adult lifespan learning. Adulthood has traditionally been a time for the development of spiritual wisdom and spiritual maturity. Most of the world's religions see the mature person becoming more "knowing" in a spiritual sense in later life. These authors relate learning, spirituality, and age to form a model of learning processes.

The second section of the book addresses the ways adults learn in the specific life contexts in which they find themselves. In chapter 10, Jack Demick and Nancy Nazzaro note that the advent of environmental psychology in the 1970s led to studies of the effects of learning environments on learning. Their chapter presents existing research on the formal learning environments of adults, discusses theoretical and methodological considerations for future research, and suggests directions for the design of optimal adult learning environments.

The specific environment of the workplace is examined by Lawrence Froman in chapter 11. He begins with the idea of a changing economy and workplace and builds on the themes of participation, choice, experience, and critical reflection. He suggests that assumptions and habitual ways of training may merit questioning if investments in human resources in the workplace are to succeed.

Noting that the average age of adults attending college has risen dramatically in the last ten years, Carolyn Harriger writes about learning factors for adults in college. In chapter 12 she discusses the fact that education is not only a preparation for life's work but also an experience that lasts a lifetime. The number of adult students over age thirty is growing at a faster rate than that of any other age group. The university may have to accommodate to these very individuated learners, a growth process that may require changes on the part of the university.

Many adults learn significant information in the "classroom" of personal growth experiences, such as psychotherapy. In chapter 13 Aaron Hogue, Laura Bross, and Jay Efran address the levels of learning that can occur in a therapeutic setting. Besides learning specific information about their own processes and behaviors, adults in therapy can learn new behaviors (Learning I), new categories of behavioral responses to the same event (Learning II), and even how new categories of behaviors can be created in response to the existential dilemma of some new life task (Learning III).

In chapter 14, Lynn Johnson writes about the difficulties faced by those trying to teach adults in international development projects such as those run by the Peace Corps and the Agency for International Development. The application of philosophical, theoretical, and practical aspects and theories to international development projects is discussed. To obtain sustainable development it may be necessary for project personnel to go beyond questions of the geography, economy, or history of a country to questions of adult learning processes themselves. This is not often done. One key process may be a true dialogue with learners.

In chapter 15, Phyllis Kahaney and Kathleen Heinrich discuss the use of a specific learning tool, journal writing. They make applications to the workplace setting. Workers were asked to solve problems by keeping a journal together. The process led to discussions of workgroup concerns, as well as to communal generation of creative objective solutions to problems.

Expert teachers are useful to adult (and child!) learning. Diane Lee, in chapter 16, considers the teacher's expertise in the realms of knowledge, imagination, and moral action. She argues that the point of intersection of these realms is governed by a postformal stage of reasoning, that is, by a way of thinking that allows for multiple, contradictory views of truth, for bridging across belief systems, and for using self-referential thought.

Laura Maciuika, Michael Basseches, and Abigail Lipson focus in chapter 17 on adults' experiences of their learning. They review four areas of work: how learners experience classroom activity, how adults organize their learning over time, how learning challenges the ways adults know themselves and their world, and research related to adults' highly individual views of their own learning experiences.

More tools for those teaching adults are found in chapter 18. Barbara Millis, Neil Davidson, and Philip Cottell describe ways to enhance adults' critical thinking skills through cooperative learning. Cooperative learning is a structured form of small group work based on positive interdependence, individual accountability, group processing, and social skills. This learner-centered environment seems to foster critical thinking.

Adults sometimes need to relearn very basic skills and need to re-remember their own histories after traumatic brain injury. Such injury may occur at any point in the lifespan, although it may also be associated with aging. Rick Parenté and Mary Stapleton describe the few theories of how such lost function might be regained, including artifact theories, anatomical reorganization, and functional adaptation, in chapter 19. Several treatment models for rehabilitation of memory are discussed.

Ariel Phillips, Abigail Lipson, and Michael Basseches in chapter 20 discuss the learning of social skills (empathy and listening skills) in the context of training programs. Empathy and listening skills develop over time, as individuals are trained. An important part of the discussion contrasts the value of didactic and experiential teaching methods in promoting these diverse families of skills.

We move next to the context of learning health-related behaviors, as discussed in chapter 21 by Renee Royak-Schaler and Patricia Maloney Alt. Adults are often admonished to exchange less useful practices for others that may extend their lifespans, yet little change seems to be learned. The authors address how and why adults learn to change their health-related behaviors, how research findings can be translated into motivating information, what barriers prevent this learning, and how health beliefs are important. The *cost* of acting upon learning is an important point of discussion here.

The last chapter in the second section, chapter 22, is a discussion by Dennis Thompson of adults learning how to read. Once again we move in the context of the Third World. Thompson seeks to examine the current state of adult literacy and the various approaches that have been used to reduce illiteracy. He attempts to name the variables most directly relevant to this type of adult learning, those that can be used by program planners and instructors. He also makes the intriguing point that we may be asking less useful, Western, developed-nation questions in teaching reading in Third World countries.

The final section surveys adult learning as it is influenced by the process of aging. Various authors look upon aging as a time-related phenomenon only, while for others it is viewed as a concept with potential confounds between time and illness (or "nearness to death"). Studies done in a laboratory setting (yet another "context" for adult learning) over the course of many years are surveyed and interpreted by David Arenberg in chapter 23. He then takes the role of devil's advocate and asks (not altogether facetiously) whether gerontology research itself has ceased learning in the laboratory. For a number of years the potential gain in understanding from such studies has been questioned. Arenberg helps explain the resurgence of such studies.

Cynthia Berg, Paul Klaczynski, Katerina Calderone, and JoNell Strough ask adult-age-differences-in-learning questions in chapter 24. They ask what strategies do older adults use to learn, and are the strategies adaptive or maladaptive for them? They do not judge those strategies to be bad or good beforehand (even if they are unlike young-adult strategies). The authors argue that training programs may sometimes fail because older adults must first unlearn their own adaptive learning strategies. If age differences in strategies are not necessarily deficiencies, we may need to study other individual-differences variables to separate age from variables related to the individual's learning style.

Alzheimer's disease is related to aging and cognitive losses, including loss of the ability to learn. In chapter 25, John Cavanaugh and Romy Nocera are clear that dementia presents us with a situation of longterm *un*learning for patients and longterm learning for caregivers. While caregivers may be learning new ways to cope, the patient is gradually losing capability. However, the disease progresses gradually, and not all patients are in the same stage. Therefore, the authors are able to describe approaches for improving outcomes in patients in earlier stages of the disease. Suggestions for research are included in this chapter, as behavioral interventions can lead to improvement for these patients.

Nancy Denney has spent years examining models of lifespan cognitive development. She uses information from training studies to support lifespan cognitive models. In chapter 26, she reviews the literature on the effects of cognitive training on basic cognitive processes. She raises difficult and important questions on the value of training studies and the learning they try to impart.

The final chapter in the third section is authored by Robin West and Jane Berry. Older learners' self-confidence about their learning ability is often low. Patterns of this self-confidence or self-efficacy may affect lifelong learning. One conclusion that can be drawn is that global estimates of one's own ability are misleading and are poor predictors of one's specific learning in one area.

The last section of the handbook addresses the future of adult lifespan learning in this time of rapid change. Chapter 28, by Jan Sinnott, attempts four things: a historical look at the range of things adults have been required to learn, a list of current problems with (or limitations of) adult learning experiences, suggestions for ways to optimize current adult learning, and a look at the future of the university as an institution in the next century. New models are proposed for the university.

Overall, this handbook presents a wide variety of original works and reviews related to currently important aspects and problems in adult lifespan learning, wherever it is found. This is an emerging and important field, and not one that can be summarized as yet by mathematical models or a clear consensus on underlying structure. We find ourselves in general at exploratory or hypothesis-creation stages, far from ready to fine-tune causal path models of relations. We find ourselves with the desire for both a clear structure to guide us and a way to let this field reflect the rich individual differences and intentions and emotions of real mature adult lives. No wonder a reader may be somewhat dissatisfied and feel that a part of what he or she sought is still missing. It is! Future work in the field(s) of adult lifespan learning may give us final theories and models that combine elegant mathematical abstraction with an awareness of rich interpersonal complexity in adulthood, ones that combine logically playful theory with the study of personally warm intentions and yearning. All these are a part of mature adulthood. Phenomenology and experimental study, mind and heart and family all come together in midlife and old age. Why not hope they can come together eventually in our final models of adult lifespan learning? You, the reader, can make it so.

THANKS

Many people helped this project reach fruition. I admit that my first reaction on being offered the chance to help create this book was (metaphorically speaking) to run the other way! It seemed like such a large project and such a huge field. It was also such an important field, in view of recent history, that I wanted the editor, whoever that turned out to be, to do it justice. In retrospect I'm glad that family and colleagues persuaded me to go forward with an outline and to see what form this handbook could take if it rested in my hands. The project turned out to be very satisfying and has led me to create other books, for example, one on the future of the university.

Let me thank, first of all, the members of the Psychology Department and other departments at Towson State University who were so free with dialogue about these ideas, with chapter topics, with chapter manuscripts, and with reviews of others' work. This kind of collegial exchange is the heart of what is so good in the university as an institution. I appreciate the assigned time and summer stipend grants from Towson State University for the purpose of completing this book. The gifts of time were invaluable. Secretarial support from the staff of the Psychology Department, including the help of Janis Carlos, Jean Foley, Kathleen Henderson, and Barbara Skinner, and support of every kind from the Chair of Psychology, Roger Fink, made this book possible. Thanks also go to reviewers and colleagues outside my university, all of whom made the *Handbook* more useful to all readers. This international crew of thinkers and doers never receives the appreciation that is its due. Thanks to Greenwood Publishing for its financial support of this effort and for the innovative and creative ideas and support of editors George Butler and Mildred Vasan. You helped make my job easier and smoother. Thanks to my family for being tolerant of my hours and moods and especially to Lynn for her visionary, yet practical awareness of the broad scope of adult learning. Finally, thanks in advance to the readers of this book who go on to learn, think, dialogue further with each other, with the authors of chapters, and with me. We will understand and create this field together, and may your work bring you as much satisfaction as I have already received.

Jan Sinnott

I. THEORIES AND MODELS

1

Chaos Theory as a Framework for Understanding Adult Lifespan Learning

John C. Cavanaugh and Lisa C. McGuire

Since the mid–1970s, scientists have made some remarkable discoveries about phenomena from everyday life to complex systems. They have shown that things such as rivers, boiling water, smoke rising from a burning cigarette, and weather patterns all have something in common—they are examples of periodically chaotic systems. To most people, chaos implies random or chance events that have no underlying systematicity. However, chaos is now understood to be a situation in which a deterministic system becomes unpredictable (Devaney, 1989; Ford, 1983).

Although a thorough discussion of chaos theory is well beyond the scope of this chapter, many of the concepts explored in that literature have considerable value for our present purposes. (A general, nonmathematical introduction of chaos theory can be found in Gleick, 1987; for a more advanced introduction, consult Devaney, 1989). Concepts in chaos theory have potentially far-reaching implications for studying human development and may provide a context for understanding lifelong learning. Indeed, some of these concepts have been applied to family transitions (Gottman, 1991); and related issues based on other new scientific paradigms have important implications as well (Sinnott, this volume).

DYNAMICAL SYSTEMS

The core concept in chaos theory is the *dynamical system* (Devaney, 1989). A dynamical system is one in which the processes and elements of the system mutually influence each other. Consequently, the key process in any dynamical system is iteration, that is, information about the current state is fed back into the system to generate its future state. In humans, this is analogous to continually updating our knowledge base, for example, with our current ongoing experiences. Some dynamical systems are rather simple; an example is *discrete dynamical systems* such as x, e^x, e^{e^x} $e^{e^{e^x}}$ and so on. Other dynamical systems are more complex; *continuous dynamical systems* are systems described by differential equations, such as population models in biology.

In general, dynamical systems tend toward some stable solution(s). For example, the particular discrete dynamical system described above quickly tends to infinity. But not all dynamical systems behave so well. For example, consider the system $f(x) = 4x(1 - x)$. If one inputs random numbers between 0 and 1 into this equation and iterates it by entering each subsequent solution as the new value for x, the system never stabilizes. Moreover, the pattern of solutions generated by the iterations varies markedly depending on the initial value. (The interested reader with a computer may want to try this.) Interestingly, if one changes the multiplier value 4 to the value 3.839, the system will settle into a pattern of the cycle 0.149888 . . . , 0.489172 . . . , and 0.959299 . . . repeated over and over again.

The solutions in the first system (with the multiplier 4) exhibit *chaos*, or unpredictability. The solutions to the second system (with the multiplier 3.839) appear to exhibit stability, but appearances are deceiving. The second system is equally unpredictable; its unpredictability is hidden by rounding (i.e., "experimental" or "measurement") error, which becomes increasingly important as precision is increased. (You can demonstrate this factor by comparing the values generated by a hand calculator with those generated by a mainframe computer that allows a higher degree of precision.) Thus, in the second case, we are deceived. We think we are dealing with a stable system when we are not. In fact, both systems are chaotic, once "error" is taken into account.

Let us consider an example from psychological research illustrating these points. Currently, there is disagreement over the stability of personality across adulthood. Some (e.g., Costa & McCrae, 1980) claim that personality remains highly stable throughout adulthood. Others (e.g., Erikson, 1982) argue that people go through a series of changes. If we accept the analogy that the different ways of measuring personality espoused by these positions correspond to the different multipliers in the preceding example (i.e., 4 and 3.839), it is possible to see how each group could draw different conclusions. Moreover, these contrary conclusions could be based on the same "data" (i.e., the same individuals) whose "values" (i.e., self-report data) are affected differently by the "multiplier" (i.e., the type of instrument used to measure personality). Note, however, that neither group would win; the stability claimed by some is illusory, and the changes espoused by others would occur at unpredictable times.

An additional important point about dynamic systems is that they are *deterministic*. That is, although the solutions to the equations behave unpredictably, the equations describing the system constrain the possible values of the solutions. No solution can be outside the boundaries ("ballpark") set by the equation; the unpredictability lives in the confines of the ballpark. For example, in the equation $f(x) = 4x(1 - x)$, no solution can be greater than 1, but the pattern of solutions is unpredictable. The result is a deterministic yet unpredictable system.

Implications for Developmental Research

The unpredictability of solutions in iterative dynamical systems leads to two important questions. What changes in dynamical systems? What becomes of the widely held belief that the goal of science is to predict the future states or values of a specific phenomenon?

The answer to the first question is relatively straightforward. What changes in a dynamical system is its *state*, that is, the interrelationships among the parts (Hirsch, 1985). Thus, understanding what happens in dynamical systems means knowing how states vary over time. Interestingly, understanding how one type of state, human behavior, changes over the finite time of the human lifespan is the raison d'être of developmental psychology.

The second question addresses a subtler and more difficult issue. To the extent that the term *predict* implies an accurate point-prediction of a future value of a state based on knowledge of previous values, then chaos theory implies that such predictions are, by definition, impossible, because of the inherent unpredictability of dynamical systems. However, if *predict* means being able to know something about the nature of interrelationships during periods of relative stability and to know that at (unpredictable) points these interrelationships will not hold, then chaos theory implies that such predictions are possible. For example, we can predict the relative interrelationships among components of somewhat complex dynamical systems such as the position of planets, in order to plot flight paths for interplanetary spacecraft. In more complex cases, however, the best we may be able to do is to identify the ballpark in which the new state (value) of a phenomenon exists. In order to know which situation holds, the long-term behavior of solutions to the equations defining the dynamical systems must be studied systematically. The only way to accomplish this in developmental psychology is to begin building a "set" of deterministic "equations" in which one of the variables is *time* (Hirsch, 1985).

Two points must be made. First, very little psychological research (even in developmental psychology) currently uses longitudinal methods. From the vantage point of chaos theory, psychologists have provided little in the way of explanations of human behavior because of their refusal to track behavioral phenomena over relatively long periods of time. Moreover, until longitudinal methods become the standard, little progress will be made.

Second, although some scientists want to study the generic behavior of the typical dynamical system (an effort analogous to studying groups of people and focusing on mean performance), this approach has been criticized on two main grounds (Hirsch, 1985): (1) generic behavior need not be stable, and (2) the definition of what constitutes generic behavior is open to debate. Consequently, although it is certainly possible to describe the generic behavior of a dynamical system, it is unclear exactly what the description means, of what it is typical, whether it changes over time, or whether it has any relevance whatsoever for understanding a specific phenomenon.

Hertzog (1990) presents essentially the same argument in the context of research on cognitive aging. He points out that we cannot build an adequate theory of cognitive aging grounded in cross-sectional research comparing mean performances of groups differing greatly in terms of age. Rather, Hertzog forcefully argues that multivariate longitudinal research, which examines the continuum of age with a focus on individual differences, is needed. We argue that this is merely the minimum necessary for beginning to build adequate theory.

STRUCTURAL INSTABILITY: THE BUTTERFLY EFFECT

The fact that dynamical systems can at times be relatively stable is especially important for lifespan developmental psychology. A dynamical system is *dynamically* or *structurally stable* if it retains the same (or very nearly the same) solutions when it is subjected to small perturbations (Abraham, 1985; Devaney, 1989). In other words, a dynamical system is stable if small errors or approximations made in the calculations (e.g., measurement error) do not fundamentally alter the solutions. In stable systems, small errors can be safely ignored. For example, if cognitive development represents a structurally stable dynamic system, then small measurement errors across different assessment batteries will make no difference in the overall evaluation of an individual's level of performance.

But, if the dynamical system is not structurally stable, even small roundings or approximations (i.e., small measurement error) could dramatically alter the solutions. The problem is that such errors may be overlooked if, as pointed out earlier, they result in apparent stability. Scientists are often quick to interpret apparent stability as if it were real stability, when in fact *structural instability* is much more likely to be the case. Indeed, most dynamical systems in classical mechanics (e.g., weather patterns, pendulums, rising cigarette smoke, and boiling water) are now recognized as structurally unstable (Abraham, 1985; Devaney, 1989; Gleick, 1987).

Structural instability in dynamical systems was first discovered by Lorenz (1963, 1979), who showed that computer models of weather systems (based on sets of deterministic equations) did not precisely replicate solutions even though they were given starting parameters generated during a previous run. Lorenz referred to this phenomenon as *sensitive dependence on initial conditions*, but it is more commonly termed the *butterfly effect*. The butterfly effect provides incontrovertible evidence that structural instability of dynamical systems cannot be ignored. The reason is that we can never be sufficiently precise (for whatever reason, e.g., technology, the uncertainty principle) in ascertaining all the values of all the variables specified in the set of deterministic equations defining the dynamical system, thereby (necessarily) introducing measurement error.

In meteorology, for example, it has been demonstrated that even the smallest imprecision due to computer hardware limitations (let alone more practical limits of trying to measure precisely all the components of weather patterns) results in huge differences in how computer models of weather systems develop. In real-world terms, the situation is like discovering that a butterfly beating its wings in Brazil changes (eventually) the weather in Texas (Lorenz, 1979). Structural instability (the butterfly effect) is the reason that local weather forecasts beyond two or three days are largely inaccurate.

Individual Differences and Replicability of Research

The butterfly effect has immediate and profound implications for developmental psychology. First, it clearly emphasizes that even the slightest difference in person-environment interactions between two people could eventually become manifested as large differences in behavior. Thus, the butterfly effect could be the major reason individual differences emerge. Something as seemingly insignificant as missing a day of school could eventually create significant differences in individuals' test scores, or slightly variant interactions with parents could create significant behavioral differences between identical twins.

Clearly, such variance in human behavior due to the butterfly effect cannot be treated as error (see a related argument in Underwood, 1975). The reality and pervasiveness of individual differences created by the butterfly effect make cross-sectional research even more suspect and raise serious questions about traditional normative longitudinal research focusing on mean performance. That is, one-shot cross-sectional studies cannot unconfound group (age) and experiential (cohort) effects, which, given the butterfly effect, are potentially more important sources of difference than previously thought. Normative studies suffer from the criticisms raised above concerning the study of generic behavior in the typical dynamical system. Along with Nesselroade and Ford (1985), we believe that a better methodological approach is ipsative (i.e., longitudinal) research, which avoids these problems by using the individual as the unit of analysis.

The second implication of the butterfly effect is that replication of psychological findings in general, and of developmental data in particular, becomes enormously difficult. The odds that two independent data sets will reveal essentially identical patterns of behavior may be extremely small. By definition, it is impossible to duplicate another researcher's study exactly because it is not possible to duplicate exactly a sample, test the new sample at exactly the same point in time, and employ exactly the same people using exactly the same methods. Given the fact of individual differences in the way the new experimenters interact with their research participants, in the equipment they use, in what hardware limits are accepted, and a whole host of other things, identical results would be the exception rather than the rule.

There is also an even subtler problem. Even if results from multiple projects appear consistent (i.e., the direction of the effects is the same), there is no guarantee that the consistency is real. The reason is analogous to the problems with apparent stability discussed earlier. In this case, measurement limitations across studies could produce apparent, but illusory, consistency in results. Only through continued replication using many types of measures over many types of individuals over extended periods of time will researchers discover whether similar results are truly consistent.

Superficially, developmental (and other) psychologists appear to accept these arguments when they invoke minor procedural, sample, equipment, stimuli, and other differences as "reasons why the present findings do not agree with previous studies." Unfortunately, we doubt that most researchers actually take such claims seriously, even though such claims are correct. Even though included in discussion sections, such claims typically tend to be dismissed as inconsequential and other claims (e.g., poor measurement or inadequate theory) are given more weight. Thus, most researchers appear not to be true believers.

The butterfly effect should produce converts. It means that such methodological claims are not only consequential and valid but may in fact be something researchers must learn to accept. It is entirely possible that theories in developmental psychology currently or previously dismissed as "untestable" or as not leading to well-replicated findings may be closer to the mark than theories perceived as "testable" or as supported by replicated findings. The reason is that psychological research methods rest on an inadequate Newtonian worldview, rendering the traditional hypothesis-testing approach inappropriate for most investigations of human behavior. Consequently, the standards by which theories have been judged (by North Americans) as testable are often inappropriate as well.

The point we wish to make is that assumptions underlying the question of whether findings are replicable or a theory is testable need to be redefined. The reconceptualization of replicability has especially important ramifications. To the extent that small differences in samples, procedures, and so forth do not matter (i.e., results from multiple independent studies are essentially identical), then the dynamical system under study (e.g., the specific behavior being examined) is structurally stable. Discovery of such stable systems has long been a goal of psychology (and other sciences), and some such systems have been tentatively identified. (We must be aware, though, that some of these apparently stable systems are really unstable ones in disguise, as discussed earlier.) However, the butterfly effect also means that a failure to replicate *does not necessarily mean that a phenomenon (dynamical system) is epiphenomenal.* On the contrary, it may indicate that the system under study is very real and is in a constant state of flux. It also means that because different teams of researchers tend to define their problems in somewhat different ways, they are destined to discover somewhat different things. The result will be multiple explanations of the same system (i.e., competing theories), all of which are somewhat accurate, but only insofar as they describe the local behavior of the system. (Of course, an even better explanation would result from the synthesis of these various explanations. How this could be accomplished, however, is beyond the scope of this chapter.)

The key to unraveling the problem of replicability appears to lie in the use of time as a (potentially explanatory) variable. It seems logical that the odds of replication improve as the number of observations of the system at relatively close points in time increases, as long as this process continues for an extended period. The longer the lag between observations, the more difficult replication becomes. It is also apparent that we need to come to some agreement on the criteria for determining successful and unsuccessful replication. As argued earlier, relying on (apparent) statistical replication of effects may be misleading. In any case, (developmental) psychology would do well to think through these issues and reemphasize (and redefine, if necessary) the role of replication in research.

MAKING THINGS HAPPEN: BIFURCATION MODELS AND CHANGE

One of the most useful potential applications of chaos theory in developmental psychology is in understanding transitions. Developmental transitions, which involve a relatively abrupt shift in behavioral competency, have been described primarily in some cognitive (e.g., Piagetian) and personality (e.g., Eriksonian) theories. One long-standing problem with transition-based theories is that the process by which individuals move from one level to another has been extremely difficult to explain. The result has often been vague appeals to ill-defined versions of an equilibrium-disequilibrium process or silence on the nature of transitions.

Chaos theory provides potentially adequate descriptions of the transition process in three ways: the apparent disruption in performance as a person moves from one way of behaving to another, the nature of qualitative changes in the knowledge base, and the way in which different styles of behaving become dominant as a result of a transition. The first two issues will be discussed here; how styles become dominant will be discussed later. To facilitate our discussion, we will focus on applications of chaos theory to cognitive developmental transitions.

Bifurcation Models

It has been known for many years that the conscious experience of transitions from one level of knowledge to another is often an abrupt, all-or-none shift. Experientially, this shift is often described as an instantaneous "aha" experience—one moment the person knows the world in one way, but the next moment brings a whole new way of looking. The aha phenomenon has been reported in widely different arenas such as Gestalt figures, world knowledge, and psychotherapy. Interestingly, the aha experience seems to be characterized by a feeling of emotional upheaval (however brief) between feelings of more certainty before and after the experience (see Sheehy, 1981, for several firsthand accounts).

This pattern of certainty followed by upheaval, followed again by certainty, is reminiscent of the pattern shown in some dynamical models, such as bifurcation models (Yorke & Li, 1975). In a bifurcation model, the number of solutions to the set of equations defining the dynamical system periodically doubles. Graphically, a periodically doubling bifurcation model looks like a branching tree diagram, where each branch represents a solution. At some point, the system loses its predictability, and an infinite number of solutions are possible; during this period, the system behaves chaotically. Graphically, it is as if lines in the tree diagram scatter all over with no systematicity. After a time, however, the system once again regains its composure and provides a small number (typically 3; see Yorke & Li, 1975) of solutions, which then undergoes periodic doubling, chaos, and so forth, thereby continuing the cycle.

Speculating a bit, it is possible that cognitive development follows a similar mode. A type of thinking or a domain of knowledge is typically limited to a few applications at first, but it becomes more extensive over time. For example, Piagetian theory includes this growth in knowledge application as the concept *horizontal decalage*. The degree to which a particular style of thinking is inculcated would be represented graphically by the number of bifurcations in the model. Few bifurcations indicate that the style of thinking is limited to usage in a small number of arenas; for example, one may be able to demonstrate an understanding of conservation with clay but not with liquids. Many bifurcations (short of chaos, of course) mean that the thinking style was available for widespread application. At some unpredictable time later, the system becomes overburdened (e.g., the current way of thinking is inadequate to solve the problems at hand) and becomes chaotic. The onset of chaos marks the beginning of a transition in development, during which one cannot predict what will happen. During this chaotic period, there may be a return to the immediately preceding style (or to a style used much earlier in life, as described in the psychodynamic concept of regression), or perhaps there may be a hint of what is to come. In any case, at some unpredictable later time the system again demonstrates stability, but now in a new way, that is, a different mode of thinking or level of understanding is evident, but one that again can be used only in a few ways. Over time, this new mode of thinking becomes applied more broadly, potentially to the point where chaos occurs again, followed by the potential emergence of yet another style of thought.

In this approach, individual differences in cognitive development are easier to understand. For example, the fact that few people achieve the highest levels of cognitive expertise could be due to differences in the rates at which different styles of thinking are generalized across content and people (i.e., individual differences in the rates of bifurcation). In turn, these differences in bifurcation rates could be due to differences across individuals in the dynamical person-environment interactions that are responsible for pushing the system. Finally, different types and degrees of usage of cognitive strategies may control the rate of bifurcation, which in turn may control the rate at which chaos and its subsequent qualitative change occur.

The Force for Change

A second important aspect of chaos theory concerning transitions is that changes in state require a "kick" to make things happen. That is, the local equilibrium of the system must be disrupted in order for a state transition to occur. In a sense, this situation is an application of the law of inertia: Things will not change unless they are made to change. One everyday example concerns boiling water. Unless heat is added continually, water in a pot will simply reach an equilibrium. The implication for human behavior is that unless a person's equilibrium is disturbed, he or she remains in a particular state (e.g., at a particular level of expertise). If the system (i.e., the individual) is not stressed to the point of chaos, then no change in behavior will occur.

This discussion is reminiscent of Piaget's description of cognitive development (e.g., 1970). In Piaget's theory, each stage is marked by a period of acquisition of new cognitive skills and a period of consolidating those skills. For example, it is widely known that such skills as conservation are not acquired in an all-or-none fashion, as argued in the previous section. Rather, conservation is initially acquired relative to a few substances and is only later generalized to others. Additionally, the notion of equilibration plays a prominent role in Piaget's theory. Ignoring the debate on the exact meaning of this concept and the lack of an agreed-upon explanation of stage transition processes in Piagetian theory, it is possible to view transitions in Piaget's theory as resulting from a disruption in local equilibrium akin to the processes described by chaos theory. Thus, phenomena already documented in cognitive development but which were not well-explained may be easier to understand given knowledge about the behavior of dynamical systems in other contexts.

ATTRACTORS (STRANGE OR OTHERWISE) AND STYLES OF THOUGHT

From the perspective of chaos theory, understanding the transition from one state to another involves another concept from chaos theory, strange attractors (Miles, 1984; Ruelle, 1980; Ruelle & Takens, 1971). One way to conceptualize strange attractors is to visualize an orbiting ball tied to a string. Given that the ball is subject to friction (e.g., from the atmosphere), the orbits over time form a spiral that eventually converges on a point where the ball will come to rest. Thus, that point "attracts" the orbits of the ball. In general, *attractors* are points toward which orbiting objects tend to gravitate.

Several aspects of attractors need to be clarified. The orbits being referred to are actually graphic representations of dynamical systems. Mathematically, such systems may be represented in what is called *phase space*, an *n*-dimensional space where *n* refers to the number of degrees of freedom in the system. The familiar Cartesian coordinate system is an example of a 2-dimensional phase space. For example, the motion of a pendulum may be represented on Cartesian coordinates, where the pendulum's angle from the vertical would be represented on the x-axis and its speed on the y-axis (Gleick, 1987).

Knowledge about a dynamical system at a specific instant in time is represented as a point in phase space. For example, the speed of the pendulum at a given angle can be plotted as a point on Cartesian coordinates. Each successive instant generates a new point. The movement of points in phase space (i.e., the function describing the points on the plot) is what is meant by an orbit. Thus, the history of a given dynamical system over time is reflected by following the moving points through its orbit. As Gleick (1987) points out, plotting change (e.g., moving pendulums) in phase space makes change easier to watch. The motion of points in phase space representing a continuously changing system like a pendulum is much like the path of a fly buzzing around a room. If the system is periodic (e.g., as a pendulum), then the plot moves in a (possibly complex) loop, passing the same position in phase space repeatedly. If certain combinations of variables are impossible (e.g., pendulums or flies moving faster than the speed of light), such situations would be represented by empty spaces on the phase space diagram (i.e., the fly never goes there). The point(s) around which plots of the motion of objects move or orbit is (are) the attractor(s) of the system.

Strange attractors involve orbits that are nonperiodic, that is, they never return to the same spot in phase space. Geometrically, this means that such an orbit drawn in phase space turns out to be an infinitely long line in a finite space that never intersects itself. Such lines are possible because they involve *fractal geometry*, a topic well beyond the scope of this paper (see Gleick, 1987, and Peitgen & Saupe, 1988, for introductions). For our purposes, it is sufficient to note that even nonperiodic systems still produce orbits around particular points, which are the strange attractors.

In some cases the changes that occur in dynamical systems converge toward or orbit more than one (strange) attractor. Graphically, the orbits exist in one area of phase space and appear to converge on one point, but suddenly "jump" to another area of phase space and appear to converge on a different point. How a system moves from one attractor to another appears to be related to the forces underlying change described earlier. That is, a dynamical system changes attractors when it receives a kick from some source. Thus, we can argue that moving from one (strange) attractor to another represents a state transition.

Attractors, strange or not, have proven extremely useful in science. For example, they provide good descriptions of the stars' orbits in a galaxy and turbulence patterns in rivers. But two characteristics of strange attractors provide considerable insight into their name. First, the plots of dynamical systems that involve strange attractors produce definite shapes in the long run, despite the fact that as new points are plotted, they scatter (apparently) randomly in phase space. That is, any two consecutive points in phase space are arbitrarily far apart, making it impossible to predict where the next one will appear. However, when many hundreds of points are plotted, a clearly definable shape emerges. (One famous strange attractor reported by Lorenz, 1963, looks like a butterfly.) Second, despite the unpredictability of the location of future points, all of them must lie on orbits around the attractor. That is, there are boundaries beyond which points (i.e., state of the system) cannot exist, making the dynamical system in question deterministic. As Gleick (1987, p. 152) states, scientists discovered "Nature was constrained. Disorder was channeled, it seemed, into patterns with some common underlying theme."

In psychology, strange attractors may have application as models of thought processes. That is, a particular style of thinking or domain of expertise may be analogous to a strange attractor, around which the dynamical system (i.e., the information-processing system) orbits. One's default mode of thinking may be the dominant strange attractor, which captures incoming problems and determines how they will be solved. Other solutions designed by other attractors are possible, but the system needs to be jolted somehow in order for these alternatives to be explored. Such a conceptualization could explain such things as functional fixedness, perseveration, absentmindedness, and processing biases. It may also explain other common cognitive phenomena as situations in which an inappropriate strange attractor was operating for a particular problem and nothing provided the kick necessary to change attractors. Individuals are capable of thinking in other ways (represented by other strange attractors), but must either be explicitly made to do so or be placed in a situation that moves the system to this alternative. This conceptualization implies that one will tend to think in certain ways, even repeating mistakes, unless there is a compelling reason not to do so.

In this view, cognitive development would be characterized by the acquisition of new strange attractors. Each acquisition process could be combined with a bifurcation model to explicate the developmental process further. This two-process account implies that cognitive development entails both *periods of enrichment*, where enrichment refers to the knowledge application (e.g., period-doubling) process involving a single attractor, and *periods of chaos*, where chaos means the simultaneous breakdown of extant attractors and the birth of new attractors. Finally, this two-process model operates in the context of the butterfly effect, thereby virtually guaranteeing substantial individual differences in the behavioral expression of the underlying knowledge as organized in the attractors.

Note that nothing in the present discussion is really new; numerous theorists have postulated that development alternates between periods of stability and transition/crisis. However, these theories have all been criticized for their lack of specificity concerning the nature of both the transition process and knowledge growth during times of stability. Our contribution is merely to point out how three concepts in a chaos-theory framework provide the specificity lacking in previous writings.

CHAOS THEORY AND LIFESPAN LEARNING

Having described some basic concepts in chaos theory and pointed out some connections between it and developmental theory, we would now like to show how the framework we have constructed advances understanding of key cognitive developmental issues. We believe that the three-process model could account for several general aspects of cognitive development: (1) why there appear to be only a relatively few levels of thinking; (2) why cognitive development tends to show spurts at a few points but relatively smooth progression most of the time; (3) why cognitive flexibility (defined as the ease with which one moves from one attractor to another in order to approach a problem in a different way) is difficult to achieve and maintain; (4) how modal ways of thinking develop; and (5) why cognitive training programs typically do not show substantial generalization effects. After first discussing some general research issues, we briefly address each of these points.

Developmental Research and Chaos Theory

It is fair to say that developmental research is heavily biased toward answering "what" rather than "how" questions about development. Furthermore, within the "what" questions there is an additional bias of avoiding "what" questions pertaining to processes of development. That is, research on "what" questions focuses much more on the *outcomes* of developmental processes than on the processes themselves. For example, we know far more about age differences in adults' scores on measures of self-efficacy than we do about age differences in the processes that produce the responses in the first place.

Adopting a chaos theory approach would force researchers to reconsider these biases. As noted earlier, chaos theory provides ways to conceptualize and model specific processes in ways never before available. This means not only that far more sophisticated versions of "what" questions could be posed but also that "how" questions could be addressed systematically as well. To begin this process requires some basic shifts in methodologies, primarily involving an emphasis on dynamic process rather than on static responses. Although this approach could most easily be implemented in studies of social interaction (e.g., see Gottman, 1991, for an excellent example), dyadic (or higher-order) interactions are not necessary (e.g., one could analyze verbal protocols generated by a single participant).

The main point is that chaos theory opens new and exciting research avenues. Certainly, the canons would need to be redefined (e.g., the meaning of "prediction" is different in chaos theory). But the outcome of this reconceptualization process would be nothing short of allowing human behavior to be examined in its full, complex glory. The solace for skeptics (and those hampered by inertia) is that physics, biology, chemistry, and other "real sciences" not only have survived the incorporation of chaos theory but also, as indicated earlier, have been able to explain phenomena that heretofore had been viewed as aberrations.

Each of the following sections raises potential research questions that could be examined within a chaos-theory framework. While these are by no means exhaustive (e.g., the change process in psychotherapy could have been added), we believe they represent some of the fundamental, but as yet unresolved, issues in human development.

Limits on Levels of Development

Over the past century, researchers studying cognitive development have gathered considerable evidence that there are probably no more than seven or so qualitatively different levels of thought. Coincidentally, research on psychosocial development and moral reasoning points to similar numbers of distinct levels. This converging evidence raises an interesting question as to whether there is an absolute limit to the number of distinct models of thinking (or feeling, or being moral).

Chaos theory per se does not place limits on the numbers of distinct levels that could develop in a particular domain. However, given the analogy between cognitive developmental level and attractor, one can build a logical case for such limits. Recall that the development and identification of an attractor requires hundreds of separate observations of discrete events. Given our analogy to cognition, this implies that several hundred discrete behavioral events are required in order for an attractor to develop. The speed with which this happens is the primary determinant of the likelihood of developing additional styles of thinking (i.e., new attractors). We argue that the rate of acquisition of new knowledge is highest during early childhood, declining over the rest of the lifespan. We argue that the knowledge-acquisition rate is important because it is related to the likelihood that chaos will occur. That is, the more quickly branches are added to a bifurcating model, the more quickly the model reaches chaos. Because chaos leads to the development of new modes of thought, any slowing in the rate of knowledge growth necessarily slows the cognitive developmental process. Moreover, we believe that the knowledge acquisition rate becomes increasingly variable across individuals as they mature, thereby providing an explanation for increasing individual differences in modes of thinking, particularly in adulthood. Indeed, the increased difficulty in tying chronological age to the achievement of new styles of thought during adulthood supports this view.

However, rate of knowledge acquisition alone is insufficient to account for the functional limit on the number of models of thought. As pointed out earlier, the development of new attractors depends critically on receiving a ''kick'' from some source. In cognitive developmental terms, new modes of thought will probably not develop unless existing modes fail to work *and* the system is pushed into (or somehow is provided a compelling reason for) creating a new way to deal with the situation. In short, the inertia that favors continuing an obsolete and ineffective way of thinking must be overcome in order for new modes of thought to emerge.

We believe that the combination of a necessary rate of knowledge acquisition and a sufficiently powerful motivation to overcome currently inadequate thinking styles happens only a relatively few times. Moreover, we believe that for most people these combinations are far more likely during childhood and adolescence than during adulthood. Those individuals who continue to develop new modes of thought during adulthood probably do so in response to complex environmental demands for continued cognitive growth. Indeed, extant research on cognitive development beyond formal operations, for example, argues that only a minority of adults develop highly abstract styles of thought (e.g., Commons, Sinnott, Richards & Armon, 1989). As our society becomes increasingly complex, however, such advanced modes of thought should become more common as more people require such modes for daily adaptation.

Developmental Spurts

The seemingly erratic course of cognitive development, as described by many researchers (e.g., Case, 1984; Fisher & Pipp, 1984; Piaget, 1970), in which periods of rapid change alternate with periods of slower progress becomes easier to understand when viewed in a chaos-theory framework. As discussed at several other points, periods of chaos are associated with subsequent instantaneous changes in state. Moreover, the periods of chaos in typical dynamical systems are substantially shorter than the periods of relative stability. This pattern of change in dynamical models maps well onto extant descriptions of cognitive development. Consequently, we argue that the reason for growth spurts in cognitive development is the same as that for other dynamical systems, namely, chaos.

Cognitive Flexibility

As argued earlier, cognitive flexibility can be viewed in a chaos framework as the ease with which one moves from one attractor to another. Such movement requires a kick from some source (as described above) to move from one thinking style to another. To the extent that a preferred mode of thought is strongly instantiated (see next section), such movement becomes more difficult because increasingly strong kicks are necessary. This implies that cognitive flexibility requires considerable effort. Whether this effort is even possible (given limits on cognitive capacity), whether the person has sufficient motivation and rationale to seek alternatives (i.e., has sufficient kick), and whether additional and appropriate alternative modes of thinking are available will determine the degree to which cognitive flexibility occurs. The difficulty in achieving cognitive flexibility is also partly responsible for the overall failure of researchers to demonstrate generalization of trained cognitive strategies, as discussed later.

One intriguing possibility is that becoming truly cognitively flexible may be the ultimate goal (endpoint) of cognitive development. That is, being able to think of (one's constructed) reality in different ways and becoming committed to one particular viewpoint while still remaining open to new possibilities may be the hallmark of cognitive maturity. In chaos-theory terms, such cognitive maturity implies that movement among attractors and the development of new attractors would happen relatively efficiently. However, we would expect such cognitive maturity to be rare and to develop only in individuals who maximize every opportunity for learning from experience and manage to escape the lure of cognitive inertia.

Modal Modes of Thinking

At several points we have referred to a modal mode of thought. To oversimplify a bit, a modal mode of thinking is simply the usual style used to generate the initial attempts at solving cognitive problems. We believe that such modal or default mode is simply the strongest attractor available. In other words, the attractor that is most fully developed (i.e., has the most branches in terms of a bifurcating model) will be the modal mode.

As a particular attractor becomes dominant, however, a trade-off occurs. On the one hand, a person may be better able to deal with many types of problems more quickly, as solutions congruent with the modal mode are more easily generated. However, the cost is a concomitant loss in cognitive flexibility, as the "gravitational pull" of the modal attractor makes leaving its "orbit" increasingly difficult. Consequently, problems that may be more appropriately solved with a different attractor may become trapped by the modal attractor and solved less adequately.

Strategy Training and Generalization

In previous papers (e.g., Cavanaugh & Green, 1990), we have argued that strategy training is unlikely to generalize unless a sufficient rationale is provided to motivate people to engage in the necessary cognitive effort. The reasons for this hypothesis can be expressed concisely in chaos-theory terms. (For an alternative view on this issue, see Berg, Klaczynski, Calderone & Strough, chapter 24, this volume.)

Strategy training consists of two general types when viewed from a chaos-theory framework. First, training may be aimed at new applications of or slightly new versions of existing attractors. This situation is analogous to adding new branches in a bifurcating model. Examples of this type of training include most memory strategies, such as rehearsal and organization. Second, training may be aimed at instantiating a whole new mode of thought that is qualitatively different from all existing attractors. Examples of this approach to training would be training conservation or hypothetico-deductive reasoning to individuals lacking the requisite attractors (concrete and formal operations, respectively).

It has been known for some time that memory strategies are easily acquired by many types of individuals, but typically generalize only to tasks or materials very much like those used in training (e.g., Borkowski & Cavanaugh, 1979). Similarly, fluid intellectual abilities trained in various settings also fail to generalize to other fluid abilities (e.g., Willis, 1990). The reasons for this are straightforward. Adding additional branches to a knowledge structure is relatively simple; individuals are predisposed to acquiring knowledge. However, strategy generalization, even though it occurs in the same attractor, requires people to make the more difficult connections across different branches. That is, strategy generalization is much like trying conceptually to connect discrete limbs on a tree where no tangible connections are possible. Just as in real life, such connections in a bifurcating model with discrete knowledge components are extremely difficult.

The situation is even more difficult when one is attempting to train a new mode of thought. In chaos terms, such training involves inculcating a new attractor. As argued earlier, chaos is the prerequisite for adding an attractor. Consequently, unless such training programs push participants into chaos (which is doubtful given the critical issue of timing as discussed earlier), acquisition, to say nothing of generalization, is impossible. Indeed, one argument in the conservation training literature has been that children who successfully acquire conservation through such programs were already "ready" for the transition to concrete operations. In other words, they were on the brink of chaos prior to participation.

In short, chaos theory casts serious doubts on the degree to which cognitive strategies acquired through a training program will generalize. Rather, chaos theory argues that only through extensive experience over time (i.e., until the strategy is firmly instantiated in an attractor) will newly acquired cognitive skills be readily applied to many other appropriate situations.

The Chaos of Lifelong Learning

In our view, chaos theory provides an important and useful framework in which to interpret lifespan cognitive development. In particular, chaos theory allows a new interpretive context for understanding lifelong learning. From a chaos perspective, learning involves adding branches to one's bifurcating models of knowledge. Most of the time, these bifurcating trees exist as highly intricate, stable systems of knowledge that allow adults to deal with a wide range of problems. Occasionally, however, the orderliness collapses and the tree structure functionally disappears. Phenomenologically, a person may feel as if he or she knows nothing and is totally confused. Quite the contrary is true, of course, as it takes substantial knowledge for a dynamical system to head into chaos. But confusion eventually abates, and new levels of understanding result from the chaos.

Merriam (this volume) and Sinnott (this volume) argue that learning across the lifespan is the basis for development and change. As applied to a chaos theory approach, their views support the idea that learning is a truly dynamic, reciprocal process that requires a non-linear analysis. For example, in optimal classroom settings, both the learner and the teacher are transformed by the dynamic learning process, leaving each with new ways of conceptualizing reality. For the learner, this may involve the creation of new attractors, the rapid growth of complex bifurcation models, or even the push into chaos. For the teacher, the process would involve at least a jump from one attractor to another, and at most an experience of chaos and the creation of new modes of thought.

What this means for adult education is profound: Educational goals need to be redefined. Increases in content knowledge alone is an inadequate outcome measure of learning. Rather, the degree to which increases in content knowledge are accompanied by experiences of chaos and restructuring of knowledge and chaos may be more appropriate. More provocative would be the suggestion that if students leave a course with more questions about the content than they had initially or with increased "confusion" about how everything fits together, then the teacher has accomplished his or her task (providing that the teacher has the skills necessary to enter into a dynamic, reciprocal learning process with students in the first place). Additionally, Merriam and Sinnott both point out that this view of learning requires fundamental shifts in teacher education; traditional emphases on classroom management and teaching styles are largely antithetical to an approach based on chaos theory.

More than anything else, applying a chaos framework to lifelong learning is like taking much of what we already know and turning it on its head. Predictability is impossible in the long run. Stability is only temporary and is ultimately illusory. Confusion may even be a good sign in the right context. Nevertheless, a chaos framework provides a parsimonious explanation for many developmental phenomena not adequately explained in other approaches. We believe that as the concepts and ideas only briefly discussed in this chapter are pursued, even more important insights will result.

NOTE

Preparation of this chapter was supported by NIA research grant AG09265 and by a research grant from the AARP Andrus Foundation to the first author. Some of the ideas in this chapter were presented at the Harvard Symposium on Adult Development, July 1989.

REFERENCES

Abraham, R. H. (1985). Is there chaos without noise? In P. Fisher & W. R. Smith (Eds.), *Chaos, fractals, and dynamics* (pp. 117–121). New York: Marcel Dekker.

Borkowski, J. G., & Cavanaugh, J. C. (1979). Maintenance and generalization of skills and strategies by the retarded. In N. R. Ellis (Ed.). *Handbook of mental deficiency* (2nd ed., pp. 569–617). Hillsdale, NJ: Erlbaum.

Case, R. (1984). The process of stage transition: A neo-Piagetian view. In R. J. Sternberg (Ed.). *Mechanisms of cognitive development* (pp. 19–44). Prospect Heights, IL: Waveland Press.

Cavanaugh, J. C., & Green, E. E. (1990). I think, therefore I can: Self-efficacy beliefs in memory aging. In E. A. Lovelace (Ed.). *Aging and cognition: Mental processes, self-awareness and interventions* (pp. 189–230). Amsterdam: North-Holland.

Commons, M. L., Sinnott, J. D., Richards, F. A., & Armon, C. (Eds.). (1989). *Adult development: Vol. 1. Comparisons and applications of developmental models*. New York: Praeger.

Costa, P. T., Jr., & McCrae, R. R. (1980). Still stable after all these years: Personality as a key to some issues in adulthood and old age. In P. B. Baltes & O. G. Brim, Jr. (Eds.). *Life-span development and behavior* (Vol. 3, pp. 65–102). New York: Academic Press.

Devaney, R. L. (1989). *An introduction to chaotic dynamical systems* (2nd ed.). Redwood City, CA: Addison-Wesley.

Erikson, E. H. (1982). *The life cycle completed: Review*. New York: Norton.

Fisher, K. W., & Pipp, S. L. (1984). Processes of cognitive development: Optimal level and skill acquisition. In R. J. Sternberg (Ed.)., *Mechanisms of cognitive development* (pp. 45–80). Prospect Heights, IL: Waveland Press.

Ford, J. (1983). How random is a coin toss? *Physics Today, 36*, 40–47.

Gleick, J. (1987). *Chaos: Making a new science*. New York: Viking Press.

Gottman, J. M. (1991). Chaos and regulated change in families: A metaphor for the study of transitions. In P. A. Cowan & M. Hetherington (Eds.). *Family transitions* (pp. 247–272). Hillsdale, NJ: Erlbaum.

Hertzog, C. (1990, March). *Methodological issues in cognitive aging research*. Invited address presented at the biennial Cognitive Aging Conference, Atlanta.

Hirsch, M. W. (1985). The chaos of dynamical systems. In P. Fisher & W. R. Smith (Eds.). *Chaos, fractals, and dynamics* (pp. 189–196). New York: Marcel Dekker.

Lorenz, E. (1963). Deterministic nonperiodic flow. *Journal of Atmospheric Sciences, 20*, 130–141.

Lorenz, E. (1979, December). *Predictability: Does the flap of a butterfly's wings in Brazil set off a tornado in Texas?* Paper presented at the annual meeting of the American Association for the Advancement of Science, Washington, DC.

Miles, J. (1984). Strange attractors in fluid dynamics. *Advances in Applied Mechanics, 24*, 198–214.

Nesselroade, J. R., & Ford, D. H. (1985). P-technique comes of age. *Research on Aging, 7*, 46–80.

Peitgen, H–O., & Saupe, D. (Eds.). (1988). *The science of fractal images*. New York: Springer-Verlag.

Piaget, J. (1970). Piaget's theory. In P. H. Mussen (Ed.). *Carmichael's manual of child psychology: Volume 1* (3rd ed., pp. 703–732). New York: Wiley.

Ruelle, D. (1980). Strange attractors. *Mathematical Intelligencer, 2*, 126–137.

Ruelle, D., & Takens, F. (1971). On the nature of turbulence. *Communications in Mathematical Physics, 20*, 167–192.

Sheehy, G. (1981). *Pathfinders*. New York: Morrow.

Underwood, B. J. (1975). Individual differences as a crucible in theory construction. *American Psychologist, 30*, 128–134.

Willis, S. L. (1990). Current issues in cognitive training research. In E. A. Lovelace (Ed.). *Aging and cognition: Mental processes, self-awareness and interventions* (pp. 263–280). Amsterdam: North-Holland.

Yorke, J., & Li, T-Y. (1975). Period three implies chaos. *American Mathematical Monthly, 82*, 985–992.

2

The Future Impact of the Communication Revolution

Lynn Johnson

Adult learning in the Western world in the twenty-first century will be affected by a redefinition of epistemology, knowledge constructs, and ways of knowing. It will also be affected by access to information, the quantity of information that will need to be processed, and the modalities that are chosen for communication. These changes are already occurring. Our future is dependent on how these changes develop and, at least in part, by the decisions made today that shape these changes. Adult learning in the twenty-first century is not an esoteric subject. Whether or not our planet continues to exist will depend on our ability as adults to learn from each other, to jointly define and solve problems, and to communicate those solutions to each other in such a way that we can adopt them and act upon them.

This chapter will mention the epistemological shift that has started to occur and the broadening affect that new ways of knowing could have on adult learning. Although an in-depth study is not possible here, this chapter will focus upon the effects of the communication revolution and how it is helping us to change our perception of reality, to question our ways of knowing, to process information, and to learn. It will also suggest that the effects of communication technologies upon the way we learn stem from three main sources: (1) their inherent characteristics, (2) their utilization, and (3) the content presented. If we are to enhance our ability to learn and thus to solve problems, we need to better understand and control these effects upon us. At the same time, we are also communicators, and it will become increasingly important that we learn to utilize the most effective form of communication for given tasks.

EPISTEMOLOGICAL SHIFTS AND NEW WAYS OF KNOWING

For the past half-century there has been a gradual shift in the way that we in the West perceive the world. This change affects how we define reality and how we as adults process information and learn. The communication revolution and its associated technological advances have enabled us to travel in space and study the macro world of the universe and the micro world of quantum physics. At the same time, communication technologies challenge our basic concepts of how the world is ordered and functions. There is a shift away from a mechanistic worldview in which all we know and experience can be explained through reasoned logic, the Newtonian laws of physics, and the scientific method. This shift is toward an organismic worldview in which everything is increasingly complex, interrelated, and interdependent. Our sophisticated technology has uncovered paradoxes that challenge our existing worldview, our basis of knowledge and knowing, our assumptions about reality and truth, and our relationships with others and with the universe.

The extent to which learning can occur in an adult is dependent in part upon the flexibility of the knowledge construct that filters new information and selectively permits the intake, assimilation, and integration of new information. If this construct is rigid, learning will be limited. Adults in the twenty-first century will need to make filters more flexible by integrating paradox into their cognitive schemata and redefining their ways of knowing and bases of knowledge. As we enter the twenty-first century and grapple with decisions that will affect the very existence of future generations, some look to Native Americans for new ways of knowing. Pamela Colorado (1992), a Native American and founder of the Worldwide Indigenous Science Network, has referred to the time since 1987 as a "window of opportunity" for Native Americans and other indigenous peoples of the world to share their ways of knowing, knowledge constructs, and wisdom with the Western world. Other people look to their own intuition, or to women's ways of knowing, to modern physicists, biologists, and mathematicians, to the Eastern mystics whose worldview is surprisingly similar to that of the particle physicists (Capra, 1975), to shamans, to Christian saints, to healers, to acupuncturists, to philosophers, and to psychologists. The upsurge in religion, spirituality, and investigations in areas as diverse as extrasensory perception, yoga, and psychic abilities can perhaps partly be attributed to this search by individuals for meaning and understanding beyond that brought by logical reasoning. Often these other ways of knowing are described as non-credible and belonging to the "fringe" and are immediately dismissed. Perhaps it is time to examine more closely other ways of knowing and allow other possibilities to increase our understanding and insight. Unless we are open to new ways of knowing and willing to restructure our thinking in a way that will permit us to integrate paradox into our own knowledge construct, we will miss this "window of opportunity" and limit our learning.

EFFECTS OF THE COMMUNICATION REVOLUTION

Inherent Characteristics of New Technologies

There has been discussion of the effects of audio and video technologies on viewers since the mid–1950s (Ellul, 1954/1967; Goldwyn & Smith, 1980; Landow, 1992). Yet the extent to which audio and video technology by their inherent nature have changed our view of reality has not, for the most part, been widely recognized or acknowledged by the average viewer. These technologies create realities that directly confront and contradict our previously held view of an objective reality, where time and space are absolute and events are continuous along a linear, chronological timeline. Some communication technologies, including virtual reality, create their own realities. Time and space can be subjectively controlled through editing, freeze frames, slow-motion, and time-lapse photography to segment actual, "real-time" events and to reorder them into the producer/director's version of reality. For example, the men's 100-meter dash did not occur immediately prior to the women's gymnastic competition in the 1992 summer Olympics, even if it was presented that way by national television coverage. Computer software can create apparent three-dimensional objects and simulate reality so that the viewer is unable to tell that it is a "created," virtual reality. Video and audio, through their presentation and juxtaposition of images and sound, carry cognitive and psychological effects that go beyond their content. One of these effects is a change in the way we perceive the world and make sense of life events. With the increased sophistication of audio and video technologies, the following have occurred: (1) time and space have become relative and fluid; (2) events are discontinuous and disconnected and only partially known; (3) observed events are in motion and transition; (4) causality is probabilistic, and cause is not necessarily antecedent and contiguous to events; (5) life events can no longer be thought of as occurring in a logical, linear progression; (6) the reality we view or hear is subjectively created; and (7) our senses are often unable to distinguish between fact and fiction.

Communication technology presents us with a multiplicity of realities, wherein fact and fantasy are interwoven. This confusion of what is real or true has become increasingly complex as video technology has become increasingly sophisticated and moved from line-drawn to computerized graphic animation. With chromakey a camera image can replace a solid color. In this way a person standing before a blue wall can appear to be one-tenth the height of an ant behind him, or a news anchorman can appear to be at the scene of an earthquake when he is actually sitting in a studio. By means of these technological tools, cartoon characters can appear to interact with real persons as in the movie "Who Framed Roger Rabbit?" This blending of reality with fiction is having a psychological and cognitive effect even if we do not fully understand or recognize what this effect is. Not only may some of the violence seen in our society today stem from an inability on the part of the perpetrator to view his or her actions as separate from similar "fictitious" actions seen on television, but it is becoming increasingly difficult for all of us to clearly separate fact from fiction. Our knowledge constructs are formulated on the premise that we can differentiate between what is real or true and what is not; yet if our criteria for making this determination depend on sensory perception, we may need to reevaluate these criteria.

There has not been an open recognition that audiovisual media cannot, by their very nature, present "objective" reality. Unfortunately, television news and other video programs have historically represented themselves as an objective presentation of actual events. A former leading anchorman's continual admonition, "That's the way it is," in concluding his newscast led us to believe incorrectly that there was one objective reality that newscasters simply reported. Television programs, even news, have always been presentations of a subjective viewpoint in which selective parts of an event have been portrayed and cut up into little pieces and rearranged by editing. Another reason that media cannot present objective reality is perhaps that objective reality, as it is popularly defined, does not exist. Studies of eyewitness memory have shown us that when more than one person view or experience an event, as many interpretations of the event follow as there are people (Loftus & Loftus, 1976).

It seems that instead of one objective reality there are a multitude of realities that are defined by, and from, each person's subjective viewpoint in relation to others (Berger & Luckmann, 1967; Schutz, 1967). We co-create reality by mutually agreeing to the aspects that define it. The implications of this assertion for adult learning and problem solving are profound. If there is no "objective" truth or reality, then every person's viewpoint is important in defining situations and problems and in resolving them (Sinnott, 1984). There can be no one person who holds all knowledge. Thus the role of the "teacher" in an adult learning situation changes to that of a facilitator who is not the sole authority. It also becomes imperative that individuals work collaboratively together to co-create reality and to solve problems instead of competing with one another.

Utilization of Media

Numerous psychological and physiological effects have been attributed to television, including sensory deprivation, apathy, violent behavior, increased heartbeat, rampant consumerism, and alienation (Mander, 1978); but it is not realistic to assume that we will throw out our communication technology and return to the world that existed in the early 1900s. We need to understand the effects of communication technology and to differentiate among those effects inherent in the characteristics of the technology, those due to the content, and those due to an inappropriate use of certain technology. More research such as that conducted by the American Psychological Association's Task Force on Television and Society (Donnerstein et al., 1992) needs to be done to document the effects of communication technology in all these areas.

More care must be given to the selection of communication media and the appropriateness of the media to the content presented. Each new technology increases our ability to receive and send information and to communicate through different modalities that are received by different senses. Some technologies rely on a mixture of aural, visual and non-verbal communication, while others may be interpreted only through one sense. If communication technologies are appropriately used, they can enhance communication and be directed to specific learning styles. Computer technology has recently broadened the ability of many disabled individuals to learn and communicate.

If, however, communication technologies are not appropriately used, miscommunication and a lack of understanding may result. It is incorrect to assume that communication technologies always increase our ability to communicate with one another. Electronic mail (E-mail) via computers cuts through hierarchical communication channels and certainly increases our access to people and the speed with which we can send and receive information. It cannot, however, communicate the nuances and subtleties that are communicated verbally, nonverbally, and visually in a face-to-face exchange. A cryptic E-mail message such as, "We need to implement a RIF, see me tomorrow," may well be misinterpreted. As our society relies increasingly on technology to communicate, the potential for miscommunication and misunderstanding also increases. Perhaps this can be avoided by combining technologies so that the same idea is communicated orally, visually, and kinesthetically.

We also need to conduct research to determine the physiological and psychological effects of the use of various communication technologies. We have not taken into account the psychological isolation and other effects that may occur with individuals who communicate only through technological tools and interact with machines instead of real people. Yet more and more people are put into this position as computers become the main mode of communication in businesses and as telecommuting, interactive video, and video teleconferencing become more popular. Thought must be given as to when and where technology is appropriate and should be used. Too often, because technologies exist, it is incorrectly presumed that they must be used and can successfully be used to meet all communication needs.

Media Content

It is essential to remember that communication technologies are simply tools that we can control and that some technologies are more successful tools than others for communicating different types of information. Computer graphics that simulate complicated phenomena that cannot be viewed in real life, such as reactions on the atomic level, can bridge experimental and theoretical models and integrate information so that it can be intuitively understood by scientists. Interactive video programs permit one to practice medical procedures numerous times before they are performed on a human. Video training programs can be used effectively to present a process that occurs over time, such as erosion in a particular valley, or to demonstrate processes, such as the preparation of a silicon chip, that would be too expensive, hazardous, or impossible to present in a classroom or board room. A talking head in front of a blackboard is, however, a very poor and inappropriate use of television.

More attention must be given to the selection and appropriate use of communication technologies in adult learning. They can be used to increase empathy and understanding, but only if we consciously decide to use them in this way. Television and video have been defined in this society as primarily entertainment. They rarely have been used as a catalyst to help people grow, interact, and learn about themselves and others. According to the *Washington Post* (Harwood, 1992) adults now spend an average of four hours and nine minutes per day watching television. With the merger of video into the computer, the development of interactive video and the potential of multimedia systems brought to the home and office over telephone lines comes the opportunity to more effectively use these tools for adult learning.

One of the newest communication-technology tools is that of virtual reality, where a separate reality is created by a computer that one can enter cognitively and affectively. Although software for virtual reality has been developed for positive uses (e.g., architects can visualize and experience their creations), sometimes its uses are not so positive. Brian D'Amato, a young New York artist, has reportedly developed a virtual reality suicide game (Hagen, 1992). In this game, one enters a reality in which one can more creatively imagine and execute ways of committing suicide.

Virtual reality, hypertext (a computerized extension of an annotated book), interactive computer novels, and other communication technologies will replace books as the dominant learning/teaching tool (Hardison, 1989). These new technologies have tremendous potential as adult learning/teaching tools, but only if they are consciously used by those who fully understand the communication process and the physiological and psychological effects associated with their use. More attention needs to be given to what we do with our communication technologies, what content is presented through them, what impacts are made with them, and what actually is communicated. The content of what is presented on television generally has been determined by a select few who have sought to insure the largest number of viewers, that is, consumers for the advertisers. This is not the criterion upon which content should be selected, whether presented on television or through some other communication technology. We must all become more concerned with the messages that media convey and personally assume responsibility for the content and utilization of communication technologies, not leave it in the hands of the few.

ACCESS

The questions of who has access, who controls access, and who controls the content to be presented through communication technologies are critical to adult learning and communication. The ways in which these questions are answered have significant consequences for adult learning and for our future. Much of the current dialogue on the communication revolution presently focuses on the legal issues of patents, copyright, and confidentiality. More of the dialogue should be focused on censorship and access (Katsh, 1989). When a politically powerful minority can legislate that information be withheld from pregnant women making a decision that will affect the rest of their lives and that of others, there is little to prevent that minority or other minorities from limiting access to information in other ways. Information control has traditionally been associated with the exercise of power. Our ability to solve problems and learn as adults depends on our access to information. If that access is limited, our solutions and capacity to learn will equally be limited.

As a result of the communication revolution, we are struggling to manipulate and assimilate vast amounts of information. Numerous databases have been developed throughout the world in order to systematize the ever-increasing amounts of data and information and make them accessible to people. Those involved in adult learning are concerned with how to categorize and access information and the process of critical thinking and problem solving. Too often we feel that we do not have enough information to make a decision, when actually we have so much information that we cannot order it to make sense of it. More research needs to be done on how people process staggering amounts of often-contradictory information.

Scientists in the new physics, the new biology, and the new cognitive sciences and mathematicians are attempting to make sense of their new knowledge, which sometimes appears contradictory, by developing new theoretical constructs that help explain and integrate this new information into even larger theories. The non-scientists are also struggling to make sense of their new world, some by ignoring and dismissing the contradictions and others by accepting and integrating them. It may be necessary to learn to restructure thinking so that we can limit and integrate the information we receive in such a way as to accept paradox and others' realities and integrate them into a larger meaning (Sinnott, 1993). This restructuring should enable one to better process information and enhance the ability to creatively solve problems. More research needs to be done in this area to understand the limiting and integrating processes of learning and to determine how to help adults expand their cognitive framework.

CONCLUSION

The communication revolution with its proliferation of technological tools has affected adult learning in numerous ways. It has helped to change our perception of reality and bring about an epistemological shift that may lead to broadening or further narrowing our selective information filters. The increasing quantity of information challenges us to change our cognitive structures so that information can be organized in new ways and contradictory information be assimilated.

With the information explosion and the increased complexity of life, the cognitive skills that adults need to possess have become those of critical thinking and problem solving across many disciplines and in a group context. This means that knowing how to access information is more important than memorization and that group collaboration is more important than competition. The teacher's role in adult learning should be that of a facilitator who can promote group interaction and direct the process of critical thinking and problem solving.

The communication revolution enables us to transfer information and communicate in many different forms and combinations of forms: aurally, nonverbally, visually, and kinesthetically. Because people vary in learning styles and sensory discrimination, this variety and combinations of presentations can enhance our learning capacities. Particularly for disadvantaged individuals it may make learning in some areas possible for the first time. The communication revolution challenges us to develop new cataloging and archival systems that can make all forms of information (i.e., computer software, audio/video recordings, interactive video, virtual reality, etc.) openly available and accessible.

There is a need for more research to explore further the psychological effects of various communication technologies on adults and to differentiate the source of these effects (i.e., those inherent to the technology form, those that are a result of the utilization of the technology, and those caused by the content presented through the technology). More research is also needed to understand further the cognitive aspects of the learning process and how adults can restructure their thinking to enhance that process.

The communication revolution and information explosion allow the wisdom and knowledge of the peoples of the world to be shared with each other. Open access to information and effective communication through a variety of media give us a window of opportunity to increase our ways of knowing. If we can enlarge our information base and restructure our thinking to synthesize and integrate the increased quantity of information, we will greatly enhance our learning potential and abilities to solve problems creatively together.

REFERENCES

Berger, P. & Luckmann, T. (1967). *The social construction of reality: A treatise on the sociology of knowledge*. Garden City, NY: Doubleday.

Capra, F. (1975). *The tao of physics*. New York: Bantam Books.

Colorado, P. (1992). Way finding and the new sun: Indigenous science in the modern world. *Noetic Science, 22*, 19–23.

Donnerstein, E., Fairchild, H., Feshbach, N., Huston, A., Katz, A., Murray, J., Rubenstein, E., Wilcox, B. & Zuckerman, D. (1992). *Report: Big world, small screen: The role of television in American society*. Lincoln, NE: University of Nebraska Press.

Ellul, J. (1967). *The technological society*. (J. Wilkinson, trans.). New York: Alfred A. Knopf. (Original work published 1954).

Goldwyn, E. (producer) & Smith, A. (host) (1980). *Goodbye Gutenberg* (videorecording)

(1980). A BBC production in association with WNET, New York. Wilmette, IL: Films, Inc.

Hagen, C. (1992, July 5). Virtual reality: Is it art yet? *New York Times*, pp. H1, H19.

Hardison, O. B. (1989). *Disappearing through the skylight: Culture and technology in the twentieth century*. New York: Viking Penguin.

Harwood, R. (1992, September 2). PBS vs. MTV: So many media, so little time. *Washington Post*, p. A21.

Katsh, M. (1989). *The electronic media and the transformation of law*. Oxford: Oxford University Press.

Landow, G. (1992). *Hypertext: The convergence of contemporary critical theory and technology*. Baltimore: Johns Hopkins Press.

Loftus, G. & Loftus, E. (1976). *Human memory: The processing of information*. Hillsdale, NJ: Lawrence Erlbaum Associates.

Mander, J. (1978). *Four arguments for the elimination of television*. New York: Quill.

Schutz, A. (1967). Concept and theory formation in the social sciences. In A. Schutz. *Collected papers*, *1*, 63–65. The Hague: M. Nijhoff.

Sinnott, J. (1984). Postformal reasoning: The relativistic stage. In M. Commons, F. Richards & C. Armon (Eds.). *Beyond formal operations: Late adolescent and adult cognitive development* (pp. 288–315). New York: Praeger.

Sinnott, J. (1993). Creativity and postformal thought: Why the last stage is the creative stage. In C. Adams-Price (Ed.). *Creativity and aging: Theoretical and empirical approaches*. New York: Springer.

3

The Educated Adult in Today's World: Wisdom and the Mature Learner

*Deirdre A. Kramer and
Weizhen Tang Bacelar*

THE INFORMATION AGE AND LIMITS OF SPECIALIZATION

Ours has been deemed the "high information age." In his book *Megatrends*, Naisbitt (1982) explores how technological advances in both the production and communication of information, coupled with the population explosion and global interdependence, have made possible vast amounts of information. One consequence is the tremendous specialization within and between disciplines. The risks of specialization include fragmented knowledge—that is, seeing the world "as through the segmented eye of a fly" (Boyer & Levine, 1981, p. 25)—and fragmented, repetitive tasks that can result in burnout. Furthermore, science and technology threaten to become the nucleus of our education. Many people believe that such professions are important channels to "the good life." The relative neglect of the social sciences, arts, and humanities creates a narrow-mindedness that may impede the ability to grasp the diverse and complex problems facing our world today. In their provocative monograph on higher education, entitled *A Quest for Common Learning: The Aims of General Education*, E. L. Boyer and A. Levine (1981) offer an antidote to the fragmentation that comes with specialization and technological sophistication. In their view, the goal of higher education is to enable the learner to transcend specific disciplinary boundaries to see connections within and between communities, the physical world, and time. The ability to transcend disciplinary boundaries, they argue, enables one to reflect meaningfully on the interdependence of all life forms and to contribute more effectively to the broader community.

Boyer and Levine trace the history of general education movements in American higher education during the last century. General education is defined in its broadest and most agreed-upon sense as the "breadth component of a college education" (Boyer & Levine, 1981, p. 2). It provides a means of moving beyond fragmented disciplinary boundaries to ensure an understanding of the connections among disciplines. Beyond that, there is considerable disagreement within the academic community with respect to both the definition of general education and means for bringing it about. Some construe it simply as the sampling of courses from a variety of areas, while others construe it more ambitiously as emphasizing the connections among seemingly disparate subject areas. Boyer and Levine believe that an awareness of connection fosters the recognition of interdependence and a sense of community. They note that each resurgence of general education has occurred during times when individualism was heightened, along with fragmentation, isolation, and apathy. An understanding of shared history, present culture, the diverse groups within given cultures, differences among cultures, and global unity may help reaffirm our sense of community. This does not, however, presuppose community at the complete expense of the individual. Rather, an inherent tension exists between the needs of the individual and that of society and is at the heart of any form of social contract within a given system. Overemphasis on either of these two dimensions results in its own set of problems, with too much emphasis on community resulting in feelings of being "herded, smothered, and restrained" and too much emphasis on the individual resulting in feelings of isolation and apathy (Boyer & Levine, p. 18). They believe that higher education can provide a vehicle for exploring these two poles, their interrelationships and their limitations. In our view, the educated, informed person who can reflect on this inherent duality and forge a dialectical synthesis will be in a position to establish meaningful and constructive ties within society.

This chapter is about the maturing and the mature adult. What characteristics would be required for the student to flourish in and contribute to an educational environment geared toward reflecting on the connections among disciplines, and what is required of an educational system in order to nurture responsible, yet self-reflective and individuated citizens? In this chapter, we consider the role of wisdom in promoting such an education. We will argue that the mature learner, already able to see interdependence among different disciplines, has a unique place in higher education and that the young, less mature learner can benefit greatly from reflecting on his or her role as both a unique individual and a member of a larger community. In doing so, we outline the tenets of Boyer and Levine's general education program and briefly present a model of wisdom, followed by an exploration of the ways in which wisdom may foster and be fostered by general education.

Six Themes in Exploring One's Relationship to the Larger Community

Boyer and Levine (1981) argue for a general education program that would emphasize six themes: (1) shared use of symbols, (2) shared membership in groups and institutions, (3) shared producing and consuming, (4) shared relationship with nature, (5) shared sense of time, and (6) shared values and beliefs. An adult who can think sensitively about these themes will be equipped to contribute to the community in ways that promote growth of the individual, the social structure, and life. He or she can place a problem or issue in its broader context, including past, present, and future, and thus make thoughtful judgments about complex dilemmas.

The first category, *shared use of symbols*, incorporates the idea that humans are uniquely able to use symbols to mediate our relationship to our surroundings. Symbols are our medium of thought. Various types of symbolic structures, as Wilber (1980) suggests, mediate and assist the emergence of a higher-order structure at each stage of the development of consciousness, which can be seen as a series of significant upward transformations. A general education curriculum would enable people to recognize the connections among different symbols and symbol systems and to understand the powerful role played by symbols in shaping our experience, attitudes, emotions, and beliefs. It would also emphasize our understanding of how different symbol systems have evolved, and perhaps evolved differently in different social settings and cultures. For example, Joan M. Erikson (1988) argues that the overemphasis on production and achievement in our culture has resulted in a loss of connection to the simple sensory experiences that open the imagination and engender creativity. This overemphasis has influenced the symbols that lie at our disposal, thus shaping and limiting our connections to our inner selves and the world around us. Our shared use of symbols may also lead us to study the modern technologies, such as television, films, and computers, used to advance them and to foster the particular symbols used in our culture. Reflection may also empower people to alter their symbol systems in order to solve problems facing the world.

The second category is *shared membership in groups and institutions*. Institutions such as family, religion, and society lie at the core of our existence. They help define our belief and value systems, our selves, our relationships with one another and the world—"those social structures that shape our lives, impose obligations, restrict choices, and provide services that we could not obtain in isolation" (Boyer & Levine, 1981, p. 39). For example, family is the primary agent for socializing emotional expression (e.g., Izard, 1971). Research on family expression of emotion (Halberstadt, 1984) indicates that "our styles of expression, skills in communication, and social perceptions are all influenced by the families we grew up in" (p. 250). A general education program would enable people to explore the evolution of institutions—their strengths, limitations, and inherent tensions—and the role the individual plays in shaping individual experience. It would also help people to acknowledge the diversity among these institutions across history, cultures, and subcultures. The better-informed person would have an enhanced understanding of how he or she is shaped by and can, in turn, shape the evolving systems in which he or she participates.

The next category with which to reflect on our relationship to a global world is that of *shared producing and consuming*. Work and leisure, along with relationships, lie at the very core of our existence. A tremendous portion of our lives and our livelihoods is devoted to these two areas. How do work and leisure patterns shape our lives? How have they evolved? What value systems are inherent in such patterns? How do they affect the emotional and moral fabric of people's lives? How do they differ from one culture to the next? No one stands alone in existence. We all have affinity with others and the world around us. An individual strives for actualization in a social context that transcends the self. One essential element of any society is interdependence, that is, accomplishing collectively for its members that which they cannot achieve individually. No one can enjoy the fruits of modern technology and the arts without depending on the contributions of others. It is through producing and consuming that our interconnections to one another become apparent, that is, that we are highly dependent upon one another (Boyer & Levine, 1981). Inquiry into the nature and function of work and leisure may help the student understand his or her relationship to the global community.

By reflecting on our *shared relationship with nature*, the fourth category, we become aware of how interconnected all living organisms are and, depending on one's standpoint, may come to believe that a spiritual essence manifests itself through all of nature. Personal intimacy with nature may help nourish harmony and balance within the self. With the advance of science and technology in modern society, our emphasis has been on domination and control of the physical world (Keller, 1985). Critical scrutiny of our relationship with nature might direct us toward greater cooperation with, rather than control of, her and the establishment of more harmonious relationships generally. Simply taking science courses does not suffice to make us aware of such interconnections. Rather, general education would help make us aware of the context in which scientific theories are tested and developed, the relationship among scientific disciplines, the responsible use of science in a global, interconnected community, the pervasive influence of science on our world, and the relationship between science and other academic disciplines (Boyer & Levine, 1981). It would also enable us to broaden our conception of truth and reality to encompass forms of knowing and experiencing that go beyond scientific disciplines.

Knowledge, culture, and civilization cannot be understood as emerging and residing in a vacuum. Rather, we are also connected to one another by a *shared sense of time*, the fifth category in Boyer and Levine's model. Our experience is colored by a past, a present, and a future that connect us with one another, our ancestors, and generations as yet unborn. A good education would allow us to explore the events and symbols that have brought us to where we are now. "More than a collection of facts, this approach would emphasize the convergence of social, religious, political, economic, and intellectual forces. . . . The chronicle of humanity . . . is an endlessly varied struggle to resolve tensions over freedom and authority, conformity and rebellion, war and peace, rights and responsibilities, equality and exploitation" (Boyer & Levine, 1981, p. 42). By exploring these inherent tensions and struggles, students would be in a better position to contribute to the decision-making processes today that will affect the world tomorrow.

Finally, a consideration of any of these issues involves exploring our *shared values and beliefs*, the sixth category of Boyer and Levine's program. Higher education should help make us aware of ourselves as human beings who are committed to particular belief systems and share particular values. "Each student should be able to identify the premises inherent in his or her own beliefs, learn how to make responsible decisions, and engage in a frank and searching discussion of some of the ethical and moral choices that confront us all" (Boyer & Levine, 1981, p. 44). Of course, this is not to imply that all people share the same beliefs—quite the contrary. Shared membership in particular groups, a shared place in history, and individual experiences will all comprise the fabric of a particular person's beliefs. It is our ability to scrutinize the contexts in which these beliefs occur and to recognize the extent to which they are shared with some and different from others, and why, that allows us to explore the connections between our own beliefs and those of others around us. Paradoxically, it is, in part, this ability to explore the connections among our beliefs that will foster an acceptance of the plurality of belief systems. Such issues relate directly to our relationships with one another and the broader community, as they help us make responsible, ethical decisions in how we choose to structure our lives.

These six categories do not function independently of one another but are connected in intricate ways. For example, the meaning of a symbol, like that of a living organism, may grow, change, and die. Our changing, dynamic symbol systems, likewise, are influenced by and in turn mediate our shared values and beliefs and our membership in institutions. In fact, our symbol systems mediate and in turn are influenced by all of the other categories, which, in turn, influence and are mediated by each other. The educational system can help the student recognize that the boundaries that separate concepts (including the ones presented in this chapter) and disciplines are cultural constructions and inherently subjective. It can also help us recognize the ways in which diverse experiences are interrelated in deep and profound ways. For example, advances in physics reveal the underlying interconnections among phenomena previously thought to be unrelated; these advances have relevance for disciplines as diverse as the natural sciences, the social sciences, medicine, philosophy, and religion.

Wisdom and the Mature Learner

Recent advances in adult cognition suggest that middle-aged and older adults may, for a variety of reasons, be well suited to the task of crossing interdisciplinary boundaries to grasp patterns, uncover underlying connections, and reflect on their relationship to the surrounding world. Work on wisdom touches on many of these issues, including the necessity for interdisciplinary connections. Csikszentmihalyi and Rathunde (1990) state:

What all the ancient thinkers seemed to realize is that without wisdom, ways of knowing are constrained by a tragic paradox: The clearer the view they provide, the more limited the slice of reality they reveal. The integrated thought of "primitive" men and women, who did not distinguish between religion, art, science, habits, and instincts, slowly gave way to more and more specialized "domains" of knowledge. Nowadays knowledge is divided into innumerable branches that appear to be unrelated to each other or to the world as we experience it. Specialization enables us to exert a powerful control on specific, limited aspects of reality. But it does not help us to know what to do with the control thus achieved. (p. 29)

One wonders, too, what feats of nature have been lost in this quest for control, such as the intimate connections with our bodies and with nature, both of which provide us with naturalistic technologies for healing (Chopra, 1989; Gerber, 1988; Jarvis, 1958). One feature of wisdom (Kramer, 1990a) that would facilitate the grasp of interconnection is that of *dialectical thinking*. Dialectical thinking orients one toward *relationship*, *interdependence*, and *non-linear causality* as central categories for understanding the world. It enables us to recognize and accept the diversity and interdependence that underlie Boyer and Levine's six themes.

D. A. Kramer (1990a) formulated a model of wisdom whereby cognition (in particular, dialectical thinking) and *affect* work in concert to allow for effective, or wise, social *action* within the life course. As a result of healthy emotional and cognitive development, the wise person can develop several wisdom-related skills, including the recognition of individuality; the recognition of context; shrewd, perceptive, and empathic interpersonal skills; an understanding of change and growth processes; and an awareness of the importance of both emotion and cognition in solving problems. These skills serve various wisdom-related, interdependent functions of resolving one's own dilemmas, advising others, managing social institutions, engaging in life review, and undertaking spiritual reflection. Wisdom is defined, then, not as a particular cognitive, affective, or behavioral state or skill, but as a process of adapting to real-life problems that involves openness to experience and subsequent growth that enables the individual to function in several wisdom-like capacities. In this view, wisdom is seen as a dynamic, never-complete process that emerges in the relationships of particular people in particular settings. It is not seen as absolute, fixed, or simply transferable from one situation to the next. Furthermore, it is not seen as detached and orderly, but as arising within affectively imbued, often conflictual and ambiguous experiences, situations, and relationships.

At the heart of the model is the developing individual. Emotional and cognitive development interact in such a way as to produce a cognitive system capable of tolerating complex, multidimensional problems characterized by contradiction, uncertainty, and change. However, for such cognitive processes to emerge in a meaningful sense—not detached from rich, interpersonal, and affective experience—the person would have to develop a healthy integration between conscious and unconscious processes. Kramer (1990a) outlined the conscious cognitive processes she believes fosters the wise understanding of oneself, other people, relationships, and social institutions and the emotional processes that accompany these. In her model, adult thinking develops toward relativistic and then dialectical thinking.

Relativistic thinking rests on the assumptions of change, subjectivity, and novelty (Kramer, 1990b). All knowledge is seen as influenced by its context, and contexts are continually changing. As one's standpoint, or context, changes, sometimes arbitrarily or randomly, prediction is seen as impossible, as all people and events are unique and continually change in potentially unsystematic ways. Consequently, irreconcilable contradiction is a central feature of understanding. There is no necessary order to a relativistic universe; any order is imposed externally or via one's cognitive framework.

Relativism, as defined here, is limited in that it does not provide a mechanism for integrating across contexts and time frames to provide for meaningful commitment to values, growth, and the like. To continue to think in a purely relativistic manner may lead to fragmentation, inability to act, or a feeling of anomie (Kramer, 1989). Therefore, it has been argued that knowledge continues to reorganize to yield a form of thinking labeled as dialectical. *Dialectical thinking* sees all knowledge and reality as engaged in continual movement and characterized by inherent contradictions. To this extent, it incorporates relativity. However, there is forward movement (i.e., growth) and the contradictions are seen as inherently interrelated—part of the same whole, rather than simply shifts in perspective—and more apparent than real. All phenomena are believed to develop as a result of an ongoing tension between events, their negation, and the resolution of that negation into momentary structures that soon give way to new tensions, initiating the cycle again, ad infinitum. The dialectical whole (i.e., the momentary structure) is characterized by emergence (i.e., it redefines and transcends its constituent elements) and reciprocity (i.e., a change in any one element in a system influences and in turn is influenced by a change in other parts of the system). Thus, in a dialectical system, all elements are interrelated and are reflections of an underlying unity.

These early modes of thinking would have an impact on how students conceptualize the subject matter presented in the classroom. However, while developmental in nature, there is also considerable individual variation within a given age group and across domains. Many people probably never reach the dialectical level; and as it develops as a result of adaptation to particular real-life demands, no one would be expected to demonstrate it across all domains or even consistently within domains or situations. This is especially true in emotionally stressful situations, which may result in the simultaneous use of multiple levels of thinking in order to resolve a problem (Haviland & Kramer, 1991). It is better to think in terms of the greater flexibility that development affords. The higher the level of development, the greater the number of reasoning tools at one's disposal. Lower levels of thinking (which are not described in this chapter because of space limitations) are sometimes more adaptive and can be seen as special cases of higher-level ones (Kramer, 1989).

It is also our assumption that these modes of thinking do not develop apart from emotion. Evidence from adolescent diaries (Haviland & Kramer, 1991; Kramer & Haviland, 1989) and the writings of Carl Rogers (Haviland, 1991) bears out this point: Cognitive development occurs in the context of emotion. A failure to recognize one's emotions appears to stunt the growth of these cognitive processes (Kramer & Haviland, 1989). Furthermore, relativistic and dialectical thinking help one to recognize the various forms of projection that stunt emotional growth, an issue that will be addressed in a later section of this chapter.

IMPLICATIONS FOR HIGHER EDUCATION

Wisdom has implications for formal and non-formal learning in adult life. In our view, there is a reciprocal, or non-linear, relationship between the learner and the material to be learned. An interdisciplinary understanding by adults of Boyer and Levine's model would foster the development of dialectical thinking, and dialectical thinking will in turn foster the ability to grasp these themes. It would enable one to recognize the constantly changing connections among disciplinary boundaries to think meaningfully about one's relationship to one's world—past, present, and future. It is our view that wisdom will be instrumental in the successful navigation of this highly technological information age and that, therefore, it is important to find ways to nurture wisdom in all members of our community. However, education well served not only will foster the cognitive requisites for exploring abstract connections among diverse disciplines but also will promote the affective development and self-understanding crucial to making such connections meaningful in a deep, interconnected, and profound way.

In this section, we will consider several ways in which wisdom and education can work in concert with one another. Mature, wise individuals provide a challenge to the college curriculum by seeking out the connections among disciplines and by calling for an integration of abstract concepts with deeply enriched, personal experience. They may see knowledge as embedded in a broader context of personal, social, and community-based experience. The educational environment, in turn, can provide them with an opportunity to reflect on their life experiences and integrate these with knowledge obtained from scholarly inquiry conducted in the context of a global community. This will foster their mastery of developmental tasks, such as generativity and ego integrity (see Erikson, 1968).

Blanchard-Fields (1986) found that young adults were poorer at integrating their newly acquired abstract reasoning skills with emotional, interpersonally embedded content. By entering a classroom where connections are made across boundaries and disciplines, the less mature adolescent or young adult student will not only be given an opportunity to further master their newly acquired abstract reasoning skills, but will be challenged to integrate these with meaningful affective and socioemotional experience. Thus, a college education would take into account the stage of development of the student and provide opportunities to grow. In doing so, it would nurture both the cognitive and emotional development of the young individual. In helping the young adult develop a strong sense of identity, firmly grounded in both cognitive and emotional development, the educational system will help prepare him or her for the psychological tasks of adult life (e.g., the achievement of intimacy and generativity) through which he or she connects with the community. Such an education would not simply foster the specialization and compartmentalization associated with a rigid career track.

There are numerous ways in which higher education can promote wisdom and in which mature, wise learners can contribute to the educational process. We will focus on six ways in which this dialectic can occur. These are not the only ways in which higher education can benefit from adhering to developmental psychological principles, and the boundaries dividing these six categories are fluid as well. These categories are (1) interdependence of cognition and affect, (2) awareness of the pervasive influence of culture and history in the construction of reality and knowledge systems, (3) questioning assumptions about so-called absolute truths handed down in Western civilization, (4) encouraging experiential and intuitive knowledge, (5) recognition of the interplay among multiple systems over time in constructing reality, and (6) recognition of global interdependence. We will consider each of these, in turn.

Interdependence of Cognition and Affect

We argued earlier that cognition and affect are inherently interdependent and that cognitive development cannot occur apart from well-integrated affective development. To the extent that cognition develops apart from affective development, it is likely to result in a distorted, fragmented conception of reality where one is wholly unaware of one's projections. Psychopathology is the likely result. In our view, an educational system that fosters the development of cognitive processes at the expense of that of the whole, integrated person fails in its mission, if the goal is, in part, to nurture people capable of contributing to the betterment of society and, indeed, all of life.

As Labouvie-Vief (1982) and Pascual-Leone (1983) point out, adolescents are already at great risk of dissociating cognition from affect. With newly developed abstract reasoning abilities in hand, little experience with the complex, contradictory, and demanding roles of adult life, and possibly a biological structure capable of subsuming a great deal of compartmentalization and denial, the adolescent's idealistic theories are often detached, lacking in relevance. Current educational practice may only escalate such detachment.

Jaques (1970), in his study of the effect of the midlife crisis on the work of creative geniuses, argued that the first half of the lifespan is geared to manic denial of one's mortality. This is reflected in both the quantity of output and the quality of themes. The midlife had a number of profound effects on both the creative process and creative products. For those whose careers spanned from pre- to post-midlife, two kinds of changes were noted. First, creative products changed from a "hot-from-the-fire" style of creativity that produces high volume to a more "sculpted" form of creativity that emphasizes the process of perfecting a product over quantity. Second, the themes changed from optimistic, idealistic ones extolling the inherent goodness of life (often in the form of comedy) toward graver ones (often in the form of tragedy), such as death, destruction, and the inherent darkness of the human condition. Jaques proposed that the early half of the lifespan represents an attempt to ward off unconscious fears about mortality by immortalizing oneself through an abundance of creative products of an optimistic nature, whereas the second half of the lifespan reflects an awareness of mortality and focuses more on quality than quantity.

One might view the first half of the lifespan as geared toward internalizing the myths and illusions of the culture and the second half of the lifespan as questioning these. This is not a new idea. Plato proposed it in his essay about the myth of the cave in *The Republic* (Plato, 1982). We have simply acquired more evidence for it. Indeed, Winegar, Renninger, and Valsiner (1989) found that mothers literally (but benignly) "lie" to their children in order to foster the development of a socially acceptable sense of control and individuality in the child. This is illustrated by an example of a mother who, upon having just helped a child in a task, exclaimed, " 'You are a big girl! You did it all by yourself!' " (Winegar et al., 1989, p. 163). We rarely question this form of encouragement, but indeed, it fosters a sense of empowerment that, while appropriate for the early portion of the lifespan, may conflict with the tasks of later life. Perhaps, too, it fosters an awareness on an unconscious level by the child that he or she has been lied to, resulting in dissociation.

The second portion of the lifespan may be geared toward the dissolution of cultural myths and illusions about reality. The shift from denial toward acceptance of fragility and mortality that Jaques observed in the content of creative works prompted him to suggest that the midlife crisis represents a resurfacing of themes of early infantile mortality. As infants, we are especially vulnerable and dependent on others (caretakers). If we are not cared for, it is literally a matter of life or death. Object relations theorists point to the profound effect early infancy has on the development of our internal emotional and psychological structure. At this time, non-mirrored (usually negative) emotional states become disowned and dissociated from one's positive emotional states and consciousness, resulting in the creation of a "false self" (see Kohut, 1978; Miller, 1981). The failure of a caretaker to provide a loving, caring response capable of mirroring the infant's emotional states can result in a disorganized, fragmented, terrifying, and potentially psychotic inner psychic life. Such inner terror and disorganization may, in the case of highly talented individuals, be masked by a high degree of social and occupational competence, often taking the form of a successful creative career (Kernberg, 1975). However, the frightened infant and child still lie within. Kernberg has found that serious psychological work on these issues often cannot begin until the midlife period in highly talented individuals.

Not all adults are so uniquely talented as the geniuses studied by Jaques or the people who are able to successfully avoid dealing with a terrifying inner life through their outstanding accomplishments. Furthermore, not all people leave infancy with a terrifying, fragmented sense of self. Nevertheless, as Miller (1981) points out, no one is completely unscathed by the travails of childhood. Levinson's (1978) and Gould's (1978) research on personality development provides evidence even in more "ordinary" human beings for a shift from an optimistic, "invulnerable," and defended self in early adulthood toward that of a more realistic, integrated sense of self where good and evil, masculine and feminine, and creation and destruction are seen as residing side by side. After the midlife, the person, sometimes through great struggle, has come to accept his or her imperfections and dark shadow side and those of others and the world around— as well as his or her finitude. One developmental task of adult life is to bring the dissociated, disavowed parts of the self into alignment with the surface, public (socialized) self.

The achievement of this developmental task would involve both conscious and unconscious processes. Earlier it was argued that dialectical thinking is fostered by and, in turn, fosters the profound task of grappling with the deepest layers of the psyche, whereby one's primitive projective identifications are owned and in time transformed. We are referring here to dialectical thinking that is based on a good sense of self and one's boundaries, an acceptance of one's limitations, and a high enough degree of ego strength to integrate the dialectical principles with emotional experience. The kind of crisis that may occur during the midlife is one where the most primitive, infantile reaches of the psyche are explored and exposed for reworking. This can result in acute disorganization and tremendous feelings of pain and loss. The feelings that emerge are likely to be inexplicable, because of their preverbal, infantile nature.

The higher educational system today in our country, with its diverse population, is faced with at least two (of many) seemingly contradictory tasks: (1) to prepare the adolescent or young adult both emotionally and cognitively for the challenging tasks that lie ahead, including the midlife crisis, and (2) to accommodate and challenge the more mature person who may have confronted these deeper layers of the psyche and perhaps recognizes the fragile, fluid, and contradictory nature of experience. Having two such disparate groups of students in the classroom can provide both a great deal of conflict and an ensuing opportunity for a synthesis of their opposing perspectives.

As for the traditional-aged college student, the educational system can go a long way toward providing a safe, yet challenging environment to explore his or her budding self in its entirety. Though the newly acquired abstract skills should be nurtured, students could also be encouraged to integrate traditional classroom principles with their own personal experiences and important social issues. Students should not, in our view, be pressured toward a particular way of integrating abstract concepts with socioemotional issues: For some the initial emphasis may be on community, while for others it may be on the self. In time, the other pole can be dealt with if and when the person is ready.

As for the seasoned adult, an educational system that is irrelevant in its presentation of presumably universal, abstract truths will in all likelihood be unsatisfying and unchallenging, and it will fail to benefit from the wisdom this non-traditional student may have to offer. The classroom environment will need to provide opportunities for this person to explore the connection between his or her deeply personal life experiences and the abstract principles being taught. In the case of both the young and the older learner, the goal is to integrate abstract ideas and personal experience. However, whereas the important task for many young learners is to assimilate personal experience into an abstract frame of reference, the task for the more mature learner may be to assimilate abstract principles into a rich personal frame of reference. This might help offset the apparent regression that occurs in some older people as they confront the limits of relativism (Kramer, 1990b), by encouraging them to integrate absolute (abstract) beliefs with relativistic ones into a more comprehensive dialectical understanding.

Encouraging Experiential and Intuitive Knowledge

One means of fostering the integration of cognition and emotion is to encourage the experiential, intuitive knowledge generated from direct, rich life experiences. Life experience is closely linked to adult learning (see Merriam, this volume). It provides a good basis for knowledge because it is direct and intimate. Experiences allow us to not only challenge our beliefs and assumptions but to know ourselves. An educational system with an overemphasis on science and technology fails to help people better "know thyself." Mastery of specialized knowledge and skills would not in itself help one to gain insight into the self or develop one's full potential, nor would it help one become integrated and wise.

Learning from life experience is a hallmark of adulthood. Life experience provides a rich context for knowing about oneself, about life, and about the interdependence of all phenomena. This culture is so engaged in evaluating products that it devalues processes, and the apparent addiction to quick solutions often creates serious social and personal problems. The process of learning from life experiences, which is never complete, is one of self-exploration: It is a process of realizing one's strengths as well as weaknesses and one's potentials as well as limitations, of finding one's unique path, of liberating one's inner child, of finding balance between community and individuality, and of relinquishing one's impossible expectations and dreams. Instead of evaluating different facets of life and knowledge as good or bad, the higher educational system might encourage students to ask such important questions as how to perceive their life experiences, how to tolerate and reconcile the inherent imperfections in reality, how to grow from pain and loss, and what promotes such growth. The seemingly good or bad events in our lives offer us great opportunities for expanding our consciousness. While here on this planet, we have an opportunity to experience life, gain knowledge and wisdom from those experiences, and construct meaning. The meaning of life may reside in experiencing life. "A hero's journey is not a courageous act but a life lived in self-discovery" (Campbell, 1988).

Life experiences provide opportunities for developing intuition. An educational system with a heavy weight on science and technology promotes rational, analytical, and logical thinking in problem solving and decision making. These are useful tools of thought. However, they have their limitations, and quite often creative answers come from a joining of rationality with intuition—one's "inner voice" or "gut feeling." Intuition, as Goldberg (1983) says, "suggests spontaneity and immediacy; intuitive knowing is not *mediated* [italics in original] by a conscious or deliberate rational process" (p. 32). It consists of subtle thoughts and impressions of the psyche, which are developed by being still, open, and receptive to subtle patterns. It involves listening to our inner voice and is a powerful tool for effective problem solving and decision making. We often encounter ill-defined, real-life problems where there is incomplete information for the problems under consideration. In such situations rational thinking alone is not adequate for problem solving. Human affairs, which involve emotions and uncertainty, are too messy to be solved by rational thinking alone and require intuition as well. Intuition not only helps us in everyday affairs but provides insight into the spiritual and psychological spheres of consciousness. For some, our inner self is seen as part of a divine, Cosmic Consciousness which connects all organisms and all natural phenomena in the universe. For others, it is a more mundane process. Either way, by continuous contact with our inner self, our consciousness may expand and evolve toward greater flexibility in its dealing with the world. By encouraging experiential and intuitive knowledge, the educational system would foster integration of rational and intuitive thought and help one find, through the expanded consciousness, the deeper layer of meaning found in our connection with all life forms.

Awareness of the Pervasive Influence of Culture and History

Most of Boyer and Levine's components of a general education program reflect, in some degree, the pervasive influence of culture and history on our constructions of reality. Whether it is through the symbols that mediate experience, the social institutions that are also mediated by those symbols and in which the symbols arise, our shared values and heritages, scientific and other forms of scholarly inquiry, our definitions of the activities and roles (e.g., work and leisure) that occupy so much of our existence, or our shared past, present, and future, culture and history pervade our every breath, our every waking moment.

At the heart of both relativistic and dialectical thinking lies the belief in the pervasive influence of cultural constructions of reality. We cannot abstract anything akin to "pure, universal knowledge" from experience. All knowledge is embedded in the particular, the actual. That actual has a past, a present, and a future. It is achieved through an ongoing process of mutual consensus, whereby the differing and often-conflicting perspectives of all life forms, human and non-human alike, engage us in a constant dialectic and process of adaptation. Talbot (1991) has even argued, based on insights from quantum physics, that physical reality as we know it has been constructed via an ongoing process of mutual consensus and shared reality of all living organisms and energy forms (human and non-human alike, atomic and subatomic, etc.). While relativistic and dialectical thinking, as defined in the present chapter, both emphasize the embeddedness of knowledge in cultural constructions, they differ in their treatment of time. Within contextualism, the cultural constructions emerge anew and are recreated with each new moment, engendering the possibility of complete discontinuity with the past. In contrast, dialectical thinking emphasizes the continuity among past, present, and future. This continuity is not purely cumulative, however; there is also a reconstructive process occurring as each new disturbance in the structure or status quo is dialectically integrated into a more encompassing structure. There may be temporary states of disorganization (such as described above in the discussion of midlife crisis) or stagnation before synthesis occurs. By fostering an awareness of the ongoing dialectic between individual organisms and the structures in which they are embedded, the educational process will further the cognitive development of adolescents and adults toward that of relativistic and dialectical thinking. Likewise, relativistic and dialectical thinking in mature learners may facilitate the creation of a dialogue within the classroom about the cultural and historical construction of reality.

Questioning of "Absolute Truth"

Despite the apparent plurality of theoretical and disciplinary perspectives in academia, there has been a great deal of acceptance of a limited body of knowledge and truths. Much of what is considered "great" in the area of ideas and "truths" is considered to derive from times of antiquity, especially the ancient Greek era. Consequently, a narrow body of discourse stemming from this era and beyond in the arts and sciences has been taken as the sine qua non of knowledge and, hence, of a good education (Schuster & Van Dyne, 1984). The entry of non-traditional students into the mainstream of academia has opened up an important dialogue about the nature of knowledge and academic discourse.

Indeed, the entire foundation of knowledge and all that we hold true in Western civilization has been challenged by recent findings and reinterpretations of old findings based on more sophisticated techniques of measurement in archeology (Eisler, 1987; Gadon, 1989; Gimbutas, 1989). Eisler (1987) has made a probing analysis of the shift from ancient Goddess cultures, which spanned the Paleolithic and Neolithic eras, c. 25,000 to 5,000 B.C. She showed how, over a period of several millennia, repeated invasions from the outside coupled with continued natural disasters resulted in a disruption, disorganization, and eventual breakdown of apparently peaceful, humanistic cultures. In these cultures the Goddess was revered, men and women may have worked together as equal partners, wealth appears to have been distributed relatively equitably, and there was a strong connection to nature. These accomplishments were not independent of technological advances, for such developments as law, religion, speaking, writing, art, and agriculture were created during this period. Perhaps most important, there is no evidence of warfare (no weapons, no pictures of warriors or weapons, no fortresses). In sum, before civilization as we know it—continually racked with violence, unequal distribution of wealth resulting in mass poverty, illness, and death—civilization may have been peaceful and social structures non-hierarchical (Eisler, 1987; see also Kramer & Bacelar, 1991).[1]

The fundamental tenets of Western civilization—its great philosophies, great religions, great theories, great science and technologies, and its wars—arose at a particular time in history, in a given historical context that has rarely been explored. Once one begins to explore this context, the fabric of history and, indeed, experience begins to unweave. One begins to question, for example, religious practices that serve to oppress certain groups (e.g., women) and to stunt sexuality and healthy psychological growth. One begins to question the belief sometimes presented in philosophy, psychology, biology, and history that war and violence are inevitable consequences of human existence. One begins to question the age-old assumptions in science that we can observe a passive physical world and dominate it at will, using as our major method that of "torturing the answers out of nature," to borrow from the words of Nobel Laureate Barbara McClintock (as cited in Keller, 1985). One begins to question the duality that underlies most of our philosophical, scientific, and theological conceptions and their relationship to sexual conflicts (Christ & Plaskow, 1979; Keller, 1985). One may even question the absolute, objective nature of physical reality altogether (Talbot, 1991).

The educational system can foster the questioning of these age-old truths and the integrating of objective, factual knowledge and subjective, experiential knowledge by promoting diversity in the classroom: where old and new ideas can be raised and enter into a dialogue. Such questioning ultimately may expand the range of choices available to people. By fostering healthy emotional and cognitive development, we can foster not only the relativistic and dialectical forms of thinking that help grasp the complex, interactive, and uncertain nature of reality but also the emotional well-being that allows one to tolerate these dimensions.

Recognition of the Interplay among Multiple Systems

Boyer and Levine's prescription for a general education encompasses the ability to recognize the interplay among different systems of reality and scholarly discourse. Just to give one example of how different systems might interact over time to influence how reality is constructed or reconstructed in any given moment, let us once again consider the shift in civilization that was "completed" approximately 5,000 years ago. If such a shift occurred, it had implications for not only one but for many, indeed all, systems of conduct, inquiry, and knowledge. Images from the old religions have been incorporated in various ways into the legends and symbols of diverse religions worldwide (Eisler, 1987; Gadon, 1989). Furthermore, the attempt to preserve elements of these older cultures has, in Eisler's view, resulted in political struggles that encompass such diverse disciplines as theology, religious institutions, medicine, and, in all likelihood, science. The widespread slaughter of at least hundreds of thousands of women (a conservative estimate) during the Middle Ages was directed at women who were self-reliant, independent, and working as healers (Eisler, 1987; Starhawk, 1982). Many people are not aware of alternative assumptions about the nature of such diverse phenomena as healing, sexuality, gender relationships, the nature of the physical world, and the nature of the divine, to name just a few.

Recognition of Global Interdependence

An educational system informed by dialectical principles will foster an awareness of the close interdependence of all life forms. Following recent theories in quantum physics and neurophysiology, Talbot (1991) likens the universe to a holographic image. Underlying physical reality may be a deeper order of reality, which is the implicate, or enfolded, order. It is this deeper order of reality that gives birth to all the objects and phenomena of the physical world, in a way similar to that in which a piece of holographic film produces a hologram. The constant, dynamic enfoldings and unfoldings between these two orders give rise to the manifestations of all forms in the universe. Thus, everything in the universe can be seen as comprised of a holographic, implicate order and is part of a continuum.

Yet, theorists of the holographic model caution that the idea of a holographic universe does not mean there are no differentiations among things in the universe or that things do not possess their own unique qualities. The idea that all things, including consciousness and life, are ensembles enfolded throughout the universe makes us aware of the dynamic interconnectedness of all phenomena and the interrelationship among all systems. With such awareness, we come to understand that we cannot treat parts of our body without affecting the whole or think of ourselves as independent and self-reliant—separate from each other and/or all of life. This society has highly valued the achievement of power, status, and material success and the accomplishment of these ends by means of competition and force. At this juncture in history, it is important for us to realize that what we do has an impact on others. In a harmonious, healthy society, where interdependence is seen as a central feature of experience, the needs and rights of each individual can be recognized and fulfilled. As a mystic said, genuine individuality is the realization of universality.

CONCLUSION

By recognizing the fluid, consensual, co-constructed, and repeatedly reconstructed nature of knowledge, we can begin to untangle the serious and infinite number of problems facing our world today. This occurs on a multitude of levels, including the psychological, scientific, philosophical, educational, spiritual, cognitive, and emotional. Through our recognition of the uncertain and fluid nature of reality, we find our empowerment. If humans, in conjunction with the rest of life, are participants in the creation of our physical, spiritual, and psychological world, then we are also in a position to engage in a dialogue to produce a significant transformation of this consensual reality. If higher education is to participate in this process, it can benefit greatly from a model of wisdom where cognition and affect are both important to the growth process. It does so, in part, by fostering a dialogue among diverse groups of adults, some young and idealistic, who have yet to confront the darkest regions of their psyches, and some older and more mature, who can directly challenge age-old, static, abstract, and sometimes irrelevant "truths." Higher education seeks to be at once both highly abstract and highly concrete, experiential. A dialectical synthesis allows one to effectively integrate these inherent polarities.

In our use of the general education concept, it is not our goal to disparage specialized knowledge or objective, rational thought. Rather, we emphasize the integration of such dualities as cognition and emotion, rationality and intuition, body and mind, to produce balanced and integrated individuals who are both specialists and visionaries. Our chapter does, however, serve as a corrective to mainstream educational practices, which foster the development of rational thought and specialized knowledge and skills often at the expense of intuition, effective interpersonal relationships, and the integration of abstract knowledge with personal experience. If we were to reorganize our educational system, a great deal of effort would have to go toward finding ways to promote a dialectical synthesis between cognition, affect, personal experience, collective experience, individual development, and community development. The classroom environment would have to allow for conflict and uncertainty to permeate it at times, which will not always be pleasant. The authority structure would not be clear-cut. A fundamental reorganization of our beliefs about education would likely occur.

Furthermore, by fostering an awareness of interconnectedness among disciplines and of all phenomena, we do not intend to ignore the differences among disciplines or levels of analysis or to mix or confuse them by claiming that they are all really the same one. Development, whether cognitive, emotional, or on the level of consciousness, fosters a higher-order structure, which is more complex and emerges through differentiation from the preceding lower-order structure. The higher-order structure includes but transcends the lower-order structure, but the opposite is not the case. As Wilber (1984) points out, "Hierarchical and asymmetrical relationships are . . . at least as important as mutual or equivalent relationships" (p. 24). Overemphasis on interrelations among all levels would oversimplify one's conclusions. The educational process could both foster a balance between the depth of specialized knowledge and the breadth of interdisciplinary knowledge and foster an awareness of the interrelatedness of all phenomena, as well as the significant asymmetrical relationships.

To do so, it would be wise to proceed on a variety of levels, taking into account a variety of students in a diverse population. This will, in itself, pose problems in the classroom. Conflicts may emerge among the needs, goals, and expectations of students at different levels of maturity. This necessitates a fundamental shift in our assumptions about education and classroom experience. Conflict and uncertainty would represent an important means of exploring one's stance on knowledge and learning from others. Knowledge would come from the sharing (and sometimes colliding) of perspectives by equal peers, in addition to being transmitted by expert figures. A certain amount of negative affect may reside alongside the enjoyment of sharing and learning. Indeed, learning would occur in a more affectively imbued environment altogether than is currently the norm in our classrooms. By embracing diversity in our classrooms, we can model and foster an awareness of the dynamic, ever-changing, interdependent, multiple, and sometimes conflicting systems of knowledge extant in our culture and, more important, in our world. Most important, we can participate in the creation and transformation of these systems.

NOTE

1. Labouvie-Vief (in press) presents an alternative view about the possible existence of peaceful, Goddess-worshipping cultures where women were accorded equal status. She argues that the vision of a peaceful, almost idyllic time represents an archetypal image, based in part on our longing for such a life. Which view is correct cannot be addressed within the confines of this chapter; in either case, exploration of the possibility of such a culture and the possibility that such a culture never existed but rather represents an archetypal image falls into the category we are discussing in this part of our chapter. The educational system should, in our view, foster such scrutiny of diverse sides of the issue of our inherited "truths."

REFERENCES

Blanchard-Fields, F. (1986). Reasoning on social dilemmas varying in emotional saliency: An adult developmental perspective. *Psychology and aging, 1*, 325–333.

Boyer, E. L., & Levine, A. (1981). *A quest for common learning*. Lawrenceville, NJ: Princeton University Press.

Campbell, J. (1988). *The power of myth*. New York: Doubleday.

Chopra, D. (1989). *Quantum healing: Exploring the frontiers of mind/body medicine*. New York: Bantam Books.

Christ, C. P., & Plaskow, J. (Eds.). (1979). *Womanspirit rising: A feminist reader*. New York: Harper & Row.

Csikszentmihalyi, M., & Rathunde, K. (1990). The psychology of wisdom: An evolutionary interpretation. In R. J. Sternberg (Ed.). *Wisdom: Its nature, origins, and development* (pp. 25–51). Cambridge, England: Cambridge University Press.

Eisler, R. (1987). *The chalice and the blade: Our history, our future*. San Francisco: HarperCollins.

Erikson, E. (1968). *Identity: Youth and crisis*. New York: W. W. Norton & Co.

Erikson, J. M. (1988). *Wisdom and the senses: The way of creativity*. New York: W. W. Norton.

Gadon, E. W. (1989). *The Once and future goddess*. New York: Harper & Row.

Gerber, R. (1988). *Vibrational medicine*. Santa Fe, NM: Bear & Company.

Gimbutas, M. (1989). *The language of the Goddess*. San Francisco: Harper & Row.

Goldberg, P. (1983). *The intuitive edge: Understanding intuition and applying it in everyday life*. Los Angeles: Jeremy P. Tarcher.

Gould, R. L. (1978). *Transformation: Growth and change in adult life*. New York: Simon & Schuster.

Halberstadt, A. G. (1984). Family expression of emotion. In C. Z. Malatesta & C. E. Izard (Eds.). *Emotion in adult development* (pp. 235–252). Beverly Hills: Sage Publications.

Haviland, J. (1991). Lifespan changes in cognition and passion: Carl Rogers. Poster presentation.

Haviland, J. M., & Kramer, D. A. (1991). Affect-cognition relations in adolescent diaries: The case of Anne Frank. *Human Development, 34*, 143–159.

Izard, C. E. (1971). *The face of emotion*. New York: Appleton Century Crofts.

Jaques, E. (1970). *Work, creativity, and social justice*. London: Heinemann.

Jarvis, D. C. (1958). *Folk medicine: A New England almanac of natural health care from a noted Vermont country doctor*. New York: Ballantine Books.

Keller, E. G. (1985). *Reflections on gender and science*. New Haven: Yale University Press.

Kernberg, O. F. (1975). *Borderline conditions and pathological narcissism*. New York: Jason Aronson.

Kohut, H. (1978). Forms and transformations of narcissism. In P. H. Ornstein (Ed.). *The search for the self: Selected writings of Heinz Kohut: 1950–1978* (pp. 427–460). New York: International Universities Press.

Kramer, D. A. (1989). Change and stability in marital interaction patterns: a developmental model. In D. A. Kramer, & M. J. Bopp (Eds.). *Transformation in clinical and developmental psychology* (pp. 210–233). New York: Springer-Verlag.

Kramer, D. A. (1990a). Conceptualizing wisdom: The primacy of affect-cognition relations. In R. J. Sternberg (Ed.). *Wisdom: Its nature, origins, and development* (pp. 279–313). Cambridge: Cambridge University Press.

Kramer, D. A. (1990b). *The measurement of absolute, relativistic, and dialectical thinking*. Unpublished scoring manual, Rutgers University.

Kramer, D. A., & Bacelar, W. T. (1991, August). Growth of wisdom in adulthood. In C. F. Alexander (Organizer). *Qualitative advances in cognition, affect, and consciousness development in adulthood*, at the 99th Meetings of the American Psychological Association, in San Francisco.

Kramer, D. A., & Haviland, J. M. (1989). Affect-cognition relations in adolescent diaries: The case of Vivienne. Unpublished manuscript, Rutgers University, New Brunswick, New Jersey.

Labouvie-Vief, G. (1982). Dynamic development and mature autonomy: A theoretical prologue. *Human development, 25*, 161–196.

Labouvie-Vief, G. (in press). Women's creativity and images of gender. In B. F. Turner & L. Troll (Eds.). *Growing Older Female*. Newbury Park, CA: Sage Publications.

Levinson, D. J. (1978). *The seasons of a man's life*. New York: Ballantine Books.

Miller, A. (1981). *Prisoners of childhood: The drama of the gifted child and the search for the true self*. New York: Basic Books.

Naisbitt, J. (1982). *Megatrends*. New York: Warner Books.

Pascual-Leone, J. (1983). Growing into human maturity: Toward a metasubjective theory of adult stages. In P. B. Baltes & O. Brim (Eds.). *Life-span development and behavior* (Vol. 5, pp. 117–156). New York: Academic Press.

Plato (1982). The myth of the cave. In P. L. McKee (Ed.). *Philosophical foundations of gerontology* (pp. 42–53). New York: The Human Sciences Press. (Reprinted from *Republic: VII*, P. Shorey [Trans.]. Cambridge, MA: Harvard University Press, 1953).

Schuster, M., & Van Dyne, S. (1984). Placing women in the liberal arts: Stages of curriculum transformation. *Harvard educational review, 54*, 413–428.

Starhawk (1982). *Dreaming the dark: Magic, sex, and politics*. Boston: Beacon Press.

Talbot, M. (1991). *The holographic universe*. New York: HarperCollins Publishers.

Wilber, K. (1980). *The atman project: A transpersonal view of human development*. Wheaton, IL: Theosophical Publishing House.

Wilber, K. (Ed.). (1984). *Quantum questions: Mystical writings of the world's great physicists*. Boston, MA: New Science Library.

Winegar, L. T., Renninger, K. A., & Valsiner, J. (1989). Dependent-independence in adult-child relationships. In D. A. Kramer & M. J. Bopp (Eds.). *Transformation in clinical and developmental psychology* (pp. 157–168). New York: Springer-Verlag.

4

Models of Collaboration and Adult Reasoning

Diane M. Lee

INTRODUCTION

The saying "Two heads are better than one" is strikingly relevant to this era. We live in the Information Age. We've witnessed increased specialization in the professions largely because what is deemed necessary knowledge changes so rapidly and is so immense that a single person is unable to keep up with it, let alone master it. Furthermore, we pose "indivisible" problems, that is, problems so big that no single person or organization can solve them (Aldrich, 1976). The problem of homeless persons is a current example. To meet the complex problems and challenges of our times, persons are working together in collaborative relationships. The purpose of this chapter is to examine two distinct models of collaboration using formal and postformal Piagetian thought. The collaborative efforts of two pairs of elementary school teachers and scientists working together as part of the ongoing mission of the Elementary Science Integration Project (ESIP) will be included to illustrate the collaborative models.

A major premise underlying this chapter is that subject-matter expertise or the presence of a specific set of skills alone cannot explain the models of collaboration that arise when persons work together. It is argued here that problem identification and styles of interrelating should be considered when examining models of collaboration. Current descriptions of adult reasoning emphasize the importance of problem finding and subjectivity in adult thought (Arlin, 1984, 1990; Sinnott, 1984, 1989, 1993; Sinnott & Cavanaugh, 1991).

ADULT REASONING: FORMAL AND POSTFORMAL OPERATIONS

Piaget's definition of formal operational thought and subsequent work by others on postformal thought offer a useful framework for studying the thinking, deliberations, problem finding, problem solving, decision making, and negotiations that occur as professionals work together.

In Piaget's definition of formal operational thought, three abilities enable thinkers to engage in scientific thinking. Formal operational thinkers can create a reversal in the relationship between reality and possibility, they can think about the nature of thinking, and they can generate abstract hypotheses and test those hypotheses by manipulating and isolating a crucial set of variables. That is, they can engage in hypothetico-deductive thought. Formal operational thinkers are capable of competent problem solving when problems are well structured.

Well-structured problems are usefully thought of as puzzles (Churchman, 1971). They are problems that have a single correct solution that can be found by applying a fixed set of rules in a logical way. The parameters of the problem are well defined or can be generated with certainty. Subjectivity is not considered relevant and is not included in the problem space.

Most likely, the problems adults encounter are not this simple, however. Many of life's everyday problems are ill structured. Ill-structured problems are identified as having multiple causes and thus require multiple solutions. There is no quick fix, no single simple solution. In dealing with such ill-structured or "wicked problems" (Churchman, 1971, p. 144), multiple perspectives and conflicting notions about what is true are to be taken into account. Thus, contradictory information enters the problem space, and disparate voices must be reconciled. Consensus, tenable solutions, and best fits are sought and enacted. Not surprisingly, with ill-structured problems priority is given to questions and problem finding as well as in arriving at the best solution(s).

Unlike well-structured problems, ill-structured problems allow for subjectivity. Persons dealing with an ill-structured problem must be aware of their own perspective and the limits of their own knowing, while being simultaneously aware of the perspectives of all others involved. Thus self-referential knowledge as well as knowledge of others comes into play as persons solving ill-structured problems set about their work.

Lastly, ill-structured problems are contextual. Each situation has certain idiosyncratic variables demanding specialized attention. What works in one situation, at one point in time, with one group, may not necessarily work in every seemingly related situation. Therefore, knowledge is seen not as fixed and static but rather as relativistic and dynamic. Consequently, working with ill-structured problems is a recursive process wherein thoughts and actions are continually monitored, evaluated, and revisited over a sustained period of time.

With ill-structured problems the limitations of formal thought are realized and characteristics of postformal reasoning are required (Lee, 1989, 1991; Sinnott,

1984, 1989, 1993). Piaget's characterization of formal operational thought and Sinnott's characterization of postformal relativistic operations are used here to study models of collaboration as illustrated by the interactions of teachers and scientists working together.

In the next section, styles of collaboration defined by these stages of adult reasoning are discussed. Descriptions of two specific pairs of teacher-scientist collaborations will follow, as they exemplify collaborative efforts in cases wherein the task was posed as a well-structured or an ill-structured problem.

COLLABORATION: CONSULTANCIES AND COLLEGIAL PARTNERSHIPS

Collaboration has become a buzzword of the 1990s. Unfortunately, it is a term that is "often carelessly used and occasionally misapplied" (Friend & Cook, 1992, p. 4). The presence of many and quite varied definitions of collaboration in the literature offers at least one viable explanation for this situation.

Collaboration is used to describe a wide variety of relationships. At one extreme, collaboration is synonymous with concepts such as consultation and teams (Idol, Paolucci-Whitcomb & Nevin, 1986; West, 1990). Collaboration as consultation is "a voluntary process in which one professional assists another to address a problem concerning a third party" (Friend & Cook, 1992, p. 17).

The notion of one professional assisting another suggests that the persons involved have different areas and/or levels of expertise. Recognizing this, one party will typically call upon the other for assistance. The relationship is hierarchical. In school-based efforts, such collaborations are typically one-shot deals that fit the pattern of a guest lecturer or what Ponticell calls "quick fix inservice workshops" and "pep talks" (1990, p. 152). Weinstein (in Lieberman, Weinstein & Trubowitz, 1990, p. 167) compares such efforts to "small tasks like worksheets in the classroom." They are short-lived, voluntary attempts to solve a specific, well-defined, and finite problem. These kinds of collaborative consultations work when formal operational thought is sufficient for solving the problem, that is, when the collaborators work together to solve a well-structured problem.

At the other extreme, however, problems posed as ill-structured require postformal relativistic thought. In these instances collaboration is a cooperative, ongoing, voluntary process involving a partnership among persons having common agendas. Partners work together, sharing power, decision making, responsibility, and status. They pool their resources and share expertise in order to build consensus and community as they work toward a common goal (cf. Friend & Cook, 1992; Ponticell, 1990; Preston, 1990; Schwartz, 1990). As emphasized by Friend and Cook (1992, p. 5), such collaboration is a style of direct interaction and thus reflects the nature of the interpersonal relationship occurring during the collaboration as well as the overall process.

In regard to the prominence of the interpersonal in such collaborative partnerships, the Charleston Faculty Practice Conference Group (1986) has high-lighted the development of collegiality among partners in collaborations of this type. Collegiality, they noted, involves "the sharing of one's innermost core identity . . . as well as the sharing of responsibility and authority" (p. 30). They quote Styles (1982, p. 143) in describing collegiality as "a spiritual brotherhood or sisterhood."

Collaboration defined this way demands interpersonal and intrapersonal know-ing; this is the subjectivity controlled for in the hypothetico-deductive logic underlying formal operations but central within postformal reasoning. Within collegial relationships partners must accept themselves and others, they must be honest and respectful, and they must be willing to argue for what they believe is essential while listening carefully to the other as negotiations progress. Dif-ferences among persons are recognized and valued as new meanings are con-structed through the collaborative experience. Postformal thought should be adaptive in these collaborations where social and emotional components are evident, because it is believed to ease communication and to encourage greater cognitive flexibility and creativity (Sinnott, 1984, 1993).

Thus, part of the collaborative process in collegial partnerships involves cre-ating a balance between unity within the group and individuals' autonomy (Wheeler & Chinn, 1984). This can be achieved only within a frame of trust and interdependence. Partners in collaborations of this sort weigh their own agendas against the common good. The power of the whole lies within the power of the collective (Wheeler & Chinn, 1984) underscoring the choice of commit-ment and responsibility within a relativistic world (Perry, 1968).

To summarize, formal operational thought characterizes the reasoning required in consultancy models of collaboration. Postformal reasoning best explains prob-lem solving when subjectivity enters the problem space, multiple perspectives are involved, contradictions arise, and consensus must be achieved. This form of reasoning is evident in collegial partnerships.

EXAMPLES OF COLLABORATION: CONSULTATION AND PARTNERSHIP

Descriptions of the collaborative efforts of the two pairs of teachers and scientists are based on responses to interviews, questionnaires, and in some cases observations, as well as on personal reflections entered in participants' journals.

A Consultation Model

The first example is of a consultation model. In this example, an elementary school teacher, Ms. Webster (names of participants are fictitious), had defined an interest in working with a chemist. A chemist, Dr. Brown, had expressed a willingness to work with a teacher. The teacher had been given the scientist's name as a willing collaborator and was to call Dr. Brown to begin a working dialogue.

The teacher was conducting chemistry experiments with students as part of the regular science curriculum. The experiments were student generated. One child had used popcorn in his project but found himself wondering if the change in popcorn from the hard, inedible kernels to the fluffy white popcorn was a physical change or a chemical change. The teacher promised to help him find the answer. The teacher called the scientist, remarking that she felt a bit awkward in doing so. Indeed, she said she felt silly and somewhat stupid. The scientist immediately put the teacher at ease, saying that it was truly a good question and one that she would have to consider carefully. The scientist then proceeded to think aloud with the teacher and over the phone gave the teacher the correct answer.

The form of collaboration depicted here is a consultation. Both participants had volunteered to participate with ESIP. They both defined the problem as one having a single correct answer that the scientist as expert could solve in conversation with the teacher. They both were working together to answer one child's specific question and, in doing so, to aid all the students' understanding of the related scientific principles. Their shared goal went one step further; they both wanted to encourage participation in scientific inquiry and the acquisition of science concepts among elementary school children and hoped that science would seem more interesting and accessible to the children. They agreed that responses to students' questions would be instrumental in achieving this goal.

The primary focus of the conversation between this teacher and scientist was informational. The conversation was basically a dialogue of report. Tannen (1990) describes report talk as:

talk that is primarily a means to preserve independence and negotiate and maintain status in a hierarchical social order. This is done by exhibiting knowledge and skill, and by holding center stage through verbal performance such as story-telling, joking, or imparting information. (p. 77)

Their dialogue of report was propositional in nature in that children were assumed to be vessels to be filled with the knowledge that can be imparted by another (Bishop & Scudder, 1990, p. 165). In this collaborative consultation, the scientist provided the teacher with information that the teacher was to share with her students. The teacher was the recipient of knowledge; the scientist was the external authority (Belenky et al., 1986).

The teacher described her thinking about working with a scientist and their initial conversation as follows: "I told her that the main thing that I was interested in now was sort of trying to find answers to some of these questions. . . . And I told her I don't have background in chemistry, . . . so to be patient. . . . I have these sort of what I call, 'idiot questions.' . . . I gave her one that day. . . . 'Is popcorn a chemical reaction or is it a physical reaction?' . . . And then she (the scientist) said, 'I'll have to think about that.' And then she said, 'Now wait a minute, no I don't. It's definitely a physical change. That's still corn. All that's happened here is that there's been a release of water.' ''

The teacher continued to describe the scientist's explanation and ended by saying, ''And she made it so simple, and there it was, and it was straightforward, and I understood it.'' Later, the teacher added, ''She had to think about it for a second, so that made me feel good.''

The teacher was clear about the way the scientist was able to help her. ''She gave me the answer. I promised [the child] I'd get the answer for him and I did.'' She was less sure about how she might give something back to the scientist. ''I don't know yet that I'm going to be able to do something to help her. . . . I still don't have a feel for what she needs or what I can do for her.'' While reciprocity was important to this teacher, she felt that the exchange thus far was one-way.

The scientist, too, described their dialogue in terms consonant with a consultation model. ''I was a resource for her (the teacher). I was able to answer her question, but we really haven't gone beyond that point yet.''

They both speak of the possibility of working together more in the future. Indeed, the teacher did speak of her plans to call on Dr. Brown when her class begins a unit on crystals. Nevertheless, at this point in time, their working relationship is consonant with a consultation model wherein one professional willingly assists another to address a problem concerning a third party (Friend & Cook, 1992, p. 17).

A Partnership Model

For a partnership model, I will describe a teacher and scientist who have been collaborating for months, beginning shortly after the school year began. The teacher was responsible for a fourth grade class. The scientist, although primarily a research scientist, also has frequent contact with children at her field site as an environmental educator. They, like the pair in the consultation model, volunteered to be in the project and began their relationship over the phone when the teacher called the scientist. During their conversation the teacher posed the problem as, ''What ought to be taught?'' This is an ill-structured problem, and they addressed it as such.

The scientist met with the teacher and looked over the entire fourth grade curriculum, not just the science curriculum prescribed by the school district. They met on several other occasions and jointly planned ways to integrate an ecological perspective throughout the curriculum. The scientist has visited the class and worked with the children. The children and teacher have taken trips to the scientist's ''lab'' (in this case, a site located on the Chesapeake Bay). Reciprocity is not problematic in this collaboration. ''We share,'' the teacher noted. They each gave, and they each reported receiving from the other. In other words, the benefits have been mutual; and, as suggested in applications of chaos theory (Sinnott, in press), the importance of each person's contribution during the process of information exchange was exhibited in their actions and attitudes.

In keeping with this spirit of mutuality, they also report friendly negotiations characterized by give and take. They respect one another "as professionals, and as persons." They realized that they could go about their shared goals many ways; and they decided on the best activities for that specific point in time, oftentimes with the children. Curricular adjustments were made as necessary, and in their refusal to adhere to one set of methods or content, they "courted chaos" (Sinnott, 1993). Both parties were constantly monitoring and evaluating their cooperative efforts.

The conversations of this teacher and scientist clearly involved a dialogue of report, in that information was shared and at times one was the expert and at other times the other was the expert. The scientist, Dr. McKay, observed, "I was able to use a lot of the scientific terms and Dee (the teacher) was able to translate my words into language the children understood. . . . We're a team." Thus, together they created a common pedagogical language.

Theirs was a conversation that could also be characterized as a language of rapport. Rapport talk involves conversation that uses language as "a way of establishing connections and negotiating relationships" (Tannen, 1990, p. 77). In rapport talk, "Emphasis is placed on displaying similarities and matching experiences" (p. 77). This theme is found in the conversations of this pair. For example, Dr. McKay noted, "We found common ground in our concern for the environment and for children. . . . We thought alike and cared about the same things . . . we care for each other." Their conversations went even further, however, as they developed collegiality. "We are soul mates," said the teacher, Ms. Rush. "We clicked immediately. . . . We talked on the phone for over an hour before we even met."

This pair used a language that calls for a changed way of being. Bishop and Scudder call this evocative language (1990, pp. 161–162). In this case, both the teacher and the scientist found that they shared roles, that is, they found themselves being both teacher and scientist. As they worked with one another, each consistently conveyed that the other was an important and competent person with something to offer the collaboration, the students, and the field in general. Together, both professionals were transformed. Ms. Rush noted, "We are able to come up with so many ways for looking at the curriculum. I'm a better teacher than I was before I met Lisa (the scientist)." Similarly, Dr. McKay commented, "I've become even more excited about what I do and even about who I am. I love working with Dee. It's fun, it's meaningful, and it's a step toward creating a whole new generation of people who will carry on our concerns for our world." Meaning was constructed by these women as each woman perceived herself as a creator of knowledge, expressed value of her objective and subjective knowing, and perceived her knowing as contextual (Belenky et al., 1986).

These partners in collaboration also used what Bishop and Scudder (1990, pp. 162–165) call expressive language, that is, language that conveys attunement to the world. Expressive language includes persons' feelings and moral appro-bations toward the world, toward someone or something. Throughout their con-versations, the teacher and the scientist spoke of their commitment to "developing an ecological concern" among the students. They were interested in exploring the environment with children in a way that called for what the scientist described "moral action." They wanted the children to learn about the relations of living organisms to one another and to themselves. They went beyond the mere sharing of information to create an agenda for action that was grounded in knowledge and moral decision making.

Using propositional, evocative, and expressive language together in dialogue is referred to as integral language (Bishop & Scudder, 1990, pp. 166–167). This is the language that underlies collaborative partnerships with persons displaying postformal reasoning. Thus the conversations of these partners includes personal as well as technical knowledge. Determining what should be taught is an ongoing debate to be considered and reconsidered. Both the teacher and scientist recognize and realize the possibilities inherent in their combined efforts. Together they are contributing to a living, dynamic way of being in classrooms.

The women in this partnership have formed a style of interaction in which each person is equally valued, where tasks may be divided along the lines of their individual strengths and areas of expertise, and yet where there is equal participation in decision making. They generously pool resources as they work toward common goals. Multiple perspectives require ongoing negotiations, which they both describe as "friendly and respectful." Their collaboration is charac-terized by postformal reasoning.

SUMMARY

Piaget's stage of formal operations and Sinnott's stage of postformal operations provided a useful framework for describing two distinct models of collaboration. Formal operational thought was sufficient to address the limited, well-structured problem posed in the consultancy model. Postformal thought was required to address the ill-structured problem posed in the collegial partnership model. In both models, however, competence involves recognition of the limitations of one's knowing and a willingness to work with others for a common good.

A consultancy model was considered a voluntary process where one profes-sional assisted another in addressing a problem concerning a third party. The relationship is hierarchical; one individual is perceived to have expert knowledge and as being able to provide insights and/or answers needed by the other in order to solve the problem the consultee could not solve alone. The dialogue between persons is primarily "report talk" (Tannen, 1990, p. 77) using propositional language. Nevertheless, there is expressed commonality of purpose, which seems to bring persons together in a respectful and cordial way.

A collegial partnership was considered as a style of interaction involving coequals engaged in shared decision making as they worked toward common goals. In this form of collaboration partners used integral language, that is, a form of speaking that unites the technical, transformative, and moral into a common language "articulating all aspects of human being and becoming" (Bishop & Scudder, 1990, p. 167). Partners are open to innovation, aware of possibilities, and not afraid to engage the uncertainties that are sure to arise when problems are posed as ill-structured and subjectivity is allowed to enter the problem space.

The call to collaborate is not likely to diminish. The complexities of modern life are nudging us toward more interdependence. The suggestion here is that postformal theories provide a useful frame for teasing out the models of collaboration that evolve as persons work together.

NOTE

This work is based upon work supported in part by The National Science Foundation under grant number TPE-8955187. Any opinions, findings, and conclusions or recommendations expressed in this material are those of the author and do not necessarily reflect the views of the National Science Foundation.

REFERENCES

Aldrich, H. (1976). Resource dependence and interorganizational relations. *Administration and Society*, *7(4)*, 419–454.

Arlin, P. K. (1984). Adolescent and adult thought: A structural interpretation. In M. L. Commons, F. A. Richards & C. Armon (Eds.). *Beyond formal operations: Late adolescent and adult cognitive development* (pp. 258–271). New York: Praeger.

Arlin, P. K. (1990). Wisdom: The art of problem finding. In R. J. Sternberg (Ed.). *Wisdom: Its nature, origins, and development* (pp. 230–243). New York: Cambridge University Press.

Belenky, M. F., Clinchy, B. M., Goldberger, N. R., & Tarule, J. M. (1986). *Women's ways of knowing*. New York: Basic Books.

Bishop, A. H. & Scudder, J. R., Jr. (1990). *The practical, moral, and personal sense of nursing: A phenomenological philosophy of practice*. Albany, NY: State University of New York Press.

Charleston Faculty Practice Conference Group. (1986). Nursing faculty collaboration viewed through feminist process. *Advances in Nursing Science*, *8(2)*, 29–38.

Churchman, C. W. (1971). *The design of inquiring systems: Basic concepts of systems and organizations*. New York: Basic Books.

Friend, M. & Cook, L. (1992). *Interaction: Collaboration skills for school professionals*. New York: Longman.

Idol, L., Paolucci-Whitcomb, P. & Nevin, A. (1986). *Collaborative consultation*. Rockville, MD: Aspen.

Lee, D. M. (1989). Everyday problem solving: Implications for education. In J. D. Sinnott (Ed.). *Everyday problem solving: Theory and applications* (pp. 251–265). New York: Praeger.

Lee, D. M. (1991). Relativistic operations: A framework for conceptualizing teachers' everyday problem solving. In J. D. Sinnott & J. C. Cavanaugh (Eds.). *Bridging paradigms: Positive development in adulthood and cognitive aging* (pp. 73–86). New York: Praeger.

Lieberman, A., Weinstein, R. & Trubowitz, S. (1990). School and university collaboration. In H. Schwartz (Ed.). *Collaboration: Building common agendas* (pp. 163–167). Teacher Education Monograph No. 10. Washington, DC: ERIC Clearinghouse on Teacher Education.

Perry, W. G. (1968). *Forms of intellectual and ethical development in the college years.* New York: Holt, Rinehart and Winston.

Ponticell, J. A. (1990). School-university collaboration: Do we share a common language and vision? In H. Schwartz (Ed.). *Collaboration: Building common agendas* (pp. 150–154). Teacher Education Monograph No. 10. Washington, DC: ERIC Clearinghouse on Teacher Education.

Preston, F. W. (1990). Implementation strategies: Policies and procedures. In H. Schwartz (Ed.). *Collaboration: Building common agendas* (pp. 49–53). Teacher Education Monograph No. 10. Washington, DC: ERIC Clearinghouse on Teacher Education.

Schwartz, H. (1990). *Collaboration: Building common agendas.* Teacher Education Monograph No. 10. Washington, DC: ERIC Clearinghouse on Teacher Education.

Sinnott, J. D. (1984). Postformal reasoning: The relativistic stage. In M. Commons, F. Richards & C. Armon (Eds.). *Beyond formal operations: Late adolescent and adult cognitive development* (pp. 298–325). New York: Praeger.

Sinnott, J. D. (Ed.). (1989). *Everyday problem solving: Theory and application.* New York: Praeger.

Sinnott, J. D. (1993). Teaching in a chaotic new physics world: Teaching as a dialogue with reality. In P. Kahaney, J. Janangelo & L. A. M. Perry (Eds.). *Theoretical and critical perspectives on teacher change.* Norwood, NJ: Ablex Press.

Sinnott, J. D. & Cavanaugh, J. (Eds.). (1991). *Bridging Paradigms: Positive development in adulthood and cognitive aging.* New York: Praeger.

Styles, M. M. (1982). *On nursing: Toward a new endowment.* St. Louis: Mosby.

Tannen, D. (1990). *You just don't understand: Women and men in conversation.* New York: Ballantine Books.

West, J. F. (1990). Educational collaboration in the restructuring of schools. *Journal of Educational and Psychological Consultation, 1(1),* 23–40.

Wheeler, C. E. & Chinn, P. L. (1984). *Peace and power: A handbook of feminist process.* New York: Margaretdaughters.

5

Expanding the Circle of Caring:
From Local to Global

John A. Meacham and Cynthia Boyd

That adults learn and continue to learn throughout the life course to care for others is quite apparent. Indeed, the facts of our caring for others through close friendships, marriage, parenthood, the assumption of civic and social responsibilities, and grandparenthood so permeate adulthood and aging that they are often regarded as merely the backdrop against which the discrete and defining acts of adult lives are played. To care for others is more than to be interested; it is to involve oneself personally in what affects others and to do so for reasons of duty and one's sense of right and wrong.

To consider the general topic of how adults learn to care, as opposed to the specific topics of how adults care in each of many contexts such as marriage and parenthood, is made challenging by the vast differences across those diverse contexts in the breadth of caring. For some individuals, the circle of caring extends to and encloses family and close friends; for other individuals, the circle encloses civic, ethnic, and religious groups, neighborhoods, genders, schools, sports teams, and workplaces; for others, the circle encloses nationalities, religious groups, races, humanity, environments, and other species. How can we describe and understand how individuals learn to expand their circles of caring, from local to global, from adolescence through adulthood and aging?

FOUR FORMS OF CARING

The organization of this chapter follows that recommended by Wohlwill (1973) for understanding developmental changes in adulthood and aging: first, describe the phenomenon; next, understand the process that underlies the phenomenon; and finally, consider whether intervention in the process is advisable and possible. The framework that will be employed to describe the forms of caring in adult-

Figure 1
A Framework for Describing Forms of Caring

```
                Cumulative                  Simple


Disjunctive (3)  A ---> AB ---> ABC   (1)  A ---> B ---> C


Conjunctive (4)  A ---> A'B ---> A'B'C (2a)  A ---> a'B ---> a'b'C

                                      (2b)  A ---> Ab' ---> Ab'c'
```

hood and aging is one that has been described more fully elsewhere (Meacham, 1980), having been derived from earlier work by Van den Daele (1969) and Flavell (1972). The letters A, B, C, and so on are taken to represent various social and psychological characteristics, with development proceeding through time from left to right.

Sequences of characteristics can be described as *simple* or cumulative, depending on whether the individual is considered to display only one or several characteristics at a given point in time. For example, a person might be single or married, but not both at the same time (simple). When change occurs, it is a matter of substitution of a new characteristic for an old one. A simple sequence can be represented by A→ B→ C. On the other hand, a person might at one and the same point in life know how to play bridge, chess, and golf (cumulative). Change is a matter of characteristics being added to (or subtracted from) the set. A cumulative sequence can be represented by A→ AB→ ABC. In addition to simple or cumulative, sequences of characteristics can be described, orthogonally, as *disjunctive*, when the relationship between characteristics is said to be one of separateness or lack of overlap (both sequences already mentioned), or *conjunctive*, when some of the earlier characteristics become included within or subordinate to later ones, as in Piaget's and Freud's theories (see Meacham, 1980, or Van den Daele, 1969, for details).

The four cells generated by the framework of simple and cumulative, disjunctive and conjunctive represent contrasting forms in the expansion of circles of caring. Consider the diversity of relationships that might exist between two people. Infatuation with the other, typical of an immature or teenage love, and captured in the "I want you, I need you" lyrics of popular music, is represented by the simple and disjunctive sequence of cell 1 in Figure 1. The focus is upon one's own identity, needs, and desires, rather than upon what the other's needs and desires might be; the other is understood merely as a reflection of oneself, rather than in terms of who he or she might really be or become. "You don't know me," responds the other, and the infatuation quickly fades, unless both individuals are equally blind to the reality of the other's needs. Although on the surface there might appear to be a shift from one object of caring to the next (to B and to C), in fact the underlying reality is that to enter into and maintain a caring relationship with any other is too threatening to one's own identity (A), so that movement through the sequence is unlikely.

The relationship represented by the simple and conjunctive sequence (cell 2) maintains the focus upon only one person's identity, needs, and desires. The relationship of conjunction, inclusion, or subordination, however, appears slightly different when viewed from the perspective of either the subordinate or the dominant partner. In the former case (2a), the identity and the possibilities for becoming of one partner in the relationship are sacrificed for the sake of maintaining the relationship ($A \rightarrow a'B \rightarrow a'b'C$). In the latter case (2b), the identity, needs, and desires of the dominant partner are maintained ($A \rightarrow Ab' \rightarrow Ab'c'$), and the circle of caring is expanded to include others when their well-being is instrumental in satisfying the needs and desires of the primary individual. Such a relationship has the potential to be abusive and destructive, with one person intent on controlling another, who may not be able to escape from the relationship. Despite the slight differences in notation from 2a to 2b, the form of the caring relationship is equivalent, that is, one of simple conjunction.

Cell 3 represents the cumulative and disjunctive relationship in which both individuals have satisfactorily defined themselves apart from the other, yet in which there is an understanding, acceptance of, and respect for, or at least a toleration of, the other. Both individuals stand equally within the circle of caring, as long as resources are sufficient to provide for both. Divorce is possible, but would not be seen as a significant loss to one's identity; the two would remain friends.

In cell 4 the relationship is cumulative and conjunctive. The commitment, devotion, and caring for the other that are unique to this cell do not stem from self-interest. Rather, because each individual is defined in terms of the other, the dichotomy of self-interest and other-interest is replaced by a commitment to enriching each other's lives, to helping the other to become all that he or she might be. Of course, it is likely that any relationship between two people includes aspects during the course of a day or week that might be typical of each of the four cells; still, one of these relationships is likely to be more typical than the other three.

FAILURE TO EXPAND THE CIRCLE OF CARING

In 1842, the Philadelphia County Board of School Controllers ordered that the Protestant King James version of the Bible be used as a reading text in the public schools (Feldberg, 1980). The controllers were reluctant to grant the same status to the Catholic Douay Bible, both because of prejudice against Catholics and the belief that the Pope and his priests would overthrow the American way of life and because of fear that angry Protestant voters would throw them out of office. As a compromise, Catholic children were permitted to leave the classroom while the Protestant Bible was read. This compromise was not satisfactory, because the Catholic Bible was still prohibited and because teachers recognized that children excused from class were not learning to read and write.

In 1844 Louisa Bedford, a Protestant teacher in the Irish Kensington district of Philadelphia, approached Hugh Clark, an Irish politician and one of the School Controllers, as he was making his weekly visit to the public schools. She expressed her dissatisfaction with the compromise, and he then suggested that she could suspend all Bible reading in her classes until the School Controllers developed a better policy. It was Henry Moore, a Methodist minister, who surprised his congregation with the news "that Clark had forced Miss Bedford against her will to 'kick the Bible out of her classroom' " (Feldberg, 1980, p. 17). This news spread rapidly. More than three thousand "nativists" gathered at a rally were reminded by political leaders that "This was and always will be a Protestant country" (Feldberg, 1980, p. 17). Encouraged, the leaders planned the next rally to be held in the Kensington neighborhood itself. Heckling, pushing, and shoving were followed by gunfire and a panic in which both Protestants and Irish Catholics were killed. Only after two hours of heavy fighting did the sheriff and his deputies arrive. The following day, the Protestants returned to Kensington, from which many of the Irish had now fled, and after a brief gunfight set fire to many of the buildings and to the Catholic church. Subsequently the Protestants returned to downtown Philadelphia and, ignoring the pleas of the mayor, burned a second Catholic church; and the city was placed under martial law for a week by the Governor of Pennsylvania.

The failure of caring shown by the adults in this historical account is like that in many contemporary conflicts in our society and around the world, in being based not only in religious prejudice but also in ethnic and class biases. The Protestant nativists saw themselves as the only "real" Americans and believed that the Catholics would maintain their ties to Ireland and never become loyal Americans. The Irish, who had been fighting against Protestant English rulers for close to 200 years, tended to live in the same neighborhoods and to socialize in their own taverns, churches, and political clubs. For the Protestants, the education of their children with the King James Bible was essential for the continued integrity of their identity and their community; for the Catholics, the education of their children with the King James Bible was a threat to the integrity of their identity and community.

The relationship of caring captured by this historical account is simple and disjunctive (cell 1). That is, for both Protestants and Catholics the choices appeared to be either to strive to maintain one's own cultural identity and community through intervention in the other's community or to abandon entirely one's own cultural identity and community. Each group feared or recognized as unworkable two other possible relationships of caring. First, either group might over time have become subordinated to and assimilated within the culture of the other. In this simple and conjunctive relationship (cell 2), the dominant group cares for the subordinate group only when it is in its interest to do so, for example, to prevent rioting or to assuage guilt. The cumulative and disjunctive relationship of caring (cell 3) is workable only when there are adequate resources to care for both parties simultaneously. This was not the case, as it was not possible to read both Bibles in the same school (consider the difficulties when three or more religions are represented in the same community). The efforts of all the educational, religious, and political leaders were to reduce the relationship of caring to the simple and disjunctive (cell 1).

Today both Catholics and Protestants live together in Philadelphia, so we can ask how the circle of caring might have been expanded in 1844 and how it has been expanded since that time. In addition to insisting on the separation of church and state provided for by the First Amendment to the Constitution of the United States, the educational, religious, and political leaders should have worked together toward better communication, should have shown greater sensitivity and tolerance, should have been prepared to sacrifice for the sake of the larger community, and should have worked to redefine their own group's identity and the sense of what the larger community could become, so that all religious and cultural groups could be welcomed with appropriate respect for diverse traditions. In general terms, there was a failure among the adults in Philadelphia in 1844 to articulate the potential of the cumulative, conjunctive relationship of caring (cell 4).

Yet merely because we now find it possible to articulate what should have been done in another historical era does not mean that we have the historical or developmental maturity to act in an appropriately caring manner in a similar context. In August of 1983, a group of black sixth-graders from Flatbush (New York City) on a graduation picnic outing to Staten Island was attacked by a group of white teenagers who threw rocks and bottles, shouted racial epithets, and broke the windows of the visitors' school bus (Blum, 1983/1988). The typical interpretation of the incident is captured in this comment by one of the sixth-graders: "They grow up in that neighborhood hating people who are strange to them. . . . Their parents taught them to hate people who are different, and now it's too late. Their parents are to blame" (Blum, 1983/1988, p. 34).

Yet here are the comments of several Staten Island parents who were interviewed following this contemporary racial incident: "We got a neighborhood to protect." "These are good kids. They're not troublemakers. They're like I was when I was growing up in this neighborhood. They're just trying to make sure the neighborhood stays the kind of place where they'll want to raise their kids someday" (Blum, 1983/1988, p. 34). "It isn't that we're prejudiced. People out here just work hard. We don't want all this destroyed. . . . We're not racists" (Blum, 1983/1988, p. 35). From the perspective of the parents of the teenagers who carried out the attack, the primary motivation was one of identification with the community and an interest in protecting it, both now and in the future. The perspective on caring, as in the Philadelphia Native American Riots of 1844, is simple and disjunctive (cell 1). For the adults in Staten Island the choices appeared to be either to care for the group with which one identifies or to abandon entirely one's own cultural identity and community.

GENDER IDENTITY AND INTERPERSONAL RELATIONSHIPS

These accounts of incidents of ethnic and racial conflict are evidence of the interpenetration of issues of caring, on the one hand, with issues of identity and community, on the other. At the extremes, one form of caring is to perceive caring for self and caring for others as an either-or proposition (cell 1); another form is to perceive caring for self and caring for others as mutually enriching (cell 4). This same interpenetration of caring, identity, and community is apparent when we consider close interpersonal relationships of caring in adulthood and aging, such as learning to live with an adult partner, rearing children, assisting teenage children to become responsible adults, and relating to one's spouse as a person. How adults engage in these caring relationships is strongly influenced by their gender-based identities (Sinnott, 1986) and by their immersion within and commitment to gender-based communities of peers. There are diverse views regarding the origin of gender-associated styles of caring.

The either-or opposition of self and other implicit in the simple, disjunctive form of caring (cell 1) may be illustrated by the approach of object relations theorists to explaining the existence of gender-associated styles of caring in terms of children's primary relationship with their mothers. Chodorow (1978) suggested that girls and boys construct their self-concepts through identifying with or rejecting their mothers. Girls, who are more similar physically to their mothers, develop their identities through a strong attachment to their mothers. Through this experience, they learn to relate to others with a flexible self-other boundary that permits intense closeness and empathy.

Boys, on the other hand, soon realize that they are different from their mothers. In order to build their identities, they must define their masculinity in terms of differentness and separateness, resulting in a less flexible self-other orientation. These developmental differences are expressed in adulthood in terms of gender-associated styles of caring: Females are better able to empathize with others while males tend to deny interpersonal relations or dependence. Thus, consistent with the simple, disjunctive form of caring (cell 1), object relations theory suggests that children may care for and identify with only the mother (A) or the father (B). There is no acceptable combination of the two, nor is it appropriate in object relations theory for a son to identify with his mother or a daughter with her father.

Such configurations imply that to be male in our culture means not to be female and, furthermore, not only that the male and female roles are incompatible in one individual but also that the only normative and natural mode of caring is through heterosexual relationships. It is not possible, within the perspective of object relations theory, to provide a sympathetic understanding of such phenomena of caring as homosexuality, bisexuality, empathic males, or caring females raised by a single male parent. In assuming a biological essence at the heart of the mother-child relationship and neglecting diverse contextual factors, object relations theory oversimplifies issues of identity and caring.

While object relations theory holds that gender-associated styles are inevitable and restricted by biological factors, another approach to identity and caring focuses on the role of society in creating gender differences. Miller (1986) argues that qualities typically characterized as feminine, such as empathy and dependence, are simply those that have been devalued in male-dominated societies and subsequently ascribed to women as the objectified others. Traditionally, success has been defined by qualities characterized as male, such as emotional independence. Consequently, women often believe that the route to respect is through identification with those male qualities, and therefore they give less emphasis to the development of their own values.

To subordinate the development of one's own values and qualities in favor of those that are imposed by or reinforced by society is consistent with the simple, conjunctive model (cell 2a). In this case, let A stand for women's true qualities and let B represent the dominant societal values. For women to be considered fully developed, they must suppress their emotional needs and present themselves as congruent with the male model of maturity (A→ a'B). Downing and Roush (1985) characterize this subordination of female qualities as passive acceptance. This simple, conjunctive form of caring also describes a relationship that is imbalanced in favor of caring for the other (B) over caring for oneself (a'). Until women move from this stage to a more assertive, self-valuing stance, through the recognition that women, too, can be valuable, they and other victims of the restrictive male value system will continue to suffer from low self-esteem and depression (Miller, 1986).

In these first two approaches to caring, one must necessarily make a choice. In object relations theory (cell 1), one must identify with either a male or female role model based upon one's own gender; and in the second case (cell 2a), one must choose to adopt either the socially accepted set of male values or the less-respected female values. It is clear that both of these approaches to caring are quite limiting, both in conceptualizing male and female qualities in terms of presumed true essences and in demanding that there must be a sacrifice of those essences in order to attain objectives of integrity and respect.

There is, however, a third alternative: androgyny. The androgyny literature claims that masculine and feminine qualities are complementary. As there are obvious advantages and disadvantages to both male and female gender roles, the solution seems to be to value both equally and integrate them within one personality (Bem, 1974). The cumulative, disjunctive model (cell 3) illustrates the androgyny theory, where A and B represent masculinity or femininity (A→ AB).

Although this might appear to be a fair approach to identity and caring, there are resource problems associated with devoting equivalent amounts of attention and energy to all possible objects of care. Minimizing gender differences diverts attention from actual societal inequities between men and women in terms of resources and power (Hare-Mustin & Marecek, 1990). For example, to deemphasize gender differences leads to equal treatment under the law. Though this may encourage gains in women's educational and vocational opportunities, it may also lead to a general discounting of women's special needs. For example, with respect to parental leave, it means that men and women should be granted the same length of time. However, while a man might benefit from only one month of leave time, a woman might require a considerably longer period in order to recuperate physically from childbirth. The concept of androgyny fails to recognize actual biological and social inequalities between men and women, raising fears about exploring these differences and their implications (Hare-Mustin & Marecek, 1990).

With the understanding that we cannot completely ignore gender differences and that inequalities for the most part have been socially constructed phenomena, the challenge has been to reframe our understanding of men's and women's identities and styles of caring. Gilligan (1982) describes the difference between male and female styles of caring as the "contrast between a self defined through separation and a self delineated through connection" (p. 35). When making decisions, women tend to choose "the solution that would be most inclusive of everyone's needs" (p. 38). She argues that women envision growth and development as the process of learning to help others while simultaneously helping oneself.

This model of caring, involving an interpenetration of concern for self and concern for others, requires rejection of the view of individuals as self-contained entities (Sampson, 1987) and adoption of a perspective in which individuals construct and transform their identities primarily through their relationships with others. The form of caring is cumulative and conjunctive (cell 4). Let A stand for the individual, and B and C for expanding circles of interpersonal relationships: close and intimate friendships, children and grandchildren, adult peers who nurture and those who are in need of nurturing, and communities and causes. As one learns to expand the circle of caring to include others, one learns to care for oneself; as one learns to care for oneself, the capacity for empathy and caring is expanded to include others. The individual is not lost within these expanded circles of caring (as in cell 2a), but to the contrary the individual's construction of a more secure and integrated identity is supported through multiple connections of caring with others ($A \rightarrow A'B \rightarrow A'B'C$) (Meacham, 1991a).

CARING FOR OTHER SPECIES AND FOR ENVIRONMENTS

There has been a marked expansion of the circle of caring in recent decades to include more than humans within the circle: prevention of needless suffering in animals and concern for the rights of animals; the protection of endangered plant and animal species; the preservation of habitats and ecosystems and land-scapes, including rocks, streams, and mountains; and a concern for the integrity of the oceans, the atmosphere, and earth's biomass. Certainly these issues as typically presented in the media appear to be following a simple, disjunctive model (cell 1), as first one and then another concern is brought to the public's attention: snail darters, spotted owls, baby seals, dolphins, the rain forest, the ozone layer, and so forth. Let A stand for humans and B and C stand for a variety of non-human concerns. Especially when the issues are characterized in terms of economic growth and jobs for humans versus protection of non-human species and wilderness environments, it must appear to many that to affirm the rights of another species is to abandon the rights of humans (A→ B). Media attention to the actions of environmental radicals, as well as to statements such as Abbey's (1968, p. 20) that he would rather kill a man than a snake, help to promote the interpretation that the choice is either humans or other species.

One criterion for choosing which plant and animal species and habitats to care for and which to abandon is to ask what value these might have for humans. The value of the rain forest is that it contains plants that may have medical uses for humans; the value of wilderness is that it provides "places for man—places big enough for backpackers to lose themselves in and for stressed city dwellers to find themselves" (McKibben, 1989, p. 174); "diversity ensures stability, especially if we err and our monocultures trigger environmental upset" (Rolston, 1989, p. 22). The relationship that humans have with other species is one of stewardship, in which humans are expected to subdue nature, to have dominion over it, and to turn nature to serve human needs (Meacham, 1991b). This developmental model is simple and conjunctive (cell 2b). Let A stand for humans and B for any plant or animal species, so that the developmental progression is for the non-human species to be subordinated to the engine of human desire: Ab'. Given the subordination of nature to humans as masters, then it becomes right for humans to do as they please (Nash, 1989, p. 89). When issues of caring for other species are phrased in terms of balancing continued economic growth against the protection of nature for future generations, the result will in the long run inevitably be a diminution of caring for nature.

Good arguments can be made for caring for each of thousands of species and their habitats, that is, one should strive to care not only for humans but also for snail darters, spotted owls, baby seals, dolphins, and so forth. This developmental model is cumulative and disjunctive (A→ AB→ ABC) (cell 3). Given the se-riousness of the threat to our environment, one is quickly overwhelmed by competing demands for attention and for resources. The relativistic nature of this model provides little guidance in choosing among the competing demands. One possible response to not being able to care for all is to reduce the circle of caring to only one, or even to care for none.

There is considerable searching and dialogue within the environmental move-ment regarding what the basis might be for an environmental ethic (McKibben, 1989; Nash, 1989; Rolston, 1989), for a circle of caring that includes both humans and other species and acknowledges the integrity and the right of each to exist. The developmental model that is being described is, in general terms, cumulative and conjunctive (cell 4). Let A stand for humans and let B and C stand for larger communities that include not only humans but also additional plant and animal species, habitats, and ecosystems. McKibben (1989, p. 172), noting that in grizzly-bear country humans are not the dominant species but merely part of the food chain, asks what it would mean to our way of life "if we began to truly and viscerally think of ourselves as just one species among many?"

McKibben (1989), Nash (1989, chapter 5), and others have elaborated upon the ideas of Albert Schweitzer, John Muir, and others to advance an ethic in which any other species has the right to exist not for the sake of human desires or needs but for its own sake (A'B'C). The contrast between the simple and cumulative conjunctive models (cells 2 and 4) is clear in the words of Leopold (1949, p. viii): "We abuse land because we regard it as a commodity belonging to us. When we see land as a community to which we belong, we may begin to use it with love and respect." The cumulative and conjunctive model is explicit in the United Nations Charter for Nature, adopted by the General Assembly in 1982 but not signed by the United States (see Nash, 1989, p. 179): "Every form of life is unique, warranting respect regardless of its worth to man, and, to accord other organisms such recognition, man must be guided by a moral code of action." And it is from the perspective of the larger community that Abbey (1968, p. 20) was able to reason that the life of a member of an endangered species would be more valuable than the life of a member of a populous species such as our own—that he would rather kill a man than a snake.

PROCESSES OF DEVELOPMENT AND FACILITATION OF CARING

Implicit in the preceding discussion has been that the cumulative, conjunctive form of caring (cell 4) is the most appropriate and developmentally mature, for within this form the extension of caring through expanding circles from close friends to communities and beyond, the enriching and transforming of one's own identity, and the securing of care for oneself are interpenetrating and mutually reinforcing processes. One well-established framework for beginning to understand the development of identity, values, and caring across the life-course is that of Erikson (1963). In Erikson's framework, young adulthood is characterized in part by the development of a strong *local* identification with family, heritage, heroic figures, nationality, and so forth (the fifth crisis, identity versus identity diffusion). Yet by middle adulthood and beyond, many individuals develop a *broader* concern for society as a whole and for the well-being of succeeding generations (not necessarily limited to one's own children) (the seventh crisis, generativity versus stagnation).

Why do some individuals develop this broader concern, while others do not?

Isn't it paradoxical that life-course development should involve the learning in young adulthood of strong local identifications such as ethnicity, nationality, or religious sectarianism that might well have to be undone in later life? Or do the earlier identifications constitute a model, for example, in terms of investment of affect, for the broader caring of later life? For example, should we expect an individual who as an adolescent developed intense loyalty and commitment to the high school football team to be less or more committed, as an older adult, to the well-being of the homeless, of succeeding generations, or of the environment? Do the latter concerns require a disengagement from the earlier commitment to the high school team, or is the process better described as a transformation of the affect as well as of the intellectual commitment? What is the nature of the learning, about oneself, about others, and about the structure of society, that is required in order for this developmental sequence or transformation to take place?

The diversity of failures of caring in adulthood and aging, in such forms as ethnocentrism, racism, child abuse, sexism, heterosexism, religious sectarianism, and speciesism, as well as the diminution of identity and self-worth of individuals trapped in less mature forms of caring, raises the question of whether it is possible to facilitate development from the less mature forms towards the more mature, cumulative, conjunctive form of caring (cell 4). What might be done to facilitate the expansion of the circle of caring, from local to global, in adulthood and aging?

The answer likely depends on how we conceptualize the relationship of conjunction, on which of the other three forms of caring the individual is currently immersed within, and—in the simple, conjunctive form of caring—on whether the individual is in the subordinate (cell 2a) or dominant (2b) position. Nevertheless, it seems clear from the present analysis that intervention cannot consist merely in calling attention to the worth and rights of those who are in need of care. The interpenetration within the cumulative, conjunctive form of caring (cell 4) of issues of caring, on the one hand, with issues of identity and community, on the other, makes clear that any intervention and facilitation of development of caring must focus at least as much on the reconstruction of the individual's own self-identity.

One possible intervention is to mobilize a process of deindividualization (Sampson, 1987), so that individuals learn to view themselves not as isolated, self-contained entities but rather as a reflection of the interpersonal relationships within which they are immersed. In order to facilitate this process and expand the circle of caring, the traditional goals of development must be restructured (Downing & Roush, 1985). Psychology has defined the goals of psychotherapy, as well as the signs of adult maturity, as self-reliance, renunciation of responsibility for others, and emotional independence. These aims are inconsistent with the cumulative, conjunctive form of caring and need to be reformulated to support individuals' needs for relationships and validate the reality of their emotional dependence on others (Hill, 1990; Sinnott, 1991). Although psychotherapy by itself may not effect a paradigmatic, societal change, it can be a part of the transforming of the current societal ideal of the isolated, self-contained individual into an ideal of individuals who become more whole through learning to be involved in and committed to expanding circles of caring for others.

REFERENCES

Abbey, E. (1968). *Desert solitaire: A season in the wilderness.* New York: McGraw-Hill.

Bem, S. L. (1974). Measurement of psychological androgyny. *Journal of Consulting and Clinical Psychology, 42*, 155–162.

Blum, H. (1983). "Bias incident" at Staten Island's Miller Field: A tale of two neighborhoods. *New York Times*, August 3. Also in P. S. Rothenberg (Ed.). *Racism and sexism: An integrated study* (pp. 31–35). New York: St. Martin's Press.

Chodorow, N. (1978). *The reproduction of mothering: Psychoanalysis and the sociology of gender.* Berkeley: University of California Press.

Downing, N. E., and Roush, K. L. (1985). From passive acceptance to active commitment: A model of feminist identity development for women. *The Counseling Psychologist, 13*, 695–709.

Erikson, E. H. (1963). *Childhood and society.* New York: Norton.

Feldberg, M. (1980). *The turbulent era: Riot and disorder in Jacksonian America* (Chapter 1, The Philadelphia Native American riots of 1844: The Kensington phase, pp. 9–23.). New York: Oxford University Press.

Flavell, J. H. (1972). An analysis of cognitive-developmental sequences. *Genetic Psychology Monographs, 86*, 279–350.

Gilligan, C. (1982). *In a different voice.* Cambridge: Harvard University Press.

Hare-Mustin, R., and Marecek, J. (1990). Gender and meaning of difference: Postmodernism and psychology. In R. Hare-Mustin and J. Maracek (Eds.). *Making a difference.* New Haven: Yale University Press.

Hill, M. (1990). On creating a theory of feminist therapy. *Women and Therapy, 9*, 53–65.

Leopold, A. (1949). *A Sand County almanac.* New York: Oxford.

McKibben, B. (1989). *The end of nature.* New York: Random House.

Meacham, J. A. (1980). Formal aspects of theories of development. *Experimental Aging Research, 6*, 475–487.

Meacham, J. A. (1991a). Conflict and cooperation in adulthood: A role for both? In J. D. Sinnott and J. C. Cavanaugh (Eds.). *Bridging paradigms: Positive development in adulthood and cognitive aging* (pp. 87–98). New York: Praeger.

Meacham, J. A. (1991b). The concept of nature: Implications for assessment of competence. In M. Chandler and M. Chapman (Eds.). *Criteria for competence: Controversies in the conceptualization and assessment of children's abilities* (pp. 43–64). Hillsdale, NJ: Lawrence Erlbaum Associates.

Miller, J. B. (1986). *Toward a new psychology of women.* Boston: Beacon Press.

Nash, R. F. (1989). *The rights of nature.* Madison: University of Wisconsin Press.

Rolston, H., III. (1989). *Philosophy gone wild.* Buffalo: Prometheus Books.

Sampson, E. E. (1987). A critical constructionist view of psychology and personhood. In H. J. Stam, T. B. Rogers, and K. J. Gergen (Eds.). *The analysis of psychological theory.* Washington, D.C.: Hemisphere Publishing Corporation.

Sinnott, J. D. (1986). *Sex roles and aging: Theory and research from a systems perspective*. New York: Karger.

Sinnott, J. D. (1991, July). The use of complex thought and resolving intragroup conflicts: A means to conscious adult development. Plenary Address at the Sixth Adult Development Symposium, Suffolk University, Boston, MA.

Van den Daele, L. D. (1969). Qualitative models in developmental analysis. *Developmental Psychology, 1*, 303–310.

Wohlwill, J. F. (1973). *The study of behavioral development*. New York: Academic Press.

6

Learning and Life Experience: The Connection in Adulthood

Sharan B. Merriam

Experience is the best teacher, so the saying goes, but this truism is rarely examined systematically for how learning from life experience actually occurs or for how we might maximize the learning potential inherent in a life experience. Interestingly, the above and other popular maxims having to do with the connection between learning and life experience are rarely applied to children who are presumed to be learning in school. Though many adults also learn in school, such formal education is often viewed as ancillary to the rest of an adult's life where "real" learning takes place. The purposes of this chapter are first to explore how learning and life experience are connected in adulthood and to review what is known about the nature of learning from life experience.

HOW THE CONTEXT OF ADULT LIFE STRUCTURES LEARNING

Learning in adult life is intricately related to the context of adult life. The learning an adult undertakes arises from roles such as parent, spouse, worker, and citizen and their related tasks, which define the person as an adult. This connection between an adult's life situation and learning can be examined from several perspectives. Three such frameworks will be explored here—work and family contexts, life events and transitions, and developmental tasks and social roles.

Work and Family

Work, family, and to a somewhat lesser extent, community and leisure are contexts that structure adult life. Most adults work at least eight hours a day and spend as many hours again tending to family, community responsibilities, and leisure. These contexts, especially those of work and family, have been shown to generate the vast majority of learning needs that adults satisfy through both formal and informal learning.

Finding a job or advancing in a present job have been reported in national surveys as the primary reasons for participating in adult education. In the most recent survey conducted by the National Center for Education Statistics (NCES), 64% of participants indicated job-related reasons for participating in adult education (U.S. Department of Education, 1987). Commenting on this link between work and learning, Cross writes:

People who do not have good jobs are interested in further education to get better jobs, and those who have good jobs would like to advance in them. Women, factory workers, and the poorly educated, for example, are more likely to be pursuing education in order to prepare for new jobs, whereas men, professionals, and college graduates are more likely to be seeking advancement in present jobs. Men are more interested in job-related learning than women are, and young people are far more interested in it than older people are. Interest in job-related goals begins to decline at age 50 and drops off sharply after age 60. (Cross, 1981, p. 91)

NCES figures account for part of the work-related learning that adults are engaged in. As most people know, a great deal of learning also occurs in the workplace itself. The workplace provides the context for much formal, work-related adult education. From on-the-job training to staff development to continuing professional education, the amount of resources put into work-related learning is staggering. One source estimates that training in America is a $210 billion business, only $28 billion less than what is spent for elementary, secondary, and postsecondary education combined (Carnevale, 1986). (For an extended discussion of adult learning in the workplace, see Froman, chapter 11, this volume.)

Though work appears to stimulate the majority of learning in adult life, family-related issues also motivate many adults to participate in adult education. A study that attempted to uncover why adults engage in adult learning experiences found that 56% of the learners were participating because of some work-related concern and that 16% were involved because of a family-related transition such as divorce and becoming a parent (Aslanian & Brickell, 1980). When the nature of the learning itself was separated from specific events that actually "triggered" the learning, it was found that 56% of the triggering events were career-related and 36% were family-related. Leisure (such as learning to play golf "triggered" by a geographical move), art, health, religion, and citizenship also structured learning but to a much lesser extent. A fuller discussion of what motivates adults to seek formal educational experiences such as in higher education can be found in Harriger's chapter in this handbook (chapter 12). Likewise, Sinnott's chapter on facilitating learning in the future addresses how we might maximize the motivations, goals, and experiences that an adult brings to the formal learning situation.

In addition to participating in formal adult education classes and activities, nearly all adults undertake informal, self-directed, personal learning projects designed to address work and family-related learning needs. The original work on learning projects was conducted by Tough, who found that 90% of the adults in his sample were involved in at least one project per year (1971, 1978). The "typical" learner conducted five projects averaging 100 hours per project. "A great many of these learning projects," according to Tough, were "related to the person's job or occupation," and to "managing a home and family" (1978, pp. 33, 35). For example, someone might spend hundreds of hours independently learning a computer software program that might be relevant to a work situation; someone else might read widely on caring for an infant in anticipation of becoming a parent. Dozens of studies replicating Tough's work have found that most adults have learning projects going on, and many of these are related to work and family issues (Merriam & Caffarella, 1991).

Whether one looks at participation in institutionally sponsored programs or at informal, self-designed learning projects, it is clear that much of adult learning is related to work and family. It is also in these two arenas that the majority of life and events and transitions—which present specific stimuli for learning—occur.

Life Events and Transitions

Within the work and family contexts occur any number of anticipated and unanticipated events and transitions that can result in learning. Though work and family are the major arenas of adult life, it is the events that take place within those arenas that structure adult life. Indeed, life events are the "punctuation marks" that shape and direct the life-course (Neugarten, 1976). Life events and life transitions thus offer an additional lens through which the connection between learning and experience becomes clear.

Life events are noteworthy occurrences that can be individual or cultural. An individual life event such as marriage, graduation, illness, or job change is a milestone in a person's life. Cultural life events such as economic depressions, disasters, and social movements shape the context in which a person lives. Both types of events stimulate learning. For example, the advent of the computer age, a general cultural phenomenon, has inspired many to learn how to use a computer. An individual may also be motivated to learn about computers because a job change requires such knowledge.

Life events can also be normative or nonnormative. Normative life events are those events assumed to occur at a particular time in people's lives. Society in general determines the timing of normative life events, and though these expectations may slowly change over time, at any particular point in time there are clear expectations. Neugarten explains:

There exists a socially prescribed timetable for the ordering of major life events: a time in the life-span when men and women are expected to marry, a time to raise children, a time to retire. This normative pattern is adhered to more or less consistently, by most persons within a given social group. . . . Men and women are aware not only of the social clocks that operate in various areas of their lives but also of their own timing; and they readily describe themselves as "early," "late," or "on time" with regard to major life events. (1976, p. 16)

Kimmel reiterates how normative life events structure our adult lives:

Not only do we tend to share implicit timetables about family events (marriage, parenthood, grandparenthood, widowhood in that order) and occupational events (first job, serious job, promotion, last chance to change jobs, reaching the peak, retirement), but we even have a timetable for death (the oldest die first). . . . We, as members of society who share these norms, tend to organize our lives in relation to these timetables, whether they fit us precisely or not. (1990, p. 83)

Normative life events lend predictability to adult life. Nonnormative events disrupt our lives, but they are also stimuli for learning. These are events that do not happen to most people and are unexpected, such as bankruptcy, winning a trip, death of a child, or a religious conversion. There is also the nonevent— one that is expected but does not occur—such as not being able to have children, not receiving an expected job promotion, and the like.

Life events, normative or nonnormative, in and of themselves are neutral phenomena. Whether the event is seen as negative or positive, as a gain or a loss, as good or bad, has to do with how the event is interpreted by the individual. Factors such as timing, cohort specificity, contextual purity, and duration determine the impact of the event on the individual. *Timing* has to do with when one expects an event to occur. A person who experiences an event that is "on time" (Neugarten, 1976) and in sequence has many resources, both personal and social, to draw upon. If events are "off-timed," such as a late-life pregnancy or being widowed at 30, there is a greater potential for crisis. *Cohort specificity* refers to the fact that an event affects different generations in different ways. The Vietnam War, for example, affected young adults differently than it did either their own children or their grandparents. The concept of *contextual purity* is used to describe the degree to which an adult's reaction to an event may be related to the extent to which the "event occurs at a relatively stable, otherwise uneventful time in a person's life" (Danish et al., 1980, p. 344). *Duration* refers to how long a person experiences an event. A long illness or the birth of a child allows time for adaptation, which can be "educative" according to Danish et al. (1980, p. 343), "in that the role, rights, expectations, and responsibilities of the impending event can be explored and learned ahead of time."

Life events are most often viewed as happenings or occurrences that "punctuate" our life course. They can also be viewed as processes having a beginning, a middle, and an ending phase. Knox (1977) for example, writes about change events as having a sequence of five periods (prestructure, anticipation, actual change event, disorganization, poststructure) with only the middle period being the actual occurrence of the event. When viewed as processes, life events are similar to the notion of transitions, which Schlossberg in fact defines as "any event or nonevent that results in change" (1984, p. 43). "Transitions take time," she writes, "and people's reactions to them change—for better or for worse—while they are under way. At first people think of nothing but being a new graduate, a new widow, a new parent or newly jilted. Then they begin to separate from the past and move toward the new role, for a while teetering between the two. A year, sometimes two years or even more pass before moving from one transition to another" (1987, pp. 74–75).

Research has demonstrated the relationship between life events and transitions and learning in adulthood. Some of the most direct evidence comes from the Aslanian and Brickell (1980) study mentioned earlier investigating why adults participate in adult education. From their national sample of adults, they found that 83% of adult learners were engaged in learning because of some past, present, or anticipated transition in their lives. They write that adults come to realize that "they will have to learn something new if they are going to make the transition successfully" (1980, p. 52). They also point out that "to know an adult's life schedule is to know an adult's learning schedule" (pp. 60–61). Schlossberg (1987, p. 74) also raises the question of how adults can be helped to "handle this journey, live through it and learn from it." She suggests taking stock of one's resources and deficits, learning problem-solving skills and techniques for coping with the transition. In a recent study of work, love, and learning in adulthood, Merriam and Clark (1991) found that the same life events that defined a person's work-and-love pattern were also identified by the participants as sources of learning. In this study, participants were asked to list formal, informal, or personal learning experiences that were especially meaningful, significant, or intense. Even though the sample was highly educated, formal learning experiences such as attending college were listed infrequently. Rather, life events such as first job, divorce, death of a loved one, travel, or job promotion were identified over 80% of the time as triggering significant learning experiences.

In summary, the concept of life events offers one framework for demonstrating the connection between life experience and learning. Whether the events are anticipated or unexpected, whether they occur suddenly or take years, they form a scaffolding for the life course. They also motivate much of adult learning.

Developmental Tasks and Social Role

Closely related to the concept of dealing with life events is the concept of engaging in developmental tasks and taking on their accompanying social roles as a catalyst for adult learning. Getting married requires taking on the role of spouse. Enrolling in a class means becoming a student. Completing one's work life leads to the role of retiree. One of the best-known models linking life events and social roles is Havighurst's (1953, 1972). In his well-known book, *Developmental Tasks and Education* (1972), Havighurst delineated what he called developmental tasks for life stages from infancy to old age. Early adulthood has eight tasks, such as starting a family and getting started in an occupation; middle age has seven tasks, such as assisting teenage children to become responsible and happy adults; and later maturity has six tasks, such as adjusting to death of spouse. There is a clear relationship between developmental task and social role, especially for adults. A social role such as "husband" or "wife" necessitates the developmental task of "getting married." Likewise, a biological drive may lead to the task of finding a mate and bearing children, which then leads to the social roles of "spouse" and "parent." These tasks and accompanying changes in social roles provide what Havighurst called the "teachable moment" (1972). That is, adults are ready to learn when faced with dealing with a developmental task, which according to Havighurst, "arises at or about a certain period in the life of the individual, successful achievement of which leads to his happiness and to success with later tasks, while failure leads to unhappiness in the individual, disapproval by the society, and difficulty with later tasks" (1972, p. 2). Havighurst wrote of the close relationship among tasks, roles, and education. "The adult educator," he notes, "can usefully see the adult part of the life cycle as consisting of a set of stages or phases which make different demands on education and offer different opportunities to the educator" (1969, p. 18).

Although certain of Havighurst's tasks and roles have been criticized for being outdated and/or biased in favor of middle-class adults, the notion of developmental tasks and changing social roles as motivators for learning is timely and receives much support in both developmental psychology and educational literature. Knox (1977), for example, speaks of a change event as something that affects one's participation in role-specific activity. He writes:

All major role change events, by definition, entail modifications of the structure of participation. When a major activity or role relationship is added, changed, or lost, there must be some alteration of the individual's time use, usually to make way for the new relationship or to fill in the time released because a relationship is lost. Often the compensation for a major role change takes the form of many minor contractions or expansions of other activities. . . . When all types of change events are distributed along the adult life cycle in terms of the age at which they typically occur, a high proportion are concentrated in early young adulthood. Furthermore, most of the change events during young adulthood entail gains of role relationships, most of those during middle age entail changes, and most of those during old age entail losses. (Knox, 1977, pp. 519–520)

Knowles (1980), who is best known for his theory of adult learning called andragogy, draws heavily upon Havighurst in one of the key assumptions of his theory: that the readiness of an adult to learn is closely related to the developmental tasks of his or her social role. This assumption has direct implications for the structuring of learning in adulthood in terms of timing and grouping of learners. New workers for example, will be more interested in how to do the job, rather than the history and philosophy of the corporation. "For some kinds of learnings," Knowles writes, "homogeneous groups according to developmental task are more effective" (1980, p. 53). A workshop designed to assist parents in coping with adolescents, for example, will appeal to adults with teenagers, just as a session on preretirement planning is most likely to be attended by a homogeneous group of adults near retirement age.

That there is a progression of tasks and accompanying social roles as we move through the life-course is a concept that undergirds much of the work in adult development. Whether dealing with hierarchical stages or age periods of ego development (Erikson, 1963; Loevinger, 1976), personality development (Levinson et al., 1978), moral development (Kohlberg, 1973; Gilligan, 1982), or cognitive development (Perry, 1981), there is the assumption that personal growth and learning are closely linked. McCoy (1977) integrated many of these developmental theories into a stage-specific educational programming response. The developmental stage of midlife reexamination (35–43 years), for example, contains such tasks as searching for meaning, reassessing marriage, reexamining work, relating to teenage children, and so on. The program response would be workshops on marriage, midcareer, and raising teenagers. The behaviors sought from these programmatic responses are outcomes such as "appropriate career decisions" and "improved parent-child relations."

Thus we can see that adult learning and experience are inextricably linked as we examine how tackling developmental tasks related to taking on new social roles both causes learning and causes a desire for learning to occur. However, while the context of adult lives and the learning that adults do can be defined by work and family, life events and transitions, and developmental tasks and social roles, it is important to note that each of these approaches are colored by the larger sociocultural context of an adult's life. Class, gender, and race shape not only the "choices, opportunities, and obstacles an adult is likely to face," but also how "those choices and obstacles are met" (Bee, 1987, p. 51). The resources that an adult has available to cope with an illness or a job loss will vary according to his or her life situation. Coping with a life event or a developmental task through learning, at least in a formal situation, may not be an option for some adults. There is in fact a lamentable middle-class bias to most of formal adult education. The reasons for this bias are complex and involve both psychological and sociological factors (Merriam & Caffarella, 1991).

Even when adults respond to a life event through informal learning, success may be limited by their life circumstances. This is in fact what Spear and Mocker (1984) found in a study of learning projects of adults with less than a high school education. "Rather than preplanning their learning projects," these self-directed learners "tend to select a course from limited alternatives which happen to occur in their environment and which tend to structure their learning projects" (p. 4). The process begins with "some change in the life circumstances. The change may be positive or negative, may happen to the individual or to someone who affects a person's life, or may be an event which simply occurs and is observed within the life space of the individual'' (p. 4). Next, ''The changed circumstance tends to provide a single or, at best, very few resources or opportunities for learning that are reasonable or attractive for the learner to pursue'' (p. 4). The learning is dictated ''by the circumstances'' and progresses ''as the circumstances created during one episode become the circumstances for the next'' (p. 5).

The first half of this chapter has demonstrated in several ways the connection between an adult's life and the learning that he or she engages in. National studies asking adults what motivated them to take a class, a workshop, or training session consistently find the primary motivation to be work-related, with family concerns secondary. Within the broad arenas of work and family, life events and transitions occur and developmental tasks arise that give structure to a person's life. These events, transitions, and tasks create changes in a person's life—changes that require new learning. Just how that learning occurs will be explored in the second half of the chapter.

THE NATURE OF LEARNING FROM LIFE EXPERIENCE

The connection between life experience and learning in adulthood seems clear. What is not so clear is how we learn from a life experience, why we learn from certain life experiences and not others, or why among those experiences from which we learn, some have a greater impact on us than others. For insights into these questions the writings of major theorists will be reviewed, as will the relatively sparse research that has examined learning from life experience.

How Experience Teaches

Some of the most thoughtful observations about the relationship between life experience and learning come from Dewey's *Experience and Education* (1938). In this classic work, Dewey examines the ''organic connection between education and personal experience'' (p. 12). He is careful to note that *not all experience educates*, by which he means that not all experiences lead to the growth of ever-widening and deeper experiences. Some experiences ''mis-educate'' in that they result in ''arresting or distorting the growth of further experience'' (p. 13). To judge whether an experience has been educative or mis-educative, Dewey poses this question: ''Does this form of growth create conditions for further growth, or does it set up conditions that shut off the person who has grown in this particular direction from the occasions, stimuli, and opportunities for continuing growth in new directions?'' (p. 29).

For an experience to be educative it must embody the principle of continuity and the principle of interaction. By continuity Dewey means that ''every experience both takes up something from those which have gone before and modifies in some way the quality of those which come after'' (1938, p. 27). The principle of interaction posits that ''an experience is always what it is because of a transaction taking place between an individual and what, at the time, constitutes his [or her] environment'' (p. 41). Based on these two interrelated principles, Dewey explains what it means to learn from experience:

To ''learn from experience'' is to make a backward and forward connection between what we do to things and what we enjoy or suffer from things in consequence. Under such conditions, doing becomes a trying; an experiment with the world to find out what it is like; the undergoing becomes instruction—discovery of the connection of things. (Dewey, cited in McDermott, 1973, p. 495).

Understanding how we learn from experience has been addressed by a number of writers since Dewey. Two models to be reviewed here built on Dewey's ideas and were developed from observations and work with adult learners. Kolb (1976, 1984), who is an educator interested in training in the work setting, has developed a four-stage cyclical model of learning from experience. In the first stage the learner is confronted by an experience; this is observed and reflected upon in the second stage. For example, an older co-worker appears to be taking credit for your ideas. This comes to your attention, and you recall specifics relevant to the situation. The third stage consists of forming abstract concepts and generalizations to explain or accommodate the experience. With regard to the co-worker problem, you might try to explain her behavior in a number of ways: maybe she is insecure about her job; maybe she feels her age and experience should count for more; and the like. The last stage involves testing the concepts in new situations, which in turn give rise to new experiences. With the co-worker example, you might confront her with what you've observed or you might ask for reassignment, and so on. Whatever action is taken in the last stage returns one to the first stage, and the cycle becomes continuous. For Kolb, learning consists of ''grasping experience and transforming it'' (Kolb, 1984, p. 41). In this process the learner ''moves in varying degrees from actor to observer, from specific involvement to general analytic detachment'' (Kolb, 1976, p. 3).

Beginning with Kolb's model but finding it too simplistic and linear, Jarvis (1987a) developed another model to explain experiential learning. Jarvis begins with the assumption that ''Life is about experience; wherever there is life there are potential learning experiences'' (1987b, p. 164). Like Kolb, he believes that learning involves transforming these experiences into knowledge, and he would add skills and attitudes. Like Dewey, he emphasizes the *potential* of learning from experience; not all experience leads to learning. In fact in his model there are nine possible responses to a life experience, three of which he categorizes as *nonlearning*. The first nonlearning response he calls presumption, by which he means those unconscious behaviors in which adults engage without much thought. Nonconsideration, the second type of nonlearning response, occurs when an adult through lack of time or interest does not attend to the experience. A third nonlearning scenario, rejection, results when the person chooses to reject learning from an experience, perhaps because it is too incongruous with one's belief system.

Jarvis classifies three other responses as *nonreflective* learning, and the last three as *reflective* learning. Under nonreflective learning Jarvis lists preconscious, practice, and memorization. Preconscious or incidental learning occurs from those daily experiences that make up the fabric of adult life but which seldom are brought to consciousness (like learning the route home from work and then not thinking about it in subsequent trips). Practice is used in the development of physical and social skills, and memorization is the means of storing knowledge so that it can be available for future use. Reflective learning can be in the form of contemplation, or intellectual reflection, or can be what he calls reflective practice, which is the development of pragmatic knowledge and can be understood as thought in action. An example of reflective practice would be thinking about or monitoring what you are doing while you are doing it. The final type is experimental, wherein the connection between knowledge and reality is demonstrated through experimentation (Jarvis, 1987a).

Dewey, Kolb, and Jarvis share the notion that life experience offers the potential for learning and agree that there is considerable variety in the way adults learn from their experience. Their theories also identify a necessary ingredient in the process of transforming experience into learning—the role of attention and reflection.

Attention and Reflection

Jarvis's model in particular makes it clear that unless we attend to our experiences, little or no learning can take place. Kolb reiterates this when he speaks of "grasping" experience (1984, p. 41). Clearly, in Dewey's thinking, one must be engaged with the experience to be able to learn from it. In addition to noticing or attending to an experience, we must also reflect upon it.

From the literature on experiential learning come two studies that focus on the importance of reflection. Boud, Keogh, and Walker (1985) define reflection in this context as "those intellectual and affective activities in which individuals engage to explore their experiences in order to lead to new understandings and appreciations" (p. 19). Their model begins with experience, consisting of behaviors, ideas, or feelings. In the reflective process, this experience is returned to and reevaluated, with attendant feelings used if they are positive or removed if they obstruct the process. Outcomes of this process can include a new perspective on the experience, a change in behavior, or a commitment to action.

Boyd and Fales (1983) studied the reflection process in a different way. They interviewed a group of counselors and educators and asked them to assess their own reflective process. They define reflection as "the process of creating and clarifying the meaning of experience (present or past) in terms of self (self in relation to self and self in relation to the world). The outcome of the process is a changed conceptual perspective" (p. 101). They identify several stages in this reflection process:

1. A sense of inner discomfort.
2. Identification or clarification of the concern.
3. Openness to new information from internal and external sources, with ability to observe and take in from a variety of perspectives.
4. Resolution, expressed as "integration," "coming together," "acceptance of self-reality," and "creative synthesis."
5. Establishing continuity of self with past, present, and future.
6. Deciding whether to act on the outcome of the reflective process. (p. 106)

Other work on reflection comes from theorists such as Schon (1983, 1987) who focus on the development of professional expertise. Similar to Jarvis's category of reflective practice, Schon has proposed that professionals carry on a dialogue with their experience, what he calls reflection-in-action. Reflection-in-action takes place when

practitioner[s] allow [themselves] to experience surprise, puzzlement, or confusion in a situation which [they] find uncertain or unique. [They] reflect on the phenomena before [them], and on the prior understandings which have been implicit in [their] behavior. [They] carry out an experiment which serves to generate both a new understanding of the phenomena and a change in the situation. (Schon, 1983, p. 68)

This description, while directed toward the development of problem-solving skills in the workplace, could also describe how attention and reflection function in learning parenting skills or coping with a job loss.

Attention and reflection are key components in understanding how a life experience becomes a learning experience. They are also critical components in theories of transformational learning, which we will turn to next for an even more thorough understanding of this process.

Meaning-Making

All of life's experiences hold the potential for learning. From the theories and models of life experience learning that we have reviewed, we can see why only certain life experiences become learning experiences. If an experience is utterly incongruous with our previous experiences, it may be rejected; if on the other hand it is too similar to previous experience it may not be noticed. Apparently an experience needs to be discomforting, disquieting, or puzzling enough for us not to reject or ignore it, but to attend to it and to reflect upon it. It is then that learning takes place. But what happens when that learning is taking place? Several writers address how meaning-making functions in learning from experience.

Kegan (1982) observes that human beings constantly attempt to render experience coherent or meaningful. The system of meanings that each person constructs defines the self. The capacity to engage in meaning-making develops across the life span. He has proposed a complex and dynamic five-stage model of this growth; at each level there is a qualitative change in how the self and the world are understood, and at each position there are constraints on rendering experience meaningful.

Also interested in growth and meaning-making is Daloz (1986). He speaks of learning as a process of "taking apart and putting together the structures that give our lives meaning" (p. 236). In learning, the self grows beyond earlier conceptions of itself and of the world. A supportive mentor figure can be particularly helpful to adults making these transitions to more inclusive meaning systems.

The most comprehensive theory to date explaining how experience, learning, and meaning are related is by Mezirow (1981, 1990, 1991). Human beings function within meaning structures, or frameworks that contain personal beliefs and values, as well as norms and expectations derived from the sociocultural context. Personal experiences are filtered through this meaning structure. A life experience congruent with the meaning structure is assimilated into the structure. If it is not congruent, it can be rejected or can lead to learning. "Learning," according to Mezirow, is "the process of making a new or revised interpretation of an experience" (Mezirow and Associates, 1990, p. 1). This process may result in a change of great magnitude—what he calls a perspective transformation. Perspective transformation is defined as "the process of becoming critically aware of how and why our presuppositions have come to constrain the way we perceive, understand, and feel about our world; of reformulating these assumptions to permit a more inclusive, discriminating, permeable, and integrative perspective; and of making decisions or otherwise acting upon these new understandings" (1990, p. 14). He goes on to point out that "more inclusive, discriminating, permeable, and integrative perspectives are superior perspectives that adults choose if they can because they are motivated to better understand the meaning of their experience" (p. 14). Mezirow sees this process as unique to adult experience and learning. Critical reflection, becoming aware of "*why* we attach the meanings we do to reality, especially to our roles and relationships . . . may be the most significant distinguishing characteristic of adult learning" (1981, p. 11).

Kegan, Daloz, and Mezirow, among others, help us understand how learning from life experience actually takes place. An experience that is attended to and reflected upon becomes transformed within our psyche; the meaning structure out of which we function has been altered. Why one life experience brings about a major transformation and another doesn't, or why the same life experience such as birth of a child, divorce, or job change affects one person and not the next, are questions only recently being investigated. Over forty years ago Carl Rogers, psychologist and educator, speculated that "a person learns significantly only those things which he [or she] perceives as being involved in the maintenance of, or enhancement of, the structure of self" (1951, p. 388). His notion has been empirically supported in a recent study by Merriam and Clark (1991, in press). Open-ended responses to a question about one's significant learning experiences were collected from 405 adults, and an additional nineteen interviews were conducted to probe more deeply about one's learning experiences and the significance they held for the learner. It was found that learning experiences considered to be significant were those that both (1) personally affected the learner and (2) were subjectively valued by the learner. The experience resulted in an expansion of skills and abilities, sense of self, or life perspective, or it precipitated a transformation similar to Mezirow's concept of perspective transformation. Furthermore, the learner is able to identify how the learning is important in his or her life; this acknowledges the fact that some of our learning from life experience may expand our repertoire of skills, for example, but may not be particularly valued and thus not be considered significant.

Psychologists and educators thus have some understanding about how adults learn from life experience. If an experience is unsettling or puzzling or somewhat incongruous with our present meaning structure, it captures our attention. If the gap is too great between how we understand the world and ourselves in it and the experience, we may choose to ignore it or reject it. If however we choose to grapple with it, learning results. Some of this learning affects us more than others. Powerful learning experiences may even transform how we think and act.

SUMMARY

Adult life is full of experiences that hold the potential for learning, learning that leads to growth and development and to an even greater capacity for learning. These life experiences shape us and influence how we think about and value both ourselves and the world around us, yet the process by which we learn from life experience is difficult to study directly. The material reviewed in this chapter first demonstrated how intricately adult life experience and learning are connected. In the second half of the chapter what we know about how this process takes place was reviewed.

Freud is reported to have said that maturity is the capacity to work and to love. The institutionalized forms of these two central forces are the workplace and the family, and it is these two arenas that structure adult life and, consequently, adult learning. National studies of why adults engage in learning transactions find work and family concerns to be the primary motivations for both formal and informal modes of learning. Individual life events and transitions within the broader framework of work and family are clearly connected to the learning adults do. Taking on a new job, coping with divorce, and moving to a new community mandate new learning, as do changes in adult social roles. The mere passage of time creates new roles for adults. The role of grandparent or retiree is qualitatively different than the role of new parent or corporate executive and requires learning new skills and knowledge. Adult life experience both stimulates and structures the nature of learning in adulthood.

For understanding how this learning takes place, we first turned to Dewey (1938), who argued that learning is characterized by dynamic interaction with the world. His problem-solving approach was developed further by Kolb, whose four-stage model documents the "grasping and transforming" of life experience (1984, p. 41). Jarvis (1987a) extends this process, outlining nine possible responses to life experiences and categorizing these as nonlearning, nonreflective learning, and reflective learning. For Dewey, Kolb, and Jarvis it is clear that all experience is potentially educative and that adults learn from it in a variety of ways.

Learning from one life experience and not another involves attending to and reflecting upon the experience. Schon applies this to professional practice and talks about reflection-in-action. Others have constructed models or stages of reflection. It is from the adult development and learning literature that we get an even clearer picture of how this learning takes place. Writers such as Kegan and Daloz speak of meaning-making, or the need to make sense out of our life experiences. Mezirow in particular documents how a meaning structure is adjusted, changed, and even transformed in the process of learning. Together these various perspectives give us a composite understanding of how life experience learning actually takes place.

Adults do in fact live and learn. While it may not be the only teacher, experience certainly is one of our more powerful teachers. The more we can understand about the connection between adult learning and life experience, the better prepared those of us in education and other helping professions can be to maximize these opportunities for growth and development.

REFERENCES

Aslanian, C. B. & Brickell, H. M. (1980). *Americans in transition: Life changes as reasons for adult learning*. New York: College Entrance Examination Board.

Bee, H. L. (1987). *The journey of adulthood*. New York: Macmillan.

Boud, D., Keogh, R., & Walker, D. (Eds.). (1985). *Reflection: Turning experience into learning*. London: Kogan Page.

Boyd, E. M. & Fales, A. W. (1983). Reflective learning: Key to learning from experience. *Journal of Humanistic Psychology, 7(4)*, 261–284.

Carnevale, A. B. (1986). The learning enterprise. *Training and Development Journal, 40(1)*, 18–26.

Cross, P. K. (1981). *Adults as learners*. San Francisco: Jossey-Bass.

Daloz, L. A. (1986). *Effective teaching and mentoring*. San Francisco: Jossey-Bass.

Danish, S., Smyer, M., & Nowak, C. (1980). Developmental intervention: Enhancing life-event processes. In P. Baltes (Ed.). *Life-span development and behavior*. New York: Academic Press.

Dewey, J. (1938). *Experience and education*. London: Macmillan.

Erikson, E. H. (1963). *Childhood and society*. 2nd edition. New York: Norton. (Originally published 1950).

Gilligan, C. (1982). *In a different voice*. Cambridge, MA: Harvard University Press.

Havighurst, R. (1953). *Human development and education.* New York: Longmans, Green.

Havighurst, R. J. (1969). Changing status and roles during the adult life cycle: Significance for adult education. In H. W. Burns (Ed.). *Sociological backgrounds of adult education: Notes and essays on education for adults.* Brookline, MA: Center for the Study of Liberal Education for Adults.

Havighurst, R. (1972). *Developmental tasks and education.* 3rd edition. New York: McKay. (Originally published 1952).

Jarvis, P. (1987a). *Adult learning in the social context.* London: Croom Helm.

Jarvis, P. (1987b). Meaningful and meaningless experiences: Towards an analysis of learning from life. *Adult Education Quarterly, 37*(2), 164–172.

Kegan, R. (1982). *The evolving self.* Cambridge, MA: Harvard University Press.

Kimmel, D. C. (1990). *Adulthood and aging.* 3rd edition. New York: Wiley.

Knowles, M. S. (1980). *The modern practice of adult education.* 2nd edition. New York: Cambridge Books.

Knox, A. B. (1977). *Adult development and learning.* San Francisco: Jossey-Bass.

Kohlberg, L. (1973). Continuities in childhood and adult moral development revisited. In P. Baltes and W. Schaie (Eds.). *Life span development psychology.* New York: Academic Press.

Kolb, D. A. (1976). *Learning style inventory technical manual.* Boston: McBer.

Kolb, D. A. (1984). *Experiential learning: Experience as the source of learning and development.* Englewood Cliffs, NJ: Prentice-Hall.

Levinson, D., Darrow, C., Klein, E., Levinson, M., & McKee, B. (1978). *The seasons of a man's life.* New York: Knopf.

Loevinger, J. (1976). *Ego development: Conceptions and theories.* San Francisco: Jossey-Bass.

McCoy, V. (1977). Adult life cycle change: How does growth affect our education needs? *Lifelong Learning: The Adult Years, 31,* 14–18.

McDermott, J. J. (Ed.). (1973). *The philosophy of John Dewey. Volume II: The Lived Experience.* New York: Putnams.

Merriam, S. B. & Caffarella, R. S. (1991). *Learning in adulthood.* San Francisco: Jossey-Bass.

Merriam, S. B. & Clark, M. C. (1991). *Lifelines: Patterns of work, love, and learning in adulthood.* San Francisco: Jossey-Bass.

Merriam, S. B. & Clark, M. C. (in press). Learning from life experience: What makes it significant? *International Journal of Lifelong Education.*

Mezirow, J. (1981). A critical theory of adult learning and education. *Adult Education, 32*(1), 3–24.

Mezirow, J. (1991). *Transformative dimensions of adult learning.* San Francisco: Jossey-Bass.

Mezirow, J., and Associates. (1990). *Fostering critical reflection in adulthood.* San Francisco: Jossey-Bass.

Neugarten, B. L. (1976). Adaptation and the life cycle. *Counseling Psychologist, 6,* 16–20.

Perry, W. (1981). Cognitive and ethical growth: The making of meaning. In A. W. Chickering and Associates. *The modern American college.* San Francisco: Jossey-Bass.

Rogers, C. R. (1951). *Client-centered therapy: Its current practice, implications, and theory.* Boston: Houghton Mifflin.

Schlossberg, N. (1984). *Counseling adults in transition*. New York: Springer.

Schlossberg, N. (1987). Taking the mystery out of change. *Psychology Today, 21(5)*, 74–75.

Schon, D. A. (1983). *The reflective practitioner*. San Francisco: Jossey-Bass.

Schon, D. A. (1987). *Educating the reflective practitioner: Toward a new design for teaching and learning in the professions*. San Francisco: Jossey-Bass.

Spear, G. E. & Mocker, D. W. (1984). The organizing circumstance: Environmental determinants in self-directed learning. *Adult Education Quarterly, 35(1)*, 1–10.

Tough, A. (1971). *The adult's learning projects*. Toronto: Ontario Institute for Studies in Education.

Tough, A. (1978). Major learning efforts: Recent research and future directions. *Adult Education, 28(4)*, 250–263.

U.S. Department of Education, Office of Educational Research and Improvement, Center for Education Statistics. (1987.) *Digest of education statistics—1987*. Washington, DC: Department of Education.

7

New Science Models for Teaching Adults: Teaching as a Dialogue with Reality

Jan D. Sinnott

We live in a time of rapid change. Teaching involves the induction of change. The "new" sciences—new physics, new biology, new cognitive science, general systems theory—focus on mechanisms for dynamic effects, that is, for changes over time. Those who attempt to teach adults, aware that this happens within the parameters of a given society, might gain useful insights about teaching and learning by examining the new sciences. What do the new sciences have to say about change and induction of change, about teaching and learning in the real adult world?

This chapter briefly examines several "new" sciences and their implications for the adult teaching/learning process. (A fifth new science model, chaos theory, is examined in chapter 1 by Cavanaugh and McGuire in this volume. Yet another complexity theory is just beginning to emerge, created by thinkers at places like the Santa Fe Institute.) These new science models seldom have been used to inform institutional change and seldom have been applied to education. Yet they have structures that would lend themselves to such an application. In a chapter in an earlier book (Sinnott, 1993), I applied them to classroom teaching of children. Some new science descriptions are reprinted here from that chapter.

The first focus of this chapter will be on the new physics and quantum theory, where I will concentrate on ideas about the nature of reality. Next I will focus on the new biology, concentrating on its theories of cooperative evolution and brain development. Finally I will investigate new cognitive sciences, concentrating on theories of Piagetian postformal thought. All these are then related to a general systems theory model (Sinnott, 1989b). One key idea of each theory will be discussed as an example of the potential richness of its approach for teaching mature adults. Each theory's potential impact on methods of teaching adults will be analyzed. Some practical application for teaching and teacher training will be outlined. I will argue that one main theme that links the new sciences' focus on change is: social, physical, or personal reality is partly *constructed* by the knower as reality is known, through principles of emergent structures, that is, order hidden within chaos. Teachers who can embrace this dialogic quality of reality empower their students to live fully and adaptively in this time of rapid change. They also more easily survive the changes in their own educational institutions.

NEW PHYSICS MODELS AND TEACHING ADULTS

Although new physics ideas (e.g., Herbert, 1986; Jeans, 1981; Pagels, 1982; Prigogene & Stengers, 1984; Sinnott, 1981; Sinnott, 1984; Wolf, 1981) have made a tremendous impact on science, technology, and philosophy, they have had a limited impact in the social sciences and everyday life. This may be true in part because new physics concepts are more difficult to grasp because they describe the less-familiar "big picture" reality. They differ from Newtonian physics concepts in that they go beyond our everyday familiar reality. However, in times of change or when one is trying to bring about change, the breadth of the big picture is needed, as small-scale descriptions have proved inadequate.

New physics ideas also seem somewhat alien to us because they do not necessarily concur with our shared Western cultural myths about reality (Campbell, 1988). In fact, these ideas are widely respected just because they overarch cultural considerations. Until we are motivated by desperation, curiosity, or cognitive shifts to explore multiple views of reality, most of us will probably avoid the challenge of new physics ideas.

In my earlier work I have described new physics ideas related to developmental psychology, change, and cognition, especially "everyday cognition" (e.g., Sinnott, 1981, 1984, 1989abc, 1990, 1991a). A table summarizing shifts in worldviews from Newtonian to new physics ideas is reprinted here (Table 1). Notice that the shifts have important implications for psychological reality. The nature of existence in psychological terms (i.e., identity), time (i.e., lifespan development), and causality (i.e., personal action, power, ability) shifts. Table 2 (Sinnott, 1984) describes the two worldviews in terms of interpersonal relations.

One conclusion that can be drawn from the new physics is that sometimes multiple contradictory views of truth are all "true" simultaneously, although they appear contradictory at first. It can be said that reality is therefore that view of truth to which we make a passionate commitment (Perry, 1975; Polanyi, 1971). Ideally, this commitment is made in awareness and with consciousness. We know that no one view of reality is, in Bronowski's (1975) words, the "God's eye view"; they are all limited by one's chosen vantage point or measuring tool. This argues that anything is known only within a region of tolerance or of error, but not absolutely. When we *share* a vantage point (stand in the same context and history), only then do we share a reality.

Table 1
Old Physics/New Physics Concepts

Old	New
Space is Euclidean.	Space is non-Euclidean, except in small regions.
Time and space are absolute.	Time and space are relative and are better conceptualized as the space/time interval.
Space is uniform in nature.	Space is composed of lesser and greater resistances.
Events are located topologically on a flat surface.	Events are located topologically on the surface of a sphere.
Undisturbed movement is on a straight line.	Undisturbed movement is on a geodesic, i.e., by the laziest route.
Events are continuous.	Events are discontinuous.
No region of events exists that cannot be known.	Unknowable regions of events exist.
Observed events are stable.	Observed events are in motion, which must be taken into account in the observation.
Formation of scientific postulates proceeds from everyday activity through generalizations based on common sense, to abstractions.	Formation of scientific postulates also includes a stage characterized by resolution of contradictions inherent in the abstractions.
Causality is deterministic.	Causality is probabilistic, except in limited space/time cases.
Cause is antecedent to and contiguous with effect.	Cause is antecedent and contiguous to event only in limiting cases. When events are grouped about a center, that center constitutes a cause.
Egocentrism is replaced by decentration during development of scientific methods.	Egocentrism and decentration are followed by taking the ego into account in all calculations.
Concepts in natural laws conform to verbal conventions.	Concepts in natural laws may appear contradictory in terms of verbal conventions.
Universe is uniform.	Universe is non-uniform-either because it is continually expanding or because it is continually being created and negated.

Source: Sinnott, 1984.

Table 2
Applications: Interpersonal Relations
Formalistic

- There is only one way to structure our relationship to reflect reality.
- Our relationship exists "out there" in reality.
- Our relationship involves only us, now.
- The relationship has just one "reality"—no need to match levels to understand.
- We can know the essence of each other.
- Role is more important than process.

Relativistic

- Our relations are logical within a set of "givens" that we choose to utilize.
- They are based on both our past relations to each other and our relations to other significant persons.
- Relating means knowing "where you're coming from" and interacting on that level.
- Relating is never knowing "You" completely, because in knowing you I am necessarily subjectively "creating" you.
- Relations are always "in process"; they cannot be described as stable until they end.

Source: Sinnott, 1984.

To create another personal or social reality (within limits), we need to change vantage points as individuals or groups. For example, in the physical world, from a small-scale, local-space vantage point, parallel lines never converge. But change vantage points to the longer history and larger context of universal space, and parallel lines always converge!

The impact of a profound idea like that of new physics in the world of adult learning can be monumental, whether we are speaking of classroom behavior, teachers confronting a changing society, development programs in Third-World countries, or other education problems. From a new physics viewpoint, different incompatible realities are not necessarily to be narrowed to one correct truth; they may each have their own correct logic. From a new physics viewpoint, learning the truths of others can teach us greater flexibility and give us more tools for working with our construction of reality.

From a new physics viewpoint, the line between teacher and learner may be a vague one. Because several truths are simultaneously valid, dialogue is more appropriate than lecture. Awareness of the new physics idea that truth is partly a choice of vantage points around which we build our reality lets the teacher begin to allow learners to use their ability to construct and experience—and be responsible for—their intellectual lives. Such awareness lets the teacher see a changing society in a more benevolent way as a society shifting from one vantage point (e.g., "Cold War") to another (e.g., "Global Village"). This is a shift that the teacher may join, go beyond, incorporate into a larger shift, and point out to learners. Meanwhile the teacher works with learners to be flexible and to see future shifts in truth as normal rather than as aberrations.

What this means is that the teacher will see his or her role as one of bridging *multiple* valued realities/truths (Johnson, 1991). Accepting shifts in reality, bridging, and dialoging between two "truths" is likely to lead to more permanent, useful, adaptive learning. Such learning is not sabotaged by a rigid world view.

NEW BIOLOGY MODELS AND TEACHING ADULTS

Proponents of some versions of the "new biology" include Augros and Stanciu (1987), Maturana and Varela (1988), and McLean (1988). Their work derives from the original data on which evolutionary theory was formed and adds the new experimental data of modern medicine and biology to attempt to answer difficult biological questions. In doing so they come to conclusions that seem to stand evolutionary theory on its head. One of their basic arguments is that, rather than modelling aggression or conflict, biological systems model synergy or cooperation. This means that species do not fight for the same niche in an environment; they evolve to fit a "free" space so that they can prevent conflict with another species. Intrapersonally, "higher," more evolutionarily recent brain centers (like the cortex and prefrontal cortex) do not so much control the instinct of "lower" centers, which are evolutionarily older. Instead, these provide clever ways both to help lower centers reach their goals and to provide a sense of community and mutual goal setting between the organism and other organisms around it. The human immune system in this new biology model is more than an army that attacks invaders; it is a sense of wholeness of mind and body, and of emotional well-being. In the new biology, opposing parts or individuals seem meant to be sympathetic rather than confrontational.

What might this finding imply for developing models for teaching adults? For one thing it implies that, although biological entities are clearly individuals, they are also part of a larger whole. Adult learners must be seen in their relatedness to others. In this theory the "whole" does not subsume the individual or make the individual unimportant. Relational reality desperately needs the individual's specialness to exist. The part or individual provides the means; the whole provides a large part of the motivation and meaning. Empty evolutionary niches go quickly out of ecological balance because they have lost touch with their meaning; they are in relation to a species. Immune systems missing appropriate connections turn on the very body that sustains them. Over and over the biological message seems to be: each part is important; each part is related; each part obtains meaning both alone and through interrelationship.

What does this theory suggest in an adult learning situation? It suggests that cooperative learning is desirable. Meacham and Emont (1989) have noted that most problem solving is social, not individual, yet classes often operate as if individuals are alone, and must learn alone. Several authors (Johnson & Johnson, 1975; Johnson, 1991) and collaborators have demonstrated the educational value of cooperative learning and group work with children and adults. Kohn (1987) has listed the detrimental effects of school competition, and even in competitive business settings, cooperative work is considered good "team building." The suggestion offered to adult educators by the new biology seems to be to capitalize on mature students' belonging to a larger whole by letting them work together. The lesson of new biology may be like the lesson of the functional family. If we form some critical mass of compassion and mutual help, external problems becomes less powerful. Teachers of adults can be facilitators of a learning team or negotiators between a community and a subject matter, in the spirit of the new biology.

NEW COGNITIVE SCIENCE MODELS AND TEACHING ADULTS

One new key area developing within cognitive science is called postformal thought. It includes cognitive epistemology (or the knowing of reality) and lifespan development. Cognitive development is theorized to be accompanied by increases in social-cognitive experience and skills and in social interaction that leads to greater cognitive development. The ideas of others challenge the reality of the knower. Postformal Piagetian thought is one theory describing this development (Sinnott, 1984, 1989abc, 1990, 1991abc). Such cognitive approaches go beyond traditional information-processing approaches; postformal thought is a complex way of solving problems, one that develops with social experience, usually not before mature adulthood. It allows a person to solve problems even in situations where conflicted formal operational belief systems and priorities overlap. In postformal thought, the solver faces multiple conflicting ideas about "what is true." The solver realizes that it is not possible to "get outside the mind" to find out which "truth" is "TRUE," but that a solution must be found to the problem anyhow. The solver then realizes that the truth system picked as true will become true, especially in relation to other people, as the solver lives it to a conclusion.

The main characteristics of these relativistic postformal cognitive operations (Sinnott, 1984) are (1) self-reference and (2) the ordering of formal operations. Self-reference is a general term for the ideas inherent in the new physics (Wolf, 1981) and alluded to by Hofstadter (1979), using the terms "self referential games," "jumping out of the system," and "strange loops." The essential notion of self-reference is that we can never be completely free of the built-in limits of our system of knowing and that we come to know that this very fact is true. This means that we take into account, in all our decisions about truth, the fact that all knowledge has a subjective component and therefore is, of necessity, incomplete. Any logic we use is self-referential logic. Yet we must *act* in spite of being trapped in partial subjectivity. We make a decision about rules of the game (nature of truth), then act based on those rules. Once we come to realize what we are doing, we then can consciously use self-referential thought.

The second characteristic of postformal operations is the ordering of Piagetian formal operations. The higher-level postformal system of self-referential truth decisions gives order to lower-level formal truth and logic systems. One of these logic systems is somewhat subjectively chosen and imposed on data as "true." For example, Perry (1975) describes advanced college students as *deciding* that a certain ethical system is "true," knowing full well that there is no absolute way of deciding the truth of an ethical system.

This is also the logic of the "new" physics (relativity theory and quantum mechanics) (Sinnott, 1981). New physics is the next step beyond Newtonian physics and is built on the logic of self-reference. It is reasonable that the development of logical processes themselves would follow that same progression (i.e., Newtonian logic, then new physics logic) to increasing complexity. As mentioned earlier, some characteristics that separate new physics thinking from earlier forms can be found in Table 1.

A new type of cognitive coordination occurs at the postformal level. Another kind of coordination of perspectives also occurs on an emotional level, taking place over developmental time (Labouvie-Vief, 1987). This coordination parallels the cognitive one and is probably engaged in a circular interaction with it. Theorists expect that postformal thought is adaptive in a social situation with emotional and social components (Sinnott, 1984) because it is hypothesized that postformal thought eases communication, reduces information overload, and permits greater flexibility and creativity of thought. The postformal thinker knows she or he is helping create the eventual TRUTH of a social interaction by being a participant in it and choosing to hold a certain view of its truth. Postformal thought has an impact on one's view of self, the world, other persons, change over time, and our connections with one another over time (Sinnott, 1981, 1984, 1989b, 1991abc). It represents the way one knows or understands ideas such as those in the new sciences, that is, in all the models we have examined in this chapter.

What is the impact of such a view of cognitive processes on teaching adults? The connections between postformal thought and learning are explored by Sinnott in this volume. In earlier work, Lee (1987, 1991, this volume) has discussed some of the points of impact of this theory on the teaching process. Johnson (1991, this volume) has examined postformal thought as it relates to the teaching/ learning process in international adult development programs. Both concluded that effective expert teachers and change agents show characteristics of postformal thought and complex cognitive processes. They can bridge across belief systems, entertain several views of truth, and work well in complex social realities. They can create the necessary chaos for the flexible change that must accompany learning. They can create cooperative learning environments in which dialogues between "teacher" and "learner" take place, dialogues that honor the truths of both parties. By modeling such thought, permitting various perspectives, and challenging any Newtonian/conflict-based/inflexible worldviews of their students, they provide the best conditions for the development of post-formal thought in students.

SPECIFIC IMPACT OF NEW SCIENCE IDEAS ON TEACHING

Example 1. Promoting Diversity and Creativity

Table 3 features some new science core principles, all related to general systems theory. All new sciences make use of systems and process ideas. The second column of the table relates each principle to a specific way in which it promotes diversity and creativity through the mediating effects of teachers' behaviors. Table 4 contains a list of activities that can be consciously undertaken by teachers of adults, to encourage more openness to diversity and more fruitful dialogue.

The dynamic of change involves interacting elements that cross boundaries between self and society, as well as boundaries between aspects of self (McLean, 1988). Kenneth Gergen, in his book *The Saturated Self* (Gergen, 1991), argues that the anguish of postmodern experience is due in part to the overwhelming number of interrelationships we experience between self and others in our lives. But this overload leads us to *see* the relativistic and self-referential quality of our own decision making about our own identities. Awareness of our role in our creation of a self can either make us very uncomfortable or lead us to a broader view of reality (Sinnott, 1991abc). Indeed, the conscious creation of this complexity of awareness has been the goal of all learning and growth traditions, including those of religious, psychotherapeutic, and mystical traditions, for millennia. The Native American learning stories described by Paula Underwood (1991) for teachers are examples of current applications of such wisdom traditions. These are some of the traditions that are learning environments for adult learners.

Going even deeper to a more basic polarity, philosophy has always juxtaposed the worldview of objective, mechanical reality against the romantic worldview of reality that is moved by emotion and mystery (Gergen, 1991). It seems that the postmodern period in which we now live is a time to unite these worldviews in a fresh union of mind and heart, objectivist and romantic, self and society. The individual as a member of the culture constructs—together with the culture— a shared reality. The shared vision becomes objectively real. The individual and the group choose to live aspects of it and incorporate them. This shared construction inevitably leads to change. The core principles of the new sciences describe the patterns in such a way that reality can be shaken up, reconstructed, and used as a reason for change. The adult learner and teacher assist each other to create this change.

The first principle noted in Table 3 is that *change can occur only if there is*

Table 3

New Sciences as a Framework for Teaching Diversity

10 Principles of New Sciences	Way They Promote Diversity
1. Change can occur only if the system includes <u>disorder</u> or <u>potential</u> or <u>unstructuredness</u>.	1. Teachers create disorder, challenge thought and rules, open up questions with no answers, reward students' adoption of alternative ways to think, be, and see the world around them, challenge interpretations.
2. Systems construct their own reality.	2. Students can construct class rules, goals, value systems.
3. An "entity" is not necessarily the result of a boundary; it is also a "consistent set of relations with others."	3. Teachers examine class members' identities as they try new and consistent styles of relating to other people or things or knowledge or themselves.
4. Systems are synergystic.	4. Students explore knowledge, cooperatively, not as competitors.
5. Systems that survive have "porous" boundaries.	5. Besides teaching criticism teachers offer students a <u>good</u> thing about every theory, viewpoint, study, philosophy.
6. Systems go through predictable "life stages."	6. Students can be taught to honor--not be anxious about--their normal stages of thinking, understanding, analysis. This permits them to learn from experience rather than fight it.
7. Rigid systems are dying systems.	7. "True believers" of any theoretical, political, social stripe are the last gasps of a dying system. (When you're sure you're "right", you're history.) (Therefore, doubt this statement).
8. To change, systems need other systems to interact with.	8. Because learning is a social experience, students learn to make good use of disagreements.
9. Systems strive for continuity.	9. Coopting an example, idea or theory is easier than destroying it, and may let you see if it works
10. Systems alter based on their context.	10. Teacher or student - remember the old saying: "Never eat with fools." Choose stimulating contexts.

Table 4
Methods for Transforming Learning Situation Conflict Experience into Change Experiences

- Purposely attempt to shift perspectives so that some other reality about the problem can be explored.
- Consciously expect conflicts in the group and make them constructive.
- Consciously expect and accept intragroup conflict (at some level of intensity) as a routine experience.
- Consciously see ourselves as "all in this together."
- Posit that "no one is to blame for this problem."
- Assume that others act in the best way they know how (but that not all their actions need be tolerated even if they mean well).
- Consciously address facts about a conflict, but don't assume that others see the same "facts."
- Convincingly create a story around the conflict, and let the conflict show you its own solution.
- Enlarge the problem space by redefining the problem or its parameters.
- Consciously shift the metatheory the group uses to frame the problem.
- Generate many "crazy" solutions to the conflict.
- Shift from focusing on a concrete solution to focusing on finding a good *process*.

potential. In teacher behaviors, this translates to opening up the meaning and possibility of things by, for example, asking questions that have no answers. Something as simple as "What is the right way to study for a test?" can lead to a discussion that shows there are many "right" ways (many realities). As one can still choose one way to actually study, though, one need not be immobilized.

The second core principle is that *systems construct their reality with the outside world.* In teacher behavior, this can mean permission from the teacher for adult students to invent a course point system on which their grades are ultimately based. As this highly charged negotiation situation *always* leads to a resolution, students can experience firsthand that diversity need not lead to immobilization or permanent indecision.

The third principle shown in the table is that *one need not be defined by a boundary, but may instead be defined by a set of relations to others.* Teacher behavior can nurture this principle and enhance change processes by creating situations in which students relate first one way, then another, to each other. In a workshop attended by the author, for example, participants took turns being "those who create structured activities" and "those who try to disrupt structured activities." Of course, all participants quickly learned about the workshop context from multiple perspectives and became much better at creating the degree of order and disorder they could tolerate!

The fourth principle is that *systems are synergistic*. Teachers of adults can allow many diverse human systems to nourish each other in the learning situation. Writing projects in which each person writes alone about a common topic, then shares that piece with others, lead to (at some point) a major leap forward in the quality of all papers and an awareness that each paper nevertheless remains unique. Principle 4 relates to principle 5, in that the *systems that survive have "porous" boundaries and can admit new information*. The teacher's behavior is the best model for adult students trying to do this; the teacher can go with the "teachable moment," for example, and be personally open to change.

Teachers can demonstrate the sixth principle—that *systems go through predictable life stages*—by pointing out developmental stages in the life of a class or group. For example, the reassurance of knowing that others initially feel anxiety about some subject and confusion over cooperative exercises, but later feel at ease, lets students feel safe enough to experiment with their thinking. The teacher can talk about personal experiences, too, demonstrating that if the teacher "made it" through anxiety like theirs, they can too. A side benefit is that power is then equalized between those taking the role of teacher and those taking the role of learner.

Principle 7 is that *rigid systems are dying*. Ironically, one of the most striking ways for teachers to teach this principle is for the teacher to *be* a rigid system. Students may be polite to a rigid teacher, but they will see the teacher as irrelevant and unworthy of imitation. Alternatively the teacher may invite the groups to abandon a failing strategy and to help create an alternative. This leads to principle 8, which lets the *teacher promote change by getting greater input (greater potential)* from others.

Systems do strive for continuity, though, according to principle 9. The teacher can provide that continuity and still induce change by showing participants how diverse ideas (old and new) link together. This linkage of ideas validates change and diversity while allowing the central project to continue.

The teacher, finally, can show that *systems change based on their context* (10). One of the most interesting ways to demonstrate this is to offer several groups the same problem to solve and to give relatively few guidelines. Groups quickly see that it is their particular "mix" of individual histories and skills that makes their product different from the other group's product.

More tools for creating conscious learning-situation tolerance of diversity and conflict along new science lines, thereby leading to acceptance of necessary change, are shown in Table 4.

Example 2. Why Is It Difficult to Change a Structured Learning Setting?

The new science core principles outlined in this chapter predict some of the roadblocks to change in any traditional learning setting. Once again, see Table 3. The first principle is that change can occur only if the system has "space" for it. This space is "potential" or "unstructuredness." Most traditional learning settings are nested in an organization with a fairly firm bureaucracy and are run in a style that is more authoritarian than dialogic. Time is to be filled by directed activity, not left open to possibility. There often is a "right" or "wrong" way to do things. Disorderly looking behavior is considered the sign of a poorly run classroom or workshop. All these attitudes and expectations militate against the nurturing of potential that is necessary for change to occur. If systems construct their reality (principle 2), change comes hard when the reality is, "We've always done it like this," and, "We (not you) know what's best."

In Table 3, principle 3 says that "identity" is a product of relations. Many teachers still have only one type of relation with students, a hierarchical one, where teachers have greater power. In a single-relationship environment, possibilities for changes in identity are stillborn. Synergy (principle 4) is not easy to use if no surprises are admitted by a teacher who is considered to be the only authority figure.

Classroom or workshop interactions are too often limited to just a few, which means that change permitted by "porous boundaries" (principle 5) is foreclosed. Even the great diversity students can find by examination of their own reactions, responses, group dynamics is often officially closed to inquiry, leading to stasis. The life stages of groups (principle 6) are often ignored in learning settings. For example, students are seldom honored for getting more knowledgeable, as people, as years go by, although a forty-year-old learner usually is very different than a twenty-year-old learner! Rigid systems are enshrined in many classrooms where nothing changes to suit adult learners.

Many structured learning settings forbid cooperative projects where knowledge is really shared. This means that there is no system/system interaction (principle 8), and significant change is less likely to occur. Since systems strive for continuity (principle 9), one way to ensure *non*-change is to imply that change will be catastrophic to the "old order." In many adult learning settings, this defensive posture is consistently maintained. Finally, if systems change based on a context (principle 10), one way to support change is to contextualize learning.

The key element in letting learning situations be open to change—both change inside the classes themselves, and change in the culture—may be to let them be led by teachers who are open to change through dialogue. Persons who have experience with adult learners as "change agents" in some other domain (for example, returning Peace Corps volunteers) might be the best teachers of adult learners. Teachers with this kind of fresh outlook could bring new ways of seeing and dialoguing.

CONCLUSION

This chapter presents very brief descriptions of four "new science" models, along with several of their general philosophical implications and several of their

Table 5

Summary Table: Some Potential Implications of New Sciences for Teaching

Concept Applied to Teaching	Implication	Prescription for Teachers
From New Physics		
-Relativity, quantum physics: Multiple contradictory realities can all be true depending on vantage points.	-Multiple truths are "true" depending on one's vantage point and choice.	-Prepare learners for multiple truths; bridge equally valid realities; have dialogues with learners.
From New Biology		
-Cooperative evolution: Species don't fight for the same niche; they evolve to fit interrelated, non-overlapping niches.	-Individual organisms are important as individuals <u>and</u> as somewhat irreplaceable members of a whole system.	-Use cooperative learning; be a fellow explorer with learner; limit competition in classroom; focus on individual in synchrony with a larger whole.
From New Cognitive Science		
-Lifespan cognitive development and postformal Piagetian thought: Mature knowers partly choose and and construct TRUTH, especially social truth.	-The learned individaul sees the relativity of realities and truth, but must make a passionate commitment to act, anyhow. This is postformal thought.	-Become a postformal thinker. Master teachers and good change agents are postformal thinkers and teachers who relate well to adult learners are postformal.

implications for teaching adult learners. A summary of those points is given in Table 5.

A key idea to note, in closing, is the clear convergence of implications of all new science models concerning the teaching process for adult learners in a changing society. The overriding message of the models is that change is a dialogue and that all voices matter. The models all suggest that we must change our traditional approaches to a greater use of dialogue and intuition if we expect our species to learn to survive in the world we are now constructing. And the construction of our world never ends.

REFERENCES

Augros, R. & Stanciu, G. (1987). *The new biology*. Boston: New Science Library.

Bronowski, J. (1975). *The ascent of man*. Boston: Little, Brown & Co.

Campbell, J. (1988). *The power of myth*. New York: Doubleday.

Gergen, K. (1991). *The saturated self*. New York: Basic Books.

Herbert, N. (1986). *Quantum reality*. New York: Doubleday.

Hofstadter, D. R. (1979). *Gödel, Escher and Bach: An eternal golden braid*. New York: Basic Books.

Jeans, J. (1981). *Physics and philosophy*. New York: Dover.

Johnson, D. (1991). Controversy and integrative negotiation. Paper presented at the annual American Psychological Association Conference, San Francisco.

Johnson, D. & Johnson, R. (1975). *Learning together and alone*. Englewood Cliffs, NJ: Prentice Hall.

Johnson, L. (1991). Postformal reasoning facilitates behavioral change: A case study of an international development project. In J. D. Sinnott & J. Cavanaugh (Eds.). *Bridging paradigms: Positive development in adulthood and cognitive aging*. New York: Praeger, pp. 59–72.

Kohn, A. (1987). *No contest*. Boston: Houghton Mifflin.

Labouvie-Vief, G. (1987). *Speaking about feelings: Symbolization and self regulation through the lifespan*. Paper presented at the Third Beyond Formal Operations Symposium at Harvard, Cambridge, MA.

Lee, D. (1987). *Relativistic operations: A framework for conceptualizing teachers' problem solving*. Paper presented at the Third Beyond Formal Operations Symposium at Harvard, Cambridge, MA.

Lee, D. (1991). Relativistic operations: A framework for conceptualizing teachers' problem solving. In J. D. Sinnott & J. Cavanaugh (Eds.). *Bridging paradigms: Positive development in adulthood and cognitive aging*. New York: Praeger, pp. 73–86.

Maturana, H. & Varela, F. (1988). *The tree of knowledge*. Boston: New Science Library.

McLean, P. (1988). *Evolutionary biology*. Paper presented at the Gerontology Research Center, National Institute on Aging, NIH, Baltimore, MD.

Meacham, J. & Emont, N. C. (1989). The interpersonal basis of everyday problem solving. In J. D. Sinnott (Ed.). *Everyday problem solving*. New York: Praeger.

Pagels, H. R. (1982). *The cosmic code: Quantum physics as the language of nature*. New York: Simon & Schuster.

Perry, W. B. (1975). *Forms of intellectual and ethical development in the college years: A scheme*. New York: Holt, Rinehart & Winston.

Polanyi, M. (1971). *Personal knowledge: Towards a post-critical philosophy*. Chicago: University of Chicago Press.

Prigogene, I. & Stengers, I. (1984). *Order out of chaos*. New York: Bantam.

Sinnott, J. D. (1981). The theory of relativity: A metatheory for development? *Human Development, 24*, 293–311.

Sinnott, J. D. (1984). Postformal reasoning: The relativistic stage. In M. Commons, F. Richards & C. Armon (Eds.). *Beyond formal operations*. New York: Praeger.

Sinnott, J. D. (1989a). Adult differences in the use of postformal operations. In M. Commons, J. Sinnott, F. Richards & C. Armon (Eds.). *Adult development: Comparisons and applications of developmental models*. New York: Praeger.

Sinnott, J. D. (1989b). Changing the known, knowing the changing. In D. Kramer and M. Bopp (Eds.). *Transformation in clinical and developmental psychology*. New York: Springer.

Sinnott, J. D. (1989c). *Everyday problem solving: Theory and application*. New York: Praeger.

Sinnott, J. D. (1990). *Yes, it's worth the trouble! Unique contributions from everyday cognition studies*. Paper presented at Twelfth West Virginia University Conference on Lifespan Developmental Psychology: Mechanisms of Everyday Cognition. Morgantown, WV.

Sinnott, J. D. (1991a). *Conscious adult development: Complex thought and solving our intragroup conflicts.* Invited presentation, Sixth Adult Development Conference, Suffolk University, Boston.

Sinnott, J. D. (1991b). Limits to problem solving: Emotion, intention, goal clarity, health, and other factors in postformal thought. In J. D. Sinnott & J. Cavanaugh (Eds.). *Bridging paradigms: Positive development in adulthood and cognitive aging.* New York: Praeger, pp. 169–202.

Sinnott, J. D. (1991c). What do we do to help John? A case study of postformal problem solving in a family making decisions about an acutely psychotic member. In J. D. Sinnott & J. Cavanaugh (Eds.). *Bridging paradigms: Positive development in adulthood and cognitive aging.* New York: Praeger, pp. 203–220.

Sinnott, J. D. (1993). Teaching in a chaotic new physics world: Teaching as a dialogue with reality. In P. Kahaney, J. Janangelo, & L. A. M. Perry (Eds.). *Theoretical and critical perspectives on teacher change.* Norwood, NJ: Ablex Press.

Underwood, P. (1991). *Three strands in the braid: A guide for enablers of learning.* San Anselmo, CA: A Tribe of Two Press.

Wolf, F. A. (1981). *Taking the quantum leap.* New York: Harper and Row.

8

The Relationship of Postformal Thought, Adult Learning, and Lifespan Development

Jan D. Sinnott

The group of scholars considering themselves to be "cognitive lifespan developmentalists" continues to grow. The general belief of these thinkers is that mature adults can continue to develop cognitively throughout life. Many of these thinkers start from a theoretical base of neo-Piagetian theory, which is organized around a constructivist worldview. Postformal theory is one key term for the idea that there are stages of "logical" complexity that are seen in the behavior and thought of mature adults, that seem like the growth of "wisdom," and that are more complex than Piaget's last stage of (adolescent onset) formal operations. Various theorists within these cognitive lifespan development/postformal traditions have separate terms and developmental sequences and outcome behaviors for their theories, and there is a lively dialogue surrounding these differences. Since this all began in the mid–1970s, the dialogue is still new, strong, vital, and occasionally caustic. In this chapter I will continue the dialogue by bridging between concepts of *learning* and *postformal thought* and by suggesting ideas for applications and research.

One would think that, if adults were continuing their cognitive development ad infinitum or at least *ad postformal thought*, they would be learning something. Perhaps they learn to be postformal. One might also think that, if these adults did demonstrate postformal cognitive growth, that such growth would influence how they learn things now.

However, those of us studying human behavior, as a science, are not exempt from behavioral laws: We form ourselves into factions that usually ignore other factions. Lifespan developmentalists tend to ignore learning theorists. As theories of learning have evolved from behavioral and educational models different from developmental models, there is little discussion of the relations between learning and postformal thought.

To make matters even worse, those studying cognitive events in *adulthood* and *aging* have generally emerged from information-processing, cognitive-experimental traditions, not from developmental traditions. Here complex processing has been studied less often, and the idea of change over time has not been an important one. Cognitive experimentalists, as a rule, are looking for processes underlying *all* human thought, not for processes unique to a developmental stage or sequence or group. The emphasis is on commonalities, not on individual differences.

Finally, there is a general predisposition on everyone's part to use young adult tasks in research with mature adults, and this tradition also complicates matters. Young adult tasks are used because they were created first and have longer histories. We know how to use those tasks, and we all know what young adulthood is like. Also, we researchers can explain "youth" to ourselves sensibly, something that many of us can't begin to do with "maturity" and "old age" because we have not yet arrived there personally. But tasks for children and young adults are specifically designed to work with simpler thinking. If we apply them to mature thinking to analyze it we may only be addressing part of whatever complex things mature adults are doing. Mature adults, in turn, may be doing only some of the simple things younger persons do. Therefore we may erroneously think we're getting "poor" adult performance, compared with youths' performance. If adults think differently as they mature, they might show less young adult thought, but do so because they are showing more mature adult thought, if only we ask about the latter. We could miss the learning connected to complex mature thought. Critiqued along these lines; the literature that says few adults reach formal, much less postformal, thought may be meaningless, as formal thought was tested with adolescents' tasks.

When we ask adults themselves how they learn and what they learn in mature adulthood and old age, we psychologists are given a blow to our egos: Adults ignore psychologists' theories, for the most part. They say things like: "I learned what was important in life," or, "I learned how to make some practical things happen," or, "I learned to love and to relax," or "I learned to get along with people better," or "I learned there is more than one right way to do things." And how did they learn? "By having a family," or, "By nearly failing at my job," they might say (see other chapters, this volume). Of course there's no reason to expect that every adult will try to resolve our theoretical controversies and speak in psychologists' terms. But there is good reason to ask ourselves why these areas of learning or processes of learning mentioned by mature adults don't seem to appear in our theories, whatever the theorists' traditions, when they do get voiced by our respondents.

Space considerations prevent elaboration upon these paradoxes in adult cognitive developmental research. The upshot of this whole situation is that "postformal" and "learning" studies are seldom joined. Roles for learning in postformal development and the effect of postformal development on learning are unclear. While neither theory seems very relevant to midlife development on the face of things, as theorists we need to ask whether learning, postformal thought, and midlife development are related and, if so, how. If the kind of cognition adults show is not related to their adaptation, we have an argument against Piagetian theory and reinforcement-related learning theories! As realists we need to ask ourselves whether the answers even matter to real people and, if so, how? The answers to these questions, if we can obtain them, should increase our understanding of everyday or basic or rare processes in adult development. Data suggests that the quality and utility of midlife thought improves when a person has access to postformal thought.

The first purpose of this chapter is to consider the potential place of learning in postformal models, models based on the behavior and ideas of mature adults. The second purpose is to examine ways in which adult learning could relate to postformal thought, stating six key principles and elaborating on them with ideas for research and applications. These suggestions may be beginning ways to bridge the anomalies in adult cognitive development research.

THE POTENTIAL PLACE OF LEARNING IN POSTFORMAL THOUGHT

Definitions and Presuppositions

Learning is typically defined in undergraduate textbooks as the processes of acquisition of information or skills through practice or experience. (Remembering, defined as the retrieval of learned information, sometimes becomes the operational definition of having learned the information.) Postformal thought (Sinnott, 1989c) is defined as a complex logical organization of thought that is characterized by the realization that knowledge and truth are not absolute but must be chosen from possible truths by the knower. For example, in a marriage, partners may ask "Is this a good marriage or not?" Formal thinkers will discuss the objective goodness of the marriage and whether they should divorce by arguing "logically" in an "either-or" way until one convinces the other that he or she is "right." These formal-thinking partners will agree that only one can be "right"; the marriage is either "good" or "bad." But postformal thinkers in a marriage will decide on the "goodness" of the marriage (and whether to divorce) by agreeing that each of them could be "right" (subjectively) about the emotional truth of the marriage, that is, it might be "good" to her and "bad" to him. They also know that they will create the truth about the next years of that marriage, partly by how they view it. A term for this kind of postformal thought is relativistic, self-referential thought (Sinnott, 1989c). It changes the way problems of adulthood are addressed or solved. It suggests that the degree of marital satisfaction is higher for partners who have access to such thought and that such partners solve marital problems differently than do their non-postformal peers.

All theories of "postformal" thought (Arlin, 1975; Basseches, 1984; Commons & Richards, 1984; Labouvie-Vief, 1984; Perry, 1975; Sinnott, 1984) more or less share the belief that such thought goes beyond Piagetian formal operations and involves a kind of commitment to one or another views of truth in order to take action. There is agreement that a person can think postformally in some areas of life without doing so in all areas of life or at all times. There is also agreement that postformal thought has practical and emotional implications, especially for interpersonal relations. In Cavanaugh's (1990) example, a postformal parent may be dealing with a formal-operational adolescent. Because of the nature of the thinking processes, if there are sharp differences of opinion, the formal thinker would never be able to see the situation from multiple perspectives and with empathy. It would be up to the postformal thinker to capitalize on his or her multiple perspective skills and reframe the situation in some way compatible with the abilities of the formal thinker so that they could begin to see the problem together. The formal thinker will not be able to reach into the reality of the postformal thinker to be flexible until the formal thinker becomes postformal. In this case, the postformal thinker becomes like the master or expert teacher (Lee, 1991).

Inherent in the entire discussion presented here is the idea that it is possible for adults to develop cognitively and in other ways and that experience or learning plays a part. Some writers hold no position on whether adults develop further because their paradigms do not encompass a generalized change like "development," focusing on lesser changes with each incidence of learning. This chapter's discussion will be less meaningful unless the reader assumes, at least for purposes of argument, that learning and development might occur in some joint way in adulthood.

There is not much evidence that writers in this field have formally linked learning, postformal thought, and development. I am currently surveying writers in the postformal tradition to determine what they personally believe to be the relation between learning, mature adult cognitive development, and midlife development. I have also examined chapters and subject indices of the following books that are important in the field, looking for evidence of a discussion of learning: Commons, Richards & Armon, 1984; Commons, Armon, Kohlberg, Richards, Grotzer & Sinnott, 1990; Commons, Sinnott, Richards & Armon, 1989; Sinnott, 1989a; and Sinnott & Cavanaugh, 1991. There have been virtually no entries related to "learning" in the subject indices of these volumes, for postformal chapters other than mine. Consequently, I can only conclude that this is an area ripe for exploration.

The Cognitive Side of Development

A prerequisite for examining the joint roles of learning and postformal development is to have in mind what mature adult development might mean. In my chapter in this volume on the future of adult lifespan learning, I describe the kinds of events that some cultures at some point in history have considered to be ''adult development'' or ''adult learning.'' We can see a tendency for adult development to include ''wisdom,'' more sophisticated interpersonal skills, concern for the group (over and above the self), deepening spirituality, and ability to deal with paradoxes whether they are within the self, among persons, or in life itself. Troll (1985) has reviewed major theories of adult development, such as Erikson's (1950). These theories all hypothesize that developed mature adults have a tendency to tie things together, to give overall meaning to life and events, to find overall purpose in one's life and death. Adult development, including postformal development, seems to mean increasing maturity, by all the definitions of maturity set out by Whitbourne and Weinstock (1979). The goal of later development seems to be to tie the individual's life to the group and to anchor both in a meaningful story that makes the struggle of existence worthwhile. This seems to require a cognitive leap to postformal thought (Sinnott, 1992; in press).

It may be useful to ask what Piaget, the originator of the theory from which postformal theory developed, might have expected postformal logical development to be like. If going from one stage to another, in his scheme, meant progressively higher-order coordination of ideas (Furth, 1969), postformal thought would lead to an adult development characterized by the ability to order *formal* thought in some more complex logical way. It would be the person's way of making sense of several different logics such as we find in the multiple ''truths'' of the everyday world.

Speculations about Learning, Postformal Thought, and Adult Development

Given the beliefs that people possess about what developing adults develop *to*, and given what writers in traditions as varied as Eastern mysticism, psychology, and gerontology expect of developing adults, we now can outline a general systems theory (Miller, 1978; Sinnott, 1989b) of the general directions of developmental tasks in mature adulthood. We can then try to place postformal thought and related learning within that flow. First, one learns to coordinate the body (Piaget's sensimotor, preoperational level) to take action in the world. Next, one coordinates facts (or abstractions from action), but, being abstractions from *action*, they are still rather concrete. Third, one coordinates the relations among those facts within a formal logical system. Finally, one coordinates the logical systems themselves and the relation of those systems to regulated emotional systems and interpersonal systems.

At each transition point between logical systems certainty is lost and one's logical order is painfully unraveled before being reordered. This means that one develops from a state of certainty, where facts and reality are clear-cut, through a period or state of "darkness," where certainty is lost in unknowing or questioning, to a new state of "light," where reality is clearer in a new, significantly improved way. After a number of these cycles, this underlying pattern reaches consciousness. One is then no longer a prisoner of the pattern, but can work with it as if it were a tool, aware of the overriding unity of the process.

To use computer-related terms, learning and development at first are data-driven. They represent a state of little order and a small data base, so that data must be "loaded in." A pattern must be created from initial data to load further data. This state, early in developmental time, would have high potential and little order in general systems theory terms. It would be very fact oriented, data driven, and very concrete. Later a balance is achieved between data-driven processing and order-driven processing. The latter "top-down" form of processing allows the initial structure to determine which available data will be taken in next. (This balance is akin to Piaget's assimilation and accommodation.) Eventually, if the program becomes more complex, it *monitors* the data-driven and top-down processes, "aware" that the balance can be altered between the two.

Postformal thought would be analogous to the last stages of the developing person and to the last state of the computer analogy just described. However, the idea of postformal thought carries the discussion of development of thought beyond the single thinker to several thinkers simultaneously participating in the knowing situation and co-creating the ensuing reality. They co-create by mutually deciding what the "reality" is. When they become conscious of this co-creation, relationships seem to get better and more mature in quality. Co-creation of reality occurs at all points of the cognitive developmental continuum. It matters more at this complex, postformal point because the knowers are several abstractions away from concrete, sensory events.

SIX RELATIONS BETWEEN LEARNING AND POSTFORMAL THOUGHT: RESEARCH AND APPLICATIONS

Although it is possible to create a book-length manuscript on potential and actual applications and research on the six principles, I will concentrate on a few examples of the way this set of principles can be operationalized. The examples come from various data sources including my own case study and experimental research. Each example shows one way of connecting learning and one theory of complex, postformal thought. The connections are linked, in turn, to theory, research, and practical applications.

Learning before Postformal Thought Can Occur

Some processes and facts must be learned before postformal thought can be shown. First, the theoretical position flowing from Piaget's original thinking

Table 1
Prerequisites for Shift from Formal Thought to Relativistic Thought

- Ability to structure inherently logical formal systems.
- Acceptance of validity of more than one logical system pertaining to a given event.
- Commitment to one set of a priori beliefs of many possible sets.
- Awareness that the same manipulation of the same variable can have varying effects due to temporal and environmental contexts.
- Awareness that the concept of causal linearity is erroneous when reality is multicausal.
- Understanding that contradiction, subjectivity, and choice are inherent in all logical, objective observations.
- Taking into account that contradictory multiple causes and solutions can be equally "correct" in real life within certain limits.
- Awareness that an outcome state is inseparable from an outcome process-leading-to-state.

Source: Sinnott, 1984.

suggests that formal operational thought must be present before postformal thought can be shown (Commons et al., 1984; Sinnott, 1984). Second, it seems necessary to learn that some problem solving involves the kind of problem that is called "ill-structured" (Churchman, 1971), where the goal of the problem and the parameters of the problem are unclear. Third, it seems necessary to gather relevant facts about the problem at hand and hold them in working memory or long-term memory long enough to see the larger complexity of the problem space (Sinnott, 1989c). These three seem to be learning prerequisite to simply *moving* to a postformal worldview in any given context. This is some of the complex material on which the manipulations of postformal thought can begin. (Of course, even more basic or primitive processes must also be present. For example, if the thinker does not know anything about relationships and their possibilities or has been virtually devoid of interpersonal encounters, he or she would have no "data" loaded in this area and would therefore be hard-pressed to think about relations in a complex way.) Table 1 (Sinnott, 1984) contains additional prerequisites for shifting from formal Piagetian thought to postformal thought. Table 2 (Sinnott, 1984) shows necessary learning in the specific context of interpersonal relations before formal thought can occur in that context.

My studies of problem solving reported in 1989 demonstrate how individual thinkers learn from probe questions that problems can be seen in more than one formal way. Using that learning, they can go on to solve other problems in more than one formal way. In a similar way, a thinker can learn that problems can have more than one goal (Sinnott, 1985, 1991) and go on to generalize that knowledge to other problems. In the case study of "John," who began to display psychotic symptoms (Sinnott, 1991), his sister could not think postformally about his condition until she learned about his behavior

Table 2
Applications: Interpersonal Relations
Relativistic

• Our relations are logical within a set of "givens" that we choose to utilize.

• They are based on both our past relations to each other and our relations to other significant persons.

• Relating means knowing "where you're coming from" and interacting on that level.

• Relating is never knowing "YOU" completely because, in knowing you, I am necessarily subjectively "creating" you.

• Relations are always "in process"; they cannot be described as stable until they end.

Formalistic

• There is only one way to structure our relationship to reflect reality.

• Our relationship exists "out there" in reality.

• Our relationship involves only us, now.

• The relationship has just one "reality"—no need to match levels to understand.

• We can know the essence of each other.

• Role is more important than process.

Source: Sinnott, 1984.

and thought, about her options, and about the formal logic being used by her father and the psychiatrist. What does the first principle mean for theory, research, and practical application? Table 3 displays one such implication for each of the six principles.

The thinker must learn there are multiple "true" views of realities. This means that more information about the complexity of a situation must be offered to the thinker. Perry (1975), for example, saw the university experience as a chance to make more complex multiple views of realities available for college students. Lee (1991) credits expert teachers with the ability to use this shift themselves and suggests that they teach it, in turn, to others (Lee, private communication). Some theorists credit intimate relationships with giving a participant in them several ways of looking at the reality of the world, courtesy of the ideas of their intimate partner (Basseches, 1984; Kramer, 1989; Sinnott, 1981, 1984, 1991). Counseling and clinical encounters seem to offer this possibility to clients as their views conflict with views of a trusted therapist (Armstrong, 1991; Benack, 1984). Problem solvers shown another person's solution to the problem they are working on, a solution different from theirs, learn to shift their realities to become more "multireality oriented" (Sinnott, 1991). Theory, research, and an application related to this second principle are shown in Table 3.

Postformal Thought Changes Learning Processes

Postformal thinkers help learners bridge conflicting "truths." Expert teachers (who are labeled as such by their peers and schools), persons good at conflict resolution, development project personnel who teach behavioral change and empowerment of project participants, and therapists working successfully with multiple personality disorder clients all seem to facilitate this bridging among conflicting truths (Armstrong, 1991; Johnson, 1991 and this volume; Kramer, 1989; Lee, 1991). It almost seems, from this, that postformal thinkers would be more likely to understand the multiple sides of themselves and be better integrated as personalities (see Chinen, 1984).

As seen in Table 3, the principle that postformal thinkers learn all truths as "definite maybes" lets us become aware of how little cognitive developmental studies teach us about knowing that shifting world. We psychologists understand too little about how we learn process and change. We have too few theories about the knowing of social realities, which shift from moment to moment as they are co-created by dyads or families or societies. In earlier problem-solving studies of my own (Sinnott, 1989ac, 1991) middle-aged and older respondents given logical problems tended to produce solutions that were actually general-izable *processes* that would bridge changing conditions from the reality of one problem to another. They had learned something new, namely, good processes. (Perhaps, in Erikson's terms, they were learning integration.) See Table 3 for theory, research, and applications related to the third principle.

For postformal thinkers, learning processes become inherently social. Once the postformal thinker knows his or her role in the creation of truth (that role being to choose a view of reality to commit to and work from), that thinker is aware of the role of others in also creating the "reality" around him or her. This social creation of reality is even true of the reality of the physical world. The postformal thinker wants to know the theory you have chosen about physics or even ordinary clock time, not to evaluate whether you are correct, but to move logically from your chosen theory to his or hers. While both positions on time grant the existence of "time" as a physical variable, you each need to know if you are talking about time with an eye toward valuing punctuality, social rules for dinner-party guests, or time/space overlap in post-Einsteinian physics. When you decide on the formal logical system each of you is using, the con-versation can proceed. The postformal thinker seems to cross over between cognition and emotion, learning with an empathy for the learned material and for others' positions on the learned material (Powell, 1984).

New social variables become important to learning when we realize the social component that exists. For example, in couples' problem solving, the adjustment of the dyad members to each other seems to influence whether postformal thought continues to be displayed over several problems or whether the couple learns to go to a simpler solution (Rogers, Sinnott & Van Dusen, 1991). Table 3 has suggestions for further research and applications.

Any learned element can be used in both postformal and non-postformal ways. Postformal and non-postformal thinkers simply use the facts like building blocks, for different purposes. Besides using learned elements in service to different logics, postformal thinkers can probably manipulate more learned facts than can non-postformal thinkers because those learned items can be combined in more

Table 3

Six Relations between Learning and Postformal Thought: Implications for Theory, Research, Applications

Principles	Theory	Research	Application
Learning Prior to Postformal Thought			
1. Basic processes (such as memory and formal operations) and basic facts (such as information about a certain context) must be learned.	1. Learning is integral to postformal thought. Use of postformal thought can be accelerated and stimulated by teaching prerequisite processes.	1. Experimentally manipulate learned material to effect change in postformal thought, e.g., teach students to recognize potential for ill-structured problems. Examine case studies of thinkers beginning to be postformal.	1. Conflicts resolution experts can teach prerequisites of postformal thought to participants in a conflict. This would accelerate resolution of the conflict. Teach parents to work in larger "problem spaces" to solve parent-child conflicts.
2. Thinker learns there can be multiple "true" views of reality.	2. Cognitive development studies begin to utilize quantum physics and general system theory change models to allow for multiple truths in cognitive change events, especially interpersonal events.	2. Perform multiperson cognition experiments to determine conditions that best teach multiple realities. For example, does group problem solving more often lead to postformal statements? Do expert therapists more often show acceptance of multiple realities?	2. Teach clients and university students how to take in and consider multiple view of reality.

Presence of Postformal Thought Alters Learning Process Thereafter

3. Postformal thinkers help new learners bridge "conflicting" realities. Postformal thinkers learn as if change is the only constant; therefore, they tend to learn processes.

4. For postformal thinkers, learning processes become inherently social.

3. The understanding of process and the awareness of changes and shifts might be key areas for further theory development in lifespan developmental psychology.

4. The multiperson nature of thought can be added to most theories of cognitive development that lack such dimensions.

3. Study the various ways cognitive development changes understanding of process. What are steps in such an understanding? Study how individuals maintain a sense of self if they see reality as (in part) commitment to a truth co-created with others and ever changing.

4. Studies of dyadic problem solving can be conducted. Studies investigating the factors influencing postformal thinkers' learning processes can be done.

3. Teach beginning therapists and new professors how to best present multiple views of reality. Teach international development workers how best to span the realities of life in economically developed countries and life in less-developed countries.

4. Cooperative learning and dialogic processes in learning settings may be useful to adult learners, who tend to be postformal.

115

Table 3 (continued)

Principles	Theory	Research	Application
5. Any learned element can be used in postformal or non-postformal ways.	5. Theory can include elements thought to determine whether a given fact will be used postformally or formally.	5. Study how persons of various ages and cognitive levels use the same facts to build formal and postformal systems.	5. Development of tests of "readiness for postformal thought."
6. Postformal thinkers and non-postformal thinkers in same situation learn different things.	6. Add cognitive development level to theories about effects of context.	6. Experimentally analyze the determinants of use of formal vs. postformal thought.	6. The elements of intragroup conflicts can be learned postformally, leading to conflict resolution.

inclusive logical hierarchies by postformal thinkers (Sinnott, 1984). This may be a way for postformals to adaptively avoid overstimulation and unnecessary reductionism when faced with too much information. Stereotyping and simplistic positions, the last resort of the overloaded non-postformal thinker, can be avoided by the postformal thinker. Of course the fact that the same learned fact can be used in postformal and non-postformal logics suggests that communication problems will occur when users of those two logics dialogue, unless the postformal among them creates a bridge. This communication challenge can be the basis for further research and postformal readiness tests (Table 3).

Postformal thinkers and nonpostformal thinkers in the same situation learn different things. Conflicts among members of a group, whether the group is a family or an organization, are not pleasant experiences. But they sometimes teach us things about ourselves and others. Experiencing those conflicts, people learn very different things from seeing the same conflict (Sinnott, 1991; 1993).

The author recently experienced the protracted conflict between a couple, one of whom showed the use of postformal thought while the other did not. The former learned to what extent *choice* influenced relations; the latter learned to blame others for problems. Marital interaction studies are one application of this principle. See Table 3.

CONCLUSION

In this chapter I have attempted to describe the newer research area of postformal thought, a theory of lifespan cognitive development, and to relate the theory to learning. I have described six basic relations between learning and postformal thought. Some research related to these principles is cited. Suggestions for theory, research, and applications of the principles have been offered. These positions may unite the paradigms of learning and cognitive development in a new way.

REFERENCES

Arlin, P. (1975). Cognitive development in adulthood: A fifth stage? *Developmental Psychology, 11*, 602–606.

Armstrong, J. (1991). Keeping one's balance in a moving system: The effects of the multiple personality disordered patient on the cognitive development of the therapist. In J. Sinnott & J. Cavanaugh (Eds.). *Bridging paradigms: Positive development in adulthood and cognitive aging* (pp. 11–18). New York: Praeger.

Basseches, M. (1984). *Dialectical thinking and adult development.* Norwood, NJ: Ablex.

Benack, S. (1984). Postformal epistemologies and the growth of empathy. In M. Commons, F. Richards & C. Armon (Eds.). *Beyond formal operations: Late adolescent and adult cognitive development* (pp. 340–356). New York: Praeger.

Cavanaugh, J. (1990). *Adult development and aging.* Belmont, CA: Wadsworth.

Chinen, A. B. (1984). *Eastern wisdom, Western aging.* Paper presented at the Annual Meeting of the Gerontological Society of America, San Antonio, Texas.

Churchman, C. (1971). *The design of inquiring systems: Basic concepts of systems and organizations.* New York: Basic Books.

Commons, M., Armon, C., Kohlberg, L., Richards, R., Grotzer, T. & Sinnott, J. (Eds.). (1990). *Adult development: Models and methods in the study of adolescent and adult thought.* New York: Praeger.

Commons, M. & Richards, R. (1984). A general model of stage theory. In M. Commons, R. Richards, & C. Armon (Eds.). *Beyond formal operations: Late adolescent and adult cognitive development* (pp. 120–140). New York: Praeger.

Commons, M., Richards, F. & Armon, C. (Eds.). (1984). *Beyond formal operations: Late adolescent and adult cognitive development.* New York: Praeger.

Commons, M., Sinnott, J. D., Richards, R. & Armon, C. (Eds.). (1989). *Adult development II: Comparisons and applications of adolescent and adult development models.* New York: Praeger.

Erikson, E. (1950). *Childhood and society.* New York: Norton.

Furth, H. (1969). *Piaget and knowledge.* Englewood Cliffs, NJ: Prentice-Hall.

Johnson, L. (1991). Bridging paradigms: The role of a change agent in an international technical transfer project. In J. Sinnott & J. Cavanaugh (Eds.). *Bridging paradigms: Positive development in adulthood and cognitive aging* (pp. 59–72). New York: Praeger.

Kramer, D. A. (1989). A developmental framework for understanding conflict resolution processes. In J. D. Sinnott (Ed.). *Everyday problem solving: Theory and applications* (pp. 133–152). New York: Praeger.

Labouvie-Vief, G. (1984). Logic and self regulation from youth to maturity: A model. In M. Commons, F. Richards & C. Armon (Eds.). *Beyond formal operations: Late adolescent and adult cognitive development* (pp. 158–179). New York: Praeger.

Lee, D. M. (1987). Relativistic operations: A framework for conceptualizing teachers' everyday problem solving. Paper presented at the Third Beyond Formal Operations Symposium at Harvard University: Positive Adult Development. Cambridge, MA.

Lee, D. M. (1991). Relativistic operations: A framework for conceptualizing teachers' everyday problem solving. In J. Sinnott & J. Cavanaugh (Eds.). *Bridging paradigms: Positive development in adulthood and cognitive aging* (pp. 73–86). New York: Praeger.

Miller, J. (1978). *Living systems.* New York: McGraw-Hill.

Perry, W. B. (1975). *Forms of intellectual and ethical development in the college years: A scheme.* New York: Holt, Rinehart, & Winston.

Powell, P. (1984). Stage 4A: Category operations and interactive empathy. In M. Commons, F. Richards & C. Armon (Eds.). *Beyond formal operations: Late adolescent and adult cognitive development* (pp. 326–339). New York: Praeger.

Rogers, D., Sinnott, J. D. & Van Dusen, L. (1991). *Marital adjustment and social cognitive performance in everyday logical problem solving.* Paper presented at the Sixth Adult Development Symposium, Suffolk University, Boston.

Sinnott, J. D. (1981). The theory of relativity: A metatheory for development? *Human Development, 24,* 293–311.

Sinnott, J. D. (1984). Postformal reasoning: The relativistic stage. In M. Commons, R. Richards, & C. Armon (Eds.). *Beyond formal operations: Late adolescent and adult cognitive development* (pp. 298–325). New York: Praeger.

Sinnott, J. D. (1985). *The expression of postformal relativistic self-referential operations in everyday problem solving performance: Adult lifespan data.* Paper presented at the Second Beyond Formal Operations Symposium at Harvard University, Cambridge, MA.

Sinnott, J. D. (Ed.). (1989a). *Everyday problem solving: Theory and application.* New York: Praeger.

Sinnott, J. D. (1989b). General systems theory: A rationale for the study of everyday memory. In L. Poon, D. Rubin, & R. Wilson (Eds.). *Everyday cognition in adulthood and old age* (pp. 59–70). New Rochelle, NY: Cambridge University Press.

Sinnott, J. D. (1989c). Lifespan relativistic postformal thought. In M. Commons, J. Sinnott, F. Richards, & C. Armon (Eds.). *Beyond formal operations II: Comparisons and applications of adolescent and adult development models (pp. 239–278).* New York: Praeger.

Sinnott, J. D. (1991). What do we do to help John? A case study of postformal problem solving in a family making decisions about an acutely psychotic member. In J. Sinnott & J. Cavanaugh (Eds.). *Bridging paradigms: Positive development in adulthood and cognitive aging* (pp. 203–220). New York: Praeger.

Sinnott, J. D. (1992). Development and yearning: Cognitive aspects of spiritual development. Paper presented at the American Psychological Association Conference, Washington, D.C.

Sinnott, J. D. (1993). The use of complex thought and resolving intragroup conflicts: A means to conscious adult development in the workplace. In J. Demick & P. M. Miller (Eds.). *Adult development in the workplace* (pp. 155–175). Hillsdale, NJ: Erlbaum.

Sinnott, J. D. (in press). Creativity and postformal thought. In C. Adams-Price (Ed.). *Creativity and aging: Theoretical and empirical approaches.* New York: Springer.

Sinnott, J. D. & Cavanaugh, J. (Eds.). (1991). *Bridging paradigms: Positive development in adulthood and cognitive aging.* New York: Praeger.

Troll, L. (1985). *Early and middle adulthood* (2nd edition). Monterey, CA: Brooks/Cole.

Whitbourne, S. & Weinstock, C. (1979). *Adult development.* New York: Holt, Rinehart & Winston.

9

Learning and Spirituality in Adulthood

Patricia S. Weibust and
L. Eugene Thomas

> I long ago lost a hound, a bay horse, and a turtledove, and am still on their
> trail. Many are the travellers I have spoken to concerning them, describing
> their tracks and what calls they answered to. I have met one or two who
> had heard the hound, and the tramp of the horse, and even seen the dove
> disappear behind a cloud, and they seemed as anxious to recover them as
> if they had lost them themselves.
>
> Thoreau, *Walden*

As we approach the topic of learning and spirituality during the adult years, we
are confronted by a vast literature ranging through the world's religions (most
especially their mystical or contemplative strains), philosophical works over the
centuries, and more recent studies and theories of psychologists. All of them
taken together, if it were possible to do so, would comprise a complex network
of ideas, a model if you will. Our aim in this paper is both more limited and,
in a sense, more ambitious. Limited, in that we will certainly not attempt to
integrate the numerous bodies of literature that relate to learning, age, and
spirituality. And ambitious, in that we would like to begin examination of the
relatively unexplored web of interrelationships among them.

It should be noted that our methodology diverges markedly from the typical
positivist paradigm upon which most social science research is based. Following
Dilthey's human science approach (the English translation of the rather forbidding
compound German name *Geisteswissenschaften*), we seek to match the method
used to the nature of the subject under investigation (Polkinghorne, 1983).
According to Wilber (1983) we must enter upon the path of the "mandalic
sciences," where one attempts to use the mind and verbal expression to discuss
the data of transcendelia. Even though we will use the best tools possible,

phenomenological and dialogical/intersubjective science, we must recognize "that we are trying to put into mental forms and concepts that which is finally transconceptual and transmental" (Wilber, 1983, p. 75). We can acknowledge this by using a different terminology—"paradoxical, translogical, or mandalic sciences" (Wilber, 1983, p. 75)—which will alert us to the fact that "rational-mental statements about Spirit or Being always eventually degenerate in contradiction or paradoxes" (Wilber, 1983, p. 75).

DISCERNING SPIRITUAL MATURITY

In seeking to understand spirituality we have chosen to follow Maslow's advice (1971), that is, to skate past philosophical complexities as fast as you can. Rather than offering a theoretical definition, we choose to approach the topic by studying exemplars of the spiritually mature or "self-actualizers." Here we follow the lead of William James, who utilized examples of extraordinary spiritual experiences in the Gifford Lectures (1902/1958) to illuminate experiences only dimly sensed by some. As Maslow (1971) has noted, the difference between the most spiritually advanced "peak experiencer" and the ordinary person is only a matter of degree, not of kind. The choice to study seemingly unique phenomena can therefore help us to understand the seemingly usual, for the extraordinary and the ordinary are one.

According to Fritjof Capra, Gregory Bateson was fond of telling the following story:

There was a man who had a powerful computer, and he wanted to know whether computers could ever think. So he asked it, no doubt in his best Fortran: "Will you be able to think like a human being?" The computer clicked and rattled and blinked, and finally printed out its answer on a piece of paper, as these machines do. The man ran to pick up the printout, and there, neatly typed, read the following words: "THAT REMINDS ME OF A STORY." (Capra, 1988, p. 77)

Capra goes on to comment, "Bateson considered stories, parables, and metaphors to be essential expressions of human thinking" (p. 78). And so, we will present in some detail the stories of two remarkable people who have reached a transcendent level of understanding.

Ann's Story

Ann, an attractive, energetic woman with a Ph.D., works as a researcher in a large insurance company. When she was in her late 40s, it was discovered that she had breast cancer. A few nights before the operation, she dreamed that she died in the hospital and saw the time of her death on her medical chart. She was so convinced of her impending demise that she gave explicit instructions to her husband on various matters she wanted taken care of after her death. The operation went well, but when she was returned to her room she was still in considerable pain. One of the doctors gave her morphine. Her daughter stopped by to look in on her and was alarmed to see that Ann looked gray. She dashed out and told the nurse, who issued an emergency code. Ann's cardiac and respiratory systems were shutting down because of an overdose of morphine. She had been given two small doses in the recovery room, and for some reason the doctor had been unaware of this when he administered a third, massive dose. For several minutes, as the emergency team worked on her, Ann had no pulse.

While the doctors and nurses were desperately trying to save her life, Ann had an out-of-body experience. All of a sudden, she was above her body and looking down at the scene. Observing in a detached way, she saw herself as a small gray body lying on the bed and the frantic efforts of the medical team. When she "heard" a nurse say, "We're losing her," Ann realized that she was dying and did not want to. She started to fight, and immediately she found herself back in her body and experiencing great pain again. She thrashed about so much that she broke a tooth.

A couple of days after surgery she experienced two more extraordinary occurrences. Ann was feeling much better physically, but she was quite shaken by her close call with death and her out-of-body experience. While her mother visited, a hospital chaplain from Ghana asked if they would like him to join them. They were grateful to see him and talked about Ann's cancer and about how low and fearful she felt while waiting for her biopsy report, which would tell if the cancer had spread. He offered to say a prayer. At first Ann was reluctant. She felt so absolutely drained that she was afraid she might break down and cry, but her mother encouraged her. During the prayer, as Ann sat in her chair, she felt a warmth begin at her feet and spread upwards to suffuse her whole body, bringing with it a sense of total peace and certainty that she was well. Immediately following, she saw the three-dimensional figure of an older woman with white hair, dressed in a pale print dress, floating through the air.

The next day, Ann's biopsy report confirmed her "sense" of being well. She slowly began to share her experiences with friends and family. It came out in bits and pieces as she recalled things she had forgotten or didn't understand and overcame her hesitation in sharing her experiences, for fear of eliciting ridicule or disbelief. She searched out books on near-death experiences. She went on retreats at a Benedictine monastery, where silence and contemplation and song are practiced. She attended church occasionally, participated in a healing service, and began to read the Bible—understanding passages in a new way, recognizing with certainty the reality of what had previously been only stories to her.

Ann noticed that her psychic abilities were becoming more pronounced. Before, she had felt a sense of intuition about various things and, of course, had had the dream about her death. But after her experience of spiritual consciousness she began to have clear mental images of something happening. To her amazement, within a short time, these images came to pass. She studied and experimented with these phenomena and learned to distinguish the genuinely psychic from ordinary hunches, concerns, or worries. For the first time in her life, she went to a medium for a psychic reading, talked with her about parapsychology, and borrowed some books.

We can end Ann's story with one rather telling event and a description of her present situation, two years after her original experience. She is finding herself increasingly sensitive to the sufferings of others, to the point where she feels she absolutely must act. It seems to her as if she takes on their suffering and is impelled to do something about it. A man at work, who has a large family, asks if he can borrow a small sum of money for the weekend. She simply gives him the money. Ann is learning about this aspect of her life by listening to her "inner voice," by acting and seeing what follows, and by reading books wherein she recognizes that the author knows about these things and adds to her understanding. She now has an immediate sense of the depth of spiritual consciousness of people she meets, and is attracted to those with whom she can share and learn—people who know.

Henry's Story

Henry, an 83-year-old retired clergyman, living with his wife in Birmingham, England, had a mystical experience at age 19 that completely changed the direction of his life. His childhood was punctuated by frequent moves from one school to another, necessitated by his father's military career. Suffering from congenital hearing problems, Henry dropped out of school at 15 in order to enter the baking trade. One day when delivering bread at a smelly butcher shop he underwent a period of ecstatic awareness. He describes it:

Suddenly a load fell—not off my back (chuckling)—but off my existential state, if you like. From a dark night of the soul to a joyful assurance of adequacy. I remember coming down those stairs with an empty basket, walking along the main street, and seeing how everything looked so different. Everything was full of glory.

It was as if a door was opened to him, and he felt drawn to the ministry. He entered night school to prepare for college, and despite the misgivings of his family and at times his own doubts, he energetically went about acting on his leading. Financing his schooling entirely on his own, Henry held a full-time job while completing his secondary and university education. After graduation he decided to apply to go overseas as a missionary. He persuaded the Archbishop of Canterbury to ordain him, only to find that his congenital hearing trouble would prevent him from going overseas. Thereafter he served a variety of chaplain jobs, working his way up to a senior chaplaincy in a psychiatric hospital.

At age 67 Henry decided to retire, not because of age as such, but because the senior psychiatrist questioned whether a hearing-impaired chaplain could adequately do his work, especially working with groups. Henry agreed that many people benefited from working in groups and sadly came to the conclusion that the individual therapy he had been doing was insufficient.

Retirement was a dark period for Henry, entailing as it did calling into question the work he had done for most of his life. It was then that he and his wife went on a spiritual pilgrimage, exploring different religions. Finally they were attracted to the silent worship of Quakers, a religion in which there are no priests or ministers. After much soul-searching they left the Church of England, and in his late 70s Henry and his wife became Quakers.

When asked if he had subsequent experiences similar to that at age 19, Henry replied:

Oh yes. Continuing. This is a kind of indescribable experience, because it is so deep that it is open to misunderstanding. It is a deep, inner experience, which continually reveals different spiritual implications. It's a very unifying experience; it gives you the awareness that life and the spirit, God, is a living God, who is in the process of causing something to happen all the time. Even when the process seems to lead you into suffering—which it does—there is joy, a feeling of unity and wholeness, in spite of the sorrow or suffering. (Interviewer: Would it be fair to say that you have a traditional view of God, then?) Well, I naturally had that early on, when I was a youngster. I understand people who have that view of the divine. The great thing is that the divine, however you conceive it, is adequate and benign, if one only responds. And one can joyfully respond. And to me that is faith. To me faith is much more than believing in things. Real faith is a response to something that is happening in the spirit, getting caught up in it, and going along and being guided by it.

UNITY CONSCIOUSNESS AS KNOWING

Both Ann and Henry had their glimpse of "the hound, the bay horse, and the turtledove," and their stories have much to tell us about learning and spirituality. It is evident from what they told us that theirs was an awareness, an immediacy and certainty of knowing, a knowledge so profound that it is difficult to express in words and subject to misunderstanding. What they experienced has been given different names by different people. Bucke calls it Cosmic Consciousness (Bucke, 1901); Wilber uses the term unity consciousness (Wilber, 1979); the Bible refers to grace; Buddhists speak of enlightenment. Yogi Ramacharaka well summarizes the perennial philosophy (Huxley, 1944) in his description of the dawning of "Spiritual Consciousness":

From the writings of the ancient philosophers of all races, from the songs of the great poets of all peoples, from the preachings of the prophets of all religions and times we can gather traces of this illumination which has come to them—this unfoldment of Spiritual Consciousness. . . . All who have experienced this illumination, even in a faint degree, recognize the like experience in the tale, song, or preaching of another, though centuries may roll between them. It is the song of the Soul, which when once heard is never forgotten. (Ramacharaka, 1903, pp. 52, 53)

To say that the "song" of Spiritual Consciousness is the same in other places and other times is, of course, the main tenet of the perennial philosophy (Huxley, 1944). Maslow (1971) expands our understanding by distinguishing the characteristics of persons who, having undergone peak experiences, have become "self-actualizing." The work of Wilber (1979, 1982) and other transpersonal psychologists further adds to our comprehension of higher stages of consciousness and enables us to better differentiate individual differences. A discussion of the levels of consciousness in Wilber's model is beyond the scope of this paper, but it is clear that both Ann's and Henry's level of consciousness is beyond that of ordinary rational functioning, reflecting the higher transpersonal level (see Thomas et al., 1993, for a discussion of Wilber's typology and an analysis of Henry's level of spiritual development). Their unity consciousness is a kind of knowing in which there is no distinction between the knowing and the known (see Wilber, 1977, p. 43).

What is interesting about both Ann and Henry is the way in which their expanded level of consciousness is reflected in their everyday lives. Rather than coming off as befuddled and otherworldly, their experiences have led them to be more grounded in the everyday and practical. Again, this reflects the teachings of most of the world's mystical traditions, as well as that of contemporary observers such as Maslow. Bateson (1972) observes that such persons are "perhaps saved from being swept away on oceanic feeling by their ability to focus on the minutiae of life. Every detail of the universe is seen as proposing a view of the whole" (p. 304). Bateson goes on to cite the famous passage from Blake's "Auguries of Innocence," as descriptive of people of this sort: "To see the World in a Grain of Sand."

This, of course, is the thrust of the mystical poetry of T. S. Eliot, that the end of our seeking is to find ourselves at the place where we began our journey and to "know the place for the first time" (Eliot, 1950, p. 145). As this concept has important implications for the learning of spirituality, it is best to state the position less poetically and more propositionally. Drawing upon a wide range of sources, Wilber notes:

The true sages proclaim there is no path to the Absolute, no way to gain unity consciousness. Says Shankara, a Hindu, "As Brahman constitutes a person's Self it is not something to be attained by that person." Says Huang Po, a Buddhist, "That there is nothing to be attained is not idle talk; it is the truth." . . . Says Krishnamurti, a modern sage, "The real is near, you do not have to search for it; and a man who seeks truth will never find it." (Wilber, 1979, p. 143)

Maslow, in his later work, echoes precisely the same sentiment, maintaining that:

The sacred is *in* the ordinary, it is to be found in one's daily life, in one's neighbors, friends and family, in one's back yard, and travel may be a *flight* from confronting the sacred. To be looking elsewhere for miracles is to me a sure sign of ignorance that *everything* is sacred. (Maslow, 1971, p. 345)

LEARNING WHAT WE ALREADY KNOW

If that which we seek to know—spiritual consciousness, enlightenment, or whatever it is called—is something that we already have, then the "learning" of that knowing becomes paradoxical. Bateson (1972), drawing upon Bertrand Russell's Theory of Logical Types, notes that when the rules of formal discourse are contravened, paradox will be generated, at which time, "the entire structure of axioms, theorems, etc., involved in generating that paradox is thereby negated and reduced to nothing" (p. 280). The famous self-referential statement, "All Cretans are liars" is an illustration of such a paradoxical statement (being a factual statement if made by anyone else, but a self-referential and therefore paradoxical statement if made by a Cretan). Learning of spirituality is just such a self-referential undertaking, if it is the case that the state of the one doing the learning already "knows" that which is to be learned, which in turn impacts on the way learning takes place.

Drawing on Russell's Theory of Logical Types, Bateson has identified three levels of learning that can help us grapple with the paradox of the self-referential nature of learning something that we already "know." Bateson begins by identifying two ordinary types of learning that are non-paradoxical. Learning I, the type of learning studied by stimulus-response psychologists, takes place where the environment remains the same. Such learning is predicated on response to certain reinforcement contingencies, and its rate of acquisition and extinction is highly predictable (at least with lower animals).

Level II learning, "learning about Learning I," is more complex. It allows the individual to generalize beyond the environment in which Learning I has taken place. Because of its broader generalizability, Learning II is very difficult to extinguish (transference in psychotherapy indicates the durability of Learning II, as well as character traits that stay with us over the years). In effect, the individual is not able to get outside his or her frame of reference, in order to effect the change. Change from this level becomes paradoxical, because the assumptions of the agent seeking the change are that which is to be changed. Because one's sense of self is a product of Learning II, in order to change this self by the efforts of the self is of the same magnitude as the eye trying to see itself or as the individual stooping over and lifting himself by his own bootstraps.

In order for an individual to be freed from the bondage of the premises of Learning II, a different kind of learning is necessary. Learning II assumptions must cease to be the spectacles through which the individual views the world; in order for them to be changed, they must become an object of one's attention. Stated somewhat differently, rather than being embedded in the assumptions brought from earlier Learning II, one takes these assumptions as the basis for further learning—one learns about Learning II, in other words. For this kind of learning, the self as the nodal point of experience must be bypassed; the self of Learning II must be seen to be irrelevant.

Compared to Learning I or II, Learning III occurs only rarely, Bateson maintains. It is not likely to happen under ordinary circumstances, but it does eventuate from time to time in psychotherapy, religious experiences, and profound reorganization of character (perhaps as exemplified by techniques of brainwashing). The major requirement for Learning III to occur is the necessity that the individual become aware of the inadequacy of a major assumption underlying Learning II, that is, of the self as a separate and unique entity. There is danger inherent in such a shift, Bateson notes, in that the individual becomes vulnerable to a complete loss of a sense of self, which in extreme cases characterizes psychosis.

The successful navigation of this transformation can lead a person to giving up the central assumptions underlying Learning II. In its simple form, this can lead to a situation "in which hunger leads directly to eating, and the identified self is no longer in charge of organizing the behavior." "These," Bateson notes, "are the incorruptible innocents of the world" (1972, p. 306). For others, who are more creative, it may lead to a merging of the self with some "vast ecology or aesthetics of cosmic interaction" (p. 306). But Bateson only gives hints as to how this change might take place, noting that it can emerge when the individual is able to resolve the "contraries" generated by Learning II.

ON BEING OPEN TO PARADOX

It is instructive to turn to the experiences of Ann and Henry, in seeking to determine what made it possible for them to move beyond Learning II of everyday consciousness. The most obvious factor in both cases is that they underwent a kind of altered state of consciousness that threw into relief the paradoxes and "contraries" of their old way of living. Henry's unitive experience was of a mystical nature, which provided a vision of a world different in every aspect from the dreary round of daily life. Ann's was more complicated in that she underwent both a spiritual and then a psychic experience, following her near-death experience. In both cases it is clear that everything did not suddenly fall into place with the original altered state of consciousness. There was much cognitive and emotional work to be done before the paths of their lives were fully changed.

In Bateson's terminology, their experience of an altered state of consciousness catapulted them into Learning III; it allowed them to see the paradoxical nature of reality and to restructure their previous assumptions about the centrality of their own egos in the scheme of things. But further, Learning II, according to these new insights, appears necessary for these insights to be incorporated into their everyday lives. This simply does not happen, Maslow observes, with the "Thursday evening turn-on that many youngsters think of as *the* path to transcendence" (1971, p. 349).

Concerning the central place that peak experiences played in Ann's and Henry's spiritual development, it is instructive to note that Maslow found that persons who were judged to be "self-actualizing" reported having had peak experiences. It is not so widely known that he discovered that high-level self-actualizers were not unique in having undergone such experiences; almost everyone he studied reported having some sort of peak experience. The main difference between them and the true self-actualizers is that such people repress their peak experiences to the extent of either denying their existence or minimizing their importance. Persons who were found to be self-actualizing, on the other hand, were fully open to experiences of altered states of consciousness and incorporated them into their lives. Again, to use Bateson's terminology, non-actualizers seem to steadfastly maintain their Learning II assumptions, rejecting any awareness of "contraries" that might confirm the existence of Learning III.

In his later work, Maslow (1971) came to discount the importance of peak experiences, in favor of what he called "plateau experiences." Peak experiences, which are "poignantly emotional, climactic, autonomic," tend to decrease with age, and to be ephemeral, in any case. Plateau experiences tend to be more voluntary than peak experiences and to have a noetic and cognitive element that is much less important in peak experiences. Whereas peak experiences can give a glimpse of another dimension, plateau experiences can allow one to "take up residence on the high plateau or unitive consciousness" (p. 349). Concerning the attainment of this level of consciousness, Maslow observes, "Plateau experiencing can be achieved, learned, earned by long work. . . . That tends to be a lifetime of effort" (p. 349).

But here we have to remember what was said earlier about the paradoxical nature of the higher spiritual states. Wilber's citation (above) of a litany of admonitions from various spiritual traditions reminds us of the widespread warning in the perennial philosophy of the impossibility of attaining higher states of consciousness by one's own efforts. One is reminded of the Buddhist teaching concerning the attainment of enlightenment by one's own efforts: It would take as long to achieve enlightenment as it would to wear down the mighty Himalayan mountains by a dove flying over them every 100 years with a silk scarf in its beak that caressed the mountain peaks as it flew over.

DISCIPLINE VERSUS PASSIVE WAITING

The issue of whether one attains higher spiritual consciousness by discipline or by passive waiting has been one of the perennial debates which reemerges throughout the centuries. The tension was present from the beginning in the Christian religion, as illustrated by the Mary/Martha dilemma of being and doing in the New Testament; it underlay the Pelagian controversy in the sixth century over free will and original sin; it surfaced again in the faith/works controversy that was the focus of the Protestant Reformation in the sixteenth century. The debate has been equally prevalent in other religions. Buddhism, for example, characterizes the issue as being the difference between the cat and monkey view of spirituality—the metaphor is that of the kitten passively carried by the nape of its neck in its mother's mouth, while the baby monkey actively holds onto its mother's fur.

This issue is clearly a representative of one of the true paradoxes of life that Schumacher (1977) refers to as a "divergent" problem. Such problems differ from "convergent" problems, where the more intelligently they are studied, the more their answers converge, "until finally they can be written down in the form of an instruction.... To make use of the solution does not require any higher faculties or abilities" (p. 125). Convergent problems tend to be those that do not involve "life, consciousness, self-awareness," in other words, they tend to be found in the physical sciences.

Divergent problems, on the other hand, are those that, even with the most intense investigation, do not "converge." Indeed, Schumacher notes, "the more they are clarified and logically developed, the more they *diverge*" (p. 122). He continues, "Divergent problems cannot be solved in the sense of establishing a 'correct formula'; they can, however be transcended" (p. 126). That is, the two sides cease to be opposites at a higher level. To put it in Bateson's terminology, the paradox can be solved only by Level III learning, which transcends the "contraries" (or "non-convergence," to use Schumacher's term) of Level II learning.

Concerning spiritual learning by means of discipline, it might be stated that the active practice of spirituality is an expression of unity consciousness (if only from a brief glance in an altered state) and at the same time creates conditions under which this consciousness is more likely to occur. Foster (1978), writing from a Christian perspective, states the general nature of the paradox:

We are tempted to believe there is nothing we can do. If all human strivings end in moral bankruptcy (and having tried it, we know it is so), and if righteousness is a gracious gift from God (as the Bible clearly states), then is it not logical to conclude that we must wait for God to come and transform us? Strangely enough, the answer is "no." The analysis is correct: human striving is insufficient and righteousness is a gift from God. It is the conclusion that is faulty, for happily there is something we can do. We do not need to be hung on the horns of the dilemma of either human works or idleness. God has given us the Disciplines of the spiritual life as a means of receiving His grace. The Disciplines allow us to place ourselves before God so that He can transform us. (p. 6)

The important point is that one must take a path, which is what Ann and Henry have done, in order to express the higher consciousness that is within. In their accounts of what transpired after their unity experiences, both of them reported that they learned to listen, to hear the still voice from within. Ann went on to seek out books, people, and religious activities to help her learn. Henry went on to a formal institution to study for the ministry and served as a chaplain for many years.

Wilber states the issue in the more general terms of the perennial philosophy:

"Even if, in our spiritual practices, it appears we are trying to attain enlightenment, we are actually only expressing it" (1979, p. 145).

So what does it mean that never, under any circumstances, at any time, through any effort, can you enter the Ultimate State of Consciousness? Only that the Ultimate State of Consciousness is already fully and completely present. . . . You therefore cannot enter It because you have always been It from the very beginning. (1983, p. 301)

Here we have clearly formulated, in propositional statements, the paradox that T. S. Eliot expressed poetically, that when we reach the finish line, we will discover that it is the starting line also, but during the journey we will have gained full knowledge of it (1950, p. 145). Interestingly, this same idea is conveyed in a moving Jewish teaching. Before a baby is born, the angel Gabriel teaches it the entire Torah. Then the angel taps the baby on the lip (which is why there is an indentation there), and at the time of birth the infant forgets all that it has been taught. The person must go about regaining this knowledge for the remainder of his or her life.[1]

Unlike "convergent" problems, which can be solved by propositional logic and concentrated effort, the paradox generated by a "divergent" problem such as this must be approached in a different way. Stated another way, a different type of learning is needed to appropriate this paradoxical domain. Before stating tentative conclusions regarding this type of learning, we will devote a final section to a consideration of the developmental nature of such learning. That is, does the ability to engage in such learning change with age? Does the nature of spiritual learning differ for the adult years, from that of childhood and young adulthood?

DEVELOPMENT AND SPIRITUAL LEARNING

Traditionally, wisdom and spiritual maturity have been associated with age. In the Hindu faith, the fourth stage, or *ashram*, of development occurs only after the obligations (*dharmas*) of career and family life are complete. Then the individual is free to become a renunciate (*sannyasi*) and devote the rest of his life to spiritual matters. Although most contemporary Indians don't actually follow this practice, the teaching still provides a normative ideal in Indian society (see Madan, 1987). Hinduism does not deny that enlightenment can come at earlier ages. But the systematic pursuit of the spiritual life, to the exclusion of other interests and obligations, is reserved for the later years, when one's duties to family and society have been completed (which, incidentally, is not seen as being so old—compulsory retirement occurs at age 55–58 in many sectors of Indian society even today).

A growing body of developmental literature helps explain such traditional and cultural assignment of spiritual learning to the later years. The earliest statement of the position, in the psychological literature, is Jung's observation that there is a normally occurring midlife reversal, a developmental movement toward inward exploration in the second half of life. At this time the pursuit of the agendas of the first half of the life cycle, "money-making, social existence . . . expansion of life, of usefulness, efficiency, the casting of a figure in social life" (Jung, 1933, p. 109, 110) no longer suffices. The agenda of the second half of life is the journey inward, of encouraging the intuitive and "wise passivity" (to use Huxley's term).

Several developmental psychologists (Hooper & Sheehan, 1977; Pascual-Leone, 1983; Labouvie-Vief, 1990), examining cognitive development in adulthood beyond formal operations, have suggested that there are actual changes in the brain (or at least in the functioning of the brain) that contribute directly to the midlife changes that Jung noticed as a clinician. Pascual-Leone, in the strongest statement of the biological deficit model, claims that the decrease in the ability to engage in abstract reasoning (fluid intelligence) reflects changes in the brain's "silent operators," or biological capacity. Ironically, these developmental deficits serve as the basis for cognitive functioning beyond formal operations. Early deficits in adulthood lead to an intermediate Dialectical Stage at approximately the same age that Jung identifies the midlife reversal (35–40), and later changes in cognitive functioning (at roughly 55–60) can lead to a final Transcendental Stage, which is characterized by metaphysical reflection.

Pascual-Leone's theory of change in brain functioning with age remains at the level of inference, but it does tie in with clinical and anecdotal reports. For instance, Jaques' (1965) study of creative productivity indicates that there is a change in the nature of artistic production with age. Young artists, like Yeats, display a type of creativity characterized by "white-hot" emotional and creative energy. The productions of older artists tend to be more philosophical and "sculpted," reflecting precisely the kind of behavior that would be predicted by Pascual-Leone's theory of cognitive change leading to the Transcendental Stage of cognitive functioning.

Returning to the cases with which we began our investigation, it is interesting that Henry had his mystical experience at age 19 and Ann underwent her altered states of consciousness at middle age. Ann's experience corresponds to Jung and Pascual-Leone's model of important psychological changes occurring at middle age (though Ann, at 48, is on the older side of the time-frame suggested by these theorists). It is also interesting that Maslow found the incidence of emotionally charged peak experiences to diminish in middle age and older, but an increase in the adult years of "plateau experiences," which are less emotionally charged and more persisting.

The apparent discrepancy in the age of occurrence of Henry's unitive consciousness experience relates to the difference in peak and plateau experiences, suggested by Maslow. Henry himself noted that although his mystical experience at age 19 led to a radical change in the direction of his life, it was only later that he came to realize the full meaning of the experience. Only in his later years did he experience the continuing feeling of equanimity and perspective that

Maslow characterizes as the plateau experience. Ann, on the other hand, was more ready to appropriate the insights of her peak experiences into her life, as they were encountered in middle age.

James Fowler (1984), whose stage theory of faith development closely parallels that of Kohlberg's stages of moral development, identified middle age as having a special place in spiritual development. He notes, "For both women and men, mid-life brings the invitations of deepening the spiritual foundations of our lives and the readdressing the issue of partnership with the Transcendent" (1984, p. 146). Fowler sees grace as present throughout the faith journey, but instances of "Saving Grace" are particularly important to movement into the last stage of "universalizing faith," in which one transcends the self.

Fowler's theory was used as the basis for a large-scale study of faith development of members of some 561 Protestant congregations (Benson & Elkin, 1990). Both qualitative and quantitative methods were used, and over 11,000 subjects were involved in their investigation. The researchers found that persons who were judged as having a mature faith (defined vertically as having had a life-transforming relationship to a loving God and horizontally as displaying a consistent devotion to serving others) were likely to be older. They concluded: "Maturity of faith is strongly linked to age, increasing with each successive decade, and is most likely to be found among those over 70" (p. 3).

Stated conceptually, transforming spiritual development appears to be age-related, but not age-determined. That is, it appears more frequently in older persons, but can be found in younger people (see Coles, 1990). The presence of elderly who show little sign of spiritual maturity, on the other hand, reminds us that the correlation with age is far from perfect.

So the paradox of learning in the spiritual sphere is that there appears to be an age-related readiness, but advanced spiritual development does not occur in all cases. Certain insights and learning are obviously possible in the earlier years. But the full fruition of spiritual maturity appears to come only after middle age. In Bateson's terminology, there can certainly be factual learning about spiritual issues in the earlier years (Learning I), and our overarching commitments and emotional affections certainly take place in earlier years (Learning II). But full spiritual maturity appears not to be accessible to logical reasoning and convergent problem-solving in Learning II. It appears to depend on a different type of openness and awareness of the paradoxical dimensions of life. Indeed, only Learning III provides the bases for calling into question the assumptions of our earlier learning (Learning II). Only then is the paradoxical learning of that which is "already known" possible.

CONCLUSION

This brief exploration of learning and spirituality in the adult years has taken us through a wide array of literature, along with an examination of the experiences of a 48-year-old woman and an 83-year-old man. We have found several general characteristics of learning and spirituality that appear to hold for the adult years: (1) There is a greater likelihood that a mature person is aware of having had a direct experience of some "peak" or spiritual consciousness. (2) Such learning, although apparently occurring spontaneously, requires continued effort and cultivation if it is to have a lasting impact on the individual's life. (3) There is a paradoxical quality of higher spiritual maturity that makes it inaccessible to effortful, rational striving, yet for the insights gained to be more than fleeting glimpses, continued effort (or Learning II) is required. (4) It is usually in the second half of life that people are able to handle the paradoxical nature of this type of learning.

We frankly find it difficult to go beyond these general conclusions. This is not to say that we, or our readers, don't know more than this. If the perennial tradition is correct, we all have had at least some acquaintance with "the hound, the bay horse, and the turtledove." But, as Polanyi (1967) reminds us, much of our knowledge is tacit, and in many areas of life we "know more than we can tell" (p. 4). If this is true anywhere, it certainly holds in the realm of spirituality. Indeed, this is the heart of the teaching of the ancient sage Lao Tzu, that "Those who know do not tell" (Wing, 56), for words alone cannot suffice.

NOTE

1. The authors are indebted to an anonymous reviewer for this story.

REFERENCES

Bateson, G. (1972) *Steps to an ecology of the mind*. New York: Ballantine Books.

Benson, P. & Elkin, C. (1990) *Effective Christian education: A national study of Protestant denominations*. Minneapolis: Search Institute.

Bucke, R. (1901) *Cosmic consciousness*. New York: Dutton.

Capra, F. (1988) *Uncommon wisdom: Conversations with remarkable people*. Toronto: Bantam Books.

Coles, R. (1990) *The spiritual life of children*. Boston: Houghton Mifflin Co.

Eliot, T. S. (1950) *The complete poems and plays: 1909–1950*. New York: Harcourt, Brace & Co.

Foster, R. (1978) *Celebration of discipline: The path to spiritual growth*. San Francisco: Harper & Row.

Fowler, R. (1984) *Becoming adult, becoming Christian: Adult development and Christian faith*. San Francisco: Harper & Row.

Hooper, F. H. & Sheehan, N. W. (1977) Logical conceptual attainment during the aging years: Issues in the neo-Piagetian research literature. In W. F. Overton & J. M. Gallagher (Eds.). *Life-span developmental psychology: Theory and research*. New York: Academic Press.

Huxley, A. (1944) *The perennial philosophy*. New York: Harper & Row.

Jaques, E. (1965) Death and the mid-life crisis. *International Journal of Psychoanalysis*, 46: 502–514.

Jung, C. G. (1933) *Modern man in search of a soul*. New York: Harcourt Brace.

Labouvie-Vief, G. (1990) Wisdom as integrated thought: Historical and developmental perspectives. In R. J. Sternberg (Ed.). *Wisdom: Its nature, origins, and development*. New York: Cambridge University Press.

Madan, T. N. (1987) *Non-renunciation: Themes and interpretations of Hindu culture*. New York: Oxford University Press.

Maslow, A. H. (1971) *The farther reaches of human nature*. New York: Viking.

Pascual-Leone, J. (1983) Growing into human maturity: Toward a metasubjective theory of adulthood stages. In P. B. Baltes & O. G. Brim, Jr. (Eds.). *Life-span development and behavior*, Vol. 5. New York: Academic Press.

Polanyi, M. (1967). *The Tacit Dimension*. London: Routledge & Kegan Paul.

Polkinghorne, D. (1983). *Methodology for the Human Sciences*. Albany: SUNY Press.

Ramacharaka, Y. (1903) *Fourteen lessons in yogi philosophy and oriental occultism*. Chicago: The Yoga Publication Society.

Schumacher, E. F. (1977) *A guide for the perplexed*. New York: Harper & Row.

Thomas, L. E., Brewer, S. J., Kraus, P. A. & Rosen, B. L. (1993) Two patterns of transcendence: An empirical examination of Wilber and Washburn's theories. *Journal of Humanistic Psychology*, *33*: 66–81.

Thoreau, H. D. (1973) *The illustrated Walden*, J. Lyndon Shanley (Ed.). Princeton, NJ: Princeton University Press.

Wilber, K. (1977) *The spectrum of consciousness*. Wheaton, IL: Theosophical Publishing House.

Wilber, K. (1979) *No boundaries*. Boston: Shambala Press.

Wilber, K. (1982) *A sociable God*. New York: McGraw-Hill.

Wilber, K. (1983) *Eye to eye*. New York: Anchor/Doubleday.

Wing, R. L. (Ed.). (1986) *The Tao of power*. New York: Dolphin.

II. LEARNING IN SPECIFIC LIFE CONTEXTS

10

Adult Learning Environments: Perspectives from Environmental Psychology

Jack Demick and Nancy A. Nazzaro

Much of adult learning occurs in formal learning environments (Gifford, 1987). Such learning environments—whose objectives usually emphasize a traditional body of knowledge, the learner's quantity of learning, and his or her verbal and analytic skills—include those associated predominantly with formal learning institutions such as schools, military settings, and training programs in business and industry (see Froman, chapter 11 this volume).[1] In this important regard, adult learning may be understood as similar to most learning across the lifespan. However, our knowledge of the interrelationships between formal learning environments and adult behavior and experience is still in its rudimentary stages. This is probably related to several factors.

First, it was not until the advent of environmental psychology in the 1970s (Proshansky, Ittelson, & Rivlin, 1976; Sommer, 1983) that psychologists and allied professionals (e.g., anthropologists, architects, economists, geographers, gerontologists, planners) exhibited a formal interest in studying the effects of physical environmental factors on human behavior (as harbingers of this move-ment, see Barker & Wright, 1955; Brunswick, 1943; Lewin, 1943). Although this subfield has more recently been broadened to include the ways in which not only physical but also interpersonal and sociocultural aspects of the environment affect, and are affected by, individuals' behavior and experience, as well as to see itself as a general conceptual approach to any psychological analysis (Pat-terson, 1989; Wapner & Demick, 1991a), the study of specific environmental contexts—for example, home, school, urban, vacation, and workplace environ-ments—has barely a twenty-year history.

Second, while extensive research on formal learning environments has since been generated within the field of environmental psychology, the majority has examined aspects of the formal school environments of children and adolescents (e.g., Bell, Fisher, Baum & Greene, 1990; Gifford, 1987; Gump, 1987; Weinstein, 1981). As our society spends vast sums of money to educate individuals of all ages, why then has research on the learning environments of adults paled in comparison?

Apart from the obvious answer that formal learning environments constitute a more central part of children's lives, environmental psychologists have historically been concerned more with the environmental contexts of older adults than of other adults. That is, although environmental psychologists (e.g., Carp, 1987; Howell, 1980; Lawton, 1990) have, to date, amassed an impressive body of literature on the environments of aging individuals, including hospitals, nursing homes, and residential housing complexes, they have typically held the tacit assumptions that (1) adults, particularly older adults, are not intricately involved in formal learning environments and that (2) adult learners, particularly those in young and middle adulthood, do not transact with their (learning) environments in ways that are fundamentally different from those of children and adolescents. However, are such assumptions correct? What is the prevalence of adults engaged in formal learning environments? Are the goals of the adult learner similar or dissimilar to younger students?

Currently, between 12% and 30% of the total adult population is involved in some sort of adult education in formal learning environments; the estimate, however, drops to 5% among adults over the age of 54 years (Cross, 1981). While some adults take formal classes for credit, most are engaged in formal noncredit classes sponsored by continuing education/extension programs or community agencies (Schaie & Willis, 1991). Further, the typical goals of adults in formal learning environments have been reported to be different from those of younger students. For example, Stagner (1985) has documented that the educational goals of adults are most often related to the types of transitions experienced in young and middle adulthood. These transitions typically involve either *career advancement* (e.g., formal courses leading to entering or reentering the work force, to upgrading or changing one's occupational status, and/or to continued professional certification) or *personal development* (e.g., formal courses such as computer literacy to understand recent technological changes and/or nutrition and exercise to increase one's well-being during the aging process).

Though the demographic characteristics of the current student body in American colleges and universities have already changed to include more older and part-time students (American Council on Education, 1984), recent trends have suggested that the number of adults in formal learning environments may well be on the rise. First, Kozol (1985) has suggested that, as increased literacy is required to deal effectively with today's high-tech job market, some of the 35% of our adult population with inadequate levels of reading, spelling, and/or mathematics will be forced to reenter formal learning environments. Second, recent research on adaptation to retirement (e.g., Atchley, 1988; Wapner, Demick & Damrad, 1988) has suggested that there is a crucial need for more formal educational programs that deal, long before retirement, with retirement preparation and financial planning. Third, one of the most well-received recent educational programs for the elderly has been Elderhostel (McCluskey, 1982). Stated simply, Elderhostel provides short-term (usually one to three weeks), on-campus (usually during the summer), college-level (usually with no homework, exams, grades, or credit) courses for older adult learners at a low cost. Begun in 1975 by a small number of colleges in New Hampshire, the program has steadily been extended to all fifty states.

In light of such trends coupled with the graying American population, it appears incumbent upon social scientists to explore more systematically than has heretofore been the case the formal learning environments of adults. Thus, the primary goals of the present chapter are (1) to present extant research on the formal learning environments of adults; (2) to discuss theoretical and methodological considerations for future research in the area; and (3) to suggest directions for the design of adult learning environments, toward maximizing the functioning of adults in their everyday lives.

THEORETICAL CONSIDERATIONS

We have chosen to present the current work on the formal learning environments of adults from within the context of our recent elaboration of Heinz Werner's (1957) organismic-developmental approach. Because little agreement has yet been reached about the most appropriate theoretical model for the study of person-environment relations (e.g., Carp, 1987), our perspective may be helpful for several reasons.[2] First, Werner's theory has been reformulated specifically for the examination of person-in-environment transactions and, as such, has figured prominently within the subfield of environmental psychology (e.g., Demick & Wapner, 1990; Wapner, 1981, 1987). Second, this approach has already demonstrated powerful heuristic potential for integrating diverse literatures and for framing a wide range of empirical inquiry (see Demick & Miller, 1993, for a review). Thus, there follows a brief description of our general elaboration[3] and a discussion of specific aspects of our elaborated approach with relevance for understanding adults in their learning environments.

We have most recently applied our elaborated approach to the study of *person-in-environment transitions across the lifespan* (e.g., Wapner & Demick, 1991a, 1991b). Here, we have attempted to delineate the regressive changes and/or progressive development of the person-in-environment system following a transition or critical perturbation to any part of the system (person, environment) at any level of organization (biological, psychological, sociocultural). Although the current reformulation is relevant most generally to the systems-oriented study of person-in-environment transactions from infancy through old age (Wapner & Demick, 1990), it has specific implications for the study of adult development and particularly of adults-in-their-environments. Examples of such studies include Demick and Wapner (1991) on cognitive functioning in adult development and aging; Hornstein and Wapner (1984, 1985) and Wapner, Demick, and Damrad (1988) on the transition to retirement; and Wapner, Demick, and Redondo (1990) on the role of cherished possessions in the adaptation of older people to nursing homes.

Prior to discussing these studies, we will now give consideration to some of our underlying assumptions that bear on the general study of adults-in-environments and on the specific study of adults-in-learning environments. Our discussion will focus, for the most part, on those individuals in the throes of adulthood, namely, those in middle and/or later adulthood.

Organismic/Holistic Emphasis

We assume that the organism-in-environment system is the unit to be analyzed. This assumption stresses that every person is inextricably embedded in some environment. Our approach thereby adopts a transactionalist and organismic perspective (cf. Altman & Rogoff, 1987; Cantril, 1950; Ittelson, 1973), which cautions against analyzing persons and environments as separate entities; rather, this perspective treats the person's "behavings, including his most advanced knowings, as activities not of himself alone but as processes of the full situation of organism-environment" (Dewey & Bentley, 1949, p. 104).

Thus, we characteristically examine the transactions (experience and action) of person-in-environment systems. We assume that, in a holistic manner, the person's (here, the adult learner's) environment in such a system is comprised of mutually defining *physical* (e.g., home, school, work), *interpersonal* (e.g., family, co-workers, teachers, fellow students), and *sociocultural* (e.g., household, work, and school rules) aspects. Analogously, the person himself or herself is assumed holistically to encompass mutually defining *biological/physical* (e.g., health), *psychological/intrapersonal* (e.g., self-esteem), and *sociocultural* (e.g., roles) aspects. These aspects of the person in conjunction with the aspects of the environment are assumed to constitute the person-in-environment system.

Related to the assumption of the person-in-environment as the unit of analysis is our assumption concerning holism and levels of integration. Specifically, we assume that the person-in-environment system operates as a unified whole so that a disturbance in one part (physical, psychological, or sociocultural aspects of the person or of the environment) affects other parts and the totality. This holistic assumption holds for functioning not only among but also within levels of integration (see Wapner & Demick, 1990). For instance, on the psychological level, such part-processes as the *cognitive* aspects of experience and action (including sensorimotor functioning, perceiving, thinking, learning, symbolizing, imagining) as well as the *affective* (feeling) and *valuative* (prioritizing) aspects of experience and action operate contemporaneously and in an integrated manner in the normally functioning adult.

Thus, from our elaborated perspective, a complete understanding of adults-in-learning environments would include consideration of a wide range of variables (listed in Table 1) and the interrelations among them. Some of the variables

Table 1
Variables Relevant to the Study of Adults-in-Learning Environments

PERSON (X ENVIRONMENT)

BIOLOGICAL/PHYSICAL

- Age
- Sex *
- Race *
- Socioeconomic Status *
- Vision
- Hearing
- General Health

PSYCHOLOGICAL/INTERPERSONAL

- Cognitive Processes
  (e.g., learning, memory,
  wisdom, metacognition)
- Affective Processes
  (e.g., need for achievement,
  past classroom experience)
- Valuative Processes *
  (e.g., priorities)

SOCIOCULTURAL

- Role (e.g., as student,
  spouse/parent, wage
  earner, retiree) *
- Status *

ENVIRONMENT (X PERSON)

PHYSICAL *

- Color
- Lighting
- Climate
- Noise
- Amount and Arrangement of Space
- Furniture
- Environmental Legibility

INTERPERSONAL *

- Family
- Instructors
- Fellow Students
- Fellow Commuters
- Co-workers

SOCIOCULTURAL *

- Learning Environment
  (e.g., transportational
  access, security)
- Sociohistorical Context
  (e.g., information explosion,
  image of adult education)

*Not examined extensively in previous research.

listed—most notably, the contextual influences on aspects of adults' cognitive functioning—have already received systematic attention in the literature to date. Others, however, still to be explored, have been identified through our holistic analysis. Further, those previously examined have typically been studied for the most part in isolation, rather than in relation to one another. To illustrate, we will briefly discuss each variable in turn and then conclude each section with some open empirical questions that consider some holistic relations among and within the different levels.

Aspects of adults: Physical/biological. Here we have included such variables as *age, sex, socioeconomic status, race, hearing, vision,* and *general health.* Age is relevant insofar as the majority of researchers have focused on aging, rather than middle-aged, individuals in formal learning environments (e.g., Elderhostel). In line with this, researchers (e.g, Whitbourne, 1985) have documented that the incidence of both impaired hearing and vision increases with each decade. By late adulthood, approximately 30% of all older adults suffer significant hearing loss with men experiencing greater loss, particularly for high-pitched sounds, than women; approximately 50% have a visual acuity of 20/70 or less, which may be worsened by inadequate lighting. However, older adults have been shown to compensate for such losses through specific techniques in their learning environments (e.g., good lighting, reading materials with larger print, sound amplification systems, closer seating to the instructor to read lip movements, instructors repeating main points). Further, we have included general health: while the relationship between aging and disease is a complex one, learning environments would benefit from assisting older adults in dealing, at the least, with the inevitable fatigue factor (e.g., rescheduling of classes and extracurricular events for maximum convenience of time and place).

We have also chosen to include sex as a relevant variable. While recent work in the field of developmental psychology has attested to differences in the behavior and experience of male versus female adults in both general (e.g., Gilligan, 1982) and educational (e.g., Goldberger, Clinchy, Belenky & Tarule, 1986) contexts, little systematic research has been conducted on sex differences in adult learning environments. Whether or not the well-documented phenomenon of the unisex of later life, that is, the tendency for each sex to move closer to a middle ground between the traditional sex roles (e.g., Troll & Perron, 1981), becomes manifest in formal learning environments is an area worthy of future empirical inquiry. Analogously, one might also include race (Graham, 1992) and socioeconomic status (Streib, 1985) as relevant variables for study here.

Though the majority of these studies have examined one or more of these variables in isolation, our holistic perspective leads to such questions as, What are the relationships among adults' participation in formal learning environments, their age, and general health status (including vision and hearing)? Do any of these relationships change dependent on adults' sex, race, and/or socioeconomic status?

Aspects of adults: Psychological/intrapersonal. We have divided aspects of adults' experience relevant to their transactions in formal learning environments into those dealing with *cognitive* (knowing), *affective* (feeling), and *valuative* (prioritizing) processes. Of these, the cognitive processes of (older) adults have received the most extensive examination in the literature. Specifically, researchers (e.g., Willis, 1985) have documented the contextual influences on adults' learning and memory, namely, that adults' cognitive skills are relevant to (1) the nature of the information to be learned; (2) the abilities, motives, and needs of the individual; and (3) the requirements of the context in which the adult is using his or her learning and memory skills. Examination of contextual requirements has typically focused on factors related to the task (e.g., pacing, comprehensible instructions) rather than to the larger environmental context (e.g., formal vs. informal learning environments) in which the learning takes place.

Further, much research has suggested that a number of other factors (e.g., those involved in mediated learning, ecologically valid learning, metacognition) has the potential to impact the cognitive functioning of adults most generally (see Schaie & Willis, 1991, for a review). Some researchers (e.g., Dittmann-Kohli & Baltes, 1990) have also focused on the development of wisdom during adulthood; however, the ways in which wisdom facilitates or hinders the dynamics of participation in formal learning environments is an open empirical question.

Also related to adult cognitive functioning is the well-documented notion of "environmental competence." Defined by Steele (1980) as "people's ability to deal with their immediate surroundings in an effective and stimulating manner" (p. 225), such competence has been shown to include sense of direction, wayfinding, knowledge of the best and worst parts of environments, and knowledge of an organization's power structure to be able to lobby for design modifications. Though there has been little empirical research on the environmental competence of adults in formal learning environments, there has been some on the general environmental competence of the elderly: for example, prior to moving to a new environment, the environmental competence of older adults may be maximized through both simulations (e.g., slides, models) and actual visits to the new locale (Hunt, 1984).

Affective processes as they relate to participation in formal learning environments have already received some consideration. Researchers have extensively documented the notion that there is a clear interrelationship between adults' cognitive and affective (e.g., needs, motives) functioning. However, much of this research has utilized older samples of adults; the ways in which the feelings of middle-aged adults (e.g., current need for achievement, feelings about past classroom experience, and/or more recent life changes) impact their behavior and experience in formal learning environments is worthy of future empirical inquiry. Further, research on adults' valuative processes in formal learning environments is almost nonexistent. While it is clear that some value education, little is known about the ways in which they prioritize the demands of their classes, families, and/or work situations.

Our perspective would suggest the following types of questions. What are some relations between adults' cognitive and affective functioning as they participate in formal learning environments? Are there circumstances under which adults' affect either facilitates or compromises their cognition? What roles do adults' values play in the formal learning environment, and how do they interface with their cognition and affect? What is the most efficacious manner for developing environmental competence in adult learners? How does environmental competence relate to other aspects of adults' cognitive as well as affective and valuative functioning?

Aspects of adults: Sociocultural. Here we have included the related variables of *role* and *status*, as we are sorely lacking information on the sociocultural roles and status of the adult learner. Thus, we find the following questions among those worthy of systematic empirical inquiry: How does the adult learner integrate his or her various roles of student, of family member, and/or of worker (perhaps even breadwinner)? Are there individual differences (e.g., age, sex, race, socioeconomic status) in the ways in which adults negotiate these various roles? What are the similarities and differences in the roles and status of middle-aged versus older adults' role and status in the formal learning environment per se? In what ways does participation in formal learning environments contribute to or hinder both middle-aged and older adults' status in society?

Aspects of environments: Physical. As environmental psychology was initially founded to understand the effects of the physical environment on behavior, it is not surprising that the physical aspect of learning environments has received the most attention. For our purposes, this research needs to be reviewed cautiously on several counts. First, because the majority of research has been conducted in the learning environments of children, adolescents, and college students, extrapolation from these findings to adult learning environments is necessary. Second, although environmental psychologists initially believed in architectural determinism in its strictest form (i.e., that the physical setting of learning environments could make or break education on its own), they have recently come to a more modified position. This position has maintained that the physical features of learning environments can either facilitate or impede the learning process but only in conjunction with other (person and environmental) variables. Thus, against these caveats, we have chosen to include here such relevant variables as *color, lighting, climate, noise, amount and arrangement of space, furniture design*, and *environmental legibility*, or the degree to which the learning environment and its surrounding area are easily learned or remembered.

For example, Pastalan (1982) has documented that the role of colors is generally important in the lives of older adults. Though not specifically concerned with the learning environment per se, he has found that many older adults tend to see colors as faded (e.g., cool colors such as blue and green appear to fade the most, while warm colors such as red appear to fade the least). Whether or not the fading of colors presents problems in the classroom is an open empirical issue. What may be more problematic, however, is that the blending and/or shifting of colors may dangerously obscure the necessary distinctions between, for example, floor levels and/or between stair risers and treads outside of the immediate context of classrooms.

As noted previously, good lighting may mitigate some of older adults' problems with visual acuity. That is, for individuals with bifocals or cataracts, good lighting may be used to define boundaries or edges of areas, to reduce glare, to increase the discernability of fine details, and to accent locations. Older adults also characteristically suffer from slow eye accommodation when moving from lighted to dark areas (or vice versa); this needs to be addressed when older adults move, for example, from indoor to outdoor space at night or from well-lit classrooms to dimly lit corridors.

Research on the relations between indoor classroom climate and students' behavior and experience is difficult to summarize because there are few simple, direct relationships. Since climate is composed of many possible patterns of temperature, humidity, and air patterns, Moos and Sommers (1976) have concluded that a combination of person and environmental variables most probably "mediate, transmit, modify, or resist" variations in climate. Nonetheless, Ahrentzen, Jue, Skorpanich, and Evans (1982) have provided the generalization that performance is maximized in classrooms that are cool and not humid; however, they have also acknowledged the possibility of individual differences in this relationship (e.g., amount of clothing, type of activity, cultural and experiential differences in preferred temperature). Although most of this work has been generated in the formal learning environments of children, one might speculate that sensitivity to as well as changes in temperature (e.g., when moving from one campus building to another) may tax the energy of adults (particularly older ones).

Recent research on noise in learning environments has strongly suggested that noise interferes with learning both as it occurs and, if the learner is exposed to noise for long periods of time, even after the noise is gone. Specifically, noise may impede performance by interfering with information processing, lowering perceptions of control, and increasing blood pressure. Again, however, most of this research has been conducted on children. Whether such relationships obtain for individuals in middle and later adulthood is worthy of future study. Further, the inability to locate and identify sounds as well as to discern relevant stimuli (e.g., a lecture) in light of irrelevant stimuli (e.g., an air conditioning unit) most probably imposes strain and fatigue on the older adult learner.

The amount (density) and arrangement of space in formal learning environments has been clearly shown to affect classroom behavior and performance. As most of this research has been conducted on preschoolers and grammar school children (see Weinstein, 1981, for a review), it will not be presented here. However, one concept with particular relevance for adult learning environments concerns the well-documented "zone of action," that is, students who sit in the front and center of the classroom participate more, are more attentive, and obtain higher grades than students who sit in other classroom locations (see Brooks &

Rebeta, 1991; Gump, 1987). Thus, encouraging adults to sit in the zone of action may facilitate students' integration into formal learning environments, particularly for returning students; for older adults, such seating arrangements might additionally allow them to engage in lipreading without the stigma of having to request a seat change.

Recommendations on classroom furniture design for adults, most notably extrapolated from classic research in nursing homes (e.g., Koncelik, 1977), have included the use of chairs with arms and/or benches with backs. Having to get up from low, armless seats (as is often the case in modern classrooms) may be difficult as well as embarrassing, especially for older adults wishing to conceal the beginnings of physical problems. Further, some have even observed that the shapes of older adults fit better in lounge furniture than in typical classroom furniture; this is consistent with recent research on "soft classrooms" (Sommer & Olsen, 1980; Wollin & Montagne, 1981), which has documented that relatively inexpensive changes (semicircular, cushion-covered bench seating rather than traditional row seating) have resulted in significant increases in student participation.

Outside of the classroom, some authors have reported that adults, particularly older ones, are initially concerned about the legibility of the larger learning environment. Whereas environmental psychologists (e.g., Lynch, 1960) have conducted research on the elements that contribute to the legibility of large cities (e.g., paths, edges, districts, nodes, landmarks), research on those elements with the potential to improve the legibility of smaller learning environments (e.g., architectural details, directional graphics, information services) has not yet been attempted.

We would thus be interested in the following types of questions. What is the best combination of physical classroom features for maximizing the behavior and experience of adult students in formal learning environments? Does the same combination hold for both adults in middle and late adulthood? Do the combinations vary dependent upon the sex, race, and/or socioeconomic status of the adults? Are any features of the physical environment (both in the classroom and on the larger campus) more conducive to adults' learning and/or performance than the others? What are the most efficacious means for increasing the legibility of formal learning environments?

Aspects of environments: Interpersonal. Participation in formal learning environments clearly has the potential to impact adults' social networks. That is, when an adult is engaged in a formal learning environment, he or she must transact with his or her instructor(s), fellow students, family members, peers, and often times employers and co-workers. Though little empirical research has been conducted on changes in adult students' interpersonal networks as a function of participation in formal learning environments, there has been considerable work on the related topic of the ways in which contemporary middle-aged women deal with their participation in the workforce. For example, Baruch (1984) has found that, when women are engaged in both family and work contexts, each context provides an important buffer to protect against whatever midlife strains might arise in the other. Whether learning environments function similarly to work contexts, however, remains an open empirical issue.

Thus, we are most interested in the following types of questions. What is the impact of adults' participation in formal learning environments on all system members? Is there congruence or incongruence between adult learners and system members in how adults' participation in formal learning environments was originally and continues to be viewed? Are any of these relationships moderated by adults' age, sex, race, and/or socioeconomic status? Which individuals function as social support for adult learners, and do these change over time?

Aspects of environments: Sociocultural. For the adult learner, there are relevant sociocultural aspects of the learning environment as well as of the larger sociohistorical context in which the learning environment is embedded that have bearing on his or her behavior and experience. For example, with respect to the learning environment per se, investigators (e.g., Weinstock, 1978) have documented that adults, particularly older ones, are generally concerned about *transportational access* to the learning environment as well as about *security* once on campus. *Flexible timetables* for formal classes and, for example, box offices (for extracurricular events) are an additional sociocultural characteristic of the learning environment that adults greatly appreciate. With respect to the larger sociohistorical context, adult learners must deal with, what some have termed, our society's current *information explosion* (often causing instructors to feel compelled to include as much relevant information in their lectures as possible) as well as with our society's *negative image of adult education*, which may more aptly be described as a lack of understanding of adult education.

From our point of view, we would be most interested in the following types of questions. What combination of sociocultural characteristics of formal learning environments maximizes the learning and/or performance of adult students? Does the combination vary dependent on adults' sex, race, and/or socioeconomic status? What processes underlie current societal attitudes toward adult participation in formal learning environments? How do community, societal, and particular institutional beliefs about adult education in formal learning environments (both individually and in combination) impact adult learners? Are there individual differences in the ways in which instructors deal with the current information explosion as well as differences related to class composition?

Developmental Emphasis

Our view of development transcends the boundaries within which the concept of development is ordinarily applied. For most psychologists, development is limited to ontogenesis. In contrast, we assume that "Wherever there is life, there is growth and systematic orderly sequence" (Werner, 1957, p. 125). Thus, we are concerned with the examination of both processes of formation (e.g., development of one's social network in the learning environment) and of dissolution (e.g., developmental changes in experience and action prior to and following final examinations) as adults negotiate maximally optimal relationships with their environments.

Components (person, environment), relations among components (e.g., means-ends), and part-processes (cognition, affect, valuation) of person-in-environment systems are assumed developmentally orderable in terms of the orthogenetic principle. This principle defines development with respect to the degree of organization attained by a system. The more differentiated and hierarchically integrated a system is, in terms of its parts and of its means and ends, the more highly developed it is said to be. Thus, we assume that optimal development involves a differentiated and hierarchically integrated person-in-environment system characterized by flexibility, freedom, and self-mastery (cf. Wapner, 1987; Wapner & Demick, 1990, 1991a).

In line with these teleological notions (cf. Langer et al., 1990, who favor nonsequential models of adult development), we have described four self-world relationships ranging from lesser to more advanced developmental status. These relationships—which have already been applied to the acculturation of the Puerto Rican migrant to the United States (e.g., Pacheco, Lucca & Wapner, 1985) and to the family systems of those practicing open versus closed (communication vs. no communication between biological and adoptive parents) adoption (Demick & Wapner, 1988)—are as follows: (1) *lack of differentiation between person and environment* characterized by the person's passive accommodation to the environment (e.g., after receiving negative feedback from family members concerning time away from home, the adult learner consciously or unconsciously denies that there is a problem); (2) *person differentiated yet isolated from environment* characterized by the person's disengagement (e.g., after receiving feedback, the adult learner continues in the formal learning environment, but disengages from fellow students and the institution); (3) *person differentiated from yet in conflict with environment* characterized by the person's nonconstructive ventilation (e.g., after receiving feedback, the adult learner argues that the feedback was unjust, etc.); and (4) *person differentiated from and integrated with environment* characterized by the person's constructive assertion (e.g., after receiving feedback, the adult learner approaches both the instructor and family members for discussion of ways to deal constructively with the situation). Thus, broader views of development and of the goal-directed character of the person-in-environment system such as the ones offered by our approach open up numerous empirical studies concerning adults-in-learning environments, a topic to which we now turn.

METHODOLOGICAL CONSIDERATIONS

Currently psychologists are involved in an ongoing controversy over whether the field should adhere to a "natural science" perspective (characterized by controlled experimentation and quantitative analysis, after Wundt, 1912) or a "human science" perspective (characterized by phenomenological methods and qualitative analysis, after Giorgi, 1975). While some might argue that a paradigm shift (cf. Kuhn, 1962) is well underway, our holistic/systems, developmental approach would advocate that both models have a place in psychological science. For us, choice of method depends in part on the level of integration to which the research question is addressed. For example, if we were concerned primarily in describing and understanding (e.g., the sociocultural role of the adult learner), we might opt to employ the phenomenological method. Alternatively, if we were interested in predicting (e.g., satisfaction as an adult learner), we might instead choose an experimental/quasi-experimental method. Within the experimental method, we would strongly argue for the necessary complementarity of cross-sectional and longitudinal designs to understand developmental change (cf. Wapner, 1987).

In line with our foci, we (Demick & Wapner, 1990) have suggested elsewhere that advances in holistic conceptualization might be obtained from the development of systematic, holistic constructs accounting for relations between and among levels of integration. With respect to the problem at hand, we would be most interested in such questions as: What are the mechanisms that underlie the ways in which phenomena at the sociocultural level (e.g., rules and mores of formal learning environments; societal misunderstanding of adult education) become translated into individual functioning at the psychological level (e.g., the adult's performance and/or self-esteem)? Conversely, how does the need for the quality of human functioning at the biological and psychological levels (e.g., the adult's energy level and/or self-concept) become actualized at the sociocultural level (e.g., through formalized programs in adult learning environments)? Toward illustrating some ways in which our approach frames such problems, a brief synopsis of three sets of empirical studies with relevance for adults-in-learning environments follows; this section is then concluded with a brief discussion of a framework for conceptualizing relations among the different levels.

Relations between Psychological Part-Processes: Cognition and Affect

In line with our holistic focus, we are currently documenting age differences in the processes underlying performance on the Stroop Color-Word Test (on Card A, *S* reads color names; on B, names color patches; on C, names colors of ink in which color names are printed) not only through the customary analyses of achievement (e.g., total time, total number of errors) but also through examination of types of errors as well as verbal and non-verbal strategies and mnemonics. We have employed normal subjects from 5 to 95 years of age, but our discussion here will focus primarily on older adults (see Demick & Wapner, 1991, for additional details).

These findings—when compared with those obtained from children and adolescents—suggest that adults aged 70 and older use qualitatively different strategies during task performance. That is, they typically emphasize boundaries between items, use sharper, more articulate pronunciation, and employ linguistic assertions (e.g., "er," "ah") rather than the inserted linguistic phrases characteristic of younger subjects. Very striking in their verbal strategies are shifts or changes in chunking organization (i.e., typical chunking of items by twos or threes is lost on the more difficult material).

From such analyses, we have argued that the cognitive functioning of older adults may not be characterized solely as exhibiting signs of *deterioration* (a common early finding in the literature), but rather as exhibiting signs of a *reorganization* of cognitive strategies. That is, older adults' use of less-efficient strategies (e.g., random counting on fingers, breathing patterns) seems to contribute to slower performance. Further, subjects' verbalized strategies on completion of the task (e.g., the common response of "I'm no good at concentrating") as well as erroneous (significantly greater) estimates of their total number of errors have suggested exploration into affective/cognitive processes (rather than simply cognitive deficits) as contributing factors to older learners' less-than-optimal cognitive functioning (cf. Lachman & Leff, 1989).

Such findings have also suggested that future research needs to take into account contextual factors in task administration. For example, the task performance of individuals in middle or older adulthood might be impacted by such contextual factors as the time of testing (e.g., morning vs. afternoon), the perceived purpose of testing (e.g., evaluative vs. non-evaluative), the ecological validity of the test session (e.g., laboratory vs. home), and the sex and/or personality of the subject in relation to the sex and/or personality of the experimenter (e.g., Demick, Raymond & Wapner, 1990). Such considerations likewise have parallel implications for adults-in-learning environments.

Psychological Aspect of Person and Physical Aspect of Environment

Here we (Wapner, Demick & Redondo, 1990) have attempted to demonstrate some relations between the physical aspect of the environment (cherished possessions) and the intrapersonal aspect of the person (adaptation and life satisfaction of older adults in nursing homes). We have found that (a) relative to those residents without cherished possessions, those with possessions were better adapted to the nursing home; (b) possessions served the major functions of *historical continuity*, *comforter*, and *sense of belongingness*; (c) women were more likely than men to have possessions and to associate them with self-other relationships; and (d) those residents in nursing homes above the mean on a combined criterion felt more in control, less helpless, more supported by staff, and were judged as more realistic in response to conflict than those below the mean.

When these findings are viewed together with those that suggest that the presence of cherished possessions aids in the general adaptation of children (Winnicott, 1971) and the specific adaptation of psychiatric patients to a hospital setting (Morgan & Cushing, 1966), the psychological importance of the non-human environment, particularly over the course of relocation, is clear. Analogously, the psychological importance of the non-human environment is most probably relevant to adults-in-learning environments.

Psychological Aspect of Person and Interpersonal Aspect of Environment

Again in line with our holistic focus, Hornstein and Wapner (1984) have found that the experience of "significant others" in the retiree's environment (e.g., spouse) was related to the experience of the retiree himself or herself. That is, pertinent dimensions relevant to relationships between retirees and network members included *degree of involvement* of the network person in the retiree's planning, assistance in the transition, and ongoing concern; *congruence versus incongruence* of the meaning and modes of coping with retirement as seen by the retiree and the social network members; and the *type of involvement*, that is, whether operating supportively or in opposition to the goals and values of the retiree.

Four types of relations occurred among these three factors: (1) low involvement in planning and support, a high degree of congruence between the network member and the retiree, and minimal but positive impact on the network member's life; (2) degree of involvement in planning and support low, moderate degree of incongruence, and some degree of impact, often negative, on the network member's own life; (3) high involvement in planning and strong support for the retiree, a high degree of congruence, and a moderate amount of positive change in the network member's life; and (4) high involvement in planning and support, moderate incongruence between retiree and network member, and a moderate degree of change often negative for the network member. The adaptation of retirees was greatest with the first and third of these structural relationships and least with the second and fourth.

In this same group of retirees, Hornstein and Wapner (1985) went on to identify four distinct groups, namely, those who experienced retirement (1) as a transition to old age, (2) as a new beginning, (3) as a continuation of pre-retirement life structure, and (4) as an imposed disruption. Wapner, Demick, and Damrad (1988) then assessed the stability of these four types as well as correlative measures of life satisfaction and degree of social support eight years post-retirement. Now, the majority of these retirees had shifted to the third category, which involved the resumption of work. Further, relative to retirees in Groups 1 and 4, those in Groups 2 and 3 experienced more life satisfaction and social support. Again, these studies have implications for adults-in-learning environments.

Relations among Aspects of Persons and Aspects of Environments

All three of the above studies were generated against the backdrop of our holistic perspective. Each has demonstrated that an appropriate unit of analysis is the person-in-environment. Specifically, Study 1 has illustrated that psychological part-processes must be considered in the context of total human activity; Studies 2 and 3 have demonstrated that individuals' psychological well-being depends, at least in part, on the physical and interpersonal aspects of their environments, respectively.

While we argue that such holistic analyses will shed light on the issue of adults-in-learning environments, we also acknowledge the need to go further toward developing systematic, holistic constructs that account for the relations between/among aspects of persons and aspects of environments. Some beginning attempts have been based on Wapner's (1969) earlier conceptualization of the relations among cognitive processes (i.e., sensorimotor action, perception, and conception). For instance, relations between cognitive operations may be *vicarious* (where use of one operation substitutes for use of another), *supportive* (where simultaneously occurring cognitive operations facilitate one another, making for greater efficiency in achievement of ends), *antagonistic* (where the operation of one function lessens the operation of another), and *correspondent* (where one level of functioning parallels another).

With respect to adults-in-learning environments, this conceptualization may be equally applicable. For example, relationships between the psychological aspect of the adult learner and the interpersonal aspect of his or her environment may be supportive (e.g., the majority of family members support the adult's decision to reenter the formal learning environment), antagonistic (the desires of the adult and his or her family members are antithetical), substitutive/vicarious (e.g., family members support the adult substituting his or her desires for their own), or correspondent (e.g., the wishes of the adult learner and family members coincide). Together with longitudinal analyses that assess progressive and/or regressive changes in the person-in-environment system over time, such mode of conceptualization may ultimately be of help in understanding the relations between aspects of persons and aspects of their environments.

DESIGN CONSIDERATIONS

Our most general suggestions for the design of adult learning environments are embedded in the goals of social design researchers and practitioners (e.g., Friedmann, Zimring & Zube, 1978; Holahan, 1983; Sommer, 1983), most of whom have adopted a related, though not identical, holistic perspective on person-environment relations. These goals have included (1) matching user needs and activities with the setting (e.g., is there person-environment habitability, congruence, or goodness-of-fit between the adult learner and the learning environment?); (2) user satisfaction (e.g., is the adult learner satisfied with his or her experience in the learning environment?); (3) changing user behavior (e.g., does participation in the learning environment increase the adult's fund of knowledge as well as sense of self?); (4) enhancing the user's sense of personal control (e.g., can the adult learner alter the learning environment so that it will suit his or her needs and reduce potential stress?); and (5) facilitating social support (e.g., does the learning environment provide opportunities for interaction with and support from instructors, administrators, and fellow students?).

Our more-specific suggestions for the design of adult learning environments proceed directly from our theoretical approach and, in particular, from our holistic unit of analysis. That is, during adulthood perhaps more so than at any other period of development, complex issues influence the learner: All that affects the life of the older student will impact the learning process as well as his or her behavior in and experience of the learning environment. Thus, the adult's issues and concerns should be considered an integral part of the learning process and not as isolated from it; in addition to examining those variables that directly influence the adult learner, the various influences on the learning environment that affect each other and the adult learner must also be assessed.

In light of this, specific recommendations for design encompass all those influences on the adult-in-learning environment system that touch on the biological, psychological, and sociocultural levels of integration. These recommendations include (but by no means are limited to) consideration of: the biological/physical aspect of the adult learner (e.g., good lighting, large print, sound amplification systems); the psychological/intrapersonal aspect of the adult learner (e.g., assessment of the interrelations among cognitive, affective, and valuative processes; attempts to increase environmental competence); the sociocultural aspect of the adult learner (e.g., role/status as impacting other parts of the system); the physical aspect of the learning environment (e.g., comfortable color, climate, noise level, design and arrangement of furniture; environmental legibility); the interpersonal aspect of the learning environment (e.g., information and support services for the adult learner as well as for family members; workshops for instructors concerned about teaching adult learners and/or dealing with information explosion); and the sociocultural aspect of the learning environment (e.g., good security, transportational access). In line with our approach's focus on individual differences (Wapner & Demick, 1991c), future research on adults-in-learning environments will hopefully shed light on whether such recommendations need calibration for the variables of gender, race, and socioeconomic status.

We are of the opinion that such holistic, ecologically oriented theory and praxis makes us aware of both the number and kind of interrelationships among aspects of the adult learner, of the environment, and of the systems to which he or she belongs. In addition to helping us conceptualize problems that are more in line with the complex character of daily life, such reframing has the potential to help psychology and its allied disciplines be perceived as a unified science, that is, one concerned not only with the examination of isolated aspects of human functioning but also with the study of important, everyday problems that cut across various aspects of persons and various aspects of environments such as adults-in-learning environments.

NOTES

1. This chapter focuses on formal learning environments, but much adult learning also occurs in informal learning environments (e.g., aquariums, botanic gardens, libraries, museums, nature centers, parks and zoos, practice fields). Even those contexts where learning is often seen as incidental to the primary purpose of the setting (e.g., homes) constitute informal learning environments in the most general sense of the term. For a more elaborated discussion of this type of learning environment, see Bitgood (1988).

2. That this is an acceptable strategy gains support in light of Gump's (1987) recent review of relevant literature on school and classroom environments in Stokols and Altman's *Handbook of Environmental Psychology* (New York: Wiley). Using an ecological perspective for understanding the behavior setting of the classroom (in preschools, grammar schools, high schools and, to a significantly lesser extent, colleges), Gump has focused primarily on (1) the physical milieu of schools, (2) issues of size and density, (3) activity programs of school environments, and (4) psychosocial school environments measured by questionnaires. In a similarly broad manner, our theoretical approach should encompass these and related issues concerning adult learning environments.

3. Our recent holistic, developmental, systems approach to person-in-environment functioning is based on Werner's (1957) organismic-developmental theory, which combines two perspectives in the analysis of human behavior and experience: *organismic* insofar as it implies that psychological part-processes (e.g., cognition, affect, valuation, behavior) must be considered in relation to the total context of human activity, that people are directed toward ends, and that they have at their disposal alternative means for achieving these ends; and *developmental* in that it provides a systematic principle governing developmental progression so that living systems may be compared with respect to their formal, organizational characteristics.

REFERENCES

Ahrentzen, S., Jue, G. M., Skorpanich, M. & Evans, G. W. (1982). School environments and stress. In G. W. Evans (Ed.). *Environmental stress* (pp. 29–36). New York: Cambridge University Press.

Altman, I. & Rogoff, B. (1987). World views in psychology: Trait, interactional, organismic, and transactional perspectives. In D. Stokols & I. Altman (Eds.). *Handbook of environmental psychology* (Vol. 1, pp. 7–40). New York: Wiley.

American Council on Education (1984). *Fact book on higher education.* New York: Macmillan.

Atchley, R. C. (1988). *Social forces and aging* (5th ed.). Belmont, CA: Wadsworth.

Barker, R. G., & Wright, H. (1955). *Midwest and its children.* New York: Row and Peterson.

Baruch, G. K. (1984). The psychological well-being of women in the middle years. In

G. K. Baruch & J. Brooks-Gunn (Eds.). *Women in midlife* (pp. 161–180). New York: Plenum.

Bell, P. A., Fisher, J. D., Baum, A. & Greene, T. C. (1990). *Environmental psychology* (3rd ed.). Chicago: Holt, Rinehart & Winston.

Bitgood, S. (1988). *A comparison of formal and informal learning* (Report No. 88–10). Jacksonville, AL: Center for Social Design.

Brooks, C. I. & Rebeta, J. L. (1991). College classroom ecology: The relation of sex of student to classroom performance and seating preference. *Environment and Behavior, 23(3)*, 305–313.

Brunswick, E. (1943). Organismic achievement and environmental probability. *Psychological Review, 50*, 255–272.

Cantril, H. (1950). *The why of man's experience*. New York: Macmillan.

Carp, F. (1987). Environment and aging. In D. Stokols & I. Altman (Eds.). *Handbook of environmental psychology* (Vol. 1, pp. 329–360). New York: Wiley.

Cross, K. P. (1981). *Adults as learners*. San Francisco: Jossey-Bass.

Demick, J. (1991). Organismic factors in field dependence-independence: Gender, personality, psychopathology. In S. Wapner & J. Demick (Eds.). *Field dependence-independence: Cognitive style across the life span* (pp. 209–243). Hillsdale, NJ: Lawrence Erlbaum Associates.

Demick, J. & Miller, P. (1993). Some open research problems on development in the workplace: Theory and methodology. In J. Demick & P. Miller (Eds.). *Development in the workplace* (pp. 221–240). Hillsdale, NJ: Lawrence Erlbaum Associates.

Demick, J. & Wapner, S. (1988). Open and closed adoption: A developmental conceptualization. *Family Process, 27*, 229–249.

Demick, J. & Wapner, S. (1990). Role of psychological science in promoting environmental quality: Introduction. *American Psychologist, 45(5)*, 631–632.

Demick, J. & Wapner, S. (1991). Field dependence-independence in adult development and aging. In S. Wapner & J. Demick (Eds.). *Field dependence-independence: Cognitive style across the life span* (pp. 245–268). Hillsdale, NJ: Lawrence Erlbaum Associates.

Demick, J., Raymond, N. & Wapner, S. (1990, March). Sex of subject, sex of experimenter, field dependence-independence, and moral reasoning. Paper presented at the Eastern Psychological Association annual meeting, Philadelphia, PA.

Dewey, J. & Bentley, A. F. (1949). *Knowing and the known*. Boston, MA: Beacon.

Dittmann-Kohli, F. & Baltes, P. B. (1990). Toward a neofunctionalist conception of adult intellectual development: Wisdom as a prototypical case of intellectual growth. In C. N. Alexander & E. J. Langer (Eds.). *Higher stages of human development* (pp. 54–78). New York: Oxford University Press.

Friedmann, A., Zimring, C. & Zube, E. (1978). *Environmental design evaluation*. New York: Plenum.

Gifford, R. (1987). *Environmental psychology: Principles and practice*. Boston: Allyn and Bacon.

Gilligan, C. (1982). *In a different voice: Psychological theory and women's development*. Cambridge, MA: Harvard University Press.

Giorgi, A. (1975). Convergence and divergence in qualitative and quantitative methods in psychology. In A. Giorgi, W. F. Fischer, & R. von Eckartsberg (Eds.). *Du-*

quesne studies in phenomenological psychology (Vol. 2, pp. 72–79). Pittsburgh, PA: Duquesne University Press.

Goldberger, N. R., Clinchy, B. M., Belenky, M. F. & Tarule, J. M. (1986). *Women's ways of knowing: The development of self, voice, and mind.* New York: Basic Books.

Graham, S. (1992). "Most of the subjects were white and middle class": Trends in published research on African Americans in selected APA journals, 1970–1989. *American Psychologist, 47*(5), 629–639.

Gump, P. V. (1987). School and classroom environments. In D. Stokols & I. Altman (Eds.). *Handbook of environmental psychology* (Vol. 2, pp. 691–732). New York: Wiley.

Holahan, C. J. (1983). Interventions to reduce environmental stress: Enhancing social support and personal control. In E. Siedman (Ed.). *Handbook of social interventions* (pp. 542–560). Beverly Hills, CA: Sage.

Hornstein, G. A. & Wapner, S. (1984). The experience of the retiree's social network during the transition to retirement. In C. M. Aanstoos (Ed.). *Exploring the lived world in readings in phenomenological psychology* (pp. 119–136). Carrollton, GA: West Georgia College Press.

Hornstein, G. A. & Wapner, S. (1985). Modes of experiencing and adapting to retirement. *International Journal on Aging and Human Development, 21,* 291–315.

Howell, S. C. (1980). Environments as hypotheses in human aging research. In L. W. Poon (Ed.), *Aging in the 1980s: Psychological issues* (pp. 424–432). Washington, DC: American Psychological Association.

Hunt, M. E. (1984). Environmental learning without being there. *Environment and Behavior, 16,* 307–334.

Ittelson, W. H. (1973). Environmental perception and contemporary perceptual theory. In W. H. Ittelson (Ed.). *Environment and cognition* (pp. 1–19). New York: Seminar Press.

Koncelik, J. (1977). *Designing the open nursing home.* Stroudsburg, PA: Dowden Hutchinson & Ross.

Kozol, J. (1985). *Illiterate America.* New York: Anchor Press/Doubleday.

Kuhn, T. S. (1962). *The structure of scientific revolutions.* Chicago: University of Chicago Press.

Lachman, M. E. & Leff, R. (1989). Beliefs about intellectual efficacy and control in the elderly: A five-year longitudinal study. *Developmental Psychology, 25,* 722–728.

Langer, E. J., Chanowitz, B., Palmerino, M., Jacobs, S., Rhodes, M. & Thayer, P. (1990). Nonsequential development and aging. In C. N. Alexander & E. J. Langer (Eds.). *Higher stages of human development* (pp. 114–136). New York: Oxford University Press.

Lawton, M. P. (1990). Residential environment and self-directedness among older people. *American Psychologist, 45*(5), 638–640.

Lewin, K. (1943). Defining the field at a given time. *Psychological Review, 50,* 292–310.

Lynch, K. (1960). *The image of the city.* Cambridge, MA: MIT Press.

McCluskey, H. (1982). Education for older adults. In C. Eisdorfer (Ed.). *Annual review of gerontology and geriatrics* (Vol. 3, pp. 403–428). New York: Springer.

Moos, R. H. & Sommers, P. (1976). The architectural environment: Physical space and building design. In R. Moos (Ed.). *The human context: Environmental determinants of behavior* (pp. 108–140). New York: Wiley.

Morgan, R. & Cushing, D. (1966). The personal possessions of long stay patients in mental hospitals. *Social Psychiatry, 1(3)*, 151–157.

Pacheco, A. M., Lucca, N. & Wapner, S. (1985). The assessment of interpersonal relationships among Puerto Rican migrant adolescents. In R. Diaz-Guerrero (Ed.). *Cross-cultural and national studies in social psychology* (pp. 169–176). North Holland: Elsevier Science Publishers.

Pastalan, L. A. (1982). Research in environment and aging: An alternative to theory. In M. P. Lawton, P. G. Windley & T. O Byerts (Eds.). *Aging and the environment: Theoretical approaches* (pp. 122–131). New York: Springer.

Patterson, D. D. (1989). The contribution of environmental psychology to visitor studies. In S. Bitgood, A. Benefield & D. Patterson (Eds.). *Visitor studies: Theory, research, and practice: Vol. 2: Proceedings of the first annual visitor studies conference* (pp. 80–85). Jacksonville, AL: Center for Social Design.

Proshansky, H. M., Ittelson, W. H. & Rivlin, L. G. (Eds.). (1976). *Environmental psychology: People and their physical settings*. New York: Holt, Rinehart & Winston.

Schaie, K. W. & Willis, S. L. (1991). *Adult development and aging* (3rd ed.). New York: Harper Collins.

Sommer, R. (1983). *The end of imprisonment*. New York: Oxford University Press.

Sommer, R. & Olsen, H. (1980). The soft classroom. *Environment and Behavior, 12*, 3–16.

Stagner, R. (1985). Aging in industry. In J. E. Birren & K. W. Schaie (Eds.). *Handbook of the psychology of aging* (2nd ed., pp. 789–817). New York: Van Nostrand Reinhold.

Steele, F. I. (1980). Defining and developing environmental competence. In C. P. Alderfer & C. L. Cooper (Eds.). *Advances in Experimental Social Processes, 2*, 225–244.

Streib, G. F. (1985). Social stratification and aging. In R. H. Binstock & E. Shanas (Eds.). *Handbook of aging and the social sciences* (2nd ed., pp. 339–368). New York: Van Nostrand Reinhold.

Troll, L. E. & Perron, E. M. (1981). Age changes in sex roles amid changing sex roles: The double shift. In C. Eisdorfer, (Ed.). *Annual Review of Gerontology and Geriatrics* (Vol. 2, pp. 118–143). New York: Springer.

Wapner, S. (1969). Organismic-developmental theory: Some applications to cognition. In J. Langer, P. H. Mussen & M. Covington (Eds.). *Trends and issues in developmental psychology* (pp. 38–67). New York: Holt, Rinehart & Winston.

Wapner, S. (1981). Transactions of persons-in-environments: Some critical transitions. *Journal of Environmental Psychology, 1*, 223–239.

Wapner, S. (1987). A holistic, developmental, systems-oriented environmental psychology: Some beginnings. In D. Stokols & I. Altman (Eds.). *Handbook of environmental psychology* (pp. 1433–1465). New York: Wiley.

Wapner, S. & Demick, J. (1990). Development of experience and action: Levels of integration in human functioning. In G. Greenberg & E. Tobach (Eds.). *Theories of the evolution of knowing: The T. C. Schneirla conference series* (pp. 47–68). Hillsdale, NJ: Lawrence Erlbaum Associates.

Wapner, S. & Demick, J. (1991a). Some relations between developmental and environmental psychology: An organismic-developmental systems perspective. In R. Downs, L. S. Liben & D. Palermo (Eds.). *Visions of development, the environment and aesthetics: The legacy of Joachim F. Wohlwill* (pp. 181–211). Hillsdale, NJ: Lawrence Erlbaum Associates.

Wapner, S. & Demick, J. (1991b). The organismic-developmental, systems approach to the study of critical person-in-environment transitions through the life span. In T. Yamamoto & S. Wapner (Eds.). *A developmental psychology of life transitions* (pp. 25–49). Tokyo: Kyodo Shuppan.

Wapner, S. & Demick, J. (Eds.). (1991c). *Field dependence-independence: Cognitive style across the life span*. Hillsdale, NJ: Lawrence Erlbaum Associates.

Wapner, S., Demick, J. & Damrad, R. (1988, April). *Transition to retirement: Eight years after*. Paper presented at Eastern Psychological Association annual meeting, Buffalo, NY.

Wapner, S., Demick, J. & Redondo, J. P. (1990). Cherished possessions and adaptation of older people to nursing homes. *International Journal on Aging and Human Development, 31(3)*, 299–315.

Weinstein, C. S. (1981). Classroom design as an external condition for learning. *Educational Technology, 21*, 12–19.

Weinstock, R. (1978). *The graying of the campus*. New York: Educational Facilities Laboratory.

Werner, H. (1957). *Comparative psychology of mental development* (3rd ed.). New York: International Universities Press.

Whitbourne, S. K. (1985). *The aging body*. New York: Springer Verlag.

Willis, S. L. (1985). Towards an educational psychology of the older adult learner: Intellectual and cognitive bases. In J. E. Birren & K. W. Schaie (Eds.). *Handbook of the psychology of aging* (2nd ed., pp. 818–847). New York: Van Nostrand Reinhold.

Winnicott, D. W. (1971). *Playing and reality*. New York: Basic Books.

Wollin, D. D. & Montagne, M. (1981). College classroom environment: Effects of sterility versus amiability on student and teacher performance. *Environment and Behavior, 13*, 707–716.

Wundt, W. (1912). Principles of physiological psychology. In B. Rand (Ed.). *The classical psychologists* (pp. 685–696). New York: Houghton Mifflin.

11

Adult Learning in the Workplace

Lawrence Froman

The U.S. economy faces dramatic changes. Competitive pressures resulting from global competition and technological change are forcing organizations to become more adaptive. There is a widely shared belief that we are entering a new economic order driven by the need to be ever more productive, innovative, and responsive to customer demands for quality and service (Carnevale, 1991). This new economic order, often referred to as the global economy, requires a commitment to the process of continuous learning. The purpose of this chapter is to examine adult learning and training in the context of a changing economy and workplace.

LEARNING, TRAINING, AND DEVELOPMENT

Training and development can be defined as a planned effort by an organization to facilitate the learning of job-related behavior on the part of its employees (Wexley & Latham, 1991). Job-related behaviors can include any knowledge and skill acquired by an employee that can be related to organizational goals. A training and development effort can be designed to increase an individual's level of self-awareness, skill, and/or motivation to perform his or her job well.

Although most of what is traditionally considered to be training and development deals with increasing an individual's skill, self-awareness and motivational issues become important when the broader spectrum of adult development issues are considered. Adult learning in the workplace will be examined in this context.

CHANGES IN THE WORKPLACE

The world of work is changing in ways that have direct implications for the training and development of adult workers. Three key issues are the aging of the American workforce, adapting to change, and the need for continuous learning.

Aging of the American Workforce

Between 1986 and 2000, the number of persons aged 35 to 47 will increase by 38%, the number between ages 48 and 53 will jump 67%, while the overall population growth will be only 15% (Offermann & Gowing, 1990).

This expansion in the proportion of middle-aged individuals will mean increased competition for scarce high-level jobs. The traditional lure of promotion as a motivational incentive may need to be replaced by alternate ways to keep workers committed and productive. For those individuals with the talent and motivation, the lower odds for promotion may lead them to become more entrepreneurial and seek out new business ventures. Such initiatives would be consistent with the projection that 85% of the workforce in the year 2000 will work for firms employing fewer than 200 people (Offermann & Gowing, 1990).

Another issue facing the older worker is that biases in the evaluation of their performance continue to exist despite evidence that age is typically unrelated to the performance of most jobs (Sterns & Alexander, 1988). There is also evidence that with few exceptions (e.g., jobs with heavy physical requirements or those requiring quick reaction time), productivity increases with age (Waldman & Avolio, 1986).

The current focus on competitiveness in American business suggests that workers will need to become more flexible and adaptive in their jobs. Research has suggested that training strategies that incorporate principles of self-assessment, self-pacing, and identification of personal learning styles can help the older worker make the necessary adjustments to perform effectively (Carnevale, 1991; Sonnenfeld & Ingols, 1986; Sterns & Doverspike, 1989).

Adapting to Change

Adult workers are faced with the challenge of adapting to new technologies, structures, and work arrangements. In addition to learning new skills, workers may be confronted with new types of organizational arrangements and structures that fundamentally alter the way work is performed. For example, many organizations are moving towards more decentralized structures through the use of self-directed work teams that empower employees to maximize their skills and creativity. Adapting to teams may be difficult for adult employees who are not familiar with doing work in this way. For these individuals, change can generate confusion, anxiety, and loss (Bolman & Deal, 1991). For others, however, the team structure along with other changes in the work environment can create opportunities for growth and renewal.

It was noted above that adult workers can benefit from training and development strategies that provide for self-assessment and identification of personal learning styles. These strategies can help alleviate some of the anxieties that adult workers experience because they individualize the process, provide a supportive learning climate, and can lead to a better match of the employee's job content and career path to his or her learning needs.

The Need for Continuous Learning

Economic growth, organizational effectiveness, and worker productivity are interrelated outcomes. A central thread that links these outcomes is the process of continuous learning that occurs within organizations. Economic progress depends on new learning—learning by doing, learning by using, and learning by borrowing (Carnevale, 1991). For example, as new work arrangements are implemented (e.g., work teams) organizations are investing in learning by doing. As information is obtained through customer feedback, learning by using is captured. And, as business organizations tap into their external networks (e.g., universities, government), learning that occurs elsewhere is being borrowed. The growth capacity of an organization and an economy is expanded as new learning is embedded into workplace practices.

Two key issues related to the need for continuous learning are technological change and employment security (London & Bassman, 1989).

Technological Change. Changes in technology have affected the way in which work gets done, as well as the output of work. There has been a renewed focus on using technology to improve product quality, customer service, and worker productivity—all of which can enhance a firm's competitive advantage.

Advances in computer-aided design and manufacturing systems, robotics, and office automation have enabled organizations to respond to customer needs in a more timely and flexible way (Carnevale, 1991; London & Bassman, 1989). These advances have also changed job descriptions and skill requirements. For example, the selling of high-tech equipment in the health field (e.g., pacemakers for cardiac patients) often requires a mix of marketing and technical skills that result in the development of partnership relationships with medical teams. The selling of electronic components such as computer chips might also require the development of partnership relationships to create customized products. With organizations becoming more decentralized, managers need to develop financial and human resource skills to become entrepreneur-executives. Moreover, in many organizations, decision-making authority is being delegated to self-managed work teams, which can play a pivotal role in transforming how work gets done (Sundstrom, De Meuse & Futrell, 1990). These teams require workers and supervisors to develop new skills in problem solving and communication.

Employment Security. Job security is increasingly tied to continuous learning and retraining. In a changing economy, a new employer-employee relationship is emerging that redefines the meaning of job security. There has been a shift in what the organization and the individual can expect from each other. As noted by London and Bassman (1989), in the past, especially in large organizations, the unstated expectation was that an employee could count on having a job as long as he or she showed up for work, performed satisfactorily, and did not do anything dishonest. However, in recent years, a new expectation has evolved in American companies in which the employee, in return for giving top performance, can expect not job security, but the opportunity for challenge, learning, growth, and development.

In companies in which there is a union presence, continuous learning and retraining programs have been negotiated to address the issues of employment security and employee development. The union, in partnership with management, needs to be involved because collective bargaining issues (job descriptions, work rules) are typically involved (London & Bassman, 1989).

Among the first major corporations and unions to enter into such a negotiated agreement were the Ford Motor Company and the United Auto Workers (UAW). This agreement was part of a major initiative undertaken to create a more co-operative approach to labor-management relations. The traditional adversarial relationship between labor and management had to change to give both sides the flexibility they needed to address the issues. For example, in return for agreeing to allow management to restructure the company's outdated and rigid job classification scheme, the UAW obtained Ford's commitment to establish a significant education and training program. This program includes workplace literacy, skills enhancement, retraining, tuition assistance, and retirement planning. A parallel educational fund for Ford's managers has also been established.

Another example of a negotiated agreement for retraining involves AT&T, the Communication Workers of America, and the International Brotherhood of Electrical Workers. Two critical forces—the breakup of part of AT&T's telecommunications operations into regional companies and rapidly changing technology—created the need for a renewed focus on the education and training needs of the workforce. A new organization was created through the collective bargaining agreement called the Alliance for Employee Growth and Development. Working with Alliance staff, labor-management committees have developed programs to train service technicians in customer relations and to retrain telephone operators affected by new automated technology for other jobs in AT&T. In addition, personal development courses have been designed to address such issues as stress, change, and career planning.

ADULT DEVELOPMENT AND LEARNING THEORY

Concepts of adult development have implications for continuous learning and the design of training and development programs (Leibowitz, Farren & Kaye, 1986). Many mid-career adult workers find themselves in a transition period where they question and reappraise their life and career structure. In such periods, individuals may experience conflict between the motivation to learn, on the one hand, and perceptions, fears, and habits that block change, on the other. Theories of adult development and learning can provide a framework to better understand individual differences within organizational settings and, as a result, create more effective approaches to training and development.

Adult Development

Adult development models have implications for the design of programs for mid-career employees who are in transition and faced with the possibility of changing jobs and/or careers. Building on the work of Geddie and Strickland (1984), researchers Leibowitz, Farren, and Kaye (1986) suggest that, in times of transition, adults are faced with the central task of questioning and reappraising their life and career experiences.

Some examples of emotions that block our ability to deal with midlife transition are ambivalence, hopelessness, and dependency. Perceptions such as "It's too late to change," and other employee views of reality can also block change. Leibowitz et al. suggest that specific interventions (e.g., individual and group counseling) are needed to remove such obstacles to allow individuals to achieve their goals.

Learning Theory

A number of writers in the field of adult learning emphasize the importance of participation, choice, experience, critical reflection, and critical thinking (Knowles, 1984; Marsick, 1987; Argyris & Schon, 1978; Brookfield, 1987).

Knowles (1984) suggests that adults should have greater control and choice over what and how they learn. Central to this idea is the need that adults have for self-direction and integration of their life experiences into the learning process. This need for self-direction, however, can conflict with the feelings of dependency that too often surround learning. As organizations design and implement training programs for the adult learner, greater attention should be given to learning climates that foster self-direction and not dependency. When dependency needs of adult learners are decreased, goals of training will be more effectively met.

The life experiences of adults can enrich the learning process. A key challenge for educators and trainers of adults is to tap into these experiences. In doing so, the adult learner can integrate information with experience in ways that have greater personal meaning. In effect, the adult learner is empowered to adopt a cognitive learning style that is motivating and effective in terms of achieving organizational goals.

The concept of critical reflection (Marsick, 1987) emphasizes the importance of choice and personal meaning for the adult learner. For example, Marsick suggests that training has too often been dominated by technical concerns, with not enough consideration given to the broader aspect of a worker's values, motivation, and goals. This "interpretative paradigm" could help explain why some very well designed training programs fail.

Consider the example of an organization undergoing major changes in its technology and work procedures. Under what Marsick refers to as the "technical paradigm," workers will be trained in robotics and computer-related technology. Appropriate as this might appear to be, problems may occur when employees realize that their jobs have been changed in significant ways, particularly with respect to issues of control and work-group relationships.

If these issues are not confronted during training, they will surface on the job and could very likely affect motivation and performance. Individuals thrust into this type of work environment can feel threatened, especially if they cannot see how they will fit into the new system. Therefore, if the technical paradigm is too narrowly focused, the effectiveness of training may be limited for the adult learner.

As noted earlier, change can create confusion and conflict. In the context of Marsick's "interpretative paradigm," the learning and training process should allow these issues to be dealt with through open, two-way communication between workers and management. Learning is not just about acquiring information, it is also about personal and possibly organizational change.

A process of critical reflection (Marsick, 1987) is needed for employees and managers to examine how values and assumptions that drive organizational goals and policies also affect the way people learn. According to Marsick, meaningful learning and change occur when organizations create a climate where people can question these values and assumptions and explore new paradigms for self-awareness, learning, and growth.

A related idea is offered by Argyris and Schon (1978) with their concept of single-loop and double-loop learning. In single-loop learning, the focus is on error detection and correction. This type of learning is sufficient so long as the governing values and norms that underlie certain strategies are still valid and fit the internal and external realities of the organization. These realities might include changes in external competition, regulation, and demand and internal changes in the nature of the work force (i.e., attitudes, values, and skills).

However, because organizations need to continually adapt to change, the values and norms that affect policy and strategy may have to be confronted. This is called double-loop learning. The key issue is to encourage workers and managers to examine the very norms that define organizational goals and standards of performance. Unquestioned norms may prevent the kind of critical inquiry that is needed for organizational learning and growth. With double-loop learning, learners become critically reflective and dig below the surface for the unstated values, assumptions, and attributions that govern the actions of the organization.

Argyris and Schon (1978) provide an example of an industrial firm that has set up a new division charged with the discovery and development of new technologies. Conflict arises when the corporation realizes that the new division generates technologies that do not fit its familiar pattern of operations. Specifically, a shift is required from the production of intermediate materials to consumer products. But this, in turn, requires that employees learn new approaches to marketing, managing, and advertising; that they adapt to a more rapid cycle of work activity; and, in fact, change the very image of the business they are in.

The essence of the conflict is that these requirements for change do not fit the existing corporate norm that values predictability and stability. Presented with this conflict, managers must first realize that if they conform to the imperative for growth, they must give up on the imperative for predictability. If they decide to maintain their current pattern of operations, they must give up on the imperative for growth. "A process of change initiated with an eye to effectiveness under existing norms turns out to yield a conflict in the norms themselves" (Argyris and Schon, 1978, p. 21).

As corporate managers begin to confront this conflict, they must shift the process of inquiry from single-loop to double-loop learning. They cannot continue to try out the same strategy or variations on it, because those solutions are based on norms that are incompatible with new technologies and products. The new division cannot perform effectively under existing norms. Rather a new process of inquiry must be initiated that attempts to resolve incompatible organizational norms by setting new priorities, inventing new performance strategies, or changing the norms themselves.

The key point is that management must be willing to confront the conflict and to begin a process of inquiry and create a climate where individuals can learn how to critically evaluate their underlying values and norms. This type of climate can promote individual and organizational renewal.

Strategic planning, effective decision making, creative problem solving, and team building are management concepts that are increasingly being heard these days. Each of these concepts have at their core the idea of critical thinking (Brookfield, 1987).

Strategic planning is an attempt to project alternative business scenarios and to plan responses to these. Creative problem solving "has at its core the readiness to question critically the appropriateness of accepted wisdom and to free ourselves from the habitual ways of organizing the workplace" (Brookfield, 1987, p. 138). Team building begins with members trying to understand how norms and assumptions inform each other's actions.

Critical reflection, critical thinking, and double-loop learning are ideas that all point in the same direction. They suggest the importance of creating organizational climates that support open communication, healthy debate, and critical evaluation of untested assumptions and values. In these climates, employees will have more freedom to experiment with new ideas and ways of working. As a result, options for individual and organizational learning can be expanded in ways that promote a more satisfying and productive work environment.

Another key issue presented by learning theory is the importance of individual differences in the ways people learn. Referring to the work of Kolb and Plovnick, Leibowitz et al. (1986) point out that most people develop dominant and different learning styles based on personality and past experience. For example, some people prefer to learn through abstract concepts, while others prefer concrete experience. Assessment instruments such as Kolb and Plovnick's Learning Style Inventory can help identify an individual's preferred/dominant learning style.

The advantage of using data from instruments like these is that individual learning strengths can be identified and integrated into the design of employee development programs. As a result, these programs will be better able to meet the needs of individual participants as well as those of the organization.

RETRAINING THE MID-CAREER WORKER

Although training and retraining are often used interchangeably, the latter focuses on learning new skills and knowledge to prepare for a new career direction, while the former's emphasis is on the development of one's current knowledge and skills (London & Bassman, 1989). Both address organizational productivity requirements, but retraining has the added component of career change.

Mid-Career Issues and Strategies

In an effort to reduce costs, organizations are eliminating jobs—many from the mid-level management ranks as well as those from the technical and professional areas. Job loss, whether by corporate cutbacks or precipitated by the individual's poor job performance, can be a blow to one's self-confidence. Corporate outplacement programs have been designed to deal with the need to rebuild the employee's self-confidence as well as provide a systematic and structured plan for the job search process. Although these programs often focus on mid- and top-level managers, some companies have expanded the scope of these efforts to include technical and hourly employees.

An example of this broader approach can be found in the Stroh Brewery Company's Employee Transition Services Program (SETS). A a result of a plant closing in Detroit, Stroh, in collaboration with a management consulting firm specializing in assisting displaced employees, developed a program that would deal with the needs employees might experience while in transition, including but not limited to finding a job.

Two program service centers were established for salaried and hourly employees. Key elements of the program included self-assessment, resume preparation, and counseling services to help employees deal with their feelings and attitudes toward job loss. There was also a significant job development effort to generate referrals to employers. Results of the program as measured by job placement rate were impressive. Of the 770 employee participants, 757 (98.3%) were able to find a job. Within this group, 242 employees (32%) found a job on their own, while 515 (68%) found a job through the direct efforts of program staff (Franzem, 1987).

Another key mid-career issue is plateauing, which involves either a lack of promotional opportunity from the organization or an individual's decision not to seek further advancement. Often, this decision arises when employees do not see a match between their career goals and the available career paths within the organization (London & Bassman, 1989).

Retraining can be a possible response to plateauing. However, all too often the focus of retraining efforts is on the narrow sphere of technical skill development, with not enough attention given to those mid-career employees who feel threatened because of "decades invested in career paths that are now being derailed" (Sonnenfeld & Ingols, 1986, p. 76).

Marsick's (1987) concept of the "interpretative paradigm" can be related to this issue of career plateauing. As noted earlier, training, and indeed retraining, comprise not just a technical enterprise but a broader process that deals with how employees interpret and adapt to change. Therefore, it is important that trainers clarify how retraining can facilitate movement into new career paths. The key point is that retraining and career development be integrated and linked to realistic opportunities within organizations.

Career plateauing can also trigger a reassessment of how work can be balanced with personal concerns such as values, family, and life-style. Indeed, many organizations are examining their human resource policies and practices to help their employees find such a balance. Strategies such as flexible work schedules, job sharing, and career sabbaticals have at their core the need for employees to integrate their personal and professional goals more fully (Coates, Jarratt & Mahaffie, 1990).

Beyond these strategies, other types of organizational change strategies might be explored. For example, job rotation could serve as a motivational catalyst for those employees who feel the need for some change but do not want to change careers. Certain types of routine jobs that lack variety and challenge could be redesigned to provide greater job satisfaction and performance (Hackman & Oldham, 1980). Training programs for supervisors could be developed that emphasize the increasingly important skills of coaching and mentoring (Sanderson, 1989).

Organizations have developed mentoring programs to address the needs of both new and older workers (Kram, 1985). Mid-career employees can provide their proteges with insights into the workings of the organization. They may help clarify policies, identify pathways for improved job performance, and develop strategies for career advancement. In return, mentors can derive satisfaction from encouraging the development of their colleagues while also helping the organization to become more productive.

Retraining Older Workers

With the tight supply of new entrants to the labor force, organizations will become increasingly reliant on the skills and abilities of older workers (London & Bassman, 1989). A variety of strategies are being examined to tap into the skill, experience, and motivation of these individuals. For example, companies have started programs to attract older workers who may be interested in second careers, often as part-time employees. Some organizations offer courses that upgrade the skills of older workers.

Unfortunately, driven by the need to reduce their costs, organizations are being restructured in ways that limit retraining efforts for older employees. For example, a typical cost-cutting strategy of organizations is to use financial incentives to pressure older workers to take early retirement. It would appear, judging from recent trends, that companies would rather hire younger workers at a lower salary than invest in the retraining of their older employees.

While the realities of organizational retrenchment and cost-cutting present some obstacles to retraining of older workers, other factors (e.g., aging babyboomers, shifts in government resources from defense to civilian work, investment in infrastructure—roads, bridges, high-speed rail—to create jobs) suggest that the need for retraining will increase. Organizations need to harness the talent, skill, and experience of all their employees, including older workers; and innovative retraining programs can play a critical role in this effort.

Human Resource Development Strategies

Human resource development strategies are needed that focus on the issues of commitment, resources, and flexibility. To support the retraining process, as with any change strategy, management needs to be firmly committed and be willing to allocate resources. Therefore, employer investment in training and retraining should be significantly increased. Government incentives (e.g., tax policies, grants, technical assistance) could also be developed to support this "investment in people" strategy.

In addition to increasing their financial commitment, employers will need to link training and continuous learning to organizational and strategic planning processes. Too often, human resource issues sit on the periphery and are not integrated into the core mission of the organization. Therefore, training and development managers should work closely with business strategists and organizational planners to design learning systems.

Within a framework of increased labor-management cooperation, more flexible policies and work rules are needed to provide employees with opportunities for lateral job changes and shifting among functional specialties. This gives the employer more options in how best to coordinate the skills of its work force and to provide employees with new opportunities for learning and career development. In a wider context, the competitive demands of a global economy require that organizations adapt to change—and, in so doing, design flexible work arrangements to promote the continuous learning and development of its work force.

Government, educational institutions, and private industry should form partnerships to coordinate training and development programs at the state and national level. These partnerships are needed to support research and development of curriculum and training methods in particular occupations, to support evaluation studies to identify cost-effective programs, and to encourage the design of new and innovative approaches to worker retraining.

This chapter has examined adult learning processes in the context of a changing economy and workplace. Building on the themes of participation, choice, experience, and critical reflection, trainers and adult educators can design more effective and innovative learning systems. The application of these ideas can lead to individual and organizational change, where assumptions and habitual ways of working can be questioned and where people can disengage from time-honored traditions to explore new work arrangements.

The demands of a changing workplace—one that is more culturally diverse, technologically complex, and globally competitive—will require investment in human resources. A key part of this investment will involve policies and strategies that promote adult learning in our organizations. It is through such learning that the seeds of individual growth and organizational renewal can be planted.

REFERENCES

Argyris, C., and Schon, D. (1978). *Organizational learning: A theory of action perspective*. Reading, MA: Addison-Wesley.

Bolman, L., and Deal, T. (1991). *Reframing organizations*. San Francisco: Jossey-Bass.

Brookfield, S. (1987). *Developing critical thinkers*. San Francisco: Jossey-Bass.

Carnevale, A. (1991). *America and the new economy*. San Francisco: Jossey-Bass.

Coates, J., Jarratt, J., and Mahaffie, J. (1990). *Future Work*. San Francisco: Jossey-Bass.

Franzem, J. (1987). Easing the pain. *Personnel Administrator*. February.

Geddie, C., and Strickland, B. (1984). From plateaus to progress: A model for career development. *Training*, June, 56–61.

Hackman, J., and Oldham, G. (1980). *Work Redesign*. Reading, MA: Addison-Wesley.

Knowles, M. (1984). Adult learning: Theory and practice. In L. Nadler. (Ed.). *The handbook of human resource development*. New York: Wiley, 6.1–6.23.

Kolb, D. A. and Plovnick, M. S. (1977). The experiential learning theory of career development. In J. Van Maanen (Ed.). *Organizational careers: Some new perspectives*. New York: Wiley.

Kram, K. (1985). *Mentoring at work: Developmental relationships in organizational life*. Glenview, IL: Scott Foresman.

Leibowitz, Z., Farren, C., and Kaye, B. (1986). Applying theory to practice in career development planning. In *Designing career development systems*. San Francisco: Jossey-Bass, 67–93.

London, M., and Bassman, E. (1989). Retraining midcareer workers for the future workplace. In I. Goldstein and associates (Ed.). *Training and development in organizations*. San Francisco: Jossey-Bass, 333–375.

Marsick, V. (1987). *Learning in the workplace: Theory and practice*. London: Croom Helm.

Offermann, L., and Gowing, M. (1990). Organizations of the future. *American Psychologist*, 45(2), 95–108.

Sanderson, D. (1989). Midcareer support: an approach to lifelong learning in the organization. *Lifelong Learning*, 12(7), 7–10.

Sonnenfeld, J., and Ingols, C. (1986). Working knowledge: charting a new course for training. *Organizational Dynamics*, Autumn, 63–79.

Sterns, H., and Alexander, R. (1988). Performance appraisal of the older worker. In H. Dennis (Ed.). *Fourteen steps to managing an aging workforce*. Lexington, MA: Lexington Books, 85–93.

Sterns, H., and Doverspike, D. (1989). Aging and the training and learning process. In I. Goldstein and Associates (Ed.). *Training and development in organizations*. San Francisco: Jossey-Bass, 299–332.

Sundstrom, E., De Meuse, K., and Futrell, D. (1990). Work teams: Applications and effectiveness. *American Psychologist*, 45(2), 120–133.

Waldman, D., and Avolio, B. (1986). A meta-analysis of age differences in job performance. *Journal of Applied Psychology*, 71, 33–38.

Wexley, K., and Latham, G. (1991). *Developing and training human resources in organizations*. New York: HarperCollins.

12

Adults in College

Carolyn Harriger

That adults can be found frequenting college campuses is not a new or startling notion. Over the past decade the average age of the college population has risen phenomenally. The number of students over the age of 25 increased by more than 11% between 1981 and 1986 (National Center for Educational Statistics, 1988). Rapidly changing technology, radical shifts in the economy, and the return of great numbers of women to the work force are some of the sociological factors that have influenced this change. Brockett (1987) asserts that these changes result in jobs that will change radically every ten years, necessitating that education and reeducation become the standard paradigm. Froman further discusses these changes in the work force and how society is being affected by them in chapter 11 of this volume, ''Adult Learning in the Workplace.'' Education, therefore, is no longer a preparation for a life's work, but rather an entity that is embraced throughout the lifespan.

It is predicted that by the turn of the century more than one-half of all college students will be over the age of 25 and a significant portion will be over 35. Part-time enrollments, chiefly of adults, are predicted to be the fastest-growing cohort in higher education, increasing six times more than full-time enrollments (National Center for Educational Statistics, 1991).

Adult college students are making a significant impact on society and on institutions of higher education as well. This chapter will consider the cohort of adults in college. Who is the college-bound adult learner? Why do adults go to college? How do adults fare in college? How is the institution (college or university) affected by the growing presence of the adult population on campus? What are the innovative institutions doing to help the adult student access what higher education has to offer? This chapter attempts to answer these questions.

WHO IS THE COLLEGE-BOUND ADULT?

Within any group of people under study, there are typically more differences among individuals than there are likenesses. People come in all ages, shapes, and sizes, bound by their own histories, experiences, expectations, needs, and desires. Answering the question of who the college-bound adult is, therefore, demands looking at descriptions of tendencies and propensities that have resulted from studies and research conducted with this population. Long (1990) reminds us of a fact central to understanding adult students, that one must accept the fact that physiological, psychological, and sociological diversity exists to a greater extent in adults than in children. In other words, the older the adult, the fewer the common variables. We need to focus on the more commonplace characteristics of this group, rather than a specific description of the college-bound adult. Long calls this a "realistic balance between recognition of individual idiosyncratic characteristics and identification of those normative characteristics that allow us to consider adult learners as a group" (pp. 25–26).

Demographic Characteristics

Cross (1978) suggests that the portrayals of participants in academic credit programs conveyed to us in various studies are quite consistent. Her opinion is supported by the early studies of Johnstone and Rivera (1965) and the more recent studies of Aslanian and Brickell (1980, 1988). According to these researchers, the college-bound adult is likely to be between the ages of 25 and 34. The student is apt to be already better educated than most adults, more than half already having some college experience. The college-bound adult is likely to have a family income of $30 thousand to $49 thousand. These studies further describe the average college-bound adult as a female, employed full-time in a professional, business, or technical field. She is married, with children under the age of eighteen, white, and living in or near an urban area (Aslanian & Brickell, 1988). In spite of this very specific picture of the adult learner, the reader is cautioned to keep in mind that there is no generic adult learner and that no description of adults can yield a complete view.

In fact, the number of older-adult college students is growing as well. In 1986 the U.S. Department of Education statistics showed that 13% of the adults participating in formal education were over the age of 54 (Merriam & Caffarella, 1991, p. 67). The graying of America and an increase in the lifespan of individuals is providing higher education with growing numbers of older adults still in the work force and seeking education as a means of updating job skills or of enrichment.

Qualitative Characteristics

To enhance the demographic descriptions of college-bound adults, educators and researchers have provided qualitative characteristics as well. In the literature of the past two decades, adult educators have reiterated in multiple works and studies the characteristics of adult students (Knowles, 1980; Cross, 1981; Long, 1983). With a variety of terms, adult learners have been described as problem solvers, as self-directed and pragmatic, and as life-experienced individuals. Adults bring these characteristics to college as personal resources and apply them toward their college experiences.

Knowles (1980) supports four critical assumptions about adult learners. He states that as individuals mature their self-concept moves from being a dependent personality toward being a more self-directed individual. He adds that over the years adults accumulate a growing reserve of life experiences. His third assumption is that adults are oriented increasingly toward problem solving within the arena of their life roles; fourth, he finds that they have a need to immediately apply what they have learned to their everyday lives and situations.

Cross (1978) characterizes adults in a similar manner. She says that adult students are decision makers who have most likely freely made the decision to return to school. They wish to apply newly acquired knowledge at the present time, rather than assimilate it for future use. Their life experiences are many and provide them with extensive prior learning to which new learning may be related. Cross emphasizes that adult learners tend to be quite strongly self-directed.

Part-Time Students

A salient characteristic of adults in college is the prevalence of part-time study. Nearly 38% of this nation's undergraduate students attend school on a part-time basis (National Center for Educational Statistics, 1990). Although students of all ages can be found in this group, "Part-time students are, in short, much more adult" than traditional-aged students (Bournier, 1991, p. xi), that is, are over the age of 25. Part-time enrollments climbed during the past twenty years, increasing by a total of 109% (National Center for Educational Statistics, 1989).

To study part-time rather than full-time is usually a decision that is thrust upon adults by their life situations. The most obvious reason is that of time limitations. For the most part, adult learners are working full-time or have other care-giving commitments that prevent them from studying full-time. Bournier's studies (1991) indicate that the average part-time student spends six hours per week attending class and nine hours in private study. Adding travel time to and from the institution culminates in a picture of a very busy adult.

Additionally, numbers of adults may be studying part-time—taking just a course or two—because they are testing the waters. Not having attended school for a number of years, these adults are characterized by a need for confidence-building before accelerating their academic programs. Still other adult students may be studying part-time because of limited funds and an inability to obtain financial aid.

There are indeed exceptions to any typical group of adults; however, it can be generally assumed that most of the adults seeking entrance to our college campuses are likely to have chosen freely to come to college and to be self-directed in seeking the type of education they want, as well as what they want from their education. Adult students have a wealth of life and work experiences to us as a resource for learning. Life experiences become the hooks or hangers, so to speak, for new experiences and new learning. Having looked at some of the more common traits of adult learners, we turn to the next question and some of the reasons adults choose to go to college.

WHY DO ADULTS GO TO COLLEGE?

"Demographic characteristics of learners are correlated with the causes, but are not themselves the causes of adult learning" (Aslanian & Brickell, 1980, p. 47); therefore, we must be cautious in making assumptions about why adults attend or do not attend college.

Motivation and Participation

The field of motivation research in adult education is vast. Following the landmark studies of Houle (1961), numerous other researchers expanded and refined what we know today about what motivates adults to go to college. Houle's early studies resulted in a typology that characterizes adults as being chiefly goal-oriented, activity-oriented, or learning-oriented in their motivation to participate in formal learning activities. Although his research has been criticized as giving only one perspective of the motivation to learn and as raising more questions than it answers (Courtney, 1984), Houle's typology is useful. These descriptions "provide a reasonably good practitioner's handle for thinking about individual motivations for learning" (Cross, 1981, p. 96). Some students are prone to learning for the sake of learning (learning-oriented). Others are geared toward the social aspect of participation in learning activities (activity-oriented). The remainder are goal-oriented, that is, they seek learning to fulfill a specific objective. Other researchers followed in expanding and further defining Houle's typology (Boshier, 1973; Burgess, 1971; Morstain & Smart, 1974; Sheffield, 1964).

Boshier (1973, 1977) contended that formal learning participation stems from the interaction of psychological (internal) and environmental (external) factors, searching for a goodness of fit between the participant and the educational environment. Boshier searched for "the presence of intra-self congruence" among the individual's learning-orientation, activity-orientation, and professional advancement-orientation. He found that when there was congruence between the learner's motive and the educational environment there was persistence. This places the onus of at least part of the answer to why adults come to college, and remain in college, on the higher education institutions themselves. Armed with their own personal motives, mature students come to college; their persistence in completing their education depends in some part on the institutions' response to their presence. A later section of this chapter will address how institutions meet this challenge.

Apps (1981) observed six factors in the adult's return to school. He first states that the prime motive for returning to college is in some way occupationally related. Second, Apps contends that a generation ago attendance at college frequently had a negative connotation, that is, an adult had to return to school to obtain something that should have been gotten earlier in life. Today, however, going to college is assuredly socially acceptable for adults. Apps' third factor is life enhancement, that is, adults attend college to enrich life with learning. Apps describes as his fourth factor the change in an individual's life situation, such as divorce, children leaving home, or loss of employment. Fifth, Apps attests to the premium that society places on the college degree. The degreed person is looked upon with high regard and is offered more opportunities than the person without this credential. Finally, Apps alleges that the active recruitment by institutions of higher education motivates some adults to attend college who might not otherwise do so. Although critics claim that this factor alone will not cause an adult to go to college, many colleges are admittedly involved in aggressive marketing to the adult population. Indeed, some researchers believe that college enrollments will remain stable through the 1990s only because of the increasing adult population (Hodgkinson, 1983).

Aslanian and Brickell (1980) go a step further in discerning reasons adults return to college. Surveying two thousand Americans 25 years of age and older in face-to-face interviews and telephone conversations, they found that 87% of those surveyed experienced life transitions as the stimulus for going to college. The authors cite transitional events, which they call triggers, such as a job promotion or loss, the birth of a child, bereavement, move to a new locale, and job dissatisfaction. Aslanian and Brickell confirm that 56% of those who were in transition specifically cited career events as the trigger for participation in college, corroborating Houle's goal-oriented category. These transitions fell into three categories: moving to a new job, adapting to a changing job, and advancing in a career. As Merriam discusses in chapter 6 of this volume, "Learning and Life Experience: The Connection in Adulthood," job-related reasons are the prime motivation for adults' return to college. Although trigger events are varied, it would appear that a great many college-bound adults are seekers of credentials and skills needed for employment or career enhancement.

Courtney (1991) draws from personality and life study research to conclude his theory of participation in education:

Those who appear eager and willing to participate in organized learning activities are distinguishable from those who are not by an underlying attitude which sees education as a positive force, to be equated with happiness, and finds in it also a mechanism for solving acute problems. However, . . . the person must be in a situation calling for the solution of a particular problem. This could mean situations such as obtaining promotion at work, changing jobs, or taking on new responsibilities in the family or community, or it could refer to the need to learn a new set of work skills, such as might arise in a situation like divorce or unemployment. (p. 83)

Barriers to Participation

In spite of what has been said about why adults go to college, many people, frequently those who would benefit most, do not. It may be helpful to look briefly at some of the reasons adults do not go to college, barriers that prohibit their participation.

Carp, Peterson, and Roelfs (1974) and later Cross (1981) have identified three types of barriers to participation in educational activities. Institutional barriers would include the college's or university's practices and procedures that may discourage adults from attending. Such procedures, which prevent access to education because they are not congruent with the life-styles and characteristics of the adult student, may include a lack of evening classes, in-person daytime registration, or daytime-only advising hours. Situational barriers include individual, personal considerations that a person faces, such as child-care needs or a lack of time or finances. The final type of barrier is dispositional, that is, relating to self-perception and attitudes toward learning. For instance, many people who have had unsuccessful school experiences in the past may be hesitant to return voluntarily to the scene of their humiliations. Poor self-esteem may convince a person that she or he is not capable of learning in a college classroom.

Darkenwald and Merriam (1982) refined dispositional barriers to include beliefs, attitudes, values, and perspectives that create a negative view of education and of oneself as a learner. They also added a fourth set of barriers, which they called informational, defined as a lack of awareness of the possibilities of obtaining an education.

Motivation for adult learning has been described as a mosaic or configuration of diverse needs and purposes (Darkenwald & Merriam, 1982). Indeed, there are many pieces to the motivation puzzle. In this author's research, students were questioned about why they participated in college (Harriger, 1991). In spite of the barriers inherent in their life-styles and within the bureaucratic confines of the institutions, students were ardent in reporting that they were in college for a chance to better themselves and their families, for love of learning, personal enrichment, and self-satisfaction. Granted, they initially returned to school to advance in their jobs and to further their employment opportunities; but the excitement of personal growth ranked high as the reason for their persistence. As one student stated, ''Regardless of whatever happens afterward, you've met a goal. It's more important than the job. . . . Just meeting the goal is what counts'' (p. 192).

Cross (1978) suggests that the more one experiences education the more one likes it, for both its intrinsic and its extrinsic awards. Cross also suggests that adults are basically curious and enjoy learning. As simplistic as this statement is, data seems to substantiate Cross' assertion.

Why do adults go to college? Motives are almost as varied as there are adults. Research data seems to substantiate the suggestion that jobs and career change are the basis for many decisions of adults to return to school; however, the love of learning (Houle's learning-oriented motive) seems to be at least a secondary and overlapping motive for many adults.

HOW DO ADULTS FARE IN COLLEGE?

Just as diversity characterizes any particular group of adults, likewise their performance as students is inevitably diverse. Personal characteristics, study skills, and outside responsibilities all affect how an individual student will fare in college. Some adults are quite intelligent, some are less so; some are quick to learn, some are slower; some are well-read and knowledgeable, some have much to learn; some are full of energy and confident of their abilities, some are worriers or apathetic. The very heterogeneous traits of adults can cause dilemmas in college; by the same token, their maturity can effect success. To discern how adults fare in college we look again at the commonalities found in adults' college experiences.

Cross (1978) describes adult students as responsive and highly motivated individuals. The very characteristics that they possess as adults add to effective coping with going to school and enriching themselves with what the educational process has to offer. Cross contends that, given the maturity with which they approach college, as problem solvers adults tend to successfully mesh "school" with their busy life-styles. As a result, they attend class regularly and know how to take control of their own learning. Should it become necessary to miss class, adults are apt to keep up through seeking arrangements with their instructors or other classmates. Cross continues to describe adults as being generally self-directed and thus more apt to develop their own learning plans and identify their own strengths and weaknesses. Their everyday lives and experiences have taught them how to negotiate the sometimes unfamiliar procedures that surround college administration.

It is difficult to avoid comparing the older students with their traditional-aged counterparts. Many younger students possess all or some of the same traits as adult students. But, by and large, when compared to most traditional students, most adult students are more highly motivated, more involved in studying and learning, more apt to interact with the faculty. Adults are more apt to utilize critical thinking in their learning than younger students (Ross, 1989).

The studies of Beder and Darkenwald (1982) and Gorham (1985) are consonant with Ross's findings and give a largely positive picture of how most adults fare in college. Adult students are more curious than the younger cohort of college students, causing them to be more active in the classroom, more inclined to participate and ask questions. In general, adult students are more motivated to learn. They are usually voluntary students who are financially responsible for their education and so are focused toward obtaining full value from their education experiences. Adults tend to take responsibility for their own learning, are clear about what they want to learn, and are concerned about the practical implications of their learning.

Adults generally fare very well in the classroom. Most faculty appreciate the presence of adult students because of the rich resources that they bring and their general enthusiasm for learning. Unfortunately, the dilemmas frequently occur outside the classroom, in synchronizing a multitude of life roles and demands with the formats of administrative offices and services.

Institutions are bureaucracies, and their structures seldom account for individual differences or a need for flexibility in services. Schlossberg, Lynch, and Chickering (1989) contend that:

Students, traditionally thought of as children and young adults, are assumed to be dependent on authorities and in need of expert guidance. . . . Adults, traditionally thought of as being in charge of their own and others' lives, are assumed to be trying to maintain control over their own lives, to preserve their independence. (p. 7)

Schlossberg sees an unfortunate paradox in the terms adult and student. She contends that institutions tend to dwell on the latter term, ignoring the former.

The plight of the adult student in many colleges could be summed up in this adult student quote: "We [adult students] do not want exceptions made for us; we want hospitality" (Harriger, 1991, p. 245). In other words, the adult student wants to be an integral part of the educational setting rather than an adjunct to it. Although many institutions are making changes to accommodate the adult population, there still exists on many campuses an "adjunct" feeling of second-class citizenry among adult students. In effect, the adult frequently feels a lack of hospitality within many institutions.

Although strides toward integrating the adult student population are being made on many campuses, this feeling of inhospitality is evidenced by various scenarios. On some campuses adult students are required to take time off from their jobs or other responsibilities during daytime hours to conduct college business such as registering, purchasing books, advising, and using the library, in spite of the fact that classes are offered in the evenings. Adult students are frequently limited in choice of major areas of study because not all required courses of all departments are offered in the evening hours. Often students are stymied after beginning a course of study advertised as an evening major to discover that some "evening" courses begin at 4:00 P.M. Some adult students meet with advisors and counselors well-versed in intercollegiate athletics and residence halls but not in child-care availability or other adult concerns. Success or failure in dealing with situations such as these often determines an adult's persistence in college and often determines how well the adult will fare.

Despite anxieties and difficulties created by some institutions, adults appear to compensate as a result of a strong motivation to learn and to obtain their education. Yet, Schlossberg, Lynch, and Chickering (1989) assert, "We believe that the character of the adult experience and the character of the educational institutions are out of synchrony" (p. 1). The dilemmas described by adult students are created by very heterogeneous adults and very rigid bureaucracies. This leads to the final question, how is the institution affected by the presence of adults on campus?

HOW IS THE INSTITUTION AFFECTED?

Given that adults on campus are no longer an anomaly, numerous institutions are either adapting their goals and mission statements to accommodate this change or establishing separate colleges to meet the distinctive needs of the adult college student. On all but a few college campuses, the traditional image of a student as an 18- to 22-year-old youth has been broadened to include mature adults of various ages and motivations. This adaptation to the changing population has occurred in a variety of ways and to varying degrees.

Clark Taylor (1982), addressing the topic of diversely prepared college students, uses four descriptive terms that are useful to illustrate the way in which institutions respond to the presence of adults in college: avoid, suffer, cope with, and embrace. Using Taylor's terms, it could be said that academic institutions are responding to the presence of adult students in one of these four ways.

Some institutions avoid adult students. They may do this through high admissions standards, inflexible regulations, or any number of other ways. These are generally the most selective institutions whose missions clearly do not include other than traditional students.

Some institutions suffer the presence of adults on campus. They may have broadened their enrolled population, but they have not reassessed their mission or their basic assumptions about students. Minor changes are grudgingly made within the institution as the politically correct thing to do.

Other institutions cope with the adult student, but any changes that they might make are basically add-ons. The central administration and programming of the institution remain the same, and adult students must accommodate them.

Finally, other institutions embrace the adult population. These schools redesign programs to emphasize the strengths and the needs of a diverse population. They are clear about each segment of the student population they are serving and develop programs with that population in mind. These are the schools that work toward an optimum fit (Boshier, 1977), so that adult students not only enroll in the school but also persist until completion.

It can be assumed that adults generally do not choose to attend "avoid" schools and that their needs are being met in "embrace" schools. Most institutions of higher learning lie within the parameters of the two middle categories, either suffering or coping with the presence of adult students. They are either grudgingly or willingly making efforts to adjust programs and services to adult students, with varying degrees of success.

The reflexes of many administrators in higher education have been conditioned by years of dealing with traditional-aged students. These attitudes are inadequate and often produce dilemmas in dealing with adult students. "The schools and universities have . . . standardized the ways in which learning has been carried on" (Kidd, 1973). Kidd suggests that in order to create a positive educational environment for adults there is need for a transformational process that involves the people, structure, and culture of the university. The truly embracing institutions go beyond merely making changes to examining their vision and their underlying values.

Institutions that most desire to serve adult students are those that offer comprehensive programs and services for adults from the moment they inquire about returning to school and through the process of application to graduation. This would include flexible scheduling of classes and administrative processes, evening office hours, alternative ways of earning credit including recognition of learning through prior experience, opportunities for financial aid, provision for child care, and numerous other ingredients needed by adults who would be students. Making slight, accommodating adjustments to the system without a commitment is wholly inadequate and provides little for the long term.

The greatest effect that the presence of adults in college has on colleges and universities is that it mandates that the institution examine its values, its mission, and its vision to decide whether or not it wishes to accommodate adult students. If that answer is found to be affirmative, changes are likely to be called for, not only in programs and services but in attitudes and perspectives as well.

Andragogy

Malcolm Knowles' (1980) andragogical model for effective teaching and programming for adults provides one of the most complete and practical guides to theory and practice. Countering the pedagogical model of education, which Knowles defines as the transmission of knowledge from teacher to student, Knowles popularized the concept of *andragogy*, a lifelong process of continuing inquiry. Andragogy is a model based on assumptions referred to earlier and factors that characterize adults. These factors encompass self-direction, life experience, problem solving, and performance-centeredness. Applying these assumptions to practice, Knowles' model is learner-centered and based first of all on the establishment of a positive learning climate. This climate must exist within the institution as well as within the program and the classroom. The classroom instructor in the andragogical model is a facilitator of learning, in partnership with the learner in diagnosing the learning needs, establishing specific objectives, designing appropriate learning activities, and finally evaluating the learning.

Knowles points out that andragogy is a model to use along with pedagogy, as ends of a spectrum, dependent on the learning situation. Although andragogical principles can be used in any teaching situation, with any age group, Knowles' theories and processes provide a strong basis for teaching adults in college. These principles have been applied by numerous institutions of higher learning in developing their own institutional models for serving adult students.

Adults-Only Models

A number of colleges and universities of varying sizes and complexities have chosen to embrace adult students in campus-based, adults-only models, that is, with continuing education colleges or units that serve only adults in their programs. In some cases the development of adults-only programs was a logical response to the growing number of adult students and their specific needs. In other cases, this model was developed because the numbers indicated that the adult student was rapidly becoming the traditional student on campus. Called adult degree programs, returning student programs, minicolleges, or any number of other names, these programs share the belief that adults are integral to the institution's mission. This model consists of an array of options depending upon the size, mission, history, and development of the institution.

Adults-only programs are advantageous in that the specific needs of adults can directly be addressed, faculty can gear its instruction toward a more homogeneous, at least age-wise, group of learners, and adults can thrive in the comfort of experiencing education in the company of learners in similar life situations.

Mainstream Model

Mainstreaming is the more common model found in institutions wishing to embrace adult students. Serving a mix of adult and traditional students, this model frequently makes its initial appearance without announcement, as a natural result of a rapid increase in the number of adult learners, sometimes along with a decrease in younger students. The trend toward part-time and older learners introduces to the institution new dimensions, new challenges, and the need for change. Many schools have faced the challenge and developed adult opportunities that are not peripheral, but rather in the mainstream of the institution. This model is characterized by integrated academic scheduling to assure that all courses are offered at all times and are accessible to all learners. Faculty are sensitized to the diversity of the student population and so adapt the delivery and mode of instruction to meet the needs of the learners. Colleges and universities following this model do not expect the mature students to be able to avail themselves of the same services and service patterns as the younger students. Rather, they incorporate into the mainstream publications and recruitment geared to adult learners, orientation programs and advising services scaled for adult learners, and some means of recognizing and assessing prior learning experiences.

The advantages of this model are many. As all programs and classes are open to all ages of students, there is usually more flexibility to serve the scheduling needs of all students; all major areas of study are usually open to adults as well as other students. The diversity of ages in the mainstreamed classroom can be enriching for all concerned—instructors, younger students, and mature learners as well.

External Degree Model

Both the adults-only model and the mainstream model are campus-based, although some institutions may operate off-campus centers. More unique in serving adult learners is the external degree model. External programs allow mature students to pursue a degree without coming to campus. Indeed, Edison College in Trenton, New Jersey, has no campus. Through a process of individual assessment, students are informed of the requirements needed to complete their degrees. Needed credits may be earned through taking courses at other colleges, correspondence courses, independent study, television courses, workplace study, or other sources. Credit by examination and assessment of prior learning are allowed to complete the degree program. External programs are advantageous for the adult who has extensive working experience, has previously earned college credits, and is an extremely self-directed and independent learner. These programs allow the mature learner to work at a distance without keeping to a set schedule or time frame.

Institutional Model for Serving Adult Students

Schlossberg, Lynch, and Chickering (1989) state that the current demographics will force an "educational revolution" (p. xiii); to this end, these authors present a comprehensive, integrated, institutional model for responding to the diversity of needs presented to campus administrators by adult learners. It provides higher education with "a map of a future in which adults will feel they matter each time they move in, move through, and move on from a particular learning experience" (p. 33).

In this three-pronged model, the initial stage, moving into the system, is an adult entry program that treats administrative processes as an educational experience in itself, from recruitment and initial inquiry through the registration and assessment of prior learning. At each phase the process and the individual are treated as an integrated whole to provide the learner with support and encouragement and to be "a powerful educational experience" of itself that will "improve the match between [the learner's] purposes and talents and the resources for learning we have to offer" (p. 87).

The second stage carries the adult through the actual academic experience. As adult learners move through their academic programs, they are helped in dealing with balancing their education with the other demands and stresses of their lives. The model designs integrated and comprehensive support services to help the student feel involved in the academic process, informed, and cared for. It encompasses such services as mentoring, adult-learner advocacy, and provision of places for adult students to meet on campus. Based on the assumption that adults do not spend many hours outside of class time on the campus, the model also prescribes extensive advertising of services so that adult students can become aware of and use them.

The final stage, often overlooked by other programs, supports mature learners as they face the end of the experience. The authors refer to this as moving on. Through culminating courses, career planning, and reviews with advisors and mentors, this stage assists the learner to assess what has been accomplished and to make decisions about the future. Each stage of the Schlossberg, Lynch, and Chickering model for adult learning is cohesive and provides what Daloz (1986) terms an education of care.

Institutions of higher learning are indeed affected by the presence of adults on the college campus. Innovation, adaptation, and reorganization can be a strenuous process, but one that colleges and universities who are committed to serving adults need to adopt. The most obvious adaptation is scheduling. Flexibility in class times and innovative formats such as minicourses, independent study opportunities, and weekend programs need to be extended to the mature learner. Attempts to create a hospitable environment for adults is crucial. Whether an adults-only model that could be a community in miniature or a mainstream model that espouses mature students' needs, such an environment could include any number of innovations that reach out to the adult learner. Admission and retention policies need to be considered that offer access to students who have been away from school for a period of time or who have not had College Board testing. Stopping-out programs are needed that allow a student to take a semester off without experiencing complex readmission procedures. Finally, the use of the media and technology for the delivery of programs needs to be strongly considered. As technology makes possible highly individualized, interactive, long-distance communication, institutions can better serve a wider variety of clients, both on and off campus.

Colleges and universities have an opportunity as well as an obligation to play a significant role in lifelong learning. They can accomplish this in several ways. They can intensify their efforts to meet the educational needs of adults through adapting courses, methods, and methodology. In addition, institutions must handle issues of format, location, and timing of instruction with flexibility and must adapt day-to-day procedures in order to provide access to working adults (Lynton and Elman, 1987).

SUMMARY

As the need and desire for education persist throughout the lifespan, more and more adults are enrolling in higher education. Adults in college are a diverse group with more differences than likenesses. As a result of some transition in life or a "trigger event," adults turn to higher education to seek options. Most often, the adult learner's motives for returning to school are employment- or career-related; however, enrichment and self-satisfaction are other vital reasons for persisting in spite of unwieldy institutional processes and procedures and hectic personal life-styles.

The maturity and characteristics that adults bring to college sometimes create a challenge both for the adult, in fitting school into her or his life-style and for the educational institution, in meeting the academic and service needs of the mature learner. But adult students fare well in the college classroom. It is incumbent upon the institution to examine its mission and goals and determine whether serving adults will appropriately fit the organization. If so, the institution needs to study existing models and programs and look toward change and innovation where needed.

REFERENCES

Apps, J. (1981). *The adult learner on campus: A guide for instructors and administrators*. New York: Cambridge Books.

Aslanian, C. & Brickell, H. M. (1980). *Americans in transition*. New York: College Entrance Examination Board.

Aslanian, C. & Brickell, H. M. (1988). *How Americans in transition study for credit*. New York: College Entrance Examination Board.

Beder, H. & Darkenwald, G. (1982). Differences between teaching adults and pre-adults: Some propositions and findings. *Adult Education, 32*(3), 142–155.

Boshier, R. (1973). Educational participation and dropout: A theoretical model. *Adult Education, 23*, 255–282.

Boshier, R. (1977). Motivational orientation revisited: Life space motives and the education participation scale. *Adult Education, 27*(2), 89–115.

Bournier, T. (1991). *Part-time students and their experience of higher education*. Bristol, PA: The Society for Research into Higher Education and Open University Press.

Brockett, R. (Ed.). (1987). *Continuing education in the year 2000*. New Directions for Continuing Education Series, *36*. San Francisco: Jossey-Bass.

Burgess, P. (1971). Reasons for adult participation in group educational activities. *Adult Education, 22*, 3–29.

Carp, A., Peterson, R. & Roelfs, P. (1974). Adult learning interests and experiences. In K. P. Cross, J. R. Valley, and Associates, *Planning non-traditional programs: An analysis of the issues of postsecondary education* (pp. 11–52). San Francisco: Jossey-Bass.

Courtney, S. (1984). *Visible learning: Adult education and the question of participation*. Doctoral dissertation, Northern Illinois University.

Courtney, S. (1991). *Why adults learn: Toward a theory of participation in adult education*. New York: Routledge, Chapman, and Hall.

Cross, K. P. (1978). The adult learner. In *Current Issues in Higher Education*. Washington, DC: 1978 National Conference Series, American Association for Higher Education.

Cross, K. P. (1981). *Adults as learners*. San Francisco: Jossey-Bass.

Daloz, L. A. (1986). *Effective teaching and mentoring: Realizing the transformational power of adult learning experiences*. San Francisco: Jossey-Bass.

Darkenwald, G. & Merriam, S. (1982). *Adult education: Foundations of practice*. New York: Harper and Row.

Gorham, J. (1985). Differences between teaching adults and pre-adults: A closer look. *Adult Education Quarterly, 35*(4), 194–209.

Harriger, C. (1991). *Barriers to the optimal use of prior learning assessment*. Doctoral dissertation, Columbia University, New York.

Hodgkinson, H. L. (1983). Guess who's coming to college? A demographic portrait of students in the 1990's. *Academe, 69*(2), 13–20.

Houle, C. (1961). *The inquiring mind*. Madison: University of Wisconsin Press.

Johnstone, J. W. & Rivera, R. J. (1965). *Volunteers for learning*. Chicago: Aldine.

Kidd, J. R. (1973). *How adults learn*. New York: Association Press.

Knowles, M. (1978). *The adult learner*. Houston: Gulf Publishers.

Knowles, M. (1980). *The modern practice of adult education*. Cambridge: The Adult Book Company.

Long, H. B. (1983). *Adult learning: Research and practice*. New York: Cambridge.

Long, H. B. (1990). Understanding adult learners. In M. Galbraith. *Adult learning methods*. Malabar, FL: Krieger Publishing Co.

Lynton, E. A. & Elman, S. (1987). *New priorities for the university*. San Francisco: Jossey-Bass.

Merriam, S. B. & Caffarella, R. S. (1991). *Learning in adulthood*. San Francisco: Jossey-Bass.

Morstain, B. R. & Smart, J. C. (1974). Reasons for participation in adult education courses: A multivariate analysis of group differences. *Adult Education, 24*, 83–98.

National Center for Educational Statistics (1988). *Preliminary data: Participation in adult education, 1988*. Washington, DC: Government Printing Office.

National Center for Educational Statistics. (1989). *Preliminary data: Participation in adult education, 1989*. Washington, DC: Government Printing Office.

National Center for Educational Statistics. (1990). *Profile of undergraduates in American postsecondary institutions*. Washington, DC: Government Printing Office.

National Center for Educational Statistics. (1991). *Preliminary data: Participation in adult education*. Washington, DC: Government Printing Office.

Ross, J. M. (1989). *Recruiting and retaining adult students in higher education*. New Directions for Continuing Education Series, *41* (pp. 49–62). San Francisco: Jossey-Bass.

Schlossberg, N. K., Lynch, A. Q. & Chickering, A. W. (1989). *Improving higher education environments for adults*. San Francisco: Jossey-Bass.

Sheffield, S. B. (1964). The orientations of adult continuing learners. In D. Solomon (Ed.). *The continuing learner*. Chicago: Center for the Study of Liberal Education of Adults.

Taylor, C. (1982). *A welcome for diversely prepared students*. New Directions for Experiential Learning Series, *17* (pp. 5–16). San Francisco: Jossey-Bass.

Tough, A. M. (1971). The adult's learning projects: A fresh approach to theory and practice in adult learning. *Research in Education Series, 1*. Toronto: Ontario Institute for Studies in Education.

13

Learning in Psychotherapy: A Batesonian Perspective

Aaron T. Hogue, Laura S. Bross, and
Jay S. Efran

INTRODUCTION

Psychotherapy is a specific relationship structure in which personal changes are purposefully designed and enacted. It is a social structure adults often choose when they want to revise some aspect of their interpersonal functioning. Of course, psychotherapists do not have a patent on either personal change or adult learning. There are many other occasions in a person's life that will turn out to have been educative and ''therapeutic''—a walk in the woods, a college course, a trip abroad, becoming a parent, seeing a particular film, and so on (Efran, Lukens & Lukens, 1990). The therapy context is unique only because it involves a contractual agreement to modify an element of the person's pattern of living.

One theorist who addressed the process of learning, both generically and as it applies to the context of therapy, was Gregory Bateson (1972, 1979, 1991). Bateson's theories are valuable because they connect insights derived from many different disciplines: anthropology, sociology, genetics, psychiatry, and psychology. In addition, his philosophy of science integrates issues of epistemology (the study of knowledge) and ontology (the study of being). Finally, his writings have had seminal influence on the field of family therapy, as well as on other psychotherapies that draw upon cybernetic and general systems thinking.

In this chapter, we first outline aspects of Bateson's theory of learning and then illustrate its applicability to four models of the therapeutic process. Rather than rounding up the usual suspects, we have chosen to emphasize four relatively new theories of therapy that have been vying for the attention of mental health workers: contextualistic behaviorism, functional analytic behaviorism, object relations, and systems/paradoxical approaches.

The models selected have some commonalities: They each contain constructivist elements, emphasizing that knowledge is constructed by an active organism operating within an environmental flux (Overton, 1984). Although none of these theories is a pure exemplar of constructivist thinking, each attempts to put clients in touch with self-imposed limitations—boundaries that the client has somehow mistaken for the limits of reality itself (Efran & Fauber, in press). Clients get trapped into believing that the distinctions they have created for themselves are the only ones possible. Therapy reminds them that other sets of distinctions are possible and can lead to options for living that are more attractive and effective.

BATESON'S THEORY OF STOCHASTIC CHANGE

Bateson (1979) draws a basic distinction between the world of the non-living (*pleroma*) and the world of the living (*creatura*). Most of the principles of physics were developed in connection with inanimate entities such as billiard balls, planets, and inclined planes. This is a world of bumps, shoves, forces, and automatic reactions. However, in the world of the living, other sorts of factors come into play and take on considerable importance—most importantly, the making of distinctions and the processing of information. With human beings, particularly after language emerges, change is largely about intents and meanings. When a rock is pushed, it simply travels a certain distance; a person who is pushed immediately inquires about who did it, what it meant, and whether or not it was "personal." One of the authors recalls noticing that children at summer camp complained about being hit on the arm only when the person who hit them seemed to be "serious." Otherwise, even though they were being hit hard, they seemed able to laugh it off. From Bateson's perspective, the problems humans experience can be understood only by focusing on how systems create and process information, that is, from the perspective of cybernetics.

Bateson argues that change in the domain of the living occurs in accordance with the so-called *stochastic process*, of which there are two fundamental types—learning and evolution. When the stochastic process operates at the level of the individual, it is called learning; when it operates at the species level, it is labeled evolution. At either level, the stochastic process is characterized by two components: (a) a stream of randomly generated events occurs, and (b) a selective process favors the endurance of certain occurrences over others. Consider an artist painting. He or she may place various colors in juxtaposition or randomly mix pigments to see what new shade can be produced. Eventually, the artist selects some mixtures as more aesthetically pleasing than the rest. Thus, the project develops through a process of trial-and-error learning. Evolution, too, requires both random fluctuation and selection "pressure."

In discussing these matters, Bateson (1972, 1979, 1991) cautions against thinking of the individual as an isolated entity. An organism exists always *in relation to* an environment and as part of a more inclusive system. A sophisticated treatment of this issue can be found in the work of cyberneticists Maturana and Varela (1987). They remind us that the organism and the ecological niche form an interlocking system, wherein each mutually specifies the other. Only in the world created by our language conventions do absolute cleavages between organism and environment exist (Efran, Lukens & Lukens, 1990; Watzlawick, 1984). For example, we typically distinguish between a person and the family "within which" we say he or she has been raised. We speak as if the person and the family were separate entities. However, a family is not a "housing" that exists independently of the people who live and interact there. In other words, the "person" and the "family" can be thought of as roughly the same set of human interactions viewed from two slightly different perspectives.

Systems with no random component, or with no possibility of informational transformation, cannot be said to learn. When feedback in an informational system generates more than one class of behavior—for example, *reinforced* vs. *non-reinforced* responses—it ushers in the need to describe human activity in terms of different classes of events.

For this reason, Bateson (1972, 1979, 1991) concludes that a theory of learning must incorporate Russell's Theory of Logical Types (Whitehead & Russell, 1910) or something quite similar to it. Russell's theory states that information is arranged in a hierarchic structure of discontinuous categories, such that each category logically implies the one beneath it. Within this system, a *class* is of a higher logical type than its *members*. At the same time, a class implies the existence of the members that constitute it. Moreover, no class can be a member of itself, although it may be a member of a higher-order classification—a class of classes. Learning can theoretically occur at any level—the level of individual behavior, the level of classes of behaviors, the level of classes of classes, and so on ad infinitum.

As we have already implied, learning is not an event that is confined within the skin of an organism (Rabkin, 1970); rather, it is manifested within the circuitry of the holistic organism-in-environment system. Thus, in order to define learning, one must define not only the activities of the learner but also the *context* in which learning takes place. We shall say more about contexts of learning later.

Bateson's theory also emphasizes feedback processes that are *recursive* rather than *lineal* in nature. A lineal sequence is one that does not return to its starting point (Bateson, 1979). Within Bateson's recursive learning framework, however, information is not imparted sequentially from environment to organism or from one learning level to another. Instead, information is part of the overall system; it can affect the operation of the system as a whole, including the elements that participated in its creation. For example, a son has the fleeting thought that his mother knows he is using drugs. From this perspective, he watches changes in her facial expression when a news report about a drug bust comes across her television screen. He interprets her reactions as evidence that he has, indeed, been found out. Although he first thought he was being overly cautious, he now regards his initial suspicion as fully justified. The process has come full circle.

Logical Levels of Learning

In keeping with his stochastic framework, Bateson (1972) defines change without randomness as *zero learning*: The organism is simply responding to a signal in a characteristic way. It adapts to the immediate environmental or physiological demands without any novelty of response. In Pavlovian terms, these are unconditioned responses (Mischel, 1986). There is no trial-and-error behavior, and new sets of responses are not created.

On the other hand, *Learning I* does rely on trial and error. New responses are emitted, and the probability of a given response occurring is modified by the outcomes. Responses are becoming part of a class of behaviors that are more apt to be evoked on similar occasions. Bateson lists the five most common types of Learning I as habituation, classical conditioning, instrumental conditioning, rote learning, and extinction/inhibition. Each type is characterized by a distinct selection process. The selection process at work in classical conditioning, for example, is based on contiguity in time between the unconditioned stimulus and conditioned stimulus; in instrumental conditioning, it is based on a contiguity between response and reinforcement.

It is important to note that according to Bateson's hierarchical learning theory, Learning I is a higher logical type than zero learning. It is a change in the way an organism responds to a signal. An organism capable of Learning I is not restricted to the emission of a behavior demanded by the stimulus. Instead, a variety of behaviors may be emitted. The organism "learns" whenever there is a revision in the probability of the use of one of those behaviors.

If Level I procedures result in the selection of a different behavior, Level II processes result in the selection of a different class of behaviors. Obviously, *Learning II* is one logical type above Learning I. Bateson (1972) also refers to Learning II as deutero-learning, set learning, or "learning to learn." In operant terms, Learning II involves the recognition of *occasions* upon which particular repertoires are likely to be reinforced. If it were not for Learning II, a child might expect the teacher to reward hand-raising on the playground as well as in the classroom. Generally, fewer direct conditioning "exposures" are needed once Learning II is underway; there has been change in the organism's readiness to respond. Bateson notes that an "experimental neurosis" is an example of Learning II. An experimental neurosis occurs when animals in a learning laboratory first learn the usefulness of distinguishing between two events (A and B), but are then placed in a situation in which A and B gradually become indistinguishable. Past experience, instead of being helpful, proves misleading.

Learning III is regarded as quite rare even in adult human beings. It is defined as a change, not just in the sets of alternatives from which a choice is being made (as in Learning II), but in the operation used in selecting sets. Although it is a tongue-twister (and headache-inducing besides), it can be described as "learning about learning to learn." A person, for example, does not only realize that many stories can be written and that such stories can be organized into different categories (such as farces, satires, and situation comedies). In addition, he or she grasps that, as storytellers, we can invent wholly new *categories* of story, as when modern artists shattered the prevailing notion that art had to be representational. Bateson (1972) states that organisms are sometimes driven to Learning III by contradictions and inconsistencies among Learning II premises. Some have argued that this is the essence of what happens in the therapy process. For example, as we shall see, Weeks and L'Abate (1982) argue that therapy revolves around the presentation and resolution of paradox. Paradoxes are logical inconsistencies that can be resolved only by moving to a higher logical level (Hofstadter, 1979; Varela, 1984). Apparent oppositions at one level are reconciled at the next.

Implications for Psychotherapy

Bateson's theory of learning, with its emphasis on signal information, organism-as-system, and logical types, was devised within the tradition of cybernetics. Nevertheless, Bateson (1972, 1991) recognized the implications of his learning theory for psychiatry in general and psychotherapy in particular. He regarded Learning I as a process of problem-solving: When faced with a given set of alternatives, the person does something that is likely to be reinforced. Likewise, he considered Learning II akin to the psychiatric notion of "insight": The person achieves an increased facility in understanding and recognizing sets of problems and potential solutions. Learning III can be thought of as character change: It is concerned with overarching life programs rather than immediate problems or problem-solving strategies.

The contexts of learning. Context is a collective term for all those cues that tell an organism from among what set of alternatives it must now make a behavioral choice (Bateson, 1972). Learning contexts are woven into the total social and historical system of organism-in-environment and as such are notoriously easy to ignore or overlook (Efran & Clarfield, in press). Learning II is sometimes characterized by Bateson (1972, 1991) as adaptation to context. The organism learns to orient itself to contexts it encounters during Learning I. Learning II produces a change in how a sequence of events is punctuated, truncating life into increasingly familiar units. In the process, certain responses become more readily available, and at the same time alternative options tend to be obscured.

Bateson (1991) suggests that the traditional "learning triad" of stimulus-response-reinforcement is just a special case of context. Event B is a "response" within a series that is punctuated A-B-C, but becomes a "stimulus" when the series B-C-D is being considered. In other words, the substance or content of an event is not what determines its significance to the organism. Small changes in punctuation—where series are thought to begin and end—can result in an altered context and therefore in dramatically different outcomes. There is the

Batesonian story about a child whose mother rewards her with ice cream for eating her spinach. The question Bateson raises is: What does a learning theorist need to know in order to predict whether that child, when she grows up, comes to love spinach, hate ice cream, or hate her mother? This is a question that points to the significance of punctuation and context in determining experience.

Character as context. A person's character consists of those patterns he or she exhibits across contexts, including habitual styles of punctuation. Furthermore, Bateson (1972) suggests that the "self" consists of the *aggregate* of such characterological patterns. Bateson's conceptualization of character contains a formidable challenge to the psychotherapist: Learning II premises in general, and character traits in particular, are extremely difficult to change. Learning II patterns are intractable because they are not immediately affected by individual events. Moreover, habitual punctuations can, to a large extent, become self-validating. People perceive events in such a way that their actions, as well as the behavior of others, appear to confirm their fundamental premises. Our earlier example of the youngster who thought his mother knew about his drug use was an illustration of that process.

Bateson (1972, 1991) refers to character traits as "hard-programmed," because they embody formal assumptions about relationships that can endure despite a diversity of outcomes. One of Bateson's favorite examples of a character-based Learning II process is the *transference* that psychoanalysts claim characterizes a therapeutic relationship. Transference signifies a similarity in the client's punctuation of client-therapist and child-parent relationships. Thus, Bateson, along with the psychoanalysts, construes psychotherapy as a context in which the client can learn about the structure of his or her generalized rules for interpreting interpersonal relationships.

LEVELS OF LEARNING IN THERAPY: FOUR RECENT THEORIES

As we have indicated, we regard Bateson's theory of learning to be a useful framework for understanding and evaluating the paradigms of psychotherapy. Having outlined the basics of his views, we turn our attention to a description of four particular theories of therapy.

Contextualistic Radical Behaviorism

All forms of radical behaviorism, including the contextualistic version presented by Steven and Linda Hayes (1992), describe an organism's behavior as a function of its general history of reinforcement (past contingencies) as well as the particular stimulus characteristics of the current situation. However, many behavioral formulations fail to emphasize higher-order contextual factors. For example, early Skinnerian accounts erroneously generalized certain principles that were gleaned from the performance of bar-pressing rats in constrained laboratory environments. As later workers discovered, the setting of the Skinner box precluded the investigation of important variables that affected behavior in more natural, open field settings. Moreover, experimenters later realized that rats were cueing on certain features of the apparatus, such as the clicks of the feeder motor or the noise of the electrical relays—elements that the investigator had considered irrelevant to the design of the experiment. The behavior of some animals seemed mysterious, indeed, because these presumably "extraneous" contextual factors were not initially included in the investigator's explanatory loop. The rat hadn't been told what to consider significant.

In working with human beings, contextual analysis becomes even more critical and more subtle. Yet, ironically, those who initially applied behavior analytic principles to human problems were not always sufficiently attentive to such considerations. For example, they sometimes operated on the simplistic notion that standard reinforcements could be defined—M & Ms, gold stars, and cigarettes—and used to modify responses in a wide variety of different settings. They were often disappointed at the variability of outcomes and the lack of generalizability across situations and circumstances. The use of these procedures fostered the erroneous impression that radical behaviorism is simplistic, mechanistic, and anti-humanistic, applicable only to low-functioning organisms in highly structured environments.

Hayes and Hayes (1992) have provided a corrective to these premature appraisals of behaviorism. By emphasizing the contextualistic aspects of the theory, they have combined Skinner's (1971, 1974) basic principles and those derived from Pepper's (1942) description of the contextualist world view. In fact, the viewpoint they arrive at is similar to Bateson's (1979) position concerning the "necessary unity" of behavior and environment. Walking to school is a behavior-in-context and is distinct from other acts of walking, even though the mechanics of the action may be similar.

In an earlier decade, Bandura (1965) and his co-investigators used, as a measure of aggression, a child's punching of an inflatable doll. The response *looked* aggressive to the investigators, and in that era it wasn't considered useful to explore details of the child's intent. Yet, if children are playing, testing their strength, or interested in how the doll bounces, their punches are not acts of aggression. Moreover, aggressive acts do not necessarily involve violent or vigorous activity. For example, a child's quiet refusal to eat can be very assaultive. Hayes and Hayes (1992) recognize that, particularly in the human arena, contexts and meanings must be given precedence over the superficial topology of overt responses.

The status of cognition. As we have already noted, Bateson's theory of learning implies a hierarchic structure within which change takes place at logically distinct levels. The Hayes and Hayes (1992) formulation also implies logically distinct learning levels. They recognize that, in addition to direct sensory learning, human activity operates in accordance with principles of *stimulus equivalence*. For example, a person who learns the discrimination "given A, pick B" can usually demonstrate the derived discrimination "given B, pick A." Similarly, a person who learns "given A, pick B" and "given B, pick C" may then easily infer that "given A, pick C." These are instances of knowing the world through indirect, logical means—rule-governed learning. Hayes and Hayes argue that their analysis of such phenomena, which makes consistent use of the principles of contingent reinforcement and stimulus equivalence, provides a more systematic treatment of "cognition" than most other behavioral frameworks.

Unfortunately, cognitive-behavioral therapists have tended simply to graft cognitive considerations onto preexisting behavioral schemes without fully working out the additional theoretical implications. They often construe cognition as an independent entity or process that controls other organismic functions from a privileged perch. Mahoney (1991) has criticized such dubious theorizing as the *myth of rational supremacy*. For example, Hayes and Hayes note the inappropriateness of assuming that "John does poorly because he thinks irrational thoughts" (Hayes & Hayes, 1992, p. 241). The possibility exists, in fact, that both his thinking and the other aspects of his behavior have been shaped by the very same contextual variables. In Batesonian terms, individual cognitions are often of the same logical type as the other kinds of behaviors one wants to modify. When that is the case, a change in one will not necessarily effect a change in the other. Only operations targeted at a next higher logical level can be expected to be useful (see also Coyne, 1982).

Acceptance and Commitment Therapy. Hayes and Hayes (1992) call the applied version of their theory Acceptance and Commitment Therapy (ACT). ACT therapists generally challenge the *contexts* that give rise to particular thoughts and behaviors. Where possible, they invoke Learning II processes. An example provided by Hayes and Hayes nicely illustrates the basic therapeutic philosophy of ACT: Clients often enter therapy believing that undesirable thoughts, feelings, or memories prevent them from enacting some preferred behavior. The typical assumption is that A has to be changed before B can happen, as in the thought "I can't travel! I'm too anxious!" (p. 244). The ACT therapist, however, clarifies for the client that the prior control of unpleasant emotions or cognitions is (a) a nearly impossible goal and (b) usually unnecessary. Rather than trying to change feelings, the client should simply accept whatever feelings arise within a given context until or unless these change of their own accord. Meanwhile, the therapist concentrates on engineering a context within which new experience can occur. Moreover, the relationship between client and therapist provides a metacontext sufficiently powerful to enable the client to "notice" contexts that had otherwise been taken for granted or gone unnoticed. In this manner, therapy facilitates a change in the punctuation of events.

Hayes and Hayes (1992) present several specific ACT strategies for facilitating Learning II in therapy. For example, certain clients habitually evaluate their thoughts or behaviors in a negative fashion. In those cases, ACT recommends that the therapist refrain from direct attempts to change the valence of events. Obviously, such reevaluations would constitute Level I changes and would be largely inefficient. Therefore, the therapist steadfastly refuses to evaluate happenings along the good-bad continuum. Instead, the focus is on the usefulness of the context of evaluation itself. More specifically, ACT therapists would not be very interested in why a client feels she has received inadequate feedback from a friend. Rather, they would want to know why any feedback at all is important to the client, and for that matter why friends themselves are important.

In sum, the ACT therapist operates at a logical level above the thoughts, emotions, or behaviors that the client considers problematic. Instead of focusing on maladaptive "habits" per se, the therapist's attention is on the hierarchy of contexts that maintain those habits. To this end, the therapeutic strategies employed often involve using language in a confusing, paradoxical, or surprising way in order to break the hold of literal meanings. The client-therapist interaction has the effect of freeing the client from his or her historically derived pattern of distinctions, thus making a broader perspective available (Efran, Germer & Lukens, 1986).

Functional Analytic Behaviorism

Robert Kohlenberg and Mavis Tsai (1991) also use a radical behaviorist framework to explain the process of therapeutic change. However, unlike Hayes and Hayes (1992), they adhere to a more standard model of behaviorism and do not specifically address issues of cognition or context. Moreover, they pursue only those aspects of learning that are directly observable or reportable, exhorting the therapist to critically examine the client's behavior during the therapeutic session, as that is the only sample of actual behavior to which the therapist is privy. At that point, the therapist works to reinforce alternative responses. He or she also helps ensure continuity between patterns developed in the therapist's office and those the client will confront elsewhere.

Unlike most radical behaviorists, Kohlenberg and Tsai (1991) employ a concept of the self. However, they do not treat it as an explanatory construct. Instead, they argue that the self arises from direct sensory experience and is not an a priori structure that interprets sensory experience. They propose that the self is a generalization built from basic speech units that a child acquires. The multiple units that involve "I" (*I have a rabbit, I have a tummyache, I have an idea*, or *I feel sad*) are first generalized into *I have, I feel, I want, I see, I like*, and so on, and then these broader units are finally synthesized into the common denominator *I*. Therefore, their theory of self-development echoes a Batesonian shift from Learning I to Learning II. Higher levels of awareness, including self-awareness, require recursive verbal iterations, as in "I see myself seeing the butterfly," and "I see myself seeing myself seeing the butterfly" (p. 141).

With self-awareness, the focus of therapeutic change shifts to what Bateson terms the punctuation of human experience (Learning II) rather than the shaping of individual behaviors. Only self-awareness on the part of clients will allow them to summarize and reflect upon the rules of the behavior that they emit, a process that Kohlenberg and Tsai consider critical.

Functional Analytic Psychotherapy. Kohlenberg and Tsai (1991) give systematic instructions for managing the shift from Learning I to Learning II. The primary task in Functional Analytic Psychotherapy (FAP) is to identify three types of clinically relevant behavior (CRB). All of these are to be understood solely in light of the client's presenting problems (a happy application of the notion, "If it ain't broke, don't fix it"). The first category is office behavior that is analogous to the presenting problem (CRB1). For example, a client who has difficulty making and keeping friends gets angry at the therapist for not having all the answers, or a client who has a tendency to fall in love with unavailable people develops a crush on the therapist. Category 2 (CRB2) is office behavior that represents an improvement when compared to CRB1. Examples of this would be a sexual abuse victim's finally trusting her therapist, or intimate disclosures from someone who tends to withdraw. At the start of therapy, very little of this behavior may be present, and the therapist may have to resort to principles of successive approximation to generate it.

Third, and possibly the most noteworthy of Kohlenberg and Tsai's (1991) categories, is CRB3: *client interpretations of behavior.* This behavior "refers to clients' talking about their own behavior and what seems to cause it. It includes 'reason-giving' and 'interpretations.' The best CRB3s involve the observation and description of one's own behavior and its associated reinforcing, discriminative, and eliciting stimuli" (p. 22). Kohlenberg and Tsai hold that "this kind of statement can help increase transfer of client gains in the therapy situation to daily life" (p. 22). From a Batesonian point of view, CRB3 statements are the bridge between Learning I and Learning II. As Kohlenberg and Tsai note, it is therefore very important that therapists not confuse these CRB3 repertoires (i.e., interpretations) with their behavioral referents. If they do so, they lose the Learning II advantage. To use Kohlenberg and Tsai's example, when a client with a history of maladaptive withdrawing from interpersonal affairs observes that she withdraws whenever she becomes dependent, her attention is fixed upon context at the Learning II level. When she actually withdraws, however, she is enacting the behavior at the Learning I level.

Kohlenberg and Tsai (1991) give five general rules for therapists to follow: Watch for CRBs, evoke CRBs, reinforce CRB2s, observe the potentially reinforcing effects of therapist behavior in relation to client CRBs, and give interpretations of variables that affect client behavior. Of course, this could serve as a training manual for almost any type of therapy, insofar as the joint effect of these rules will be to make Learning I behaviors salient and to bring both client and therapist to a Learning II understanding of these behavioral patterns.

Object Relations Theory

Object relations theory is concerned with the relational context of human learning. There are a number of versions of object relations therapy (Greenberg

& Mitchell, 1983); in this review, we draw heavily upon Sheldon Cashdan's (1988) description of it. Along with Bateson, object relations theorists reject the notion of a free-standing self; we are born in a dyadic relationship with our mothers and construct the idea of an object (our mother) at the same time as we construct the idea of ourselves, through processes of differentiation and integration. Differentiation refers to the discovery that something is not-self; integration refers to the assumption that something is like-self. In object relations theory, learning develops as we impose our patterns of relationship onto the world in cycles of differentiation (introjection, or accommodation) and integration (projection, or assimilation). The distinctive feature of object relations is the assumption that in the integrative, assimilative phase of these cycles, we *project* our internal patterns of interpersonal interactions—our internal model of object relations—onto the environment. (From a Batesonian standpoint, this is not remarkable: Projection of our code for organizing the world is much the same as punctuating elements of the environment.) Object relations theorists additionally argue that the differentiation phase of the cycle is associated with anxiety, whereas the projective phase is not. They hypothesize that this is why people spend as much time as possible in the projective phase and therefore are not particularly good at noticing the salient details that make one experience different from another. For instance, a person may have difficulty distinguishing the experience of "therapist" from the experience of "mother."

We are all constantly engaged in differentiation-integration cycles. For example, we read a book originally thinking it demarcates distinctions with which we are familiar (integration, or projection), only to later become aware that the book is not quite saying what we already believed (differentiation). The differentiation-integration cycle creates a thesis and an antithesis—a subject pole and an object pole (Mitchell, 1988; Overton & Horowitz, 1991). This dialectical view of psychological functioning is fully compatible with Bateson's theories of learning: We construct meaning in our world by developing patterns of punctuation through which additional experience is interpreted. For the object relations theorist, we are relational creatures *by design*, in that we are biologically born that way, and *by intent*, in that we crave relationships and operate dialectically.

Projective identification. The projective phase of a differentiation-integration cycle can sometimes have the quality of a *command*, or a demand on others. When that command is noticeable to the other person in the relationship matrix, it is called a *projective identification*. It is as if the person is no longer saying, "I see everything this way, and always have"—an act of clear ownership—but is now saying, "I see things so inflexibly that you will have to play the matching role for me"—an act of implication.

Projective identifications, then, are patterns of interpersonal behavior that induce a certain type of behavior from the other person. They were first described by Wilfred Bion as a process that compels the other participant to play "a part, no matter how difficult to recognize, in somebody else's phantasy" (1952, p. 149). The attention to patterns of behavior (rather than to the behaviors themselves) makes it clear that object relations work is anchored in Learning II level processes.

Object relations therapy. Unlike Kohlenberg and Tsai (1991), Cashdan's (1988) concern with the relationship between client and therapist focuses on higher-order metacommunications (i.e., projective identifications) rather than observable behavior. Cashdan lists four prototypic projective identifications—those organized around dependency, power, sexuality, and ingratiation—and for each he details the metacommunications, relational stances, and behaviors these are apt to induce in the other party.

The dynamics surrounding dependency provide a clear example of the process of projective identification. If a client were to come in talking about loneliness, looking for someone strong, unable to make decisions, and so forth, he or she might be considered a dependent person. If, in addition, the therapist finds himself or herself uncharacteristically offering a great deal of advice, thinking of lending the client the use of the office phone, and so on, projective identification is involved. The difference between dependency and a projective identification of dependency is the therapist's active participation in the dynamic. The projective identification of dependency entails a metacommunication of "I can't survive without you," a display of the relational stance of helplessness, and, perhaps most notably, the induction of caretaking behaviors in the other party.

Because Cashdan takes as his therapeutic focus the level of character traits (Learning II), he attends to context markers and perceived punctuations in the flow of events. Furthermore, because projective identification entails the therapist's becoming an active participant in the symptomatic dynamics of the client, the therapist is able to use his or her own experience as a source of therapeutic hypotheses. In other words, whereas Kohlenberg and Tsai are forced, by the implications of their theory, to focus primarily on the client's observable behaviors, Cashdan can use his own intuitions, including private thoughts and feelings, as evidence for the existence and classification of client punctuations.

Cashdan believes that the object relations therapist should actively and willingly participate in the projective identification that develops, thereby temporarily relinquishing aspects of his or her own character style (see also Ogden, 1982). From a Batesonian perspective, then, Cashdan is requiring the therapist to attain (at least occasionally) the level of Learning III, which is admittedly difficult for any individual to achieve or sustain. In a sense, therapists must be able to retain a firm sense of self while simultaneously allowing aspects of their self-definition to "drift." Perhaps this is why object relations therapy is considered by many to be more demanding and personally "hazardous" to the mental health worker than those forms of therapy that do not involve encounters of such intensity.

Paradoxical Psychotherapy: A Theory of Dialectical Change

Gerald Weeks and Luciano L'Abate (1982) offer a comprehensive, integrated theory of change within the philosophical and psychological tradition of general systems theory (see also Brendler, Silver, Haber & Sargent, 1991; Haley, 1987; Neill & Kniskern, 1982). Systems theory maintains that the whole is more than just the sum of its parts. A system is a set of elements operating as a unit, such that the behavior of the whole can be understood only in terms of the interdependent relationships that exist among the elements.

Like Bateson, Weeks and L'Abate (1982) emphasize the recursive nature of living systems, in which *negative* feedback and *positive* feedback are the primary mechanisms of change. Negative feedback utilizes novel information to promote *first-order change*—a behavioral response by the system that maintains existing relationships among the parts of the system. In Batesonian terms, first-order change is actually an instance of zero learning—the receipt of information results in a characteristic response by the system in connection with situational demands. However, there is no correction in how the system is organized to process future information. In other words, it is, more or less, business as usual.

Positive feedback, on the other hand, promotes *second-order change*, which Weeks and L'Abate (1982) also refer to as *dialectical change*: Novel information induces a structural reorganization of the relationships among the various parts of the system. They describe second-order change as a "quantum jump in the system to a different level of functioning" (p. 19). Second-order change involves a discontinuous restructuring of the system at the level of relationship.

Weeks and L'Abate (1982) suggest that the way to facilitate second-order change is through the use of paradoxical psychotherapy. True to the Batesonian refusal to view units in isolation, Weeks and L'Abate construe the problems of all clients, including those who present themselves for individual therapy, as due to *transactional pathology*. The transactional view holds that pathology is a multi-person event that occurs within an interpersonal context. Therefore, an individual cannot be expected to improve unless there is a change in the overall relationship system.

Paradoxical intervention. Weeks and L'Abate (1982) state that their brand of therapy is based on the paradoxical principle that a person often changes by trying to remain the same. Actually, from their point of view, a person's frantic attempts to be different frequently make matters worse. In fact, it is specifically in those instances in which ordinary change efforts have failed that the person seeks the advice of a therapist. A paradoxical directive, then, asks the client *not* to change a symptom, thereby invoking a so-called *therapeutic double-bind*. In designing such paradoxical injunctions, the symptom itself becomes a fulcrum for producing change.

The possibility of a double-bind is inherent in Bateson's framework and has been highlighted by Weeks and L'Abate. In his early work with schizophrenic individuals and their families, Bateson (1991) developed the concept of *pathogenic* double-binds (see also Hampden-Turner, 1982). These occur when a response that seems warranted at one level of communication is simultaneously invalidated by a message at another level. For example, a mother verbally asks her son for a kiss, but simultaneously turns her cheek away, non-verbally communicating her distaste for the gesture. The child is thus caught in a metacommunicational bind, in other words, damned if he does and damned if he doesn't. Furthermore, there is the additional injunction against attempts to clarify the matter. The implicit, cardinal rule is, "We aren't supposed to talk about that."

Empirical research on the *schizophrenic* double-bind has been equivocal (Berger, 1978), but many find that the general notion is still useful. *Therapeutic* double-binds are, of course, attempts to reverse the effects of the original double-bind by engineering suitable counter-ploys. One category of these are so-called *symptom prescriptions* (Efran & Caputo, 1984; Haley, 1987; Weeks & L'Abate, 1982). The therapist asks the client to continue behaving in symptomatic fashion, or even to increase the frequency and intensity of the symptomatic behavior. In some circumstances, the client is urged to "do the symptom" at particular times or in particular places. In each instance, the client is placed in a sort of "no-lose" situation—the therapeutic double-bind. For instance, a person who has trouble falling asleep partly keeps himself or herself up worrying about sleep loss. Thus, trying to fall asleep usually makes matters worse. However, if one stops trying, the element of rumination is removed, and, paradoxically, falling asleep becomes easier. To take another example, a couple that is fighting but instructed to "fight more" usually finds it virtually impossible to keep the fight going. Something that seemed involuntary is now being enacted by design, which subtly changes the nature of the context. In other words, explicitly naming the game changes the game (Efran & Heffner, 1991). The additional element introduced by the paradoxical directive disrupts the existing patterns and relationships, paving the way for new adaptations.

Weeks and L'Abate (1982) outline the most frequently used sequence of interventions in paradoxical therapy. First, the therapist *positively connotes* the problematic symptom. In other words, something that was considered negative is described in favorable terms. For example, a couple's quarrels are offered as evidence of how much each person cares about the other. A child who refuses to go to school is described as attempting to stay with his mother in order to protect her from an untimely visit from her estranged, drug-addicted, sometimes violent husband. By "reframing" problems in these ways, the therapist rearranges the alliances in the system as a whole. Reframes alter system punctuations, opening the door to useful Level II changes.

After the reframing, a paradoxical directive is given. Finally, when change has occurred, the therapist typically predicts a relapse. This helps ensure that the system will not revert to its former mode of operating. For example, a person who has given up cigarettes may be told that she will definitely smoke again the next time she is under pressure. That dire prediction rearranges motives and, ironically, makes it less likely that smoking will recur. Many clients report that under these circumstances they abstained just to prove that the therapist was wrong!

Weeks and L'Abate hold that insight in the form of a client's *understanding* of systemic properties and relationships is not a prerequisite for therapeutic change. Paradoxical therapy works at the contextual level. Therapists who work this way do not subscribe to the notion of rational supremacy. Instead, they assert that a system must be "jarred" into changing, whether or not the members of the system have an intellectual understanding of what is happening.

CONCLUSION

In this chapter we have outlined a number of different theories of therapy. Each theory has had to grapple with issues of relationship and context. Bateson (1972) describes therapy as being like two canasta players not playing canasta, but instead discussing the rules of canasta and then using a modified set of rules for future games. In other words, most therapy operations involve at least Learning II processes, and some of them tip toward the deep transformations characteristic of Learning III. The traditional writings on therapy, such as those by Rogers, Freud, Ellis, and Adler, tend to describe problems as pathologies contained within individuals. The newer viewpoints, including all those described here, have broken away from such medical-model constraints and have adopted a genuinely ecological perspective that coincides with Bateson's emphasis on "the pattern that connects." One of the virtues of the object relations perspective, for example, is that it reconstrues symptoms originally considered to be "in a person's head" and explicates the transactional elements that serve to sustain them. Behavioral viewpoints also began with the intensive study of organisms in isolation, usually in a restricted laboratory setting. However, the newer therapies derived from these positions have become more sophisticated and now take into account the interpersonal matrix in which human problems exist.

Moreover, in all of these attempts to describe the essence of the therapeutic encounter, there is a renewed appreciation for the importance of linguistic and symbolic processes (Efran, Lukens & Lukens, 1990). Language, including the exchange of symbols, can be construed as a higher-order coordination of actions within a social community. Without the advanced form of coordination that language represents, the kind of problems a person brings to a therapist wouldn't exist. (Animals, after all, do not seem to seek or require psychotherapeutic assistance. They may have stressful circumstances, but not "problems.") Again, the genius of Bateson was that he anticipated that habits of symbolic distinction-making and punctuation underlie most of what ails the human spirit. In that sense, therapeutic learning is less about recounting or changing "facts" than about increasing the range of meanings that can be constructed from them. George Kelly (1969), one of the first to devise a constructivist theory of therapy, quotes a client who found therapy helpful as saying, "In many ways *things* are the same as they were before, but how differently I see them!" (p. 227).

NOTE

The authors wish to thank Elsa R. Efran and Michael E. Remshard for their assistance in the preparation of this chapter.

REFERENCES

Bandura, A. (1965). Vicarious processes: A case of no-trial learning. In L. Berkowitz (Ed.). *Advances in experimental social psychology*, Vol. 2, pp. 1–55. New York: Academic Press.

Bateson, G. (1972). *Steps to an ecology of mind*. New York: Ballantine Books.

Bateson, G. (1979). *Mind and nature: A necessary unity*. New York: Bantam Books.

Bateson, G. (1991). *A sacred unity: Further steps to an ecology of mind* (R. Donaldson, ed.). New York: HarperCollins.

Berger, M. M. (Ed.). (1978). *Beyond the double-bind: Communication and family systems, theories and techniques with schizophrenics*. New York: Brunner/Mazel.

Bion, W. R. (1952). Group dynamics: A review. In W. R. Bion (Ed.). *Experiences in groups and other papers* (pp. 141–192). New York: Basic Books.

Brendler, J., Silver, M., Haber, M. & Sargent, J. (1991). *Madness, chaos, and violence: Therapy with families at the brink*. New York: Basic Books.

Cashdan, S. (1988). *Object relations therapy: Using the relationship*. New York: W. W. Norton.

Coyne, J. (1982). A critique of cognitions as causal entities with particular reference to depression. *Cognitive Therapy and Research, 6*, 3–13.

Efran, J. S. & Caputo, G. C. (1984). Paradox in psychotherapy: A cybernetic perspective. *Journal of Behavior Therapy and Experimental Psychiatry, 15*, 235–240.

Efran, J. S. & Clarfield, L. E. (1993). Context: The fulcrum of constructivist psychotherapy. *Journal of Cognitive Psychotherapy: An International Quarterly, 7*, 171–180.

Efran, J. S. & Fauber, R. L. (in press). Radical constructivism: Questions and answers. In R. A. Neimeyer & M. J. Mahoney (Eds.). *Constructivism in psychotherapy*. Washington, D.C.: American Psychological Association.

Efran, J. S., Germer, C. K. & Lukens, M. D. (1986). Contextualism and psychotherapy. In R. L. Rosnow & M. Georgourdi (Eds.). *Contextualism and understanding in the behavioral sciences: Implications for research and theory* (pp. 169–186). New York: Praeger.

Efran, J. S. & Heffner, K. P. (1991). Change the name and you change the game. *Journal of Strategic and Family Therapy, 10*(1), 50–65.

Efran, J. S., Lukens, M. D. & Lukens, R. J. (1990). *Language, structure and change: Frameworks of meaning in psychotherapy*. New York: W. W. Norton.

Greenberg, J. & Mitchell, S. (1983). *Object relations in psychoanalytic theory*. Cambridge, MA: Harvard University Press.

Haley, J. (1987). *Problem-solving therapy* (2nd ed.). San Francisco: Jossey-Bass.

Hampden-Turner, C. (1982). *Maps of the mind*. New York: Macmillan.

Hayes, S. C. & Hayes, L. J. (1992). Some clinical implications of contextual behaviorism: The example of cognition. *Behavior Therapy, 23*, 225–249.

Hofstadter, D. (1979). *Gödel, Escher, Bach: An eternal golden braid*. New York: Basic Books.

Kelly, G. (1969). *Clinical psychology and personality: The selected papers of George Kelly* (B. Maher, Ed.). New York: Wiley & Sons.

Kohlenberg, R. & Tsai, M. (1991). *Functional analytic psychotherapy: Creating intense and curative therapeutic relationships*. New York: Plenum Press.

Mahoney, M. (1991). *Human change processes: The scientific foundations of psychotherapy*. New York: Basic Books.

Maturana, H. & Varela, F. (1987). *The tree of knowledge: The biological roots of human understanding*. Boston: Shambhala Press.

Mischel, W. (1986). *Introduction to personality: A new look* (4th ed.). New York: Holt, Rinehart & Winston.

Mitchell, S. (1988). *Relational concepts in psychoanalysis: An integration*. Cambridge, MA: Harvard University Press.

Neill, J. & Kniskern, D. (1982). *From psyche to system: The evolving therapy of Carl Whitaker*. New York: Guilford.

Ogden, T. (1982). *Projective identification and psychotherapeutic technique*. Northvale, NJ: Jason Aronson, Inc.

Overton, W. (1984). World views and their influence on psychological theory and research: Kuhn, Lakatos, Laudan. *Advances in Child Development and Behavior* (Vol. 18, pp. 191–226). New York: Academic Press.

Overton, W. & Horowitz, H. (1991). Developmental psychopathology: Differentiations and integrations. In D. Cicchetti & S. Toth (Eds.). *Rochester Symposium on Developmental Psychopathology* (Vol. 3, pp. 1–42). Hillsdale, NJ: Erlbaum.

Pepper, C. (1942). *World hypotheses*. Berkeley: University of California Press.

Rabkin, R. (1970). *Inner and outer space: Introduction to a theory of social psychiatry*. New York: W. W. Norton.

Skinner, B. F. (1971). *Beyond freedom and dignity*. New York: Alfred A. Knopf.

Skinner, B. F. (1974). *About behaviorism*. New York: Alfred A. Knopf.

Varela, F. (1984). The creative circle: Sketches in the natural history of circularity. In P. Watzlawick (Ed.). *The invented reality* (pp. 309–323). New York: W. W. Norton.

Watzlawick, P. (1984). Epilogue. In P. Watzlawick (Ed.). *The invented reality* (pp. 325–332). New York: W. W. Norton.

Weeks, G. & L'Abate, L. (1982). *Paradoxical psychotherapy: Theory and practice with individuals, couples, and families*. New York: Brunner/Mazel.

Whitehead, A. & Russell, B. (1910). *Principia mathematica*. Cambridge: Cambridge University Press.

14

Nonformal Adult Learning in International Development Projects

Lynn Johnson

This chapter will discuss the application of philosophical, theoretical, and practical components of nonformal adult education to international development projects and recommend that they be more formally incorporated into the design and methodology of such projects. It will also suggest that the theories underlying nonformal education are particularly relevant to understanding the adult learning and behavioral change processes in international development project, as are Lindeman's theory about adult learning (1926), the educational psychologist's andragogical model (Knowles, 1990), and Carl Rogers' (1969) facilitator of learning concept. These theories and their applications appear to be critical factors in the success or failure of international development projects and their sustainability.

SUSTAINABLE DEVELOPMENT

Goals

Millions of dollars have been spent every year since the end of World War II on international development projects for less economically developed countries throughout the world. In the past decade, there has been a movement by the Agency for International Development, the largest federal agency that funds U.S. international development projects, toward sustainable development (National Research Council, 1992). This means that international development projects are being designed, planned, and implemented with the entire ecosystem in mind. This approach seeks to provide for the needs of current and future generations of people living in less-developed countries (LDCs) while conserving their natural resources and a systemic balance. During the past forty-seven years, there have been numerous approaches to international development projects. New theories have emerged in an attempt to understand the developmental process and to explain the failures that have occurred. The stated goal of most international development projects is to raise the economic level and quality of life for the majority of people living in LDCs. Yet most people in LDCs are poorer and worse off today than they were a decade ago; and input-intensive systems (introduced in large part by international development projects) have often led to soil degradation, depletion of aquifers, contamination of ground water and surface waters, pest resistance, deforestation, and overall environmental decline (Byerlee, 1990; Lal, 1988; Ruttan, 1988). This new approach of sustainable development calls for participant involvement in all phases of the research from problem identification and the establishment of priorities to evaluation and dissemination of results (National Research Council, 1992). Lip service has been paid to participant involvement for many years, but if the participants are not wholly involved and empowered to implement changes in their lives, it is unlikely that any sustainable change will occur (FAO, 1987a; Harrison, 1987; O'Sullivan-Ryan & Kaplun, 1981). About 95% of the current growth in population is occurring in LDCs, and the percentage of global population living in LDCs is projected to increase from 77% in 1990 to 84% in 2020 (Royal Society of London & U.S. National Academy of Sciences, 1992). With a doubling of the world's population in the next sixty years (ibid.), it is essential that the developed world work with the LDCs to improve the quality of life and income levels for those who live in the LDCs.

Measurements of Success

In an attempt to assess the success of international development projects and to explain the failures, a body of literature including individual project case studies and theories of international development has evolved. Yet often the lessons learned from one project go unheeded, and mistakes are repeated. This may happen because development projects occur in a particular time and place and the successes and failures are often not generalizable to other times and geographical locales. Additionally, donor and recipient countries often have different goals and objectives and tend to define success or failure from their particular perspective. Likewise, evaluators of international development projects have generally evaluated the project from their own disciplinary perspective and have focused on causal and influencing factors peculiar to their own way of looking at the world. There is a growing consensus across disciplines that international development projects involve complex processes and that there are a multitude of interdependent factors at the individual, project, societal/regional, and national/international levels that affect a project's success or failure.

Factors Affecting the Behavioral Change and Learning Processes

No one objective criterion can be universally applied to define success or failure in all development projects. Yet a common feature of successful international development projects seems to be the occurrence of specific, behavioral change by a critical number of participating adults that continues beyond the length of the development project. This acceptance and adoption of change is usually a consequence of a nonformal adult learning process. (Unlike the formal educational process, if measurable behavioral change in an intended direction does not occur, the project cannot be considered successful.) It is not enough that adult learning has taken place if that learning does not manifest itself in action by a sufficient number of people to sustain the changed behavior. This learning process is very complex, difficult to measure, and dependent upon numerous factors. Whether or not behavioral change will occur as an outcome of the learning process is even more problematic, as it is not an automatic outcome but rather a process as well with its own set of determinant factors. Table 1 is an attempt to focus on the learning and behavioral change processes of the adult participants of international development programs and identify those factors that hinder or enhance these processes. The variables are grouped by type into four major categories: participant characteristics, characteristics situational to the specific international development project, societal or regional characteristics, and those that occur at a national or international level.

Perhaps because adult learning and behavioral change are so complex, they are rarely a stated focus, goal, or objective of a development project's plan of work. Hence these processes are invisible, misunderstood, or ignored; and success is generally measured in more easily quantifiable terms that the donor and recipient government can understand. If we are to understand the development process on a national or global scale, we must also understand the processes of adult learning and behavioral change as they occur in groups of individuals. In a world system where all variables are related and interdependent to each other, each affects the other.

Adult Learning, the Key to Sustainable Development

Most development literature has attempted to simplify and reduce the causal factors and components of change processes to an understandable and manageable level. From a practical point of view, only so many factors can be taken into account in the planning and implementation stages of an international development project. If it is assumed that only a select number of factors are important, however, some variables will be overlooked, which may impair the change process. This has been all too obvious in international development programs where the multiplicity of factors has not been acknowledged, and programs have

Table 1
Factors Affecting the Learning and Behavioral Change Processes in Adult Learners in International Development Programs

TYPE	PARTICIPANT	PROJECT	SOCIETAL/ REGIONAL	NATIONAL/ INTERNATIONAL
Educational	Educational level, literacy	Technical expertise of staff		
	Skill/technical abilities	Technical training to participants - role of facilitator		
	Learning style, pace	Appropriate technology		
	Communication to staff	Two-way communication		
	Understandable, relevant communication	Appropriate communication skills		
	Perceived needs	Perceived needs by staff		
Cultural/ Psychological	Belief systems	Belief systems of staff		
	Norms & values	Norms & values of staff		
	Past experiences	Past project experiences		
	Perceived threats	Perceived threats to project		
	Self-esteem, self-directedness			
	Problem solving skills	Problem solving skills of staff		
	Motivations	Motivations of staff		
	Interpersonal skills	Interpersonal skills of staff		
	Receptiveness to change			

	Individual	Project	Community / Institutional	National (LDC)
	Realizable power to affect change	Realizable power to affect change		
Physiological	Level of reasoning	Complex reasoning abilities		
	Energy level			
	Health status			
	Emotional state			
Socio-political	Ethnicity Familial/household structure	Relationship of staff to participants	Social structure- kinship, patronage, formal and informal leaders, ethnic groups	LDC socio-political structure
	Status in community	Status of project in community	Division of labor, decision-making patterns	LDC policies on ownership of land & resources
	Membership in formal and informal gourps	Relationship of project to other groups, local, regional, governmental	Formal & informal organizations	LDC policies on local leadership, local organizations
	Perception of governmental intervention	Amount of governmental intervention	Political structures - intervention at local and regional level	LDC policies on subsidies, taxes, research, extension
	Goals/aspirations	Project Goals		LDC political relation to multinational corporations & donor countries
Economic	Access to resources	Availability of resources- land, labor, capital	Natural resources	Natural resources

Table 1 (continued)

TYPE	PARTICIPANT	PROJECT	SOCIETAL/ REGIONAL	NATIONAL/ INTERNATIONAL
	Cash flow, barter system - obligations	Assets and cash flow	Prices of inputs, services, land, labor, capital	LDC economic relation to donor country & world economy
	Perceived and real economic benefit	Local price controls Access to credit	Consumption patterns	Price structuring
	Access to markets	Access to markets & processing facilities	Marketing - role of cooperatives & intermediaries	Role of government in marketing. Access to international markets
Infrastructure/ Geographical	Access to services	Access to services	Availability of services	Level of infrastructure
	Availability of clean water, power, sanitation	Water control, energy extension, health, education	Production conditions- irrigation, drainage, power source	Production conditions
	Ability to transport goods	Ability to transport supplies, equipment, goods, products	Transportation infrastructure-roads, bridges	Transportation
Physical/Ecological	Sensitivity to ecological balance	Environmental - pests & diseases, ecosystem	Ecology - soils, topography, hydrology, flora & fauna, climate Demography	Climate Use of resources Environmental policies Natural disasters

Sources: Doorman, 1983; Doorman, 1991; Galjart, 1968; Mendez & Doorman, 1984; Nweke, 1981; Rogers, 1969; Shaner, Phillip & Schmehl, 1982.

failed because a critical factor such as an environmental restriction, financial liability, or cultural taboo has been ignored. Perhaps the key to successful sustainable international development projects does not lie in the manipulation and management of variables that might directly or indirectly affect such a project. Success may center on whether the principles of adult learning can be incorporated into the methodology and implementation of the development project such that the participants in groups are able effectively to handle whatever changes may occur.

ADULT LEARNING

The adult education theories first developed in the United States in the 1920s were based on a philosophy of individualistic democracy. Their appeal and applicability, however, are more universal because they are also grounded in the right to human dignity. They challenge the static definition of intelligence, an elitist system of education, and the traditional role of the teacher who maintains knowledge and power over the learner.

Individual over Structure

In 1926, Eduard Lindeman laid the foundation for a systemic theory of adult learning by identifying key assumptions about adult learners. He believed that the individual was more important than the educational structure and that curriculum should be built around the adult learner's needs and interests. He felt that adults were motivated to learn by the need to solve problems from life experiences. If the adult learner did not see the problem's relevance to life experiences, learning would not occur. He saw the role of the teacher as engaging in a process of mutual inquiry with the learner, and he viewed adults as possessing a deep need to be self-directing. He also thought that individual differences among people increased with age and that the learning context needed to conform with the individual learner's differences in style, pace, and timing. Lindeman's characteristics of adult learners (Lindeman, 1926) appear to be as relevant to participants in international development projects as to adult learners in other contexts.

Maximizing Adult Learning

Carl Rogers (1951, p. 144) took the insights that he had gained from clinical psychology and developed a set of five hypotheses that could be applied to adult education:

1. We cannot teach another person directly: we can only facilitate his learning.
2. A person learns significantly only those things which he perceives as being involved in the maintenance of, or enhancement of, the structure of self.

3. Experience which, if assimilated, would involve a change in the organization of self tends to be resisted through denial or distortion of symbolization.

4. The structure and organization of self appear to become more rigid under threat; to relax its boundaries when completely free from threat. Experience which is perceived as inconsistent with the self can only be assimilated if the current organization of self is relaxed and expanded to include it.

5. The educational situation which most effectively promotes significant learning is one in which (a) threat to the self of the learner is reduced to a minimum, and (b) differentiated perception of the field is facilitated.

Motivation in Adult Learners

Malcolm Knowles (1990) enlarged upon Lindeman's assumptions in the development of his andragogical model. Not only do adults learn what they need to know, but it is often the facilitators' task to help the adult learner to an awareness of a "need to know." Adults are self-directed and feel responsible for their lives and for their decisions. Adult learners have a great diversity and quality of experiences that they can utilize in the learning process. These experiences define who they are as individuals. If this experience is denigrated, it results in rejection of the person. This results in low self-esteem, and learning is negatively affected. Adults are life centered, and their orientation to learning is through problem solving in a real context. Adults are motivated to learn and change by many factors externally and internally. Through his research, Tough (1979) discovered that all adults are motivated to keep growing and developing and that this motivation is intrinsic and powerful. It is blocked, however, when they lack the resources, time, energy, accessibility of opportunities, or negative self-esteem.

The model of andragogy and Lindeman's and Roger's student-centered teaching have profound implications for international development projects. Many international agricultural extension programs have embraced, at least in part, adult education practices. Likewise, the relatively new client-centered management approach to organizational development and the training of trainers model and strategic and institutional planning projects incorporate adult education principles. International development projects in these areas, although they share much of the same theories, philosophies, and techniques that also form the foundation for adult education, do not specifically state such principles or formally incorporate them into the methodology. As has been apparent in many international development projects, the pedagogical approach that utilizes the traditional formal educational model of a vertical dominant relationship between the development project staff or change agent and its participants will not lead to sustained behavioral change (FAO, 1987b). It may be very helpful to revisit the adult education approaches prominent in the 1960s community development and antipoverty empowerment programs in the United States and to apply the lessons taken from that experience and other adult learning contexts to international development projects.

NONFORMAL EDUCATION

Nonformal education is defined by LaBelle (1975) as organized educational programs that are given outside of a formal educational context and are designed to provide specific learning experiences to a specific target population. Nonformal education is usually associated with international development projects in LDCs and is characterized by programs in agricultural extension, community development, family planning, consciousness raising, vocational/technical training, literacy, and basic education for the adult learner. In the 1950s and 1960s, U.S. international development program planners and staff tended to disregard the participant, usually a rural subsistence person, and focused on the information to be communicated and the transference technique. Since the 1970s, there has been a growing assumption that every individual participant is capable of responsible decision making if he or she has sufficient self-esteem, the resources and necessary tools to define and solve problems, and the freedom to do so. Howard Ray and Jose Luis Monterroso (1971) outline basic principles for the transfer of technology in international development programs through nonformal education. Essentially, they believe that providing a participant with information is only the first step of the adult learning and behavioral change process and that numerous other factors will determine the adoption of the innovation. They think of participants as individuals who are rational decision makers and recommend that any change agent should understand what the participant is currently doing and why, before attempting to change it. The participants' situation is never static and is affected continually by change factors, some of which are within his or her control and others that are not. They conclude that the ability of the participants to adapt to changing circumstances is the linchpin to the success or failure of the project.

TWO-WAY COMMUNICATION

It could be argued in many development projects in LDCs that the participants are not self-directed. This may occur because they do not feel that they have control over their lives, nor can they identify and solve problems because they lack sufficient resources, skills, or self-esteem. This lack has been ascribed to personal characteristics of the individuals involved (Rogers, 1983), but it may be that this lack of self-directedness is a consequence of the culture and/or the attitudes communicated by the development project staff. Unfortunately, there are development projects where the staff believe that they cannot learn anything from LDC rural subsistence peasants (Johnson-Dean, 1986). Yet, as long as this attitude persists and communication is a one-way process, the disparate power relationships will remain and the participants will learn inaction, apathy, and appeasement, not empowerment and control over their lives and future.

To enhance the adult learning and behavioral change processes that lead to successful international development projects, ongoing two-way communication with the participants is essential. It appears that two-way communication is always important in adult learning, but perhaps this is even more true when communication is cross-cultural and when the potential for miscommunication is high.

THE FACILITATOR

Role

In some international development projects the role of the information expert has been redefined as that of a facilitator who works with participants in groups to help enhance the participants' self-esteem, resources, and problem-solving skills (Srinivasan, 1990; Svendsen & Wijetilleke, 1988). This consciousness-raising process generally involves a group-oriented, ongoing dialogue between the participants and a facilitator.

The role of such a person is to introduce information to the participants, to receive their feedback and input through a two-way communication exchange, and to act as a resource for them and as a facilitator of change. Some international development projects devote substantial time to the establishment of cooperative groups (Kindervatter, 1987). Technical information and innovations are then introduced by the facilitator to these groups. The facilitator seeks through group processes to insure that the participants not only acquire the information but can implement it and apply it to their lives. Although the facilitator initially possesses the knowledge of the new information or innovation, the participant possesses the knowledge of context, and together they can achieve the best implementation. The focus in these projects is on the ability of the group to identify their needs and problems and work toward a resolution of them. These types of projects, where power and information have been transferred to the participants, have generally been more successful, that is, have resulted in more behavioral change than has occurred in projects that do not do so.

Characteristics

The role of a facilitator in a group context is very different from that of the traditional expert who transferred information unilaterally, and the requisite skills are different (Johnson, 1991a). The facilitator and his or her interpersonal skills, cognitive ability, level of empathy, and communication skills are a critical component of the success of a project. This requirement, however, is often overlooked, and the facilitator is chosen for reasons other than his or her attributes. It is recommended that the facilitator also be the change agent with technical knowledge, although the facilitator could be a person who solely specializes in group processes including conflict resolution, team building, action planning, and empowerment. If there is a separate technical expert, she or he must also have good interpersonal skills and be able to act as a facilitator to the participants. Any technical information must be presented in such a way that it relates to the previous knowledge or skill level of the participant. For behavioral change to occur, such information must be incorporated into the participant's cognitive framework and acted upon. This means that there must be a two-way communication exchange between the facilitator and participants. The facilitator must also understand the level of the participants' self-esteem, self-directedness, skills, and levels of reasoning.

The facilitator must also realize that information is not value free. All information is conveyed and perceived through individual filters that are determined by experiences, health, emotions, values, beliefs, cultural system, and context. For information to be communicated so that the majority of what is sent is what is received, the information must be at least somewhat acceptable to the receiver's belief, value, and cultural systems. To further complicate the communication process, individual filters are not static but change according to context and over time. A woman who has just found out that she is pregnant or a man who has gastroenteritis may not hear a word that is said by the facilitator. The facilitator should be able to bridge disparate worldviews and values, beliefs, and cultural systems. She or he must be sensitive to group dynamics and the participants' emotional and health states. One way of bridging different perspectives is by creating a dialogue through two-way communication and by empathizing with another's feelings and outlook. Perhaps this can most effectively be done through guided group interaction and discussion, which can provide a forum for participants to share their own views and listen to others. An effective facilitator should be able to reason in complex ways, to adopt multisystem perspectives of reality, to empathize with, listen to, and understand other views, to communicate complex ideas and technical information in simple ways that can be understood at different levels, and to establish and maintain interpersonal relationships built on trust and respect (Sinnott, 1984). These are not the skills that traditionally have been sought in selecting international development experts or project staff.

TRAINING OF TRAINERS

International development project staff who utilize adult education techniques as they train trainers can be among the most effective change agents. To overcome problems associated with the transference of information cross-culturally, the trainer trains opinion leaders in the community in a particular innovation. They, in turn, train others. This is an effective model, if two-way communication occurs and if the trainer of trainers (ToT) measures success by how well trainees can replicate the product. The ToT, however, is imparting a product, not a process. The facilitator approach, unlike that of the ToT model, enables partic-ipants to cope with the complexities of sustainable development over time.

CONCLUSION

Adult Learning and Behavioral Change in International Development Projects

What has been learned about the adult learning and behavioral change pro-cesses that occur in international development projects? These processes are complex and interrelated, although separate. Learning can take place without behavioral change occurring. Adult learning and the encoding of information are dependent upon the perceptual filters of the learner (Sternberg, 1988). These filters are determined by the learner's cognitive framework, which is shaped by experiences, values, beliefs, and culture and by the learner's emotions, health, and relationships to the world and others at a given time in a specific context. The medium used to communicate information may either facilitate or retard the learning process. Information needs to be presented in a familiar context and must be at least somewhat acceptable to the learner's belief, value, and cultural systems for encoding to occur. During the communication process, that which is sent is often not what is received. Communication should be a two-way process so that there is a dialogue and agreement on what is communicated. Two-way communication is essential to the adult learning process and changes the rela-tionship between teacher and learner. In adult learning, there should be no power differential between teacher and learner; they both learn from each other (Sinnott, this book). Behavioral change will not occur unless that which is learned is integrated into the learner's existing cognitive framework. The factors that un-derlie an individual's decision-making process that results in behavioral change, or not, are extremely complex and interrelated parts of an overlapping and integrated system.

Success in International Development Projects

Even if one could identify all of the factors that affect such processes, this does not mean that such factors could necessarily be controlled or that devel-opment projects could be planned or implemented in a way to take these into account. Thus what is the point in identifying the multitudinous factors that affect the learning and behavioral change processes in international development proj-ects?

Perhaps the key to success in international development projects does not lie in the identification and manipulation of factors that affect the decision-making process or the implementation of behavioral change, but rather in the realization that these are very complex processes that occur and that it truly is impossible to identify all such factors. Perhaps the orientation of the development planners should not be to determine what technological innovation will economically benefit a developing country but rather to help provide the people of a developing country with the tools, resources, and information to identify and solve their own problems. The difficulty with empowering people to change their lives is that they might do it, and do it in a way that they (rather than the planners) perceive as beneficial. Empowerment destroys existing power relationships, even between change agent/teacher and participant/learner. If you help people learn how to think critically and solve problems, then they are much more adaptable to change and more likely to try to improve their lives in creative ways. They are also much less likely to give others power over their lives. Paolo Freire discusses this power reversal in his *Pedagogy of the Oppressed* (1971). These are words of revolution and may well not be what the national government or donor country had in mind.

Transference of Power

The U.S. Agency for International Development (USAID) supports "democratization" or those international development projects that will help support or develop democratic governments. It should be realized that it is not possible to build a democracy without a transference of power from development experts and the larger society to the participants of a development project. This should occur as part of the adult learning process. The choice between status quo and change and between societal and individual good is an issue that must be addressed and resolved by international development planners, those who implement the projects, and those national governments who host them. In the design phase of the international development project, it is essential that all parties agree on who will benefit from the project. Will an outcome of international development projects be to raise the economic level and quality of life for the majority of people in LDCs? Or will it be to raise the level of a select few who will maintain the current power structures that bring economic benefit to the donor countries at the expense of the majority of the LDCs' populations? If it is the former, it cannot be done without understanding how adults learn and modify their behavior.

It is hoped that some of the insights that have been gained in adult learning and behavioral change processes in international development projects may be useful to other areas of adult learning and behavioral change. Development planners when designing, implementing, and evaluating projects should consider the research undertaken and the lessons learned in other fields of adult learning and behavioral change as reported in other chapters of this book and in the literature of other disciplines. Likewise, as the adult learning process is examined in other chapters of this book, it is hoped that the knowledge imparted there may well benefit future international development programs through an understanding of the change processes that occur.

REFERENCES

Byerlee, D. (1990). *Technical change, productivity, and sustainability in irrigated cropping: Emerging issues in the post-Green Revolution era*. CIMMYT Working Paper 19–7. Mexico: Centro International de Mejoramiento de Maiz y Trigo.

Doorman, F. (1983). Adopción y adaptación en el uso de tecnología en la producción de arroz. Resultados del estudio de casos en el cultivo de arroz entre pequeños productores de la región de Nagua, Leiden, the Netherlands. (IDC Microform Publishers). Wageningen, the Netherlands: Wageningen Agricultural University.

Doorman, F. (1991). A framework for the rapid appraisal of factors that influence the adoption and impact of new agricultural technology. *Human Organization, 50*(3), 235–244.

Food and Agriculture Organization of the United Nations (FAO). (1987a). *Pioneering a new approach to communication in rural areas: The Peruvian experience with video for training at grassroots level*. Rome: FAO, Development Support Communication Branch Information Division.

Food and Agriculture Organization of the United Nations (FAO). (1987b). *Report of FAO expert consultation on development support communication*. Rome: FAO.

Freire, P. (1971). *Pedagogy of the oppressed*. New York: Herder and Herder.

Galjart, B. (1968). *Itaguai. Old habits and new practices in a Brazilian land settlement*. PhD thesis. Wageningen, the Netherlands: Wageningen Agricultural University.

Harrison, P. (1987). *The greening of Africa*. New York: Penguin Books.

Johnson, L. (1991a). A case study of positive adult cognitive development during an international development project. In J. Sinnott & J. Cavanaugh (Eds.). *Bridging paradigms: Positive development in adulthood and cognitive aging* (pp. 59–71). New York: Praeger.

Johnson, L. (1991b). *Change in international development programs*. (ERIC Report No. RC 018 108). Baltimore, MD: Towson State University. (ERIC Document Reproduction Service No. ED 330 543).

Johnson-Dean, L. (1986). *The effectiveness of videotape programs as a communication tool in the small-scale livestock for rural farming women project, Honduras*. Master's thesis. (ERIC Report No. RC 018 027. ERIC Document Reproduction Service No. ED 334 030). Las Cruces, NM: New Mexico State University.

Kindervatter, S. (1987). *Women working together for personal, economic, and community development* (2nd ed.). Washington, DC: OEF International.

Knowles, M. (1990). *The adult learner: A neglected species* (4th ed.). Houston: Gulf Publishing Co.

LaBelle, T. (1975). Liberation, development and rural non-formal education. *Council on Anthropology and Education Quarterly, 6*(4).

Lal, R. (1988). Soil degradation and the future of agriculture in sub-Saharan Africa. *Journal of Soil and Water Conservation, 43*(6), 444–451.

Lindeman, E. C. (1926). *The meaning of adult education*. New York: New Republic.

Mendez, F. & Doorman, F. (1984). *Diferenciación y adaptación en la producción de arroz. Resultados del estudio de casos en el cultivo de arroz entre pequeños productores en la región de Nagua*. (IDC Microform Publishers). Wageningen, the Netherlands: Wageningen Agricultural University.

National Research Council. (1992). *Toward sustainability: A plan for collaborative re-*

search on agriculture and natural resource management. Washington, DC: National Academy Press.

Nweke, F. (1981). Determinants of agricultural progressiveness in the small-holder cropping system of southeastern Nigeria and consequences for research and extension administration. *Agricultural Administration, 8*, 163–176.

O'Sullivan-Ryan, J. & Kaplun, M. (1981). Communication methods to promote grassroots participation. A summary of research findings from Latin America. *Communication and Society, 6*, 62–137. Paris: UNESCO.

Ray, H. E. & Monterroso, J. L. (1971). The Basic Village Education Project: Transfer of technology. In R. Niehoff (Ed.). *Report of conference and workshop on nonformal education and the rural poor.* Michigan: Institute for International Studies, Michigan State University.

Rogers, C. R. (1951). *Client-centered therapy.* Boston: Houghton-Mifflin.

Rogers, C. R. (1969). *Freedom to learn.* Columbus, OH: Merrill.

Rogers, E. M. (1969). *Modernization among peasants: The impacts of communication.* New York: Holt, Rinehart and Winston.

Rogers, E. M. (1983). *Diffusion of innovations.* New York: The Free Press.

Royal Society of London & U.S. National Academy of Sciences. (1992). *Population growth, resource consumption, and a sustainable world: A joint statement.* Washington, DC: National Academy of Sciences.

Ruttan, V. (1988). Sustainability is not enough. *American Journal of Alternative Agriculture, 3*, 28–130.

Shaner, W. W., Phillip, P. F. & Schmehl, W. R. (1982). *Farming systems research and development: Guidelines for developing countries.* Boulder, CO: Westview Press.

Sinnott, J. D. (1984). Postformal reasoning: The relativistic stage. In M. L. Commons, F. A. Richards & C. Armon (Eds.). *Beyond formal operations: Late adolescent and adult cognitive development* (pp. 298–325). New York: Praeger.

Sinnott, J. D. (1993). Teaching in a chaotic new physics world: Teaching as a dialogue with reality. In P. Kahaney, L. Perry, J. Janangelo (Eds.). *Teachers and change: Theoretical and practical perspectives.* Norwood, NJ: Ablex Publishing Co.

Srinivasan, L. (1990). *Tools for community participation: A manual for training trainers in participatory techniques.* New York: PROWWESS/UNDP.

Sternberg, R. J. (1988). *The nature of creativity.* New York: Cambridge University Press (pp. 125–147).

Svendsen, D. S. & Wijetilleke, S. (1988). *NAVAMAGA: Training activities for group building, health and income generation.* Washington, DC: OEF International.

Tough, A. (1979). *The adult's learning projects* (2nd ed.) Toronto: Ontario Institute for Studies in Education.

15

Journal Writing as Social Interaction: Writing to Learn in the Workplace

Phyllis Kahaney and Kathleen Heinrich

Freud tells us that the importance of work in the lives of adults is rivaled only by the importance of love. Adult educators would add a third passion to these two—that of learning. Adults are lifelong learners who are just as apt to continue their learning outside of formal education as within it (Tough, 1984). We know from studies in education that learning is both interactive and social (Vygotsky, 1986), and that writing enhances learning (Bizzell, 1982; Britton, 1970). According to the literature on adult learning, adults are pragmatic and problem-centered learners (Lewis, 1985); they appear to learn best when there is a sense of choice and personal meaning in their work environment (Froman, chapter 11, in this volume). Because adults are known to be pragmatic meaning-makers and storytellers, journal writing is an inspired way for adults to make meaning of their experiences by giving voice to their stories. Based on our experiences as educators of adults and on the initial findings of a pilot project, we found that adults use journals not only as a method of intrapersonal discovery and exploration but also as an interpersonal communication tool. Journal writing, traditionally viewed as a way for individuals to make meaning of their personal, relational, or academic lives, can also be used by mature adults to reflect on, identify, and resolve problems in their work lives throughout the adult lifespan.

In this chapter, we intend to show how adults' journals can be both an act of individual learning and a medium for communication. We describe a pilot project that we initiated to illustrate how to create groups for journal writing that can improve adults' work lives. This article will review the extant literature, describe a pilot project designed as a follow-up to a workshop, and discuss implications for practitioners and researchers who wish to use journal writing as a form of social interaction between and among adults.

REVIEW OF THE LITERATURE

The plethora of popular literature detailing how to keep journals for everything from psychological insight to spiritual awareness attests to a burgeoning interest in journal writing. Sharing this enthusiasm, educators in all fields have begun to integrate journal writing into their classes (Leahy, 1985) with both traditional-aged and adult learners. In classrooms, journals have been used to foster personal development, to encourage thinking "shaped at the point of utterance" (Vygotsky, 1986), to develop cognitive processes, and to "write to learn" (Britton, 1970). Educators believe that writing skills are thinking skills (Bazerman, 1981; Odell, 1980; Kinneavy, 1980). They say that journal writing not only improves students' reading and writing skills (Graves, 1978), but actually organizes thought and thereby facilitates analysis and synthesis of ideas (Emig, 1977). Journaling can deepen journalists' abilities to reflect on their lives and help them develop an understanding of perspective and the importance of context in the creation of knowledge (Macrorie, 1976). The old "learning to write" paradigm of writing as recording thought needs to shift to a "writing to learn" paradigm whereby writing is seen as developing thinking (Allen, Bowers & Diekelmann, 1989). Journal writing can be a powerful entry into this writing-to-learn paradigm. Moffett (1982) indicated that journal writing develops skills in introspection, reflection, self-conversation, and dialogue.

For adult learners in pre-professional training and professional schools, journal writing has been used to link and translate theory into practice (Allen, Bowers & Diekelmann, 1989). In all these ways, journal writing outside classrooms over the past twenty years has helped educators and clinicians come to understand more clearly how writing can be a tool in the development of an individual capacity for reflection and in coming to understand emotional processes.

However, only one study in the literature spoke to using journal writing with adults to help them understand their work lives and to communicate with fellow workers. Joanne Cooper and Diane Dunlap's (1989) qualitative study involving women administrators in government, business, and education found that most women "never mentioned they were diary or journal keepers until they were asked directly. This underscores the peculiarly private nature of this process" (p. 9).

The women administrators they studied used journals in three ways. The first was sorting, naming, and framing—an activity that helped the participants in the study to make sense of the chaos they found in their jobs. These administrators used a writing method called freewriting (Haviland, 1980) to explore unconscious processes, such as recording dreams. Second, the subjects in the study also used journal writing to generate and evaluate possible solutions to problems. Finally, the participants used their journals as records of successful past problem solving; this recording function Cooper and Dunlap called "support through documentation of past problem solving."

In short, we discovered on reviewing the literature that most uses of the journal were related either to education or to psychology. With the exception of Cooper and Dunlap, no one else addressed the journal as a social mechanism, as a springboard for interactive communication.

BACKGROUND

Phyllis Kahaney, in addition to her faculty position in the Department of English, teaches a "Writing across the Curriculum" course to faculty in all disciplines at the University of San Diego. Kathleen Heinrich, a faculty member in the School of Nursing, had, in her work as a psychotherapist, kept a personal journal and used journal writing as a strategy with clients, but she had never used journal writing in the classroom. Excited by the potential of journal writing to increase students' self-awareness and help them make links between classroom theory and professional practice, Kathy began to use journal writing with both the undergraduate and the graduate nursing students in her classes.

Because Phyllis and Kathy's dissertations dealt with adult learning issues, they were charged by the University of San Diego's Internship and Experiential Education Committee with developing a journal workshop for university staff and faculty. They were interested in helping participants develop an awareness of the possibilities of journal writing as a way of enhancing their work lives and their workplace. As luck would have it, a synchronistic event helped Phyllis and Kathy develop a specific focus for the workshop. One evening, Phyllis saw an interview on the local television evening news with a man in his late 50s who described how he had used a journal to help himself get through a horrible year of unemployment. She immediately contacted the station and, through them, contacted him and asked to read his journal. He mailed us the journal immediately and, as we both read, we became aware that his joy at finally getting work by using his journal to think through issues had become an inspiration for us. We decided to explore this type of journal writing in a workshop with other adults in the work world. This incident stimulated our interest in finding out whether journal writing would be useful to adults outside of a traditional classroom or therapeutic setting.

Our questions for the proposed workshop centered around the ways adults would use journals socially. Because the educational and psychological literature on journal writing focuses attention on individual development and rarely explores the role of journals in discovering more about how individuals interact socially with the environment, we knew we would find few answers to our questions in the literature. In fact, we found only one article that discussed the ways a secretary used journal writing to attempt to organize and improve communication in her office (Fulwiler, 1987). In order to find out more about how journal writing might be used by adults in the workplace in learning about their own processes of reflection, in solving problems, and in enhancing communication, we developed the workshop on journaling as an action research project.

THE WORKSHOP

Action research is research done by practitioners with the intent of making links between theory, practice, and research (Bogdan & Bikle, 1982). In order to connect theory and practice, we designed a "Use of Journal Writing in the Workplace" workshop as an action research project that would serve the dual purpose of meeting the participants' needs as learners and our own needs as researchers. To this end, we opened the workshop with two objectives we made explicit—to introduce participants to models of journal writing that might enhance their work lives and to invite the workshop participants to identify a journal-writing project related to their work.

We next explained that there were various ways of looking at writing by looking at both its purpose and its audience. We used Strackbein and Tillman's (1987) distinctions among logs, diaries, and journals to illustrate this point by clarifying how journal writing differed from other kinds of writing. They say that logs develop journal writers' abilities to write with scientific objectivity; diaries are introspective exercises written for the self, whose sole audience is the self; and journals are written dialogues between the self and a chosen audience of teachers, mentors, or colleagues. While diaries are strictly private, journals are often seen as public discourse that may be shared with teachers and sometimes with other writers (Simmons, 1989). Journals are written dialogues between the self and a chosen audience (Strackbein & Tillman, 1987). By definition, journal writing is an introspective exercise in which journal writers record their thoughts, feelings, and experiences. "Ideally journals are a . . . personal, unstructured exploration—an opportunity to write freely" (Zimmerman, 1990, p. 70). Journal writing is writing in the first person about things the journalist cares about.

While journals are written mainly for the self, the fact that they are shared with a specific audience creates an intimate link between inner dialogue and outer dialogue with another person. Journals are referred to by different names depending on the ways that they are used. The "dialogue journal" is a term coined to indicate a journal written in a friendly, letter-writing format that forms a dialogue between two parties (Mikkelsen, 1985; Oberlin & Shugarman, 1989). We explained during the workshop that we hoped that the dialogue journal would be useful in modeling the kind of journal writing some participants might wish to experiment with after the workshop was over. We then identified from participants' responses five general categories that journal writing might comprise— intrapersonal issues, interpersonal issues, organizational issues, skills development, and documentation. Dividing the responses into these categories, we hypothesized, might allow participants to reflect more clearly on how they could apply journal writing to their own work lives. For example, although some people had kept some form of journal in their lives (even diaries when they were teenagers) that had allowed them to focus on intrapersonal issues, few had tried journal writing in a social context, to see how they could communicate in this format with others. In the same way, no one had tried journal writing to improve their work skills, to try to solve an ethical or a work-related problem, or to document the history of problems and how they became resolved.

The act of listing the possibilities gleaned from the participants' own writing caused many of the people at the workshop to consider the extensive possibilities of journal writing. They agreed during this discussion, though, that if an office or group of professionals were thinking of using a work journal then "everyone must participate and everyone needs to buy in." These words were to be prophetic when some participants attempted to implement journal writing in their workplaces.

Our final workshop activity was to describe our action research project. We asked if participants would be willing to participate in helping us learn more about journal writing as a social activity in the context of the workplace. We indicated that we were as interested in learning from failures as from successes, and we encouraged them to experiment freely. If they were willing to participate, we wanted each of them to identify a journal writing project that fit one of the five categories generated from the group discussion. They spent the last part of the workshop organizing this. After the workshop, they were to implement the journal in their workplaces for a month and meet with us for lunch at the end of that month to report back. All participants agreed to participate in this project, and we set a date and time to meet.

Follow-up Session

Based on their enthusiastic responses on the workshop evaluations, we were surprised when, one month later, only three of the thirteen participants showed up for lunch. Two people called in sick, two others cancelled for other reasons, and the others simply did not show. (The lunch, by the way, was on us!) Only one of the women who came to the lunch said the journal writing in the workplace had been successful.

When we contacted the remaining participants by phone, we discovered that there were very good reasons that the journal they had envisioned at the workshop had not worked for them at their job. One of the secretaries said that the office was swamped with work that month and no one in the office was willing to spend precious time creating a work journal. One woman who worked in the volunteer literacy office said that she had tried three times to initiate a journal that would let others know what was going on in the office and would let her co-workers share their work problems with her. That office was divided into three locations, and although the workers all agreed that the journal was a good idea, they were too busy to make the journal a priority. A research librarian was laid off from her job during the time blocked out to try the journal writing project and so had had no opportunity to see how it would play out in her workplace. Another person was engrossed in her dissertation. We were unable to contact the others by phone or by letter.

Discussion of Findings

We were intrigued to find that the ways that Cooper and Dunlap (1989) said administrators in their sample used journals were the ways participants in our study actually used or tried to use journals. That is, whether they were using the journal intrapersonally or interpersonally, we found that they identified and worked through problems in their journal writing. We applied Cooper and Dunlap's ways of using the journal: "sorting, naming and framing," generating and evaluating possible solutions to problems, and using the journal to record events in their work lives. In the following section, we will show how Aubrey Jones, the man we saw interviewed on television, used journal writing in intrapersonal ways to solve problems and how Pam Keene, one of our workshop participants, used journal writing in interpersonal ways with her fellow workers. Both names have been changed to protect the participants' confidentiality.

INTRAPERSONAL JOURNAL BECOMES A METAPHOR FOR A SOCIAL PROBLEM

Aubrey Jones is a man in his late 50s who used a journal to help him get through a horrible year of unemployment. The journal, he said, had kept him going in the face of unimaginable financial woes and legal problems. He explained that the writing of the journal helped him keep track of where he had been and where he was going in his search for work. When in desperation he was unable to find a job, he went public with his journal on the evening news, and his story became a metaphor for the numerous people who are out of work. He was kind enough to send us his journal, along with several newspaper articles about his experiences and journal, and gave us permission to use entries from his journal for this chapter. The quotations from the journals are his, without editing for spelling or punctuation.

Mr. Jones's own perception of what journal writing has accomplished for him is encapsulated in this early entry:

This journal has defined my desires, objectives, & has painted a picture of my achievements. It feeds my will to act upon my desires, has kept me from giving up, from acting stupid. It started the day I made my first entry. It has grown tuching the public through [television reporter] of the *Star News*.

A later entry states that: "For the last week I have focused on a new resource, 'using my journal' to develop a informative artical, including the *Star News* artical, the letter to President Bush." He ends the entry with "Get afermative action!"

The above excerpts from Aubrey Jones's journal entries eloquently trace the movement of his journal from a dialogue with himself—initiated to help him reach his goal of retirement security—to the decision to use his journal as a public document of the pain and despair of losing his employment and being unable, despite Herculean efforts, to become re-employed in these difficult financial times.

Sorting, Naming, and Framing

Cooper and Dunlap (1989) found that participants in their study used writing to "sort through the often chaotic experiences in which they found themselves" (p. 9). The first step in this process identified by Cooper and Dunlap is "sorting, naming and framing." Mr. Jones's entry entitled "Highlights of the Last Several Years of My Life" (7/3/91) fits into this category; in this entry, Mr. Jones identifies specific problems and puts his struggles into perspective. In this entry, he recounts how he has been:

the primary caregiver for my mother, age 87. . . . My mother's health not good and needing help I found it practical to live with her, in her home alowing me to maintain the home and watch her state of health. In 1988 she had a stroke, increasing my responsibilities as a care giver.

In June 1989 my employment with _____ had changed from full time to part time. I took a security position with _____.

The position was good by my transportation changed. My car became unsafe to drive & I could not aford to repair or replace it.

No public transportation at the end of my shift; "2 A.M." As a result I was riding a bicicle and two night would stay on [work site] property until first bus at 5 A.M.

Riding the bicicle street people jumped out in front trying to stop me; three times. On one occasion while waiting to make a bus transfer a gang-fight erupted and one started to turn on me with a knife.

After I started caring a 22 automatic in self defence. Only to be victom of a station attendance suspension and charged with concealed wepon.

May 1990 I was informed I could not stay at [worksite] after hours.

I made a effert to transfer to day shift but was unable. Making it necessary to leave employment.

I have been active in job development programs. . . .

Not having a car has limited my ability for job serch. To overcome the probem I have mailed over 40 resumes.

The firearms charge has prevented my consideration for employment several times.

Generates and Evaluates Problems

Mr. Jones "generates and evaluates problems" (Cooper and Dunlap, 1989) throughout his highly pragmatic, problem-centered journal. The central problem and the impetus for his keeping a journal stemmed from his efforts to seek gainful employment. Mr. Jones's New Year's (1/1/91) entry reads:

Coming into 1991 with a desire backed with a positive state of mind; to build retirement security by 6/21/97.

To do I need a stable cash flow.

Employment in electronics can be that cash flow with groth potential. I will study electronic, it's products, manufacturing mathods and marketing. I will explore all resorces related to my enployment and advancement.

As Cooper and Dunlap found in their study, personal and professional issues are intertwined in people's journals, as they are in Aubrey Jones' journal. In his 1/14/91 entry, Jones identifies relationship difficulties with his infirm mother and his brother that are distracting him from his "immediate problem":

Due to negative critism, demands from mom & brother, though with good intentions expressed so forceful with a negative impact, they destroy my ability to keep focus on solving my imidate problem. . . .

I need a clear head to do so I must find shelter elsewhere in the street if need be.

On 1/25/91, he again intertwines his personal life with his professional life when he notes:

Getting ready for the interview! I bought new shoes & (3) shirts/$60.00

This act may not sell well at home as I am not as yet contributing to food and bills. But it is necessary for a successful interview.

On 4/24/91, Aubrey Jones notes a relationship in his personal life that is enhancing his resolve to find a job:

Dinner with Nina tonight. The friendship that we share is the mental chemistory of our common desire. It is creating a new feeling about myself. Maney of my values that had been put on the shelf so to speek are now comming before me and demanding attention and action. I am seeing change, feeling its effect, creating a new cofidance and faith never before experienced.

On 1/22/91, he reframes the job search from a problem to call it

The most positive part of my life in two years. I am learning to look at my education & skills rather than job title, learning to use resources to match the employer to my skills.

The problem of shelter & its state of priority is present; I am so involved with job search . . . [and] transpertation I have not been able to fully focus on new shelter.

Mr. Jones often begins to identify and focus on a new issue that emerges from his reflection on old problems, as he does in his entry of 2/24/91, when he says, "It is time to refocus time management," and identifies his long-term and immediate goals. In a later entry (7/22/91), he is able to articulate a problem he has had during his entire work life that enables him to seek help. He says:

I find after one week I am still having problems making serious mistakes. I freeze up in simple rutines and loosing concentration. "Getting lost" when pushed under stress. I have had this problem all my life but this is the first time I've defined it. I need answers as to how to cope with it. Is it corectable?

After successfully identifying this problem, he spoke to the job resources person and worked it out with her.

Support Through Documentation of Past Problem Solving

Mr. Jones uses the journal as a supportive mechanism to document what he calls his "priorities," to record the resources he is contacting to find jobs, to further educate himself, and to identify and resolve his setbacks. By 5/9/91, Mr. Jones notes in his journal:

Housing is established a nice apt at a afordable rate. I now need to focus on transpertation. Working on cash flow and transpertation.

On 5/12/91, he describes how he "brought the motorcycle home," and on 5/22/91 he is hired for a security position.

Aubrey Jones also uses his journal to document the ideas he gets from speaking with resource people and from attending workshops for those seeking employment. On 6/13/91, he notes how he is

Coming into 1991 with a desire I defined as retirement security by 6/21/97. I organized a plàn for its achievement. I now am able to put that plan into action.

The security position I have been offered is the tool to achive my final objective, retirement security. . . . Using the same principles I used to prepair myself for the oppertunity will help me achive my long term desire.

Not in 20 years but in the 6 years I have left befor retirement. My achivment since January 1, 1991 is the substance of my faith that I can achive my desire.

I have altered my resorce as needed but never my objective

The frustration, anger, and despair of defeat is clear in Mr. Jones's 6/15/91 entry entitled "stop light," where he writes that he was "denied security job due to a firearms charge." Later, he states, "I have given my all. . . . I have done my best to fullfil socitys expectations. Do not turn your back on me!"

In his entry of 7/13/91, he hatches a brilliantly creative action plan:

Thought: Not knowing what would be the effect of taking my story to *Star News*. It is another resource. I was surprised by its acceptance and coverage.

I have not as yet achived employment but it has restored my fath in socity giving me new resources and ideas.

If I am not working by the first of August I will probley recive an eviction notice. I will give it to the *Star News* for a follow up.

I have another thougth: to take my story to the govenor and president.

It is evident from his journal that Mr. Jones has been able to identify his priorities, clarify problems, and arrive at creative solutions by writing out his thoughts and reflecting on his actions. He turned his journal into an instrument of social action when he brought his journal to the local news. Clearly, Aubrey Jones uses his journal in very creative ways to overcome adversity.

INTERPERSONAL USES OF THE JOURNAL

Journals can be used as a means not only to dialogue with oneself but also to dialogue with others. Although Aubrey Jones wrote in his journal as a way to solve his own problems, many of the participants in our workshop worked in settings where communication among staff members was problematic. As they interacted with each other and with us, these people began to see the possibility of using journal writing as a way to identify common issues in the workplace and to resolve them more efficiently by actively soliciting group input through writing back and forth to each other.

One of the workshop participants, Pam Keene, decided to bring this idea of interactive journal writing to the nursing staff at her in-patient psychiatric unit. For one month, the nursing staff agreed unanimously to participate. Their initial journal entry read:

Welcome to the . . . communication log. Several nurses have expressed a desire to have a means to pass along information from shift to shift—So here goes!!

As is implied in the preceding entry, the impetus for keeping such a journal came from identifying a problem—the perceived problem that communication among nursing shift staff members was breaking down. At times, the journal was used purely as a way of sharing information; in these cases, no response or dialogue was required. An example of such an information-sharing entry:

Restraints
I ordered 4 complete sets of brand new restraints . . . today. They should be here in about 2 weeks according to the supervisor.

However, the more common use of the journal among this staff focused around identification of problems.

Sorting, Naming, and Framing Problems

Problems were sorted, named, and framed throughout the interpersonal working journal that this group of nurses created. Such problem identification elicited the sharing of information and observations. If the problem was repeatedly written about, indicating general concern, then it was either resolved by an administrative decision or placed on the agenda to be discussed at a staff meeting. Caffeine was the first topic on the "Topics for Discussion" agenda for the next unit staff meeting, and the minutes noted that "no caffeinated beverages on the locked unit were to be allowed." The genesis of this "no caffeine" policy began during the following interactive journal dialogue:

Entry #1—Caffeine policy—This weekend was a trying time as far as pts [patients] & visitors bringing in caffeinated drinks. It caused some anxiety among staff as pts tried to push staff apart by pointing out the inconsistencies. So let's please be consistent and support each other. No caffeinated soft drink while pt is on closed unit. If pt orders them—We can hold them for them until they go to open unit/discharge. I appreciate your support in enforcing this. Thanks. MH

Entry #2—Please put this in an official . . . policy to be consistent. Because as of this date it's only being directed at one pt. Others are being allowed sugar free sodas with caffeine in them.

Entry #3—Staff Meeting
Topics for discussion
1. Caffeine

Entry #4—Meeting [Minutes]
1. No caffeinated beverages on locked unit

Entry #5—Regarding the "no caffeine" policy on the locked unit, are the patients being informed in the community meeting? Is it going to be written in the patients' handbook? Several pts ordered pizza and diet Coke this eve and stated they didn't know about no caffeine. They did not get it anyway. Please clarify.

Entry #6—Caffeine on the Unit—I put a note in the community log under "staff announcements" regarding informing pts of the staff not allowing caffeinated drinks. Hopefully "forewarned" will be forearmed as well as keeping anxiety level down amongst staff and pts. Thanks.

Entry #7—Items such as above need to be included in the Patient Handbook. Which incidentally needs updating. Do we have a volunteer for this project? It would look good on your performance evaluation.

Generates and Evaluates Problems

From these journal entries, it became evident that these people wrote about their intrapersonal issues and that these issues in turn became the source of an interpersonal dialogue. The dialogue often began with an issue that one staff member noted and then moved into more organizational issues as members identified differences of opinions between and among staff members and called for consensus and/or policy statements. The fact that these issues became discussion topics in the staff meetings where staff could discuss them face-to-face attested to the value of keeping staff journals to identify issues and to solve problems.

An example of using the interpersonal journal to generate and solve problems emerged from this group in the form of developing the policy around coffee:

Entry #1—Can we expedite getting a coffee pot for the pts? Let's see if Volunteers has one that works. MH Never mind—I understand the pot works—but we need to have the hasp for the lock replaced—and what happened to the lock?

Entry #2—We the PM staff prefer not having a coffeepot. The spilled H20 and/or coffee presents a potential danger of slipping for our patients and we noticed that . . . Pts do not seem to miss it.

Entry #3—Leadership on [unit], we need a coffee policy on coffee. It's unclear what this policy is and is a source of conflict among staff and pts. Perhaps 3 coffee allotments a day between meals. . . .

Entry $4—Coffee pot—Personally, I feel that giving pts access to hot water is no different than giving them any other weapon. Also, I understand that at least 2 staff members have had hot water thrown on them! This, along with many nurses coming to me on an individual basis saying they feel a lot safer now and only 1 pt even missed the pot (& just happened to be the pt who broke it in the 1st place!). So the majority wants no pot and that's what I'm going with. Mary

Mary, the administrator of the unit, made an administrative decision based on her observations, reports from staff members included in the journal, and information on patients. Therefore, the topic of the coffee pot never moved to the agenda of the staff meeting.

It is clear both from the interactive discussions about whether to allow patients to use the coffee pot and whether to allow patients to have caffeinated beverages that the group of nurses working on this psychiatric ward used journal writing to help them identify and resolve problems. Although no formal agenda or protocol was drawn up beforehand about how the journal would work, it is clear that this group of professionals made the journal work for them in a practical way. We as researchers noted repeatedly that as problems were described by the personnel on one shift, personnel on other shifts joined the dialogue to help create the groundwork for a uniform policy for everyone concerned. We noticed, also, that the journal inspired action. The usual resolution for these issues was either by discussion at a staff meeting or by an administrative staff decision. Because of what we saw happening when journal writing was used in this manner, we have come to believe that dialogue journal writing is a mode of communication that could be successfully implemented in many different work environments with equal success.

ALTERNATE CREATIVE USES OF JOURNALS IN THE WORKPLACE

Besides using the journal as Aubrey Jones did—to actively problem-solve so that he would become gainfully employed—or as Pam Keene and her co-workers did—to dialogue about problems facing them on different shifts in a nursing ward—we discovered other ways that the journal might be used in the workplace to solve work-related problems. One woman described a "bulletin board" journal in which a law professor and a student publicly wrote back and forth as they debated a controversial ethical question on a bulletin board reserved for faculty-student communication. When others read the debate they joined in, so that the debate eventually included many people at all levels in the law school. We believe that such a debate could take place in many workplaces. The dialogue could be open as it was in this case, or it could be anonymous, but the results would be the same—to open discussion about an important topic to all who might be interested. Such a discussion could stand on its own, or it might eventually be included on the agenda of a staff meeting. Important questions and concerns could be brought up in this way, and problems could be solved.

One secretary described the way that the secretaries in the university community used E-mail to communicate with each other. They used it to request data that could be printed out, like student transcripts, or they used it to help each other solve problems, such as how to use a computer program or how to fill out a certain form. We believe that computer dialogues are an as-yet untapped resource for dialogue journal writing, one that could eventually be used to great advantage in problem resolution and communication.

Finally, one woman described how in her workplace the workers used a work journal with three different practical applications. The first was the "Problem Journal," where people wrote about things that were worrying or angering them. The second was the "Rumor Journal," in which workers discussed personal issues or ideas that needed to be clarified. Finally, there was the "Scheduling Journal," which this woman said had made an enormous difference in everyone's lives since a calendar was drawn up for the year and made public so everyone knew well ahead of time when vacations would be, who they could trade with for time off, and the like.

WHAT WE LEARNED FROM UNSUCCESSFUL PARTICIPANTS

From the large number of participants who failed to follow through with journal writing during the month following the workshop, we learned that increased support from us for the duration of the project would be necessary if we wanted people to try out a new concept like journal writing in the workplace. There are two reasons for this. We came to realize that we were asking the workshop participants not only to change their own ways of communication, but to be a catalyst for change in the communication patterns of others at their workplace. When we factored in the complexity of any workplace situation and the complexities and demands of writing, we realized that what at first might have seemed like a relatively minor task—writing in a journal—in fact had the effect of potentially upsetting the established balance in the system.

WHAT WE LEARNED FROM OUR EXPERIENCE

What did we learn from this experience of moving journal writing from the private domain of individuals interacting with their own thoughts to using journaling in the more public domain of the group? What do we believe happens when adults engage in a public writing activity in the workplace? We noted that the three categories identified by Cooper and Dunlap (1989) in their research were replicated here. Whether participants were using the journal for intrapersonal or interpersonal use, their usage in the workplace revolved around identifying and solving problems. Whether the journal was used as a tool for exchanging information about patients and patient care on a psychiatric unit or interacting with colleagues in a secretarial pool, writers of dialogue journals sketch out the patterns of problems as they write to and for each other over time. In this way, they sort out, name, and frame. In the act of writing in the journals, several participants said they found out things they would not have known otherwise; they commented that it seemed to them that "the pen thought for itself." This seems to be a good description of "writing to learn"—finding out what it is one thinks or knows in the activity of writing. Journaling, then, became an act of discovery—first of discovering what it was that the writer thought and later coming to know what the community thought when reading the entries in the journal about a certain issue. While journal writing in the workplace solved some problems, it helped define others or bring difficult issues to light.

These journals generated varied and creative solutions to problems in the workplace. In fact, the activity of collective journal writing went beyond simply communicating ideas and issues to one's colleagues. It would appear that the collective activity of journal writing—of noting issues as they arose or reading and responding to other people's concerns—went a long way toward creating order out of chaos. Considering the mass of information, problems, and issues that most people must deal with in offices, hospitals, nursery schools, and universities—indeed, in most workplaces—getting those ideas and problems down on paper and keeping a public record of what is said tends to allow the participants in that journal-writing process the possibility of seeing patterns emerge. This emergence of patterns was evident in the journals we read. It is our belief that when patterns/problems become clearly delineated and obviously shared by more than just one or two individuals, problems can be identified more accurately and dealt with in ways that are more effective so that misunderstandings and friction in the workplace decrease.

We would further argue that when a community of workers shares in this way—when they take time from a busy day to communicate in a journal—their participation in the process binds them together by building a community based on making history together. Just as partners in any social relationship build their commitment to each other by talking, spending time together, and overcoming problems, so do the workers and staff in a work setting build a history when they construct among themselves a shared record-keeping system, in this case a journal. At the follow-up luncheon, one of the participants noted that writing is a lost art and that the act of taking time to write down one's thoughts so they can be shared with the community is a very special and very caring act.

We believe that this sharing, problem solving, and idea generation facilitates learning. By fostering adult learning outside of a structured classroom setting, the job at hand can become more interesting and stress levels can be reduced. When Rita, a dean's secretary, reported that using journaling in the dean's office helped reduce scheduling conflicts, she said that everyone in the office felt afterward that their own needs were being met. This sense of well-being led to a willingness to discuss other issues.

We also believe that journal writing in the workplace serves as a record of successful problem solving. It actually allows the participants to make meaning and to participate in the shaping of their own reality. The collective journal is a tool for discovery about both the self and the work world, and the process of writing oneself and responding to colleagues' writing allows a person to struggle to solve problems and to discover meaning. We believe that the form of the interactive journal—informal, unstructured—involves a kind of learning and develops an understanding of self and others that is both integrative and synergistic.

REFERENCES

Allen, D. G., Bowers, B. & Diekelmann, N. (1989). Writing to learn: A reconceptualization of thinking and writing in the nursing curriculum. *Journal of Nursing Education, 28*(1), 6–11.

Bazerman, C. (1981). What written knowledge does: Three examples of academic discourse. *Philosophy of the Social Sciences, 11*(3), 361–387.

Bizzell, P. (1982). Cognition, convention and certainty: What we need to know about writing. *Pre-text, 3*(3), 213–243.

Bogdan, R. C. & Biklen, S. K. (1982). *Qualitative research for education: An introduction to theory and methods.* Boston, MA: Allyn & Bacon, Inc.

Britton, J. (1970). *Language and learning.* New York: Penguin Books.

Cooper, J. E. & Dunlap, D. M. (1989). *Journal keeping as an example of successful reflective practice among administrators in government, business and education.* Paper presented at the American Educational Research Association. San Francisco, CA.

Emig, J. (1977). Writing as a mode of learning. *College Composition and Communication, 28*(2), 122–128.

Fulwiler, T. (Ed.). (1986). *The journal book*. Upper Montclair, NJ: Boynton/Cook-Heinemann.

Fulwiler, T. (1987). The argument for writing across the curriculum. In A. Young and T. Fulwiler (Eds.). *Writing across the disciplines: Research into practice* (pp. 21–33). Upper Montclair, NJ: Boynton/Cook.

Graves, D. (1978). *Balance the basics: Let them write. A report to the Ford Foundation*. New York: New York Ford Foundation.

Haviland, C. P. (1980). Writing discovery journals: Helping students take charge. *College Composition and Communication*, 39:84–85.

Kinneavy, J. (1971). *A theory of discourse*. Englewood Cliffs, NJ: Prentice-Hall.

Kinneavy, J. (1980). *A theory of discourse*. New York: Norton.

Leahy, R. (1985). The power of the student journal. *College Teaching*, *33*(3), 108–112.

Lewis, L. (1985). *Characteristics of adult learners*. Lecture delivered at the University of Connecticut, Storrs.

Macrorie, K. (1976). *Telling writing*. Rochelle Park, NJ: Hayden Book Company, Inc.

Mikkelsen, N. (1985). Teaching teachers: What I learn. *Language arts*, *62*(7), 742–753.

Moffett, J. (1982). Writing, inner speech and meditation. *College English*, *44*(3), 231–246.

Oberlin, K. J. & Shugarman, S. L. (1989). Implementing the reading workshop with middle school LD readers. *Journal of Reading*, *32*(8), 682–687.

Odell, L. (1980). The process of writing and the process of learning. *College Composition and Communication*, *31*(1), 42–50.

Simmons, J. (1989). Thematic units: A context for journal writing. *English Journal*, *78*(1): 70–72.

Strackbein, D. & M. Tillman (1987). The joy of journals—with reservations. *Journal of Reading*, *131*(1): 28–31.

Tough, A. (1984). *Major learning efforts: Recent research and future directions*. Toronto: Ontario Institute for Studies in Education.

Vygotsky, L. (1986). *Thought and language (Alex Kozulin, Ed.)*. Cambridge: MIT Press.

Zimmerman, J. (1990). Journal as dialogue. *Synergist, National Center for Service Learning, ACTION*, *10*(2), 46–50.

16

Becoming an Expert: Reconsidering the Place of Wisdom in Teaching Adults

Diane M. Lee

INTRODUCTION

> Foresight, vision and value constitute the major part of wisdom; the task of
> the educator is thus revealed as rooted neither in convention, nor in craft,
> nor in caprice, but in a wisdom that unites knowledge, imagination and the
> good.
>
> Scheffler, *Of Human Potential*

Recent reports on the state of education conclude that a crisis in education does
indeed exist and that the key to educational reform lies in the expertise of our
nation's teachers. As noted by Shulman (1987), the investigations, deliberations,
and debates regarding what teachers should know, should know how to do, and
should do have never been more active.

Scheffler's words situate the debate on the place of expertise in teaching within
three contexts: (1) within the realm of knowledge deemed essential to good
teaching; (2) within the realm of imagination, that is, within creativity, possibility, and play; and (3) within the realm of moral action. It is toward these
three "places" that I will direct my comments. I will argue that the intersection
of expert knowledge, imagination, and ethical decision is governed by a postformal stage of reasoning, that is, a way of thinking allowing for multiple,
contradictory views of truth, for bridging across belief systems, and for privileging subjective and self-referential thought. In conclusion, I will suggest some
implications for teaching adults consonant with this conceptualization.

THE PLACE OF KNOWLEDGE

Underlying the Holmes Group (1986) and Carnegie Task Force (1986) reports is the assumption that there is a codifiable knowledge base for teaching. There appears to be general agreement that teachers must have content area knowledge, pedagogical knowledge, and practical knowledge in order to be most effective. In this chapter I will emphasize the knowing that escapes easy codification. I will emphasize personal, embodied knowing as it relates to knowledge of content, persons, and practices.

Teaching is often depicted metaphorically as a shared journey (Berman et al., 1991). Teachers have a unique responsibility in this journey as they are presented the task of guiding others through a landscape that may be known as well as unknown, comfortable as well as in "upheaval" (Stimpson, in Berman et al., 1991, p. vii). Decisions must be made carefully, thoughtfully, as teachers determine when they should guide from a position of authority, that is, from the front; from a position of a co-equal, that is, side-by-side; or from behind, that is, as a learner nudging students forward. Ultimately, teachers are responsible for determining what discourse will be allowed, what content will be covered, and how it will be presented.

Codifiable Knowledge

Responsible decisions demand that teachers be well informed about the content to be taught, the ways of representing and formulating the content so that it is made comprehensible and meaningful to students, and the " 'materia medica' of pedagogy" from which teachers choose curricular alternatives and materials available for instruction (Shulman, 1986b, p. 10). Shulman (1986a, 1986b, 1987) refers to these categories of content knowledge as subject matter content knowledge, pedagogical content knowledge, and curricular knowledge respectively.

In this categorization, Shulman is placing emphasis on the body of codifiable knowledge available to teachers. Subject matter content refers to the "conceived world that the teacher seeks to bring to the student" (Rivkin, in Berman et al., 1991, p. 72). It includes facts and information, the many ways the concepts and principles are organized, and the rules and objective standards for determining the validity of this knowledge. Pedagogical content knowledge connects what can be known about a discipline with what is known about learners. Pedagogical content knowledge necessarily incorporates what can be known based upon representations of persons in theory and research with practiced and reasoned ways of watching and listening to learners in classrooms. Curricular knowledge is represented in texts, equipment, defined teaching methods, worksheets, guides, outlines, questions, objectives, and goals. Human development, educational psychology, anthropology, and curriculum and instruction are a few fields among many that do provide accessible means for integrating what is to be known with ways of teaching and the needs of those to be taught.

In Shulman's explication of the knowledge underscoring expertise in teaching, he suggests three forms of knowledge for "classifying both the domains and categories of teacher knowledge . . . and for representing that knowledge" (1986b, p. 10). The forms are propositional, case, and strategic knowledge. He refers to propositional knowledge acquired through disciplined empirical or philosophical inquiry, practical experience, and moral or ethical reasoning. The propositions are known as principles, maxims, and norms. Case knowledge is acquired from specific, well-documented, thick descriptions of events. Cases, Shulman notes, exemplify theoretical principles, communicate principles of practice through maxims, and convey norms and values through parable. Propositional and case knowledge can be confirmed by research, analysis, and common agreement. Strategic knowledge renders the unilaterality within propositional and case knowledge problematic. Strategic knowledge is developed as contradictions in principles and practices arise and are acknowledged. Wisdom applies here when action is grounded in choice, when alternatives are weighed in a rational, logical, and well-reasoned way.

Embodied Knowledge

My purpose here is not to argue with Shulman's conceptualization of the knowledge base of teaching. Indeed, I included as much of it here as I did out of respect and a belief that Shulman has encapsulated much of the current thinking on the place of knowledge in teacher expertise (see also Berliner, 1986; Rosenshine & Stevens, 1986; Yinger & Clark, 1983). Rather, my purpose here is to suggest we decenter our focus on knowledge that is easily codified and articulated in traditional forms of research and teacher lore. In its place, I call for a hermeneutic turning which commits us to being-in-the-world (Heidegger, 1962), that brings to the fore teachers' tacit knowing (Polanyi, 1958) that reveals the deeply embedded and personal thoughts, beliefs, values, desires, doubts, uncertainties, and questions that situate teacher responsibility in the "consciousness (of) being the incontestible author of an event or object" (Sartre, 1956, p. 440).

Thus the focus is on being, and not only on knowing or doing. It is toward embodied knowledge that we now turn in thinking about expertise in teaching. To know this way, we must bring forth the "speech within" that calls us back to our selves (Grange, 1989, p. 171) and listen authentically in a way that involves the totality of our selves (Fiumara, 1990; Levin, 1989). This focus on being is a call for self-referential thought present in postformal reasoning (Kitchener & King, 1981; Kitchener & Kitchener, 1981; Sinnott, 1984).

To listen to our selves and to others "is not simply an activity of applied thinking" (Fiumara, 1990, p. 115) or receiving a signal; it is hearing in the sense of hearkening and heeding. In hearkening, listening and feeling are closely connected to our total being, pointing us toward the feminist critique. Indeed, the call here is the feminist voice arguing for the cultivation of listening in receptiveness, responsiveness, care, and the aesthetic (see Belenky et al., 1986; Berman, 1977; Erdman, 1990; Gilligan, 1982; Greene, 1988; Grumet, 1988; Miller, 1990; Noddings, 1984; Rich, 1979). It is a feminine spirit that takes us to the place within us where unity is carefully inscribed within difference, where the intertwining of self and other is both enlightening and emancipatory, and where the vibrations of reflection, recollection, thoughtfulness, and mindfulness create an openness to a sonorous way of being long exiled in the patriarchal landscape of rationality.

This inner place where rational analysis as a favored way of coming to know is set aside for "that deep realm of intuitive knowledge which some theologians call ontological reason" (Daly, 1973, p. 39). Intuition begins with looking, as evidenced in its etymological roots. It is derived from *intueri*, the Latin verb "to look upon," initially positioning sight as the critical sense. It has come to mean "the ability to perceive or know things without conscious reasoning" (*Webster's New World Dictionary*, 1984, p. 740), and all the senses are given an operative role in creating knowledge. "Intuition," note Noddings and Shore (1984, p. 57), "is that function that connects objects directly in phenomena. This direct contact yields something we might call 'knowledge.' " Intuition leads us to be fully present in genuine encounters. As Buber (1970) describes in *I and Thou*, such knowing is a way to gain the world "by seeing, listening, feeling, forming. It is in encounter that the creation reveals its formhood; it does not pour itself into senses that are waiting but deigns to meet those that are reaching out" (p. 77). This statement is reminiscent of Noddings and Shore's (1984) position attributing intention and will to intuitive thought. They write of intuition as a conscious process, a process to be called upon as persons go about making sense of their world. "To do this kind of work takes a capacity for constant active presence, a naturalist's attention to minute phenomena, for reading between the lines, watching closely for symbolic arrangements, decoding difficult and complex messages left for us by women of the past" (1984, p. 14). This process is integral in the feminist mandate for a multifocal, relational perspective in education wherein women as well as men, those marginal as well as mainstream, have voice.

Voice and Harkening

The concept of voice has gained special attention in the educational discourse of this decade. It has become the calling card for true equality among all those demanding entry into the conversations regarding "what ought to be taught." Language and voice represent power and a lack of power among those usually silenced. Students and teachers distanced from curriculum and the happenings in schools voluntarily and involuntarily are drawn into a culture of silence (Shor & Freire, 1987). The call for inclusion here extends beyond the popular invitation to those traditionally silenced (women, people of color, children and teenagers, the underclass, and all those marginal individuals who "walk the edges," as M. Lynne Smith, 1990, describes). The invitation here is also to the voice within, the voice of being.

In this way of being, voice is chosen and silence needn't be a tool of domination. Rather, silence may be a self-chosen place where the "silent reserve of Being" may be unconcealed (Levin, 1989, p. 254) and, in its creative function, where the challenge of transcendence is conceived. As noted by Sciacca (cited in Fiumara, 1990, p. 101), "With silence we express the most varied and conflicting states, sentiments, thoughts and desires. Silence is meaningful. . . . Silence is anything but an 'absence.' " Thus it is in silence that adults are most likely to synthesize disparate voices, to find the order within chaos, to put themselves fully into the task of sense-making in an increasingly complex world.

Silence chosen also has a communicative function. Silence, Sciacca reminds us, is "not an interval . . . but the bridge that unites sounds" (cited in Fiumara, 1990, p. 102). Again, silence thus conceived brings us back to our selves, to our persona, "the person sounding through, resonating" (Caputo, 1987, p. 289). It leads us to dwell in "a tensionality of contrapuntal interplay, a tensionality of differences" (Aoki, in Berman et al., 1991, p. xiii).

Listening fully, hearkening, and heeding the call to silence chosen can support the hermeneutic and phenomenological efforts called for here. Meanings created and understood in solitude can help us establish links to meanings created in community. This internal language, however, is difficult to translate and escapes measurement. My claim here is that it is within this existential posture that we are drawn from the dominant paradigm and stretched beyond the limits of rational knowing. To listen and to come to know, as described above, is to deny the traditional conception of rationality privilege, for the solitary, self-contained, self-sufficient cogito is essentially disembodied, therefore not capable of being fully present or of authentic listening (Levin, 1989, p. 130). Yet it is this form of knowledge that dominates the discourse in teacher expertise.

To see teaching in its widest, most revealing sense, as it is and as it may be, I feel requires a partnership between the natural, the social, the rational, the phenomenological, the existential, and the hermeneutic. It calls upon the reflexive and pre-reflexive, the conceptual and pre-conceptual, the logical and pre-logical structures that undergird all experience. My leanings toward alternative paradigms are, in part, a response to the conspicuous absence of such alternatives amid much of the mainstream educational literature regarding teacher knowledge. The boundaries of traditional discourse must be expanded and the positioning of personal ways of knowing centered if we are to understand better the place of knowledge in teacher expertise.

THE PLACE OF IMAGINATION

The origin of the word *imagination* lies in the Latin *imago*, referring to imitation or copy. Common usage today emphasizes a visual representation of someone or something not actually present. The focus is on creativity, specifically on creating that which has never been experienced or on creating by combining previous experiences (*Webster's New World Dictionary*, 1984, s.v. "imagination"). This usage meshes meaningfully with the mission of educators.

The Latin word *educare*, from which *education* is derived, means to bring forth, to lead out from darkness into light. The delicate work of educators is to bring forth or surface what persons know and then "to make present what is absent, to summon up a condition that is not yet" (Greene, 1988, p. 16). It is imagination in education that draws us toward the unexplored, the mysterious, the possible. "Nothing on earth is more gladdening than knowing we must roll up our sleeves and move back the boundaries of the humanly possible once more" (Dillard, 1990, p. 51). Education conceived this way presents "the lure of the transcendent" (Huebner, 1984, p. 114), and imagination provides the bridge between what is present and what might be. Thus, imagination is a point of departure, notes Riddell (1971), "it is the potentiality of a future" (p. 56).

Toward Possibility

Imagination is a point of departure throughout the entire educational journey. Imagination prompts detour, the kind of turning inviting wonder (see Hultgren in Berman et al., 1991; Roderick in Berman et al., 1991). In classrooms, this wonder is exhibited in true inquiry. Teachers, knowledgeable and confident in the worth of the journey itself and in their many positions from which to guide, stand humbly before the questions students raise. A form of disciplined inquiry results wherein students' queries give shape to the unfolding curriculum. Such purposeful inquiry often leads to woodpaths (Heidegger, in Krell, 1977, p. 34), that is, a kind of meandering through thick unmarked woods where light is muted and sound muffled. But these poorly delineated paths eventually lead to clearings, and it is in these openings that speculative thinking is granted passage. Heidegger claims the clearing "free for brightness and darkness, but also for resonance and echo, for sounding and diminishing of sound. The clearing is the opening for everything that is present and absent" (1986, p. 250). Inquiry takes us to the unknown, mysterious, unpredictable, and uncertain. To inquire is to accept the invitation imagination sends forth.

Imagination creatively connects our dreams with reality, our passions with experience, and our reasoning with play. In this regard Le Guin (1989) recounts Virginia Woolf's image of a woman writing:

She was not thinking; she was not reasoning; she was not constructing a plot; she was letting her imagination down into the depths of her consciousness while she sat above holding on by a thin but quite necessary thread of reason. (p. 227)

The woman Woolf describes was holding onto intellectual inheritances but working imaginatively, playfully, freely beyond them. Thus, it is toward the imaginative, toward openings and freedom that expert teachers lead their students.

Toward Freedom

"Imagination is first characterized by liberation. By exercising imagination, we are freed from the ordinary," says Brimfield (1988, p. 253). The emancipatory function of imagination calls into question the stale exercises of mind that rely upon a priori givens and pure logic in sense-making. Imagination involves a flash of originality, the dissonant twist, a disruption of the predictable, and the potential for new connections (Brimfield, 1988, p. 255). It is a release from convention, regimentation, and compulsion. "To think creatively is to walk at the edge of chaos," says Grudin (1990, p. 15). To think creatively is to find the order within disorder, the patterns within chaos, and the iterative processes that regulate chaotic systems. Creativity is not expressed in a rule-governed, mechanistic relation between thought and action, but rather resides in receptivity, openness, freedom, curiosity, and the subjective relation between thought and action.

Toward Play

It is through receptivity, individual desire, and the openings created by imagination that persons are drawn into play. The open region is in play, declares Heidegger (1986, p. 249). We speak of playing with ideas, toying with preconceived notions, and losing ourselves within daydreams. Such play disciplines persons to carry out the critical task of "transcending the what-is to reach for what might be" (Berman, 1977, p. 255). Such play is a personal expression of our humanity, of the connections between our inner and outer selves. Imaginative play brings us to the province where we create ourselves, and herein lies a paradox. As noted by Kierkegaard (in Manheimer, 1977), it is in choosing our selves that we reveal a continuity with others and the essence of our relationship with others. So it is in this place, too, that we find the genesis of community and our ethical calling.

THE PLACE OF MORAL ACTION

To be in community, Berman (1991, p. 149) reminds us, is to "share a common abode," the root meaning of ethics. If we are to truly dwell in community and inhabit our world, we will meet one another in genuine encounters as Buber (1970) describes and face-to-face as Levinas (1985) describes. We will meet the other within the moral imperative requiring radical responsibility for self and the other.

In assuming such responsibility as teachers, we must come to teaching with such confidence in our knowledge of subject, pedagogy, and self that we are released to be responsive with learners. Confidence must be tempered by humility, however. We must be present to ourselves and honestly confront the limits of our knowing, the bases of our values, and the ways we are willing to recreate ourselves and others. It is humility that allows for revisioning, for discarding the irrelevant, for wonder, for harkening.

The tension between confidence and humility is represented in concern, in care. Care for self, for others, for self as a professional, for others as learners, for the profession of teaching itself, and the content to be taught. To care this way is to conceive of teaching as ethical action.

Responsibility

Considering teaching as ethical action this way leads us away from the patriarchal hierarchy of rights to a feminist perspective on ethics, that is, to dual notions of responsibility embedded in care (Gilligan, 1982, 1986; Lyons, 1990; Noddings, 1984). The first responsibility is to our selves. We must live as thoughtfully, freely, imaginatively, playfully, and attentively as we possibly can. The second responsibility is to others. We must enable, encourage, and empower others to live as we should. This way of being in community engages all persons in mutual responsibilities. The boundaries of community then are not to restrict persons within, as Heidegger recognized (1977, p. 332), but rather are the horizons from which essential unfolding begins.

The words and metaphors used to contemplate knowing, teaching, learning, imagination, creating, and play here demand that persons attend to the ethical consequences of their being. "Being," notes Heidegger (Krell, 1977, p. 196), "presides over thinking and hence over the essence of humanity." Teaching cannot be relegated to technical expertise. Teaching as being must be sensitively conceived as a moral craft (Tom, 1984) where propositional knowledge is insufficient for judging right or wrong, good or bad. Judgment must also involve compassion, responsiveness, and responsibility. Matters of value and goodness are the portion of every educational enterprise, and to this enterprise teachers must commit and profess their entire being.

The claim here is that knowledge in teaching must always project toward possibility—possibility manifested in embodied knowing, imagination, and responsibility. Teachers and students alike should realize possibility as *my* possibility. An appeal to such subjective awareness is a call for each individual to constitute her/himself deliberately. Such an engagement should restore spontaneity, authenticity, and genuine encounters between teacher and student. It should release persons from subordination to preconceived notions developed "out there" or from placement in an existing hierarchical system. It encourages persons to recall their original vision of things, to listen with a "third ear" to the diversity of meanings generated in community.

The claim here is for wholeness of being, for knowledge that brings a sense of unity to existence. Thus integrity is prized. Risks are to be taken as new insights, new ideas, new callings endanger prior assumptions. Inspirational leaps over the logical steps of reasoning have a place in classrooms as we are beckoned by the call of freedom. The seeming paradox between childlike attunement to the world and the form of wisdom implied in the most complex forms of mature adult thought comprises the space in-between, where true expert teachers dwell. It is to this place that our conversation leads us now.

THE SPACE IN-BETWEEN: CHILDLIKE ATTUNEMENT AND MATURE ADULT THOUGHT

Merleau-Ponty (1962) speaks in ways reminiscent of the wisdom discussed above when he suggests a return to the core of primary meaning in which a person's knowing originates. He recalls the perceptual consciousness through which a child first comes in contact with the environment, before the child is capable of logical thought. He suggests a return to "primordial perception," that is, to the things themselves before they are filtered through expectation or intention (p. ix). This is the active engagement of children in play, exploring, observing, inquiring. This is bodily-felt listening released from previous understandings and bent toward enchantment and not comprehension alone. This childlike attentiveness is a way of being that Annie Dillard (1974) so eloquently describes as innocence in *Pilgrim at Tinker Creek*. "What I call innocence is the spirit's unself-conscious state at any moment of pure devotion to any object. It is at once a receptiveness and total concentration" (p. 82). "Self-consciousness is the curse of the city . . . the novelist's world, not the poet's" (p. 81). To turn a deaf ear to the child within would be like "violating truth and, perhaps even worse, extinguishing both thought and wonder" (Gould, 1990, p. 111). This childlike presence is a way of being that privileges embodied knowing. It is a way of being consonant with Sinnott's portrayal of postformal reasoning.

Postformal thinkers, as Jan Sinnott reminds us in this volume and other publications (see Sinnott, 1984 and 1993), are capable of recognizing multiple and contradictory forms of truth, are able to deal with the diversity, turbulence, paradoxes, and the rapid and often unpredictable changes underlying chaos. They are not held to a priori givens but rather engage freely and creatively in the conscious breaking-away from the conventional, agreed-upon canons perpetuating the mundane and the status quo. Postformal thinkers restore the "essential notion of self-reference" (Sinnott, chapter 8 of this volume) in problem posing and problem solving and consciously use self-referential and subjective knowing to create and recreate self and others. As persons are aroused to their own subjective awareness, they choose their journey and their place among sojourners. They create spaces for freedom (as Maxine Greene describes, 1988), invite imagination into their deliberations, and consider the ethical meanings of their actions and personal encounters. They do all this—I believe they turn toward their original selves—as they listen with their total being to the many voices without and harken to the interior voice and silence within. Thus, postformal thinkers acknowledge the interrelatedness of all experience and adopt a metasystemic or reflective and integrative approach to thinking (Csikszentmihalyi & Rathunde, 1990, p. 31) and being.

THE PLACE OF WISDOM IN TEACHING: IMPLICATIONS FOR TEACHING ADULTS

A constructive outcome of placing wisdom at the fore of our thinking about expert teachers lies in the implications for teaching, especially when working with adult learners. Teaching, consonant with the intricate details of wisdom described here, would be democratic, dialogic, and ecologically valid. The suggestions that follow are focused on the adult learner, but they are not necessarily exclusive to adult learners.

Democratic Teaching

Democracy, Dewey wrote (1916, p. 90), is "more than a form of government; it is primarily a mode of associated living, of conjoint communicative experience." In this conceptualization the classroom is represented as a community and thus, from the feminist perspective, emphasizes sensitivity to and inclusiveness of all persons: women, people of color, minorities, poor persons, and those with lesser status and power as well as those traditionally privileged (Erdman, 1990, p. 175).

In democratic teaching, teachers and learners are full partners in the educational enterprise. Everyone is responsible for creating and sharing knowledge. Teachers do have a unique responsibility, however, to plan and orchestrate classroom events. A form of hierarchical positioning is not necessary; rather, the teacher's role is an expression of care as responsible teachers ensure that everyone does have voice and that knowledge is not used to intimidate or overwhelm. Ultimately, the teacher is responsible for making sure that the curriculum is not trivialized, that is, oversimplified, uncritical, shallow, fragmented, or requiring little judgment (Short, 1990). Knowledge and meaning should be magnified in a true, interactive human community.

The interactive and equitable approach advocated here is found in cooperative models. The concept of letting adults work together is particularly salient. The conditions of learning Knowles describes as necessary for adult learners depict an environment characterized by mutual trust and respect, mutual helpfulness, freedom of expression, and acceptance of differences (1980, pp. 57–58). Furthermore, Knowles defines adult education as problem centered. Most problem solving is a social task, involving the joint efforts of persons working in concert toward a common goal (Meacham & Emont, 1989). Democratic and cooperative models of education are essentially dialogic forms of teaching and learning.

Dialogic Teaching

Education is perceived here as a disciplined dialogue between teachers and students about something (Scudder & Mickunas, 1985). Teachers must know the subject content matter so well that they may serve as a bridge between students' experiences, their own experiences, and the field itself. Yet, true dialogue is open, as Witherell and Noddings (1991, p. 7) remind us, so "conclusions are not held to be absolute by any party at the outset." Rather, they continue, "The search for enlightenment, responsible choice, perspective, or means to solve a problem is mutual are marked by appropriate signs of reciprocity."

Such reciprocity rejects "authoritative discourse" viewing knowledge as received and static, as a set of givens to which allegiance is demanded. In its place is "internally persuasive discourse" wherein each individual, teacher and student alike, is invited to selectively assimilate the words of others (Bakhtin, 1981, pp. 341–342). Thus, neither teacher nor student nor text is an infallible authority.

The struggle between forms of discourse, that which holds a place of privilege and power and that which provisions dismantling of the taken-for-granted, invites multiple perspectives, contradiction, and the placement of self in a dynamic world. As each voice in dialogue attempts to make what is known and is being created her or his own, spaces for improvisation, creativity, risk, play and what Sinnott (in press) calls useful disorder must be made.

Dialogue journals, narrative, and personal story create such spaces. The literature on adult learning consistently points toward the meaningfulness of learning when the varied and rich life experiences of adult learners are affirmed (Aslanian & Brickell, 1980; Dewey, 1916; Knowles, 1980). Reflections on one's life bring integrity to the classroom and provide unique opportunities for the expression of connected knowing, that is, for links between the interior voice of reflection and the public voice of oral speech and written text. Thus, dialogue journals, narrative, and story integrate the affective, cognitive, and moral dimensions of experience, providing the perfect vehicle for experiments in self-discovery, reality testing, and ethical debate. They bring a sense of wholeness to adults living and shaping their lives through dialogue and text.

Ecologically Valid Teaching

The essence of ecologic teaching is in "relatedness and receptivity" (Noddings, 1984, p. 192). In thinking about teaching adults as being ecologically valid, it is useful to consider the origins of the term: "Eco" from the Greek *oikos* for house, "logic" from the Greek *logikos* for speaking or reasoning. "Eco" in the combining form means environment or habitat. Classrooms for adults should be gathering places where inhabitants create a curriculum through dialogue, autobiographical activity, story, and narrative. Ecology also deals with the relations between living organisms and their environment; the relations among persons willing to open themselves to others, to become aware of the limits of their own thinking, and to use their own voices will necessarily be grounded in mutuality, trust, compassion, and care. The curriculum created in community should be sufficiently flexible to "celebrate each person's unique characteristics" (Brimfield, 1988, p. 262) while accommodating difference. Teaching and learning that is ecologically valid will point toward the interconnectedness, interdependency, and interrelatedness between that which is to be known and the knower, toward a nonfragmented knowledge of being and becoming.

Thus, classes for adult learners should be integrative and directed toward dynamic knowing. Openness to the possibility that phenomena and information may take on new meanings in the context of discursive interplay and acknowledgment that such cognitive flexibility will be tempered by responsibility and self-reflection often result in mature action directed toward the common good. Adult learners often expect immediacy in application as they construct and reconstruct their experiences; curricula must be relevant to their lives.

CONCLUSION

Teachers whose practice is based upon ''wisdom that unites knowledge, imagination, and the good'' (Scheffler, 1985, p. 12) are most likely to be at the postformal stage of reasoning. They are also likely to be sensitively attuned to the polyphony of voices so that, with their students, they will move toward possibilities not yet realized.

Adults, as teachers and learners joining together to create knowledge and self, are like the quilters of long ago. Their stitching becomes a quilt ''stitched of the careful insights, the living experiences reflected into ideas, the weighted remark, the forgiving touch, the tolerance, the faithfulness, the moments saved and cherished'' (Rivkin, in Berman et al., 1991, p. 75).

NOTE

This work was supported by a University of Maryland Baltimore County DRIF grant.

REFERENCES

Akoi, T. (1991). Toward curriculum for being: Voices of educators. Albany, NY: State University of New York Press.

Aslanian, C. B. & Brickell, H. N. (1980). *Americans in transition: Life changes as reasons for adult learning.* New York: College Board.

Bakhtin, M. M. (1981). *The dialogical imagination.* Austin: University of Texas Press.

Belenky, M., Clinchy, B., Goldberger, N. & Tarule, J. (1986). *Women's ways of knowing.* New York: Basic Books.

Berliner, D. (1986). In pursuit of the expert pedagogue. *Educational Researcher, 15*(7), 5–13.

Berman, L. M. (1977). Curriculum leadership: That all may feel, value, and grow. In L. Berman & J. Roderick (Eds.). *Feeling, valuing, and the art of growing: Insights into the affective.* Washington, DC: Association for Supervision and Curriculum Development.

Berman, L. M., Hultgren, F. H., Lee, D., Rivkin, M. S. & Roderick, J. A. (1991). *Toward curriculum for being: Voices of educators.* Albany, NY: State University of New York Press.

Brimfield, R.M.B. (1988). Imagination, rigor, and caring: One framework for educational reform. *Journal of Curriculum and Supervision, 3*(3), 253–262.

Buber, M. (1970). *I and Thou*. Translated by Walter Kaufman. New York: Charles Scribner's Sons. (Original work published c. 1923).

Caputo, J. (1987). *Radical hermeneutics: Repetition, deconstruction, and the hermeneutic project*. Bloomington: Indiana University Press.

Carnegie Task Force on Teaching as a Profession. (1986). *A nation prepared: Teachers for the 21st Century*. Washington, DC: Carnegie Forum on Education and the Economy.

Csikszentmihalyi, M. & Rathunde, K. (1990). The psychology of wisdom: An evolutionary interpretation. In R. Sternberg (Ed.). *Wisdom: Its nature, origins, and development* (25–51). New York: Cambridge University Press.

Daly, M. (1973). *Beyond God the father*. Boston: Beacon Press.

Dewey, J. (1916). *Democracy and education*. New York: Macmillan.

Dillard, A. (1990). The stunt pilot. In J. Kaplan & R. Atwan (Eds.). *The best American essays 1990* (48–59). New York: Ticknor & Fields.

Dillard, A. (1974). *Pilgrim at Tinker Creek*. New York: Harper's Magazine Press.

Erdman, J. I. (1990). Curriculum and community: A feminist perspective. In J. T. Sears & J. D. Marshall (Eds.). *Teaching and thinking about curriculum: Critical inquiries* (172–186). New York: Teachers College Press.

Fiumara, G. C. (1990). *The other side of language: A philosophy of listening*. Translated by Charles Lambert. New York: Routledge.

Gilligan, C. (1983). Do the social sciences have an adequate theory of moral development? In N. Haan, R. Bellah, P. Rabinow, & W. Sullivan (Eds.). *Social science as moral inquiry*. New York: Columbia University Press.

Gilligan, C. (1982). *In a different voice: Psychological theory and women's development*. Cambridge, MA: Harvard University Press.

Gilligan, C. (1986). Remapping the moral domain: New images of self in relationship. In T. Heller, M. Sosna, & D. Wellbery (Eds.). *Reconstructing individualism: Autonomy, individuality, and the self in Western thought*. Stanford, CA: Stanford University Press.

Gould, S. J. (1990). The creation myths of Cooperstown. In J. Kaplan & R. Atwan, (Eds.). *The best American essays 1990* (99–111). New York: Ticknor & Fields.

Grange, J. (1989). Lacan's other and the factions of Plato's soul. In A. B. Dallery & C. E. Scott (Eds.). *The question of the other: Essays in contemporary continental philosophy* (157–174). Albany: State University of New York Press.

Greene, M. (1988). *The dialectic of freedom*. New York: Teachers College Press.

Greene, M. (1985). Imagination and learning: A reply to Kieran Egan. *Teachers College Record, 87* (Winter), 167–171.

Grudin, R. (1990). *The grace of great things*. New York: Ticknor & Fields.

Grumet, M. R. (1988). *Bitter milk: Women and teaching*. Amherst: University of Massachusetts Press.

Heidegger, M. (1986). The end of philosophy and the task of thinking. In M. C. Taylor (Ed.), *Deconstruction in context: Literature and philosophy* (242–255). Chicago: University of Chicago Press.

Heidegger, M. (1962). *Being and time*. J. Macquarrie & E. Robinson (Trans.). New York: Harper & Row.

The Holmes Group (1986). *Tomorrow's teacher: A report of the Holmes Group.* East Lansing, MI: Author.

Huebner, D. (1984). The search for religious metaphors in the language of education. *Phenomenology and Pedagogy, 2*(2), 112–123.

Kitchener, K. S., & King, P. M. (1981). Reflective judgment: Concepts of justification and their relation to age and education. *Journal of Applied Developmental Psychology, 2*, 89–116.

Kitchener, K. S. & Kitchener, R. F. (1981). The development of natural rationality: Can formal operations account for it? In J. A. Meacham & N. R. Santilli (Eds.). *Social development in youth: Structure and content.* Basel: S. Karger.

Knowles, M. (1980). *The modern practice of adult education.* Chicago: Association Press/Follett Publishing Co.

Krell, D. F. (Ed.). (1977). General introduction: "The Question of Being." In *Martin Heidegger: Basic writings from Being and Time (1927) to The Task of Thinking (1964)* (1–35). New York: Harper & Row.

LeGuin, U. K. (1989). The fisherman's daughter. In Ursula K. LeGuin, *Dancing at the edge of the world: Thoughts on words, women, places* (212–237). New York: Grove Press.

Levin, D. M. (1989). *The listening self: Personal growth, social change and the closure of metaphysics.* New York: Routledge.

Levinas, E. (1985). *Ethics and infinity.* Translated by R. A. Cohen. Pittsburgh: Duquesne University Press. (Original work published 1982).

Lyons, N. (1990). Dilemmas of knowing: Ethical and epistemological dimensions of teachers' work and development. *Harvard Educational Review, 60*(2), 159–180.

Manheimer, R. (1977). Kierkegaard as educator. Berkeley: University of California Press.

Meacham, J. A. & Emont, N. C. (1989). The interpersonal basis of everyday problem solving. In J. D. Sinnott (Ed.) *Problem-solving: theory and application.* New York: Praeger.

Merleau-Ponty, M. (1962). *Phenomenology of perception.* Translated by C. Smith. London: Routledge and Kegan Paul.

Miller, J. (1990). Teachers as curriculum creators. In J. T. Sears & J. D. Marshall (Eds.). *Teaching and thinking about curriculum: Critical inquiries* (85–96). New York: Teachers College Press.

Noddings, N. (1984). *Caring: A feminine approach to ethics and moral education.* Berkeley: University of California Press.

Noddings, N. & Shore, P. (1984). *Awakening the inner eye: Intuition in education.* New York: Teachers College Press.

Polanyi, M. (1958). *Personal knowledge.* Chicago: University of Chicago Press.

Rich, A. (1979). *On lies, secrets, and silence: Selected prose 1966–1978.* New York: W. W. Norton & Company.

Rich, A. (1979). Foreword: On history, illiteracy, passivity, violence, and women's culture. In A. Rich, *On lies, secrets, and silence: Selected prose 1966–1978* (9–18). New York: W. W. Norton & Company.

Riddell, J. N. (1971). Stevens on imagination: The point of departure. In O. B. Hardison, Jr. (Ed.). *The quest for imagination.* Cleveland: Press of Case Western Reserve University.

Rosenshine, B. & Stevens, R. S. (1986). Teaching functions. In M. C. Wittrock (Ed.). *Handbook of research on teaching* (3rd ed., 376–391). New York: Macmillan.

Sartre, J. (1956). *Being and nothingness*. Translated by Hazel E. Barnes. New York: Philosophical Library.

Scheffler, I. (1985). *Of human potential: An essay in the philosophy of education*. Boston, MA: Routledge & Kegan Paul.

Scudder, J. R. & Mickunas, A. (1985). *Meaning, dialogue and enculturation: Phenomenological philosophy of education*. Washington, DC: University Press of America.

Shor, I. & Freire, P. (1987). *A pedagogy for liberation*. South Hadley, MA: Bergin & Garvey.

Short, E. C. (1990). Challenging the trivialization of curriculum through research. In J. T. Sears & J. D. Marshall (Eds.). *Teaching and thinking about curriculum: Critical inquiries* (197–210). New York: Teachers College Press.

Shulman, L. S. (1986a). Paradigms and research programs for the study of teaching. In M. C. Wittrock (Ed.). *Handbook of research on teaching* (3rd ed., 3–36). New York: Macmillan.

Shulman, L. S. (1986b). Those who understand: Knowledge growth in teaching. *Educational Researcher, 15*(2), 4–14.

Shulman, L. S. (1987). Knowledge and teaching: Foundations of the new reform. *Harvard Educational Review, 57*(1), 1–22.

Sinnott, J. D. (1993). Teaching in a chaotic new physics world: Teaching as a dialogue with reality. In P. Kahaney, J. Janangelo, & L.A.M. Perry (Eds.). *Theoretical and critical perspectives on teacher change*. Norwood, NJ: Ablex Press.

Sinnott, J. D. (1984). Postformal reasoning: the relativistic stage. In M. L. Commons, F. A. Richards & C. Armon (Eds.). *Beyond formal operations: Late adolescent and adult cognitive development* (298–325). New York: Praeger.

Smith, M. L. (1990). Walking the edges: Reading and writing in the lives of low SES, urban high school student/parents, their parents, and their children. Unpublished doctoral dissertation, University of Cincinnati, May, 1990.

Stimpson, C. R. (1991). *Toward curriculum for being: Voices of educators* (vii–ix). Albany, NY: State University of New York Press.

Tom, A. (1984). *Teaching as a moral craft*. New York: Longman.

Webster's New World Dictionary. (1984). New York: Simon & Schuster.

Witherell, C. & Noddings, N. (Eds.). (1991). *Stories lives tell: Narrative and dialogue in education*. New York: Teachers College Press.

Yinger, R. J. & Clark, C. M. (1983). *Self-reports of teacher judgment* (Research Series No. 134). East Lansing: Michigan State University, Institute for Research on Teaching.

17

Exploring Adult Learning from Learners' Perspectives

Laura V. Maciuika, Michael Basseches, and Abigail Lipson

In this chapter, we explore recent theory and research on adult learning informed by adult learners' perspectives on their own learning. This literature cuts across education and psychology, theory and practice; linking these areas is an effort to understand adults' experiences of learning and to present the findings while staying close to adults' own terms.

We have organized this review into four somewhat-overlapping areas. In the first, cognitive approaches to adult learning, we review work on how learners experience classroom activities such as reading, writing, and lectures. The second area on developmental perspectives includes research that focuses on how adults organize or structure their learning and knowing over time. In the third area, adult learning as transformation, we explore work on how learning challenges the ways in which adults know themselves and their relational, sociopolitical, and cultural contexts. Finally, we review innovative research in adult education that describes a variety of adults' learning experiences, including researchers' perspectives on their own learning.

Many of the authors presented here critique the dominant natural science orientation within much educational and psychological research on learning. This orientation tends to privilege the conceptual frameworks that researchers bring to their inquiry, while downplaying or ignoring how learners themselves describe their learning experiences. A carryover from the natural sciences, this approach tends to emphasize researchers' language and worldviews, often by overt or covert claims that there is no framework or worldview, but rather only "objective observation." We pay special attention in this review to work that critiques this dominant orientation and that demonstrates alternative approaches to exploring learning that allow learners to voice their own experiences and perspectives (see also Phillips et al., chapter 20, in this volume).

COGNITIVE APPROACHES TO LEARNING

Within the Western tradition of cognitive approaches to educational psychology, a shift occurred during the mid–1970s among educational psychologists in Great Britain and Sweden. Noel Entwistle (1985) of Edinburgh writes that, before 1975, Western educational psychologists explored adult students' entry qualifications, exam outcomes, or memory tasks, focusing on learning as a product while largely ignoring students' learning as a process. *How Students Learn*, published in 1975 and edited by Entwistle and Dai Hounsell, contained essays exploring adults' learning processes informed by learners' own perceptions and experiences. Since then, two networks of educational psychologists, one in Great Britain and the other in Sweden, have examined "realistically complex student learning in natural settings" (Entwistle, 1976, p. 1), maintaining a cognitive approach to learning and allowing adults' experiences of their own learning processes to inform data analysis and theory building.

These researchers reject imposing predetermined categories on learners and using experimental laboratories for learning research. Instead, they seek to keep research on adults' learning in context, creating categories from information gathered qualitatively using action research (Entwistle & Hounsell, 1979), a grounded theory approach (Entwistle, 1984, 1985), or a phenomenographical approach (Marton, 1981, 1982). These researchers explore not, "How much is learned?" but rather, "What is learned?" (Dahlgren, 1984, p. 24) and emphasize, in Entwistle's phrase, that the verb "to learn" takes the accusative—that *something* is learned by *someone*, potentially in a variety of ways (1976). Below is a sample of studies conducted by these educational psychologists.

Learning from Written Texts

Examining how adult students learn from a given written text, Ference Marton and Roger Säljö (1976, 1984) interviewed thirty educational psychology students (no ages, genders, socioeconomic status, or racial/ethnic backgrounds reported[1]) in one study, and forty students (all women; no other background data provided) in another, who answered comprehension questions in qualitatively different ways after reading the provided texts. One result, which the researchers termed "astonishingly simple," was that "*the students who did not get 'the point' did not do so simply because they were not looking for it*" (Marton & Säljö, 1984, p. 39, original emphasis). They found that some adults described reading the text as if trying to memorize it, as if they saw themselves as "empty vessels, more or less, to be filled with the words on the page" (1984, p. 40). This approach was termed a "surface approach" to reading and learning, as contrasted with the "deep approach" taken by those whose reading process included looking for relationships between the text and their experiences. Learners using the deep approach "seemed to have seen themselves as creators of knowledge" (1984, p. 40) and reported reflecting on the text from their own experience. Surface approach learners reported being more anxious, skimming the text essentially trying to memorize it, not looking for and therefore not finding "the point," and being conscious of time pressures. Marton and Säljö (1976) found that the deep approach was associated with clear articulations of the author's main point, while the surface approach was associated with less coherent expressions of the point or missing the point altogether.

Learning from Lectures

Maintaining that most knowledge about lecturer effectiveness has been determined through pre- and post-test designs ignoring students' perceptions, Vivien Hodgson (1984) looked into college students' experiences of lectures. With a sample of thirty-one adults (no genders or backgrounds reported), she conducted playback sessions of lectures with students individually, interviewing them about their thoughts and feelings during the lectures. Hodgson found that these students experienced the relevance of lecture content in three ways: *extrinsically* (corresponding to the surface approach); *intrinsically* (corresponding to the deep approach); and *vicariously*, assuming the lecturer's enthusiasm for the material, or finding one example interesting, rather than the overall issue under discussion. Hodgson suggests that the vicarious response may be transitional between extrinsic and intrinsic understanding. She adds that the vicarious experience of lecture relevance helps to clarify the link between traditional studies' findings of lecturer enthusiasm and rapport as "effective" in student learning, and learners' actual experiences.

Learning through Essay Writing

Dai Hounsell (1984) researched thirty-three students' experiences of essay writing in history and psychology courses through two sets of semi-structured interviews about essay content and writing process (no genders or other background data reported). He found that students held three distinct conceptions of essay writing, which cut across preparation, content, and writing procedures: *the essay as viewpoint*, when the essay is seen as an ordered presentation of an opinion; *the essay as arrangement*, when the essay is considered to be an ordering of both facts and ideas; and *the essay as argument*, when the essay is seen as a presentation of an argument supported by evidence (1984). Hounsell notes that within academia, the argument approach is promoted and rewarded. He suggests that students who maintain the arrangement orientation may do so out of sheer workload, or may not share premises of knowledge with teachers. He also suggests that students maintaining the viewpoint approach seem to value self-expression and originality over doing the assignment in the expected argument form. However, Hounsell goes no further in exploring the more political implications of how educators may emphasize a "right way" of writing over originality and self-expression.

ADULT LEARNING FROM DEVELOPMENTAL PERSPECTIVES

Underlying many developmental explorations of learning is the Piagetian notion that individuals create meaning. Eleanor Duckworth writes: "Meaning is not given *to* us in our encounters, but it is given *by* us—constructed by us, each in our own way, according to how our understanding is currently organized" (1987, p. 112, original emphasis). Researchers reviewed in this section seek to understand how adults construct their learning and knowing over time.

Learning and Ways of Knowing

William Perry (1968) conducted an early inquiry into young adults' development. Interested in "the variety in students' response to the impact of intellectual and moral relativism" of the twentieth century (p. 10), Perry and his colleagues held 464 interviews with college students at the ends of four academic years (no background data included). Perry noticed patterns in how students structured their understandings of the world, identifying these as epistemological "positions" (1968). The Perry scheme includes nine developmental positions, ranging from a dualistic construction of experience and a search for right answers held by Authority, to increasing perception of relativism of knowledge and Authority's answers, toward a perception of all knowledge as relative, and responsibility within a relativistic world.[2]

Perry's research remains a landmark in demonstrating how the subjective, constructed experience of any learner influences how information is received and in documenting these experiences longitudinally. Perry (1968) illustrates how learners at different developmental positions may construct the same lecture, book, or discussion very differently. He also argues that what may be assumed to be differences in ability, intelligence or personality in educational settings may in fact reflect developmental process.

Dialectical Thinking

Michael Basseches (1984) also studied learning in the context of higher education, focusing on the cognitive structures adults use in constructing their understanding and experience of education. He interviewed a sample of college students and faculty members regarding their understanding of the nature of education and their experience of education in their common college setting (no background data given). His goal was to explore whether dialectical thinking— a cognitive structure able to hold multiple, interacting ideas at once—could be identified in subjects' responses.

Though within the Piagetian tradition, Basseches extends Piaget's study of knowing into adulthood. In addition, he criticizes Piaget's work for equating mature thought with an overly formalistic approach to problem solving. Basseches offers dialectical thinking as a conceptualization of postformal adult thinking in which systematization is appreciated, but where limitations of any system are recognized and the processes of system transformation are fundamental. His data illustrate dialectical thinking in adults' understanding of learning processes as more transformative in contrast to formal thinkers' image of learning as incorporation of powerful theories and methods.

Like other cognitive developmentalists, Basseches holds that adults develop through challenges that upset existing equilibria of thought. What then becomes important in *educational* settings is for instructors to promote adults' development through engaging with existing structures of thought, challenging those structures to their limits, being careful not to reach the point where learners experience this as an attack and react defensively. Basseches calls this balance of challenge and support an "optimal mismatch" (p. 304) and remarks that this stance in education is complicated further by the fact that any instructor also can experience upset of his or her cognitive equilibrium.

Learning and Ego Development

Jane Loevinger's (Loevinger, Wessler & Redmore, 1970; Loevinger, 1976) theory of ego development was another early framework to include adults as developing human beings. Here, "ego" is considered to be the underlying organizing principle of the self, including cognitive and interpersonal styles, impulse control, and character development. Individuals begin at the Presocial/ Symbiotic level, moving through the Impulsive, Self-Protective, Conformist, Self-Aware, Conscientious, Autonomous, and the rarely seen Integrated levels (see Loevinger, Wessler & Redmore, 1970).

As within Perry's developmental positions, individuals' experiences of education and educational settings within ego levels are qualitatively different (see also Kegan, 1982). Loevinger (1976) posits constructions of education across ego levels through analyses of the "Education is . . . " sentence stem given as part of the Sentence Completion Test. Within the Self-Protective level, education is a thing to get and then have; at the Conformist level it is the number of years of schooling, and is important for getting a job; at the Conscientious level, education affects inner life; while at the Autonomous level, education has intrinsic value and supports understanding.

Depending on ego level, then, one's experience of and attitude toward *education* necessarily varies. While Loevinger herself does not explore people's experiences of *learning* in more depth, others have applied her framework to learning in adults. Harry Lasker and Cynthia de Windt's mode (in Keeton and Associates, 1976; Weathersby, 1976) posit that adults within the Self-Protective level construct knowledge as something provided by external authority, while motivation to seek education is to *get* X. The learning process is constructed as *demonstration*, with authorities showing one how to do things. At the Conformist level, knowledge is constructed as objective truth, with the learning process constructed as one of *revelation* of truth by experts; here, education is sought in order to *be* X. From within the Conscientious level, knowledge is viewed as practical skills for problem solving, with learning constructed as *discovery* of right answers through analysis, acknowledging but not necessarily embracing multiple views; education is pursued to *do* X. At the Autonomous level, individuals construct knowledge as insights into life and its processes, with knowledge viewed as being gained through reflection on one's own experiences. The learning process becomes one of *examining personal insights and experiences*, with education pursued to *become* X.

Further examinations of the Loevinger framework as relevant to adults and learning were undertaken by Rita Weathersby (1977) and Jill Tarule (1978). Weathersby (1977) hypothesized that adults at different developmental levels would have varying conceptions of knowledge, authority, and responsibility in educational settings. Part of her research examined whether adults' reasons for enrolling in formal education, and their conceptions of education and their learning environments, would differ in ego level-related patterns.

Weathersby's (1977, 1980) interviews with sixty-seven adults (approximately 75% women, 25% men, age range 21 to 81; no other backgrounds given) provided the first data on developmental stages in adults within formal education. She found patterns by ego level in adults' reports of the supportive elements of their learning environments, as well as in their reasons for seeking a degree. Specifically, she found a qualitative shift in adults' constructions of learning at the Individualistic level: adults at this level and beyond seemed to "consciously appropriate their own process of learning" (1977, viii), and took more responsibility for their own learning. These adults also tended to appreciate learning from life experiences in contrast to educational settings.

Learning and the Process of Change

Jill Tarule (1978, 1980) examined the process of change itself with college students (no backgrounds given). She argues that developmental theory has focused on inter-stage differences in order to describe stages, and that descriptions are needed of what adults experience during intra-stage transitions. Tarule (1978, 1980) found distinct experiences during transitions, which did not demonstrate patterns by ego level, life cycle stages or gender. She hypothesized four steps during transitions, which may occur in a variety of speeds and sequences or with skipped steps.[3] These steps she called *diffusion*, marked by confusion as individuals' old ways of creating meaning are challenged; *dissonance*, in which individuals gained clarity about what was happening and could name and work with it; *differentiation*, in which individuals began to rebalance and integrate new perspectives; and definition, later called *coherence* (1980), in which there was less activity and an experience of greater integration or holding steady.

Learning and Women's Ways of Knowing

A study specifically exploring adults' experiences of learning was conducted by Mary Belenky, Blythe Clinchy, Nancy Goldberger, and Jill Tarule (1986). This examination of women's experiences of self, voice, and mind in learning and knowing drew on the work of Carol Gilligan (1979, 1982) on women's voices and their absence within the field of psychology and Perry (1968) on adults' ways of knowing based primarily on a male sample. They chose to interview only adult women in order to pursue whatever alternative patterns of development interviewing women might present. Continuing Perry's commitment to understanding experiences from the research participants' points of view, they interviewed 135 women from a variety of socioeconomic and racial backgrounds and formal educational experiences, although their resulting scheme is not broken down by these areas.

Belenky et al. (1986) present five main epistemological categories. They maintain that Perry posited potentially universal developmental *positions* because of his homogenous sample, similar in gender, race, socioeconomic status, and formal educational experiences. In contrast, Belenky et al. (1986) suggest that "When the context is allowed to vary . . . universal developmental pathways are far less obvious" (p. 15). These researchers therefore describe *perspectives* from which women know their worlds. While the perspectives resemble a developmental framework, because the work was not longitudinal the researchers acknowledge that further work will determine whether the perspectives on ways of knowing are developmental, categorical, or something else.

The five epistemological perspectives posited are *silence*, in which women experience themselves as voiceless and without internal experiences of authority; *received knowledge*, in which women construct themselves as able to receive knowledge from external authorities but as incapable of creating knowledge; *subjective knowledge*, in which women construct knowledge as primarily created subjectively or known intuitively and as personal; *procedural knowledge*, in which women construct themselves as capable of learning and applying procedures for gaining and communicating knowledge; and *constructed knowledge*, in which women conceive of themselves as creators of knowledge, value both objective and subjective knowing, and perceive knowledge as contextual.

As in other frameworks above, these women described experiencing learning and knowing in qualitatively different ways. Of the 135 women interviewed, almost half constructed experience from within the subjectivist perspective. Interestingly, the researchers heard women of all ages and backgrounds reporting "the discovery of subjective truth as the most recent and personally liberating event of their lives at the point at which we interviewed them" (p. 54). In other words, women across age, race, socioeconomic status, and educational groups named as important their shift from accepting *external* authority as truth to orienting towards their own *internal* authority as truth. The researchers note that constructing experience from the subjectivist perspective is double-edged.

Though experiencing inner truth as valid can be a breakthrough in learning and development, Belenky et al. (1986) note that "Women subjectivists are at a special disadvantage . . . when they go about learning . . . in the public domain" (p. 55), given current Western values trivializing personal knowledge.

Women's experiences from the procedural knowing perspective included more systematic approaches to knowledge. Belenky et al. heard two constructions, which they termed "separate" and "connected" knowing, using terms posed by Gilligan (1982) and later by Lyons (1983) describing experiences of self in relation. Belenky et al. (1986) use these terms to describe two epistemological orientations within the procedural position, with some individuals using separate knowing as engaging truth through "impersonal procedures," and those using connected knowing taking a stance in which "truth emerges through care" (p. 102). Although women used both orientations, those from traditional elite colleges tended to use predominately separate knowing orientations. This may reflect the training they received in generating knowledge through distanced stances, given the status this approach is accorded in traditional academia.

Most women within the constructed knowledge position had balanced separate and connected knowing in a new way, combining their own sense of what was important within knowledge stated by others to be important or true. They also perceived authorities in qualitatively different ways: while expertise was respected, only authorities acknowledging the complexity of contexts and maintaining some humility about their own perspectives were valued.

One finding of Belenky et al.'s work points to an important direction for research. When asked to describe important learning experiences, a majority of women who were mothers responded that childbirth had been a key learning experience, causing them to reevaluate how they saw themselves and experienced their own creativity. This highlights the need for explorations of what learning adults consider to be important in their own experience in order to better support adults' continued learning and growth (also see Maciuika, 1992).

LEARNING AS TRANSFORMATION

Theorists and researchers reviewed in this section explore learning that adults experience as challenging their perceptions, values, and assumptions, or ways of relating to others, themselves, or their environment.

Significant Learning

Psychologist Carl Rogers (1969) describes two types of learning along a spectrum. On one end he placed learning nonsense syllables for memorization and recall. On the other end was "significant learning," with learning connecting with a learner's life in meaningful ways. Rogers (1969) advocated the promotion of significant learning through an experiential approach.[4] He also highlighted the importance of being able to *learn how to learn* in order to live and love creatively in a society in which rapid change is a given. Throughout his career, Rogers (1977, 1980) continued to advocate what he came to recognize as a radical stance in both education and therapy: acknowledging learners as experts on their own experiences. Rogers recognized that this could threaten "experts" in both fields; acknowledging the primacy of learners' or clients' unique experiences can challenge educators' and therapists' authority. Yet, with such a stance, adults on both sides of classrooms or clinical offices become more open to exploring the differences and similarities they hold understanding their worlds. Rogers challenged educators to explore multiple realities and called on therapists to cease being originators of change in clients and instead be "midwives of change" (1977, p. 15). Rogers was one of the first North Americans to pose these challenges to psychology and education and also one of the first to examine the potentially radical implications of exploring learning from the learners' perspective.

Intrinsic Learning

Rogers' contemporary, Abraham Maslow (1968, 1971), also called for greater attention to learning that addresses individuals' experiences. Maslow (1971) described learning on a spectrum from extrinsic learning, having to do with skills and information, to intrinsic learning, having to do with character, personality, and soul. He argued that learning in formal educational settings holds little intrinsic value for learners. Instead, he supported inquiry into "character-change learning" (1968, p. 39), including the complexities of human experience from learners' understandings of their own growth and change.

In his explorations of adults' most important learning experiences, Maslow (1968) reports individuals' frequent descriptions of changes that resulted from tragedy or a sudden insight, "which forced change in the life-outlook of the person and consequently in everything he [sic] did" (p. 39). This linking of knowledge and action is one powerful implication of exploring authentic learning. Like Rogers, Maslow (1968) was aware of the radical consequences of exploring individuals' experiences, as once adults know their own experience "fully and completely, simple action follows automatically and reflexly" (p. 66). Intrinsic learning is therefore potentially threatening to those in power, as individuals examining their own experiences may be moved to action. Thus both Maslow and Rogers named the inherently political nature of such learning, maintaining that power structures in any situation may be challenged and changed through meaningful learning experiences.

Learning as Developing Critical Consciousness

Paolo Freire (1971, 1973; Shor & Freire, 1987) defined learning as adults exploring their experiences in social context, developing his ideas through literacy work in his native Brazil and in Chile. For Freire, one of the fundamental flaws in most formal education is its reliance on "banking" education (1971), in which the instructor deposits empty facts into students, who passively receive it. In contrast, Freire (1971, 1973) supports developing critical consciousness, supporting learners in developing knowledge connected to their own realities, and thereby becoming active subjects of their learning.

Freire (1972) states that any human being is by nature *in relationship* with others and with the world, and therefore creates reality only *through interaction* with others and with the world. Critical consciousness is developed through "conscientization," or critically examining given situations, relationships or norms. Such learning is by nature transformative; by engaging in critical dialogue, individuals become aware of their own contexts, increasingly becoming able to change their relationship to previously accepted truths about themselves and their contexts. In critical educator Ira Shor's (1980) term, learners take on a "de-socialization" process (p. 268). The vehicle for transformative learning of this nature is dialogue. Shor and Freire (1987) discuss dialogical education as an "epistemological position" (p. 100), from which both educators and learners explore the object of learning and the ways it is known, with educators re-learning along with students.

Learning as Critical Thinking

Stephen Brookfield (1986, 1987a, 1987b) has criticized adult education and learning research in the United States for holding the arrogant assumption that individuals who do not participate in formal education settings are disadvantaged in some way. Along with Belenky et al. (1986), Brookfield (1986) notes that most adults' important learning occurs outside of formal educational settings. He marks the complexity in the learning adults experience in family, work, and other settings and holds that this complexity has been ignored by most adult learning theorists and practitioners.

For Brookfield (1987a), learning to think critically in the contexts of relationships, work, and political involvements is "one of the most significant activities of adult life" (ix). This learning includes more than the logic skills often taught in critical thinking courses. Instead, critical thinking involves "calling into question the assumptions underlying our customary, habitual ways of thinking and acting and then being ready to think and act differently" (p. 1). Critical thinking is a creative ongoing process that increases active engagement in life and promotes the appreciation of diversity. The process may be initiated by trigger events, causing an adult to reappraise how he or she understands the world. But Brookfield (1987a) does not assume that critical thinking is sparked only by trauma, and he cites individuals' reports of peak experiences, falling in love, or feeling that things fit together as triggers for reassessing priorities and assumptions.

Brookfield notes that adults in his learning workshops often name learning about oneself as their most important form of learning (Brookfield, 1987a). Adapting Rogers' (1969) phrase, Brookfield (1987a) calls "significant personal learning" a critical reflection into underlying assumptions and alternative ways of living within relationships. This learning brings on questioning of one's assumptions about relating, and results in redefinition of some aspect of oneself. Along with Rogers, Maslow, and Freire, Brookfield (1987a) acknowledges the difficulty of this kind of learning. He states that questioning our assumptions is "psychologically explosive," since the frameworks through which we have been making sense of the world "can come crumbling down" (p. 30). Brookfield (1987a), along with other psychologists and educators (Belenky, Clinchy, Goldberger & Tarule, 1986; Kegan, 1982; Maslow, 1968; Morimoto, 1973; Perry, 1968; Rogers, 1969) recognizes the difficulty of losing familiar ways of knowing and being in the world, as old ways are left behind and new ways of being are explored.

Learning as Perspective Transformation

Jack Mezirow (1978, 1989) termed "meaning perspectives" the ways in which one's cultural and psychological assumptions influence understanding and relating to oneself and others. Perspective transformation involves developing the awareness that one is influenced by culture and context and the reexamination of one's assumptions (see also Gilligan, Brown, & Rogers, 1990). Mezirow (1978) states that different cultures, or the same culture at different times, will differ in terms of the opportunities provided for this kind of reassessment on a collective level. He cites the women's movement in the United States during the 1960s, during which time thousands of women engaged formally or informally in consciousness-raising activities, examining their assumptions about social and personal contexts. (Mezirow [1978] notes that this movement never found its way into the adult education literature.)

Mezirow (1978) explored community colleges that support women's reentry into formal education as contexts promoting individual perspective transformation. He developed thirty-six case studies of such reentry programs nationally, concluding that "the identification of perspective transformation [is] the central process occurring in the personal development of women participating in college re-entry programs" (p. 7). Along with Tarule (1978, 1980) and others examining adult learning as change and development, Mezirow (1978) noted patterns in self-descriptions of personal change, describing this process as a "transformative cycle" (p. 12). Phases might include a disorienting dilemma, engaging in self-examination, exploring new ways of being, building competence in new roles, and reintegrating into society based on new assumptions and new perspectives. Mezirow (1978) also noted psychological patterns within the reentry process and described eight different groups of learners. By defining and describing these processes of learning, Mezirow's work provides one model for adult learning as transformation, especially through phenomenological and ethnographic research.

Learning as a Change in Worldview

Canadian educational psychologist John Osborne (1985) describes learning as "increased receptivity to new experiences" (p. 196), a change in personality, or an increase in the novelty of experience. This learning involves a change of one's relationship to the world or one's "worldview" and includes a primary focus on an individual's "lived (phenomenological) experience within the learning context rather than observable behavioural and environmental correlates of that experience" (p. 196). This focus on internal experience and internal change has profound implications for research on learning. Osborne (1985) reviews the work of psychologists and philosophers who have considered learning as a change in worldview and describes human experiences that include worldview shifts, such as existential crises or a profound reciprocity in love relationships. Overall, Osborne holds that redefining learning as a change in worldview is "a more comprehensive way of conceptualizing learning that includes aspects of being-in-the-world that are usually neglected by natural science" (p. 204). Such a reconceptualization requires an explicit focus on *individual experiences* of learning, posing a challenge for natural science orientations, which often focus on behavioral manifestations of learning, failing to take into account learners' own experiences of their learning.

Learning as Growth of Consciousness

Canadian educator John Weiser (1987) explored adults' experiences of learning as a growth of consciousness. Citing work by Mezirow (1978) and Osborne (1985), as well as Roberto Assagioli's (1965) work on subpersonalities, Weiser suggests that individuals' changes in meaning perspectives, or their growth of consciousness, occurs in vertical and horizontal dimensions. With growth of consciousness in the vertical dimension, learning includes recognition of new connections among things that previously seemed unrelated, often occurring as a *Gestalt* experience, grasping a whole without reflecting on the parts. By contrast, the horizontal dimension of growth of consciousness is more a step-by-step process through small shifts of information and insight, rather than through immediate comprehension of a whole idea or experience.

Weiser studied several graduate students who were involved in qualitative research (no genders or backgrounds given) to examine their *own* growth of consciousness through the research process. Each researcher was involved in investigating participants' experiences of difficult situations. Weiser observed the extent to which researchers identified with their participants' difficulties. Those researchers who identified more closely with their participants experienced learning or growth of consciousness that was vertical, deeper, or more profound. These researchers became "co-participants," sharing a mutual process of learning with their research participants.

LEARNING IN ADULT EDUCATION

Recently, a number of researchers in adult education have reconceptualized inquiry into adults' experiences of learning. Despite varied interests, these researchers hold common commitments to (a) including themselves and their experiences in their research, (b) allowing adult learners to describe their own experiences of learning, and (c) adding unexplored areas of adult learning to the adult education literature.

Reexamining Self-Directed Learning

Marilyn Taylor (1987) examined self-directed learning from learners' perspectives after noticing that existing research was presented from educators' perspectives alone. She hypothesized that an ''inside-out'' investigation of the factors facilitating learning would allow both educators and learners to support learning more effectively. Taylor followed two men and six women (age ranges from 24 to 50; no other backgrounds given) through a graduate course on ''basic processes in facilitating adult learning.'' She interviewed each adult fourteen times, creating a conceptual framework from patterns she noticed in the data.

Taylor's learning pattern parallels those described by Tarule (1978, 1980) and Mezirow (1978, 1989). Taylor (1987) names phases of learning that she found in consistent order around particular themes. The phases were *disconfirmation* with a major discrepancy between expectations and experience); *disorientation* (with confusion and withdrawal from anyone associated with that confusion); *naming the problem* (without blame of self or others); *exploration* (relaxed inquiry into the issue at hand); *reflection* (private review); *reorientation* (synthesizing experiences, developing new approaches); *sharing the discovery* (trying out new understandings); and *equilibrium* (refining and applying new approaches). Adults proceeded through this cycle at different paces, experiencing initial disorientation at different times and for a variety of reasons during the course.

Intuitive Learning

In an effort to describe non-linear kinds of learning, Margaret Denis and Ingrid Richter (1987) explored intuitive learning, described as a ''thread,'' identifiable as an entity, but stronger when woven with other threads. They suggest that intuitive learning is stronger when used with other modalities of learning, but should not be overlooked as a modality in and of itself.

These authors discuss eighteen dynamics of intuitive learning identified through research conducted earlier by Denis (1979). Among these are remaining open to the unexpected, a sense of multiple realities, awareness of the dynamics of the unconscious, and recognizing revelation in the learning process. Denis and Richter also discuss ways of further developing a vocabulary of intuitive learning in order to allow for more complex descriptions of the qualities of intuitive learners and intuitive learning.

A related study was conducted by Lanie Melamed (1987) examining play and its connection to adults' experiences of learning, in an effort to add play and playfulness into the arena of adult learning research. She conducted semistructured interviews with nine white, middle-class women in their forties who considered themselves playful, using a grounded theory approach with the data. She discovered that, for these women, play was a way of being in the world, as opposed to an activity. She also found that those characteristics that make play possible also make openness to learning possible, as both involve risk, new connections, and remaining open to the unknown. Melamed describes five areas compatible with a playful approach to living and learning: *relational* (the capacity for connectedness); *experiential* (the ability to learn from experience); *metaphoric* (intuitive thinking); *integrative* (valuing organic connectedness); and *empowering* (facilitating transformation in oneself and in others). She concludes that both play and learning are potentially transformative, both leading learners from what is to what could be.

Authority and Power in Teaching and Learning

Seeking to explore "interdependence,"where mutual learning and co-created knowledge are supported and valued, Gwyneth Griffith (1987) engaged in an average of six hours of conversation with each of twenty-two adults. These were twenty women and two men (no ages or other backgrounds given), all in a graduate school group in which participants determined their own learning goals, planned the curriculum, and facilitated their own sessions. According to Griffith (1987), all of these learners had some unlearning to do in order to become more interdependent in their approach, but the needed unlearning differed depending on each learner's relationship to authority. As the group developed, she notes, the most fundamental change had to do with the transformation of authority and power. The facilitators ceased to hold and distribute knowledge exclusively; instead, knowledge became co-created by participants and facilitators. In short, paralleling Freire's stand on learning and Brookfield's ideas on critical thinking, Griffith states that in interdependent adult learning, a transformation occurs in which learning and teaching become one process.

The Researcher as Learner

Peter Reason and Judi Marshall (1987) hold that inquiry must be a process that is participatory, or "enquiry *with* people, rather than research *on* people, a personal process pursued in relation to others" (p. 113, original emphasis). They examine research as a process of personal development, offering examples of personal development and learning in four case studies created in collaboration with their own research students. These students speak about their experiences with choosing research questions, struggles in communicating with people in academic and work settings, and questioning the meaning of working toward a doctorate. Reason and Marshall reflect on ways to support students and colleagues in their inquiry, mindful that inquiry is partly a process of personal learning— and they invite researchers and supervisors to consider personal learning in their own work.

Learning as a Process of Experiencing Difference

Thelma Barer-Stein (1986) explored the idea that adult learning involves a process of experiencing differences between the familiar and the unfamiliar. She initially interviewed nine English as a Second Language teachers in Toronto in two studies (no genders or backgrounds given). She continued in-depth interviewing with one teacher, whom she called Elizabeth, exploring her process of learning as experiencing difference.

Barer-Stein (1986) offers a framework within which to understand learning as an experience of difference in general, as well as Elizabeth's learning in particular. She frames this process as one of volitional and cumulative phases including *observing, acting-in-the-scene,* and *involving oneself,* with a key intermediary phase of *confronting difference,* which determines whether or not involvement will occur. She also identifies four possible outcomes of confrontation with difference: *meeting and passing, engaging in conflict, withdrawing into oneself,* and *engaging oneself.* Barer-Stein holds that while the first outcome is passive and the others require action, only the last is a positive outcome, allowing an individual to be engaged; paradoxically, once involved, differences increasingly are taken for granted, until learning by experiencing difference begins anew.

DISCUSSION

The previous sections present four organizing themes for exploring adult learning from learners' own perspectives. The first, cognitive approaches, included cognitive researchers who present early moves in education and psychology toward taking an interest in adults' own perceptions of their learning. More fundamentally, their work acknowledges methodologically that there are adult learners engaged in learning. Their discussions, however, fail to pursue questions raised by some of these researchers themselves about the biases favoring certain discourses within higher educational settings. Nor do these researchers specify genders or backgrounds of their research participants. Given recent psychological and educational research discussing the implications of differences in a variety of settings (Belenky, Clinchy, Goldberger & Tarule, 1986; Delpit, 1988; Gilligan, 1982; Gilligan, Brown & Rogers, 1990; McCarthy, 1988), it seems crucial to us to include explicit discussions of how formal educational experience, gender, race, and socioeconomic background can influence adults' relationships to knowledge and authority.

Developmental perspectives constituted our second organizing theme, highlighting the various ways individuals experience the same learning situations. Basseches (1984), Perry (1968), and Loevinger (1976) examine underlying organizing principles of learning and knowing. Weathersby (1977, 1980), Tarule (1978, 1980), and Belenky et al. (1986) focus on narratives of learning and knowing, while building on earlier theories. Tarule's (1978, 1980) inquiry into the process of change itself during learning relates to that of Taylor (1987), as each describes initial periods of disorientation or confusion, gradually moving toward new understanding and balance.

Learning as transformation, our third organizing theme, highlights the notion that important learning involves connecting oneself to one's context in new ways. Psychologists such as Maslow (1968, 1971) and Rogers (1969, 1977, 1980) hold that the most import learning has intrinsic value to the learner. Both note the political implications of this stance, as it questions the nature of power in formal education and therapeutic relationships. Freire (1971, 1973) discusses the political activities of dialogue and conscientization as being by nature educational, causing learners to reflect in new ways about themselves and their sociopolitical contexts. Brookfield (1986, 1987a, 1987b) takes up the related theme of critical thinking, focusing on individuals' learning about the self-in-social-context, in contrast with the intrinsically community-oriented nature of Freire's work. Mezirow (1978, 1989) and Osborne (1982, 1985) reflect reconceptualizations of adult learning as a transformational process. Their theoretical discussions, as well as research by Weiser (1987), seek to broaden the definition of learning in adults and to examine that learning from learners' own perspectives.

Work in the area of adult education provided our fourth perspective. Although this literature overlaps with other themes, we find it interesting that these researchers all deliberately place their work within adult education. They challenge others to broaden their conceptions of adult education and learning, as well as the methodologies appropriate to exploring adult learning in greater depth. They also hold a common commitment to placing themselves and their experiences in their work, from explaining how their questions are important to them to relating their own processes in conducting their research.

The works within all four of the perspectives reviewed, then, represent varying degrees of departure from what has been the dominant, natural science approach within adult learning research. Common to all areas reviewed here is a break from methodologies borrowed from the natural sciences, using categorization and interpretation without participants' actual participation in naming the terms of their experience. We believe, along with many of the authors cited here, that such methods are poorly suited to exploring human experience, as they lead researchers to place complex experiences into predetermined and often reductionistic coding schemes and to guess at or ignore what meanings individuals' experiences hold for them. Such an approach may serve well in examining discrete, clearly-defined areas of human experience. However, for the less explored territory of adult learning from learners' perspectives, we join some of the authors here in suggesting that broadening learning research to include qualitative, exploratory approaches brings research participants into true participation, allowing them to voice their own experiences through their own terms and understandings.

Regardless of learning "area," then, many researchers in this review made a variety of methodological moves that allowed learners to name their experiences within research settings. We believe such moves are vital if adult learning and other human experiences are to be understood in their true-to-life complexity, creating knowledge grounded in terms informed and defined by adult learners. Along with broadening the definition of adult learning, listening to learners' perspectives challenges the fields of psychology and education to take into account complex stories of difference, rather than treating difference as a fixed variable to be controlled, as a problem or as a non-issue. By listening to learners' own perspectives on learning, by privileging learners' knowledge rather than researchers' frameworks, issues of difference and complexity enter discussions of theory as well as practice and thus challenge researchers and practitioners to take the role of learners themselves.

NOTES

1. Throughout, we will note background data given on research participants; we will also note the absence of reports on gender, age, socio-economic, educational, and racial/ethnic background. We do not suggest that including this information means results generalize to all members of a group, nor do we assert that these descriptors are exhaustive. Rather, our effort is to emphasize the importance of acknowledging the complexity of adults' contexts and background experiences, especially in exploring complex experiences such as learning.

2. While Perry interviewed both Harvard men and Radcliffe women, illustrations and validations for this study were taken almost exclusively from the men's data. This raises questions about the application of the scheme to both women and men, in addition to its relevance to populations outside of privileged university students (see Perry, 1968; Gilligan, 1982; Belenky, Clinchy, Goldberger & Tarule, 1986).

3. Compare these to stages of transformation posited by James Loder (1981), and elaborated on by Sharon Parks (1986).

4. Rogers' work (and the ideas of John Dewey, Kurt Lewin and Jean Piaget) generated a school of learning called "experiential learning," which we will not discuss here. Although it advocates an approach concentrating on learners' experiences, much of it is theoretical rather than applied (see Keeton & Tate, 1978; Kolb, 1984; and Walter & Marks, 1981, for discussions of experiential learning from a variety of perspectives).

REFERENCES

Assagioli, R. (1965). *Psychosynthesis*. New York: Viking.

Barer-Stein, T. (1986). Learning as a process of experiencing difference. Doctoral dissertation, University of Toronto, Ontario.

Basseches, M. (1984). *Dialectical thinking and adult development*. Norwood, NJ: Ablex.

Belenky, M. F., Clinchy, B. M., Goldberger, N. R. & Tarule, J. M. (1986). *Women's ways of knowing*. New York: Basic Books.

Boud, D. & Griffin, V. (Eds.). (1987). *Appreciating adults learning: From the learners' perspective*. London: Kogan Page Ltd.

Brookfield, S. D. (1986). *Understanding and facilitating adult learning*. San Francisco: Jossey-Bass.

———. (1987a). *Developing critical thinking*. San Francisco: Jossey-Bass.

———. (1987b). Significant personal learning. In D. Boud & V. Griffin (Eds.). *Appreciating adults learning: From the learners' perspective*, pp. 64–75. London: Kogan Page Ltd.

Dahlgren, L. Outcomes of learning. (1984). In F. Marton, D. Hounsell & N. Entwistle (Eds.). *The experience of learning*, pp. 19–35. Edinburgh: Scottish Academic Press.

Delpit, L. D. (1988). The silenced dialogue: Power and pedagogy in educating other people's children. *Harvard Educational Review*, *58*(3), 280–298.

Denis, M. (1979). Development of a theory of intuitive learning in adults based on descriptive analysis. Doctoral dissertation, University of Toronto, Ontario.

Denis, M. & Richter, I. (1987). Learning about intuitive learning: Moose-hunting techniques. In D. Boud & V. Griffin (Eds.). *Appreciating adults learning: From the learners' perspective*, pp. 25–36. London: Kogan Page Ltd.

Duckworth, E. (1987). *The having of wonderful ideas*. New York: Teachers College Press.

Entwistle, N. J. (1976). Editorial introduction. *British Journal of Educational Psychology*, *46*, 1–2.

———. (1984). Contrasting perspectives on learning. In F. Marton, D. Hounsell & N. Entwistle (Eds.). *The experience of learning*, pp. 1–18. Edinburgh: Scottish Academic Press.

———. (1985). Contributions of psychology to learning and teaching. In N. Entwistle (Ed.). *New directions in educational psychology: 1. Learning and teaching*, pp. 3–8. London: Falmer.

Entwistle, N. J. & Hounsell, D. (Eds.). (1975). *How students learn*. Lancaster, U.K.: Institute for Research and Development in Post-Compulsory Education.

Entwistle, N. J. & Hounsell, D. (1979). Student learning in its natural setting. *Higher Education*, *8*, 359–363.

Freire, P. (1971). *Pedagogy of the oppressed*. New York: Herder & Herder.

———. (1973). *Education for critical consciousness*. New York: Seabury Press.

Gilligan, C. (1979). Woman's place in man's life cycle. *Harvard Educational Review*, *49*, 431–446.

———. (1982). *In a different voice*. Cambridge, MA: Harvard University Press.

Gilligan, C., Brown, L. M., & Rogers, A. (1990). Psyche embedded: A place for body, relationships, and culture in personality theory. In A. Rabin, R. Zucker, R.

Emmons & S. Frank (Eds.). *Studying persons and lives*, pp. 86–147. New York: Springer.

Griffith, G. (1987). Images of interdependence: Authority and power in teaching and learning. In D. Boud & V. Griffin (Eds.). *Appreciating adults learning: From the learners' perspective*, pp. 51–63. London: Kogan Page Ltd.

Hodgson, V. (1984). Learning from lectures. In F. Marton, D. Hounsell & N. Entwistle (Eds.). *The experience of learning*, pp. 90–102. Edinburgh: Scottish Academic Press.

Hounsell, D. (1984). Understanding teaching and teaching for understanding. In F. Marton, D. Hounsell & N. Entwistle (Eds.). *The experience of learning*, pp. 103–123. Edinburgh: Scottish Academic Press.

Keeton, M. T. & Associates (1976). *Experiential learning: Rationale, characteristics, and assessment*. San Francisco: Jossey-Bass.

Keeton, M. T. & Tate, P. J. (Eds.) (1978). *Learning by experience: What, why, how*. Vol. 1. San Francisco: Jossey-Bass.

Kegan, R. (1982). *The evolving self*. Cambridge, MA: Harvard University Press.

Kolb, D. A. (1984). *Experiential learning: Experience as the source of learning*. Englewood Cliffs, NJ: Prentice-Hall.

Loder, J. E. (1981). *The transforming moment*. San Francisco: Harper & Row.

Loevinger, J. (1976). *Ego development*. San Francisco: Jossey-Bass.

Loevinger, J., Wessler, R., & Redmore, C. (1970). *Measuring ego development*. Vol. 1 & 2. San Francisco: Jossey-Bass.

Lyons, N. (1983). Two perspectives on self, relationships and morality. *Harvard Educational Review, 53*, 125–145.

Maciuika, L. (1992). "When their world has been rocked": Profound learning and psychological change in adults. Doctoral dissertation. Harvard University Graduate School of Education, Cambridge, MA.

Marton, F. (1981). Phenomenography: Describing conceptions of the world around us. *Instructional Science, 10*, 177–200.

———. (1982). Towards a phenomenography of learning. III: Experience and conceptualization. *Reports from the Department of Education*. Vol. 8. University of Gothenburg, Sweden.

Marton, F. & Säljö, R. (1976). On qualitative differences in learning. III: Outcome and process. *British Journal of Educational Psychology, 46*, 4–11.

———. (1984). Approaches to learning. In F. Marton, D. Hounsell & N. Entwistle (Eds.). *The experience of learning*, pp. 36–55. Edinburgh: Scottish Academic Press.

Marton, F., Hounsell, D. & Entwistle, N. (Eds.). (1984). *The experience of learning*. Edinburgh: Scottish Academic Press.

Maslow, A. H. (1968). *Toward a psychology of being*. 2nd ed. New York: Van Nostrand.

———. (1971). *The farther reaches of human nature*. New York: Viking.

McCarthy, C. (1988). Rethinking liberal and radical perspectives on racial inequality in schooling: Making the case of nonsynchrony. *Harvard Educational Review, 58*(3), 265–279.

Melamed, L. (1987). The role of play in adult learning. In D. Boud & V. Griffin (Eds.). *Appreciating adults learning: From the learners' perspective*, pp. 13–24. London: Kogan Page Ltd.

Mezirow, J. (1978). *Education for perspective transformation.* New York: Center for Adult Education, Teachers' College, Columbia University.

———. (1989). Transformation theory and social action: A response to Collard & Law. *Adult Education Quarterly, 39*(3), 169–175.

Morimoto, K. (1973). Notes on the context for learning. *Harvard Educational Review, 43*(2), 255–256.

Osborne, J. W. (1982). The hegemony of natural scientific conceptions of learning. *American Psychologist, 37,* 330–332.

———. (1985). Learning as a change in world view. *Canadian Psychology, 26*(3), 195–206.

Parks, S. (1986). *The critical years: The young adult searches for a faith to live by.* New York: Harper & Row.

Perry, W. G., Jr. (1968). *Forms of intellectual and ethical development in the college years.* New York: Holt, Rinehart and Winston.

Reason, P. & Marshall, J. (1987). Research as personal process. In D. Boud & V. Griffin (eds.), *Appreciating adults learning: From the learners' perspective,* pp. 112–126. London: Kogan Page Ltd.

Rogers, C. R. (1969). *Freedom to learn.* Columbus, OH: Charles E. Merrill.

———. (1977). *Personal power.* New York: Delacorte.

———. (1980). *A way of being.* Boston: Houghton Mifflin.

Säljö, R. (1979). Learning about learning. *Higher Education, 8,* 443–451.

———. (1984). Learning from reading. In F. Marton, D. Hounsell & N. Entwistle (Eds.). *The experience of learning,* pp. 78–89. Edinburgh: Scottish Academic Press.

Shor, I. (1980). *Critical teaching and everyday life.* Boston: South End Press.

Shor, I. & Freire, P. (1987). *A pedagogy for liberation.* South Hadley, MA: Bergin & Garvey.

Tarule, J. M. (1978). Patterns of transition in adulthood: An examination of the relationship between ego development stage variation and Gendlin's experiencing levels. Doctoral dissertation, Harvard Graduate School of Education, Cambridge, MA.

———. (1980). The process of transformation: Steps toward change. In E. Greenberg, K. M. O'Donnell & W. Bergquist (Eds.). *New directions for higher education: Educating learners of all ages.* No. 29. San Francisco: Jossey-Bass.

Taylor, M. (1987). Self-directed learning: More than meets the observer's eye. In D. Boud & V. Griffin (Eds.). *Appreciating adults learning: From the learners' perspective,* pp. 179–196. London: Kogan Page Ltd.

Walter, G. A. & Marks, S. E. (1981). *Experiential learning and change.* New York: John Wiley & Sons.

Weathersby, R. (1976). A synthesis of research and theory on adult development: Its implications for adult learning and postsecondary education. Qualifying paper, Harvard Graduate School of Education, Cambridge, MA.

———. (1977). A development perspective on adults' uses of formal education. Doctoral dissertation, Harvard Graduate School of Education, Cambridge, MA.

———. (1980). Education for adult development: The components of qualitative change. In E. Greenberg, K. M. O'Donnell & W. Bergquist (Eds.). *New directions for higher education: Educating learners of all ages*, pp. 9–22. San Francisco: Jossey-Bass.

Weiser, J. (1987). Learning from the perspective of growth of consciousness. In D. Boud & V. Griffin (Eds.). *Appreciating adults learning: From the learners' perspective*, pp. 99–111. London: Kogan Page Ltd.

18

Enhancing Adult Critical Thinking Skills through Cooperative Learning

Barbara Millis, Neil Davidson, and Philip Cottell

One of the "Seven Principles for Good Practice in Undergraduate Education" identified by a thirteen-member team of education researchers from various institutions calls for "Cooperation among Students." Chickering and Gamson (1987) elaborate on this principle:

> Learning is enhanced when it is more like a team effort than a solo race. Good learning, like good work, is collaborative and social, not competitive and isolated. Working with others often increases involvement in learning. Sharing one's ideas and responding to others' reactions improves thinking and deepens understanding. (p. 1)

Even though, as Diane Lee has noted elsewhere in this volume, collaborative learning has become a common buzzword, many scholars have recognized (Gere, 1987; Goodsell, Maher, Tinto, Smith & MacGregor, 1992) that collaboration in the classroom has a long history. Those who relish the challenges of teaching adult learners have long recognized the value of small group work. Malcolm Knowles (1980), for example, has for years advocated the use of small groups, suggesting that "with larger groups the ideal situation can be approximated . . . by an imaginative use of subgroupings" (p. 226). Stephen Brookfield (1986) specifically notes: "The distinct tradition in the facilitation of adult learning is that of adults meeting as equals in small groups to explore issues and concerns and then to take action as a result of these explorations" (pp. 14–15). Motivation for learning can be enhanced by a student-centered, facilitative approach, one that actively engages adults as participants in the learning process. When well structured, small group work provides experiential instruction, respects and capitalizes on adults' prior learning, offers active problem-solving opportunities, fulfills facilitative needs, and contributes variety to learning activities. Because small group work, however, often is not well orchestrated, recent attention has focused on a more structured form of collaborative learning in small groups, known as "cooperative learning."

Cooperative learning might be considered a subset of collaborative learning because, by definition, all cooperative learning activities involve collaboration. But as William Whipple (1987) admits, collaborative learning embraces an "extraordinarily wide range of programs, projects, pedagogical techniques and classroom strategies" (p. 3). It can include a variety of classroom approaches, including the use of case studies, problem-centered instruction, peer teaching, and editing. Cooperative learning, on the other hand, differs from collaborative learning by focusing on group work using, as Jim Cooper (1990) notes, "structures designed to ensure student-student interdependence" and by emphasizing "individual accountability" through "individually completed tests and papers, rather than undifferentiated group grades for team work" (p. 1). Unlike collaborative learning, cooperative learning is, according to Robert Slavin (1989–1990b), "one of the most thoroughly researched of all instructional methods" (p. 52). Johnson, Johnson, and Smith (1991) conclude:

During the past 90 years, over 575 experimental and 100 correlational studies have been conducted by a wide variety of researchers in different decades with different age subjects, in different subject areas, and in different settings. . . . Far more is known about the efficacy of cooperative learning than about lecturing, . . . the use of technology, or almost any other facet of education. (p. 28)

Furthermore, although much of the research has been conducted at the K–12 level, Natasi and Clements (1991) conclude that the benefits of cooperative learning, described as "enhance[d] academic achievement and cognitive growth, motivation and positive attitudes toward learning, social competence, and interpersonal relations," seem to be universal. They emphasize that:

Cognitive-academic and social-emotional benefits have been reported for students from early elementary through college level, from diverse ethnic and cultural backgrounds, and having a wide range of ability levels. . . . Furthermore, cooperative learning has been used effectively across a wide range of content areas, including mathematics, reading, language arts, social studies, and science. (p. 111)

Thus, cooperative learning is also one of the most versatile educational strategies available. It can be used effectively in virtually any setting that involves adult learning, ranging from college and university classrooms to informal adult learning groups.

WHAT IS COOPERATIVE LEARNING?

Several researchers, such as Schmuck (1985) and Davidson (1990), trace the philosophical basis of cooperative learning to John Dewey's emphasis on experiential learning and the role of the schools in preparing students for life in a cooperative, democratic society. Hassard (1990) finds its roots "in the work on synergy by Ruth Benedict and Margaret Mead and in the psychological models developed by Abraham Maslow and Carl Rogers" (p. viii). Sherman (1990) sees it evolving from Kurt Lewin's impact on the group dynamics movement of the early 1940s, influenced in particular by Lewin's student Morton Deutsch, with his interest in "applied" social psychology. Brown and Palincsar (1989) believe that several different research traditions have influenced the cooperative learning movement, including Piagetian and Vygotskian theories in developmental psychology.

Cooperative learning tends to be more carefully structured and delineated than most other forms of small group learning. Cooper and Mueck (1989) describe it as "a structured, systematic instructional strategy in which small groups work together toward a common goal" (p. 1). Most experts agree that several components distinguish cooperative learning from other small group procedures, including collaborative learning.

Positive interdependence occurs, according to Kagan (1989), "when gains of individuals or teams are positively correlated" (p. 4:3). The Johnson brothers in numerous publications use the expression "sink or swim together." Basically, all members of a learning team contribute to each other's learning. Through careful planning, positive interdependence can be established by (a) mutual goals, such as reaching a consensus on a problem's solution; (b) mutual rewards, such as team grades based on a composite of each member's improvement or on a random selection of one team member's paper or quiz to represent the team score; (c) structured tasks, such as a report with sections contributed by each team member; and (d) interdependent roles, such as group members serving as discussion leaders, organizers, recorders, and spokesperson.

A second component, *individual responsibility*, tends to eliminate "free riders/coasters/sandbaggers" and "workhorses" or "dominators." Because of carefully structured activities and assignments, adult students have a vested interest in helping teammates, but if grades are involved, they reflect individual learning, not undifferentiated group grades. Most adults are mature enough to recognize the intrinsic value of cooperating in learning teams. Those enrolled in non-credit programs or, to use Alan Knox's (1986) term, "proficiency-oriented adult learning" are even more inclined to cooperate in order to reach their educational goals. The literature on adult education emphasizes the strong motivation of self-directed learners. Cooperative learning also empowers adults, including women and diverse students, who would lose their voices in traditional learning situations where the teacher, however well-meaning, dominates.

Appropriate grouping is also essential. Researchers such as Kagan (1989) and Johnson, Johnson, Holubec, and Roy (1984) recommend heterogeneous teams, reflecting varied learning abilities, ethnic and linguistic diversity, and a mixture of the genders. Elizabeth Cohen (1986), on the other hand, advocates random grouping because of the adverse status effects of heterogeneous grouping. In a semester-length academic course, most practitioners recommend teacher-selected learning teams of four whose composition can be changed every six weeks or so. In briefer situations, short-term teams focusing on specific learning goals are appropriate; depending on the task and the group members, these teams can be homogenous. Because adults are workplace oriented and because most employers value cooperation and teamwork, heterogeneous teams provide opportunities to prepare for or to reinforce practices needed in the "real world." The Total Quality Management (TQM) movement, for example, has spread from industry to academe (Marchese, 1991).

A fourth component, *group processing*, helps build team skills, allows adults to reflect on the learning process and outcomes, and provides facilitators with continuous feedback. Teachers and students monitor group and individual progress. After an assignment or activity, for instance, adult participants could respond to questions such as: "Did all members of the group contribute?" "What could be done next time to make the group function better?" or "What were the most important things I learned today?"

Social skills are also important in cooperative learning, but may not need to be taught directly to adults as they often are to younger learners. Some orientation is needed, however, to help adult students recognize the importance of cooperative interaction and mutual respect. Adult learning facilitators should model appropriate social skills, including ways of providing constructive feedback or eliciting more indepth responses through probing questions. They may also reinforce these social skills by publicly complimenting students who use them effectively.

Would-be practitioners are reassured by the fact that cooperative learning techniques rarely replace, in toto, traditional approaches to learning such as the lecture or teacher-directed discussion. Cooper (1990) notes that most college and university faculty use cooperative learning techniques only about 15% to 40% of the total class time available (p. 2). As Slavin (1989–1990a) cautions, "Successful [cooperative learning] models always include plain old good instruction; the cooperative activities *supplement* but do not replace direct instruction" (p. 3). The integration of cooperative learning techniques into traditional delivery methods such as lecture does emphasize the facilitative approach most adults welcome. Power is shifted from the authority figure of the instructor to the adult students, who then become actively involved in their own learning and in the learning processes of their peers. In informal terms, the teacher becomes not the "sage on the stage" but "the guide on the side." This approach is particularly effective in short adult-centered seminars. Cooperative learning structures can provide a framework for learning if students are given enough "think time" to foster critical reflection.

For college settings, evaluation remains, as always, an area of crucial concern for both adult students and faculty. Because cooperative learning approaches must be integrated into course content and philosophy, they are sometimes linked with noncompetitive grading practices such as learning contracts or mastery learning, practices particularly suited to adult learners. Malcolm Knowles (1980), in fact, regards contract learning as "a truly magical way to help learners structure their own learning" (p. 243). Evaluation can be done also through traditional methods such as in-class or take-home tests or quizzes, group projects, homework, self-evaluation, and peer evaluation, provided that the grades reflect individual accountability and that all groups have had an opportunity to master the assigned material. Practices such as grading on the curve can sabotage cooperative group efforts because they set up an "I win, you lose" mentality as students compete for the scarce commodity, As.

COOPERATIVE LEARNING STRATEGIES

Flexibility is a key virtue of cooperative learning. Although the work of Robert Slavin (1986) and his colleagues at Johns Hopkins University has focused on curriculum-and-domain-specific learning, most cooperative learning structures can be used at all grade levels (K through graduate school) in virtually all academic disciplines. They are extremely effective in all types of situations involving adult learners, including such diverse cases as a church Bible-study group, continuing education opportunities for certified public accountants, faculty development efforts, and actor training studios. Some of the structures best suited to adult learning are:

Think-Pair-Share: In this activity, developed by Frank Lyman (1981), the facilitator/instructor poses a question, preferably one demanding analysis, evaluation, or synthesis, and gives students/participants a brief period to think through an appropriate response. This "wait time" can be spent writing, also. Students then turn to their partners and share their responses. During the last stage, responses can be shared with a learning team, with a larger group, or with an entire class during a follow-up discussion. The caliber of discussion is enhanced by this technique, and all students have an opportunity to learn by reflection and by verbalization.

Corners: Based on a teacher-determined criterion such as their stands on a controversial issue, students divide themselves into several large subgroups, each with a common interest or belief or preference. For example, in a political science class, students might group themselves according to their favorite presidential candidate. This technique, called corners simply because facilitators usually point to a section of a room where students are to meet, provides a quick way to group adults homogeneously.

Three-Step Interview: Common as an ice-breaker or a team-building exercise, this structure can also be used to share ideas promoting critical thinking, such as reactions to a film or article or the sharing of prior knowledge, experience, or informed opinions. In this structure, adults interview one another in pairs, alternating roles as speakers and listeners. They then share in a four-member learning team, composed of two pairs, the information or insights gleaned from the paired interview. Prior learning experiences, important for adults, can be highlighted in this exercise.

Numbered Heads Together: Members of learning teams, usually composed of four individuals, count off: 1, 2, 3, and 4. The teacher poses a question, sometimes factual in nature, but requiring some higher-order thinking skills. Students discuss the question, making certain that every group member knows the answer. The instructor calls a specific number, and the designated team members (1, 2, 3, or 4) respond as group spokespersons. Again, adults can enhance their critical thinking skills from the verbalization, and the peer coaching helps both the high and the low achievers master concepts and content. Less time is wasted on inappropriate responses, and all adult students become actively involved with the material. Because no one knows which number the teacher will call, all team members have a vested interest in being able to articulate the appropriate response. Furthermore, because it is a team and not an individual response, adults who might not otherwise speak up in class are far more willing to participate.

Roundtable: In this brainstorming technique, adults in a learning team take turns writing on a single pad of paper, saying their ideas aloud as they write. As the tablet circulates, more and more information is added until various aspects of a topic are explored. This exercise validates the contributions of all group members, but also emphasizes the need for interaction in generating ideas, a good reinforcement for critical thinking.

Co-op Cards: In this procedure, useful for memorization and review, students coach each other using flashcards. Each student prepares a set of flashcards with a question on the front and the answer on the back. When a student answers a question correctly, the partner hands over the card; they continue going through the set until all questions have been answered correctly. The pair then reverses roles, using the second set of questions and answers prepared by the other partner until both students have mastered both sets of questions.

Pass-a-Problem: Each group or team identifies or is given a specific issue to focus upon. The groups independently brainstorm solutions to their particular issues, inserting their ideas into a manila folder or envelope. The folder or envelopes are passed to another group, so that each team now has a second issue to consider. The groups—without looking inside—then brainstorm again and put their solutions to the new issue in the folder or envelopes, which are passed for a third time. This time each team reads the solutions posed by the two other groups, adds any of their own, and then stars the top two solutions. This activity promotes active problem solving and builds positive interdependence.

Expert Jigsaw: The faculty member or facilitator divides an assignment or topic into four parts with one person from each "home" learning team volunteering to become an "expert" on one of the parts. Four expert teams with members from each home team with the same topic then work together to master their fourth of the material and to discover the best way to help others learn it. All experts then reassemble in their home learning teams, where they teach the other group members. This strategy, which fosters higher-order thinking and results in peer teaching, was originally described by Aronson (1978).

COOPERATIVE LEARNING AND ADULTS

In a review of the research literature on teaching and learning in the college classroom, McKeachie, Pintrich, Lin, and Smith (1986) conclude: "The best answer to the question, 'What is the most effective method of teaching?,' is that it depends on the goal, the student, the content, and the teacher. But the next best answer is, 'Students teaching other students' '' (p. 63). Hassard (1990) summarizes some of the benefits of cooperative learning:

Educational theorists such as David and Roger Johnson, Robert Slavin, and Spencer Kagan reported that cooperative learning resulted in high academic achievement; provided a vehicle for students to learn from one another; gave educators an alternative to the individual, competitive model; and was successful in improving relationships in multiethnic classrooms. (p. viii)

Cooper, Prescott, Cook, Smith, Mueck, and Cuseo (1990) in "The Case for Cooperative Learning in the College Classroom" explain the research basis for cooperative learning's ability to develop higher-level thinking skills; promote student learning and achievement; increase student retention; enhance student satisfaction with the learning experience and promote positive attitudes toward subject matter; develop student skill in oral communication; develop students' social skills; promote student self-esteem; and promote positive race relations.

Cooperative learning techniques are particularly suitable for adult, self-directed learners. Patricia Cross's (1981) "Characteristics of Adults as Learners" (CAL) model makes it relatively easy to see that cooperative learning methods can operate across all three of the continua (physical, sociocultural, and psychological) by creating a "warm, and accepting environment on the physiological dimension; a cooperative, adventuresome environment on the life-phase continuum; and a challenging environment for stimulating developmental growth on the developmental-stage continuum" (p. 240). Indeed, by its very nature, cooperative learning complements perfectly current theories on adult learning. Philip Candy (1991) emphasizes, for instance: "Adult education is distinguished by the extent to which it arises naturally as a result of, and takes place within, social contexts" (p. 22). Donald Schon (1990) urges educators to serve as coaches who provide the "freedom to learn by doing in a setting relatively low in risk" (p. 17). The recent work of Jack Mezirow (1990; 1991) on transformative and emancipatory learning also encourages adult educators to serve as mentors who are committed to helping learners "become more imaginative, intuitive, and critically reflective of assumptions; to become more rational through effective participation in critical discourse; and to acquire meaning perspectives that are more inclusive, integrative, discriminating, and open to alternate points of view" (1991, p. 224). Such learning cannot occur through traditional delivery methods with "authority figures" lecturing to passive adults. In fact, as Giezkowski (1992) points out, the large influx of adult students into colleges and universities—because they are focused and pragmatic and bring with them a wealth of life experiences—has often revitalized the learning environment. Faculty or facilitators are challenged to juggle the conflicting expectations they may have. Versatility is the key. Successful teaching depends on "the flexibility of a college instructor's teaching repertoire and his or her readiness to draw on a range of teaching styles for a variety of ends" (Adams, 1992, p. 15). Varied learning approaches, including cooperative learning, are critically important, Cross (1991) argues, because of what we know of learning:

What do students already know, and how can new learning be framed to make meaningful connections? The more teachers can develop analogies and metaphors to relate to the backgrounds of students, the more likely new knowledge will become integrated into the schemata or knowledge structure that represents the student's understanding. (p. 28)

Cooperative learning, by allowing time for reflection, rehearsal, and peer teaching, can stimulate adults and those who facilitate their learning.

INFORMAL COOPERATIVE LEARNING IN ADULT LIFE

This stimulation can occur in virtually any setting where adults gather to explore meaningful topics. Cooperative learning techniques, because of their versatility and flexibility, can be extremely effective outside formal college classrooms as well, as the following examples illustrate.

Church Bible Study Group

Phil Cottell developed a cooperative learning structure to replace the traditional leader-dominated model of Bible study. Named Cooperative Bible Study (CBS), the structure is a hybrid of the Think-Pair-Share and the Three Step Interview.

In CBS the leader, rather than the participants, reads the passage of scripture, allowing them to listen to the passage instead of worrying about their reading skills. It also avoids inevitable problems caused by the diverse translations now in use.

The leader allows a time of silence and reflection after the reading. The importance of think time in structured small group work is well documented. Moreover, a time for reflection and meditation in Bible study is important in seeking a deeper understanding of scripture.

After the moments of silence, the leader pairs participants into heterogeneous dyads (pairs) based on experience and gender. Each person is asked to tell the partner what the passage of scripture says to him or her personally. The leader permits time for this to occur and may circulate among groups or share with a partner, also.

At a prearranged signal, the pairs reassemble into the group as a whole. The leader asks the group members to share not their own perspectives but instead their partner's. The leader also encourages people to avoid the views of "authorities" or commentators.

The CBS has many advantages over the traditional Bible study. Listening skills are enhanced by the scripture recitation and by reporting a partner's perspective. As one does not bring one's own views or the views of commentators to the discussion, participants are less likely to become adamant about defending those views.

CBS promotes bonding and caring in small Bible study groups, because one-on-one interaction between group members is structured into meeting times. People hear their views expressed and respected by others in the larger group interaction. Even those persons shy about sharing their religious views in a small group find that the intimacy of the pair gives them a voice. Thus, far greater participation occurs with CBS than with traditional studies.

The leader receives additional benefits. He or she no longer has to play the role of the scripture "authority," but can be a more relaxed group member.

Continuing Education for Certified Public Accountants

Hugh Hoyt is the administrative partner of a firm (AHI) that provides continuing professional education programs for local and regional CPA firms across the nation. Hugh has developed teaching techniques that employ structured small group work in numerous staff training programs offered by AHI over a period of twenty years.

When introduced to the recent literature on cooperative learning in college classrooms, Hugh recognized that structured group work meshed closely with techniques used in AHI's programs. Cooperative learning gave Hugh a more precise terminology, such as "numbered heads," to describe the effective teaching methods employed by his company.

Cooperative learning structures increase the enjoyment and attention span of the Certified Public Accountants who attend AHI's staff training programs. The high ratings received by AHI discussion leaders provide evidence of the success of the cooperative learning methods employed by Hugh. To Hugh, the most important benefit of cooperative learning comes from the fact that participants in staff training programs learn more and retain this learning longer.

Actor Training Studio

Janice Dean, head of the Actor Training Program at Miami University, conducts a studio for men and women who aspire to be professional actors. Structured small group work plays an integral part in the training of Janice's acting students.

In one effective structure, students study Stanislavski's Actor Training Model as an out-of-class assignment. Janice then pairs students into teams whose assignment is to develop a script that illustrates a portion of the model. Finally, these pairs act out the script before their peers. This structure replaces traditional lecture about the Actor Training Model.

Janice also uses the Meisner Technique to teach aspiring actors the need to be aware of fellow actors in a play. In this technique paired students develop their ability to concentrate on their peers by means of an in-class exercise. Janice has the students begin in random pairs who look into the eyes of each other and call out what they see. As students develop this ability, they progress to in-class, impromptu script playing where their fellow actor has differing goals.

Students respond to these in-class exercises enthusiastically and express disappointment on days when time does not permit all of them to participate. Acting ability improves markedly, and students frequently make a major break-through in performance during class periods.

Many other examples can be drawn from other areas. Many people, for example, spend hours sitting around long tables in non-productive meetings conducted by authority figures. Instead of this format, groups wishing to stimulate problem solving and creative brainstorming can adopt cooperative learning techniques such as Roundtable or Pass-a-Problem.

COOPERATIVE COGNITION

One of the key uses of cooperative learning is to stimulate both critical and creative thinking. In education, business, and government, memorization of masses of information is not an adequate goal; in fact, with the doubling of the world's stores of information every few years, it becomes impossible for any individual to keep up with all this information even in a narrow field. Much more important are the abilities to locate information when needed, to process it, and to apply it in problem solving and decision making.

A book by Davidson and Worsham (1992) presents numerous strategies for fostering cooperative problem solving and decision making. The intellectual power of a group far outstrips that of individuals in addressing such complex tasks as a challenging research problem in mathematics or science, the design of new technology for a computer system or stereo system, or a social issue such as disease control or crime prevention.

In business and industry, there is a new emphasis on cooperation and teamwork (Hilt, in Davidson and Worsham, 1992). Many of the leading corporations are moving towards the use of facilitative management practices involving cooperation and teamwork. The movement toward total quality management incorporates development of cross-functional work teams, quality circles, and a host of other small group techniques as a means of fostering continuous improvement in quality and timeliness of work.

In recent years a host of books have been written about cooperation and teamwork in the business world (for example, Kinlaw, 1990). The emphasis on teamwork in business and industry parallels the emphasis on cooperation learning in schools, colleges, and continuing education. Students of all levels who are learning skills in interpersonal communication, conflict resolution, group problem solving, and group decision making are being prepared appropriately to function in the contemporary business world.

The cries for educational reform and the challenges facing higher education and society in general are well known. "Today's professors are challenged to teach a student population increasingly diverse in age, levels of academic preparation, styles of learning, and cultural background. Professors are now expected not only to 'cover the material,' but also to help students to think critically, write skillfully, and speak competently" (Ekroth, 1990, p. 1). Faculty teaching adults are especially challenged. They must learn to help build the "supportive and active learning environment" advocated by Knox (1986). They must learn to celebrate student diversity—minorities, older students, part-time learners, underprepared underachievers—and to find ways to both motivate and educate adults for the twenty-first century.

REFERENCES

Adams, M. (1992). Cultural inclusion in the American college classroom. In Chism, N.V.N. & Border, L.L.B. (Eds.). *Teaching for diversity*. New Directions for Teaching and Learning, no. 49, San Francisco: Jossey-Bass.

Aronson, E. (1978). *The jigsaw classroom*. Beverly Hills, CA: Sage Publications.

Astin, A. W. (1991, July 24). VMI case dramatizes basic issues in the use of educational research. *Chronicle of Higher Education*. Point of View, *37*(44), A36.

Brookfield, S. D. (1986). *Understanding and facilitating adult learning*. San Francisco: Jossey-Bass.

Brown, A. L. & Palincsar, A. S. (1989). Guided, Cooperative Learning and Individual Knowledge Acquisition. In L. B. Resnick (Ed.). *Knowing, Learning, and Instruction: Essays in Honor of Robert Glaser* (pp. 391–451). Hillsdale, NJ: Lawrence Erlbaum.

Candy, P. C. (1991). *Self-direction for lifelong learning*. San Francisco: Jossey-Bass.

Chickering, A. W. & Gamson, Z. F. (1987). Seven principles for good practice in undergraduate education [special insert]. *The Wingspread Journal*, *9*(2).

Cohen, E. (1986). *Designing groupwork: Strategies for the heterogeneous classroom*. New York: Teachers College.

Cooper, J. L. & Mueck, R. (1989). Cooperative/collaborative learning: Research and practice (primarily) at the collegiate level. *The Journal of Staff, Program, and Organization Development*, *7*(3), 149–151.

Cooper, J. L. (1990). What is cooperative learning? *Cooperative Learning and College Teaching*, *1*(1), 2.

Cooper, J., Prescott, S., Cook, L., Smith, L., Mueck, R., & Cuseo, P. (1990). *Cooperative Learning and College Instruction: Effective Use of Student Learning Teams*. Long Beach, CA: California State Health Foundation.

Cross, K. P. (1981). *Adults as learners*. San Francisco: Jossey-Bass.

Cross, K. P. (1991, October). Effective college teaching. *ASEE Prism*, 27–29.

Davidson, N. (1990). The small-group discovery method in secondary and college-level mathematics. In N. Davidson (Ed.). *Cooperative learning in mathematics: A handbook for teachers* (pp. 335–361). Menlo Park, CA: Addison-Wesley.

Davidson, N. & Worsham, T. (1992). *Enhancing Thinking through Cooperative Learning*. New York: Teachers College Press, Columbia University.

Deutsch, M. (1960). The effects of cooperation and competition upon group process. In D. Cartwright and A. Zander (Eds.), *Group Dynamics: Research and Theory*. New York: Harper and Row.

Ekroth, L. (1990). Why professors don't change. In L. Ekroth (Ed.), *Teaching Excellence:*

Toward the Best in the Academy (Winter-Spring). Stillwater, OK: Professional and Organizational Development Network in Higher Education.

Gere, A. R. (1987). *Writing Groups: History, Theory, and Implications.* Carbondale: Southern Illinois University Press.

Giezkowski, W. (1992). The influx of older students can revitalize college teaching. *The Chronicle of Higher Education, 38*(29), 133–134.

Goodsell, A., Maher, M., Tinto, V., Smith, B. & MacGregor, J. (1992). *Collaborative Learning: A Sourcebook for Higher Education.* University Park, PA: National Center on Postsecondary Teaching, Learning, and Assessment.

Hassard, J. (1990). *Science experiences: Cooperative learning and the teaching of science.* Menlo Park, CA: Addison-Wesley.

Johnson, D. W., Johnson, R. T., Holubec, E. J. & Roy, P. (1984). *Circles of learning: Cooperation in the classroom.* Alexandria, VA: Association for Supervision and Curriculum Development.

Johnson, D., Johnson, R. & Smith, K. (1991). *Cooperative learning: Increasing college faculty instructional productivity.* ASHE-ERIC Higher Education Report No. 4. Washington, DC: George Washington University, School of Education and Human Development.

Kagan, S. (1989). *Cooperative learning resources for teachers.* Laguna Niguel, CA: Resources for Teachers.

Kinlaw, D. (1990). *Developing superior work teams.* New York: Free Press.

Knowles, M. (1980). *The modern practice of adult education: From pedagogy to andragogy.* Chicago: Follett.

Knox, A. B. (1986). *Helping adults learn: A guide to planning, implementing, and conducting programs.* San Francisco: Jossey-Bass.

Light, R. J. (1990). *Harvard assessment seminars, first report: Explorations with students and faculty about teaching, learning, and student life.* Cambridge, MA: Harvard University Graduate School of Education and Kennedy School of Government.

Lyman, F. (1981). The responsive classroom discussion. In A. S. Anderson (Ed.). *Mainstreaming Digest.* College Park, MD: University of Maryland College of Education.

Marchese, Ted. (November 1991). TQM reaches the academy. *AAHE Bulletin, 44*(3), 3–9.

McKeachie, W. J., Pintrich, P. R., Lin, Y. & Smith, D. A. (1986). *Teaching and learning in the college classroom: A review of the research literature.* Ann Arbor: University of Michigan.

Merriam, S. B. & Caffarella, R. S. (1991). *Learning in adulthood.* San Francisco: Jossey-Bass.

Mezirow, J. (1991). *Transformative dimensions of adult learning.* San Francisco: Jossey-Bass.

Mezirow, J. & Associates. (1990). *Fostering critical reflection in adulthood: A guide to transformative and emancipatory learning.* San Francisco: Jossey-Bass.

Natasi, B. K. & Clements, D. H. (1991). Research on cooperative learning: Implications for practice. *School Psychology Review, 20*(1), 110–131.

Schmuck, R. (1985). Learning to cooperate, cooperating to learn: Basic concepts. In R. Slavin, S. Sharan, S. Kagan, R. Hertz-Lazarowitz, C. Webb & R. Schmuck (Eds.). *Learning to cooperate, cooperating to learn* (pp. 5–15). New York: Plenum Press.

Schon, D. A. (1990). *Educating the Reflective Practitioner*. San Francisco: Jossey-Bass.

Sherman, L. (1990, March). Cooperative Pedagogies in Psychology: Implications from Social Psychology for Active Learning Experiences. Paper presented at the Fourth Annual Conference on Undergraduate Teaching of Psychology, Springfield, MA.

Slavin, R. E. (1986). *Using student team learning: The Johns Hopkins team learning project*. Baltimore, MD: Johns Hopkins University.

Slavin, R. E. (1989–1990a). Guest editorial: Here to stay—or gone tomorrow? *Educational Leadership*, *47*(4), 3.

Slavin, R. E. (1989–1990b). Research on cooperative learning: Consensus and controversy. *Educational Leadership*, *47*(4), 52–55.

Whipple, W. R. (1987, October). Collaborative learning: Recognizing it when we see it. *AAHE Bulletin*, *40*(2), 3–7.

19

Recovery of Memory after Traumatic Brain Injury

Rick Parenté and Mary Stapleton

Memory and cognition are fragile faculties that can be lost entirely or seriously impaired as a result of life experiences. For example, thinking and memory are clearly diminished as a result of degenerative disease, and they are typically impaired after traumatic brain injury. In many cases, these faculties may never improve. In some cases, however, certain therapies may improve the person's memory and other cognitive skills to the point where he or she can function independently, return to gainful employment, or at least do most things that were once possible.

This chapter describes the recovery of memory functions after injury to the brain or as the brain degenerates with age. Indeed, there are few theories of recovery of function, and most do not have any implications for treatment. Nevertheless, it is possible to group the existing theories into three broad classes: "artifact theories," "anatomical reorganization," and "functional adaptation," each of which is discussed in this chapter.

The authors' literature review revealed little discussion of cognitive restoration in the adult lifespan. Therefore, the chapter presents several treatment models that summarize common approaches to rehabilitation of memory and, implicitly, describe a common developmental process of recovery. These models are not theories per se. That is, they are not intended to explain the physiological mechanisms of recovery. They simply suggest a particular sequence of therapies that will produce the most rapid recovery. The chapter ends with a discussion of the authors' developmental model of recovery.

THEORIES OF RECOVERY

Anatomical Reorganization

The notion of brain plasticity is, perhaps, the oldest of the recovery models (Munk, 1878; Rosner, 1974). The concept assumes that the brain can reorganize its functions after injury and that undamaged portions assume the functions of the damaged areas. The various areas of the brain are not functionally specific but rather are structured from lowest to highest levels. After injury, each of the higher levels can take on the functions of the lower levels with more or less success. However, if the higher levels are damaged, the lower levels may not be able to assume their functions with the same degree of sophistication. Therefore, the person may never recover all of his or her functions (Taylor, 1931).

Munk (1878) was one of the first to discuss brain plasticity and its relationship to recovery of function. Although the basic idea was the same as those outlined above, his theory placed more emphasis on the specialization of brain functions. The various areas would assume the functions of another as best they could, but only if the damaged areas were still in a state of recovery. However, the functions once controlled by the damaged areas gradually returned as those areas recovered.

Functional Adaptation

Alexander Luria (1963) was the first to assert that recovery of cognitive function is largely a process of learning new ways to reach the same goals. He called this model functional adaptation. There was no assumption of brain plasticity, but rather recovery was viewed as a compensatory process whereby we learn new ways of doing what we did before. Although the brain plasticity and functional adaptation notions share certain similarities, the latter requires fewer assumptions. For example, there is no need to assume that brain structures reorganize or change their functional status. The only assumption is that humans can learn compensatory behaviors and that brain functions are flexible and can accommodate this type of change. The degree of flexibility along with the extent of the damage largely predicts recovery. Perhaps the major advantage of the functional adaptation model is that it has clear implications for treatment. Accordingly, treatment should emphasize teaching the person new ways of doing what he or she did before.

Artifact

According to Miller (1984), artifact theories assume that damage to the brain produces irreversible effects. Moreover, there are secondary and temporary disturbances that occur in other parts of the brain. Recovery may seem to occur because the disturbances in these secondary areas resolve, which produces rapid return of function. Nevertheless, the areas of primary loss will never recover, which results in permanent impairment of certain functions. This theory assumes that some types of cognitive impairments are transient.

Von Monakow (1914) discussed one type of transient phenomenon of recovery called *diaschisis*. Although the exact mechanism of diaschisis is unclear, the basic idea is that injury to the brain produces a site of primary damage as well as secondary damage to collateral sites. The secondary damage results in temporary reduction of cognition, and the type of dysfunction may not resemble that which would normally be associated with the primary lesion site. It is as if the primary damage causes a shock wave that traverses the brain and causes damage as it passes through the tissue (Uzzell, 1986).

As the collateral areas begin to regenerate, the person begins to experience some amount of recovery. However, recovery may never be complete. Therefore, recovery is not assumed to result from regrowth or regeneration of receptors, the regeneration of damaged mechanisms, or the reorganization of brain functions. Because the damage is caused by a severe wave motion, which, in turn, disturbs the various connections between cells as it passes through the brain, these tissues are not destroyed but only temporarily disabled. Moreover, what seems to be global dysfunction may quickly resolve, leaving only minor but relatively permanent disorders. Unfortunately, there is little the artifact model can do to predict the extent of the diaschisis effect, and it provides even less in the way of functional suggestions to expedite recovery.

Miller (1984) has provided the most lucid summary of artifact, anatomical reorganization, and functional adaptation theories of recovery. He asserted that there are many similarities between these positions and that they are best described as interesting notions that are still in the early stages of development. Each explains certain aspects of recovery; however, none is obviously superior to another. Indeed, the major problem is that most lack implications for planning treatment. The various models of recovery simply describe ways therapists can conceptualize cognitive dysfunction.

PHYSIOLOGY OF RECOVERY

After head injury, a person's development and recovery is mediated by a variety of physiological mechanisms. Most involve changes in the cells or the interrelationship among cells as they regenerate. The mechanisms of change, however, are not well understood and will not be discussed in detail. None of the mechanisms discussed here is clearly the most viable description of physiological changes after injury to the brain. Indeed it is likely that all of the mechanisms play a role in recovery. Because of space limitations, only the basic concepts that underlie each process are discussed. The reader is referred to Miller (1984) for a thorough review.

The first three processes, silent synapses, cell regeneration, and sprouting, describe the regeneration or extension of existing cells to recreate the damaged interface. The last three processes, denervation supersensitivity, substitution, and vicaration, describe the increase in excitability in the cells to compensate for the lessened area of cortical synapse resulting from brain damage.

Silent synapses are hypothetical connections that only begin to function after the existing cells are damaged. Brain injury is therefore assumed to activate dormant synapses or to remove inhibition that, in turn, allows the silent synapses to take over the functions of the damaged cells.

Cell regeneration occurs when neurons that were damaged regenerate their connections to other neurons to which they were previously connected. Although it is unclear exactly how this occurs, the basic idea is that certain cells multiply and later guide new fibers to their former connections.

Sprouting is a process whereby nerve fibers in the cortex that were left intact after brain injury begin to grow branches spontaneously. These extensions then occupy the spaces left by lesioned axons, and the fibers that were not originally linked to the original lesion sites extend and occupy these areas. The process is quite rapid, usually occurring in a matter of days after the injury.

Denervation sensitivity occurs when nerve fibers in the brain become hypersensitive to their neurotransmitters because the number of receptors at the neural synapse increases. The result is that more receptors become available and respond to stimulation (Ungerstedt, 1971). The spared synapses are literally supersensitive, and the neurotransmission is increased to compensate for the reduction in the number of synapses. The process is especially apparent in the young (LaVere, 1975, 1980).

Other mechanisms may mediate recovery, but little is known about their physiology. Vicaration occurs when the function of a damaged area of the brain is assumed by another area that is not heavily used. An area directly adjacent to the damaged area takes over the functions of the damaged area. Re-routing involves establishing new connections after the cell's normal pathways are disrupted. Although these mechanisms provide hope that the brain can regenerate its neural connections, there is little evidence that re-routing or vicaration occurs beyond the site of the original insult. Moreover, these mechanisms are generally uncommon outside of the realm of younger, developing organisms. Moreover, there is little evidence that any of the processes discussed above can overcome the sequelae of degenerative events that typically follow injury to the brain or occur after the onset of a degenerative disease.

There are several types of degenerative events that limit recovery. Scar tissue results from astocyte activity in the damaged area. Scarring also results from large calcium deposits that typically occur after stroke. Also, many of the cells' axons in the lesioned area are damaged or severed. This produces death of the cells bodies and dendrites. Moreover, the neurons that were connected to the damaged cells may die and the connections between damaged cells' dendrites may shrink or atrophy, which limits transmission to other cells. There are few surgical or preventative methods that can limit these processes or reverse them.

In conclusion, no single physiological process or dominant theory of recovery explains most of the available research data. It is safe to say, however, that artifact theory, especially edema resolution, probably accounts for the majority of early recovery. The functional adaptation theory of recovery is the only model with clear predictions for therapeutic intervention. Anatomical reorganization is more useful as a model of recovery in developing systems, for example, in young children with traumatic brain injury (Miller, 1984).

INTERVENTIONS AND RECOVERY

A variety of interventions designed to improve cognition after damage to the brain have been proposed. They include surgical intervention and tissue transplants, nutrient therapy, and drug treatments. As time and space do not permit a full discussion of these areas, the reader is referred to the appropriate references in each of the following sections. It is important to note, however, that most of these intervention strategies produce only modest improvement.

Surgical Interventions

Sprouting and regeneration, discussed above, could conceivably expedite recovery if a new medium were provided that would permit growth of the axons. Some research findings suggest that, indeed, fetal tissue transplants can provide this medium and can also facilitate these two recovery processes (Low et al., 1982). It is possible to transplant embryonic tissue directly into the site of the lesion, and the regenerating fibers can subsequently grow through this tissue bridge and reconnect with cells. In essence, the new tissue permits and facilitates regeneration and sprouting. Low et al. and Zimmer (1981) have found that this technique can partially facilitate memory restoration in lesioned animals.

Stein (1987) reported that transplanted tissue was not a necessary condition for collateral sprouting or regeneration. His research focused on extracting certain enzymes from transplant tissue and then injecting them directly into the lesion site. This procedure seemed to produce the same effect previously found in the transplant studies. Stein's work suggests that enzyme injections may one day be used as a treatment for anyone who has suffered brain injury.

Nutrient and Drug Interventions

Pharmacological interventions are especially interesting areas of recovery research. One of the earliest was proposed by Alexander Luria (1963). He hypothesized that certain drug treatments would accelerate recovery of function by reducing cholestrenase levels after head injury. This would, correspondingly, increase production of certain neurotransmitters such as acetylcholine. Luria reported that using galanthomine and/or neostigmine had this desired effect. Choline drugs have been found to improve memory functioning in patients with degenerative diseases such as Alzheimer's. Indeed, a wide variety of nutrient treatments have been proposed to supplement conventional cognitive rehabilitation therapies.

According to Pelton (1989) and Dean & Morgenthaler (1990), phosphatidyl choline is a source of a major neurotransmitter, acetylcholine. Lecithin, a phospholipid, is sometimes taken in large doses to provide enough choline to enhance acetylcholine, thereby improving cognition. Lecithin and choline substances have been used to treat a variety of cognitive deficits including Huntington's chorea, Parkinson's disease, and tardive dyskinesia (Gelenberg, 1979; Goldberg, Gerstman & Mattis, 1982). Sitaram and Weingartner (1978) reported that a single treatment of choline versus a placebo substance yielded a measurable improvement in cognitive functioning with traumatically brain injured patients.

Pelton (1989) also discussed a variety of herbal formulas that have been shown to improve cognitive functioning. Ginkgo biloba is an oriental herb that relaxes the microcapillaries in the brain. It also increases the blood flow, with resulting increase in attention and concentration (Allard, 1986; Auguet, 1986; Hindmarch, 1986; Taillandier, 1986). Ginkgo biloba significantly improves working memory functions (Hindmarch, 1986) and it has also been shown to inhibit cerebral deterioration due to aging and Alzheimer's disease (Allard, 1986; Warburton, 1986).

Dimethyl-amino-ethanol is another substance that has been shown to improve memory and cognition (Pfeiffer, 1957). Dimethyl-amino-ethanol is a naturally occurring substance found in anchovies and sardines. After several weeks of use, it tends to reduce daytime fatigue and to increase attention span (Murphree, 1960).

According to Zasler (1990), different categories of drugs have been found to improve memory and cognition. These include cholinergic agonists (Goldberg et al., 1982), monoamines (Clark, Geffen & Geffen, 1986), psychostimulants (Coper & Herrmann, 1988; Evans & Gualtieri, 1987), neuropeptides (Greidanus, van Wimersma & Wied, 1985; Zagler & Black, 1985), and nootropics (Poschel, 1988). The nootropics are, perhaps, the most exciting area of research. Nootropic drugs act on the forebrain and are known to improve learning, memory, and cognition in animals and humans (Diamond & Browers, 1976; Giurgea, 1973; Mindus, 1976). Piracetam is a nootropic compound that has been used successfully as a treatment for dyslexia (Chase, 1984; Conners, 1984; Dilanni, 1985; Wilsher, 1987). Treatment with vinpocetine resulted in significant improvements on cognitive tests with patients suffering from dementia (DeNoble, 1986). Studies with two other substances, oxiracetam and pramiracetam have also shown improvement in cognitive functions (Ferrero, 1984; Murray & Fibiger, 1986).

Several studies have demonstrated improvement in memory and concentration after treatment with vasopressin (Gold, 1979; Legros, 1978; Oliveros, 1978). Hydergine has been used for years to treat memory dysfunction after senile dementia (Exton-Smith, 1983; Hughes, 1976; Yoshikawa, 1983). Elderly patients typically notice improvement after two weeks of treatment (Yesavage, 1979).

In conclusion, tissue transplants and nutrient/drug treatments are especially attractive to most patients and clinicians because they provide what seems to be an immediate cure. Transplant surgery is still unproven with humans, although there is some literature that documents dramatic improvement after certain types of drug treatments. Nutrients such as ginkgo biloba, ginseng, and DMAE are generally available without prescription. Most of the drugs discussed in this chapter, however, have not been approved by the FDA. With the exception of Hydergine, none are commonly prescribed by physicians in the United States. Choline and lecithin may eventually improve cognitive functioning, but it may take several months of mega dosage before the treatment produces a therapeutic blood level and clear improvement results. Perhaps the greatest improvement in memory and cognition may result from simple life-style changes such as a well-balanced diet, enough rest, and avoiding drugs and alcohol and stimulants such as caffeine and nicotine.

COGNITIVE REHABILITATION

One of the oldest and most controversial methods of intervention involves direct retraining of memory and cognition (Parenté & Anderson-Parenté, 1991). Most of these techniques are not based in theory but are simply descriptions of various types of treatment strategies that may be appropriate with certain patients. For this reason, they are best described as "treatment models" to emphasize the fact that they are not necessarily grounded in physiological or learning theory. Gross and Shutz (1986) provided a cogent summary of these intervention models of recovery and offered useful suggestions and considerations that would help a treating therapist select the appropriate treatment.

Orientation-Remediation

In the initial stages of recovery, a patient may be confused, disoriented, and unable to maintain attention and vigilance. It is therefore necessary to begin treatment with simple orientation-remediation processes. Ben-Yishay, Piasetsky, and Rattok (1987) developed the Orientation Remediation Modules (ORM) to provide therapy appropriate for a patient at this level of recovery. The patient proceeds through a series of tasks designed to improve simple orientation and attention gradually. The sequence is arranged hierarchically, from simple reaction time training to exercises that train more complex discrimination and memory skills.

The first stage uses a device called the Attention Reaction Conditioner to train the patient to react to simple visual and verbal signals. This simple reaction-time device measures the person's speed of responding to simple stimulation.

In the second stage, the Zero Accuracy Conditioner, which is similar to a clock, activates a sweep hand that the person stops by depressing a button. Once the sweep hand is started, the person must stop the sweep hand when it reaches certain markers on the dial. The goal is to decrease errors of approach. In the third stage, the Visual Discrimination Conditioner is used to train vigilance. This device contains a display of digits and colored lights. The therapist controls the display of color/number combinations, and the patient must scan the display for certain combinations. The fourth stage of training involves time estimation. The person simply estimates the passage of certain amounts of time on a special stopwatch by activating a lever. In the final stage, the Rhythm Synchrony Conditioner is used to train anticipatory attention. The person responds to a series of Morse code-like tones and eventually learns to anticipate certain rhythms and respond in sequence.

Each of the above tasks may seem quite simple. In the early stages of recovery from traumatic brain injury, however, the patient may find them to be extremely difficult. Successive tasks gradually become more difficult in preparation for the next stage of recovery, which involves complex attention, concentration, and memory. Perhaps the oldest and best-researched model of attention training was proposed by Sohlberg and Mateer (1987). Parenté and Anderson-Parenté (1991) have proposed a seven-level model of attention training that subsumes the Sohlberg and Mateer model. Both models assume a hierarchical structure of recovery and propose certain therapeutic exercises that are appropriate at each stage.

Sohlberg and Mateer (1987) developed the Attention Process Training program (APT) as a five-stage therapy. The first stage involves Focused Attention. Similar to the ORM model outlined above, this stage provides simple reaction time and vigilance training. The second stage provides additional Sustained Attention training, which is similar to the concept of vigilance. Selective Attention training is a set of exercises that trains activation or inhibition of specific responses. Alternating Attention Training requires moving back and forth between mental tasks. Finally, Divided Attention Training requires doing more than one thing simultaneously.

Both of the above training models illustrate the sequential nature of recovery from brain injury. It is necessary that the person move through a structured set of activities that require progressively more cognitive effort. These activities also illustrate a tedious and often frustrating aspect to cognitive retraining. Attention training may take months or even years before noticeable improvement occurs. However, other therapies will have only limited effect until the person can attend and concentrate.

Environmental Control

The environmental control approach modifies the person's physical and social environment to facilitate or train adaptive behavior. This type of intervention also is used to suppress undesirable behavior. The model assumes that the environment can be used to modify behavior and that modifications can also facilitate independence. For example, the family could install a single switch that turns off all electrical appliances to reduce the possibility of a fire and to eliminate the obsessive and compulsive checking of the various appliances that commonly results from poor memory.

Prosthetic Device Model

The prosthetic device approach to rehabilitation literally replaces a lost memory or cognitive function. The goal is similar to that of the environmental model because both emphasize external aids to memory and cognition. The two models differ, however, because the various prosthetic devices are things the person may take with him or her outside of the home. Most are electronic aids that obviate the problem rather than retrain a lost function. For example, an elderly person may use a beeping pillbox to signal when it is time to take medications. Simple devices such as checklists can be used to remind the person of certain things that must be completed each day. The person may also use a small dictation tape recorder to remember complex messages, telephone conversations, or instructions.

Stimulus-Response Conditioning

A reinforcement theory of learning is based on the assumption that behavior depends on the effect it produces. Accordingly, behavior therapists first identify rewards that are effective with a particular person, then provide or withhold those rewards to change some desired behavior. The next step is to determine if the behavior can be broken down into smaller parts that can be trained separately. Complex behaviors are best viewed as sequences of simpler ones that are conditioned with appropriate rewards. Once learned, the behaviors are then combined into wholes. The goal is to condition specific behaviors and to shape a complex behavioral repertoire.

Cognitive Skills Training

The cognitive skills training model assumes that complex mental abilities are made up of smaller skills or processes that can be trained separately. The therapist focuses treatment on specific processes. Presumably, improved performance on the training tasks strengthens the underlying cognitive processes, which in turn will transfer to activities of daily living. The model assumes that there are a limited number of skills that permeate a greater number of specific behaviors. For example, teaching visual scanning by having the person follow a moving target on a computer screen should transfer to other activities that also require visual scanning such as reading.

Cognitive skills form a hierarchy, with simple processes such as impulse control, orientation, and attention at the bottom. Complex skills such as reasoning, judgment, and planning are at the top. Clearly, it is necessary to train less complex skills before training those that are more complex. Regardless of the type of skill, the therapy is usually done on a computer or with paper-and-pencil materials. The model assumes that simply practicing tasks that require these skills is sufficient to retrain them. In essence, doing hierarchically structured "mental pushups" is assumed to be the most expedient means of regaining lost function.

Strategy Substitution Model

The strategy substitution model also teaches cognitive skills. However, the person is taught cognitive sets or ways of organizing and remembering rather than doing mental pushups. These cognitive sets are thought to generalize to a variety of different situations. For example, training the person to use imagery to memorize shopping lists will apply to any shopping excursion. Training the person to use a simple mnemonic such as "i before e except after c" will improve spelling of any word that contains a combination of i and e.

Parenté and Anderson-Parenté (1991) have shown that traumatically brain-injured people can learn memory strategies. These strategies also improve memory functioning significantly. The authors pointed out that the art of training memory strategies is to choose the strategies wisely so that the person sees their relevance and usefulness. Further, the person must consciously apply the strategies in their everyday life. It is not sufficient simply to demonstrate the strategies and expect the person to use them spontaneously.

The Cognitive Cycle Model

Gross and Shutz (1986, p. 191–192) have proposed the following five-step model, which is designed to train complex executive skills such as problem solving and decision making.

Step 1: Self-Identification of Goals. The person identifies exactly what he or she wants to achieve in any situation.

Step 2: Conditional Thinking. The person learns to generate options, ideas, or behaviors that may produce the goals identified in Step 1.

Step 3: Planning. This step involves generating a plan of action that stems from Step 2. The person learns that goals are obtained by following a specific behavioral action plan.

Step 4: Action Initiation. The person identifies the trigger for his or her action plan and subsequently initiates activity.

Step 5: Feedback and Cycling. If the person does not achieve the goal, then he or she cycles through the entire process once again, until the goal is achieved.

The cognitive cycle model teaches a recursive process that requires the person to anticipate the future consequences of his or her actions and to evaluate results to determine if the goal was achieved. The person must also exhibit executive thinking, that is, he or she must be able to self-initiate and self-monitor his or her behavior. This is a relatively high-level skill for most brain-injured individuals. The cognitive cycle model is therefore usually appropriate only for those who are in the later stages of recovery.

Conclusion

Each of these models of retraining is designed for persons who are at different levels of recovery. Common to all the models, however, is the assumption that the person can learn, can transfer newly learned skills, and can generalize these skills to novel situations. If the person cannot learn rapidly, then the only applicable model of rehabilitation may be the environmental control system. If the person does learn rapidly, then the S-R training or strategy substitution models are applicable. Training to use prosthetic devices may help when the person can learn but shows limited ability to generalize his or her knowledge. If the person can learn and can generalize, the therapist has several additional treatment options, including cognitive skill training already mentioned. If the person can self-monitor and demonstrate a modicum of executive behavior, then the cognitive cycle system is worth trying.

DEVELOPMENTAL MODEL

Parenté and Anderson-Parenté (1991) have proposed a developmental model of recovery that describes the change in function as the person recovers. It also describes an optimal sequencing of different treatments. This is not a formal theory of recovery per se. It is a description of the stages of recovery that a typical brain-injured person ascends. The developmental model of recovery subsumes most of the training models outlined above. It is, in essence, a description of successive therapeutic steps, with specific training at each step that will facilitate the next.

Arousal-Orientation Training

The arousal-orientation training usually occurs in the acute care hospital. A person at this stage of recovery may not know his or her name, recognize loved ones, know what time it is, or why he or she is in the hospital. The person may be confused, disoriented, or perhaps violent or combative. At this stage, the therapist can orient the person in time and place and to person and can also retrain recognition memory of family and friends via repetition of names and faces and biographical information. Gradually, the person relearns to recognize what was once familiar. He or she becomes less combative and verbally abusive as a sense of personal identity is reformed. The ORM training methods may also be useful at this stage of recovery (Rancho Level 2–3).

Attention and Concentration

Once the person is oriented in time and place and to person, then he or she is capable of relearning attention and concentration skills. Retraining attention involves practice orienting correctly for sustained periods. The therapy teaches the person to do mental work while attending. The Sohlberg and Mateer program may be especially useful at this stage of recovery. None of these types of training requires memory. For example, the person may simply play video games that involve active decision making but do not require remembering past events or outcomes.

Rehearsal Training

Rehearsal training is designed to teach the person to sustain information in memory so that he or she can eventually work with it. However, rehearsal training may be effective only after the person has relearned how to attend and concentrate. Usually, the person cannot rehearse information automatically and must relearn how to do so at a conscious level. Rehearsal training is extremely important because the person must rehearse in order to maintain relevant information in memory long enough to encode it for effective retrieval. It is critical that the person learn how many times he or she will have to rehearse most information in order to remember it in the long term.

Encoding

Encoding is the process whereby a person transforms information into easily retrievable units. Training to encode involves teaching skills such as mnemonics, imagery, and other types of memory strategies. The quality of the encoding determines the ease of retrieval. Learning memory strategies is virtually useless until the person can rehearse effectively. Indeed, the authors have found that teaching memory strategies is effective only after an initial period of rehearsal training. Rehearsal and encoding are therefore correlated processes. The person must first be able to sustain information in memory in order to encode it. A breakdown in either of these functions limits the ability to retrieve information from memory.

Recovery of Episodic Memory

Episodic retention is the ability to recall the novel episodes of life. This stage involves training the person to apply newly learned encoding strategies to everyday life. Training the brain-injured person to use memory strategies and to form memory cues is more than doing "mental pushups." The majority of cognitive rehabilitation therapies focus on training abstract cognitive skills that exercise the mind but do not necessarily teach new ways of performing old mental functions. They are based on the assumption that mental functions will improve if the person practices doing different activities that require that particular skill. Teaching strategies, however, is based on the assumption that the person benefits most from learning a new way of remembering. The goal is, therefore, not simply to make the person practice remembering, but to teach him or her a new way of remembering.

Cognition

After the person has regained the ability to encode, the next step is to stimulate the active input/output of the encoded information between the working memory and the long-term store. This process involves presenting real-life information to the person and requiring that he or she rehearse, encode, and generate an appropriate cue for the information. At this stage, it is important to use therapy materials that are relevant to the person's activities of daily living. The general model involves identifying the types of things the person has to remember, then developing encodings for those materials and providing practice using them. For example, the person may have a hard time remembering a specific sequence of actions to operate a certain appliance around the home. The therapist may therefore develop a mnemonic that reminds the person how to perform this task.

Recovery of Social Competence

Recovery of social competence is a process whereby subtle social skills are relearned. This is an especially important area of recovery because it has an impact on every area of the person's social life. For example, the training may involve recognizing subtle social cues such as a person's constantly checking a watch while conversing. The relearning process usually requires active participation such as roleplaying or modeling, and it may also require new learning of social cues such as body language. For this reason, it is best carried out in a group setting.

Conclusion

The progression of recovery through the various stages is seldom rapid or consistent from person to person. Some persons may never reach the higher stages. Some may plateau at the first or second stage. It is important, however, to reemphasize that the stages are developmental. The therapist cannot skip any stage.

SUMMARY

Several theories of recovery after brain injury were presented. Artifact theories assert that brain damage is permanent and that most recovery results from the return of spared skills that were only temporarily disabled after the injury. Anatomical reorganization theories, otherwise known as brain plasticity models, assume that other areas of the brain can and will take over the functions of damaged portions. The functional adaptation model is not a theory per se. It does suggest, however, that the most expedient route to recovery involves teaching the person new ways of doing things that he or she used to do. Several physiological mechanisms of recovery were also discussed.

A number of intervention strategies were discussed, including surgical tissue transplants as well as different drug and nutrient treatments. Various nutrients have been found to improve memory and concentration with brain-injured adults and Alzheimer's patients. These substances include ginkgo biloba, ginseng, and dimethyl-amino-ethanol. Certain drugs may also be effective for improving cognition after brain injury. These include nootropics, psychostimulants, monoamines, and neuropeptides.

Different models of recovery underlie the treatment programs typically used to restore function. The models are hierarchical and emphasize the gradual regaining of skills. Two structured therapy programs were described that retrain orientation and attentional processes. The Orientation Remediation Modules are especially effective for retraining simple cognitive processes during the initial stages of recovery. The Attention Process Training program is useful after the person has become oriented in time and place and to person and before more complex memory strategy training is initiated.

Both orientation and attention process training systems are necessary precursors to memory skills training. This type of therapy typically involves retraining rehearsal skill, the ability to manipulate information in memory, and the ability to transform information for effective retrieval and to develop appropriate memory cues. Stimulation therapy and cognitive skills training are, perhaps, the most frequently used as prevocational memory training programs. These usually involve paper-and-pencil and computer training that provides practice performing certain skills. The therapy assumes that this type of practice will gradually restore functioning.

The prosthetic memory model emphasizes teaching the person to use different devices that obviate memory problems. For example, the person may learn to use devices such as checklists and tape recorders that literally replace the defective memory. The biggest advantage to prosthetic memory training is that it provides rapid solutions to nagging problems.

A developmental model of recovery was also presented that emphasizes return of function across a broader time span. Several stages were identified including orientation, attention, rehearsal, encoding, cognition, and social competence.

Different therapy procedures were described that are appropriate at each stage of recovery.

Recovery after stroke or traumatic brain injury is a complex and unpredictable process. The most effective remediation efforts include highly individualized treatment, training the client to use prosthetic devices, and realistic expectations by the client and therapist. Clients and their families must accept the reality that recovery is seldom rapid or complete. Therapists must understand that there are no commercially available treatment packages with proven efficacy. This chapter outlines several avenues of therapy which can help this burgeoning patient population. The authors are optimistic that, in the not-too-distant future, scientist/ practitioners will combine these techniques into a generally accepted treatment model.

REFERENCES

Allard, M. (1986). Treatment of old age disorders with ginkgo biloba extract. *La Presse Medicale, 15*(31), 1540.

Auguet, M. (1986). Bases of pharmacologiques le impact vascularie de l'extrait de ginko biloba. *La Presse Medicale, 15*(31), 1524.

Baburin, E. F. (1986). On the effect of eleutherococcus senticosius on the results of work and hearing acuity of radio-telegraphers. In I. I. Brekhamm (Ed.). *Eleutherococcus and the adaptogens among the Far Eastern plants* (pp. 179–184). Vladivostok, Soviet Union: Far Eastern Publishing House.

Ben-Yishay, Y., Piasetsky, E. & Rattok, J. (1987). A systematic method for ameliorating disorders in basic attention. In M. Meier, A. Benton & L. Diller (Eds.). *Neuropsychological rehabilitation* (pp. 165–181). New York: Guilford Press.

Chase, C. H. (1984). A new chemotherapeutic investigation: Piracetam effects on dyslexia. *Annals of Dyslexia, 34*, 272–278.

Clark, C. R., Geffen, G. M. & Geffen, L. B. (1986). Role of monoamine pathways in the control of attention: Effects of droperiodol and methylphenidate in normal adult humans. *Psychopharmacology, 89*, 234–238.

Conners, C. (1984). Piracetam and event related potentials in dyslexic children. *Psychopharmacology Bulletin, 20*, 667–673.

Coper, H. & Herrmann, W. M. (1988). Psychostimulants, analeptics, nootropics: An attempt to differentiate and assess drugs designed for the treatment of impaired brain functions. *Pharmacopsychiatry, 21*, 211–217.

Dean, W. & Morgenthaler, J. (1990). *Smart drugs and nutrients*. Santa Cruz, CA: B & J Publications.

DeNoble, V. (1986). Vinpocetine: Nootropic effects on scopolamine-induced and hypoxia-induced retrieval deficits in step through passive avoidance response in rats. *Pharmacology, Biochemistry & Behaviour 24*, 1123–1128.

Devor, M. (1982). Placticity in the adult nervous system. In L. S. Illis, E. M. Sedgwick & H. J. Glanville (Eds.). *Rehabilitation of the neurological patient*. Oxford: Blackwell.

Diamond, S. J. & Browers, E.Y.M. (1976). Increase in the power of human memory in normal man through the use of drugs. *Psychopharmacology*, *49*, 307–309.

Dilanni, M. (1985). The effects of piracetam in children with dyslexia. *Journal of Clinical Psychopharmacology*, *5*, 272–278.

Diller, L. & Gordon, W. A. (1981). Rehabilitation and clinical neuropsychology. In S. B. Filskov & T. J. Boll (Eds.). *Handbook of Clinical Neuropsychology*. New York: John Wiley & Sons.

Evans, R. W. & Gualtieri, C. T. (1987). Psychostimulant pharmacology in traumatic brain injury. *Journal of Head Trauma Rehabilitation*, *2*, 29–31.

Exton-Smith, A. N. (1983). Clinical experience with ergot alkaloids. *Aging*, *23*, 323.

Ferrero, E. (1984, August). Controlled clinical trial of oxiracetam in the treatment of chronic cerebrovascular insufficiency in the elderly. *Current Therapeutic Research*, *36*(20), 298–308.

Gelenberg, A. (1979). Lecithin for the treatment of tardive dyskinesia. *Nutrition and the Brain*, *5*, 285–290.

Giurgea, C. E. (1973). The nootropic approach to the pharmacology of integrative activity in the brain. *Conditioned Reflex*, *8*(2), 108–115.

Gold, P. (1979, November). Effects of 1-desamo–8-arginine vasopressin on behavior and cognition in primary affective disorders, *Lancet*, 992–994.

Goldberg, E., Gerstman, L. J. & Mattis, S. (1982). Effects of cholinergic treatment on post-traumatic anterograde amnesia. *Archives of Neurology*, *38*, 581.

Greidanus, T., van Wimersma, B. & Wied, D. (1985). Hypothalamic neuropeptides and memory. *Acta Neurochirugica*, *75*, 99–105.

Gross, Y. & Shutz, L. E. (1986). Intervention models in neuropsychology. In B. P. Uzzell & Y. Gross (Eds.). *Clinical neuropsychology of intervention*. Boston: Martinus Nijhoff.

Hindmarch, I. (1986). Activity of ginkgo biloba extract on short-term memory. *La Presse Medicale*, *15*(31), 1592.

Hughes, J. R. (1976). An ergot alkaloid preparation (Hydergine) in the treatment of dementia: A critical review of clinical literature. *Journal of the American Geriatrics Society*, *24*, 490–497.

Iljutjecok, R. J. & Tjaplygina, S. R. (1978). *The effect of a preparation of eleutherococcus seticosus on memory in mice*. Novosibirsk, Soviet Union: Academy of Sciences, Department of Physiology.

LaVere, T. E. (1975). Neural stability, sparing, and behavioral recovery following brain damage. *Psychological Review*, *82*, 344–358.

LaVere, T. E. (1980). Recovery of function after brain damage: A theory of the behavioral deficit. *Physiological Psychology*, *8*, 297–308.

Legros, J. J. (1978, January). Influence of vasopressin on learning and memory. *Lancet*, 41–42.

Low, W. C., Lewis, P. R., Bunch, T., Dunnett, S. B., Iverson, S. D., Bjorklund, A. & Stenevi, Y. (1982). Function recovery following neural transplantation of embryonic septal nuclei in adult rats with septohippocampal lesions. *Nature*, *300*, 260–261.

Luria, A. (1963). *Recovery of function after brain injury*. New York: Macmillan.

Miller, E. (1984). *Recovery and management of neuropsychological impairments*. New York: John Wiley & Sons.

Mindus, P. (1976). Piracetam-induced improvement of mental performance: A controlled study on normally aging individuals. *Acta Psychiatrica Scandinavia, 54,* 150–160.

Munk, H. (1878). Weitere Mettheilungen zur Physiologie der Grosshirnrinde. *Archives of Anatomy and Physiology, 3,* 581–592.

Murphree, H. B. (1960). The stimulant effect of 2-Dimethylamino ethanol (Deanol) in human volunteer subjects. *Clinical Pharmacology and Therapeutics, 1,* 303–310.

Murray, C. L. & Fibiger, H. C. (1986). The effect of pramiracetam (CI–879) on the acquisition of a radical arm maze task. *Psychopharmacology, 89,* 378–381.

Oliveros, J. C. (1978). Vasopressin in amnesia. *Lancet,* 42.

Parenté, R., and Anderson-Parenté, J. K. (1991). *Retraining Memory: Techniques and Applications.* Houston: CSY Publishers.

Pelton, D. (1989). *Mind food and smart pills.* New York: Doubleday.

Petkov, V. (1987). Effects of standardized ginseng extract on learning, memory and physical capabilities. *American Journal of Chinese Medicine, 15*(1), 19–29.

Pfeiffer, C. (1957). Stimulant effect of 2-Dimethyl-1 aminoethanol: Possible precursor to brain acetylcholine. *Science, 126,* 610–611.

Poschel, B.P.H. (1988). New pharmacologic perspectives on nootropic drugs. *Handbook of Pharmacology,* 11–18.

Rosner, B. S. (1974). Recovery of function and localization of function in historical perspective. In D. G. Stein, J. J. Rosen & N. Butters, (Eds.). *Plasticity and recovery of function in the central nervous system.* New York: Academic Press.

Schacter, D. L. & Glisky, E. (1986). Memory remediation: Restoration, alleviation, and the acquisition of domain-specific knowledge. In B. Uzzell & Y. Gross (Eds.). *Clinical neuropsychology of intervention.* Boston: Martinus Nijhoff.

Sitaram, N. & Weingartner. (1978). Human serial learning: Enhancement with acetylcholine and choline and impairment with scopolamine. *Science, 201,* 275–276.

Sohlberg, M. M. & Mateer, C. A. (1987). Effectiveness of an attention training program. *Journal of Clinical and Experimental Neuropsychology, 9,* 117–130.

Stein, D. (1987). Physiological mechanisms of recovery from brain injury. Paper presented at the annual meetings of the Connecticut Head Injury Foundation. Hartford, CT.

Taillandier, J. (1986). Traitement des troubles vu viellissement cerebral par l'extract de ginkgo biloba. *La Presse Medicale, 15*(31), 1583.

Taylor, J. (1931). *Selected writings of John Hughlings Jackson.* London: Hodder & Stoughton.

Ungerstedt, U. (1971). Post synaptic supersensitivity after 6 hydroxy-dopamine induced degeneration of nigrostriatal dopamine system. *Acta Physiologica Scandinavia, Supplement 367,* 69–93.

Uzzell, B. P. (1986). Pathophysiology and behavioral recovery. In B. P. Uzzell & Y. Gross (Eds.). *Clinical neuropsychology of intervention.* Boston: Martinus Nijhoff.

von Monakow, C. (1914). *Die Lokalisation in Grosshirn und der Function durch Kortikale Herde.* Wiesbaden: J. F. Bergmann.

Warburton, D. M. (1986). Clinical psychopharmacology of ginkgo biloba extract. *La Presse Medicale, 15*(31), 1595.

Wilsher, C. R. (1987). Piracetam and dyslexia: Effects on reading tests. *Journal of Clinical Psychopharmacology, 7*(4), 230–237.

Yesavage, J. (1979). Dihydroergotoxine: 6 Mg vs 3 Mg dosage in the treatment of senile dementia; preliminary report. *Journal of the American Geriatrics Society, 27* (2), 80–82.

Yoshikawa, M. (1983). A dose-response study with dihydroergotoxine mesylate in cerebrovascular disturbances. *Journal of the American Geriatrics Society, 27*, 80–82.

Zagler, E. L. & Black, P. M. (1985). Neuropeptides in human memory and learning processes. *Neurosurgery, 17*, 355–369.

Zasler, N. (1990, September). Pharmacologic approaches to cognitive and behavioral dysfunction after traumatic brain injury: Selected bibliography. In *Proceedings: Cognitive Rehabilitation & Community Integration* (pp. 233–240), Richmond, VA.

Zimmer, J. (1981). Lesion induced reorganization of central nervous system connections: With note on central nervous system transplants. In M. W. van Hoff & G. Mohn (Eds.). *Functional recovery from brain damage*. Amsterdam: Elsevier.

20

Empathy and Listening Skills: A Developmental Perspective on Learning to Listen

Ariel Phillips, Abigail Lipson, and Michael Basseches

Teachers in many contexts of adult learning value the ability to listen and respond well. Training programs in fields as diverse as business, counseling psychology, education, negotiation, and medicine reflect a concern with interpersonal communication, and many professionals in those fields have devoted considerable thought and effort to the question of how to teach it. For example, some medical schools (Weihs & Chapados, 1986) and teacher training programs (Tolle, Cooney & Hickam, 1989) include interpersonal communication as part of their curricula, and some descriptions of negotiation skills mention the importance of careful listening (Fisher & Ury, 1981). A program designed in part to help college students learn to take others' perspectives and appreciate cultural diversity emphasizes the value of listening (Thorsheim & Roberts, in collaboration with Basseches, 1991).

Despite the frequent use across time and in various contexts of terms related to communication and listening, the meanings of some of these terms remain muddy, along with their implications for learning and teaching. "Skills" and "empathy" are examples. Some authors writing about interpersonal communication and some programs designed to teach it stress what they call "listening skills," while others stress "empathy." Some imply that one precedes the other, or that one is a subset of the other, and some use these terms interchangeably.

The field of interpersonal communication training has been hampered by a tendency to refer to "empathy" and "skills" as if their meanings were agreed upon. We believe the field would be strengthened by a broader recognition that teachers and students bring to their efforts a diversity of constructions of meaning, including diverse understandings regarding key concepts in interpersonal communication.

This chapter explores the meanings of "listening skills" and "empathy," using a framework of lifespan psychological development. We begin with a review of current uses of these terms and then move to a discussion of developmental theory as it sheds light on the teaching and learning of listening. We introduce a six-part model describing how learners with different modes of learning to listen may construe their roles as listeners. Following this, we consider different approaches to teaching listening as they might be experienced by different adult learners. In conclusion, we discuss some implications for learning and teaching.

LISTENING SKILLS AND EMPATHY: WHAT IS THE DIFFERENCE?

The use of the terms ''listening skills'' and ''empathy'' has taken a number of turns in the past several decades. As the following examples show, these terms appear together and separately in many contexts, and their meanings vary considerably.

Writing in 1952, Rogers and Rothlisberger discussed the obstacles and pathways to communication in a business context (reprinted in 1991). Their emphasis at that time was on the value of ''listening''—by which they mean taking the perspective of the other person in a dialogue—and letting the other person know she or he is being understood. They discuss impeding and facilitating factors in interpersonal communication, referring to what they call ''listening with understanding'' (p. 106).

In 1980, Rogers reflected on an evolution that he had observed in his own thinking about the meaning of empathy. Between 1959 and 1980, he moved away from thinking of empathy as a *state* and toward considering empathy as a process of sensing the other's experience and communicating that sense, as well as checking one's understandings with the other. Thus, Rogers shifted from an emphasis on understanding toward a concern with responding and then further, to include the element of the speaker's experience of being understood.

During the 1970s, the term ''active listening'' gained popularity, partly through its use by Thomas Gordon (1970) in ''Parent Effectiveness Training,'' although in practice it bore a strong resemblance to Rogers' (1980) description of empathy. Many employee training programs of that period taught people that listening involves more than just passive hearing; it requires the listener to restate the speaker's words so that the speaker is satisfied that she or he is understood (Gabarro, 1991).

This use of ''listening'' and ''listening skills'' in a way that resembles some descriptions of ''empathy'' continues in the present. In a response almost forty years later to the Rogers and Rothlisberger article, Gabarro (1991) notes that most business schools still stress the importance of making judgments, rather than listening non-judgmentally (empathically). He reaffirms the value of non-judgmental listening, but also notes that managers must be able to both listen and judge if they are to be effective. They must recognize the importance of suspending judgment in order to make more accurate judgments later. Writing about the training of counseling psychologists, Doyle (1982) proposes that certain interpersonal skills, such as making eye contact, reflecting content and feeling, and paraphrasing are a means of conveying empathic understanding to the client. In an article about psychiatric training in Britain, Cobb and Lieberman (1987) use the term *skills* to include "empathic statements" and "open questions, silence and reflections" (p. 590).

When the term *empathy* is used, its meaning can vary considerably from author to author. For example, Margulies (1989) refers primarily to empathy rather than to skills, and he differentiates between two types of empathy: "resonant" and "imaginative" (p. 18). Resonant empathy is more passive, more echoing, and Margulies associates it with Carl Rogers. Imaginative empathy is more active, and Margulies invokes the philosopher Martin Buber's description of "a bold swinging, demanding the most intensive stirring of one's being, into the life of the other" (quoted in Margulies, p. 18).[1] According to Margulies, a complex form of empathy arises from the dialectic between these two ways of empathizing. "As I become engaged with the inner life of another, I experience a growing sense of familiarity with a built-up internal landscape. Oftentimes this is not so conscious to me. I enter a private world constructed from associations and images stimulated by my patient and drawn from my own personal past experience" (p. 53).

Gladstein (1983) also differentiates between two kinds of empathy—not the same two as Margulies, however—and his work lends support for the view that different authors and researchers use the term "empathy" differently. He describes two stages of empathy to partially account for the differences that he perceives in the literature. First, there is an "emotional stage," which essentially involves automatic, unwilled identification (p. 475). Following that is a "cognitive, conscious" stage that involves a more deliberate effort to understand the other person. Gladstein found that the clients he questioned wanted their therapist to be empathic, but they preferred therapists who exemplified the more conscious, deliberate empathy over those who exemplified the more emotional, automatic empathy.

Two other views, Ivey's (1988) and Bolton's (1979), suggest that empathy can be learned through the acquisition of skills, which can themselves be taught. A number of training programs are based on a model of "microskills" put forth by Ivey, who states that empathy is "experiencing the client's world as if *you* were the client. This means moving into the client's frame of reference" (p. 128). His approach emphasizes the teaching of individual behavioral skills, and he suggests that "attending skills," such as paraphrasing, reflection of feeling, and reflection of meaning, are deeply involved in developing basic empathy (p. 128).

Ivey offers a five-level scale for rating empathic responses, starting with responses that simply disagree with the client, which he terms "subtractive," progressing through responses that essentially echo the client, and culminating in "additive" responses, which Ivey considers to be the most empathic because of the addition of thoughts and questions from the listener. In additive empathy, the counselor or interviewer uses "influencing skills" and adds congruent ideas and feelings from another frame of reference to facilitate client exploration (p. 128). Here is an example of the most empathic type of response:

Client: I don't know what to do. I've gone over this problem again and again. My husband just doesn't seem to understand that I don't really care anymore. He just keeps trying, but it doesn't seem worth bothering with him anymore.

Response: I sense your hurt and confusion and that right now you really don't care anymore. Given what you've told me, your thoughts and feelings make a lot of sense to me. At the same time, you've had a reason for trying so hard. You've talked about some deep feelings of caring for him in the past. How do you put that together right now with what you are feeling? (p. 128)

Here we can see that, for Ivey, empathy consists of reflecting not only what the client says, but also what the client does not say, including elements of the client's history that may have given rise to immediate experience.

Clearly, then, the terms "empathy" and "listening skills" are used in various ways. Are there consistent differences between the two phenomena? Do the terms refer to different phenomena? One way to approach this issue is through an example. Let us consider an imaginary conversation between two people, Rob and Jane:

Jane: I'm so frustrated about my life right now!

Rob: (Leaning forward slightly, looking at Jane's eyes) Something is really not right . . . ?

Jane: Yeah, I just can't ever feel good about anything, kind of like I'm in a rut.

Rob: As if you're sort of stuck or trapped. . . .

Jane: (Emphatically) Or, like, I just can't take charge. And I feel like I should be able to, but sometimes I almost don't want to, I guess. . . .

Rob: Like you should, but you can't or won't . . . ?

To summarize some of the most obvious elements of this interchange, Rob is listening and responding to Jane. He makes paraphrasing-type responses, at one point he makes eye contact, and he asks some questions about the nature of her experience. A shared understanding seems to be developing. Is this an example of listening skills? Is it an example of empathy?

Let us first consider this dialogue as an example of listening skills. There are some obvious skills at work here. Rob makes eye contact, leans forward slightly to show he is listening, paraphrases what Jane has said, and verifies his understanding. He says things that encourage her to talk more, and her responses seem to become increasingly specific about her experience.

Now let us interpret the conversation in terms of empathy. Rob takes Jane's perspective, steps into her shoes. He tries to understand and to show her *how* he understands her. His responses are tentative, and he gives her room to clarify her meanings. She feels as if he is with her, and she continues to share her experience.

There are some similarities between these two interpretations. Both describe an interpersonal exchange that is both verbal and non-verbal. According to both, the focus is primarily on the nature of the dialogue, rather than, for example, an analysis of Jane's motives. But is there a difference between these two views? This question goes right to the heart of the issue of learning to listen. The primary difference between the two interpretations is that the first focuses primarily on Rob's behavior; his use of skills that are relatively observable and quantifiable. The second interpretation centers on the participants' experiences of empathy and perspective-taking, which do not necessarily correspond to specific behaviors. That is, Rob may be empathizing with Jane even if he doesn't make eye contact or use specific forms of speech, even if he looks at his hands, remains silent, or exhibits any number of gestures. The first perspective focuses on skills manifest in observable behaviors, the second focuses on conscious and unconscious events, experience both observable and unobservable.

Clearly, many dialogues, like the one between Jane and Rob, can be construed in terms of either listening skills or empathy; it is a matter of perspective. The terms are not interchangeable, nor do they refer to entirely separate phenomena. One's interpretation rests largely on which aspects of the dialogue one notices; the listener's behavioral gestures and types of responses or the listener's inner experience and sense of the speaker's experience.

LISTENING SKILLS OR EMPATHY: WHICH COMES FIRST?

Not only can a conversation look different depending on whether one focuses on listening skills or empathy, but the process of learning to listen, and therefore the appropriateness of different training methods, looks different, depending on the focus, as well. One view suggests that learning to listen involves developing one's capacity for empathy, with the expectation that the development of empathy will result in more skillful responses. In this view, one learns to enter another's world through making associations and experiencing one's own past. Such an internal journey leads to an authenticity of response that is more heartfelt and automatic than it is calculated and deliberate.

Margulies (1989), Rogers (1961), and Benjamin (1981) all suggest that empathy arises through a personal journey that allows the learner eventually to respond to another with authentic interest and compassion. Through this introspective and intuitive process, learners come to sense and feel a vivid picture of both their own experience and that of the speaker. They may find themselves expressing their empathic understanding via observable listening behaviors, such as making eye contact and paraphrasing. But, the main idea is that one learns capacities for empathy first and that skilled listening follows naturally.

The contrasting view, exemplified by Ivey (1988), Carkhuff, Berenson, and

Pierce (1976), and at times Bolton (1979),[2] focuses on behavioral skills, such as body language, eye contact, and specific forms of speech, with the expectation that these skills will lead to empathy. According to this view, learning to listen and respond is an incremental process in which one gradually becomes more conscious of one's own behavior and adds skills to one's repertoire, which in turn contributes to increasing amounts of accurate understandings, or empathy. Skills are learned first, and empathy follows.

Bolton expresses another possible relationship between listening skills and empathy in which empathy neither arises from nor gives rise to skills. He proposes that a person's positive attitudes—for example, a basic respect and appreciation for others—might be unseen or misunderstood if the person doesn't have appropriate expressive skills. In this view, it is as if the learner learns to prevent inappropriate behaviors from interfering with preexisting empathic feelings.

It seems that the meanings of the terms "empathy" and "listening skills" are deeply intertwined and that there are differing views of their temporal relationship to one another. In the following section we will discuss how developmental theories can help account for these different meanings and views.

DEVELOPMENTAL THEORY AND LEARNING TO LISTEN

In the group of theories of adult development sometimes called "structural" or "constructive-developmental" (see Basseches, 1984, for a thorough presentation), there is much that bears directly on how adults learn to listen and respond. These theories assume an ongoing process of sense-making in which qualitatively different organizations of meaning evolve sequentially. Each organization has a more complex structure than the previous one and is capable of including, differentiating among, and integrating a more diverse range of experience and phenomena within it. While every person's meaning-making has its unique characteristics, constructive-developmental theories attempt to describe common patterns. Terms such as "stages," "positions," or "levels" are used to refer to these common patterns—structural features of the sequentially-arranged organizations of meaning. Each stage describes a different lens through which individuals make sense of others, themselves, and many aspects of life.

Constructive-developmental theories shed considerable light on the questions that concern us here with regard to the teaching and learning of interpersonal communication. How does a "listener" at different developmental stages construe his/her role? How are the concepts "skills" and "empathy" understood? And how do students at different developmental stages experience various educational or training interventions? The model we present below, drawing on the work of such constructive-developmental psychologists as Basseches (1984), Kegan (1982), Kohlberg (1981), Loevinger (1977), Perry (1970), and Piaget and Inhelder (1969), represents how learning to listen might be experienced differently from the perspective of six different organizations of meaning-making, which we call "Modes of Learning to Listen."

Perhaps it goes without saying that we must maintain a tentativeness about our ideas. The process of learning to listen involves the interaction of complex intrapsychic and interpersonal phenomena, only some of which we can observe directly. Add to that the individual's interactions with one or more other individuals (such as teachers and fellow students), each with unique and dynamic organizations of meaning, and the picture becomes more complex at a rate that makes even modest comprehension difficult. We find that it helps to remember Perry's comment: "Just as a map is always smaller than the territory it covers, the theory is always smaller than the person" (W. G. Perry, Jr., personal communication, 1982). The danger of any typological theory is that it tends to belie the complexity of the territory it attempts to describe. With this in mind, we encourage the reader to regard our model as a map of phenomena that remain far more textured and multidimensional than our model can describe.

We have chosen to use the term *mode* rather than the more common but also more ambiguous term *stage*. Stage is taken by some to mean a unitary stance toward the world—a set of meanings and a degree of cognitive complexity that are stable across time and context, except when an individual is in transition between stages. Others understand stage to mean that, although an individual's way of making sense and the complexity with which she or he experiences vary across different moments and contexts, there are patterns of development (For a more thorough discussion of stage as non-unitary, see Basseches, 1989; Phillips, 1989). While our understanding of stage is more like the second than the first of these interpretations, we wish to focus here, not on individuals in terms of their overall growth, but on coherent ways of experiencing. Our choice of the term mode reflects this orientation. A Mode of Learning to Listen describes an individual's experience in a given context at a particular moment in time; the same individual may be in another Mode in another context or at another moment. Through our discussion of modes, we are attempting to focus on the integrity of experience within a limited time frame and in the context of learning to listen.

SIX MODES OF LEARNING TO LISTEN

Listening Because I Have To

Central to this mode are two conflicting concerns: (a) a desire to comply with authority in order to avoid punishment or hurt and (b) a desire to differentiate oneself from others, including those in authority. A student might, for example, want to comply with the demands of a teacher or the expectations of a peer in order to avoid negative consequences (a concern Kohlberg, 1981, associates with his Pre-Conventional stages of moral development), while simultaneously wanting to avoid being "pushed around."

These concerns bear directly on the way individuals in this mode would construe their role as students or listeners. Let us imagine a young student in such a program. Because her sense of herself as a separate being is relatively fragile, a training program that encourages her to focus on a speaker's experience may appear to her as a requirement to feel what the speaker feels—to merge with the speaker. She feels she must resist such a threat to her own separateness or integrity, but she decides to go through the motions of learning in order to avoid punishment or censure. The student grasps at the more concrete aspects of a training program; she tries to make eye contact and repeat what the speaker says, but more-abstract aspects such as taking another person's perspective appear vague and unnecessary.

When students operating in this mode experience difficulty in a program, externalizing blame ("This program is stupid") serves to maintain the differentiation between themselves and others, while self-rejection ("I'm stupid") serves to appease authority. Individuals may experience these responses in varying combinations at overt and covert levels. Whatever the combination, learners in this mode may tend to act out the central conflict in ways that instructors find annoying and disruptive. (This tendency toward hostility is described by Loevinger, 1977, as part of the Self-Protective Stage.)

One way that many students resolve the tensions of this mode on their way toward the next, Listening as a Way of Fitting In, is this: They come to identify with a group in opposition to authority. Instead of being primarily concerned with avoiding punishment, they come to crave a sense of belonging. Consequently, students in a training program who are approaching this point in their development are increasingly affected by the degree to which their program offers them the opportunity to develop this sense of group belonging. Lasker's (1978) study of workers in Curaçao indicates that, as individuals at Loevinger's Self-Protective Stage develop, they begin to be powerfully motivated to belong to a group, a central feature of the subsequent Conformist Stage.

For this reason, a training program that requires students functioning in this mode to compete with one another, work separately, and meet unilateral demands of the teacher is likely to be met with resistance by students who are moving toward the next mode. On the other hand, a training program that encourages group work and collaboration gives students at this developmental juncture a sense of belonging and a degree of authority over themselves, which leads to the next mode, Listening as a Way of Fitting In.

Listening as a Way of Fitting In

Central to this mode is the implicit desire to conform to group norms and a tendency to see oneself and others in terms of stereotypes. Inner life is understood simplistically, in clichés such as "sad" and "happy." The individual experiencing the world in this mode is uncomfortable with conflict and interpersonal differences, striving to be like and be liked by others. As a listener, the individual may recognize that he or she has a different opinion from a speaker, but will tend to consider his or her own view as objective and the speaker's view as mistaken.

A student's relationship with authority in this mode is captured in part by Perry's (1970) account of the Multiplicity position. The student sees the teacher as the authority to whom she or he must submit in order to avoid ostracism and punishment, but may value the opinions of peers just as highly. To the extent that students feel a need to conform to peer norms, they are likely to be more motivated to learn if their peers somehow sanction the learning. If sanctioning is clear, students will often be able to master some of the skills described by Carkhuff, Berenson, and Pierce (1976) and by Ivey (1988). As this is a mode in which the person places high value on being part of a group, the individual is especially vulnerable to feeling shame or embarrassment when criticized or ridiculed by others.

Because individuals operating from this mode are concerned with being like and liked by peers, approved of by teachers, and affiliated with the patients or clients to whom they listen, they have difficulty in responding to conflict and negative feelings. Using the earlier dialogue between Jane and Rob as an example, a student/listener might understand Jane's first remark as simply ''feeling bad'' and have a strong urge to cheer her up or otherwise get rid of her difficulty. When a teacher explicitly encourages a student to acknowledge a speaker's experience, the student may make an attempt to do so. Nonetheless, the student's responses may sound mechanical because they go against the grain of this mode's concern with minimizing conflict and difference.

Listening as Doing Good and Doing Well

A concern central to this mode is a sense of pursuing one's systematic life agenda and a growing appreciation of others' efforts to do the same. The individual is less concerned with appearing to conform to norms and is able to take the perspective of another to a greater degree. Other people are seen as having motives and feelings, although personality is often understood in terms of static traits rather than in terms of development and past experience.

In this mode, learning to listen is understood as a matter of mastering a set of skills in order to achieve personal competence, while living up to personal standards of fairness and good relations. Students want to do well for the sake of doing well, not primarily to conform; and they feel guilty when they fail to meet their own standards.

As in Loevinger's (1977) Conscientious Stage, and in contrast with earlier modes, one's standards are now more consciously chosen and self-evaluated. Yet, as in earlier modes, these standards are often assumed to be superior, and others' differing standards are not yet easily tolerated. A listener can accept a speaker's mixed feelings more easily than in the previous mode, but feelings that are ambiguous or cast doubt on the logic of the listener's system of meanings will be less well tolerated than those that are unambiguous and syntonic with the logic of the listener's system. Basseches' (1984) description of "formalism" is applicable to this mode. Within a formalistic framework, specific situations are "governed by rules and laws which can be stated at a general or universal level, with no reference to the content of the particulars" (p. 142).

A listener in this mode might paraphrase Jane's statement to reflect a broader sense of her experience: "You're saying something is really not going well." Such a paraphrase may sound like careful listening, but the listener will find it difficult, if not impossible, to refrain from offering, in the interest of being helpful, his or her own perspective as a better one. In response to Jane's statement, "Or, like, I just can't take charge. And I feel like I should be able to, but sometimes I almost don't want to, I guess," a listener in this mode will have difficulty recognizing and acknowledging her ambivalence. The listener is likely to respond to the unambivalent part and offer advice from his or her own experience: "You feel you should be able to take charge. Have you tried just taking it easy on yourself?" Speakers tend to experience such a listener as having an agenda or as waiting for a chance to speak.

Listening Because People Are Individuals

In this mode, perspective-taking has developed to the point where the individual is able to see connections among various aspects of his or her own experience as well as others'. As Loevinger (1977) says about the transition from the Conscientious to the Autonomous Stage, tolerance blooms "out of the recognition of individual differences and of complexities of circumstances" (p. 22). For example, difficulty in decision-making is understood in this mode as partly a matter of internal conflict, rather than simply a result of external demands.

In this mode, the individual has come to appreciate that "truth" depends on one's perspective, and one's context plays a primary role in determining that perspective. Perry (1970) refers to the loss of certainty that accompanies such an appreciation of relativism; when there is no sure stance from which to identify the "truth," it is difficult or impossible to exercise choice. A listener in this mode might therefore find it daunting to choose, for example, which aspects of Jane's experience to respond to. At the same time, the listener will be motivated to try to understand how Jane's experience is part of her individuality.

The listener in this mode may respond to Jane in a way that reflects genuine interest in how Jane came to feel the way she does, for example, "I wonder how it came to feel so frustrating." Note that this is not the same as the response from the previous mode, "You're saying something is really not going well," which has a more certain tone and uses a standard figure of speech found in many training programs, "You're saying————." The beginning, "I wonder————," represents instead a departure from the standard phraseology and indicates the listener's interest in the nature of the speaker's experience. Also more likely in this mode are responses that affirm the intensity of the speaker's internal conflict and feelings, both positive and negative. The speaker tends to sense from such responses that the listener is offering permission and encouragement for the speaker to attend in some depth to his or her own experience.

Listening To Be in a Complex Relationship

In this mode, simple curiosity and tolerance have given way to the ability more fully to appreciate and even to embrace others' separate identities and experiences. The listener can take the perspective of another in richly differentiated terms, while maintaining a sense of the differences between self and other. Added to this is a recognition of development and change over time. Loevinger (1977) speaks of this recognition in her description of the Autonomous Stage, in which "the person sees himself and others as having motives that have developed *as a result of past experiences*" (p. 23, emphasis added). Whereas a powerful motive in the earlier mode of Listening as Doing Good and Doing Well was the desire to achieve personal competence and autonomy, now the liabilities of autonomy are also seen: Autonomy can mean being so self-sealing that one experiences a sense of invulnerability to and disconnection from others, with the consequent loss of many opportunities for growth through interdependence. In this mode, while respect for the other is seen as necessary to making relationships safe and supportive, it is respect for the transformative potential of relationships that provides the motivation for listening. Concern for others as complex beings combines with a sense that one's own development as a complex being depends on one's relationships.

In this mode, potential responses in a given situation become richly varied and many-faceted. The listener's responses reflect a wish to better sense the depth and breadth of a speaker's experience, rather than an attempt to paraphrase in concrete terms what the speaker just said. Because of an awareness of the complexity and diversity of experience and meanings, the listener may be very reluctant to assume understanding, putting responses in tentative terms: "As if you just feel caught somehow?"

The listener in this mode is more aware than ever before of his or her own past and present experience and consequently is more aware of the speaker as having potentially different past and present experiences. In learning how to listen, students in this mode demonstrate a complex recognition of the dynamic between two people, including both the potential misunderstandings and the ways in which each person might be transformed through the interaction. Such a recognition is reminiscent of some of the more complex forms of "dialectical" reasoning described by Basseches (1984) and others.[3]

Listening to Life

In this mode, listening to another person is seen as a window on the ongoing process of life, poignant and infinitely complex, but a process of which both speaker and listener are parts. Listening is felt as an opportunity to bridge what sometimes seems to be an infinite chasm between people by participating in a shared and dynamic experience. It is important to note, however, that this mode's appreciation of the value of shared experience is not simplistic or reductive; it does not deny the complexity and flux of relationships and the limitations these impose on communication. Rather, this mode incorporates the previous mode's ability to comprehend multiple systems and contexts and to think dialectically (Basseches, 1984) in terms of mutual change and development. As in the previous mode, listening is understood to serve the functions of connection and communication, aspects of the overall process by which people transform one another via their interactions. One's own and others' intrapsychic voices are heard in their complexity, while nevertheless understood to coexist within the larger whole of life.

Now, with the ability to mentally juxtapose complex realities, the individual notes paradoxes and ironies that accompany life's pain, pleasure, and ennui. Contradictions may be relished as aspects of life at its most stubborn and its most vivid. The process of learning to listen may itself become grist for the existential amusement that Loevinger (1977) associates with the Integrated Stage in her theory. Students may experience their training as a delicate process punctuated by moments of deep discomfort, delight, and poignant humor. (Note that it is not others' pain or struggle that at times appears amusing, but rather the process of learning itself.) Their recognition of the complexity of life is balanced by their sense of the preciousness of life as a whole. For this reason, students in this mode are more likely to appreciate the concrete aspects of skills-training (practicing specific techniques, for example) if these aspects are presented with adequate recognition of the complexity and uniqueness of human experience.

In the foregoing description, we have seen six ways that the activity of listening and the process of learning to listen may be experienced differently, depending on one's Mode of Learning to Listen. Benack (1981) documents the very different meanings that one college counseling course held for different students. Using the Perry (1970) scheme of development, she explores the differences in students' understandings of the course's content. Although Perry's scheme includes nine positions, Benack was particularly interested in Perry's distinction between "dualistic" and "relativistic" frameworks. Dualism refers to the tendency of individuals at the earliest positions in Perry's scheme to make sense of the world in polar terms—things are either right or wrong. Relativism refers to the ability, found in Perry's later positions, to make sense of the world in ways that acknowledge that rightness and wrongness are dependent on assumptions and context.

The course Benack studied was designed to teach students the deeper kind of responsiveness or empathy, beyond simply the skills that empathy involves. She compared students whose perspective was essentially dualistic with those whose perspective was relativistic. A primary finding was that dualistic students tend to be able to learn skills, but not a deeper kind of empathy. Their responses carry a certain, non-tentative tone, or they seem to be driven by a hope of getting the right answer, as if on an examination: "So, then, what you're feeling is *happy*?" (Benack, p. 288). It is as if "the client's experience was treated as a fixed entity or state, like a disease to be diagnosed, and that the client's role in the interaction was to provide information about this entity to the counselor. The counselor then tried to build a theory of the client's experience, to hand back a diagnosis" (p. 288).

In contrast, relativists seemed immediately to understand the idea of taking the other person's perspective and incorporated such perspective-taking into their responses. Their responses tended to be tentative, as if they would be reluctant to assume they knew what the client was feeling, but rather wanted to try to get a sense of the client's overall experience from the client's perspective. The relativists were quick to understand and incorporate the "form and the spirit of accompanying-reflective counseling" (p. 285). By the time they had made their second tape for the course, they had "essentially stopped asking questions, giving suggestions, [and] making interpretations" (p. 285).

HOW STUDENTS UNDERSTAND TWO TEACHING
FOCUSES

In any given training program, there are likely to be moments when the teacher's attention will be primarily focused on what we have been calling "listening skills," and other moments when the teacher's attention is primarily focused on what we have been calling "empathy." Table 1 shows how each of these moments in teaching listening might be understood by students with different understandings regarding the *nature* of listening. That is, for each Mode of Learning to Listen, Table 1 describes the learner's understandings of and basic questions regarding the two teaching focuses, skills or empathy.

For example, how would students whose mode is Listening as a Way of Fitting In hear the different moments in a training program? When a teacher talks a good deal about eye contact, the importance of paraphrasing, and other skills, students in this mode of listening might feel that they understand the subject quite well, and they would evaluate their understanding in terms of their own behavior, such as eye contact, repeating words, and so forth. One of their central questions would be, "Am I doing anything that will make me look foolish to the others?"

But when the teacher talks primarily about the importance of building a sense of the speaker's inner world and about the value of recognizing the complex interrelationship between the speaker's and the listener's past experience, students in the mode of Listening as a Way of Fitting In might feel differently. They might feel that the meaning of empathy is too vague and hard to grasp. The standard of evaluation would appear unclear ("Do they just want me to nod my head and be nice?") and consequently threatening in the degree to which it makes a student vulnerable to looking foolish.

We can now see how the difference between "listening skills" and "empathy"

Table 1

The Learner's Experience of the Teacher's Attention to Skills or Empathy by Mode of Learning to Listen

Mode of Learning To Listen	Focus of Teacher's Attention	
	Skills	Empathy
Listening Because I Have To	**Understanding:** I have to look at the person's eyes and be quiet most of the time. I have to say back what they say. **Question:** Is there some way I can get out of this without getting into trouble?	**Understanding:** Maybe I am supposed to feel what the other person feels, but I don't want to. **Question:** How can I act like I'm doing it, but escape?
Listening as a Way of Fitting In	**Understanding:** I am supposed to maintain eye contact, repeat back other's words, etc. **Question:** Am I doing anything to make myself look foolish?	**Understanding:** I guess they want me to feel what the other person feels, but this is confusing, unclear. **Question:** Am I supposed to be nice?
Listening to Do Good and Do Well	**Understanding:** I am proud of building these skills successfully, and I can help others make sense better. **Question:** Am I doing it right?	**Understanding:** This idea seems wishy-washy and imprecise. **Question:** How can I get this right when I don't know what to do?
Listening Because People Are Individuals	**Understanding:** Eye contact and things like that make sense to me as a way of helping people talk, but sometimes the skills seem artificial. **Question:** Am I really helping?	**Understanding:** I can see how it helps another person to feel understood, and it makes sense to me as a way of letting other people be themselves. **Question:** I don't know if this is enough. Can it work?

Table 1 (continued)

Mode of Learning To Listen	Focus of Teacher's Attention	
	Skills	Empathy
Listening to be in a Complex Relationship	**Understanding**: Listening skills do seem to be part of a relationship, and I can see how it helps people feel closer to each other and less alone. **Question**: How will speakers react to this "technique?"	**Understanding**: The back and forth of relating oneself to another's experience seems to be a good way of building a relationship. **Question**: What protects a relationship from our distorting projections about one another?
Listening to Life	**Understanding**: Focusing on skills is one way of engaging in a relationship. I can see the utility, but they seem limiting. **Question**: How does this integrate with the larger picture?	**Understanding**: This process helps me see beyond the complexity and struggle of life to its integrity, and I can feel myself and the speaker as part of that. **Question**: Can I share this process with others in a way that doesn't substitute proselytizing for listening myself?

as concepts relates to the discussion of students' developmentally determined conceptions of listening. The relationship can be summarized as follows: There is a complex form of attending to another person that is often understood as "empathy." If an observer watched someone who was attending in this complex way, they could easily assume that the attending was solely comprised of a collection of behaviors, such as eye contact, asking open-ended questions, and so forth. They might also assume that the behaviors were sufficient to convey to the speaker a sense of being heard. However, these behaviors, often called "listening skills," are not equivalent to more complex, empathic attending. It is important to differentiate between learning listening skills on the one hand and learning perspective-taking or empathy on the other because of the developmental processes involved in both. Although the learning of skills and the learning of empathy may both take place to some extent in any given course, students in different modes will experience skills-training and empathy-training differently. Some students may be unable to learn the complex perspective-taking involved in empathy-training, while others may find that skills-training is artificial or otherwise unsatisfying unless it involves a recognition of the complexity of experience and the tentative nature of understanding.

IMPLICATIONS FOR TEACHING AND LEARNING

Clearly, the sense that students make of the act of listening is defined and constrained by what we have called their "Mode." This raises a dilemma with regard to the orientation of our teaching/training effort. Should our fundamental orientation be toward teaching a student in those ways or with those methods that are most accessible to the student, within the boundaries of whatever mode he or she is operating in? Or should our orientation be toward stretching the boundaries of what is accessible and challenging him or her to develop more complex modes?

This dilemma has arisen before within the broader arena of constructive developmental theory and practice. Some have argued that education should not aim directly to promote stage development. Others have argued that it is precisely the educator's job to challenge students to move on to the next developmental stage. (See Kohlberg and Meyer, 1972, for a discussion of this issue. For additional reading on the application of developmental theory to teaching, see Copes, 1982; Knefelkamp, Widick & Parker, 1975.) How any educator resolves this dilemma depends on both the teacher's basic value commitment and the pragmatic context of the training. However, it seems clear that whichever value orientation one believes to be the proper focus of education, an understanding of and careful attention to students' Mode of Learning to Listen is a prerequisite for effective teaching of interpersonal communication.

We will now discuss four areas of specific implications of the model we have proposed here for teaching and learning: risks and benefits of skills-oriented training, risks and benefits of empathy-oriented training, multiple roles and layers of complexity, and implications for specific training arenas.

Risks and Benefits of Skills-Oriented Teaching

A teaching approach that emphasizes listening skills has several potential benefits: (a) If students accumulate enough skills, according to some advocates of skills-training, they *will be* empathizing. (b) By developing these skills, students may *eventually learn* to take another's perspective. (c) Learning listening skills may provide a means of expressing the compassion that the students already feel but may not know how to convey. (d) Having exercised some listening skills that, at the very least, encourage the speaker to keep talking, the student may become well enough acquainted with the speaker to develop some empathy for and begin to engage in a deeper relationship with the speaker.

However, according to our understanding of development, teaching that primarily emphasizes skills also carries some risks. For the learner in a later mode, paying attention to skills may not be at odds with understanding the depth of another's experience, but it may be a distraction in that it represents a different orientation, a different internal process. For example, when listeners are concerned with monitoring their behavior against a checklist of behaviors, they may find it difficult to get a personal sense of another's experience. William Kreidler, of Educators for Social Responsibility, a group that trains adults in conflict resolution, believes that teaching "active listening" and "I-messages"[4] tends to draw the learner's attention away from the speaker's experience. He believes that when the teaching focus is on learning specific behavioral skills, feelings and intuition tend to be neglected because the learner's attention is on the skills, not on the speaker's point of view (W. J. Kreidler, personal communication, February 28, 1992). Taking the other's perspective requires more of an effort to "step into the other's shoes," which in turn requires an internal freedom to cast attention to that other person's experience rather than one's own checklist of specific behaviors.

There are also risks that arise from the developmental complexity, not of the listener, but of the person being listened to. A client who has a complex grasp of the potential chasms of misunderstanding that exist between people (in Perry's terms, a relativist) may be more likely to feel "missed" by a listener who is oriented to a list of skills. A complaint from a counseling client about being "psychologized" may sometimes be a response to being listened to in a mechanical way that measures behavioral skills as evidence of deeper empathy. Armstrong (1991) makes a strong case for the importance of matching the complexity of a psychiatric patient's experience with a therapist who can think in similarly complex terms.

Risks and Benefits of Empathy-Oriented Teaching

A teaching focus that emphasizes perspective-taking and empathy also carries both potential benefits and risks. For example, a course that for many years was a mainstay of the counseling program at Harvard's Graduate School of Education attempted to foster students' development, including their development of self-awareness and empathy.[5] Its teaching process emphasized the discovery and examination of the learner's own assumptions about responding through role play and listening to audiotaped recordings of "as if" counseling sessions. The teaching focus was on helping learners understand the speakers' experience as the speakers experienced it. The teaching in this course fostered a process in which listeners were asked to attend to the felt experience of the speakers (as the listeners heard it) and then tentatively check that understanding with the speakers. For instance, the course invited students to ask themselves questions such as, "What is the world like for this person?" "What is the nature of their pain?"

Through this course, students had the opportunity to develop and express their genuine interest in and concern for the experience of the other. They also had the opportunity to explore their own experience as listeners and, through that exploration, discover their own tacit assumptions. The hope implicit in this kind of teaching focus is that students will gain the ability to be with others in more genuine and empathic ways. This teaching focus rests on the assumption that a student listener's genuine interest will lead to many of the overt behaviors that are on the skills checklist, but that the listener's primary concern is with the speaker's experience, not the checklist.

A focus on empathy rather than skills has particular benefits for the *relationship* between speaker and listener. Only when listeners are free to leave behind their concerns about measuring their responses against a behavioral checklist can they become fully interested in the other person's experience, and the feeling of this difference is often clear for both listener and speaker. For speakers, it may feel as if they are being kept company, as if they are being offered a moment of freedom to go even further inward, knowing that their companion will try to follow. It may be a great relief to feel, at long last, that there is someone who has some sense of their experience. For listeners, it may feel as if the speaker's experience is becoming vivid and compelling. They may find themselves with strong feelings, almost as if they were standing in the shoes of the speaker, enabling them to perceive and acknowledge not only the emotional aspects, but also the coherence and integrity of the speaker's experience. The listener experiences associations between the speaker's expression, the listener's understanding of the speaker's experience, and the listener's other associations and feelings.

Teaching that is primarily empathy-oriented carries risks as well as benefits. Because it fosters students' recognition of interpersonal differences and similarities, it serves to encourage many students to shift from earlier modes, such as Listening as Doing Good and Doing Well, toward later modes, such as Listening Because People Are Individuals. However, those students who are the most uncomfortable with ambiguity and who want concrete, measurable tasks may find this kind of encouragement difficult to understand. To the extent that these students are motivated largely by a desire to avoid censure or punishment or to perform well, rather than by curiosity or a desire to enhance relationships (both of which become prominent in later modes), they will experience empathy-oriented teaching as confusing.

Teaching that focuses primarily on empathy may also be inappropriate or inaccessible for those teachers who understand the listening process only in concrete, behavioral terms. Additionally, some teachers may be uncomfortable with or even opposed to a course that invites intrapersonal searching and interpersonal sharing to the degree that an empathy-oriented focus often does.

Moreover, some teachers and administrators may find that the time involved in such in-depth teaching of listening is prohibitive. If it takes only a few sessions to convey specific skills sufficiently for students to replicate many of them, whereas an empathy-oriented program may take several weeks or even months to be useful (particularly if students enter the course with a Listening-as-a-Way-of-Fitting-In or a Listening-as-Doing-Good-and-Doing-Well orientation), it is tempting to see skills training as more immediately practical. However, students who primarily learn skills may not be able to provide the kind of listening that some speakers find most helpful. In addition, as the following discussion emphasizes, adopting one approach to the exclusion of the other risks missing some students.

Multiple Roles and Layers of Complexity

No doubt the reader has noticed that we have used the term "listener" to refer to people in several different roles. For example, a "listener" might be a student listening to another student in a classroom role-play, a student listening to a teacher of listening skills, a teacher listening to a student's understanding of "listening skills," or a trainer listening to teachers talk about understanding their students. Interpersonal communication is ubiquitous, and any individual may at the same time or at different times operate in the role of listener or speaker, teacher or learner.

The problem of how to teach listening is more complicated than simply matching the approach of the course with the type of student in it. A teacher is faced with a class composed of students with diverse ways of understanding. Some students may benefit more from a listening-as-skills approach, and others from an approach that emphasizes taking the perspective of the other. To disregard such diversity and teach to some idea of an "average" student, or to teach only to those who have the most difficulty, or to teach only to those who can empathize most easily, all make the course content inaccessible to some students. Instead, we suggest listening to students for their diverse ways of understanding the material and responding within their frameworks. There are many opportunities for this kind of attending and responding through interactive journals and during individual and group discussions. When such attending occurs in a group, the teacher implicitly communicates to students that they have different ways of making sense, which fosters their self-awareness and awareness of others' experience, two hallmarks of development.

Implications for Specific Training Arenas

We see implications for specific training arenas, as well, such as the training of psychotherapists, teachers, and negotiators. In the training of counselors, psychologists, and psychiatrists, programs can be fruitfully designed to take into account the developmental diversity of students. Such programs offer students opportunities to explore their own assumptions and feelings about their work, as well as offering discussions of behavioral skills. Armstrong (1991) proposes an idea aimed more directly at promoting development:

Training, supervision, and consultation ought not only to focus on imparting concrete information, specific techniques, and abstract theory, but also on presenting therapeutic dilemmas in ways that encourage postformal problem solving. Therapeutic errors in treatment can also be understood in cognitive developmental terms. They may represent difficulties in entertaining the idea of alternative reality systems, or problems in bridging these systems, or the experience of becoming cognitively overwhelmed in a relativism that has many alternatives and no priorities. (pp. 15–16)

Armstrong's proposal explicitly considers students' level of developmental complexity as an aspect of their training.

Teacher training is another area related to our discussion. One way to think about the dilemma confronting teachers is to picture the complexity of the scene with which they are faced: a classful of students with diverse, often overlapping systems for making sense, a range of emotions, and a wide variety of life contexts. Moreover, the teacher in such a classroom hopes to communicate about issues that themselves vary in complexity. Daunting as it is, we think that the difficult task of responding to students' differing ways of making sense can at least partly be addressed by attending to teachers' development. Teachers who themselves have had the opportunity to develop forms of sense-making that are sufficiently complex to permit dialectical thought will be better able, if not eager, to take students' perspectives and understand their ways of making sense, a skill that is highly valued in classroom teaching (Saphier & Gower 1987). This implies preparing teachers through fostering their development; it means helping them to discover themselves as having assumptions, feelings, and perspectives that may differ from those of their students, while helping them to listen for the integrity of their students' experience.

In the field of negotiation, perspective-taking is already understood by many to be important. Negotiators who are able to take the perspectives of others are better equipped to negotiate a solution that is mutually acceptable (Fisher & Ury, 1981). Although a capacity for perspective-taking can be developed to some extent via skills training, a program that promotes the development of empathy will have greater value. A negotiator who genuinely tries to understand and even appreciate the other party's interests is more likely to be experienced by the other party as taking those interests into account. In contrast, a negotiator who is absorbed in performing skills will tend to be experienced by the other party as being manipulative. Moreover, through coming to understand the other's point of view, negotiators may find themselves shifting in their own position, transforming their previously adversarial role into a more collaborative one. An empathy-oriented approach to teaching negotiation must offer frequent opportunities for student negotiators to explore their own assumptions about the other party's feelings and thoughts as well as their own. For example, it is important to provide opportunities for role-playing so that students can try out different kinds of response styles and hear how they affect another person. Such an approach will also include opportunities for students themselves to be heard so that they can discover through their own experience the power of being heard by a genuinely interested listener.

A fairly new field, that of conflict resolution training, could also make use of the ideas in this chapter by attending to differences in mode among learners. A program designed to train adults to manage conflict would take care to challenge those who immediately understand the idea of perspective-taking, while also speaking to those who are concerned with the more concrete aspects of interpersonal communication, such as specific forms of speech and eye contact. Conflict resolution training, like other forms of training in interpersonal communication, would thus require a multilayered teaching process, fostering both skills and empathy.

CONCLUSION

In this chapter, we have introduced a developmental model of learning to listen and integrated it with ideas about the learning and teaching of interpersonal communication. In addition to development and teaching orientation as factors in learning to listen, there are, of course, other factors too numerous to mention here, some of which profoundly effect the learning experience. As Hogue, Bross, and Efran indicate in chapter 13 of this volume, learning is a complex interaction between organism and context.

One contextual factor is a pedagogical one: the choice of a didactic or an experiential format is likely to make a critical difference in the way students make sense of a course on listening skills. The didactic approach—which consists primarily of lectures, with little opportunity for learners to interact with the material or with one another—has several advantages, such as its efficiency. The straightforward lecture format can be employed in large classes. Further, the material can be read to students by instructors who are not very familiar with the content.

The didactic format carries a number of risks, however, a primary one being that the subject matter may be learned superficially or abstractly and may not become integrated with students' current experience and beliefs. Lipson (1988) observes that learning that brings the learner into personal relationship with the subject matter is far more likely to be integrated into the learner's meaning-making system and thus be better remembered than learning that is experienced as unconnected and impersonal. To quote Perry, "If I say, 'So, what you were feeling was anger,' that's a concept. *Experience* is in the present tense and unfolding, in motion. A *concept* is fixed" (personal communication, November 12, 1992). Didactic teaching gives students concepts *about* listening, but they are not learning listening. Accordingly, it would not be surprising for them to feel general acceptance of the *concepts* of empathy or listening skills but to have little ability to actually exercise empathy or employ listening skills.

In contrast, the experiential format provides opportunities for personal learning. Such a format may, for example, feature participation in and observation of role playing in which learners converse with each other, learning more about perspectives different from their own and receiving feedback on their interpersonal communication. In chapter 28 of this volume, writing on the future of adult lifespan learning, Sinnott emphasizes the importance for adults of learning about multiple perspectives "through sharing truth with others and hearing their truths." Through its hands-on nature, an experiential format offers opportunities for students explicitly to connect the subject matter to their current beliefs and experience and to hear about the nature of others' experience.

A drawback of this format is that it can take more time than a didactic format. In addition, it may not be welcomed by faculty who view teaching as an information-transmitting function. Nevertheless, we are convinced that the long-term advantages of the experiential format outweigh the short-term disadvantages of the time required and that interpersonal communication is an area in which competence is best acquired through practice, rather than through the passive receipt of information.

Communication is a complex process, and basic assumptions about what it means to "listen" shift over time and across contexts. Learners of interpersonal communication benefit from teaching that implicitly recognizes the different ways in which students interpret the listening process. At times, some students will benefit from a focus on well-defined listening skills. Other students are sometimes better served by a focus that fosters their ability to empathically take the perspective of the speaker. However, there may be times when all of these students benefit from the alternative teaching focus. Every training group or class is in some degree of flux with respect to these variables. In this developmentally complex and dynamic situation, we see value in distinguishing empathy, in the broader, deeper sense, from the set of specific behavioral skills that may spring from (or lead to) it.

NOTES

1. The original context of this quote is Buber (1965), *The Knowledge of Man*, New York: Harper and Row, p. 81.

2. Despite his basic support of the skills-first sequence, Bolton cautions against going too far in adherence to the learning or teaching of specific skills, becoming "legalistic about them" (p. 273).

3. In chapter 4 of this volume, Lee describes a collaboration between a teacher and a scientist that reflects this kind of mutual transformation.

4. An "I-message" is a statement of one's own feeling, such as "I feel hurt," as opposed to a "You-message," which is usually an evaluation of the other person, such as "You are thoughtless." For a more complete description, see Gordon (1970), pp. 115–138.

5. This is the course mentioned previously on which Benack based her work. For more detailed descriptions of this course, see Benack (1981) and Phillips (1985, pp. 36–37).

REFERENCES

Armstrong, J. (1991). Keeping one's balance in a moving system: The effects of the multiple personality disordered patient on the cognitive development of the therapist. In J. D. Sinnott and J. Cavanaugh (Eds.). *Bridging paradigms: Positive development in adulthood and cognitive aging*. New York: Praeger.

Basseches, M. (1984). *Dialectical thinking and adult development*. Norwood, NJ: Ablex Publishing.

Basseches, M. (1989). Toward a constructive-developmental understanding of the dialectics of individuality and irrationality. In D. Kramer and M. Bopp (Eds.), *Transformation in clinical and developmental psychology*. New York: Springer-Verlag.

Benack, S. (1981). The development of relativistic epistemological thought and the growth of empathy in late adolescence and early adulthood. Doctoral dissertation. Harvard University.

Benjamin, A. (1981). *The helping interview*. Boston: Houghton Mifflin.

Bolton, R. (1979). *People skills: How to assert yourself, listen to others, and resolve conflicts*. New York: Simon and Schuster.

Buber, M. (1957). Elements of the interhuman. *Psychiatry, 20*, 105–113.

Carkhuff, R. R., Berenson, D. H. & Pierce, R. M. (1976). *The skills of teaching: Interpersonal skills*. Amherst, MA: Human Resource Development Press.

Cobb, J. P. & Lieberman, S. (1987). The grammar of psychotherapy: A descriptive account. *British Journal of Psychiatry, 151*, 589–594.

Copes, L. (1982). The Perry developmental scheme: A metaphor for teaching and learning mathematics. In *For the Learning of Mathematics, 3*(1), 38–44.

Doyle, R. E. (1982). The counselor's role communication skills, or the roles counselors play: A conceptual model. *Counselor Education and Supervision, 22*(2) 123–131.

Fisher, R. & Ury, W. (1981). *Getting to yes: Negotiating agreement without giving in*. Boston: Houghton Mifflin.

Gabarro, J. J. (1991). Retrospective commentary. *Harvard Business Review, 69*(6), 108–109.

Gladstein, G. A. (1983). Understanding empathy: Interpreting counseling, developmental, and social psychology perspectives. *Journal of Counseling Psychology, 30*, 467–482.

Gordon, T. (1970). *Parent effectiveness training: The tested new way to raise responsible children*. N.Y.: Penguin Books.

Ivey, A. E. (1988). *Intentional interviewing and counseling*. Pacific Grove, CA: Brooks/Cole.

Kegan, R. (1982). *The evolving self: Problem and process in human development*. Cambridge, MA: Harvard University Press.

Knefelcamp, L. L., Widick, C. & Parker, C. A. (1975). The counselor as a developmental instructor. *Counselor Education and Supervision, 14*(4), 286–296.

Kohlberg, L. (1981). *The philosophy of moral development: Essays in moral development*. New York: Harper and Row.

Kohlberg, L. and Meyer, M. R. (1972). Development as the aim of education. *Harvard Educational Review, 42*, 449–496.

Lasker, H. (1978). Ego development and motivation: A cross-cultural analysis of *n* achievement. Doctoral dissertation. University of Chicago.

Lipson, A. (1988). Academic Amnesia. *Harvard Magazine*, Jan./Feb., 47–50.

Loevinger, J. (1977). *Ego development: Conceptions and theories*. San Francisco: Jossey-Bass.

Margulies, A. (1989). *The empathic imagination*. New York: W. W. Norton & Company.

Perry, W. G., Jr. (1970). *Forms of intellectual and ethical development in the college years: A scheme*. New York: Holt, Rinehart and Winston.

Phillips, A. (1985). Self-appreciation and internal dialogue: A review of literature. Qualifying paper, Harvard University.

Phillips, A. (1989). Inner voices, inner selves: A study of internal conversation in narrative. (Doctoral dissertation, Harvard University, 1989). *Dissertation Abstracts International*, 90–00877.

Piaget, J. & Inhelder, B. (1969). *The psychology of the child*. New York: Basic Books.

Rogers, C. R. (1980). *A way of being*. Boston: Houghton Mifflin.

Rogers, C. R. (1961). *On becoming a person*. Boston: Houghton Mifflin.

Rogers, C. R. & Rothlisberger, F. J. (1991). Barriers and gateways to communication. *Harvard Business Review*, 69(6), 105–111. (Originally published in *Harvard Business Review*, July-August, 1952).

Saphier, J. & Gower, R. (1987). *The skillful teacher: Building your teaching skills*. Carlisle, MA: Research for Better Teaching.

Sue, D. W. (1991). A conceptual model for cultural diversity training. *Journal of Counseling and Development*, *70*, 99–105.

Thorsheim, H. I. & Roberts, B. B., in collaboration with Basseches, M. (1991). *Listening to each other's stories, seeing through each other's eyes: A workbook for pairs of students working together to build skills for cross-cultural understanding*. Northfield, MN: St. Olaf College.

Tolle, S. W., Cooney, T. G. & Hickam, D. H. (1989). A program to teach residents humanistic skills for notifying survivors of a patient's death. *Academic Medicine*, *64*(9), 505–506.

Weihs, K. & Chapados, J. T. (1986). Interviewing skills training: A study. *Social Science Medicine*, *23*(1), 31–34.

21

The Process of Health Behavior Change: Individual Factors and Planning Models

Renee Royak-Schaler and
Patricia Maloney Alt

Since the early 1970s, American health professionals, researchers, and policy-makers have been concerned with the relationship between health practices and longevity. Early research informed us that individuals could influence their health status and the onset of chronic disease through changes in diet, exercise, smoking, and alcohol consumption (Belloc & Breslow, 1972). Findings from controlled intervention trials described cost-effective methods to reduce morbidity and mortality in the adult population. Research emphasized the importance of health promotion and monitoring for improving the health of American adults (Breslow & Somers, 1977).

How and why do adults learn to change their actions in beneficial or harmful ways? Can research findings on the value of preventive practices be translated into terms that adults will not only comprehend but act upon? What are the barriers to behavior change that prevent or limit our living healthier lives? These are critical questions for understanding health behavior. Our awareness of our own mortality leads to a high level of emotional investment in health learning. Affective responses are often more important than factual information in shaping behavior. As in "new science," we construct our own reality and then react to it (Sinnott, chapter 7, in this volume).

As a nation, we have responded to the threat of heart disease and cancer with an approach emphasizing both individual and environmental control through behavior change and public legislation. The main reduction in mortality from heart disease during the past fifteen years has resulted from controlling risk factors through behavior change. Interventions have focused on increasing exercise, dietary management, smoking cessation, stress management, and controlling hypertension. These strategies are considered to be "health protective behaviors,'' undertaken by people to promote, protect, or maintain their health, regardless of their health status (Harris & Guten, 1979).

Those individuals who engage in indirect preventive health behaviors such as medical checkups and screenings, immunizations, and seatbelt use do not necessarily engage in such direct preventive health behaviors as smoking cessation, exercise, and healthy diet (Langlie, 1977). The 1985 Health Interview Survey, for example, found that only 34% of women examined their breasts more than six times per year, only 42% of adults reported exercising or playing sports regularly, and only 32% wore seat belts most of the time (Thornberry, Wilson & Golden, 1986). It appears that individuals who practice direct preventive health behaviors are those who have a strong sense of control over health, value preventive health actions, and usually belong to higher socioeconomic groups. Those who follow rigorous exercise regimens to promote their health may not, however, be committed to healthy diet or stress management. Health protective behavior is complex and multifaceted, with different individuals committed to different sets of health practices (Levine & Sorenson, 1984).

Although we are a people who believe that we can remain healthy through appropriate health actions and personal control, this control is paradoxical (Brownell, 1991). Personal control over health can produce positive consequences for individuals who make behavior changes and for society in reducing rates of disease. The perception of personal control over health can lead to more self-initiated preventive health care, better emotional health, and the ability to make desired behavior changes (Seeman & Seeman, 1983; Thompson & Spacapan, 1991). It can also be a factor that delays seeking medical care when care is seen as a threat to personal control (Timko, 1987). There is, however, a danger of holding individuals responsible for their poor health, blaming them for not making the changes society expects of them, while excusing public policies that limit their ability to change (Becker, 1986; Marantz, 1990; Kenkel, 1991).

In promoting an integrative understanding of health behavior this chapter focuses first on the cognitive, behavioral, emotional, and social factors that influence individual life-style. Next, it discusses frameworks that describe health behavior in individuals and communities, used in planning effective behavior change and health promotion programs. Finally, the behavior change process itself is examined. Our purpose is to describe adult learning processes in health behavior choices and the impact of educational efforts on those choices.

FACTORS INFLUENCING INDIVIDUAL HEALTH BEHAVIORS

The practice of individual health behavior and the process of behavior change are influenced by five types of factors: social factors, emotional factors, cognitive factors, access to medical care, and perceived symptoms. Social factors that contribute to health practices include social approval and peer influence, family rearing practices, and cultural values of particular groups. The health practices we were raised with as children strongly influence our adult patterns in everything from brushing our teeth to eating red meat and fatty foods.

Emotional factors affect eating and exercise habits; they also play a very significant role in addictive behaviors such as smoking and alcohol and drug use. Emotions influence individual willingness to obtain health screenings. Women with a family history of breast cancer who are very anxious about their high-risk status, for example, are less likely to have regular mammograms and clinical breast exams and to perform breast self-examination than those who are less anxious (Kash, Holland, Halper & Miller, 1991; Royak-Schaler & Benderly, 1992).

Cognitive factors also affect personal health practices, usually in the form of thinking that a particular health practice will be beneficial. Thinking that lowfat diet and exercise will contribute to reducing the likelihood of heart disease can incline individuals from high-risk family backgrounds to modify their diets and exercise regularly. These behaviors can also serve to reduce the individual's feelings of vulnerability.

Education and income are crucial factors determining individual access to medical care; Those with more education and higher income are more likely to receive immunizations, have regular physicals when they have no symptoms, obtain preventive dental care, get Pap smears, and respond to breast-cancer screening programs (Kirscht, 1983). Women of lower socioeconomic status (SES) have 25% higher death rates from breast cancer and 2.8 times higher cervical cancer mortality rates than higher-SES women (USDHHS, 1990).

Perceived symptoms, both in oneself and in friends and family members, often serve as cues to take health actions. Finding a breast lump will encourage a woman to seek medical care for this immediate situation and will serve as a reminder for follow-up screenings. Developing a persistent cough can serve as a reminder to the individual who smokes that it might be time to actively pursue stopping smoking.

Some of the factors that influence health behavior can be modified through educational interventions. These include personal factors that restrict or enhance the potential for change, social and systemic factors that diminish possibilities for behavior change, and reinforcing factors that serve as incentives or disincentives to change. Individual, environmental, organizational, and community factors that facilitate or inhibit changes in health behaviors will be discussed next in the context of frameworks for understanding health behavior.

FRAMEWORKS FOR UNDERSTANDING HEALTH BEHAVIOR

The primary models or frameworks that have been used to understand and predict health behavior are the Health Belief Model (Becker, 1974; Rosenstock, Strecher & Becker, 1988), the PRECEDE framework (Green, Kreuter, Deeds & Partridge, 1980), Social Cognitive Theory (formerly called social learning theory;

Bandura, 1977, 1986), Health Locus of Control measures (Wallston, 1992), and Fishbein and Ajzen's Theory of Reasoned Action (Ajzen, 1987; Ajzen & Timko, 1986; Timko, 1987). They are all in current use.

Each of these theoretical approaches acknowledges that health behavior change is a complex process; that no one model will predict all behaviors; that the change task is different when one is adopting new healthy behaviors than when unlearning chronic behavior patterns; that interventions, treatments, and measures of change must be tailored to particular problems and individual needs; that people, both individually and in groups, need to "own" their problem and its solution; and that perceived self-efficacy or self-control are critical elements in understanding and maintaining health-promoting behaviors (Rosenstock et al., 1988; Bandura, 1986; Wallston, 1992; Ajzen & Timko, 1986).

Health Belief Model

The Health Belief Model originally theorized that individual health behaviors can be understood on the basis of three factors: health motivation or sufficient concern and interest in health, the perception and belief that one is vulnerable to a serious health problem or threat, and the perception and belief that following a particular health practice will effectively reduce the health threat. The benefits of health actions are weighed against perceptions of physical, psychological, financial, and other barriers inherent in the health efforts. From this perspective demographic, social, structural, and personality factors have been viewed by some researchers as modifying factors, since they influence health behavior (Becker, 1974).

This model was developed in the early 1950s to help understand the failure of individuals to use screening tests for the early detection of asymptomatic disease (Becker, 1974). It was later applied to patients' responses to symptoms, compliance with prescribed medical regimens, such preventive health actions as breast self-examination, and changing such chronic health habits as smoking and dieting (Becker, 1974; Langlie, 1977; Hallal, 1982). In recent work, its authors have pointed out the original model's limitations in explaining change in existing chronic behaviors, rather than the addition of new preventive practices (Rosenstock, Strecher & Becker, 1988).

A review of forty-six studies using the Health Belief Model found that the factor "barriers to action" was the best predictor of both preventive health behavior and sick-role behavior (Janz & Becker, 1984). In breast self-exam studies, for example, perceived barriers such as "fear of finding a lump, lack of confidence in one's abilities, forgetting, and thinking it is not necessary" have been the factors most consistently associated with breast self-exam infrequency (Champion, 1987; Rutledge & Davis, 1988).

The Health Belief Model has been found to be most useful with higher-SES individuals who have extensive health knowledge and value health. The Fishbein/Ajzen theory of reasoned action has been used by some researchers to add the dimension of social normative influences to the Health Belief Model. This emphasizes the importance of considering a person's beliefs that significant others in the environment think she or he should or should not perform a health behavior (Ajzen & Fishbein, 1980; Janz & Becker, 1984; Lierman et al., 1990). Assessing a person's belief about what her smoking co-workers will think about her quitting smoking and what her mother and sister think about her performing monthly breast self-exam are examples of adding this dimension.

The basic Health Belief Model is limited to explaining health behaviors on the basis of attitudes and beliefs; it does not account for other forces that influence health actions. A study in which the health belief model was compared with PRECEDE and the Fishbein/Ajzen theory of reasoned action as predictors of changes in smoking, exercise, and sweet- and fried-food consumption, found that such demographic characteristics as age, gender, and ethnicity were important predictors of health behavior over and above the components of the models (Mullen, Hersey & Iverson, 1987). Older respondents, for example, exercised less and were less likely to attempt to quit smoking. Black smokers were less likely to attempt to quit. Younger respondents were the most frequent consumers of sweet foods, and women exercised less frequently than men. The importance of age, gender, and ethnicity in these predictions emphasized the need to target messages to particular audiences.

PRECEDE

The PRECEDE framework extends the Health Belief Model in providing a comprehensive approach to health problems and health behavior change. It was developed by Green as a method for evaluating health education programs and later expanded to a diagnostic framework for health education and health promotion planning (Green et al., 1980).

PRECEDE is an acronym for "predisposing, reinforcing, and enabling constructs in educational diagnosis and evaluation." The model focuses on three types of factors that are assumed to influence health behavior and to be modifiable by educational intervention. Predisposing factors include knowledge, attitudes, beliefs, values, and interest. They serve as a motivational force prior to deciding to take health action (Green, 1984).

Enabling factors include skills and other resources necessary to carry out health actions, regardless of motivation. Educational methods aimed at enabling factors involve building a repertoire of skills through training or drilling, allowing for automatic recall of information and recognition of symptoms. This involves self-care skills on the individual level, and factors in the community and environment that facilitate health-promoting behavior.

The third group, reinforcing factors, arise from social and peer influences and include rewards and punishments that realistically follow a behavior or are anticipated as a result of it. Smoking, drug abuse, and sexuality among adolescents, for example, have been successfully approached by reinforcing students for demonstrating skills in resisting the offer of a cigarette or pressure to engage in sexual activity against their better judgment (McAlister & Gordon, 1980; McAlister et al., 1980). Women community-health workers have served as successful role models and reinforcing agents in promoting regular breast and cervical cancer screenings among minority, low-income women (Royak-Schaler, 1991).

The PRECEDE model is applied by first assessing the quality of life and/or a specific health problem in a target population. Next, health behaviors important to the health problem under investigation are identified; non-behavioral factors—economic, environmental, and genetic—influencing the health behaviors are also identified. Predisposing, enabling, and reinforcing factors are considered to evaluate the probability of change and potential approaches given available resources. Health-promoting interventions are designed, matched to resources and administrative capabilities. The intervention is then carried out and evaluated. The main contribution of the PRECEDE model is its emphasis on organizational, community, and institutional factors. Effective health promotion programs combine learning experiences directed at the three groups of factors (predisposing, enabling, reinforcing) that influence behavior, based on diagnosis of the predominant variables in each category for the target population. Health behavior may be highly motivated and reinforced socially; however, individuals must be enabled to initiate and maintain behavior change. Conversely, a motivated and skilled individual who meets with social criticism and ridicule rather than reinforcement will have a difficult time maintaining newly initiated behaviors (Green, 1984).

Social Cognitive Theory

Research demonstrates that individuals who have the skills to perform a particular health behavior and who believe that the behavior will lead to a particular outcome still will not change their behavior or maintain a change they have already made. Bandura's Social Cognitive Theory proposes self-efficacy as the cognitive mechanism that mediates behavior change (Bandura 1977, 1986). Perceived self-efficacy involves individuals' beliefs that they can control their motivation, behavior, and social environment. People's beliefs in their abilities to perform certain behaviors influence (1) their choice of behavior and what they attempt or avoid, such as performing breast self-exam, starting an exercise program, or attempting to quit smoking; (2) the effort they expend in attempting a task, because people devote more energy to a task they believe they can succeed at; (3) how long they persist in the face of difficulties, as in maintaining an exercise program or diet; (4) engaging in encouraging or defeating self-statements (in undertaking still another attempt to quit smoking or to lose weight, for example); and (5) emotional reactions they experience, such as anxiety or depression, when confronted with stressful situations (Bandura, 1990; Lawrence & McLeroy, 1986).

Self-efficacy has been examined in a variety of addictive behavior problems, such as smoking, alcoholism, and obesity. Self-efficacy is a better predictor of smoking abstinence and relapse than physiological dependence, coping history, motivation to quit, confidence in treatment, and expectancies concerning the rewards of smoking. This appears to be the case regardless of treatment methods, methods of measuring self-efficacy, and the populations being studied (Di-Clemente, 1981; DiClemente, Prochaska & Gilbertini, 1985; Lawrence & McLeroy, 1986; Marlatt & Gordon, 1980). It has also been used in examining a variety of behaviors from eating disorders to pain tolerance during dental treatment and childbirth and in response to tension headaches (Chambliss & Murray, 1979; Weinberg et al., 1984; Holroyd et al., 1984; Klepae, Dowling & Hauge, 1982; Manning & Wright, 1983). Individuals' belief in the ability to affect their health increases adherence to a multitude of medical regimens. While self-efficacy theory represents an important contribution to understanding the process of health behavior change, contributing factors from both the Health Belief Model and PRECEDE remain critical for effectively researching health behavior.

Theory of Reasoned Action/Planned Behavior

The central factor in the Fishbein and Ajzen theory of reasoned action is an individual's intention to perform a behavior. Three conceptually independent factors determine these intentions. The first is attitude toward a particular behavior and the individual's favorable or unfavorable evaluation of it. Second is a social factor called the subjective norm, which includes social pressure to perform or not to perform the behavior. Third is individual perception of behavioral control, based on past experiences as well as anticipated impediments and obstacles. The theory of planned behavior asserts that particular actions can best be understood by examining attitudes, subjective norms, and perceived behavioral control *for specific actions*, rather than by any global perceptions about health or efficacy. They also found that perceived behavioral control can predict action even better than stated intentions (Ajzen, 1987; Ajzen & Fishbein, 1980; Ajzen & Timko, 1986; Timko, 1987).

Application of compatible health behavior models allows for comprehensive collection of data on individual health beliefs, including self-efficacy and perceived behavioral control, as well as data relevant to particular groups and communities. People's failure to comply with medical advice and to undertake health-promoting behavior must be understood in the context of poor health motivation and incentives, feeling that they are not susceptible to particular health conditions and that developing the condition would not seriously affect their lives, believing that prevention or control of the condition is not likely through their personal actions, and believing that the effort they need to make to prevent the condition exceeds the benefit they will get from doing so (Rosenstock, Strecher & Becker, 1988). Applying this information allows professionals to effectively plan health promotion programs targeted to the needs of specific individuals and populations and facilitate health behavior change.

FACILITATING INDIVIDUAL HEALTH BEHAVIOR CHANGE

Fundamental to the process of individual behavior change are factors that are within individuals' control, such as self-efficacy, decision-making, choosing goals that one feels personally capable of achieving in a specified time frame, and the change process itself. More static factors such as age, education, income, gender, race, and health status are less susceptible to control but contribute to the development of health practices. Both dynamic and static factors are therefore considered in the following discussion of the change process.

Prochaska and DiClemente (1986) describe the addictive behavior change process in their five-stage transtheoretical model, developed from their work in the area of smoking cessation. The stages represent constellations of attitudes, intentions, and behaviors that are relevant to an individual in the process of change. Each stage also represents a period of time and a set of tasks needed for movement to the next stage. Although people may spend a variable amount of time at each stage, the tasks to be accomplished do not vary.

Precontemplation is the earliest stage in which people are not seriously thinking about changing in the next six months. To move ahead in the change cycle, precontemplators must own the health problem they are having, increase awareness of the negative aspects of the problem, and evaluate their self-change capacities. The next stage is *contemplation*, in which people are seriously thinking about changing an unhealthy behavior in the next six months. Those contemplating smoking or alcohol cessation are more upset about these behaviors than precontemplators; however, they are not prepared to take action at the present time.

Following contemplation is *preparation*. Individuals in this stage are on the verge of taking action, giving up cigarettes or beginning a weight-loss program, for example, but need to make firm commitments to follow through on their actions. The *action* stage involves the overt modification of the problem behavior. Individuals in this stage need the skills to interrupt their habitual patterns of behavior and adopt more productive patterns. Awareness of pitfalls that undermine continued effective action is critical at this stage.

Maintenance is the final stage in the change process. Maintenance requires sustained behavior change activity after the initial action. Relapse appears to be the norm for most addictive behavior change attempts, although most relapsers cycle back into contemplation. Smokers who are able to quit completely require on the average three revolutions through the cycles of change before they are able to live relatively free from temptations to smoke (Prochaska & DiClemente, 1986).

The four most common patterns of change identified in smoking cessation research by DiClemente, Prochaska, and colleagues were (1) linear profile, in which individuals progress directly from one stage to the next; (2) cyclical profile, in which individuals begin to take action and relapse, followed by further contemplation and action before improvements are maintained; (3) unsuccessful cyclical profile; and (4) nonprogressing profile, in which individuals remain stuck in precontemplation or contemplation without improving over time (Prochaska & DiClemente, 1986).

Perceived self-efficacy accurately reflects people's status as smokers and non-smokers. Smokers have significantly lower self-efficacy scores than short-term quitters (up to six months after cessation), who in turn have significantly lower scores than long-term quitters (more than six months of maintenance). Self-efficacy relates to the ability to achieve and maintain smoking cessation, and it increases over time in the maintenance cycle. This operates similarly for those who quit on their own and those who use programmed assistance (DiClemente et al., 1985).

Successful and lasting behavior change is most likely to occur when people believe that they can control their motivation, behavior, and social environment. Self-efficacy and social modeling affect what people choose to do, how much effort they mobilize, how long they persevere in the face of difficulties, whether they engage in encouraging or debilitating thought patterns, and the amount of stress and depression they experience in taxing situations. All stages of the personal change process—from contemplation to action to maintenance—are influenced by individuals' beliefs in their capabilities, their self-efficacy, and their perceived behavioral control.

CONCLUSIONS

Social, emotional, cognitive, and behavioral factors are important in the process of understanding, predicting, and changing health behaviors. Factors that influence health behavior and can be modified by educational interventions include personal factors that restrict or enhance potential for change, social and systemic factors that diminish or support possibilities for behavior change, and reinforcing factors that serve as incentives or disincentives to change.

While people may have the skills to perform a particular health behavior and believe that the behavior will lead to a particular outcome, they still may not be willing to change their behavior or maintain a change they have already made. Social Cognitive Theory proposes self-efficacy as the cognitive mechanism that mediates behavior change, while the Theory of Planned Behavior describes the importance of perceived control.

Application of health behavior models allows for comprehensive collection of data on individual health beliefs, including self-efficacy of data on individual health beliefs, including self-efficacy, as well as data relevant to particular groups and communities. Applying this information allows professionals effectively to plan health promotion programs targeted to the needs of specific individuals and populations and to facilitate health behavior change. For behavior change to succeed, people must have a reason to take action, feel concerned about their current behaviors, and believe that a specific kind of change will produce a valued outcome at an acceptable cost. Most important, people must feel capable of making and maintaining that change.

REFERENCES

Ajzen, I. (1987). Attitudes, traits and actions: dispositional prediction of behavior in personality and social psychology. In L. Berkowitz (Ed.). *Advances in experimental social psychology* (pp. 1–63). San Diego, CA: Academic Press.

Ajzen, I. & Fishbein, M. (1980). *Understanding attitudes and predicting social behavior.* Englewood Cliffs, NJ: Prentice-Hall.

Ajzen, I. & Timko, C. (1986). Correspondence between health attitudes and behavior. *Basic and Applied Social Psychology, 7,* 259–276.

Bandura, A. (1977). *Social learning theory.* Englewood Cliffs, NJ: Prentice-Hall.

Bandura, A. (1986). *Social foundations of thought and action: A social cognitive theory.* Englewood Cliffs, NJ: Prentice-Hall.

Bandura, A. (1990). Perceived self-efficacy in the exercise of control over AIDS infection. *Evaluation and Program Planning, 13,* 9–17.

Becker, M. H. (1974). *The Health Belief Model and Personal Health Behavior.* Thorofare, NJ: Slack.

Becker, M. H. (1986). The tyranny of health promotion. *Public Health Reports, 14,* 15–25.

Belloc, N. B. & Breslow, L. (1972). Relationship of physical health status and health practices. *Preventive Medicine, 1,* 409–421.

Breslow, L. & Somers, A. R. (1977). The lifetime health-monitoring program: A practical approach to preventive medicine. *New England Journal of Medicine, 296,* 601–610.

Brownell, K. (1991). Personal responsibility and control over our bodies: When expectation exceeds reality. *Health Psychology, 10,* 303–310.

Chambliss, C. A. & Murray, E. J. (1979). Efficacy attribution, locus of control and weight loss. *Cognitive Therapy and Research, 3,* 349–353.

Champion, V. L. (1987). The relationship of breast self-examination to health belief model variables. *Research in Nursing and Health, 8,* 375–382.

DiClemente, C. C. (1981). Self-efficacy and smoking cessation maintenance: A preliminary report. *Cognitive Therapy and Research, 5,* 175–187.

DiClemente, C. C., Prochaska, J. O. & Gilbertini, M. (1985). Self-efficacy and the stages of self-change of smoking. *Cognitive Therapy and Research, 9,* 181–200.

Green, L. W. (1984). Health education models. In J. D. Matarazzo, S. M. Weiss, J. A. Herd, N. E. Miller & S. M. Weiss (Eds.). *Behavioral health: A handbook for health enhancement and disease prevention* (pp. 181–198). New York: Wiley.

Green, L. W., Kreuter, M. W., Deeds, S. G. & Partridge, K. B. (1980). *Health education planning: A diagnostic approach.* Palo Alto, CA: Mayfield.

Hallal, J. C. (1982). The relationship of health beliefs, health locus of control, and self concept to the practice of breast self-examination in adult women, *Nursing Research, 31,* 137–142.

Harris, D. & Guten, S. (1979). Health protective behavior: An exploratory study. *Journal of Health and Social Behavior, 20,* 17–29.

Holroyd, K. A., Penzien, D. B., Hursey, K. G., Tobin, D. L., Rogers, L., Holm, J. E., Marcille, P. J., Hall, J. R. & Chila, A. G. (1984). Change mechanisms in EMG biofeedback training: Cognitive changes underlying improvements in tension headache. *Journal of Consulting and Clinical Psychology, 52,* 1039–1053.

Janz, N. K., & Becker, M. H. (1984). The health belief model: a decade later. *Health Education Quarterly, 11,* 1–47.

Kash, K. M., Holland, J. C., Halper, M. & Miller, D. G. (1991). Women at high genetic risk of breast cancer: Surveillance behavior and psychological distress. Paper presented at American Society of Preventive Oncology, Seattle, WA.

Kenkel, D. S. (1991). Health behavior, health knowledge, and schooling. *Journal of Political Economy, 99,* 287–305.

Kirscht, J. P. (1983). Preventive health behavior: A review of research and issues. *Health Psychology, 2,* 277–301.

Klepac, R. K., Dowling, J. & Hauge, G. (1982). Characteristics of clients seeking therapy for the reduction of dental avoidance reactions to pain. *Journal of Behavior Therapy and Experimental Psychiatry, 13,* 293–300.

Langlie, J. K. (1977). Social network, health beliefs, and preventive health behavior. *Journal of Health and Social Behavior, 18,* 244–260.

Lawrence, L. & McLeroy, K. R. (1986). Self-efficacy and health education. *Journal of School Health, 56,* 317–321.

Levine, S. & Sorenson, J. R. (1984). Social and cultural factors in health promotion. In J. D. Matarazzo, S. M. Weiss, J. A. Herd, N. E. Miller & S. M. Weiss (Eds.). *Behavioral health: A handbook of health enhancement and disease prevention* (pp. 222–229). New York: John Wiley & Sons.

Lierman, M., Young, H. M., Kasprzyk, D. & Benoliel, J. Q. (1990). Predicting breast self-examination using the theory of reasoned action. *Nursing Research, 39,* 97–101.

Manning, M. M. & Wright, T. L. (1983). Self-efficacy expectancies, outcome expectancies, and the persistence of pain control in childbirth. *Journal of Personality and Social Psychology, 45,* 421–431.

Marantz, P. R. (1990). Blaming the victim: the negative consequence of preventive medicine. *American Journal of Public Health, 80,* 1186–1187.

Marlatt, G. A. & Gordon, J. R. (1980). Determinants of relapse: Implications for the maintenance of behavior change. In P. Davidson & S. Davidson (Eds.). *Behavioral medicine: Changing health lifestyles* (pp. 424–452). New York: Brunner/Mazel.

McAlister, A. L. & Gordon, N. (1980). Prevention during early adolescence. In W. Bukowski (Ed.). *Prevention evaluation* (National Institute on Drug Abuse). Washington, DC: U.S. Government Printing Office.

McAlister, A., Perry, C., Killian, J., Slinkard, L. A. & Maccoby, N. (1980). Pilot study of smoking, alcohol, and drug abuse prevention. *American Journal of Public Health, 70,* 719–721.

Mullen, P. D., Hersey, J. C. & Iverson, D. C. (1987). Health behavior models compared. *Social Science and Medicine, 24,* 973–981.

Prochaska, J. O. & DiClemente, C. C. (1983). Stages & processes of self-change of smoking: toward an integrative model of change. *Journal of Consulting and Clinical Psychology, 51,* 390–395.

Prochaska, J. O. & DiClemente, C. C. (1986). Toward a comprehensive model of change. In Miller, W. R. & Heather, N. (Eds.). *Treating addictive behaviors: Processes of change* (pp. 1–27). New York: Plenum Press.

Rosenstock, I. M., Strecher, V. J. & Becker, M. H. (1988). Social learning theory and the health belief model. *Health Education Quarterly, 15*, 175–183.

Royak-Schaler, R. (1991, August). Promoting preventive health practices among low-income, minority women: Breast and cervical cancer interventions for the 1990s. Unpublished manuscript presented at American Psychological Association annual convention.

Royak-Schaler, R. & Benderly, B. L. (1992). *Challenging the breast cancer legacy: A program of emotional support and medical care for women at risk.* New York: Harper-Collins.

Rutledge, D. N. & Davis, G. T. (1988). Breast self-examination compliance and the health belief model. *Oncology Nursing Forum, 15*, 175–179.

Seeman, M. & Seeman, T. E. (1983). Health behavior and personal autonomy: A longitudinal study of the sense of control in illness. *Journal of Health and Social Behavior, 24*, 144–160.

Thompson, S. C. & Spacapan, S. (1991). Perceptions of control in vulnerable populations. *Journal of Social Issues, 47*, 1–21.

Thornberry, O. T., Wilson, R. W. & Golden, P. (1986). Health promotion and disease prevention provisional data from the National Health Interview Survey: United States, January-June, 1985. *NCHS Advance Data, 119*, May 14.

Timko, C. (1987). Seeking medical care for a breast cancer symptom: Determinants of intention to engage in prompt or delay behavior. *Health Psychology, 6*, 305–328.

U.S. Department of Health and Human Services (USDHHS) (1990). *National Center for Health Statistics. Health, United States, 1989.* (DHHS Publication No. PHS 90–1232). Washington, DC: U.S. Government Printing Office.

Wallston, K. A. (1992). Hocus-pocus, the focus isn't strictly on locus: Rotter's social learning theory modified for health. *Cognitive Therapy and Research, 16*, 183–199.

Weinberg, R. S., Hughes, H. H., Critelli, J. W., England, R. & Jackson, A. (1984). Effects of preexisting and manipulated self-efficacy on weight loss in a self-control program. *Journal of Research in Personality, 18*, 352–358.

22

Adult Education in the Third World: The Case of Adult Literacy

Dennis N. Thompson

In many parts of the world today, the major focus of adult education has been to address the issues and problems behind adult illiteracy. As a major social concern, literacy has come to be seen as a requirement for complete development of the individual and full participation in public life. While the debate continues as to the extent of the role that literacy plays in the economic and social development of Third World nations, it has become accepted that literacy is, if not an end in itself, a necessary condition for continued economic development.

Throughout the developing world since the end of World War II, literacy projects and campaigns of every kind have been undertaken. Some have focused on the village level, while others have involved whole nations. There have been Freire-style consciousness-raising approaches and other, more traditional approaches. There have been programs stressing the mother tongue, while others have limited the definition of literacy to an official national language. The range of strategies and approaches has resulted in virtually complete success in some instances and near-total failure in others. And while a broad consensus exists as to the factors that lead to success, the best conclusion from past experience is that no universal solution will be successful in every context and in every situation.

This chapter will seek to examine the current state of adult literacy found in Third World settings and the various approaches that have been used to reduce illiteracy. An attempt will be made to identify variables most directly relevant to education that can be used by program planners, instructors, and administrators to improve success rates.

DEFINITIONS AND DEMOGRAPHICS

Much debate has focused on the definition of literacy. Opinions vary in the literature across time and location. In some cases, an individual who is able to read the alphabet is considered literate; but in other, more-developed countries an individual incapable of reading written instructions of a highly technical nature may be considered functionally illiterate. As groups of people achieve skills formerly defined as literacy, new circumstances render the old definitions obsolete, and new definitions replace old ones as new goals are set.

Although there is no one commonly accepted definition of adult literacy, the United Nations Educational, Scientific, and Cultural Organization (UNESCO) has sought to address these issues by differentiating general literacy from "functional" literacy. General literacy is seen in terms of an adult's reading and writing ability without regard to social context. According to UNESCO a person is illiterate "who cannot with understanding both read and write a short, simple statement in his everyday life" (UNESCO, 1978). This ability is regarded as a first step on the way to developing a more acceptable level of skills. Functional literacy, on the other hand, refers to an individual's ability on reading and writing tasks relative to the environment and the culture in which the individual needs to function. According to UNESCO, a functionally literate person must be able to "engage in all those activities in which literacy is required for effective functioning of his group and community" (UNESCO, 1988). (Functional literacy as defined here is different from the functional literacy of the Experimental World Literacy Program discussed later).

Because of rapid technological changes throughout the world, literacy thresholds are likely to be in a continuing state of change. These varying interpretations of literacy have created problems for attempts to compare statistics from various countries or simply to state the number of illiterates in the world today. Nonetheless, in spite of necessary precautions when interpreting demographic data on world literacy, significant trends can safely be discerned.

Of an estimated 857 million illiterates aged 15 and above in 1985, all but 20 million were located in developing countries. Reason for hope and reason for concern are found among the existing statistics. There is reason for hope because the illiteracy rate throughout the world has steadily declined since the end of World War II, declining from 44% in 1950, to 33% in 1970, and to 28% in 1985 (see Carcalles, 1990, for a review).

On the other hand, there is reason for concern because the number of illiterates in the world has been steadily rising from 760 million in 1970, to 857 million in 1985, a relative increase of 12.8%. This absolute increase is generally attributable to two major factors. The first is the enormous population increase in many developing countries, outpacing current literacy efforts. The second is the continuing poor state of elementary education for children in many developing countries. Coombs (1985, p. 269) presents statistics that indicate that as many as one-half of all children in developing countries never enter school, with approximately one-third of the population graduating from elementary school.

It is important to remember that the illiteracy rate throughout the world is a general figure, and large differences exist across population groups. The vast majority of illiterates, approximately 75%, live in Asia, primarily in India and China. But the highest rates of illiteracy are in Africa. In 1990, twenty-three African countries had illiteracy rates in excess of 50% (UNESCO, 1990).

Throughout the world, illiteracy typically affects the least-privileged groups. The highest rates are in rural areas, often accompanied by extreme poverty. But vulnerable groups also include the urban unemployed, migrant workers and their families, nomadic people, and refugees. Much attention has focused on the fact that women are more likely than men to be illiterate, accounting for 60% of the illiterate population. Evidence also indicates that the number of female illiterates has increased, perhaps because of the slow rate of change in the perception of women's roles in many developing countries (Ramdas, 1989).

We must bear in mind, however, that though illiteracy is largely a problem of the Third World, the problem is also found in industrialized Western nations. In recent years research from the United States and other countries has alerted us to the fact that there exist native-born adults who are unable to deal with daily literacy demands. Although differences appear in the literature as to the severity of the problem, one UNESCO document observed that an individual

> need only stand at the counter of a post office, bank, tax office or social security office ... to realize that functional illiterates are legion. They have more or less mastered the rudiments of reading and writing ... but in the jungle of bureaucracy they are lost, entangled in the red tape and incapable of understanding the instructions or filling in forms (UNESCO, 1981, as cited in Coombs, 1985, p. 281).

In this regard, Coombs (1985) observes that the need for literacy is not limited to developing countries. In industrialized countries as well as in the Third World, the literacy as obtained in school is not always congruent with the functional literacy required for everyday life.

THE RECENT PAST

Until the 1920s literacy was almost always taught through the education of children in school. Even in the West, adult education, if addressed at all, was given extremely limited attention (see Stubblefield & Keane, 1989, for a review).

The first mass adult literacy campaign was initiated in the USSR in December 1919, shortly after the 1917 revolution. All individuals aged 8 through 50 were required to read in Russian or in their native tongue. Government employees not already motivated were given the option of learning to read or losing their job. Though the campaign goal to eradicate illiteracy by the tenth anniversary of the revolution was not accomplished, 20 million people were made literate by the program's end in 1939. This program is also important historically, in that both men and women were educated and that the program was not limited to one official language.

Outside the notable programs in Turkey (1928–1935) and in Mexico (1944), it was not until the end of World War II that literacy campaigns at the national level were developed in large numbers. The explanation for this appears to be in the political changes that took place following World War II, most particularly in the independence gained by so many new Third World countries.

Founded in 1945, UNESCO has become the single most important policy influence behind literacy programs in developing countries. While still in its infancy, UNESCO abandoned the classical concept of literacy, which limited training to reading and writing skills. By 1946, the concept of "fundamental education" was adopted. This approach combined literacy training with training in practical skills, community development, and education for basic needs. In these programs the mother language, rather than an official language, was stressed. Numeracy, however, was not yet seen as part of the definition.

UNESCO changed its strategy in 1964 by launching the Experimental World Literacy Program (EWLP), in which a new "functional literacy" approach was initiated. This remains UNESCO's most substantial applied program in literacy. As defined in this program, functional literacy stressed economic growth and increased productivity. Each literacy program was designed to be linked to a specific economic project in industry or agriculture. It was reasoned that individuals in key economic areas would have the greatest need and motivation to become literate.

The EWLP programs were intensive efforts of limited duration. In this approach to literacy, traditional teaching methods were abandoned in favor of the adult-oriented approaches of Malcolm Knowles, Alan Knox, and others. In all, over one million persons were enrolled in eleven participating countries. Notably, a majority of the participants were women (55%). The program's emphasis on economic development eventually came to be viewed as too narrow, but among its successes was a high student-attendance rate averaging 80%, with 24% of participants remaining through the final stages of the program (see UNESCO, 1976, for its own assessment of these programs).

Since 1974, UNESCO has taken a much broader approach to literacy than the economic approach of the EWLP. This, it is argued, gives UNESCO a far more flexible program by providing situation-specific advice to member states. According to Jones (1990), what has emerged is the implementation of regional literacy strategies that can be developed on a case by case basis.

APPROACHES AND OUTCOMES OF RECENT LITERACY STRATEGIES

In addition to the effort launched by UNESCO through the EWLP, Lind and Johnston (1986) have identified three other approaches to adult literacy. These are the conscientization approaches originated by Paulo Freire, the various forms of the mass campaign approach, and large-scale general literacy programs. Each of these approaches has its own strategy for achieving literacy as well as its own set of strengths and weaknesses.

The conscientization approach to literacy was formulated in Brazil in the early 1960s on the theoretical foundation of the work of Paulo Freire. During the 1970s Freire's educational theory gained a wide audience, particularly among more radical educators (see Freire & Macedo, 1987, for a recent review).

Freire's approach aims at making it possible for illiterates, perceived as oppressed, to become aware that they can change their situation. A major task of the adult educator is to initiate a process referred to as "cultural reflection," which is believed to result in action and change on the part of the student and the necessary motivation to learn to read and write. Pedagogical principles are learner-centered, but Freire does not provide any practical guidance as to how to organize a literacy project or how it should be maintained or evaluated. Moreover, the teacher's responsibility to promote the learner's participation is extremely demanding and often difficult to achieve, especially with teachers of limited educational backgrounds themselves. Nevertheless, Freire's approach has been widely adopted, most notably in Latin America where, Brookfield (1986) has argued, there hardly exists any government literacy program that is not based on Freire's principles.

The mass campaign approach to literacy is characterized by a very intense, large-scale effort to enable all adult individuals in a nation to reach literacy within a particular, usually brief, period of time. They are often seen as most successful when political will is strong, as in post-revolutionary societies. Among the most notable examples of the mass campaign approach are Cuba in 1961, where adult illiteracy was reduced within a few months from 24% to 4%, and Nicaragua, in 1979–1980, reporting a reduction from 50% to 13%.

A variation of the mass campaign approach emphasizes a series of large-scale campaigns each with a specific target population and its own timetable. The most noted examples of this approach include the campaigns in the USSR, Vietnam, China, Iraq, and Ethiopia. As with other mass literacy campaigns, political mobilization and sensitization are seen as critical factors in success. But this sequential approach is much more attractive where population numbers are large, and reaching target groups all at once would be extremely difficult. This is especially true when finding adequate numbers of teachers is also a consideration. In addition, the series approach is more frequently seen in heterogeneous societies, especially where there is a diversity of languages to contend with.

On the other hand, one risk in developing a serial version of the mass campaign is that interest may lag after two or three successful campaigns. To keep interest at optimal levels, two things seem to be necessary: to clearly identify new priorities for each campaign and to create a spirit of continued progress among potential participants. In this regard, Bhola (1983) stresses the creation of a strong political base structure with responsibility for encouraging continued participation and enrollment.

Finally, there are what Lind and Johnston (1986) refer to as the large-scale general literacy programs. These programs also emphasize the use of literacy for purposes of economic growth, but motivation is based on a concept of providing literacy to adults who want it, rather than on a spirit following revolution or rapid political change. Lind and Johnston (1986) argue that the majority of the nationwide literacy programs during recent years most readily fall into this category.

In many of the countries that have employed this approach, illiteracy is concentrated among the rural poor and the unemployed. The economy has developed to a point that individuals perceive realistic opportunities for employment or promotion as a result of becoming literate. An additional incentive is often expressed as a result of the large-scale migration to cities in many developing nations, with the desire to write to loved ones who have relocated.

These programs are usually organized at the national level through the nation's Ministry of Education. The government is likely to be involved through making public statements of support and may initiate a large-scale advertising campaign, but the primary initiative comes from local literacy personnel. In a number of countries such as Turkey in recent years, the initiative for these literacy efforts also originates out of adult education programs in the universities. In any event, the motivation for these programs is usually intrinsic, and little social pressure is operating. In contrast to the mass literacy campaigns, where small classes are the norm and dropouts are not a problem, these large-scale literacy programs are characterized by high initial enrollments, followed by a high dropout rate. Lind (1985) reports that continued support from highly respected local officials can be very effective in addressing this problem.

The curriculum in these programs is oriented around subjects of interest to adults (e.g., agriculture, child care, conservation). However, Lind and Johnston (1986) argue that, out of a desire to make curriculum interesting to adults, there is a risk that these programs will become ''swamped'' with too many goals and too much subject matter. On the other hand, because the motivation for learning lies largely with the individual, it is in these types of programs that curriculum design and methodology fall under the closest scrutiny and the quality of teaching becomes a particularly important factor.

EDUCATIONAL VARIABLES BEHIND ADULT LITERACY SUCCESS

In a review of the literature, Coombs (1985) argued that there are significant differences between the fervor expressed by the developers of modern literacy programs and the realities faced by most current countries. Developers from industrialized areas are often unaware of what life is really like for people living in poverty in remote rural locations. In many cases, these rural villages lack any reading materials and are essentially oral societies. After the first few meetings in a literacy class, it becomes clear to participants that learning to read and write takes considerable time and effort and class size dwindle. There is little reason to make the investment, as the only thing to read in the villages is the dull literacy primers.

The overwhelming concern throughout the literature on adult literacy, from mass campaigns to the voluntary efforts of the general literacy programs, focuses on generating appropriate levels of motivation. While methods vary, in Laubach's words, the two most typical methods to inspire literacy motivation are "making it easy, and making it necessary" (Laubach, 1947).

From a purely educational standpoint, it is far more practical to concentrate on Laubach's first approach rather than on his second. Laubach in his pioneering work identified several reasons that adults in developing countries are often reluctant to participate in literacy programs. Among these, he reported the widespread belief among adults that only children can learn. Adults in these societies see themselves as too old and incapable of taking on new tasks. Such sentiments of self-doubt are often expressed by adults in industrialized countries as well. Peterson (1983) presents a review of the Western literature on this topic. Second, Laubach noted that adults often equate education with the tedious and often rote learning approaches used in many Third World elementary school classrooms. In this regard, Laubach saw teachers' attitudes in the effort to improve literacy as essential for encouraging participation and for maintaining motivation. In his thinking, he moved away from the techniques of the elementary school classroom and was an early advocate for modern adult educational techniques.

In addition to maintaining appropriate levels of motivation, other variables under the control of planners of adult literacy programs include the recruitment and training of teachers, program decisions regarding the size and scope of the effort, and strategies to retain competency among the newly educated literates.

This recruitment and retention of adequate numbers of teachers remains one of the most talked-about topics in the literature. Although television and computers have been introduced to education all over the world, no replacement has been found for the presence of an instructor whose task it is to motivate as well as teach. In most countries, no literacy staff is available prior to the campaign, and senior staff must be selected from people from a variety of backgrounds in the community.

Generally, teachers come from one of three sources: from professional, generally elementary, school teachers; from technical experts who are "enlisted" to teach literacy; and from volunteers in the community. Each approach has its advantages and disadvantages.

Professional teachers have background in methods of instruction for children, but often have difficulty in adapting to methods that work effectively with adults. They may also define literacy narrowly and concentrate on the rote memorization of materials. If elementary teachers are used, classes may be limited to communities in which there is a school.

Another approach is to call on the technical staff (those individuals teaching agriculture, family planning, etc.) or the community-development assistant. These teachers have often already learned to cater to learners' needs and can be effective in motivating the learner. In Mali, for example, during UNESCO's EWLP, professional teachers rarely became effective in teaching technical activities, but the technicians became highly effective in teaching literacy. This led one observer to conclude that it is easier to make a literacy instructor out of an agricultural expert than to make an agricultural expert out of a school teacher (Hamadache, 1986, p. 85).

The third approach used to locate successful teachers is to draw on volunteers, often from among villagers who have recently completed literacy programs. This appears to be an effective method, especially in rural areas, where teachers from urban locations may not be well integrated into the community and may not speak the local language. In Ethiopia for example, the program was structured into two short intensive phases, the first for the entire target group and a second for those who had passed the first phase. This allowed faster learners to graduate quickly, while volunteers from the first phase could be used to provide slower learners with smaller classes and more attention.

Volunteer teachers are also often drawn from the population of students attending universities. Though this approach can generate large numbers of enthusiastic teachers, several cautions must be raised. One is that, because of the fairly strict age-grade norms that exist in many Third World countries, adults are often put off by young instructors. On example occurred in India, where literacy staff members were often young unmarried students. Particular problems arose when the content of the literacy class included materials on family planning and child care. Another problem concerns the overall availability of college students as teachers. In Burma, for example, programs had to be scheduled during times when college students were available, often limited to university holidays. Because these volunteers can usually serve for only a short period of time, extensive training is usually not practical (Ryan, 1981, p. 210).

Perhaps the most important responsibility of the teacher is to maintain a classroom atmosphere appropriate for adult learners. An appropriate attitude on the part of the instructor is seen as essential for participation and for sustaining motivation. Most adult educators argue that a democratic, open, and involved attitude that treats the learner as an equal, conducted in a supportive atmosphere, will have the most positive results with the adult learner (see chapter 14 by Lynn Johnson in this volume for a review of the literature on teaching styles appropriate with adult learners).

A major factor in determining the scope and extent of a literacy program involves identification of the target population to be reached (e.g., adult women, older men, automobile-mechanic apprentices). Obviously, accurate statistics are desirable concerning the number and distribution of the target population, but frequently fundamental decisions are based on highly approximate figures. In a review of the literacy programs in Iran, Burma, Thailand, and India, John Ryan

(1981) stresses that the content of the primers used in most literacy programs in the Third World is based on the interests of the target population. Ryan maintains that a simple survey may be all that is needed to determine what these interests are. On the other hand, he maintains that attention is often limited to identifying "core" interests in the population such as farming methods or child care. The possibility of differential interests based on sex, social class, occupation, and other variables is given little attention. In addition, other researchers have pointed out that, though potential participants may express a wide range of interests when responding to a survey, they may not actually show much enthusiasm for these topics when the actual programs are offered (see Peterson, 1983, for a review of the Western literature on this subject).

Closely related to the makeup of the target population is the question of the language in which literacy is offered. Except in rare cases, where there is only one national language, this is often a critical and difficult choice. In light of experience from past literacy programs, it is clear that literacy programs that teach reading and writing in the participants' spoken language are successful in far shorter periods of time than programs that stress an official language. Teaching literacy in an official language, which is foreign to the individual, means that the student has to learn the vocabulary and grammar of the language, in addition to the mechanics of reading and writing. On the other hand, if the local language is used exclusively, it is not very functional in a national sense (e.g., finding jobs) and may be perceived as providing an inferior education. Some countries have adopted bilingualism, with initial literacy achieved in the native language, followed by instruction in the official national language. In his analysis of this issue, Hamadache (1986, p. 80) finds that the acquisition of the mechanics of reading and writing in one's native language actually serves to facilitate the acquisition of a second language.

An issue related to both the number of teachers available and the scope of the program is that of class size. In the politically intense atmosphere of mass literacy campaigns, small classes are the norm. For example, the 3-to-1 student-teacher ratio found in Cuba represents one of the lowest ratios reported to date. With most modern programs, however, a higher ratio is effective and cost efficient, with class size usually falling in the range between 25 and 30 to 1. Though lower ratios may seem ideal, it is important to note that, in the general literacy programs discussed earlier, dropout ratios are high, often exceeding 50% over the first few weeks. If too low a ratio is used at the beginning of the program, it can quickly threaten the very existence of the group (see Hamadache, 1986, for a review of this area).

Finally, followup is extremely important for consolidating literacy skills and for preventing a relapse into illiteracy. Often adults who finish literacy programs are only marginally literate, and the main concern of a post-literacy program should be a "better" literacy program (Carron & Bordia, 1985).

Efforts to involve and motivate the newly literate take place in a number of ways. Most countries have tried to produce accessible and inexpensive reading materials such as books, newspapers, and magazines. In Turkey, for example, the Ministry of Education has developed a network of village reading libraries that distribute newspapers, magazines, vocational bulletins, and other material of local interest directed at the newly literate. This is especially important in remote village locations which previously had been largely oral societies (Gedikoğlu, 1991).

SOME CONCLUSIONS

After summarizing across the many and diverse programs that have been used to teach literacy, a few conclusions seem to follow.

Adult education in the Third World has often come to be equated with adult literacy. The causal link between literacy and development remains ambiguous at best. Most theories, including the current view of UNESCO, subscribe to a dialectical view, that the relationship between literacy and socioeconomic development is mutual and cumulative.

Although many nations have directed their efforts toward disadvantaged populations, promoting change for many members of minority populations is still slow. Among these groups, women remain vulnerable. Women represent approximately 60% of the world illiterates. As a group, illiterates are seen as worse off in terms of life expectancy, infant mortality, nutrition, health care, and income.

Noteworthy successes have been achieved in the wake of revolution or the winning of independence. But in the absence of national mobilization, methods, approaches, and teaching style become critically important.

Literacy training materials for adults should be adapted to the environment and the local interests of the community. In modern approaches, careful attention is placed on integrating literacy with the simultaneous learning of subjects of utility to individual learners. In terms of classroom atmosphere, learners play a role with the teacher in deciding on their most urgent concerns and what they are most interested in learning.

Initial literacy skills need to be followed by readily available reading material of interest to the new learners. The post-literacy phase involves the establishment of stable foundation for the long term. This may include libraries, brochures, booklets, and the like of continued interest to the target population.

While these conclusions follow from the existing literature, perhaps there is one additional point to be made. Much of the available literature comes from Western researchers and observers, using Western research methods, to test Western hypotheses. Indeed the fields of education and psychology themselves are largely an English-language business. As an example, the author was recently visiting a large academic library in Ankara, Turkey. In a review of a list of 320 journal subscriptions in psychology, it was surprising to note that 300 of the titles were in English.

An important goal for practitioners in the field of literacy should be that the available research be rooted in the populations toward which these efforts are directed. It is important to support the research capabilities in the countries themselves, and even more important to facilitate the distribution of research undertaken by Third World researchers. Being closely grounded in the field of practice, future practitioners will find themselves a little closer to making their visions a reality.

REFERENCES

Bhola, H. (1983). *The promise of literacy campaigns, programs and projects.* Baden-Baden: Nomos Verlagsgesellschaft.

Brookfield, S. (1986). *Understanding and facilitating adult learning.* San Francisco: Jossey-Bass.

Carcalles, G. (1990). World literary prospects at the turn of the century: Is the objective of literacy for all by the year 2000 statistically plausible? *Comparative Education Review, 34,* 4–20.

Carron, G. & Bordia, A. (1985). *Issues in planning and implementing literacy programs.* Paris: UNESCO Press.

Coombs, P. (1985). *The world crisis in education.* New York: Oxford University Press.

Freire, P. & Macedo, D. (1987). *Literacy: Reading the word and the world.* South Hadley, MA: Bergin and Garvey.

Gedikoğlu, S. (1991). *Türkiye' de yaygin eğitimden çağdaş halk eğitimine.* [Contemporary adult education in Turkey]. Ankara: Kadioğlu Matbaasi.

Hamadache, A. (1986). *Theory and practice of literacy work: Policies, strategies and examples.* Paris: UNESCO Press.

Jones, P. (1990). UNESCO and the policies of global learning. *Comparative Education Review, 34,* 41–60.

Laubach, F. (1947). *Teaching the world to read.* New York: Friendship Press.

Lind, A. (1985). *Adult literacy in the Third World: A literature review.* Stockholm: University of Stockholm.

Lind, A. & Johnston, A. (1986). *Adult literacy in the third world: A review of objectives and strategies.* Stockholm: Swedish International Development Authority.

Peterson, D. (1983). *Facilitating adult education for older learners.* San Francisco: Jossey-Bass.

Ramdas, L. (1989). Women and literacy: A quest for justice. *Prospects, 19,* 519–530.

Ryan, J. (1981). Design and development of literacy programs. In Alexander Charters (Ed.). *Comparing adult education worldwide* (pp. 196–217). San Francisco, Jossey-Bass.

Stubblefield, H. & Keane, P. (1989). The history of adult and continuing education. In Sharan B. Merriam and Phyllis M. Cunningham (Eds.). *Handbook of adult and continuing education* (pp. 26–36). San Francisco: Jossey-Bass.

UNESCO. (1976). *The experimental world literacy program: A critical assessment.* Paris: UNESCO Press.

UNESCO. (1978). *Records of the General Conference, Resolutions,* Vol. 1. Paris: UNESCO Press.

UNESCO. (1988). *Compendium of statistics on illiteracy.* Paris: UNESCO Press.

UNESCO. (1990). *Statistical yearbook.* Paris: UNESCO Press.

III. THE INFLUENCE OF AGING ON LEARNING

23

Aging and Adult Learning in the Laboratory

David Arenberg

Has gerontological research ceased learning in the laboratory? This question is not intended to be entirely facetious. It raises at least two related issues—the quantity of publications in recent years and potential gain in knowledge/understanding.

A count of annual publications about learning and aging since World War II would be instructive but tedious for the reader and even more so for the writer. A few observations may serve instead to convey the changes over that period. In a handbook edited by Birren (1959), three chapters were either devoted to reviewing the literature on learning and aging or featured that literature extensively. In the first edition of the *Handbook of the Psychology of Aging* (Birren & Schaie, 1977), separate chapters were assigned to learning and memory; the chapter on learning included animal research (Arenberg and Robertson-Tchabo, 1977). In the second edition, learning research was subsumed under memory in the chapter entitled "Differences in Human Memory with Aging: Nature, Causes, and Clinical Implications" (Poon, 1985). In addition, a substantial section on the adult learner appeared in the chapter on educational psychology (Willis, 1985). The most recent edition of that handbook included two chapters with learning in their titles, which were divided into animal (Woodruff, 1990) and human (Hultsch & Dixon, 1990) research. Although the latter is entitled "Learning and Memory in Aging," the term "learning" appears in the title of only two of the more than one hundred references; and neither of those publications is about aging! In a recent book entitled *Cognitive Development in Adulthood* (Howe & Brainerd, 1988), five of the nine chapters are about memory and aging; but the term "learning" does not appear in the subject index. Some part of this is attributable to the varied use of the terms "learning" and "memory." For example, in the eight experiments reported in Howe's (1988) excellent chapter on storage and retrieval in the Howe and Brainerd volume, lists of sixteen words were studied (and tested) until a criterion of two consecutive errorless trials was attained. Some investigators would consider those to be learning experiments, and they are reviewed in this chapter. It is quite clear, however, that much of the shift from learning to memory in recent cognitive research in aging represents a substantial change not only in paradigms but, to some extent, in processes of interest as well.

The focus of this chapter is on recent research in verbal learning and aging in the laboratory. Although learning and memory are closely related, the distinction suggested by Craik (1977) is maintained here; in studies of learning, the material to be learned is presented for several trials, whereas in memory studies, the material is presented once. The area of memory and aging has been reviewed extensively (see, e.g., Kausler, 1982, 1990; Light, 1992; Salthouse, 1985; Craik & Jennings, 1992; as well as chapters cited previously). That literature and other areas such as conditioning, motor learning, and animal learning are cited only when helpful in elucidating and understanding higher-level human learning and aging. Much of the recent research in this area involves retention and forgetting; therefore, a substantial portion of this chapter is devoted to those findings.

Kausler's (1990) introductory comments to his excellent review of the findings in the literature capture the importance of learning and of the study of learning and aging. "Learning is obviously critical for adaptations to our environments . . . [and it] is just as important for elderly adults as it is for younger adults. Fortunately, learning has no age barrier. . . . Of course, to say that learning occurs in late adulthood is not to say that it occurs without losses in proficiency. . . . The critical importance of learning to human adaptability makes it essential that we discover the extent to which learning proficiency is affected by human aging and that we understand the reasons why it is so affected'' (pp. 189–190).

Much of the early research directed toward that goal was in the domain of verbal learning. Virtually all of the cross-sectional studies in the literature found age differences between learning performance of young and elderly adults. Because age and birth cohort are totally confounded in cross-sectional designs and individual changes can be measured only in longitudinal designs, we begin with the few longitudinal studies of adult learning in the literature.

Changes in performance over time in the same individuals, especially late in life, were reported in those studies (Arenberg & Robertson-Tchabo, 1977; Gilbert, 1973; Robertson-Tchabo & Arenberg, 1985). Those reports included only two times of measurement. The studies of paired-associate learning and serial learning in the Baltimore Longitudinal Study of Aging (BLSA) (Shock, Greulich, Andres, Arenberg, Costa, Lakatta & Tobin, 1984) were concluded with three times of measurement; those data were analyzed recently and are summarized here.

VERBAL LEARNING STUDIES IN THE BLSA

Beginning in 1960, paired-associate and serial learning performance were obtained from the men in the BLSA. They are, for the most part, educated, white, and employed in (or retired from) professional or managerial positions. All are volunteers who visit the Gerontology Research Center of the National Institutes of Health in Baltimore, Maryland, periodically (the goal interval has varied during the study—12, 18, or 24 months, at times) for two or three days for extensive examination and physiological, anthropometric, and behavioral measurements (Shock et al., 1984).

At the time those studies were initiated, there was considerable interest in the effect of pacing on age differences (and, in this case, on changes with age, as well). Much of that interest stemmed from the general slowing hypothesis that postulated that at least some part of age differences and age changes in cognitive performance was attributable to physiological slowing. Therefore, three different anticipation intervals were used in each study. The anticipation interval is the time a participant is given to respond to each stimulus. Details of the procedures were reported in Arenberg (1967b). The second and third learning measures were nominally six and twelve years after the first, but those intervals were exceeded by as much as two and a half years.

Paired-Associate Learning

In this procedure, each item consists of a stimulus component and a response component. In the BLSA study, the stimuli were two consonants and the responses were familiar adjectives (e.g., TL = INSANE). An eight-item list was presented visually in several different orders until the criterion of one errorless trial was reached. The performance measure was the sum of the errors across all the trials. The list for the first administration of the procedure was the same as that used by Gladis and Braun (1958). The lists for the second and third administrations were constructed in the same way. The anticipation interval (the stimulus letters were displayed) was 1.9 seconds, 3.7 seconds, or subject paced; each participant was assigned to one of these three paces for all trials and all three lists. For all participants, the study interval (both the stimulus and response components were displayed) was 1.9 seconds and the inter-item interval (nothing displayed) was 1.8 seconds.

Analyses of incomplete data for the first administration and for participants with two data points at least six years apart have been reported previously (Arenberg, 1967b; Arenberg & Robertson-Tchabo, 1977; Robertson-Tchabo & Arenberg, 1985). Typically, age differences and changes with age have been substantial only late in life, and these age effects were greater at the short anticipation interval than at the longer interval or under the subject-paced condition.

A summary of all the three-point paired-associate data are reported in Table

Table 1
Paired-associate Learning: Means of Total Errors and Slopes: Baltimore Longitudinal Study of Aging

Age at Time 1	N	Time 1	Time 2	Time 3	Mean Slope
			Short Interval		
20–29	7	65.6	68.1	46.3	− 1.02
30–39	30	66.0	75.3	65.7	0.02
40–49	36	55.0	90.3	88.1	2.34
50–59	28	72.6	106.6	109.8	2.67
60 +	15	133.4	173.1	170.9	2.82
			Long Interval		
20–29	14	28.9	29.8	23.8	− 0.35
30–39	31	43.5	54.7	45.1	0.15
40–49	30	54.0	86.1	66.7	0.89
50–59	32	59.4	66.6	65.4	0.46
60 +	18	86.2	106.9	133.7	3.63
			Subject-paced		
20–29	15	26.1	42.1	28.5	0.24
30–39	23	35.2	37.5	26.7	− 0.60
40–49	36	35.1	46.9	37.1	0.20
50–59	22	45.1	49.4	36.2	− 0.66
60 +	13	41.5	77.6	65.4	1.91

1. Means are listed for five groups based on age at first administration (between 1960 and 1974, when the men ranged in age from 21 to 76). (They were between 34 and 89 at the third administration). The results are similar to the earlier analyses; changes over the twelve years or more between the first and third measures are small or even show improvement for the youngest groups and show substantial decline only for the oldest groups. Performance changes of the groups who were in their fifties at the time of their first measure are especially instructive. The men in that age group who learned at a short anticipation interval performed almost as well as the two youngest groups initially; but twelve years later, when their ages were between 62 and 72, that group declined substantially, while the youngest groups improved. In contrast, the groups in their fifties initially who learned at the longer anticipation interval or responded at their own pace declined very little or improved over that same period.

With three data points for each participant, it is possible to calculate individual regressions over time, that is, rates of change. Means of the regression coefficients, expressed as change in errors per year, are also shown in Table 1. The correlations between initial age and regression are .25, .31, and .19 for the groups who learned at the short anticipation interval, at the longer interval, and subject-paced respectively. Clearly, age is related to magnitude of change in paired-associate learning at all three pace conditions. The older the learner, the greater the increase in errors over a more-than-twelve-year interval; and this occurs in paired-associate learning whether time to respond is short, long, or under the control of the subject.

Serial Learning

In this procedure, each list consisted of twelve familiar nouns presented in the same order on every trial. Each word served as the stimulus to respond with the word that followed. (An asterisk was the signal to respond with the first word.) As in the study of paired associates, three anticipation intervals were used. The words (and the asterisk) appeared for 2.0 seconds. For the two paced groups, each word was followed by a blank period of 1.8 seconds or 3.6 seconds. For the subject-paced group, the blank period was a minimum of 1.8 seconds or until a response occurred. As a result, the anticipation intervals were 3.8 seconds, 5.6 seconds, or subject paced. The performance measure was the total number of errors until the criterion of one errorless trial was attained.

As in paired-associate learning, cross-sectional and two-point longitudinal data over six-plus years have shown substantial age differences and changes with age in serial learning only late in life (Arenberg, 1967b; Arenberg & Robertson-Tchabo, 1977). Means of the three-point data for five groups based on age at the first administration are shown in Table 2. The only groups that decline during the twelve or more years from the first to third administrations are the men who were at least 60 years old initially (and at least 72 at the time of the third measure). All other groups show some improvement. Surprisingly, only the old group that learned at the long anticipation interval shows a substantial mean decline.

Individual regressions were calculated for everyone with three data points, and the means of the regression coefficients are also shown in Table 2. The correlations between age and regression are .21 for the group that learned at the short anticipation interval, .34 for the group at the longer interval, and .04 for the subject-paced group. For the two groups that learned under paced conditions, age is positively related to magnitude of decline; the older the learner, the greater the increase in errors. Unlike paired-associate learning, however, the oldest group who learned at the self-paced condition do not decline over the same twelve-year-plus interval. Furthermore, serial learning does not decline for the other age groups, even those who were at least 62 at the third administration.

A RECENTLY REPORTED LONGITUDINAL STUDY

A small-scale longitudinal study of multitrial free recall was reported recently by Howe (1990). As with all of his studies of learning and aging, the procedure was tailored to allow a mathematical model to be applied to the data, providing

Table 2
Serial Learning: Means of Total Errors and Slopes: Baltimore Longitudinal Study of Aging

Age at Time 1	N	Time 1	Time 2	Time 3	Mean Slope
			Short Interval		
20–29	7	64.1	44.1	48.1	−1.32
30–39	27	102.6	76.3	62.5	−2.87
40–49	37	105.0	87.1	92.7	−0.81
50–59	29	111.0	102.8	102.9	−0.54
60+	17	167.9	180.1	173.8	0.50
			Long Interval		
20–29	13	41.0	38.7	30.3	−0.79
30–39	30	47.7	50.6	42.9	−0.33
40–49	29	76.7	65.5	57.7	−1.29
50–59	28	59.1	49.9	50.4	−0.68
60+	19	100.0	117.3	157.3	4.24
			Subject-paced		
20–29	14	49.6	41.2	42.5	−0.48
30–39	26	50.2	42.1	42.4	−0.63
40–49	39	368.6	49.7	53.7	−1.08
50–59	23	66.3	64.4	58.3	−0.60
60+	14	70.0	53.9	71.8	0.07

estimates of parameters to be compared between age groups. The cross-sectional studies of normal aging of Howe and Hunter (1985, 1986) and Howe (1988) are reviewed later in this chapter, and the parameter comparisons are discussed. For the longitudinal study, however, only the global performance measure, proportion correct, is discussed here (although changes in the parameter estimates are reported in Howe's 1990 chapter).

Two-point longitudinal data were reported for twenty-five participants measured at two calendar times 8 to 12 months apart. The participants were between 63 and 79 years of age. The task was to learn sixteen-item lists of either related (eight words from each of two categories) or unrelated words. Unlike the studies previously reported by this group, in which all subjects learned to a stringent criterion of mastery, three study trials and four test trials were administered for each of two lists at each time of measurement. A distractor task preceded each test trial. The items were presented at a 10-second rate.

Surprisingly, given the short interval between the two times of measurement, changes in proportion correct were found. Even more surprising is that unrelated lists showed a decline, but related lists showed a small improvement. This longitudinal project was termed "ongoing" in this report; perhaps an explanation of these findings will become available at a later time.

It is clear that over a period of twelve or more years, mean declines in learning performance occur late in life. (The unusual findings for the short-term longitudinal study by Howe (1990) may be attributable to learning-to-learn processes rather than to aging.) These longitudinal results indicate that at least some part of cross-sectional age differences in learning in the literature is attributable to intra-individual decline.

CROSS-SECTIONAL STUDIES

Pacing

The effects of pacing on age differences in learning were studied rather extensively during the heyday of studies of learning and aging in the 1960s and early 1970s. Canestrari (1963) reported a striking effect of pacing on paired-associate learning. At a fast pace, the age difference was at least twice as great as at a slower pace and at least four times as great as at the subject-paced condition. In that study, the anticipation interval was confounded with the study interval. For example, at the fast pace, both the anticipation interval (time to respond) and the study interval (study time) were 1.5 seconds; similarly, at the slow pace, both intervals were 3.0 seconds. Therefore, it was not possible to disentangle the effects of time to respond from the effects of time to study the pairs.

In a serial-learning study conducted at about the same time, Eisdorfer, Axelrod, and Wilkie (1963) also showed that pace was an important variable. When the groups that were learning at a fast pace were switched to a slower pace, the old group showed a sudden improvement in performance. This suggested that they had learned more than they had been able to demonstrate at the fast pace. In the study of Eisdorfer et al. (as in typical serial learning procedures), however, study time and time to respond are identical; they are the same interval.

Arenberg attempted to determine whether time to respond alone (unconfounded with study time) could account for age differences in studies of both paired-associate (1965, 1967b) and serial (1967b) learning. In the paired-associate study with well-educated men (1967b), the stimulus component was either 1.9 seconds or 3.7 seconds; but the study interval was the same, 1.9 seconds, for both pace conditions. The difference in errors to reach criterion was small for the groups at the short and long anticipation intervals who were under 35 years of age but increased rather systematically with increasing age to a large difference for the groups over 75. The results were similar for the serial learning study with virtually the same participants. In that study, the words were displayed for 2.0 seconds for both pace groups, but at the short anticipation interval, 1.8 additional seconds were provided to respond whereas at the long anticipation interval, 3.6 additional seconds were available to respond. Again, the pace differences were small for the youngest groups and largest for the groups over 60.

A paired-associate study with two age groups of less-educated men (Arenberg, 1965, Study II) was designed to determine whether the effect of the anticipation interval was on learning or was due to insufficient time to respond even when the items had been learned. Standard confirmation trials (each item consisted of both a response and a study component) were alternated with self-paced performance trials without feedback. In the latter, the stimulus components (two consonants) were displayed until the participant responded; but the correct responses (familiar nouns) were not shown. These trials were intended to determine how much had been learned with no time pressure to respond but also with no further opportunity to study. The usual interaction between age and pace was found, that is, the age difference was larger at the short interval than at the longer interval. More important, this was true of the self-paced trials alone. Very few of the errors committed by the old group under the fast-paced condition were attributable to insufficient time to respond with learned responses. This study provides evidence that learning, not merely performance, is affected by the anticipation interval in paired-associate learning.

In another paired-associate experiment, Hulicka, Sterns, and Grossman (1967) alternated study trials (no responding) with test trials similar to the nonlearning trials in the experiment by Arenberg (1965) described above. They varied time to study the items in the study trials. No interaction was found; the age difference was not greater when study time was short than when it was long. In an experiment by Monge and Hultsch (1971), both the anticipation interval and the study interval were varied. They found an interaction with age for the anticipation interval but not for the study interval, that is, the age difference was largest when time to respond was shortest and small when more time was available to respond, but the age differences were unaffected by the variation in study time.

Neither general slowing nor the total time hypothesis, in which total time per item is the important variable, can account fully for these findings. The evidence from these studies indicates that time to respond is a critical variable, but study time per se does not contribute to age differences. The reason for this has not been established. There is, however, some indication that opportunity to access and respond correctly strengthens learning; additional test trials without further study improves performance (see, e.g., Slamecka & Katsaiti, 1988). It is possible that this beneficial effect increases with increasing age.

It was the hope among some investigators that increases in time would bring the performance of the old up to that of young adults. It is clear, however, that even when subjects are given as much time as they need to respond, age differences occur (see Salthouse, Kausler & Saults, 1988, for recent large-scale studies of paired-associate learning with subject-paced test trials). Another variable that held some hope that there may be conditions that produce equivalent performance across the adult age range was variations of providing mediators or instructions to use them.

Mediators

Several studies of the effects of providing mediators or instructions in their use were conducted in attempts to understand age differences in paired-associate learning. These studies have been reviewed both intensively and extensively in Poon, Walsh-Sweeney, and Fozard (1980) and in Kausler (1990).

Hulicka and her colleagues reported that older learners use some kind of associative connection to link a stimulus with its response far less frequently than do their young adult counterparts (Hulicka, 1965; Hulicka & Grossman, 1967). Furthermore, when mediators are used by the elderly, they tend not to involve imagery, which is often the most effective for learning. Several studies have shown that providing mediators or giving instructions to use mediators improves performance for the old groups; and sometimes the improvement is greater for old than for young adults (Canestrari, 1968; Hulicka & Grossman, 1967; Rowe & Schnore, 1971; Treat, Poon, & Fozard, 1978; Treat & Reese, 1976).

Treat and Reese (1976) factorially varied both pace and the mediator variable and found that the combination of a long anticipation interval and mediators that were subject generated produced equivalent learning for the old and young groups; under these conditions, no age difference occurred. Another finding of note is that, with practice, the old develop a mediator strategy. By the last session of a three-session study (Treat, Poon, & Fozard, 1978), the old control group was performing about as well as the old groups that were instructed to use their own mediators or were provided mediators by the experimenters. There is little doubt that many elderly learners do not use effective mediators spontaneously; but with instruction or with practice, that strategy is adopted and is beneficial to learning.

Storage and Retrieval

Although registration/encoding, storage, and retrieval processes typically have been foci of age studies in memory of material presented once, Howe and his colleagues have used a two-stage model to separate these processes in learning and retention using multitrial procedures (Howe, 1988; Howe & Hunter, 1985, 1986). They argued that fixed-trial designs confound age and completeness of learning; and only when learning continues to an equivalent level for all age groups can the effect of manipulated variables on age differences in storage and retrieval be measured. Those differences are assessed by comparing estimates of parameters derived from a mathematical model. The first stage of acquisition in the model "involves learning to encode and store items in memory, and the second stage involves learning to retrieve stored traces from memory" (Howe & Hunter, 1985, p. 133).

Two studies of multitrial free recall were designed to determine the effects of item concreteness on age differences in storage learning (first stage) and retrieval learning (second stage) (Howe & Hunter, 1985). In both studies, all participants learned sixteen-item lists until mastery as indicated by two consecutive errorless test trials. In Experiment 1, subjects learned a list of objects presented visually either as words or as pictures. Study trials in which each item was presented for 5 seconds were alternated with test trials in which subjects were given as much time as they needed to respond with all the words they could recall from the list. A distractor task also preceded each test trial to avoid short-term memory effects. Standard analyses of the data, termed "qualitative findings" by the investigators, yielded an age difference for each list and a list difference for each age but no interaction. The young committed fewer total errors than the old, and pictures were learned with fewer errors than words, but the age difference was unaffected by the type of list.

The results of the comparisons of estimates of storage (subsuming encoding) and retrieval components based on the model were somewhat different, however. The young group was superior to the old at storing both words and pictures and also at retrieving pictures, but the old were superior to the young at retrieving words.

Experiment 2 was similar except that the lists were either concrete or abstract nouns (although the lists did not differ in meaningfulness or rated frequency). Age and list effects were found in the "qualitative analysis," and the interaction was also significant. Again, the young committed fewer errors than the old group, and concrete words were learned with fewer errors than abstract words; but the age difference was much larger for the abstract list than for the concrete list. The results from the analysis of parameter estimates were quite similar to the results in Experiment 1. The young group was superior to the old at storing both concrete and abstract words and at retrieving abstract words, but the old group was superior at retrieving concrete words.

In another report, Howe and Hunter (1986) included analyses of the model parameters for both acquisition and retention one week later. (The retention findings are reviewed in the section on forgetting.) In this study, paired-associate items were formed of concrete concepts—two words, two pictures, or a word and a picture (in either order). The twenty-item lists were presented at a 5-second rate, and study trials were alternated with test trials until the criterion of three consecutive errorless test trials was attained.

Analysis of total errors showed only an age difference favoring the young adult group. Neither a list effect nor an interaction between list and age was found. Analyses of the estimates of the model parameters, however, were much more revealing. Those findings were rather complex, but two points were emphasized in the summary of the acquisition results. A pictorial superiority effect was found at storage for both age groups, and the major age differences were found in retrieval processes.

A subsequent report of eight experiments also was designed to permit age comparisons of parameter estimates with the two-stage mathematical model

(Howe, 1988). In all eight experiments, the task was to learn a sixteen-item list of words to a criterion of two consecutive errorless test trials. On the study trials, items were presented at a 5-second rate; but in the test trials, subjects had as much time to respond as they needed. As in the previous experiments, study trials were alternated with test trials, and each test trial was preceded by a distractor task.

Concrete words were used in Experiments 1 and 2, and abstract words were used in Experiments 3 and 4. In all four experiments, meaningfulness was an independent variable. Analyses of total errors per item showed age differences favoring the young group in all four experiments. Comparisons of the parameter estimates indicated that the young group was superior to the old in establishing a stable trace in long-term memory. The young were also superior at learning to access the information they had stored. These results were similar to those reported previously (Howe & Hunter, 1985).

Experiments 5 through 8 were designed to identify the model parameters that differ for young and old adults when organizational variables are manipulated. It was pointed out that previous research had indicated "that elderly adults tend to engage in spontaneous organizational restructuring of information less frequently and less effectively than younger adults . . . [but] age differences do not disappear under enhanced conditions" (Howe, 1988, p. 54). A free-recall procedure was used in Experiments 5 and 6, and cued recall was used in Experiments 7 and 8. In Experiments 5 and 7, lists consisted of two categories with eight items in each; in Experiments 6 and 8, lists consisted of four categories with four items in each. As in the first four experiments, an age difference favoring the young group also was found for total errors per item in these four experiments.

Some of the results of the parameter comparisons were similar to those found in Experiments 1 through 4. The young groups were superior at establishing a stable trace in long-term memory and also at learning to access that information. Unlike the first four experiments, however, Experiments 5 through 8 found larger age differences in retrieval than in storage.

Howe cautioned that the age declines did not generalize to all aspects of storage and retrieval in the model. For a more detailed description of the nuances of the model and the age differences in the subcomponents, the reader is referred to the original reports.

Early studies of memory and learning that were designed to unravel age differences in storage and retrieval for the most part were disappointing because retrieval failures could not be interpreted as completely independent of encoding and storage. Some investigators have advocated abandoning this effort. Recently, however, Howe and his colleagues have applied to age studies of multitrial learning a sophisticated mathematical model that overcomes many of the methodological and measurement problems inherent in the designs of previous research. The model separates storage and retrieval processes and provides parameter estimates of these components of learning. The investigators have already demonstrated the utility of their approach by showing that age differences in these components and their subcomponents are quite complex and merit further study to enhance our understanding of the learning processes involved in aging.

Retention and Forgetting

The dominant theory of forgetting in the 1950s and 1960s involved interference. Forgetting was attributed to proactive interference, the effects of previous cognitive activity, or to retroactive interference, the effects of cognitive activity between learning new material and recalling or relearning that material at a later time. Welford (1958), in his review of the meager findings to that time, concluded that much of the age differences in forgetting was due to the greater susceptibility of the old to interference.

Not surprisingly, the early studies of aging and forgetting/retention used interference paradigms. Gladis and Braun (1958) reported no age difference in retroaction when age differences in initial and interpolated learning were taken into account statistically. In another retroaction experiment, however, Wimer and Wigdor (1958) reported an age decrement in relearning the first list after learning an interpolated list. Both of those studies used paired associates, but one of the many differences in procedure was the duration of the anticipation interval, the time to respond to each stimulus. Gladis and Braun allowed four seconds, whereas Wimer and Wigdor required responding in one second. Subsequently, Arenberg (1967a) attempted to determine whether the difference in anticipation interval contributed to the difference in findings of those two studies. He found an age difference in relearning at a short interval but not at a longer one. Arenberg (1965, Study II) had demonstrated that not only is performance of the old especially diminished when the anticipation interval is short but they actually learn less effectively. Subject-paced test trials (with no confirmation) alternated with standard paired-associate trials showed that even when the old had ample time to respond, they recalled fewer correct words when the standard confirmation trials required fast responding than when those trials provided twice as much time to respond. This suggests that, in retroaction studies, when the anticipation interval is short, learning to criterion may not represent the same level of "true" learning for the old as learning to the same criterion when more time is provided to respond to each item.

Several other age studies of interference were reported around that time with rather mixed results and are summarized in Arenberg (1973). Kausler (1982) not only provides an excellent review of those and later studies but gives the reader a solid understanding of interference paradigms and how they were applied in studies of aging. With the accrual of further evidence, it became clear that interference was not the primary mechanism for age differences in forgetting (if such differences exist). Smith (1980), on the basis of both the learning and memory literature, concluded, ''In summary, little evidence supports the view that older age groups are more vulnerable to interference effects'' (p. 26); and Kausler agreed.

Not everyone, however, was prepared to abandon susceptibility to interference as an age-related phenomenon. Although the evidence at that time from studies of divided attention and attention switching was not conclusive and apparently continues to be mixed (see McDowd & Birren, 1990), Arenberg (1980) argued that distraction (diversion of attention) is a type of interference that may be a source of difficulty for older individuals. He predicted age differences in recalling unfamiliar telephone numbers following an interruption between input and final dialing, and there is now evidence for that kind of distraction. West and Crook (1990, Experiment 2) reported that, although little decline was found from early adulthood to late life in dialing 7-digit telephone numbers, redialing performance after a busy signal declined monotonically with age.

In laboratory studies of retroactive interference, the activities between initial learning and subsequent recall are tightly controlled so that forgetting can be attributed to the interpolated (interfering) activities. In most studies of retention and forgetting, however, the retention period is frequently hours or even days; and the interpolated activities occur outside the laboratory. Interpretations of the underlying mechanisms of forgetting based on activity between acquisition and retention are, therefore, rarely made.

There has been a flurry of papers recently on how best to measure forgetting rate (see Bogartz, 1990a, 1990b; Loftus, 1985; Loftus & Bamber, 1990; Slamecka, 1985; Wixted, 1990). The argument seems to have originated when Loftus criticized Slamecka and McElree (1983) for using interactions in analysis of variance to test for group differences in forgetting rate. Slamecka and McElree were studying the effects of a difference in original learning on forgetting rates. They argued that if performance means of two groups converge or diverge over the retention period, then they are forgetting at different rates; and an interaction between groups and time should reflect this. Loftus proposed that a difference in forgetting rate should be evaluated by whether or not groups decline from one specific level of performance to another specific level in the same time. As time is typically plotted on the abscissa, Loftus referred to these differences in forgetting time as ''horizontal differences.'' The performance differences compared with an interaction test in ANOVA were dubbed ''vertical differences.''

It is interesting to note that several of the early studies of aging and retention had avoided this problem by matching age groups in initial learning. They were attempting to minimize the possibility that age differences during or at the end of the retention period could be attributable to age differences that existed at the beginning of that period. It turns out that when groups are equivalent at the beginning of the retention period, a subsequent divergence in performance can be interpreted as a difference in forgetting rate with either horizontal or vertical difference criteria.

In several early studies of paired associates in which acquisition was continued to a criterion of one errorless trial, recall was measured hours or even days after initial learning (Hulicka, 1965; Hulicka & Rust, 1964; Hulicka & Weiss, 1965; Wimer, 1960). The typical result was no age difference in recall after learning to criterion. A somewhat more recent study by Thomas and Ruben (1973) described in Poon's review chapter (1985) reported substantial forgetting at one hour by the old group that learned paired associates under standard instructions, but the age difference at one hour did not increase at 4, 8, 12, or 16 months. The generality of this and other findings was questioned by Poon, Walsh-Sweeney, and Fozard (1980) because the items consisted of two three-letter words that were alphabetically contiguous; and it was possible that some unknown number of subjects in each age group used this structural information in recall.

There are two methodological problems shared by all of the studies cited above. Whenever all participants learn to a criterion of one or more errorless trials, those subjects who require many trials to attain that criterion are exposed to much overlearning of items they learn on early trials. If those overlearned items are relatively resistant to forgetting, then the old group (consisting of a higher proportion of the slower learners) may not manifest the same amount of forgetting as would occur without the overlearning. In addition, paired-associate-learning procedures usually include a relatively few number of items, especially in studies of aging. As a result, it is necessary to test all items at every retention time in order to obtain reasonably reliable measures. In studies with multiple retention times, the same items are repeatedly tested. It is possible that repeated testing of items helps to retain those items thereby reducing the apparent forgetting effects.

Several recent retention studies of picture recognition avoided those problems. Picture recognition typically does not produce age differences in acquisition; immediately after presentation of all the pictures, recognition memory is quite good for old as well as young adults. No age difference in overlearning should occur. In addition, high recognition performance is maintained even with many pictures. As a result, it is possible to test different subsets of acquisition pictures at each retention time. No items that appear in earlier subsets are repeated in later subsets.

In two of those studies (Park, Royal, Dudley & Morrell, 1988; Rybarczyk, Hart & Harkins, 1987), the same subjects were tested at all retention times. Recognition performance was equivalent for the two age groups until 48 hours; but at 1, 2, and 4 weeks, the young adults correctly recognized a higher proportion of the pictures. In the study by Mitchell, Brown, and Murphy (1990), independent groups were tested at each retention time. Although no statistically significant interaction between age and retention time was found, the age difference increased from 1 to 7 to 21 days, results not dissimilar from the other two studies. It is possible that the loss of power resulting from using independent groups accounted for the failure of the increased age differences to yield a statistically significant interaction effect. Based on these picture recognition studies, it appears that age differences in forgetting occur only after 48 hours.

Two recent verbal-learning studies included unusual approaches to identifying age differences in retention/forgetting. Howe and Hunter (1986) used a two-stage mathematical model to identify the storage and retrieval processes that contribute to age differences in retention of paired associates. Giambra and Arenberg (in press) included a large-scale experiment of forgetting that was designed to provide age comparisons of time to forget the same amount of sentence information. The acquisition segment of the study by Howe and Hunter (1986) was described in the section on storage and retrieval. An age difference was found in mastering twenty-item lists of paired associates, but the experimental manipulation of list type yielded no differences for either age group. In the retention phase of the study, the same items were tested four times one week after the acquisition phase. No further study trials were given. Half the subjects who had learned each list type (word-word, word-picture, picture-word, and picture-picture) were given the same cues during retention trials: the other half were given the cues in the other format; for example, if the cues in the acquisition list were words, then comparable pictures were the cues at retention. The 5-second rate used during acquisition was used in retention as well.

Standard analysis of total errors in the four retention trials yielded main effects of age, list type, and cue type; in addition, age interacted with each of the other two variables. The young retained more than the old group in all eight conditions. The change in cue type had no effect on the young adults, but the old groups retained far less when the cues were changed compared with when they were the same as during acquisition. Furthermore, list type had no effect on retention for the young; but the old retained less than the young on all but the word-picture list.

The results for the comparisons of parameter estimates were even more complicated, and only a few major findings can be reported here. An age difference in ability to retain traces in storage was found at retention, a difference not found at acquisition. In addition, the superiority of the young in retrieval at acquisition was much less evident at retention. The investigators concluded that generalizing age differences in storage and retrieval processes at acquisition to age differences in long-term retention is unwarranted and that these results are quite difficult to interpret within any framework that attributes cognitive declines in aging to a single underlying mechanism.

Three experiments conducted by Giambra and Arenberg (in press) were designed to elucidate age differences in forgetting of sentence information. In all of these experiments, the sentences consisted of five words with the structure of this example: "The slave entered the village." Many sentences were studied and for several trials. (Details about number of study trials, study time per item, number of items, and so on in each experiment are available from the investigators.) In all three experiments, a subset of the acquisition sentences was tested immediately after the acquisition trials and a different subset was tested at each of one or three more times subsequently. The primary task was a form of paired associates in which the predicate was to be recalled for each two-word subject, for example, write "entered the village" after the cue "The slave. . . . " In Experiments 1 and 2, there were two age groups, and the retention times were 3, 6, and 24 hours after acquisition. In Experiment 1, an age difference was found, but this difference did not increase in magnitude during retention. This result was similar to many findings from the paired-associate studies of the 1960s.

In Experiment 2, the old group was given more time than the young to study each sentence during the acquisition trials to match the performance of the two age groups immediately after learning. A small divergence was found as early as three hours later; the young recalled more sentence predicates than did the old group. There was evidence of a small age difference in forgetting, and that difference was apparent much earlier than the age differences became apparent in the picture-recognition studies.

Those two experiments involved rather small groups at two ages. In contrast, Experiment 3 included 440 subjects whose ages ranged from 18 to 74 years. Each subject was randomly assigned to a retention interval from 10 minutes to 7.5 hours to determine how early the age difference in forgetting could be detected. In addition to performance comparisons at various intervals, the experiment was designed to provide comparisons of time to forget for subjects with equivalent performance (See Loftus, 1985, for an argument for this type of comparison). There was evidence of an age effect on forgetting as early as 10 minutes after acquisition. Furthermore, age was related to time to forget for subjects with equivalent performance both immediately after acquisition and at retention. The results of these experiments indicate that there are small age differences in forgetting rate, and they occur soon after acquisition.

The prevailing finding from these recent studies is that age differences in retention and forgetting definitely occur two days after acquisition, and small differences may occur as early as 10 minutes after acquisition. Although the studies with multiple retention intervals do not always find evidence of increasing age differences over time, the overall picture does suggest just that.

FINAL COMMENT

At the beginning of this chapter, it was suggested that the hiatus in age studies of human learning during the 1970s and into the 1980s was attributable, at least in part, to a communal recognition that the potential gain in knowledge/understanding from such a pursuit had diminished. Recent studies, especially in retention and forgetting, indicate a renewed interest in this area; and the application of sophisticated mathematical models to identifying specific storage and retrieval processes underlying age differences in acquisition and retention are especially exciting.

In this spirit of optimism, it may be prudent to note Schonfield's (1989) concerns about the plethora of gerontological research and its value. If we are at the beginning of a resurgence in productivity in learning and aging, we should join him in the hope that the results will be not only of interest to the investigators in the field but will lead to an increase in broad principles. As Schonfield wrote, "Framing more principles with wider implications should be a major aim," and "Principles constitute the bridge between academia and professionals" (p. 507). Perhaps that goal will be realized to a greater extent in the next edition of this volume.

REFERENCES

Arenberg, D. (1965). Anticipation interval and age differences in verbal learning. *Journal of Abnormal Psychology, 70*, 419–425.

Arenberg, D. (1967a). Age differences in retroaction. *Journal of Gerontology, 22*, 88–91.

Arenberg, D. (1967b). Regression analyses of verbal learning on adult age at two anticipation intervals. *Journal of Gerontology, 22*, 411–414.

Arenberg, D. (1973). Cognition and aging: Verbal learning, memory, and problem solving. In M. P. Lawton & C. Eisdorfer (Eds.). *The psychology of adult development and aging* (pp. 74–97). Washington: American Psychological Association.

Arenberg, D. (1980). Localization of decline and the role of attention in memory. In L. W. Poon, J. L. Fozard, L. S. Cermak, D. Arenberg & L. W. Thompson (Eds.). *New directions in memory and aging* (pp. 19–22). Hillsdale, NJ: Erlbaum.

Arenberg, D. & Robertson-Tchabo, E. A. (1977). Learning and aging. In J. E. Birren & K. W. Schaie (Eds.). *Handbook of the psychology of aging* (pp. 421–449). New York: Van Nostrand Reinhold.

Birren, J. E. (Ed.). (1959). *Handbook of aging and the individual*. Chicago: University of Chicago Press.

Birren, J. E. & Schaie, K. W. (Eds.). (1977). *Handbook of the psychology of aging*. New York: Van Nostrand Reinhold.

Bogartz, R. S. (1990a). Evaluating forgetting curves psychologically. *Journal of Experimental Psychology: Learning, Memory, and Cognition, 16*, 138–148.

Bogartz, R. S. (1990b). Learning-forgetting rate independence defined by forgetting function parameters or forgetting function form: Reply to Loftus and Bamber and to Wixted. *Journal of Experimental Psychology: Learning, Memory, and Cognition, 16*, 936–945.

Canestrari, R. S., Jr. (1963). Paced and self-paced learning in young and elderly adults. *Journal of Gerontology, 18*, 165–168.

Canestrari, R. S. (1968). Age changes in acquisition. In G. A. Talland (Ed.). *Human aging and behavior* (pp. 169–188). New York: Academic Press.

Craik, F.I.M. (1977). Age differences in human memory. In J. E. Birren & K. W. Schaie (Eds.). *Handbook of the psychology of aging* (pp. 384–420). New York: Van Nostrand Reinhold.

Craik, F.I.M. & Jennings, J. M. (1992). Human memory. In F.I.M. Craik & T. A. Salthouse (Eds.). *Handbook of aging and cognition*. Hillsdale, NJ: Erlbaum.

Eisdorfer, C., Axelrod, S. & Wilkie, F. L. (1963). Stimulus exposure time as a factor in serial learning in an aged sample. *Journal of Abnormal and Social Psychology, 67*, 594–600.

Giambra, L. M., & Arenberg, D. (in press). Adult age differences in forgetting sentences. *Psychology and Aging*.

Gilbert, J. G. (1973). Thirty-five year follow-up study of intellectual functioning. *Journal of Gerontology, 28*, 68–72.

Gladis, M. & Braun, H. W. (1958). Age differences in transfer and retroaction as a function of intertask similarity. *Journal of Experimental Psychology, 55*, 25–30.

Howe, M. L. (1988). Measuring memory development in adulthood: A model-based approach to disentangling storage-retrieval contributions. In M. L. Howe & C. J. Brainerd (Eds.). *Cognitive development in adulthood: Progress in cognitive development research* (pp. 39–64). New York: Springer-Verlag.

Howe, M. L. (1990). Development of a mathematical model of memory for clinical research applications in aging. In M. L. Howe, M. J. Stones & C. J. Brainerd (Eds.). *Cognitive and behavioral performance factors in atypical aging* (pp. 3–36). New York: Springer-Verlag.

Howe, M. L. & Brainerd, C. J. (Eds.). (1988). *Cognitive development in adulthood: Progress in cognitive development research*. New York: Springer-Verlag.

Howe, M. L. & Hunter, M. A. (1985). Adult age differences in storage-retrieval processes: A stages-of-learning analysis of developmental interactions in concreteness effects. *Canadian Journal of Psychology, 39*, 130–150.

Howe, M. L. & Hunter, M. A. (1986). Long-term memory in adulthood: An examination of the development of storage and retrieval processes at acquisition and retention. *Developmental Review, 6*, 334–364.

Hulicka, I. M. (1965). Age differences for intentional and incidental learning and recall scores. *Journal of the American Geriatrics Society, 13*, 639–649.

Hulicka, I. M. & Grossman, J. L. (1967). Age-group comparisons for the use of mediators in paired associate learning. *Journal of Gerontology, 22*, 46–51.

Hulicka, I. M. & Rust, L. D. (1964). Age-related retention deficit as a function of learning. *Journal of the American Geriatrics Society, 12*, 1061–1065.

Hulicka, I. M., Sterns, H. & Grossman, J. L. (1967). Age-group comparisons of paired-associate learning as a function of paced and self-paced association and response times. *Journal of Gerontology, 22*, 274–280.

Hulicka, I. M. & Weiss, R. L. (1965). Age differences in retention as a function of learning. *Journal of Consulting Psychology, 29*, 125–129.

Hultsch, D. F. & Dixon, R. A. (1990). Learning and memory in aging. In J. E. Birren & K. W. Schaie (Eds.). *Handbook of the psychology of aging* (3rd ed., pp. 258–274). San Diego, CA: Academic Press.

Kausler, D. H. (1982). *Experimental psychology and human aging*. New York: John Wiley.

Kausler, D. H. (1990). *Experimental psychology, cognition, and human aging* (2nd ed.). New York: Springer-Verlag.

Light, L. (1992). The organization of memory in old age. In F.I.M. Craik & T. A. Salthouse (Eds.). *Handbook of aging and cognition* (pp. 111–165). Hillsdale, NJ: Erlbaum.

Loftus, G. R. (1985). Evaluating forgetting curves. *Journal of Experimental Psychology: Learning, Memory, and Cognition, 11*, 397–406.

Loftus, G. R. & Bamber, D. (1990). Learning-forgetting independence, unidimensional memory models, and feature models: Comment on Bogartz (1990). *Journal of Experimental Psychology: Learning, Memory, and Cognition, 16*, 916–926.

McDowd, J. & Birren, J. E. (1990). Aging and attentional processes. In J. E. Birren & K. W. Schaie (Eds.). *Handbook of the psychology of aging* (3rd ed., pp. 222–233). New York: Academic Press.

Mitchell, D. B., Brown, A. S. & Murphy, D. R. (1990). Dissociations between procedural and episodic memory: Effects of time and aging. *Psychology and Aging, 5*, 264–276.

Monge, R. H. & Hultsch, D. F. (1971). Paired-associate learning as a function of adult age and the length of the anticipation and inspection intervals. *Journal of Gerontology, 26*, 157–162.

Park, D. C., Royal, D., Dudley, W. & Morrell, R. (1988). Forgetting of pictures over a long retention interval in young and older adults. *Psychology and Aging, 3*, 94–95.

Poon, L. W. (1985). Differences in human memory with aging: Nature, causes, and clinical implications. In J. E. Birren & K. W. Schaie (Eds.). *Handbook of the psychology of aging* (2nd ed., pp. 427–462). New York: Van Nostrand Reinhold.

Poon, L. W., Walsh-Sweeney, L. & Fozard, J. L. (1980). Memory skill training for the elderly: Salient issues on the use of imagery mnemonics. In L. W. Poon, J. L. Fozard, L. S. Cermak, D. Arenberg & L. W. Thompson (Eds.). *New directions in memory and aging* (pp. 461–484). Hillsdale, NJ: Erlbaum.

Robertson-Tchabo, E. A. & Arenberg, D. (1985). Mental functioning and aging. In R. Andres, E. L. Bierman & W. R. Hazzard (Eds.). *Principles of geriatric medicine* (pp. 129–140). New York: McGraw-Hill.

Rowe, E. J. & Schnore, M. M. (1971). Item concreteness and reported strategies in paired-associate learning as a function of age. *Journal of Gerontology, 26*, 470–475.

Rybarczyk, B. D., Hart, R. P. & Harkins, S. W. (1987). Age and forgetting rate with pictorial stimuli. *Psychology and Aging, 2*, 404–406.

Salthouse, T. A. (1985). *A theory of cognitive aging.* Amsterdam: North-Holland.

Salthouse, T. A., Kausler, D. H. & Saults, J. S. (1988). Utilization of path-analytic procedures to investigate the role of processing resources in cognitive aging. *Psychology and Aging, 3*, 158–166.

Schonfield, D. (1989). Conflicting conclusions, gerontological theories and applications. *Canadian Psychology, 30*, 507–515.

Shock, N. W., Greulich, R. C., Andres, R., Arenberg, D., Costa, P. T., Jr., Lakatta, E. G. & Tobin, J. D. (1984). *Normal human aging: The Baltimore Longitudinal Study of Aging* (NIH Publication No. 84–2450). Bethesda, MD: The National Institutes of Health.

Slamecka, N. J. (1985). On comparing rates of forgetting: Comment on Loftus (1985). *Journal of Experimental Psychology: Learning, Memory, and Cognition, 11*, 812–821.

Slamecka, N. J. & Katsaiti, L. T. (1988). Normal forgetting of verbal lists as a function of prior testing. *Journal of Experimental Psychology: Learning, Memory, and Cognition, 14*, 716–726.

Slamecka, N. J. & McElree, B. (1983). Normal forgetting of verbal lists as a function of their degree of learning. *Journal of Experimental Psychology: Learning, Memory, and Cognition, 9*, 384–397.

Smith, A. D. (1980). Age differences in encoding, storage, and retrieval. In L. W. Poon, J. L. Fozard, L. S. Cermak, D. Arenberg & L. W. Thompson (Eds.), *New directions in memory and aging* (pp. 23–45). Hillsdale, NJ: Erlbaum.

Thomas, J. C. & Ruben, H. (1973). Age and mnemonic techniques in paired-associate learning. Presented at the Gerontological Society meeting, Miami, FL.

Treat, N. J., Poon, L. W. & Fozard, J. L. (1978). From clinical and research findings on memory to intervention programs. *Experimental Aging Research, 4*, 235–253.

Treat, N. J. & Reese, H. W. (1976). Age, pacing, and imagery in paired-associate learning. *Developmental Psychology, 12*, 119–124.

Welford, A. T. (1958). *Aging and human skill.* Oxford: Oxford University Press.

West, R. L. & Crook, T. H. (1990). Age differences in everyday memory: Laboratory analogues of telephone number recall. *Psychology and Aging, 5*, 520–529.

Willis, S. L. (1985). Towards an educational psychology of the older adult learner: Intellectual and cognitive bases. In J. E. Birren & K. W. Schaie (Eds.). *Handbook of the psychology of aging* (2nd ed., pp. 818–847). New York: Van Nostrand Reinhold.

Wimer, R. E. (1960). A supplementary report on age differences in retention over a twenty-four hour period. *Journal of Gerontology, 15*, 417–418.

Wimer, R. E. & Wigdor, B. T. (1958). Age differences in retention of learning. *Journal of Gerontology, 13*, 291–295.

Wixted, J. T. (1990). Analyzing the empirical course of forgetting. *Journal of Experimental Psychology: Learning, Memory, and Cognition, 16*, 927–935.

Woodruff, D. (1990). Mammalian models of learning, memory, and aging. In J. E. Birren & K. W. Schaie (Eds.). *Handbook of the psychology of aging* (3rd ed., pp. 234–257). San Diego, CA: Academic Press.

24

Adult Age Differences in Cognitive Strategies: Adaptive or Deficient?

Cynthia A. Berg, Paul A. Klaczynski,
Katerina S. Calderone, and
JoNell Strough

A strategy has been defined as "one of several alternative methods for performing a particular cognitive task" (Salthouse, 1991, p. 197) and "a procedure that is nonobligatory and goal directed" (Siegler & Jenkins, 1989, p. 11). Adult age differences in strategy use have been explored as a possible locus for the deficient performance of older adults on a wide array of cognitive tasks. Older adults have been found to use different strategies than young adults on tasks involving memory (e.g., Hultsch, 1969; Sanders et al., 1980; see Smith, 1980 for a review), spatial cognition (e.g., Evans, Brennan, Skorpanich & Held, 1984; Hertzog & Yuasa, 1987; Waddell & Rogoff, 1981; see Kirasic, 1989, for a review), laboratory problem solving (see Denney, 1989, and Reese & Rodeheaver, 1985, for reviews), and everyday problem solving (see Denney, 1989, for a review).

The idea that such age "differences" in cognitive strategies represent "deficiencies" on the part of older adults has been a rather longstanding view in the adult developmental literature (see Salthouse, 1991, for a review). Older adults are posited to be deficient in their strategy use as they are less likely to use strategies that young adults use spontaneously (e.g., Murphy, Sanders, Gabriesheski & Schmitt, 1981), and the strategies that older adults do use have been deemed ineffective (e.g., Reese & Rodeheaver, 1985). More recently, a different approach to developmental comparisons of strategy use has been advanced (see also Bjorklund & Green, 1992). Rather than view age differences in cognitive strategies as representing deficiencies in older adults, this approach has focused on the adaptive nature of older adults' strategies as they relate to the context of older adult life (e.g., Adams, Labouvie-Vief, Hobart & Dorosz, 1990; Gould, Trevithick & Dixon, 1991).

These two views of age differences in cognitive strategies, deficient versus adaptive, have important consequences for adult life-span learning. That is, the view that older adults' strategies are deficient has led to numerous training programs to encourage older adults to use more effective strategies (see Willis, 1987, for a review). Such intervention studies have demonstrated that training produces improvement on the task for which training was directed but does not typically extend to other tasks. However, the view that older adults' strategies are adaptive leads to different types of interventions, namely, those that help older adults hone the strategies that they are already using (e.g., Lachman, Weaver, Bandura, Elliott & Lewkowicz, in press). In fact, these interventions often show improvements in performance similar to those of interventions that are directed at teaching new cognitive strategies (e.g., Baltes, Sowarka & Kliegl, 1989; Lachman et al., in press), and may possibly lead to greater generalization and maintenance over time (see Blackburn, Papalia-Finlay, Foyce & Serlin, 1988).

In this paper we will briefly review work on cognitive strategies that adopts this more recent adaptive view of older adults' strategies. A broad array of cognitive tasks will be included in the review focusing on memory, laboratory problem solving, and everyday problem-solving tasks to illustrate that this view guides the study of numerous types of problem-solving and intellectual tasks. We will then present our work examining the adaptive nature of cognitive strategies for solving spatial-verbal cognitive and everyday problem-solving tasks. Our research suggests that cognitive strategies vary not only as a function of age, but also as a function of numerous other individual (e.g., cognitive abilities) and contextual characteristics (e.g., task demands, training instructions). In addition, cognitive strategies may relate to how such individual and contextual characteristics are reflected in the individuals' interpretation or definition of the problem (see also Berg & Calderone, in press; Klaczynski, Laipple & Jurden, 1992; Sansone & Berg, 1993; Sinnott, 1989). We will conclude by drawing implications for lifelong learning of these views of adult developmental differences in strategies.

VIEW OF AGE DIFFERENCES AS ADAPTIVE

Recently, researchers have argued that age differences in cognitive strategies do not necessarily represent deficiencies or deficits in the cognitive capabilities of older adults. The impetus for this work comes from numerous directions, including work on expertise and aging (see Charness & Bieman-Copland, 1992, for a review) and work within the neo-Piagetian (see Labouvie-Vief, 1992, for a review) and contextualist perspectives to cognitive development (see Dixon, 1992, for a review). Much of this research examines how older adults may compensate for decrements in some cognitive components by using substitutable components or strategies to maintain overall levels of cognitive performance. Therefore, the strategies used by older adults, although different, are not deficient, but adaptive in light of changing experiences and demands present in the contexts of adults across the life span.

Numerous studies in the area of expertise and aging reveal that older experts maintain proficient performance on a skilled task, through the development of cognitive strategies that compensate for losses in lower-level cognitive skills (see Charness & Bieman-Copland, 1992, and Salthouse, 1987, for reviews). Thus, in some sense older adults may adapt to perceived and actual losses in cognitive functioning by developing cognitive strategies that allow for a better fit between themselves and the demands of the cognitive task. For instance, Salthouse (1984) examined skilled typists between the ages of 19 and 72 to explore relations among age, performance on basic cognitive abilities, and numerous components of typing skill. He found age differences on most measures of basic cognitive abilities (e.g., finger-tapping, choice reaction time, memory span) and yet no age differences on measures of typing performance. Older typists seemed to compensate for decreases in speed of response through the use of a strategy that allowed them to plan further ahead, by anticipating words further along in the to-be-typed string.

Work within the expertise literature has also demonstrated that older adults may be better able to execute strategies that both young and older adults use to approach skilled tasks. For instance, Charness' work with chess experts (1981) and bridge players (1983) demonstrates that older adults may maintain high levels of performance by a more efficient search of the problem space, which may compensate for decrements in other basic-level cognitive processes (e.g., memory, inefficient chunking processes). Similar results have been obtained by Walsh and Hershey (in press) in a decision-making task involving how much money an individual should invest in an Individual Retirement Account or in a 401k plan. Older adults and experts considered a smaller subset of variables in reaching a decision and considered these factors in a more goal-directed and efficient fashion than did young adults and novices.

Researchers from a neo-Piagetian perspective have also examined adaptive strategy use by young and older adults (e.g., Labouvie-Vief, 1982; Sinnott, 1989). For instance, Adams, Labouvie-Vief, Hobart, and Dorosz (1990) examined the story recall style of young and older adults to determine whether differences in story recall style could account for older adults' typically poorer memory performance on text-processing tasks. They hypothesized that the style of processing adopted by young adults, remembering for propositional content, is best suited to the demands of most scoring schemes on text-processing tasks. However, an interpretative style of processing concerned more with the metaphorical and psychological implications of the text, hypothesized to be used more by older adults, would place individuals at a disadvantage when typical scoring schemes value remembering propositional content. They argue that the interpretative style used by older adults may have adaptive significance in providing an efficient means of storing information and transmitting that information to other generations. Their results support, in part, the idea that older adults adopt a strategy that is more integrative or interpretive than do young adults, whose strategy was based on remembering text-based and factual information. Similar results pointing to the more interpretative style of older adults have been found by Gould, Trevithick, and Dixon (1991) and Dixon and Backman (1992).

Sinnott's work (1983, 1989) explores a similar locus for the age differences in cognitive performance on Piagetian reasoning problems. Older adults typically perform poorly on Piagetian combinatorial and proportional reasoning problems, using strategies that do not test for all possible combinations in the most efficient fashion, even when such problems are couched in terms of real-life demands. For example, one problem involved constructing all possible pairs of letters, another involved allocating pairs of visiting relatives to sleeping quarters. Sinnott found that older adults interpret real-life logical problems in a greater variety of ways than do younger adults, focusing on the social and interpersonal components of the problem. Their strategies fit with such interpretations in that older adults used pragmatic strategies for the solution of such problems (e.g., a grandfather and a daughter couldn't sleep in the same bed). Young adults, however, interpreted such problems as formal logic problems and used strategies that were consistent with such interpretations (e.g., viewed all possible logical combinations as equally valid).

Similar results have been reported by Laipple (1991). He presented young and older adults versions of Kuhn and Brannock's (1977) "house plants" task. The house-plants task involves determining which variables are responsible for a plant looking unhealthy or healthy. After presenting the task to participants, participants were asked to administer the task back to the experimenter. These verbal protocols were then used to categorize interpretations as formal (i.e., based solely on the information given), pragmatic (i.e., based on experience to the exclusion of formal task demands), or mixed. Older adults were more likely to interpret the problem as pragmatic, which had consequences for how they solved the logical problem. With type of interpretation controlled, age differences in performance disappeared. The experience-based interpretations of the older adults were thought to be adaptive as the use of experience might conserve mental energy or alternatively be more effective in general in dealing with adult demands outside of the school context.

Folkman, Lazarus, Pimley, and Novacek (1987) also examined the fit between strategies and problem appraisal by exploring the adaptive nature of young and older adults' coping strategies for dealing with life stressors. They found that older adults were somewhat more likely to use emotion-focused strategies (i.e., those that changed the problem solver's subjective reaction to the problem) than young adults, who were more likely to use problem-focused strategies (i.e., those aimed at changing the objective conditions of the problem situation to fit better with the problem solver's needs and goals). Folkman et al. caution against viewing such differences as reflecting deficiencies on the part of older adults, as such coping patterns fit with the way in which problems were appraised (i.e., older adults viewed their problems as less changeable than did young adults).

In sum, recent researchers have uncovered age differences in cognitive strategies but have not interpreted such differences as deficiencies in the performance of older adults. Rather, this research seeks to understand whether such differences serve specific adaptive functions for young and older adults, given the cognitive and pragmatic demands faced at different points in development. This research also uncovers variables other than age that may impact strategy use, including individuals' experience and individuals' interpretations of problem-solving tasks. We will now turn to a discussion of several of our own studies that illustrate how developmental differences in strategy use may serve adaptive functions. Consistent with the work described in this section, our work suggests that age is only one of many factors that impact strategy use.

INDIVIDUAL AND TASK CHARACTERISTICS THAT IMPACT STRATEGY USE

In two different lines of research we have sought to understand how individual differences in strategy use are influenced by a number of individual and contextual factors. The first line of work explores whether the typical age differences found on tests of spatial abilities (e.g., Kirasac, 1989) could be due, in part, to older adults using different strategies than young adults. Two studies will be described that examined the adaptive nature of strategy use by exploring whether strategies were consistent with individuals' underlying perceived and measured cognitive abilities and were flexibly fit to particular task conditions, including conditions of training and different features of structurally similar tasks. The second line of work explores adult age differences in strategies for solving everyday problems. A study will be discussed in which we examined the strategies that young and older adults used in solving their own everyday problems. This study illustrates that although young and older adults may report using different kinds of strategies, such differences do not result in differences in the rated effectiveness of their strategies. The last study explores one mechanism that may help explain why young and older adults differ in their strategies for solving everyday problems, namely, that they may hold different interpretations or definitions of their everyday problems. Taken as a whole, these studies indicate that a more complete understanding of individual differences in strategy use involves numerous individual characteristics in addition to age (e.g., underlying cognitive abilities, self-efficacy, the individual's interpretation of the problem) as well as characteristics of the context and/or task.

Spatial-Verbal Cognitive Tasks

Individual differences in strategy use and training. The first study explored whether older adults' poorer performance on spatial tasks could be due to older adults using different strategies than young adults. Many of the spatial tasks used to examine adult age differences in spatial ability are thought to be solved via some spatial imaging strategy. However, such spatial tasks can be approached with a variety of strategies, some of which rely on different types of verbal and visual approaches (e.g., Cohen & Faulkner, 1983; Just & Carpenter, 1985; Lohman & Kyllonen, 1983). Winograd and Simon (1980) suggested that older adults may rely more on verbal modes of dealing with spatial problems because they have difficulty in forming and manipulating visual representations. Numerous studies have found that older adults' performance was facilitated more than young adults' by the use of verbal codes as opposed to visual codes (e.g., Arenberg, 1977; Clarkson-Smith & Halpern, 1983; Elias & Kinsbourne, 1974).

The goal of the study (Berg & Rodin, 1991) was to understand the nature of age differences in verbal versus visual strategies for solving a spatial cognitive task by examining how such strategies fit with adults' verbal and spatial abilities, and whether such strategies were flexibly changed when the instructions encouraged a different strategy. We anticipated that older adults would be more likely to employ a verbal strategy than young adults. Further, we anticipated that adults' strategy use would be adaptive in that it would relate to their perceived and measured spatial and verbal abilities, with those adopting a visual strategy having higher spatial abilities and perhaps lower verbal abilities than those adopting a verbal rehearsal strategy. We also explored the flexibility with which individuals could adopt a strategy different from their own strategy, when instructed to do so, and whether age differences would occur in adopting alternative strategies.

The spatial cognitive task developed for the study was patterned after the sentence verification task used by MacLeod, Hunt, and Mathews (1978), based on work of Clark and Chase (1972). The task involved viewing a pair of sequentially presented stimuli (either of which could contain verbal statements or a picture) and verifying whether the stimuli were the same or different. Individuals were given a set of verbal statements (e.g., Go south on Mix Street for two miles, turn west for 2 miles on State St., the college is straight ahead) or a picture that directed them to a particular location. Similar to the work of MacLeod et al. (1978) on the sentence verification task, the present task could be approached via at least two different strategies. Individuals who adopted a verbal rehearsal strategy compared stimuli by rehearsing sentences and recoding pictures into their relevant sentences to compare. Individuals who adopted a visual imaging strategy recoded the sentences into a pictorial representation and compared their pictorial representation to the relevant pictures. These two strategies were discriminable on the basis of differential patterns of reaction times to study and verify sentence versus pictorial stimuli.

Twenty-four young and twenty-five older adults performed this spatial cognitive task under three conditions. Individuals were first instructed to perform the task with any strategy that they wished. Individuals then performed the task under specific training instructions that encouraged the use of either the verbal rehearsal or the visual imaging strategy. To examine the relation between strategy use and perceived and measured spatial and verbal abilities, participants were asked to rate their efficacy at various spatial and verbal tasks (e.g., reading a map, vocabulary) and were given psychometric measures of verbal (Primary

Mental Abilities [PMA] Verbal Meaning Test, Thurstone, 1960) and spatial abilities (PMA Figures Test and Educational Testing Services' Building Memory Test).

The results indicated that adults could be classified as using one of three strategies for performing the task: a verbal rehearsal strategy, a visual imaging strategy, and a mixed strategy (that consisted of using both the verbal rehearsal and visual imaging strategies). Age differences were found in performance such that overall older adults were slower and less accurate in performing the task. Age differences were also found in spontaneous strategy use such that more young adults used a visual imaging strategy, whereas more older adults adopted a verbal rehearsal strategy. Although such strategies were discriminable on the basis of differential patterns of reaction times to study and compare different types of stimuli, neither the visual imagery nor the verbal rehearsal strategy was overall more effective in solving the task. That is, no differences in overall reaction time or error rate were found in comparing individuals who used verbal rehearsal with those who used visual imaging strategies.

To explore whether spontaneous strategy use was related to individuals' un-underlying perceived and actual verbal and spatial abilities, individuals' self-efficacy ratings and psychometric performance were examined. Those adopting the visual imaging strategy had higher Building Memory Scores and higher PMA Figures Test scores than those using the verbal rehearsal strategy. These two groups did not differ on the PMA Verbal Meaning Test. In addition, participants' own ratings of their ability to use maps did differ: Individuals classified as using the visual imaging strategy rated themselves higher than did those using the verbal rehearsal strategy. Thus, individuals' spontaneous strategy choice was well fitted to their perceived and measured spatial abilities.

Finally, individuals' ability to change strategies in response to training was examined to see whether older adults were less flexible in fitting their strategies to changing task demands when instructed to do so. The results indicated that both young and older adults were able to use the trained strategy equally effectively. Although individuals could adopt the trained strategy, they did retain some of the advantages of their spontaneous strategy use. For instance, across the training conditions, individuals who spontaneously used the visual imaging strategy continued to be much faster at studying pictures than individuals initially using the verbal rehearsal strategy.

These results are consistent with the literature indicating that older adults are less likely to use visual strategies to approach spatial cognitive tasks than young adults and rely instead more on verbal modes of dealing with spatial problems. In addition, these results are also consistent with work showing decrements in fluid intelligence and maintenance of crystallized intelligence across the life span (see Horn & Cattell, 1967). We do not consider such strategy differences as deficiencies on the part of older adults, as both young and older adults' strategies fit with their perceived and measured spatial abilities and both strategies were equally effective in solving the task. In addition, both young and older adults were able to adapt their strategies to specific training instructions that encouraged the use of a different strategy. The results from this study indicate that the factors that lead individuals to use a verbal or visual strategy involve more than simply age and may involve both individual and task characteristics.

Individual differences in strategy consistency across two cognitive tasks. A second study was conducted (Berg, 1991) to examine further the influence of task characteristics on spontaneous strategy use. Spontaneous strategy use on the cognitive maps task, used in the first study, was examined in relation to spontaneous strategy use on a structurally similar, although less spatial task, the sentence verification task. Of particular interest was whether individuals would adopt similar strategies across the two tasks or whether individuals would fit their strategies to particular features of the two tasks. The sentence verification task developed by Clark and Chase (1972) and used by MacLeod et al. (1978) to examine individual differences in verbal and visual strategy use, involves viewing a sentence (e.g., star above plus) and verifying whether it matches a picture that is subsequently presented of a star and a plus. MacLeod et al. (1978) found individual differences in strategy use with individuals adopting one of two types of strategies, linguistic or pictorial, that are again discriminable on the basis of differential reaction times, much like the cognitive maps task. Individuals were presented with four types of sentence-picture stimulus pairs (true affirmative, false affirmative, true negative, and false negative), which are posited to take different amounts of time, depending on the linguistic complexity of the sentences, for those using a linguistic strategy. Thirty-two young and thirty-three older adults performed the cognitive maps task and the sentence verification task in order to examine strategy consistency across the two tasks.

The results indicated that older adults were slower and less accurate in performing both the cognitive maps and the sentence verification tasks. Similar to the Berg and Rodin (1991) study discussed above, more young adults adopted a visual imagery strategy, whereas more older adults adopted a verbal rehearsal strategy on the cognitive maps task. However, no age differences were found in strategy use on the sentence verification task. Analyses conducted to examine whether individuals consistently used the same strategy across these two tasks indicated that individuals were not using similar strategies across the two tasks. Strategy consistency did not differ by age group.

These results indicate that young and older adults do not always differ in their strategy use for tasks that can be construed as spatial in nature (see also Cohen & Faulkner, 1983). Although older adults were less likely than young adults to use visual strategies to approach the cognitive maps task, no strategy differences were found for the sentence verification task. The lack of consistency in strategy use across these two cognitive tasks for both age groups indicates that strategy choices, verbal and visual, may not be cognitive styles that adults use across cognitive tasks. Rather, strategy choices may involve a complex interplay between task characteristics (e.g., salience of spatial information, difficulty level) and individual characteristics (e.g., age, abilities). This research suggests that participants in our studies may not see the similarity in task structure that we as experimenters see our tasks as containing (see also Lave, 1989). Such task and individual characteristics must be carefully examined before generalizations about the strategy use of older adults can be made with confidence.

Everyday Problem-Solving Tasks

We have also been exploring the adaptive nature of adult age differences in strategies on tasks that are less laboratory based and more practical and everyday in nature. Previous work by Denney and colleagues (see Denney, 1989, for a review) and Folkman et al. (1987) indicated that young and older adults differed in the strategies they perceived to be effective and actually used to deal with everyday problems. However, disagreement existed as to whether such age differences represented deficiencies on the part of older adults (see Denney & Palmer, 1981) or were adaptive given the larger context in which adult problem-solving takes place (see Folkman et al., 1987). The first study to be described in this section examines the strategies that young and older adults use to solve their own everyday problems and their view of how effective they were in dealing with the problem. The second study explores a potential mechanism for why young and older adults report using different sorts of strategies, namely, that they interpret or define problems differently.

Strategies adults report using to solve their own everyday problems. The data reported here are part of a much larger ongoing project investigating individual and contextual features of everyday problems and experiences in both child and adult development (see Berg, Calderone & Gunderson, 1990; Sansone & Berg, 1993). The data reported concern everyday problem solving in 110 young college students and 98 older adults (i.e., 60 years and older). The goal of these analyses was to further understand the types of strategies adults use to solve their own everyday problems and whether young and older adults differ in the perceived effectiveness of their strategies.

Adults were asked to think about a recent problem (hassle, conflict, challenge) they had experienced and to describe the problem in as much detail as possible. They were asked to relate any problem that came to mind. This very open-ended method was used so that individuals could select the types of problems that were most salient to them (Higgins, King & Mavin, 1982) and thereby give us a sense of what has prominence in their own view of the context of everyday problem solving. This methodology yielded results indicating that certain domains of problems were differentially salient for young and older adults. For instance, the most salient types of problems mentioned by older adults dealt with family and health, whereas younger adults mentioned a variety of types of problems (e.g., family, friends, romantic relationships), with no one single domain being overly prominent.

In order to assess the strategies individuals use in dealing with their problems we asked them to describe what they did to deal with the problem as specifically as possible. Adults' responses to this question were coded into four distinct categories. These strategies were designed to capture two ways that problem solvers might deal with their problems. First, problem solvers could adapt to their problem environment by changing some aspect of themselves, either their cognitions or their behavior. Second, problem solvers could produce some change in their problem environment, by changing either other individuals in the environment or some physical aspects of the environment. This distinction was used for two primary reasons: (1) it follows from a contextual perspective to everyday problem solving (see Berg & Calderone, in press), which posits that individuals actively modify their problem solving in order to meet the demands the context presents and simultaneously modify aspects of the context to meet their personal goals, and (2) it is similar to other distinctions found in existing strategy coding schemes (e.g., Band & Weisz, 1988; Berg, 1989; Cornelius & Caspi, 1987; Folkman et al., 1987). Four distinct categories were examined. *Cognitive self-regulation* involved thoughts of the problem solver directed at regulating how he or she thinks about the problem (e.g., should pay more attention, not let Frank bug me). *Behavioral self-regulation* involved self-initiated action by the problem solver to make his or her behavior conform with the demands of the problem (e.g., study harder, exercise more). *Regulation or inclusion of others* involved attempts by the problem solver to shape and change other people's behavior, beliefs, or feelings so that the problem situation fit better with the problem solver's needs and goals (e.g., get Jane to see my point of view, ask Tim to fix my car). *Regulation of the physical environment* involved shaping and changing physical aspects of the environment so that the problem environment fit better with the problem solver's needs and goals (e.g., get the junk food out of the house, buy a lock for the front door).

Two coders categorized 25% of all strategies into these categories with 74% agreement. Disagreements were resolved between the two coders, and one coder categorized the rest of the data. Each strategy adults reported using to solve their problem was coded. Thus, any individual could have multiple strategy codes, if multiple strategies were mentioned. The number of strategy codes given to an individual's response ranged from one to five; however, most individuals reported using a single strategy. In order to assess the perceived effectiveness of individuals' strategies, we asked them to rate on a seven-point scale how well they thought they dealt with the problem.

The results indicated that adults used a variety of strategies for dealing with their own problems. The most frequently used strategies were regulation or inclusion of others (mentioned by 38% of individuals), followed by behavioral self-regulation (33%) and cognitive self-regulation (20%). Regulation of the physical environment was the least frequently used strategy (9%). In addition, age differences were found in strategy use. Young adults were more likely than older adults to use regulation or inclusion of others and cognitive self-regulation. Older adults were more likely than young adults to use regulation of the physical environment to deal with their problems.

To see whether such age differences in strategy use had consequences for the perceived effectiveness of such strategies, we also examined the relation between perceived effectiveness of strategies and the strategies individuals used for dealing with the problem. Results indicated that although young and older individuals used different strategies to deal with their problems, there were no overall age differences in the perceived effectiveness of their solutions for dealing with the problem (see Camp, Doherty, Moody-Thomas & Denney, 1989, for similar results). Strategies were, however, perceived as differentially effective. Individuals in both age groups saw strategies of regulating the physical environment as most effective in dealing with their problems, followed by behavioral self-regulation and cognitive self-regulation. Regulation or inclusion of others was seen to be least effective.

The results of this study are consistent with those of Denney (1989) and Folkman et al. (1987), described above, in that young and older adults differed in the strategies they used to solve everyday problems. However, in the present study such differences do not necessarily represent deficiencies on the part of older adults, as young and older adults did not differ in the perceived effectiveness of their strategies (see also Camp et al., 1989). Although one might question the accuracy of problem solvers' own effectiveness ratings as a measure of the effectiveness of strategies, other measures of strategy effectiveness derived by experimenters are not without their problems as well (see Camp et al., 1989). The problem solvers' own view of the effectiveness of their solutions takes into account numerous aspects of the problem-solving environment that may not be available to an outside viewer (e.g., the problem solver's past history of problem solution, contextual constraints, and the like) and is not logically less legitimate than experimenters' judgements of effective strategies.

We are currently using this data set to explore how individuals' strategies may be influenced by a complex interplay of other individual (e.g., goals) and contextual characteristics (e.g., domain of problem). The question remains regarding the source of the observed age differences in strategies. We now turn to a study that explores how such individual and contextual characteristics may be reflected in the individuals' interpretation of the problem environment, which may subsequently lead to individual differences in strategy use. If this is true, then one possible explanation of age differences in strategy use is that the different strategies of young and older adults reflect different underlying interpretations of the problem situation.

Age differences in problem interpretations. Other recent work in our laboratory (Klaczynski & Berg, 1992) has used individuals' problem interpretations to understand age differences in strategy use and the potentially adaptive nature of these age differences. The basis for this approach is that, at least in the domain of everyday problem solving, the different strategies used by young and older adults may arise not only from differences in underlying abilities but also from other individual characteristics. In particular, individuals embedded in distinct life and developmental contexts, faced by various developmental tasks, may solve everyday problems with different strategies because the meaning of the problems for their daily functioning is different. That is, because everyday problems lend themselves to a wide array of possible interpretations, the age differences in strategy use reported in the previous section may not reflect inevitable differences associated with increased age but instead may result from the different meaning or interpretations young and older adults attach to everyday situations. Rather than using age per se as the primary independent variable, age differences in strategies may be mediated by differences in problem interpretations. Interpretations, in turn, also may influence or be influenced by expectations for control in particular problem situations, perceptions of problem difficulty, and beliefs regarding the efficacy of using acquired knowledge or experience in solving the problem. Together with problem interpretations, these perceptions are likely to influence strategy use.

To provide initial data bearing on this question, 76 young and older adults were presented a range of everyday problems in one of two highly scripted routine events. One-half of the participants received problems that could occur when going to a doctor's office; the other half received problems that could arise at a dinner party. These two situations were selected because they were familiar to both age groups and because both groups could, potentially, have a highly elaborated knowledge base from which problem interpretations could be drawn.

After reading each problem, individuals were asked to describe in detail the "real" problem in the situation. Interpretations for both the "doctor" and the "dinner party" problems were coded into four primary categories that were empirically derived and were hypothesized to relate to individuals' perceptions of control. *External-social interpretations* occurred when participants believed that a problem situation was caused by the behavior (or failures to behave) of other social agents (e.g., "The problem is that the people [at the dinner party] are not getting along or having any fun"). *Internal-affective interpretations* occurred if participants believed that a personal emotion or emotional state was the underlying problem (e.g., "The problem is that you're going to a party, and you really don't like the people that will be there"). *Internal-cognitive interpretations* involved describing a problem situation in terms of mental operations, such as decision-making, selections between alternative possibilities, and planning (e.g., "The problem is you showed up [at the party] too early because you forgot what time it was supposed to be and you need to revise your plans accordingly"). *Internal-social interpretations* occurred when a problem was attributed to both the behavior of the self and the behavior or reactions of others (e.g., "The problem is that your sibling is aware of past disasters with her cooking and so wants to change her image. You want to see her succeed but don't want to hurt her sensitive feelings"). Interrater agreement on classifications was 81%.

After providing an interpretation, individuals rated on seven-point scales the perceived difficulty of each problem, the extent to which they could use experience with visiting physicians or attending dinner parties to solve the problem, and the extent to which solving the problem would depend on internal, external, and chance factors.

Age differences were found in some aspects of how problems were interpreted. For the doctor's office problems, results indicated that older adults were more likely than younger adults to interpret the problems as external-social. That is, older adults were more likely to attribute these problems to factors in the social surround rather than to themselves (e.g., the doctor should be more flexible). A different pattern of results emerged on the dinner party problems. Older adults were more likely than younger adults to interpret the problems as internal-cognitive and were less likely than young adults to interpret the problems as internal-affective.

Analyses of the relationships between problem interpretations and perceived control, perceived usefulness of experience, and perceived difficulty revealed that, for the dinner party problems, individuals who made external-social and internal-social interpretations were more likely to believe that successfully solving the problems depended on factors external to themselves. This relation did not hold for doctor problems.

Although this work is in its preliminary stages, it illustrates that everyday problem solving involves a host of variables that generally have been neglected in the cognitive aging literature. The manner in which individuals interpret problems is likely to contribute to the types of strategies they select to solve the problems. Further support for this idea comes from two recent studies of adolescent everyday problem solving (Berg & Calderone, in press; Klaczynski et al., 1992) and adult logical problem solving (see Laipple, 1991). On both everyday and traditional problems, then, the way a problem is interpreted may mediate the type of strategy selected to solve the problem. Our current work in progress extends this idea to the everyday problem solving of older adults.

SUMMARY AND CONCLUSIONS

In this article we have argued that adult age differences in strategies do not necessarily represent deficiencies on the part of older adults, but may be adaptive in light of changing cognitive and pragmatic demands faced by adults throughout the life span. Our research and the work of others suggests that strategies are influenced not only by age but by a complex interplay of individual (e.g., age, abilities, experience, interpretations) and task characteristics (e.g., training conditions, salience of spatial information). In the two studies exploring age differences in spatial cognitive problems we found that individual differences in strategies were influenced by age, individuals' measured and perceived spatial abilities, and by conditions of the task such as training instructions and stimulus materials. Our work examining age differences in solving everyday problems reveals that an individual's interpretation of an everyday problem may be an important factor in understanding age differences in cognitive strategies. Individuals' problem interpretations may not only be useful in understanding age differences in everyday problem solving, but differences in laboratory-based problem solving as well (see Gould, Trevithick & Dixon, 1991; Johnson, 1990).

The results of our studies have numerous implications for adult learning. The fact that individuals often differ in their strategies for solving both traditional and everyday problems should caution researchers away from assuming that there is a single best strategy for performing any task. Individual differences in strategy use are often overlooked in cognitive aging work (see also Hertzog, 1985). Such neglect of individual differences is apparent in numerous intervention studies that involve explicit training on the use of a single strategy for performing intellectual and problem-solving tasks (e.g., Willis, 1987). This work often makes conclusions on the basis of the outcome of training as to whether adults of different ages can adopt the trained strategy. Based on our research, however, for many adults training to use a specific strategy may involve not only practice with the strategy but also suppression of one's spontaneous strategy. This may explain why training programs that simply allow older adults to practice on their own are often as successful as programs that teach a specific strategy (e.g., Lachman et al., in press).

Although young and older adults are clearly capable of adopting strategies that are not their own, a more fruitful approach to intervention may be to tailor training to features of individuals that may impact strategy use. Such individual characteristics may include individuals' underlying cognitive abilities, their experience, and their interpretation or definition of the problem environment. Such tailored instruction has proven fruitful in the educational literature.

Our results also point to the importance of task and/or contextual characteristics in influencing strategy use. The finding that individuals did not use similar strategies across the two structurally comparable tasks (i.e., the cognitive maps and sentence verification task) is consistent with numerous intervention studies that reveal a lack of transfer of training procedures across similar tasks (e.g., Baltes & Willis, 1982; Bassock & Holyoak, 1989). It is possible that adults' interpretations of such problems might help us understand why participants perform differently on tasks that we design to be analogous. For instance, young and older adults' problem interpretations of the cognitive maps and sentence verification task might help to unravel why adults did not show consistency in strategy use across these structurally similar tasks.

In conclusion, the view that adult age differences in strategies do not necessarily represent deficiencies in the performance of older adults makes us search for factors other than simply age that lead individuals to different strategies. Such a search for the adaptive nature of adult strategies may mean that we as cognitive psychologists need to examine factors that we are not accustomed to including in models of strategy implementation (e.g., problem interpretations, context). However, such a search may help us to unpack what has been represented by "age" differences in strategy use. These factors may eventually lead us to a greater understanding of how best to facilitate the learning process for adults.

NOTE

Studies 1, 2, and 4 were supported by grants from the University of Utah Research Committee awarded to Cynthia A. Berg. Study 3 was supported by HD25728 from the National Institute of Child and Human Development and the National Institute of Aging awarded to Cynthia A. Berg. We would like to thank Janet Williams, Nancy Hill, and Quang Dang for their help in various phases of data coding and preparation.

REFERENCES

Adams, C., Labouvie-Vief, G., Hobart, C. J. & Dorosz, M. (1990). Adult age group differences in story recall style. *Journal of Gerontology: Psychological Sciences, 45*, P17–P25.

Arenberg, D. (1977). The effects of auditory augmentation on visual retention for young and old adults. *Journal of Gerontology, 32*, 192–195.

Baltes, P. B., Sowarka, D. & Kliegl, R. (1989). Cognitive training research on fluid intelligence in old age: What can older adults achieve by themselves. *Psychology and Aging, 4*, 217–221.

Baltes, P. B. & Willis, S. L. (1982). Plasticity and enhancement of intellectual functioning in old age: Penn State's adult development and enrichment project (ADEPT). In F.I.M. Craik & S. E. Trehub (Eds.). *Aging and cognitive processes* (pp. 353–389). New York: Plenum.

Band, E. & Weisz, J. R. (1988). How to feel better when it feels bad: Children's perspectives on coping with everyday stress. *Developmental Psychology, 24*, 247–253.

Bassock, M. & Holyoak, K. J. (1989). Interdomain transfer between isomorphic topics in algebra and physics. *Journal of Experimental Psychology: Learning Memory and Cognition, 15*, 153–166.

Berg, C. A. (1989). Knowledge of strategies for dealing with everyday problems from childhood through adolescence. *Developmental Psychology, 25*, 607–618.

Berg, C. A. (1991). Individual differences in strategy shifts across two spatial cognitive tasks. In C. Berg & M. Johnson (Chairs). Age differences in cognitive strategies: New approaches to an old problem. Symposium presented at Gerontological Society, San Francisco, CA.

Berg, C. A. & Calderone, K. S. (in press). The role of problem interpretations in understanding the development of everyday problem solving. In R. J. Sternberg & R. K. Wagner (Eds.). *Mind in context: Interactionist perspectives on human intelligence*. New York: Cambridge University Press.

Berg, C. A., Calderone, K. & Gunderson, M. (1990, November). Strategies young and old adults use to solve their own everyday problems. Paper presented at the meeting of the Gerontological Society, Boston, MA.

Berg, C. A. & Rodin, J. (1991). Individual differences in young and old strategies in a spatial cognitive task. Manuscript, University of Utah, Salt Lake City, UT.

Bjorklund, D. F. & Green, B. L. (1992). The adaptive nature of cognitive immaturity. *American Psychologist, 47*, 46–54.

Blackburn, J. A., Papalia-Finlay, D., Foyce, B. F. & Serlin, R. C. (1988). Modifiability of figural relations performance among elderly individuals. *Journal of Gerentology: Psychological Sciences, 43*, 87–89.

Camp, C. J., Doherty, K., Moody-Thomas, S. & Denney, N. W. (1989). Practical problem solving in adults: A comparison of problem types and scoring methods. In J. D. Sinnott (Ed.). *Everyday problem solving: Theory and applications* (pp. 211–228). New York: Praeger.

Charness, N. (1981). Aging and skilled problem solving. *Journal of Experimental Psychology: General, 110,* 21–38.

Charness, N. (1983). Age, skill, and bridge bidding: A chronometric analysis. *Journal of Verbal Learning and Verbal Behavior, 22,* 406–416.

Charness, N. & Bieman-Copland, S. (1992). The learning perspective: Adulthood. In R. J. Sternberg & C. A. Berg (Eds.). *Intellectual Development.* New York: Cambridge University Press.

Clark, H. H. & Chase, W. G. (1972). On the process of comparing sentences and pictures. *Cognitive Psychology, 3,* 472–517.

Clarkson-Smith, L. & Halpern, D. F. (1983). Can age-related deficits in spatial memory be attenuated through the use of verbal coding? *Experimental Aging Research, 9,* 179–184.

Cohen, G. & Faulkner, D. (1983). Age differences in performance on two information-processing tasks: Strategy selection and processing efficiency. *Journal of Gerontology, 38,* 447–454.

Cornelius, S. W. & Caspi, A. (1987). Everyday problem solving in adulthood and old age. *Psychology and Aging, 2,* 144–153.

Denney, N. W. (1989). Everyday problem solving: Methodological issues, research findings, and a model. In L. W. Poon, D. C. Rubin & B. A. Wilson (Eds.). *Everyday cognition in adulthood and late life* (pp. 330–351). New York: Cambridge University Press.

Denney, N. W. & Palmer, A. M. (1981). Adult age differences on traditional and practical problem-solving measures. *Journal of Gerontology, 36,* 323–328.

Dixon, R. A. (1992). Contextual approaches to adult intellectual development. In R. J. Sternberg & C. A. Berg (Eds.). *Intellectual development* (pp. 350–380). New York: Cambridge University Press.

Dixon, R. A. & Backman, L. (1992). Reading and memory for prose in adulthood: Issues of expertise and compensation. In S. R. Yussen & M. C. Smith (Eds.). *Reading across the lifespan.* New York: Springer-Verlag.

Elias, M. F. & Kinsbourne, M. (1974). Age and sex differences in the processing of verbal and nonverbal stimuli. *Journal of Gerontology, 29,* 162–171.

Evans, G. W., Brennan, P. L., Skorpanich, M. A. & Held, D. (1984). Cognitive mapping and elderly adults: Verbal and location memory for urban landmarks. *Journal of Gerontology, 39,* 452–457.

Folkman, S., Lazarus, R. S., Pimley, S. & Novacek, J. (1987). Age differences in stress and coping processes. *Psychology and Aging, 2,* 171–184.

Gould, O. N., Trevithick, L. & Dixon, R. A. (1991). Adult age differences in elaborations produced during prose recall. *Psychology and Aging, 6,* 93–99.

Hertzog, C. (1985). An individual differences perspective. *Research on Aging, 7,* 7–45.

Hertzog, C. & Yuasa, M. (1987). *Adult age differences in the speed and accuracy of mental rotation.* Manuscript. School of Psychology, Georgia Institute of Technology, Atlanta, GA.

Higgins, E. T., King, G. A. & Mavin, G. H. (1982). Individual construct accessibility and subjective impressions and recall. *Journal of Personality and Social Psychology, 43*, 35–47.

Horn, J. L. & Cattell, R. B. (1967). Age differences in fluid and crystallized intelligence. *Acta Psychologia, 26*, 107–129.

Hultsch, D. F. (1969). Adult age differences in the organization of free recall. *Developmental Psychology, 1*, 673–678.

Johnson, M.M.S. (1990). Age differences in decision making: A process methodology for examining strategic information processing. *Journal of Gerontology, 45*, 75–78.

Just, M. A. & Carpenter, P. A. (1985). Cognitive coordinate systems: Accounts of mental rotation and individual differences in spatial ability. *Psychological Review, 92*, 137–171.

Kirasic, K. C. (1989). The effects of age and environmental familiarity on adults' spatial problem-solving performance: Evidence of a hometown advantage. *Experimental Aging Research, 15*, 181–187.

Klaczynski, P. A. & Berg, C. A. (1992, April). What's the real problem: Age, perceived control and perceived difficulty as predictors of everyday problem definitions. Presented at Cognitive aging conference, Atlanta, GA.

Klaczynski, P. A., Laipple, J. S. & Jurden, F. H. (1992). Educational context differences in practical problem solving during adolescence. *Merrill-Palmer Quarterly, 38*, 417–439.

Kuhn, D. & Brannock, J. (1977). Development of the isolation of variables scheme in experimental and "natural experiment" contexts. *Developmental Psychology, 13*, 9–14.

Labouvie-Vief, G. (1982). Dynamic development and mature autonomy: A theoretical prologue. *Human Development, 25*, 161–191.

Labouvie-Vief, G. (1992). A Neo-Piagetian perspective on adult cognitive development. In R. J. Sternberg & C. A. Berg (Eds.). *Intellectual Developmental*. New York: Cambridge University Press.

Lachman, M. E., Weaver, S. L., Bandura, M., Elliott, E. & Lewkowicz, C. J. (in press). Improving memory and control beliefs through cognitive restructuring and self-generated strategies. *Journal of Gerontology: Psychological Sciences*.

Laipple, J. S. (1991). Problem solving in young and old adulthood: The role of task interpretation. Doctoral dissertation, West Virginia University.

Lave, J. (1989). *Cognition in Practice*. New York: Cambridge University Press.

Lohman, D. F. & Kyllonen, P. C. (1983). Individual differences in solution strategy on spatial tasks. In R. F. Dillon & R. R. Schmeck (Eds.). *Individual differences in cognition* (pp. 105–135). New York: Academic Press.

MacLeod, C. M., Hunt, E. B. & Mathews, N. N. (1978). Individual differences in the verification of sentence-picture relationships. *Journal of Verbal Learning and Verbal Behavior, 17*, 493–507.

Murphy, M. D., Sanders, R. E. Gabriesheski, A. S. & Schmitt, F. A. (1981). Metamemory in the aged. *Journal of Gerontology, 36*, 185–193.

Reese, H. W. & Rodeheaver, D. (1985). Problem solving and complex decision making. In J. E. Birren & K. W. Schaie (eds.). *The handbook of the psychology of aging* (Vol. 2, pp. 474–499). New York: Van Nostrand Reinhold.

Salthouse, T. A. (1984). Effects of age and skill in typing. *Journal of Experimental Psychology: General, 113,* 345–371.

Salthouse, T. A. (1987). Age, experience, and compensation. In C. Schooler & K. W. Schaie (Eds.). *Cognitive functioning and social structure throughout the life course* (pp. 142–157). Norwood, NJ: Ablex.

Salthouse, T. A. (1991). *Theoretical perspectives on cognitive aging.* Hillsdale, NJ: Erlbaum.

Sanders, R. E., Murphy, M. D., Schmitt, F. A. & Walsh, K. K. (1980). Age differences in free recall rehearsal strategies. *Journal of Gerontology, 35,* 550–558.

Sansone, C. & Berg, C. A. (1993). Adapting to the environment across the life span: Different process or different inputs? *International Journal of Behavioral Development.*

Siegler, R. S. & Jenkins, E. (1989). *How children discover new strategies.* Hillsdale, NJ: Erlbaum.

Sinnott, J. D. (1983). Individual strategies on Piagetian problems: A thinking aloud approach. Paper presented as part of the symposium "Understanding of problem solving from a gerontological perspective: Today's status, tomorrow's research, and some new ideas," L. Giambra, chair, sponsored by the Gerontological Society, San Francisco.

Sinnott, J. D. (1989). A model for solution of ill-structured problems: Implications for everyday and abstract problem solving. In J. D. Sinnott (Ed.). *Everyday problem solving: Theory and applications.* New York: Praeger.

Smith, A. D. (1980). Age differences in encoding, storage, and retrieval. In L. W. Poon, J. L. Fozard, L. S. Cermak, D. Arenberg & L. W. Thompson (Eds.). *New directions in memory and aging* (pp. 23–45). Hillsdale, NJ: Erlbaum.

Thurstone, L. L. (1960). *Primary mental abilities.* Chicago: University of Chicago Press.

Waddell, K. J. & Rogoff, B. (1981). Effect of contextual organization on spatial memory of middle aged and older women. *Developmental Psychology, 17,* 878–885.

Walsh, D. A. & Hershey, D. A. (in press). Mental models and the maintenance of complex problem solving skills into old age. In J. Cerella & W. Hoyer (Eds.). *Adult information processing: Limits on loss.* New York: Academic Press.

Willis, S. L. (1987). Cognitive training and everyday competence. In K. W. Schaie (Ed.). *Annual review of gerontology and geriatrics,* Vol. 6 (pp. 159–188). New York: Springer.

Winograd, E. & Simon, E. W. (1980). Visual memory and imagery in the aged. In L. W. Poon, J. L. Fozard, L. S. Cermak, D. Arenberg & L. W. Thompson (Eds.). *New directions in memory and aging* (pp. 485–506). Hillsdale, NJ: Erlbaum.

25

Cognitive Aspects and Interventions in Alzheimer's Disease

John C. Cavanaugh and Romy Nocera

When confronted with the prospect of cognitive aging, most people tend to think first of the normative changes occurring with age. Even if people view these changes through the lens of social stereotypes, the view is not altogether negative. Indeed, what actually happens, at least in terms of the normative changes described elsewhere in this volume, is often substantially less bleak than stereotypes portray. However, there is another and much darker set of cognitive changes than often come to mind when people speculate about their own cognitive aging—the prospect of succumbing to dementia.

Probably no other condition associated with aging is more feared than dementia. In dementia people may literally lose their minds, being reduced from complex, thinking, feeling human beings to confused, vegetative victims unable even to recognize their spouse and children. Approximately 4.4 million older Americans, or roughly 15% of people over age 65, have some type of dementing disorder (Davies, 1988). Estimates are that the number may double in the next fifty years because of the increase in very old adults (Crook, 1987). Incidence of dementia is age-related; fewer than 1% of the people are afflicted at age 65, but the incidence rises sharply to 20% of those over 80.

The term *dementia* does not refer to a specific disease but, rather, to a family of diseases with similar symptoms. About a dozen forms of dementia have been identified. All are characterized by cognitive and behavioral deficits involving some form of permanent damage to the brain (American Psychiatric Association, 1987).

Dementias can be classified in several ways. The most important is to group dementias on the basis of whether they are treatable. Some dementias can be treated effectively, while others cannot. This distinction between reversible and irreversible dementias has profound implications for the patient. In this chapter we will focus on irreversible and degenerative dementias. Given this focus, we wish to emphasize two points. First, the cognitive changes we will describe occur in only a minority of older adults. Second, the changes we discuss should be compared to the normative changes described in several other chapters in order to appreciate more fully the differences between normal and abnormal cognitive aging.

Because the most common and widely known form of dementia is Alzheimer's disease, we begin by describing the changes occurring in this disorder. Subsequently, we will discuss various types of cognitive interventions that have been attempted with Alzheimer's disease patients.

Prior to our review, however, we need to emphasize two points. First, the topic of this chapter represents the flip side of lifelong learning. In a very real sense, dementia represents lifelong unlearning, that is, the unrelenting progression of cognitive loss observed in dementia can be viewed as unlearning the information amassed over a person's lifetime. Lost first is information learned most recently; eventually, even what one has learned about one's own basic identity is gone. Thus, the inclusion of this chapter in this volume reflects a recognition that lifelong learning may not always be an outcome of old age.

Second, although a few ways have been found to temporarily address the cognitive declines in dementia (examples of which are reviewed later), the situation is quite different than that discussed in Parenté and Stapleton's chapter in this volume on recovery of memory after traumatic brain injury. The former case involves a progressive and ultimately irreversible disease, whereas the latter does not (see Parenté and Stapleton, chapter 19, this volume). This difference is extremely important and needs to be kept in mind when comparing techniques with cognitive impairments with different etiologies. Nevertheless, some of the approaches described by Parenté and Stapleton may have potential applicability for dementia patients early in the course of the disease.

ALZHEIMER'S DISEASE

Alzheimer's disease is the most common form of progressive, degenerative dementia, accounting for perhaps as many as 70% of all cases of dementia (Davies, 1988). However, only over the past quarter century have we realized how common Alzheimer's disease is, and in what age groups it is most likely to occur. For sixty years after Alois Alzheimer's initial description of the disease in a 51-year-old, physicians believed that the disease was very rare and that it was a form of presenile dementia (i.e., dementia occurring before age 65). However, it was not until Tomlinson, Blessed, and Roth (1970) showed that the same kinds of changes occurred in both early onset and late onset of the disease that physicians realized that Alzheimer's disease could occur across adulthood. Although research has shown that a common set of neurological changes underlies Alzheimer's disease irrespective of age, recent evidence suggests that age is correlated with the severity and speed of progression in the disease (Morgan, 1992).

Although we will focus on Alzheimer's disease, it should be recognized that other forms of dementia exist as well, such as Pick's disease, multi-infarct dementia, Huntington's disease, Lewy body disease, and dementia associated with Parkinson's disease, among others. In many cases, clinical behavioral symptoms of these other forms of dementia are similar to those observed in Alzheimer's disease, especially early in the disease course. However, the underlying neurological changes of these various diseases are different. Readers interested in learning more about the differential diagnosis of these other forms of dementia should consult Raskind and Peskind (1992), who provide an introduction to these issues.

Neurological Changes in Alzheimer's Disease

The changes in the brain that characterize Alzheimer's disease are microscopic. This means that definitive diagnosis of the disease can be done only at autopsy; brain biopsies are an alternative, but the risks are so high that they are rarely performed (Crook, 1987). The microscopic changes that define Alzheimer's disease are neurofibrillary tangles, neuritic plaques, and granulovacuolar degeneration.

Neurofibrillary tangles are accumulations of pairs of filaments in the neuron that become wrapped around each other; when examined under a microscope, these paired filaments look like intertwined spirals. Neurofibrillary tangles occur in several areas of the brain, and the number of tangles is directly related to the severity of symptoms (Farmer, Peck & Terry, 1976). Neuritic plaques are spherical structures consisting of a core of amyloid protein, surrounded by degenerated fragments of dying or dead neurons. The plaques are also found in various parts of the brain and are related to the severity of the disease (Blessed, Tomlinson & Roth, 1968). Degeneration of neurons in some areas of the brain results in the formation of vacuoles, or spaces that become filled with fluid and granular material. Although granulovacuolar degeneration is a defining characteristic of Alzheimer's disease, its relationship to the severity of the disease is still unknown.

In addition to these three changes, atrophy of various parts of the brain has been found in Alzheimer's disease. However, brain atrophy alone is not a reliable indicator, as it is associated not only with Alzheimer's disease but also with many other diseases as well as normal aging (Crook, 1987).

Considerable research has uncovered specific deficits in neurotransmitters in Alzheimer's disease. Most notable is a marked decrease in the enzyme choline acetyltransferase, a marker for acetylcholine, a neurotransmitter involved in learning and memory (Davies & Maloney, 1976). The decline in acetylcholine appears to be caused mainly by the degeneration of the nucleus basalis of Meynert and surrounding structures in the base of the brain (Dekker, Connor & Thal, 1991). These changes may be the cause of the drastic declines in cognitive functions associated with Alzheimer's disease. Other studies have revealed decreases in other neurotransmitters, including noradrenaline (Bondareff, Mountjoy, & Roth, 1982), serotonin (Gottfries, Roos, & Winblad, 1976), and dopamine (Gottfries, Gottfries, & Roos, 1969). Changes in these neurotransmitters may be related to other symptoms, such as agitation, sleep disturbances, and perceptual difficulties.

Although the changes occurring in the brains of Alzheimer's victims are substantial, we must use caution in assuming that they represent qualitative differences from normal aging. They may not. Gottfries (1985) notes that all of the changes seen in Alzheimer's disease, from cognitive changes to the changes in neurotransmitters, are also found to some degree in normal elderly people. To be sure, the changes in Alzheimer's disease are much greater. But the important point is that Alzheimer's disease may be merely an exaggeration of normal aging and not something qualitatively different from it.

Clinical Symptoms and Diagnosis

The major symptoms of Alzheimer's disease are gradual changes in functioning: declines in memory, learning, attention, and judgment; disorientation in time and space; difficulties in word finding and communication; declines in personal hygiene and self-care skills; inappropriate social behavior; and changes in personality (Crystal, 1988; Davies, 1988). These symptoms tend to be vague in the beginning, and they mimic other psychological problems such as depression or stress reactions. For example, an executive may not be managing as well as before and may be missing deadlines more often. The symptoms worsen gradually. Eventually, an executive who once could easily handle millions of dollars will be unable to add two small numbers. Emotional problems also become increasingly apparent, manifesting themselves as depression, paranoia, and agitation. As the disease progresses, the patient becomes incontinent and increasingly dependent on others for care, eventually becoming completely incapable of even such simple tasks as dressing and eating. Throughout the course of the disease, symptoms are worse in the evening than in the morning, a phenomenon referred to as sundowning.

Cognitive Symptoms. In the initial stage of the disease, the Alzheimer's patient typically complains of simple memory loss, such as forgetting where he or she placed familiar objects, and an inability to recall names he or she formerly knew well. If given a clinical evaluation at this point, the individual may perform somewhat below average. It is important to note, however, that it is extremely difficult to tell whether these symptoms are an early sign of Alzheimer's disease as opposed to normal changes in memory with age. As the disorder continues, however, the impairment in recent memory ability becomes increasingly worse; for example, the individual experiences an increased inability to remember the names of persons to whom he or she was just introduced. Additionally, the victim may retain very little information from reading a newspaper article and show variation in recall of recent events, recalling some events well and forgetting others. Regarding the latter, the context and related circumstances surrounding the event are also usually forgotten. At this point, the individual is typically demonstrating decreased performance at work, may begin to become lost in previously familiar locations, and is experiencing mild to moderate anxiety. In a clinical evaluation, performance on standardized intelligence and memory tests may be below average (Department of Health & Human Services, 1984). However, the individual may still obtain a perfect score on a mental status exam (described later).

As the disease continues, more serious decline occurs. There are noticeable deficits in concentration and decreased knowledge of recent events, both in the context of one's personal life and with regard to the outside world. The individual's ability to travel alone decreases. He or she has difficulties in managing personal finances and does not perform complex tasks accurately or efficiently. At this stage, denial is a dominant defense mechanism; additional characteristics include social withdrawal, flattening of affect, and loss of initiative, tact, and judgment. From a clinical perspective, the patient in this stage typically makes three to nine errors on the MMSE. However, it is sometimes possible for the patient to function safely in a limited, familiar environment and to follow familiar daily routines (Department of Health & Human Services, 1984).

As decline in abilities continues, patients cannot function without assistance. For example, they cannot remember their home address, phone number, or names of close family members. Disorientation is frequent, and the individual loses the ability to reason (Henig, 1985). Patients may show poor judgment in choosing proper and appropriate clothing. Interestingly, however, toileting and eating activities tend to remain unimpaired, and patients can still remember their own names and those of their spouses and children. During this time, there are some episodes of lucidity, during which the patient may seem like his or her "old self."

Eventually, lucid periods occur less often and grow shorter in duration. The patient occasionally forgets his or her spouse's name and experiences increased unawareness of recent life events. Victims become unaware of environmental surroundings and time. Diurnal rhythms become disturbed. Sleep disturbances and nocturnal wandering are common. There may be episodes of incontinence. Also, the individual tends to demonstrate significant personality and emotional changes, such as delusional and paranoid behavior, obsessive symptoms, anxiety, and agitation, and may become violent or abusive (Department of Health & Human Services, 1984). From a self-orientation perspective, it is commonly observed that the patients begin to lose their unique qualities, identity, and individuality (Henig, 1985). They are also often unable to initiate appropriate action, as they cannot retain a thought long enough to make appropriate choices and act. In addition, when compared to age-matched normal controls, Alzheimer's patients show far greater deficits in reality monitoring (Shimamura, 1990).

Continued deterioration results in the loss of all verbal abilities. For example, Shimamura (1990) reported that only Alzheimer's patients, when compared to patients with Huntington's Disease, Korsakoff's Syndrome, and age-matched controls, showed impaired word-completion priming late in the disease. Shimamura further noted that lexical and semantic representations are particularly affected by Alzheimer's disease as the disease progresses. (However, some patients appear relatively unimpaired even relatively late in the disorder; see Grosse, Wilson & Fox, 1990; Nebes & Brady, 1990.) By now, incontinence typically becomes a continual problem, and the individual invariably needs assistance in toileting and eating. In some cases, patients lose the ability to walk. Victims experience a great deal of confusion and disorientation, and there may be more frequent episodes of irrationality and emotional outbursts (Henig, 1985). At this point, in a clinical evaluation the patient typically answers all items on the MMSE incorrectly.

Finally, patients typically lose the ability to communicate, and all memories, including personal identity, appear to be lost (Henig, 1985). Many individuals are placed in nursing homes or other similar institutions by this point.

It is extremely important to note that the rate of the cognitive deterioration just described in Alzheimer's disease is highly variable from one victim to the next, although progression is usually faster when onset occurs earlier in life (Bondareff, 1983). It is important to reiterate that many other diseases also cause the problems observed early in Alzheimer's disease. In fact, fewer than 10% of those individuals showing signs of mild memory impairment will subsequently develop serious cognitive impairment (Reisberg, Ferris, Anand, de Leon, Schneck & Crook, 1985). However, severe cognitive deficits clearly indicate the presence of the type of decline characteristic of Alzheimer's disease (Reisberg et al., 1985).

Clinical Diagnosis. Although a definitive diagnosis of Alzheimer's disease depends on an autopsy, clinicians can make reasonably accurate diagnoses of probable Alzheimer's disease based on the number and severity of behavioral changes observed (Crook, 1987). The key to early diagnosis, though, is a comprehensive and broad assessment. Table 1 provides the set of guidelines developed by a work group convened by the National Institute of Neurological and Communicative Diseases and Stroke (McKhann et al., 1984). Note that a great deal of the diagnostic effort goes into ruling out other possible causes for the observed cognitive deficits. This point emphasizes the fact that all possible treatable causes for the observed symptoms must be eliminated before a diagnosis of Alzheimer's disease may be made. Unfortunately, many clinicians do not conduct such thorough diagnoses.

As noted in Table 1, the clinical diagnosis of Alzheimer's disease consists of noting the history of the symptoms, documenting the cognitive impairments, conducting a general physical exam and neurological exam, performing laboratory tests to rule out other diseases, obtaining a psychiatric evaluation, performing neuropsychological tests, and assessing functional abilities (Crystal,

Table 1
NINCDS-ADRDA Criteria for the Diagnosis of Probable Alzheimer's Disease
1. Criteria for clinical diagnosis of *probable* Alzheimer's disease include

- Dementia established by clinical examination and documented by Mini-Mental State Test (Folstein, Folstein & McHugh, 1975) or some similar examination and confirmed by neuropsychological tests
- Deficits in two or more areas of cognition
- Progressive worsening of memory and other cognitive functions
- No disturbance of consciousness
- Absence of systemic disorders or other brain diseases that in and of themselves could account for progressive deficits in memory and cognition

2. Diagnosis of *probable* Alzheimer's disease is supported by

- Progressive deterioration of specific cognitive functions, such as language (aphasia), motor skills (apraxia), and perception (agnosia)
- Impaired activities of daily living and altered patterns of behavior
- Family history of similar disorders, particularly if confirmed neuropathologically
- Laboratory results of normal lumbar punctures as evaluated by standard techniques, normal patterns or nonspecific changes in EEG, such as increased slow-wave activity, and evidence of cerebral atrophy on CT with progression documented by serial observation

3. Other clinical features consistent with diagnosis of *probable* Alzheimer's disease, after exclusion of causes of dementia other than Alzheimer's disease, include

- Plateaus in course of progression of illness
- Associated symptoms of depression; insomnia; incontinence; delusions; illusions; hallucinations; catastrophic verbal, emotional, or physical outbursts; sexual disorders; and weight loss
- Other neurological abnormalities in some patients, especially with more advanced disease and including motor signs, such as increased muscle tone, myoclonus, or gait disorder
- Seizures in advanced disease
- CT normal for age

4. Features that make diagnosis of *probable* Alzheimer's disease uncertain or unlikely include

- Sudden, apoplectic onset
- Focal neurological findings such as hemiparesis, sensory loss, visual field deficits, and uncoordination early in the course of the illness
- Seizures or gait disturbance at onset or very early in the course of the illness

5. Clinical diagnosis of *possible* Alzheimer's disease are

- May be made on the basis of dementia syndrome, in absence of other neurological, psychiatric, or systemic disorders sufficient to cause dementia and in the presence of variations in onset, in presentation, or in clinical course

Table 1 (continued)

• May be made in presence of second systemic or brain disorder sufficient to produce dementia, which is not considered to be cause of dementia

• Should be used in research studies when single, gradually progressive severe cognitive deficit is identified in absence of other identifiable cause

6. Criteria for diagnosis of *definite* Alzheimer's disease are

• Clinical criteria for probable Alzheimer's disease

• Histopathological evidence obtained from biopsy or at autopsy

7. Classification of Alzheimer's disease for research purposes should specify features that may differentiate subtypes of the disorder, such as

• Familial occurrence

• Onset before age 65

• Presence of trisomy–21

• Coexistence of other relevant conditions, such as Parkinson's disease

1988). The history or progress of the disease should be obtained from both the patient, if possible, and a family member. The questions asked must cover when the problems began, how they have changed, what the patient is capable of doing, and other medical problems.

The cognitive impairments are typically documented through a mental status exam, which is a brief series of questions tapping orientation ("What day is this? Where are you?"), memory, arithmetic ability (counting backwards), ability to follow directions, motor skills (copying a design), and general information ("Who is the president now?"). One of the most widely used mental status exams is the Mini-Mental State Exam (MMSE; Folstein, Folstein & McHugh, 1975). Individuals who score poorly on a mental status exam should be examined more carefully; typically this entails thorough neuropsychological examinations.

The general physical exam and neurological exam help rule out other causes such as cardiovascular disease, nutritional problems, or strokes. A series of laboratory tests must be conducted to rule out additional causes of the observed behaviors. Blood tests look for evidence of chronic infections and for abnormal levels of vitamin B_{12}, folic acid, and thyroid hormone. An EEG should be performed to rule out subtle seizures and to verify that the characteristic diffusely slow EEG pattern in Alzheimer's disease is present. Brain imaging techniques such as computed tomography (CT), magnetic resonance imaging (MRI), positron emission tomography (PET), or single photon emission computed tomography (SPECT) may be used. However, none of these imaging techniques provides conclusive evidence; at best they can rule out the presence of tumors, strokes, or other abnormalities (Crystal, 1988).

A psychological evaluation must be conducted to rule out any serious emotional problems that may be causing the observed deficits. Chief among these is depression, which if severe may mimic the early signs of Alzheimer's disease. The likelihood of diagnostic confusion between depression and Alzheimer's diminishes over time based on whether the cognitive symptoms continue to worsen. As noted earlier, cognitive problems increase in number and severity in Alzheimer's disease while in depression they typically do not. The patient's functional abilities must be evaluated as well; these include instrumental daily activities, such as cooking and housekeeping chores, and personal self-care skills, such as dressing and bathing.

Putting Symptoms in Context: Effects on Everyday Life

Understanding the impact of a degenerative disease such as Alzheimer's means being able to place it in its proper context. While the description of symptoms and the diagnostic process described above provide a quick clinical overview, they do not furnish a context in which to view the disease's impact on everyday life. In order to understand much of the motivation underlying intervention efforts, such a context is necessary. From this perspective, the disorder changes every aspect of the patient's everyday life. The cognitive changes alone cause major disruptions: being unable to remember a neighbor's name, how to dial a once-familiar phone number, or how to dress oneself would be serious problems for anyone. The patient and his or her family and friends all experience disruption in everyday life. Living situations, understanding and communication between the patient and others, and ultimately all relationships are inevitably affected by the continual deterioration caused by Alzheimer's disease. In short, the symptoms of the disorder are manifested in routine activities and have a great deal of impact on daily life (Aronson, 1988).

Consider, for example, Aronson's (1988) description of a typical scenario. As memory problems increase, family members and friends may feel hurt or angry when the patient forgets a birthday, anniversary, or other important date or feel annoyed at having to continually repeat information to the patient. In addition, there are potentially dangerous situations associated with memory loss, as when the patient forgets to turn off the stove or to properly extinguish a cigarette. Deficits in language skills cause the patient to experience difficulty in self-expression and in following directions and make it increasingly laborious for others to communicate with him or her. Changes in language ability are progressively debilitating and are especially difficult problems for family members to deal with. Additionally, visual-spatial symptoms can cause disturbances in the ability to operate household appliances, such as the stove, and in finding one's way around a new environment, such as a relative's home (Aronson, 1988). As disorientation to time, place, and person ensue, the individual can easily become lost, have difficulty in keeping appointments, and call people by the wrong names.

Further deficits in calculation abilities and the increasing incidence of poor judgment, confusion, and unpredictability can lead to difficulties in handling money (such as balancing the checkbook), inappropriate behavior, sloppiness, carelessness, misplacing of objects, and erratic or impulsive behavior. Close family members especially experience the impact of these deficits, as the person with Alzheimer's disease may mishandle and lose joint monies, accuse others of stealing objects that he or she actually misplaced, or accuse them of being strangers or intruders in the house (Aronson, 1988).

Personality changes, too, become apparent to persons in the patient's surroundings. Such changes cause interactions with the patient to be quite demanding, in that he or she may behave in a manner totally different from long-established patterns or may exhibit behaviors that may shock or upset individuals who knew the patient prior to the onset of the disease. An example from our own research fits this latter category. We encountered a female Alzheimer's disease patient in whom the disease was quite advanced. Upon our initial entrance to the special care unit of the nursing home in which she lived, the woman approached one of our team with the greeting, "My, what a tall handsome man you are!" Upon questioning, family members revealed that previously the woman had been quite shy and reserved, especially with men. Prior to the onset of the disease, it would have been extremely unlikely that she would have made such a comment to a man.

It is quite common for patients to display delusional thinking; several of the participants in our research projects have (incorrectly) claimed to have been physicians, Peace Corps volunteers, famous dancers, and so forth when asked about what they had done for a living. Interestingly, many of these individuals present very convincing stories, complete with relevant (and often accurate) information. Where such stories originate, however, remains a mystery. In any case, individuals may change so dramatically that they essentially become strangers to their family and friends (Aronson, 1988).

One of the most interesting and underresearched phenomena about the everyday impact of Alzheimer's disease concerns the patient's awareness of his or her problems. In our experience, patients often seem quite aware of their declining abilities. While this may not seem surprising in individuals early in the disease process, we have observed what we believe to be similar signs of awareness much later. For example, several participants in our research in both home settings and on a special care unit sometimes decline to respond to questions on cognitive tests. Participants tested in home settings sometimes frankly admit that they are unable to do the task or state that they just don't want to try. Nursing home participants sometimes show outbursts of temper, frustration, and crying episodes or outright refusal. One nursing home resident repeatedly insisted that he had "more important things to do" when a researcher attempted to initiate an evaluation.

Although we have no direct evidence linking such behaviors to personal insight, we believe that they are at least suggestive of such awareness. We argue that patients refuse to participate in order to avoid embarrassment, frustration, or other negative feelings caused by their inability to answer questions they once would have perceived as simple. As previously stated, denial is a defense mechanism found frequently in Alzheimer's patients; every incorrect response may serve to remind the patient of his or her declining abilities.

As an additional piece of anecdotal evidence, we observed an interesting behavioral pattern in our nursing home sample. Residents appeared to cycle through periods of good cooperation and periods of absolute refusal. That is, residents would be cooperative on all aspects of the cognitive assessment for several weeks, then suddenly become angry or obstinate when confronted with them. But within a few days or weeks, these same residents would once again become cooperative. Most intriguing was the pattern of performance across these periods of cooperation. Invariably, the uncooperative periods were followed by substantive drops in scores once residents became cooperative again. A very interesting research question is whether the simultaneity of the uncooperative period and a drop in performance represented mere coincidence or an emotional signalling of patients' awareness that they were deteriorating further.

INTERVENTION STRATEGIES FOR COGNITIVE DEFICITS IN ALZHEIMER'S DISEASE

As indicated earlier, the most serious and consistent problems in Alzheimer's disease patients are the various types of cognitive difficulties. Chief among these are the progressively serious memory losses. Memory intervention programs have been used with many different populations, including both normal and clinical groups of older adults (Kotler-Cope & Camp, 1990). Persons with Alzheimer's disease constitute one of the most interesting clinical target groups, largely because of the progressive decline and changing nature of patients' memory ability.

Memory interventions with Alzhemier's disease typically take two main forms. First, some interventions are aimed at altering the physical environment of Alzheimer's disease patients and are often incorporated into nursing home design and caregiver education programs. For example, one relatively common practice in nursing homes is to color-code halls and to label a resident's room with both a printed name and a photograph of the individual at the entrance. Recently, a growing number of researchers are attempting to develop training programs using paradigms that have strong empirical bases in the literature on normal cognitive aging. Unfortunately, few investigators have examined the efficacy of such training programs for everyday functioning. In particular, researchers have not extensively studied the degree to which cognitive training of Alzheimer's disease patients generalize from training settings to real-world (e.g., home) settings. Additionally, virtually no work has focused on the various strategies caregivers generate in attempts to provide cognitive support for their affected family member. Our own research is an attempt at addressing this latter point.

Environmental Interventions

Much of the emphasis over the years in terms of cognitive interventions has focused on practical suggestions for circumventing the increasing memory difficulties experienced by Alzheimer's disease patients (e.g., Zgola, 1987). Although many of these suggestions appear to make sense intuitively, few have any supporting empirical evidence concerning efficacy.

Two general types of environmental intervention strategies have been developed. One involves the actual redesign of living space to accommodate individuals with cognitive impairments (Regnier & Pynoos, 1992). This approach has been adopted most by long-term care and other institutions whose residents are cognitively impaired. Our focus is on the second type of environmental intervention, which entails making minor modifications in home settings, for example, in order to provide cognitive support for the individual with cognitive impairment.

As a rule, environmental interventions of this latter type designed to address memory impairments are begun as the patient experiences serious recent-memory problems. These types of interventions consist of altering or manipulating the physical environment in order to provide as much contextual support as possible. For example, common strategies include posting labels on kitchen and other cabinets that provide information about their contents, placing frequently used objects in plain view, writing instructions for daily routines (e.g., making a cup of tea) in simple step-by-step fashion, and providing clearly understandable calendars and clocks. To the extent possible, these manipulations should be implemented as they are needed. That is, caregivers should monitor the level of memory impairment and only provide the level of support absolutely necessary in order to avoid frustration and to provide a safe environment. In particular, caregivers should avoid providing too much support (i.e., underestimating the patient's abilities), as this may negatively affect the patient's self-esteem.

Environmental interventions are implemented in nursing homes and adult day-care centers that have cognitively impaired clients, and some forms of therapy utilize such interventions. For example, reality orientation is a technique based on repetition and relearning that was developed for moderately confused residents (Stephens, 1975). The key to reality orientation is that it is a 24-hour program that is integrated into the entire environment. The goal is to keep the resident in touch with what is going on in the world in every way possible.

Implementing a reality orientation program in a nursing home, for example, involves several things. Residents are addressed by a title such as Mr. or Mrs. unless they specify otherwise. Plenty of clocks and bulletin boards with calendars are placed in prominent locations. Name cards are used at meals. Activities are interesting and diversified and are announced on the public address system. Birthdays are recognized individually, and special meals are served on holidays. Visiting hours are liberal, and volunteers are encouraged to visit. Color-coded rooms and hallways are used. Independence is encouraged as much as possible.

In short, everything that occurs in the institution is geared to keeping residents in touch with reality.

Research findings on the effects of reality orientation are mixed. It appears to be most beneficial for mildly disoriented individuals (Spayd & Smyer, 1988). Overall, reality orientation appears to improve individuals' knowledge of basic orienting facts (e.g., day, month, time) rather than providing them with a set of transferrable skills for dealing with different environments (Hart & Fleming, 1985).

In our view, it appears that many of the suggestions for environmental intervention make intuitive sense. Moreover, some (e.g., providing cues for the contents of cabinets) appear grounded in sound principles of cognitive psychology (i.e., organizational or category cues). However, too little empirical evidence is currently available to evaluate the efficacy of these interventions, especially in view of the progressive nature of Alzheimer's disease. It seems obvious that such interventions should work better at earlier stages of the disease, but when and under what circumstances the techniques become ineffective remains anybody's guess.

Empirically-Based Programs

The lack of a substantial empirical literature on cognitive remediation in Alzheimer's disease has motivated some researchers to examine the problem. The point of departure for this work is the mainstream cognitive literature, with the goal of inculcating memory strategies that will assist the Alzheimer's disease patient in dealing with memory problems that cause personal embarrassment.

One of the most difficult situations for Alzheimer's disease patients is the inability to remember people's names. In a very interesting series of studies, Camp (see Camp & McKitrick, 1991) showed that people with Alzheimer's disease can successfully be taught the names of staff at day-care centers and nursing homes. His technique involves spaced retrieval, which consists of progressively increasing the amount of time between the recall trials of the target information (i.e., a person's name). This technique has been examined for many years in the mainstream cognitive psychology literature as a way to assist normal young adults learn new information (Landauer & Bjork, 1978). In the procedure, the trainer shows the client a photograph of a person and says that person's name. After an initial recall interval of 5 seconds, the trainer asks the client to remember the name. As long as the client remembers correctly, recall intervals (in seconds) are increased to 10, 20, 40, 60, 90, 120, 150, and so on. If the client forgets the target name, the correct answer is provided; and the next recall interval is decreased to the length of the last correct trial. During the interval, the trainer simply engages the client in conversation to prevent active rehearsal of the information.

Camp and McKitrick (1991) report that even people who previously could not retain new information for more than 60 seconds can remember names taught via spaced retrieval for intervals up to 5 weeks. Although there are individual differences in how long people with Alzheimer's disease remember information learned this way and how well they transfer new learning from photographs to the real people, these results are extremely encouraging. The intervention requires no drugs, can be done in any setting, and involves social activity. The training can even be inserted into everyday activities such as playing games or normal conversation, making it comfortable and unintervention-like for the client. Although more work needs to be done to refine the technique, it appears that spaced retrieval represents a very promising, easy-to-use intervention method.

Interventions such as this that are strongly grounded in theory and the larger cognitive aging literature are greatly needed. Clearly, it remains to be seen how many names individuals can learn using spaced retrieval and whether names learned this way will generalize from one setting to another. Still, the demonstration that people whose recent memory shows severe impairment can nevertheless demonstrate new learning represents a major break-through.

Caregiver-Generated Strategies

An important issue overlooked in both environmental intervention and empirically-based work is the natural evolution of caregiver-provided strategies. That is, little attention has been paid to the kinds of cognitive strategies that caregivers learn to provide to their relatives with Alzheimer's disease. Over the past few years, we have been attempting to address this knowledge gap. In particular, we have developed a set of tasks both on well-researched standardized tests and traditional laboratory memory tasks that allow us to document the kinds of strategies spousal caregivers provide. Our short-term goal in this research is to gain understanding of the degree to which caregivers spontaneously provide cognitive support to their affected spouses. In the long run, we hope to develop an empirically based set of recommendations that could be implemented in caregiver training programs.

Our first foray into this area (Cavanaugh et al., 1989) was aimed at accomplishing two things: development of a reliable coding system of caregivers' verbalizations and demonstration that this system could be applied to a dyadic problem-solving task. In this and subsequent work, we utilized videotaped records of caregiver-patient interactions. In this first project, we based on efforts on an interactive version of the Block Design subtest from the WAIS-R (Wechsler Adult Intelligence Scale-Revised). The task entailed having the caregivers instruct patients in how to construct the designs. Caregivers were free to provide any instruction they wished, with the constraint that they were not allowed to

Table 2
Verbal Behavior Coding Categories for Block Design Task

Category	Behavioral Definition
1. Location	Cues concerning a specific (top, right) or general (here, there) location for a block or token
2. Reminder[a]	Reference to what was just done, what the task is all about, or what is to be done next
3. Goal Direction[a]	Reference to the desired end state by drawing attention to the picture that depicts the final design
4. Strategy	Reference to a systematic method of doing the task efficiently (telling how to turn a block or token; suggesting ways to manipulate block or token)
5. Color/Form/Shape	References to the color, shape, or orientation of the blocks (red; square; right side up)
6. Justification	An answer to a "why" question
7. Motivation	Praise, reward, encouragement
8. Restriction	Interrupt verbally and take over instructions, or says "no" or "don't"
9. Feedback[a]	Reference to whether block or token has been put in the right place, or whether progress is being made
10. Requests[b]	Care-recipient asks for help or feedback

[a]Coded for caregivers only
[b]Coded for care-recipients only

touch the blocks. Caregiver-patient dyads were compared to normal dyads in order to document systematic differences in instructional techniques.

Based on careful analyses of the dyadic interactions, we identified ten discrete verbal behaviors that could be coded reliably. These behaviors are listed in Table 2. Each incidence of a codable verbalization was recorded; the recording period lasted 10 minutes per dyad. As can be seen, caregivers provided a large number of strategies. In general, strategies tended to be concrete (focusing on perceptual features or location). Additionally, caregivers provided much positive feedback, most of which was unconditional (given whether the patient did the correct thing or not). However, subsequent analyses revealed substantial individual differences in the number and type of verbalizations, leading us to wonder about important correlates of such behaviors.

Given the success of our initial study at reliably documenting caregivers' attempts at providing cognitive support, we have subsequently expanded our efforts. We have developed three additional tasks that allow us to address two important limitations of the first study. Specifically, we wondered whether the number of strategies caregivers tried was related to caregivers' basic ability to give instructions, and whether the number of strategies provided was a function of the type of task. Thus, we systematically manipulate the degree to which caregivers' instructions are constrained and whether the task explicitly involves verbal memory.

The four tasks we are investigating include two nonverbal and two verbal tasks. One task in each group allows caregivers to generate any strategy they choose, while the other requires them to work from a specific script (either the actual standardized administration instructions or an experimenter-generated set of instructions). The constrained nonverbal task is the Token Test, a relatively widely used standardized neuropsychological test. The unconstrained nonverbal task we used is the Block Design, the task used in our first investigation. The constrained verbal memory task is the Sort Task, a standard laboratory task involving the learning of a categorizable list of items. The unconstrained verbal memory task is a variation on this theme, which we call the Kitchen Cabinets Task. This task involves learning a categorizable list of kitchen items that caregivers may sort into representations of kitchen cabinets (actually cardboard boxes).

These manipulations provide information useful for interpreting individual differences in caregivers' verbalizations. Refinements in our coding scheme to include additional categories for patients' verbalizations will also help in this regard. Additionally, important correlates such as caregiving hassles and marital satisfaction are being examined as other possible explanations of individual differences.

Preliminary results reveal that caregivers tend to be fairly consistent across different types of tasks in the kinds and numbers of cognitive support strategies they provide. This implies that whatever types of verbal strategies caregivers develop, they tend to apply them fairly consistently across situations in which tasks share certain properties. For example, to the extent that caregivers are not limited in the types of verbal cognitive strategies they can provide (as in the Block Design and Kitchen Cabinets tasks), they attempt to use elaboration-based approaches (e.g., attempt to tie to-be-learned items in the Kitchen Cabinets Task with previously encountered situations). Interestingly, these results indicate a tendency to generalize memory strategies in ways not typically found in laboratory-based training studies (Cavanaugh & Green, 1990). If replicable, these findings would have important implications for training. That is, it may be easier for people to see how strategies apply in different settings when in a position of instructing others than when instructing oneself.

RESEARCH RECOMMENDATIONS

Compared with research on other aspects of Alzheimer's disease (e.g., biomedical, caregiver stress), little attention has been paid to cognitive interventions aimed at providing support for declining abilities. In our view, future work should be targeted at four important issues: (1) establishing which of the many well-researched cognitive strategies that have been shown to be effective with nondemented elderly (both normal and brain-injured) also improve performance with demented elderly; (2) specifically examining the efficacy of the many recommendations made by support groups and related associations; (3) including strategy training comparison conditions in drug studies (for a review of the pharmacological research, see Parenté and Stapleton, this volume); (4) comparing experimenter-generated with caregiver-generated strategies to determine which work better under which conditions; and (5) examining all of these issues as functions of severity of the disease in order to map out the boundaries of each type of intervention.

An aggressive research program on these issues is overdue and will provide invaluable information about potentially powerful and effective behavioral interventions. We believe that cognitive-aging researchers have the training and technology to offer viable alternatives to pharmacological studies. Moreover, cognitive training interventions avoid the specter of serious side effects that often accompany such medications (e.g., liver toxicity). Finally, we argue that such interventions could and should be developed so that caregivers could be the instruments of change. If we are able to design these types of intervention programs, then cognitive aging researchers will have truly made a major contribution to the field.

NOTE

Preparation of this chapter was supported by NIA research grant AG09265 and by a research grant from the AARP Andrus Foundation to the first author.

REFERENCES

American Psychiatric Association (1987). *Diagnostic and statistical manual (DSM III-R)*. Washington, DC: Author.

Aronson, M. K. (1988). Patients and families: Impact and long-term management implications. In M. K. Aronson (Ed.). *Understanding Alzheimer's disease* (pp. 74–88). New York: Scribner's.

Blessed, G., Tomlinson, B. E. & Roth, M. (1968). The association between quantitative measures of dementia and of senile changes in the cerebral grey matter of elderly subjects. *British Journal of Psychiatry, 114*, 797–811.

Bondareff, W. (1983). Age and Alzheimer's disease. *Lancet, 1*, 1447.

Bondareff, W., Mountjoy, C. Q. & Roth, M. (1982). Loss of neurons or origin of the adrenergic projection to cerebral cortex (nucleus locus ceruleus) in senile dementia. *Neurology, 32*, 164–168.

Camp, C. J. & McKitrick, L. A. (1991). Memory interventions in DAT populations: Methodological and theoretical issues. In R. L. West & J. D. Sinnott (Eds.). *Everyday memory and aging: Current research and methodology*. New York: Praeger.

Cavanaugh, J. C., Dunn, N. J., Mowery, D., Feller, C., Niederehe, G., Frugé, E. & Volpendesta, D. (1989). Problem-solving strategies in Alzheimer's patient-caregiver dyads. *The Gerontologist, 29*, 156–158.

Cavanaugh, J. C. & Green, E. E. (1990). I believe, therefore I can: Self-efficacy beliefs in memory aging. In E. A. Lovelace (Ed.). *Aging and cognition: Mental processes, self-awareness, and interventions* (pp. 189–230). Amsterdam: North-Holland.

Crook, T. (1987). Dementia. In L. L. Carstensen & B. A. Edelstein (Eds.). *Handbook of clinical gerontology* (pp. 96–111). New York: Pergamon.

Crystal, H. A. (1988). The diagnosis of Alzheimer's disease and other dementing disorders. In M. K. Aronson (Ed.). *Understanding Alzheimer's disease* (pp. 15–33). New York: Scribner's.

Davies, P. (1988). Alzheimer's disease and related disorders: An overview. In M. Aronson (Ed.). *Understanding Alzheimer's disease* (pp. 3–14). New York: Scribner's.

Davies, P. & Maloney, A.J.F. (1976). Selective loss of central cholinergic nuerons in Alzheimer's disease. *Lancet, 2*, 1403.

Dekker, J.A.M., Connor, D. J. & Thal, L. J. (1991). The role of cholinergic projections from the nucleus basalis in memory. *Neuroscience and Biobehavioral Reviews, 15*, 299–317.

Department of Health and Human Services. (1984). *Report of the Secretary's Task Force on Alzheimer's Disease* (DHHS Publication No. ADM 84–1323). Washington, DC: U.S. Government Printing Office.

Farmer, P. M., Peck, A. & Terry, R. D. (1976). Correlations among neuritic plaques, neurofibrillary tangles, and the severity of senile dementia. *Journal of Neuropathology and Experimental Neurology, 35*, 367–376.

Folstein, M. F., Folstein, S. E. & McHugh, P. R. (1975). Mini-mental state: A practical method for grading the cognitive state of patients for the clinician. *Journal of Psychiatric Research, 12*, 189–198.

Gottfries, C. G. (1985). Alzheimer's disease and senile dementia: Biochemical characteristics and aspects of treatment. *Psychopharmacology, 86*, 245–252.

Gottfries, C. G., Gottfries, I. & Roos, B. E. (1969). The investigation of homovanillic acid in the human brain and its correlation to senile dementia. *British Journal of Psychiatry, 115*, 563–574.

Gottfries, C. G., Roos, B. E. & Winblad, B. (1976). Monoamine and monoamine metabolites in the human brain post mortem in senile dementia. *Aktuelle Gerontologie, 6*, 429–435.

Grosse, D. A., Wilson, R. S. & Fox, J. H. (1990). Preserved word-stem-completion priming of semantically encoded information in Alzheimer's disease. *Psychology and Aging, 5*, 304–306.

Hart, J. & Fleming, R. (1985). An experimental evaluation of a modified reality orientation program. *Clinical Gerontologist, 3*, 34–45.

Henig, R. M. (1985). *The myth of senility: The truth about the brain and aging.* Glenview, IL: Scott, Foresman.

Kotler-Cope, S. & Camp, C. J. (1990). Memory interventions in aging populations. In E. A. Lovelace (Ed.). *Aging and cognition: Mental processes, self-awareness and interventions* (pp. 231–261). Amsterdam: North-Holland.

Landauer, T. K. & Bjork, R. A. (1978). Optimal rehearsal patterns and name learning. In M. M. Gruneberg, P. E. Morris & R. N. Sykes (Eds.). *Practical aspects of memory* (pp. 625–632). London: Academic Press.

McKhann, G., Drachman, D., Folstein, M., Katzman, R., Prince, D. & Stadlam, E. M. (1984). Clinical diagnosis of Alzheimer's disease: Report of the NINCDS-ADRDA

Work Group under the auspices of the department of Health and Human Services Task Force on Alzheimer's disease. *Neurology, 34*, 939–944.

Morgan, D. G. (1992). Neurochemical changes with aging: Predisposition towards age-related mental disorders. In J. E. Birren, R. B. Sloane & G. D. Cohen (Eds.). *Handbook of mental health and aging* (2nd ed., pp. 175–199). San Diego, CA: Academic Press.

Nebes, R. D. & Brady, C. B. (1990). Preserved organization of semantic attributes in Alzheimer's disease. *Psychology and Aging*, 574–579.

Raskind, M. A. & Peskind, E. R. (1992). Alzheimer's disease and other dementing disorders. In J. E. Birren, R. B., Sloane & G. D. Cohen (Eds.). *Handbook of mental health and aging* (2nd ed., pp. 477–513). San Diego, CA: Academic Press.

Regnier, V. & Pynoos, J. (1992). Environmental interventions for cognitively impaired older persons. In J. E. Birren, R. B. Sloane & G. D. Cohen (Eds.). *Handbook of mental health and aging* (2nd ed., pp. 763–792). San Diego, CA: Academic Press.

Reisberg, B., Ferris, S. H., Anand, R., de Leon, M. J., Schneck, M. K. & Crook, T. (1985). Clinical assessment of cognitive decline in normal aging and primary degenerative dementia: Concordant ordinal measures. In P. Pinchot, P. Berner, R. Wolf & K. Thau (Eds.). *Psychiatry* (Vol. 5, pp. 333–338). New York: Plenum.

Shimamura, A. P. (1990). Aging and memory disorders: A neuropsychological analysis. In M. L. Howe, M. J. Stones & C. J. Brainerd (Eds.). *Cognitive and behavioral performance factors in atypical aging* (pp. 37–65). New York: Springer-Verlag.

Spayd, C. S. & Smyer, M. A. (1988). Interventions with agitated, disoriented, or depressed residents. In M. A. Smyer, M. D. Cohn & D. Brannon (Eds.). *Mental health consultation in nursing homes* (pp. 123–141). New York: New York University Press.

Stephens, L. R. (Ed.). (1975). *Reality orientation* (rev. ed.). Washington, DC: American Psychiatric Association.

Tomlinson, B. E., Blessed, G. & Roth, M. (1970). Observations on the brains of demented old people. *Journal of the Neurological Sciences, 11*, 205–242.

Zgola, J. M. (1987). *Doing things: A guide to programming activities for persons with Alzheimer's disease and related disorders*. Baltimore: Johns Hopkins University Press.

26

The Effects of Training on Basic Cognitive Processes: What Do They Tell Us about the Models of Lifespan Cognitive Development?

Nancy W. Denney

A large body of research on age differences in cognitive abilities in adults indicates that while some abilities tend to be fairly well maintained throughout adulthood at least until the very latest adult years, some abilities exhibit decline beginning in early or middle adulthood (e.g., Denney, 1982a; Labouvie-Vief, 1985). The abilities more likely to be maintained tend to be verbal (e.g., vocabulary) and informational facts about the culture. The abilities that decline tend not to be verbal and factual but, rather, to be spatial, abstract, and perceptual motor abilities. A variety of explanations have been proposed to explain why the two general types of abilities take different developmental courses across the adult years. John Horn (1970), using Cattell's (1963) distinction between crystallized and fluid abilities, reported that crystallized abilities tend to be maintained or increase across the adult years while fluid abilities tend to decline. Crystallized abilities involve "the perception of relations, eduction of correlates, abstraction, etc. in materials in which past appropriation of the collective intelligence of the culture would give one a distinct advantage in solving the problems involved" (Horn, 1970, p. 462). Fluid abilities, on the other hand, involve "the ability to perceive complex relations, educe complex correlates, form concepts, develop aids, reason, abstract, and maintain span of immediate apprehension in solving novel problems in which advanced elements of the collective intelligence of the culture were not required for solution" (Horn, 1970, p. 462). Horn suggests that crystallized abilities are maintained or increase throughout adulthood as individuals continue to be exposed to the "intelligence of the culture," whereas fluid abilities decrease with age because they are dependent on the neurophysiological status of the individual, which declines with age.

Denney (1982a), on the other hand, drew a distinction between exercised and unexercised abilities. She suggested that it is not the type of ability that determines whether it will be maintained, increase, or decrease with age. Rather, she suggests that it is the extent to which an ability is used throughout the adult years that will determine its developmental function. Abilities that are exercised frequently will be relatively well maintained, and those that are not exercised during the adult years will exhibit early decline. In addition, Denney suggests that all abilities, even highly exercised abilities, will eventually exhibit some decline if the individual lives long enough. This inevitable decline is a result of neurophysiological decline that accompanies aging.

Baltes and his colleagues (e.g., Baltes, Dittmann-Kohli & Dixon, 1984) proposed yet another explanation for the differential developmental courses of different abilities. They made a distinction between two types of processes they called the "mechanics" and the "pragmatics" of intelligence. The mechanics of intelligence are "the basic cognitive operations and cognitive structures that are associated with such tasks as perceiving relationships, classification, and logical reasoning" (p. 63). These operations and structures are content free. The pragmatics of intelligence, on the other hand, include "(1) systems of knowledge that are fairly generalized, (2) specialized dimensions of knowledge, and (3) knowledge about factors of performance, i.e., about skills relevant for the activation of intelligence in specific contexts requiring intelligent action" (p. 63). The pragmatics of intelligence deal with the context-related application of the mechanics of intelligence. Baltes and his associates predict that, with increasing age, the mechanics of intelligence will exhibit decline because of age-related declines in biological functioning while the pragmatics of intelligence may continue to increase with age because of the continued experience.

As a result of the age-related declines in cognitive functioning during the adult years, many investigators have attempted to facilitate the performance of middle-aged and elderly adults via a variety of intervention techniques. These attempts were made for both practical and theoretical reasons. The purpose of this chapter is, first, to review the literature on the effect of cognitive training on basic cognitive processes across the adult years and, second, to discuss the implications of this research for the general models of lifespan cognitive development. Because of limited space, this review will not include a review of the literature on memory intervention studies (see Kotler-Cope & Camp, 1990, and Yesavage, 1985, for reviews of memory intervention research. Also see chapters by Cavanaugh & Nocera and Parenté & Stapleton in this volume).

TRAINING ON BASIC COGNITIVE PROCESSES

Noncognitive Factors

A number of investigators have attempted to improve cognitive performance in elderly adults by manipulating noncognitive factors thought to be important in determining elderly adults' performance. These investigators have tried to facilitate elderly adults' performance by manipulating factors such as response speed (e.g., Denney, 1982b; Hoyer, Labouvie & Baltes, 1973; Hoyer, Hoyer, Treat & Baltes, 1978–79), motivation (Denney, 1980), self-confidence (Denney, 1980), strategy planning time (Denney, 1980), social contact with the experimenter (e.g., Willis, Cornelius, Blow & Baltes, 1983) and noncontingent social praise (Mergler and Hoyer, 1981). In earlier reviews (e.g., Denney, 1979; Denney, 1982a; Denney, 1990) it has been demonstrated that these attempts to modify cognitive performance by manipulating variables other than cognitive variables tended to be ineffective.

More recently, Hayslip (1989) reported that a stress inoculation procedure facilitated performance of older adults on tests of fluid abilities. However, because the stress inoculation procedure was confounded with practice on the types of tests that served as dependent variables and because it is well established that practice effects on fluid ability tests are fairly robust (as will be discussed later), future research will be needed to determine whether stress inoculation alone actually does facilitate performance.

Thus, it appears that there is no good evidence that the manipulation of noncognitive variables has an effect on cognitive performance in the elderly. Rather, it appears that more direct cognitive interventions are necessary to effect real change in cognitive performance. This suggests that the declines in performance that are obtained with some cognitive abilities during the later adult years are a result of cognitive deficits/changes rather than a result of noncognitive variables such as motivation, self-confidence, and the like. Of course it is possible that other manipulations of noncognitive variables might prove more effective in the future. However, because it currently appears that noncognitive interventions are not very effective, this review will be limited to a review of the intervention research that has focused directly on cognitive variables.

Cognitive Factors

Much of the research on direct cognitive interventions has appeared in earlier reviews (e.g., Denney, 1979; Denney, 1982a; Denney, 1990). In these reviews it was clear that a variety of cognitive training techniques yield significant improvement in the cognitive performance of elderly adults. For example, research indicates that modeling efficient strategies is effective in facilitating cognitive performance. In the modeling studies the subjects observe a model perform the cognitive task in an efficient manner. Modeling has been demonstrated to be an effective training technique on problem-solving tasks (e.g., Denney & Denney, 1974), classification tasks (e.g., Denney, 1974), concept-learning tasks (e.g., Meichenbaum, 1972), and a card-sorting task (e.g., Crovitz, 1966).

Likewise, research indicates that direct instruction has proven an effective means of facilitating performance on cognitive tasks. In direct instruction studies, the experimenter simply tells subjects how to perform the task in an efficient manner rather than actually showing them how to do it as is done in modeling studies. Direction instruction studies have yielded improved performance on set induction tasks (e.g., Heglin, 1956) and nonverbal search tasks (e.g., Young, 1966).

Providing subjects with feedback regarding the correctness of their responses also appears to be an effective method of facilitating performance on cognitive tasks in the elderly. Feedback effects have been demonstrated to increase performance on spatial egocentrism (Schutz & Hoyer, 1976), concept learning (Sanders, Sterns, Smith & Sanders, 1975) and conservation (Hornblum & Overton, 1976).

Thus, in the early 1980s it was fairly well established that strategy modeling, direct instruction, and response contingent feedback are all effective methods for facilitating the cognitive performance of older adults. Since that time, what has intervention research demonstrated?

More recent research has supported the finding that modeling, feedback, and direct instruction intervention techniques facilitate the cognitive performance of elderly adults on a variety of fluid abilities. Many of these more recent studies have employed cognitive training programs that have combined the training techniques that proved effective in earlier research. Schaie and Willis (1986; see also Willis & Schaie, 1986) demonstrated that they could facilitate the performance of elderly adults on either inductive reasoning or spatial organization problems with five one-hour training sessions. Their training involved components of direct instruction, modeling, feedback, and practice. Using a similar comprehensive training procedure, Baltes, Dittmann-Kohli, and Kliegl (1986) subjected older adults to five one-hour sessions aimed at training on figural relations problems and to five one-hour sessions aimed at training on induction problems. They found that performance on both figural relations and induction problems improved in comparison to a no-contact control group. Blackburn, Papalia-Finlay, Foye, and Serlin (1988) also reported that five hours of training modeled on the training procedure employed by Willis and Schaie (1986; Schaie & Willis, 1986) facilitated figural relations performance in older adults. Finally, Denney and Heidrich (1990) demonstrated that significant training effects could be obtained on Raven's Progressive Matrices in only one short training session.

Thus, early research indicated that modeling, feedback, and direct instruction training techniques can be used to facilitate the performance of elderly adults on the types of tasks on which they typically perform relatively poorly. More recent research has tended to focus on comprehensive cognitive training techniques that include all three of these training components—direct instruction, feedback, and modeling. This research has supported the finding that these techniques can be used to improve performance in elderly adults on the types of tasks on which they typically show relatively early declines with age.

Further, while the earlier cognitive training research tended to involve short, one-session training procedures, the more recent research has typically involved extended training procedures, often involving up to five one-hour sessions. However, the Denney and Heidrich study, as well as much of the research conducted before 1980, indicates that significant training effects can be obtained with short, one-session procedures. This suggests that the extended training employed in the studies conducted by Willis, Schaie, Baltes, and their colleagues may not have been necessary. It is possible that the same degree of improvement could have been obtained in a much shorter time period. To test this possibility, one would need to compare the effectiveness of short, one-session procedures with longer, five-hour procedures in the same study.

Practice

In addition to the beneficial effects of various types of cognitive training, it appears that practice alone, without any cognitive training component, may, at least in some circumstances, have a beneficial effect on the cognitive performance of elderly adults on the types of tasks on which relatively large age-related declines are typically obtained. In earlier reviews (e.g., Denney, 1979; Denney, 1982a) it was reported that, while there was some indication that practice may facilitate the cognitive performance of elderly adults (e.g., Labouvie-Vief & Gonda, 1976; Panicucci, 1975), there were also studies that found no evidence that practice alone might result in improved performance (e.g., Hoyer, Hoyer, Treat & Baltes, 1978–79; Sanders, Sterns, Smith & Sanders, 1975; Schutz & Hoyer, 1976).

More recent research appears to indicate more consistently that practice alone, without any direct instruction, feedback, or modeling, in certain circumstances does result in improved performance in elderly adults. For example, in a study of elderly adults, Hofland, Willis, and Baltes (1981) reported significant practice effects on figural relations and induction tests. They presented their subjects with eight practice sessions, each of which included a figural relations test and an induction test. The tests were administered under standard timed conditions and no feedback was given. Hofland et al. found significant improvement on both figural relations and induction post-tests. Similar practice effects were also reported by Schaie and Willis (1986) in a study of inductive reasoning and spatial orientation.

Anderson, Hartley, Bye, Harber, and White (1986) also demonstrated that practice alone could improve performance in only one training session. Anderson et al. subjected both young and elderly adults to one of three practice-only conditions on the Raven Progressive Maze. Some of the subjects were prompted by questioning to attend to all components of the matrix stimuli, some were prompted to consider all the components of the stimuli as well as their relationships, and others were given practice without any prompting. Significant improvement was found in all three groups from pre-test to post-test, and there were no significant differences in performance between the three groups. Further, the performance enhancement effects did not differ as a function of age.

In another study of elderly adults, Baltes, Sowarka, and Kliegl (1989) demonstrated that performance could be enhanced on figural relations tasks with practice alone. They compared an experimenter-guided, rule-based training condition and a self-guided practice condition with a no-training control condition. Both the experimenter-guided and the self-guided conditions included five one-hour sessions. Their results indicated that their practice-only condition resulted in just as much improvement as their rule-based training condition. Baltes, Kliegl, and Dittmann-Kohli (1988) found that practice alone was even more effective than experimenter-guided training in a study in which elderly adults were given either practice or experimenter-guided training on both figural relations and induction tasks. They also reported that more generalization to other types of tasks were obtained in the practice-only condition than in the experimenter-guided training.

Blackburn, Papalia-Finlay, Foye, and Serlin (1988) also reported that practice significantly facilitated the performance of elderly adults on figural relations tasks. In their study of the effect of a comprehensive cognitive training program on elderly adults' performance, they included a group that was not given any training but rather was told to use the practice materials and learn on their own. This group was given as many practice problems as the subjects who were given the cognitive training. Following practice with the test materials, the participants discussed the strategies they had developed and reported the answers they derived from the strategy they used. They were then told whether their answers were correct or incorrect. Though the authors discuss this condition as a practice-only condition, it is clear that the subjects were given feedback as to the correctness of their answers. This is different from the practice-only control groups used by others. Blackburn et al. found that this condition facilitated performance and, in fact, that the improvement obtained in this condition was maintained over time better than in their more intensive training condition.

In summary, the results of the research prior to about 1980 yielded inconsistent results regarding the effectiveness of practice only to enhance the performance of elderly adults on the type of tasks on which they typically perform less well than younger adults. More recent training studies that have included practice-only groups have more consistently indicated that the performance of the subjects in the practice-only conditions is enhanced by the practice. One difference between the early and the later studies is in the extensiveness of the practice. In the early studies, the training procedure tended to consist of only one rather short training session. This meant that the practice-only conditions tended to be rather short as well. In the more recent studies, as the training has tended to be more extensive, the practice conditions have had to be more prolonged as well. It may be that very short practice sessions are not extensive enough to produce consistently reliable improvement in performance.

Although the more extended cognitive training procedures are not necessary to yield improvement in elderly adults' performance and may not even yield more improvement than the shorter cognitive training procedures, it appears that more extended practice may be necessary to obtain reliable improvement. More research will be needed to determine the relationship between the duration and extent of practice and the degree of improvement obtained as well as the generalizability and duration of any obtained improvements. Recent research suggests that extended practice-only conditions may yield more generalization to other types of tasks and more generalization over time than the more direct cognitive training procedures. Further research will be needed to determine the reliability of these effects.

Generalization

Studies conducted prior to 1980 demonstrated that a variety of techniques could be used to facilitate the performance of elderly adults on a variety of cognitive tasks. One question that arose as a result of those early studies was whether the improvement in performance obtained on the type of task on which training was given would generalize to other types of cognitive tasks. As a result, many of the studies conducted after 1980 included tests of generalization to other types of tasks. Another question that arose was whether the improvement in performance that resulted from the various training programs would be maintained across time. A number of the studies conducted in the 1980s addressed this issue as well.

Most of the training studies that have investigated generalization across tasks indicate that training on one particular type of cognitive task does not generalize to other types of tasks. For example, Schaie and Willis (1986) found no generalization from extended training on induction to spatial orientation and vice versa. They further found that training on induction and spatial orientation did not generalize to perceptual speed or numeric and verbal abilities. Likewise, Baltes, Dittmann-Kohli, and Kliegl (1986) found that extended training on figural relations and induction did not generalize to Raven's Progressive Matrices and tests of perceptual speed and vocabulary. Baltes, Sowarka, and Kliegl (1989) reported that extended training and practice on figural relations tests did not generalize to other types of abilities, including Raven's Progressive Matrices, induction, and vocabulary. Willis, Cornelius, Blow, and Baltes (1983) trained elderly adults on the Underwood Number Counting Test, the Stroop Color Interference Test, a letter-matching test, a continuous paired-associate recall task, a semantic recall task, a concentration task, and a word-recognition task. They found significant training effects on some of the abilities on which training was given, but they found no evidence of generalization to memory span, perceptual speed, or measures of fluid and crystallized intellectual abilities.

Though no generalization has been found in the majority of the studies, there is one exception. Blackburn, Papalia-Finlay, Foye, and Serlin (1988) reported that they obtained some generalization. They investigated the effect of an extended training program on elderly adults' performance on figural relations tests. They looked at generalization on the following tests: a culture fair test, Raven's Progressive Matrices, formal operations, induction, identical pictures and vocabulary. They found some evidence of generalization to the culture fair and formal operations tasks. However, because they performed separate statistical analyses comparing each of the two training groups to the control group for eight different tasks rather than doing one overall analysis, it is difficult to know how to interpret their results.

It seems that the safest conclusion at this point is that extended training on a particular type of cognitive task does not generalize to performance on other types of tasks. But what about generalization over time?

In one study, Blieszner, Willis, and Baltes (1981) trained elderly adults on an inductive reasoning task and then administered post-tests at one week after training, one month after training, and six months after training. They found significant training effects at one week and at one month, but not at six months. A similar finding was reported by Baltes, Dittmann-Kohli, and Kliegl (1986). They found that the gains exhibited as a result of their induction and figural relations training lasted for their first two post-tests, which occurred one week and one month after training, but that by the six-month post-test the effect was no longer evident.

On the other hand, Willis, Blieszner, and Baltes (1981) found that the training effects they obtained on a figural relations task lasted up to six months after training was completed. Willis, Cornelius, Blow, and Baltes (1983) also found significant training effects lasting as long as six months. They trained elderly adults on the Underwood Number Counting Test, the Stroop Color Interference Test, a letter matching test, a continuous paired-associate recall task, a semantic recall task, a concentration task, and a word recognition task, and they found significant training effects on some of the abilities on which training was given. Further, they found that most of the training effects lasted up to at least six months after the training, when their last post-test was administered.

Blackburn, Papalia-Finlay, Foye, and Serlin (1988) also looked at generalization over time. They investigated the effect of extended training on elderly adults' performance on figural relations tests. Though these authors did not report the statistical analyses that would be required to determine whether there were significant training effects at their post-test, which occurred one month after training, the authors reported that their training effects lasted at least one month.

In summary, it appears as if many of the more extended cognitive training programs result in improved performance that lasts up to one month and, in some cases, even up to six months. However, it does appear that the gains obtained with cognitive training tend to decline over the first six months after training. Although little generalization occurs to tasks other than the one on which training was given, training effects do tend to be maintained over at least short periods of time.

Individual Differences

Finally, some of the training research conducted in the 1980s included assessments of individual differences in individuals' response to cognitive training. Schaie and Willis (1986) reported that in subjects between 64 and 95, improvement in response to training on inductive reasoning and spatial organization did not vary as a function of age, education, or income. However, training effects were greater for individuals who had declined over the previous fourteen years in the particular ability on which they were given training than for those who were stable over the previous fourteen years. Training effects were also greater for women than for men. Willis and Nesselroade (1990) also found that training effects on figural relations were unrelated to age in adults 63 years of age and older and unrelated to education in older adults who were in good health.

No relationship between age and response to cognitive training was found in studies in which younger adults were included along with elderly adults. Anderson et al. (1986) included young and elderly adults in their study of the effect of practice on the Raven Progressive Matrices. They found no relationship between age and training gains. Further, Denney and Heidrich (1989) found no significant difference in the response of young, middle-aged, or elderly adults to cognitive training on Raven's Progressive Matrices.

It seems clear that there may be some individual differences in response to cognitive training; there may be sex differences, and differences as a result of one's previous history with a particular type of ability. However, it appears that training gains may not be predicted by age, education, or income. Further research will be needed to determine the reliability of these findings and to extend our understanding of the relationship between responsiveness to training and other individual difference variables.

Summary and Conclusions

Recent research on the effect of training on cognitive abilities in the elderly tended to use comprehensive training programs based on the effective treatment techniques that were demonstrated to be effective in the research conducted prior to 1980. Further, they tended to involve more extensive training procedures. This more recent research, not surprisingly, indicated that all of the individual training techniques that proved effective in facilitating the performance of the elderly were also successful when combined and presented in more time-intensive training programs. However, these studies also provided new information. They indicated that even with as many as five- to ten-hour training sessions, training on one task is unlikely to generalize to different types of tasks. They indicated that training produced in the more-extended training programs tends to last at least a month and in some cases up to six months. It may last even longer, but the research has only included tests over months rather than over years to test the durability of training effects. Two questions remain. Future research might be focused on the length of the training and the resultant strength and durability of the training effects. Do the more extended training programs produce stronger training effects? Do they produce more durable training effects?

The post–1980 research also demonstrated that on the types of tasks on which there are large age-related declines, elderly adults' performance improves as a result of practice alone. In fact, there is some indication that practice alone might produce improvement that is more durable over time and more likely to generalize to other tasks than the more direct training procedures that have typically been used.

Finally, the research conducted in the 1980s indicated there do not appear to be significant relationships between age (among elderly adults), education, and income and the degree to which individuals benefit from training. There is, on the other hand, indication that there may be gender differences in response to training, with older women showing more gains than older men. Further, individuals who have exhibited decline in a particular ability tend to benefit more from training than individuals who have been stable on the particular ability.

Thus, the research conducted in the last decade has been informative and has resulted in an increased understanding of the effects of cognitive training and practice in elderly adults. An important question is what the theoretical and practical significance of these new findings is. Both will be discussed in the following section.

THEORETICAL IMPLICATIONS

What do these research findings indicate in terms of the various models of lifespan cognitive development? All three of the models of lifespan cognitive development discussed in the beginning of this chapter provide descriptions and explanations of both the types of abilities that tend to be maintained during most of the adult years and the abilities that tend to exhibit more decline during the adult years. There are some commonalities and some differences in the explanations that are provided for the differential developmental courses taken by these two types of abilities. In all three models, continuing experience is the explanation given for the stability or, in some cases, even increases observed in some abilities. Horn (1970) suggests that these abilities are maintained or increase because of the individual's continued exposure to the "intelligence of the culture." Denney (1982) suggests that these abilities tend to be maintained or even increase because they are abilities that are frequently exercised throughout the adult years. Baltes and his colleagues (Baltes, Dittmann-Kohli & Dixon, 1984) suggest that these abilities may continue to increase because of the individual's continued experience and resultant increase in knowledge systems. All three theorists suggest that it is the continued practice of, and experience with, these abilities that is responsible for their relative maintenance during the adult years.

While all three theorists are in agreement on the reason for the stability of the abilities that are well maintained, the three theorists differ in their explanation for the observed decline in other abilities. Horn suggests that those abilities that decline do so because they are highly dependent on, or highly associated with, the neurophysiological functioning of the individual, which declines with age. Likewise, Baltes and his colleagues suggest that the abilities that exhibit the most and earliest decline do so because they are more affected by the biological declines that occur with age. They suggest that age-related declines in performance "will be manifested primarily in functioning at 'maximum' and difficult levels of performance" and that "most fluid intelligence tasks are more difficult than crystallized tasks. Similarly, memory and information-processing tasks that often show negative age differences are those that could be characterized as more difficult." (p. 44). They suggest that age-related biological declines set limits on maximal levels of performance and thereby set limits on performance on difficult tasks.

Horn's and Baltes's positions are very similar. Both suggest that certain abilities are highly dependent on the biological or neurophysiological functioning of the individual and that when the inevitable age-related biological declines occur during the adult years, these abilities are necessarily affected. Denney's position is quite different from that of both Horn and Baltes. She suggests that the abilities that display the greatest decline do so simply because they are not exercised much during the adult years. She does not believe that the abilities that demonstrate the most age-related decline are more highly associated with neurophysiological functioning, as Horn has suggested. Nor does she believe that the tasks which exhibit the most decline do so because they are more difficult, as Baltes has proposed.

What does the training research indicate with respect to the cause of the decline in those abilities that diminish most rapidly during the adult years? First, the training research indicates that it is easy to obtain marked improvement in these abilities. Significant improvement can usually be obtained in a very short time period, often in only one training session. This fact suggests that the decline in these abilities is not a result of their being highly dependent on neurophysiological functioning, which declines with age, as both Horn and Baltes have suggested. Although it is true that neurophysiological decline does occur with age during the adult years, there is no reason to believe that the abilities that typically show the earliest and most drastic declines with age would be more affected by that decline than the abilities that are relatively well maintained throughout most of the adult years. Both types of abilities would, after all, be totally dependent on neurophysiological functioning.

Further, there is no reason to believe that the abilities that decline the most with age do so because they are measured by tasks that are more difficult than those typically used to measure the abilities that do not show much age-related deterioration. Many of the abilities that have been discussed in this chapter are measured by subtests of intelligence tasks, and typically those subtests are at least roughly equated in difficulty. More importantly, however, the ease with which significant improvements can be obtained in performance on these tasks provides further evidence that they are not particularly difficult. If they were very difficult, one would expect that more intensive training would be needed to facilitate performance.

It seems likely that if performance on a particular task decreased primarily as a result of neurophysiological decline, it would take longer to remediate. Further, it seems likely that if performance on a particular task declined because the task was extremely difficult, it would take much longer and more intensive training to ameliorate. The fact that significant training effects can be obtained in only a matter of minutes suggests that the primary cause of the decline is not based in irreversible neurophysiological decline or the extreme difficulty of the tasks.

Denney's model, on the other hand, predicts that the abilities that decline most drastically during the adult years will also be the ones that are the most responsive to training effects. She suggests that the abilities that show the most age decline do so because they are not exercised during the adult years. She further suggests that those are the abilities that would be the most responsive to training because most individuals are not close to their maximum potential in those particular abilities. As a result, there is a lot of room for improvement (see Denney, 1982a, for a more complete discussion). Clearly the training research confirms this prediction; the abilities that are most likely to decline with age are extremely responsive to a variety of training techniques.

Denney's model predicts that the abilities that decline the most with age would be very responsive to training, and it also predicts that the abilities that tend to be maintained throughout most of the adult years will be much less responsive to training efforts. This prediction is made because of the assumption that most individuals' levels of performance on measures of such highly exercised abilities are much closer to their maximum potential and there is, therefore, less room for improvement. As Willis (1987) has pointed out, "Virtually all training research has focussed on cognitive domains that show the largest age differences or greatest age-related decline. . . . Little is known regarding the potential for further enhancement of cognitive domains that exhibit little normative decline" (p. 160). The lack of research on the effects of training on abilities that tend to be fairly stable may be, at least in part, a consequence of researchers' knowing at an intuitive level that such training would be much less effective. For example, one of the abilities that tends to be relatively well preserved across age is vocabulary. Though it is almost certainly true that an effective training program would result in improved vocabulary scores, it is also obvious that the degree of training required to yield significant training effects would be massive compared to what is required to produce significant training effects in the abilities that show much earlier decline. Thus, it is the abilities that exhibit the most decline that are the most responsive to training effects, just as the Denney model predicts. Neither Horn's nor Baltes's model can account for these differential training effects.

The fact that practice alone is also effective in increasing the level of elderly adults' performance provides further support for Denney's contention that performance on those abilities is low primarily because of a lack of exercise. If the abilities declined primarily as a result of declines in neurophysiological functioning, one would expect that if the declines could be reversed at all, it would require more than a relatively short period of practice. The fact that practice alone is so effective is consistent with the position that elderly individuals are not performing well on those types of tasks because they have not been using the abilities; when they begin to use them, they show substantial improvement without any direct instruction or training. If adults had been using those particular abilities and their performance had still declined, then practice alone would not be expected to have much effect on performance.

Thus, the fact that very short-term cognitive training is so effective at improving performance on the types of tasks on which age-related decline is typically obtained and the fact that practice-alone is also effective is consistent with Denney's model. Both of these findings are explicitly predicted by the model. Neither Horn's nor Baltes's model predicts that the abilities that show the most decline with age will be the most responsive to training or that practice alone will be an effective method of facilitating performance. These findings are not only not predicted by these researchers' models but are also inconsistent with their positions as described previously.

Not only does Denney's model account for the main findings of the training research, but it also accounts for the phenomenon known as "terminal drop," the decline in typically well-maintained abilities that occurs in the very latest adult years. Denney predicts that those abilities that are highly exercised will tend to be maintained during the adult years until one's maximum potential, which declines with age, falls below the level at which the individual has been functioning. At that point the individual's performance will be limited by the age-related decline in biological potential (see Denney, 1982a, for a more complete discussion). Horn states that crystallized abilities increase with age, and Baltes proposes that the pragmatics of intelligence increase with age. Neither model provides an explanation for the terminal drop phenomenon. If terminal drop occurs because the individual's performance is being limited by a biologically determined decline in maximum potential, then it is unlikely that training procedures would be very effective in improving performance very much. Future research will be needed to determine whether training is less effective for individuals who have already begun to experience terminal drop than for individuals who have not.

The fact that the manipulation of noncognitive factors has proven to be ineffective in increasing performance on cognitive tasks also is consistent with Denney's model. According to Denney's model, the abilities that exhibit the most decline during the adult years do so because they are not practiced much during the adult years. As a result, either direct training or instruction would be expected to facilitate performance. But, the manipulation of noncognitive factors such as motivation, self-confidence, social contact with the experimenter, and social praise would not be expected to have a very large effect on performance on such tasks.

In summary, Denney's model of lifespan cognitive development accounts for all of the major findings of the training research reviewed in this chapter. It predicts that training effects will be larger for the abilities that decline most with age than for those that tend to be maintained. It predicts that both direct cognitive training and practice alone will facilitate performance. It predicts that direct cognitive training or practice would be much more likely to facilitate performance than the manipulation of various noncognitive variables. In addition, it predicts that cognitive training and practice would be least effective on the abilities that tend to be relatively stable after the point at which an individual begins to exhibit terminal drop. Denney's model is the only one of the three models that predicts all of the above outcomes. Thus, at least for the research findings available to date, it appears that Denney's model is the most useful model.

PRACTICAL IMPLICATIONS

Given that elderly adults' performance on a variety of types of tasks can be significantly improved by training and/or practice on the particular task of interest, many investigators have suggested that such training may have important practical applications. This view was expressed recently by Lerner (1990), who discussed ways in which training programs might result in durable changes in cognitive abilities and how elderly adults could be motivated to participate in such programs:

Training, to have enduring effects, may require either a longitudinal series of "booster shots" (i.e., a sequence of repeated exposures to the training regimen) or application of a set of services or experiences supportive of continued enhanced functioning (Willis & Nesselroade, 1990). The issue of maintaining enhanced functioning becomes, then, a matter of learning how to motivate people to participate in training programs or services (which must be ecologically valid) and of determining the content and the timing of the longitudinal series of intervention sessions or supportive experiences needed to retain (or, ideally, to increase) gains in particular aspects of cognition. (p. 913)

Although the training research reviewed in this chapter has made very important theoretical contributions to the field, Denney's model of lifespan cognitive development predicts that the practical contributions of this research will be less substantial. According to Denney's model, training will have its greatest impact on those abilities that are infrequently used during the adult years. Given that the abilities for which training will be most effective are ones that tend not to be used during the adult years, there seems little reason for providing adults with training on such abilities. Such training would stimulate only a temporary increase in performance on the abilities for which training was provided. After a number of months the training gains would be lost, as a result of a lack of exercise. Though "booster shots" of training could periodically be given (see Willis & Nesselroade, 1990), according to Denney's model there would be no reason to provide such training. Why should efforts be made to increase elderly adults' performance on abilities that they do not use?

Denney's model suggests that training will be less effective in facilitating performance on abilities that adults frequently use in their daily lives. Because these abilities are highly exercised, adults' performance on these abilities are much closer to their maximum potential. As a result, there is less room for improvement as a function of training. Though training would certainly have an effect on these abilities, the amount of training required to produce small performance gains would, in all likelihood, be rather large. It would, for example, take massive amounts of training to significantly improve adults' vocabularies. Would the gains be worth the time, effort, and money required to secure these gains? How much benefit would it be to adults to have larger vocabularies? Though some small benefits might accrue to most adults if they had larger vocabularies, the small benefits would in all likelihood not be worth the cost of instituting and administering vocabulary training programs. Adults already know the vocabulary words they need to use in their daily lives. Knowing additional vocabulary words might be desirable, but certainly not enough to justify massive training programs.

The time in an individual's life when abilities that are frequently used and that are necessary for functioning in daily life begin to decline is the time when training would be of some practical use. However, this is the time, according to Denney's model, when training would be the least effective. When individuals begin to lose abilities that are frequently used, that means that the biologically based decline in his or her maximum potential has fallen below the level at which he or she has been performing. If the maximum potential level limits performance, then the effects of training and practice should be limited. It is when the individuals most need the practical benefits of training that training is the least likely to be effective.

In summary, according to Denney's model, the practical applications of training on cognitive abilities in adults are limited. Training will be most effective on abilities that are not frequently used during the adult years. If these abilities are not used, why should adults be given training on them? Training will be only somewhat effective on those abilities that are frequently used. However, the amounts of training needed to yield significant training effects on frequently used abilities would be massive and the beneficial effects would be minimal. Thus, training on such abilities would not be very cost effective. Finally, training will be least effective on those abilities that are frequently used but that have begun to exhibit terminal drop. When the need for training is the greatest, the actual effectiveness of training would be minimal. Altogether, these predictions suggest that cognitive training programs will have limited practical usefulness.

REFERENCES

Anderson, J. W., Hartley, A. A., Bye, R., Harber, K. D. & White, O. L. (1986). Cognitive training using self-discovery methods. *Educational Gerontology, 12*, 159–171.

Baltes, P. B., Dittmann-Kohli, F. & Dixon, R. A. (1984). New perspective on the development of intelligence in adulthood: Toward a dual-process conception and a model of selective optimization with compensation. In P. B. Baltes & O. O.

Brim, Jr. (Eds.). *Life-span development and behavior* (Vol. 6). New York: Academic Press.

Baltes, P. B., Dittmann-Kohli, F. & Kliegl, R. (1986). Reserve capacity of the elderly in aging-sensitive tests of fluid intelligence: Replication and extension. *Psychology and Aging*, *1*, 172–177.

Baltes, P. B., Kliegl, R. & Dittmann-Kohli, F. (1988). On the locus of training gains in research on the plasticity of fluid intelligence in old age. *Journal of Educational Psychology*, *80*, 392–400.

Baltes, P. B., Sowarka, D. & Kliegl, R. (1989). Cognitive training research on fluid intelligence in old age: What can older adults achieve by themselves? *Psychology and Aging*, *4*, 217–221.

Blackburn, J. A., Papalia-Finlay, D., Foye, B. F. & Serlin, R. C. (1988). Modifiability of figural relations performance among adults. *Journal of Gerontology*, *43*, 87–89.

Blieszner, R., Willis, S. L. & Baltes, P. B. (1981). Training research in aging on the fluid ability of inductive reasoning. *Journal of Applied Developmental Psychology*, *2*, 247–265.

Cattell, R. B. (1963). Theory of fluid and crystallized intelligence: A critical experiment. *Journal of Educational Psychology*, *54*, 1–22.

Crovitz, E. (1966). Reversing a learning deficit in the aged. *Journal of Gerontology*, *21*, 236–238.

Denney, N. W. (1974). Classification abilities in the elderly. *Journal of Gerontology*, *29*, 309–314.

Denney, N. W. (1979). Problem solving in later adulthood: Intervention research. In P. B. Baltes & O. G. Brim (Eds.). *Life-span development and behavior* (Vol. 2). New York: Academic Press.

Denney, N. W. (1980). The effect of the manipulation of peripheral, noncognitive variables on problem-solving performance among the elderly. *Human Development*, *23*, 268–277.

Denney, N. W. (1982a). Aging and cognitive changes. In B. B. Wolman & G. Stricker (Eds.). *Handbook of Developmental Psychology* (pp. 807–827). Englewood Cliffs, N.J.: Prentice Hall.

Denney, N. W. (1982b). Attempts to modify cognitive tempo in elderly adults. *International Journal of Aging and Human Development*, *14*, 239–254.

Denney, N. W. (1990). Adult age differences in traditional and practical problem solving. In E. A. Lovelace (Ed.). *Aging and Cognition: Mental Processes, Self Awareness and Interventions* (pp. 329–349). Amsterdam: Elsevier Science Publishers.

Denney, N. W. & Denney, D. R. (1974). Modeling effects on the questioning strategies of the elderly. *Developmental Psychology*, *10*, 458.

Denney, N. W. & Heidrich, S. M. (1990). Training effects on Raven's Progressive Matrices in young, middle-aged and elderly adults. *Psychology and Aging*, *5*, 144–145.

Hayslip, B. (1989). Alternative mechanisms for improvements in fluid ability performance among older adults. *Psychology and Aging*, *4*, 122–124.

Heglin, H. J. (1956). Problem solving set in different age groups. *Journal of Gerontology*, *11*, 310–317.

Hofland, B. F., Willis, S. L. & Baltes, P. B. (1981). Fluid intelligence performance in the elderly: Intraindividual variability and conditions of assessment. *Journal of Educational Psychology*, *73*, 573–586.

Horn, J. L. (1970). Organization of data on life-span development of human abilities. In L. R. Goulet & P. B. Baltes (Eds.). *Life-span developmental psychology: Research and theory*. New York: Academic Press.

Hornblum, J. N. & Overton, W. F. (1976). Area and volume conservation among the elderly: Assessment and training. *Developmental Psychology*, *12*, 68–74.

Hoyer, F. W., Hoyer, W. J., Treat, N. G. & Baltes, P. B. (1978–79). Training response speed in young and elderly women. *International Journal of Aging and Human Development*, *9*, 247–253.

Hoyer, W. J., Labouvie, G. & Baltes, P. (1973). Modification of response speed and intellectual performance in the elderly. *Human Development*, *16*, 233–242.

Kotler-Cope, S. & Camp, C. J. (1990). Memory interventions in aging populations. In E. A. Lovelace (Eds.). *Aging and cognition: Mental processes, self-awareness and interventions*. Amsterdam: Elsevier Science Publishers.

Labouvie-Vief, G. (1985). Intelligence and cognition. *Handbook of the Psychology of Aging*. New York: Van Nostrand Reinhold Company.

Labouvie-Vief, G. & Gonda, N. J. (1976). Cognitive strategy training and intellectual performance in the elderly. *Journal of Gerontology*, *31*, 327–332.

Lerner, R. M. (1990). Plasticity, person-context relations, and cognitive training in the aged years: A developmental contextual perspective. *Developmental Psychology*, *26*, 911–915.

Meichenbaum, D. (1972). Training the aged in verbal control of behavior. Paper presented at the International Congress on Gerontology, Kiev, Russia.

Mergler, N. & Hoyer, W. (1981). Effects of training on dimensional classification abilities: Adult age comparisons. *Educational Gerontology*, *6*, 135–145.

Panicucci, C. L. (1975). *The effect of training on inductive reasoning behavior in young and old adults*. Paper presented at the 28th annual meeting of the American Gerontological Society. Louisville, KY, October 1975.

Sanders, J. C., Sterns, H. L., Smith, M. & Sanders, R. E. (1975). Modification of concept identification performance in older adults. *Developmental Psychology*, *11*, 824–829.

Schaie, K. W. & Willis, S. L. (1986). Can decline in adult intellectual functioning be reversed? *Developmental Psychology*, *22*, 223–232.

Schutz, N. R. & Hoyer, W. J. (1976). Feedback effects on spatial egocentrism in old age. *Journal of Gerontology*, *31*, 72–75.

Willis, S. L. (1987). Cognitive training and everyday competence. *Annual review of gerontology and geriatrics*, *7*, 159–188.

Willis, S. L., Blieszner, R. & Baltes, P. B. (1981). Intellectual training research in aging: Modification of performance on the fluid ability of figural relations. *Journal of Educational Psychology*, *73*, 41–50.

Willis, S. L., Cornelius, S. W., Blow, F. C. & Baltes, P. B. (1983). Training research in aging: Attentional processes. *Journal of Educational Psychology*, *75*, 257–270.

Willis, S. L. & Nesselroade, C. S. (1990). Long-term effects of fluid ability training in old-old age. *Developmental Psychology*, *26*, 905–910.

Willis, S. L. & Schaie, K. W. (1986). Training the elderly on the ability factors of spatial orientation and inductive reasoning. *Psychology and Aging*, *1*, 239–247.

Yesavage, J. A. (1985). Nonpharmacological treatments for memory losses with normal aging. *American Journal of Psychiatry, 142*, 600–605.

Young, M. L. (1966). Problem-solving performance in two age groups. *Journal of Gerontology*, 1966, *21*, 505–509.

27

Age Declines in Memory Self-Efficacy: General or Limited to Particular Tasks and Measures?

Robin Lea West and Jane M. Berry

The potential for lifelong learning has been demonstrated clearly in research on problem solving, prose recall, and other measures of mental skill (Reese & Puckett, 1993; Sinnott, 1989). However, there are factors that may serve as barriers to lifelong learning for older adults (see Arenberg, chapter 23 in this volume). Among others, these factors include age changes in attentional or memory capacity (e.g., Salthouse, 1991), declines in memory self-confidence or change in memory beliefs (e.g., Berry, West & Dennehy, 1989), and reduced opportunities for education and training (e.g., Rebok & Offermann, 1983). This chapter focuses on self-report or subjective beliefs about memory.

A growing literature points to the relationship between subjective factors (e.g., memory complaints, self-efficacy, locus of control) and age-related memory performance differences (Cavanaugh & Green, 1991; Hertzog, Dixon & Hultsch, 1990; Lachman, Steinberg & Trotter, 1987). One factor that has received considerable attention is self-efficacy, which is defined as an individual's level of confidence and assessment of his or her ability to perform successfully on a particular task or domain of tasks. Self-efficacy has been an important factor in investigations of aging and metamemory (e.g., Hertzog, Hultsch & Dixon, 1989), and an independent measure of memory self-efficacy, the MSEQ, has been developed and validated (Berry et al., 1989). Take together, the evidence indicates that global measures of self-efficacy show age differences, with older adults having less self-efficacy and greater concern about their performance than younger adults (Berry et al., 1989; Hertzog et al., 1989).

The existing literature, however, has not sufficiently explored two compelling questions: (1) the scope or generality of age differences in efficacy and (2) the nature of the relationship between older adults' lower memory self-efficacy and their lower memory task performance (see Berry & West, 1993). This investigation focuses on the former question.

Numerous authors have argued that efficacy per se is an important issue for investigation by gerontologists (Cavanaugh & Green, 1991; Hertzog, 1992). There are both theoretical and applied reasons for studying the breadth and depth of age differences in memory self-efficacy. Reduced efficacy could occur only for highly difficult tasks or only for unfamiliar tasks, or it could extend to more familiar, everyday memory activities, and even to simple memory tasks. Investigation of the generality of age decline in memory self-efficacy is important because a negative self-evaluation that is not limited but extends to many types of memory activities is more likely to have consequences for the individual's behavior, affecting memory performance in many contexts and situations (Bandura, 1977, 1986).

From an applied perspective, it is also important to examine the generality of lowered efficacy. Many investigators have suggested that self-doubt can lead to self-fulfilling failure; that is, a low self-evaluation could result in self-limiting actions that further reduce competence (e.g., Bandura, 1986). As a result, older adults' beliefs about memory have themselves become the focus of intervention research (Rebok & Balcerak, 1989; Weaver & Lachman, 1989; West, Bramblett, Welch & Bellott, 1992). To develop effective interventions, applied psychologists must know whether negative attitudes about memory among older adults are limited (existing only for specific types of tasks) or widespread. Self-evaluation instruments that assess general beliefs or single tasks cannot show whether efficacy judgments apply to a wide range of tasks and measures. More refined measures are needed to study generality. Before examining some data, a theoretical framework for efficacy aging will be outlined.

Self-efficacy refers to an individual's sense of mastery of particular tasks in a given behavioral domain. Personal efficacy evaluations are derived from past performance accomplishments, vicarious experience, social expectations, and physiological arousal. Efficacy evaluations are expected to serve as mediators between competence and performance, affecting a person's on-task behavior (Bandura, 1986).

There has been considerable discussion of the way in which aging may be related to lower self-efficacy. Age changes in memory performance can result in increased memory errors (i.e., performance accomplishments occur less often). In terms of self-efficacy, this age-related memory change leads to a reevaluation of personal capabilities. At the same time, stereotypes about aging (i.e., social expectations) lead older adults to question their abilities and to be vigilant about memory errors. When memory errors by older adults are noticed (including errors by themselves and by similar others), the societal stereotypes are reinforced. Thus, memory deficits and social stereotypes combine to reduce older adults' sense of efficacy. Theoretically, this reduced efficacy can result in avoidance of learning opportunities and reduced memory effort, which in turn limit performance capabilities. This interactive model has been explained elsewhere (Bandura, 1981, 1986). In the domain of phobic behavior, similar models have been tested extensively (e.g., Bandura, Reese & Adams, 1982), but there are relatively few studies of aging and memory. Rebok and Offermann (1983) have discussed how changes in self-efficacy might discourage older adults from participating in educational programs or might limit their opportunities to learn. In addition, the presence of age differences in general self-efficacy confirms aspects of this theoretical framework (Berry et al., 1989; Hertzog et al., 1989), as does evidence showing that lowered self-efficacy sometimes leads to reduced memory effort among older adults (see Berry & West, 1993).

Up to now, the research has focused on two types of memory self-report measures—prediction on single tasks and general measures based on factor scores from lengthy questionnaires. The single-task prediction studies have yielded some interesting data, showing, for example, that postdiction is more accurate than prediction (e.g., Devolder, Brigham & Pressley, 1990) and that older adults tend to overestimate their scores on specific tasks (e.g., Lachman & Jelalian, 1984). Single-task predictions, however, do not represent typical self-efficacy items (Berry & West, 1993), and they do not provide information concerning the generality of age declines in self-confidence across tasks or measures. The same is true for the more general approach that uses factor scores. The findings obtained with this approach have highlighted general age differences in memory self-evaluation (e.g., Cavanaugh & Poon, 1989; Hertzog et al., 1989; Zelinski, Gilewski & Anthony-Bergstone, 1990).

An alternative methodology, designed to examine the generality of age differences in memory self-efficacy, requires a task-specific questionnaire and multiple indicators of efficacy. Bandura, in fact, recommends this more refined analysis. He endorses the use of microanalysis of self-efficacy, rather than global, omnibus tests (Bandura, 1986). A task-specific, microanalytic approach requires that many different activities and multiple levels of difficulty are described within the same task domain, with an assessment of confidence for each task at each difficulty level. Such an approach permits the examination of individual task variations in efficacy.

THE MEMORY SELF-EFFICACY QUESTIONNAIRE

The Memory Self-Efficacy Questionnaire (MSEQ) permits microanalysis of self-efficacy, by reliably assessing a wide range of memory tasks at varying levels of difficulty (Berry et al., 1989). Many converging dependent measures can be gleaned from the MSEQ, but they have not been systematically studied with respect to the generality of age differences in efficacy and potential age-by-task interactions. In this paper, archival data compiled by the first author are used to examine these issues.

The breadth of age differences in self-efficacy can be revealed by examining self-efficacy across different types of memory tasks. The MSEQ is a paper-and-pencil questionnaire used to obtain a memory self-evaluation for ten memory tasks (Berry et al., 1989, Study 1). The MSEQ describes four tasks from the domain of everyday memory (recall of a grocery list, object locations, phone numbers, and directions), four tasks from the domain of laboratory memory (word list, picture, digit, and route recall), and two filler tasks. A sample page from the MSEQ is given in Table 1. If age differences in memory self-efficacy are a general, widespread phenomenon, they should be present across all tasks in these two domains and thus show breadth or generality of effects.

At the same time, multiple dependent measures of efficacy can be used to examine the depth of age differences in memory self-efficacy. If age differences in efficacy are pervasive, they should be present on a number of different dependent measures derived from the MSEQ. The traditional measures proposed and used by Bandura are self-efficacy strength and level (Bandura et al., 1982). Subjects respond "yes" or "no" to indicate if they can perform the described memory task. The number of "yes" responses reflects self-efficacy level (SEL), which varies from 0 to 5 on each task. For each "yes" response, subjects are asked to circle a confidence value (10%–100%). These are averaged, with "no" responses counted as 0, to get a self-efficacy strength score (SEST). Thus, "no" responses act to lower SEST. SEST and SEL are expected to decrease with age.

Two other aspects of self-efficacy should be examined, to focus more on those tasks that adults feel capable of doing. The five items describing each task are presented in a descending hierarchy, with more difficult levels occurring first. CONF1 is the confidence value (10% to 100%) circled for the item representing the most difficult level to which the person responded "yes." CONF1 is expected to be higher when a person lacks secure beliefs in their abilities. That is, the uncertain person may show a response bias and not respond "yes" until confidence is high. This measure should be higher for older adults than younger adults, because older adults' abilities are changing. Changing abilities lead, in turn, to uncertainty and unstable self-evaluations (Bandura, 1981).

The second new measure is the person's average confidence for "yes" responses only, ranging from 10% to 100% (CONF-YES). CONF-YES can be compared to SEST. SEST is calculated for all responses at all levels (five levels for each task), and a "no" response is given a value of 0; CONF-YES is based only on "yes" responses, and the number of "yes" responses may vary from task to task. Items with responses of "no" are excluded. It should be noted that individuals who never respond "yes" on a given scale are considered as missing scores for that scale for CONF1 and CONF-YES.[1]

TESTS OF GENERALITY ACROSS TASKS AND MEASURES

Sample 1

To examine the issue of generality of self-efficacy ratings, we selected a sample of forty-eight older (60 to 80 years) and twenty younger (18 to 25 years) adults

Table 1
Sample Task Scale from MSEQ

PHONE Task

---

(5) -If I looked up 3 phone numbers in the phone book at the same time, I could remember 3 complete phone numbers.

NO YES 10%   20   30   40   50   60   70   80   90   100%

(4) -If I looked up 3 phone numbers in the phone book at the same time, I could remember 2 complete numbers.

NO YES 10%   20   30   40   50   60   70   80   90   100%

(3) -If I looked up 3 phone numbers in the phone book at the same time, I could remember 1 complete number plus the first 3 digits in one other phone number.

NO YES 10%   20   30   40   50   60   70   80   90   100%

(2) -If I looked up 3 phone numbers in the phone book at the same time, I could remember 1 complete number.

NO YES 10%   20   30   40   50   60   70   80   90   100%

(1) -If I looked up 3 phone numbers in the phone book at the same time, I could remember the first 3 digits of one phone number.

NO YES 10%   20   30   40   50   60   70   80   90   100%

Note: The numbers in parentheses indicate the performance level represented by each item, with (1) as the lowest performance level. These numbers were not present on the actual questionnaire.

from a self-efficacy data archive. Participants ranged in education level from 8 to 20 years, with higher education levels for younger (M = 15.2) than older (M = 12.2) adults, $F(1,66)$ = 17.3, $p < .0001$, ω^2 = .21. As analyses using education as a covariate did not change the pattern of significant effects, the basic analyses without the covariate are reported below.

A preliminary multivariate analysis of variance (MANOVA) was conducted, with scores calculated across all four laboratory scales (e.g., total number of "yes" responses across the four laboratory scales yields a laboratory SEL score) and across all four everyday scales (e.g., confidence for all "yes" responses is averaged across the four everyday scales to yield an everyday CONF-YES score). One older adult responded "no" to all items on one scale and therefore was a missing case for CONF1 and CONF-YES (multivariate N = 67). Age (young-old) was a between-subjects factor and domain (laboratory, everyday) was a within-subjects factor in this MANOVA with the four dependent measures described above: SEL, SEST, CONF1, and CONF-YES. Significant effects were obtained for age (multivariate $F(4,62)$ = 5.9, $p < .0001$) and domain (multivariate $F(4,62)$ = 12.1, $p < .0001$), and there was no significant interaction, indicating that the pattern of age-group differences (younger adult scores higher than older adult scores) generalized across the two domains. Self-efficacy for the four everyday tasks was higher than that for the four laboratory tasks. Tasks from the two domains were then examined separately to evaluate generality across individual tasks.

Laboratory Domain. A mixed design MANOVA was used to investigate the potential interaction of age and task differences. The four dependent measures were SEL, SEST, CONF1, and CONF-YES, with age as a between-subjects factor and task as a within-subjects factor (word, picture, digit, and route scales). Pillai's Trace statistic was used for all multivariate F calculations. The MANOVA showed significant age effects (multivariate $F(4,62)$ = 4.9, $p < .005$), no significant interaction of age and task, and significant multivariate differences across tasks ($F(12,582)$ = 6.2, $p < .0001$).

Follow-up univariate tests were conducted to examine the effects of age and task on the individual dependent measures. These were mixed analyses of variance conducted for each dependent measure with age (between: old, young) and task (within: word, picture, digit, route) as independent variables. As expected, significant age differences in efficacy were obtained for SEL [$F(1,66)$ = 12.2, $p < .001$, ω^2 = .10] and SEST [$F(1,66)$ = 10.0, $p < .005$, ω^2 = .08]. Significant task differences (all dfs = 3,198) occurred for SEL (F = 15.5, $p < .0001$, ω^2 = .05), SEST (F = 23.7, $p < .0001$, ω^2 = .07), and CONF-YES (F = 6.6, $p < .0001$, ω^2 = .03). In general, the digit efficacy scores were lower than scores for the other laboratory tasks in post hoc comparisons (see Table 2). The results showed no significant interactions of age and task for SEST, CONF1, or CONF-YES; but the interaction was significant for SEL ($F(3,198)$ = 3.82, $p < .05$). The means are presented in Table 2. Post hoc comparisons using Tukey's tests ($p < .05$) revealed that this interaction was due

Table 2
MSEQ Means for Laboratory and Everyday Tasks

Laboratory Tasks	Young	Old	Everyday Tasks	Young	Old
		SEL (Range	= 0 to 5)		
WORD[a]	4.2	3.2	GROCERY[cb]	4.6	3.5
PICTURE[a]	4.2	3.3	LOCATION[c]	4.6	4.0
DIGIT[b]	3.6	2.2	PHONE[ba]	4.2	3.1
ROUTE[a]	4.0	3.5	MAP[a]	3.8	2.9
		SEST (Range	= 0 to 100)		
WORD[a]	68.4	49.2	GROCERY[b]	73.2	54.8
PICTURE[a]	64.8	52.2	LOCATION[c]	76.6	66.2
DIGIT[b]	51.5	32.0	PHONE[ab]	67.8	50.2
ROUTE[a]	60.6	50.4	MAP[a]	59.1	43.6
		CONF1 (Range	= 10 to 100)		
WORD	56.0	58.5	GROCERY	55.5	60.0
PICTURE	51.0	61.5	LOCATION	58.5	66.0
DIGIT	46.5	57.9	PHONE	59.0	65.2
ROUTE	51.5	52.1	MAP	54.0	56.2
		CONF-YES (Range	= 10 to 100)		
WORD[a]	79.9	76.4	GROCERY[ab]	79.1	78.2
PICTURE[a]	78.3	78.9	LOCATION[b]	81.9	81.4
DIGIT[b]	70.5	72.3	PHONE[b]	81.5	80.4
ROUTE[b]	74.8	70.3	MAP[a]	75.5	73.7

Note: Means that represent significant task differences for a particular variable have different superscript letters. A complete table, with standard deviations, is available upon request.

to the fact that the younger adults showed no task differences in SEL. Task differences were significant, however, for the older adults, who had lower SEL scores for digit than the other tasks.

To summarize the results for the laboratory domain, there were significant task differences on two measures for the younger adults and on three measures for the older adults. Age differences were present for the traditional measures that reflected the total pattern of "yes" and "no" responses on the MSEQ (age differences in SEL and SEST scores were significant on all tasks), but not for the other confidence measures based only on "yes" responses (CONF-YES and CONF1).

Everyday Domain. A mixed design MANOVA examined the four dependent measures (SEL, SEST, CONF1, and CONF-YES) as a function of task (grocery, location, phone, and map—within-subjects) and age (young or old—between-subjects). Significant age differences were evident on these everyday measures [multivariate $F(4,63) = 4.9, p < .005$]. Multivariate task differences [$F(12,591) = 4.1, p < .0001$] were also significant, but not the interaction of age and task.

Scores for the everyday tasks were then examined with univariate mixed analyses of variance, in separate analyses for each dependent measure (SEL, SEST, CONF1, CONF-YES) using age (between) and task (within) factors. The pattern of effects was similar to that obtained in the laboratory domain.

Task differences (all $df = 3,198$) were evident for SEL ($F = 12.0, p < .0001, \omega^2 = .06$), SEST ($F = 13.7, p < .0001, \omega^2 = .07$), and CONF-YES ($F = 5.0, p < .005, \omega^2 = .02$), but not CONF1. In general, the map task showed the lowest self-efficacy and location the highest (see task differences indicated in Table 2). No age by task interactions were significant, indicating that age effects were generally consistent across the four everyday tasks.

With respect to age differences, the older adults had lower efficacy on both measures that reflected the total pattern of "yes" and "no" responses: for SEL, $F(1,66) = 16.0, p < .0001, \omega^2 = .10$; for SEST, $F(1,66) = 10.4, p < .005, \omega^2 = .07$. The other measures, CONF1 and CONF-YES, showed no age differences in efficacy.

These results show that self-efficacy varies considerably among individual tasks within the domains of everyday and laboratory memory. Task differences were evident, but patterns of age differences did not change across tasks. For most laboratory and everyday tasks, older adults showed lower self-efficacy whenever they were asked a simple "yes-no" question about their ability to perform a task. At the same time, these older adults were not less confident than younger people in their ability to perform those tasks to which they responded "yes." Whereas the traditional measures showed consistent age effects, the two new measures of confidence did not. In both domains, this group of older adults did not show higher confidence than younger adults on their first "yes" response (CONF1), nor did they show overall lower levels of confidence on the tasks that they felt that they could perform (CONF-YES).

Although age differences in CONF1 scores were expected, this measure did not vary significantly as a function of age. The means in Table 2 show that the trend was in the predicted direction, with older adults showing higher levels of confidence for their first "yes" on picture, digit, location, grocery, and phone tasks than the young. However, the overall difference was not significant.

The results from Sample 1 demonstrated an interesting qualification for age differences in efficacy. The four dependent measures did not converge to show consistently lower efficacy. Although older adults feel that they cannot perform at a level as high as that endorsed by younger people and are less confident overall, their confidence is not substantially lower than that of the young for the tasks that they feel they *can* perform (those marked "yes"). These results validate the importance of examining multiple measures and multiple tasks to clarify the relationship between aging and efficacy.

These results provide a useful illustration, but replication is needed. It is possible that the findings were due to the particular set of task descriptions that were used on the MSEQ. For example, five of the eight tasks represented relatively simple memory tests, with ten to twelve items to recall. It is possible that more difficult tasks would yield age by task interactions. A second analysis was therefore conducted with a new sample, and new task descriptions, to further examine the generality of efficacy aging across tasks and measures.

Sample 2

The second archive sample was limited to individuals who had finished high school and not yet college, to make the older (N = 68, mean age = 67.3, mean education = 13.2 years) and younger (N = 68, mean age = 18.7, mean education = 12.6) adult subject groups more comparable. Unlike Sample 1, overall educational differences in this sample favored the older group [$F(1,135)$ = 11.2, $p < .001$, ω^2 = .08]. Analyses using education as a covariate resulted in a similar pattern of effects. Therefore, the results reported here are based on the analyses without the covariate.

A larger number of subjects was included in this sample, as compared to Sample 1, to increase the power of the statistical tests. Also, the memory task descriptions were modified to ensure that the observed domain and aging effects were not limited to the particular task descriptions used on the MSEQ. The A-MSEQ was administered. In comparison to the MSEQ used in the first study, the task descriptions in the A-MSEQ generally describe more difficult tasks. For instance, the grocery scale in the A-MSEQ described an eighteen-item grocery list (task descriptions are given in Berry et al., 1989, Study 3), whereas the MSEQ grocery scale described a twelve-item list. We expected higher self-efficacy scores for the younger participants on the two traditional self-efficacy measures (SEL and SEST) and on the new measure of confidence, CONF-YES. As explained previously, confidence for the first "yes" response, CONF1, was expected to be higher for the old than for the young.

As before, preliminary analyses were used to see if domain differences interacted with age. A multivariate analysis was conducted using the four dependent measures (SEL, SEST, CONF1, CONF-YES). Each dependent measure used a summary value calculated across the four scales within the everyday domain or the laboratory domain. The multivariate analysis showed main effects for age [multivariate $F(4,117) = 10.2, p < .0001$] and domain [multivariate $F(4,117) = 28.8, p < .0001$] and no interaction. Age effects generalized across both domains.

Laboratory Domain. Task analyses were then conducted, examining tasks from the two domains separately. Multivariate analyses were conducted first, followed by univariate analyses. The MANOVA used four dependent measures— SEL, SEST, CONF1, and CONF-YES—examined across age groups and four tasks within the laboratory domain (word, digit, cubicles, and wordpair). Ten older adults and one younger adult were missing values for at least one task scale for CONF1 or CONF-YES because they responded "no" to all five items on that scale. This reduced the multivariate sample to 125 cases. There were significant age group differences [multivariate $F(4,120) = 8.2, p < .0001$] and task differences [multivariate $F(12,1104) = 10.8, p < .0001$], but no significant interaction.

Mixed analyses of variance with age as a between-subjects factor and task as a within-subjects factor were then carried out in univariate analyses, one analysis for each dependent measure. No age-by-task interactions were significant, but task differences were significant for each analysis: for SEL, $F(3,402) = 26.4$, $p < .0001$, $\omega^2 = .07$; for SEST, $F(3,402) = 42.3, p < .0001, \omega^2 = .11$; for CONF-YES, $F(3,369) = 23.6, p < .0001, \omega^2 = .06$; and for CONF1, $F(3,369) = 3.5, p < .02, \omega^2 = .01$. Post hoc analyses of these task effects showed that wordpair self-efficacy was generally higher than digit and cubicles self-efficacy (see significant task differences noted in Table 3).

The self-efficacy measures for the four laboratory tasks also showed significant age group differences: for SEL, $F(1,134) = 8.2, p < .005, \omega^2 = .03$; for CONF-YES, $F(1,123) = 7.2, p < .01, \omega^2 = .03$; and for CONF1, $F(1,123) = 30.8, p < .0001, \omega^2 = .07$, but not for SEST, $p < .10$. As predicted, the older adults had higher CONF1 and lower SEL scores than the younger adults. Contrary to expectation, CONF-YES values were actually higher for the older adults than for the younger adults. That is, considering only those tasks to which individuals responded "yes," the old showed higher levels of confidence than the young.

Everyday Domain. Multivariate analyses showed significant age group differences across the four dependent measures for the everyday tasks [multivariate $F(4,125) = 11.9, p < .0001$], significant task differences [multivariate $F(12,1149) = 7.1, p < .0001$], and no significant interaction.

The four tasks in the everyday domain—grocery, location, route, and phone— were also examined with mixed univariate analyses of variance using four tasks (within) and two age groups (between). Separate analyses were conducted for each dependent measure. Task differences were present on SEL [$F(3,402) = $

Table 3
A-MSEQ Means for Laboratory and Everyday Tasks

Laboratory Tasks	Young	Old	Everyday Tasks	Young	Old
SEL (Range = 0 to 5)					
WORD[b]	3.8	3.3	GROCERY[c]	4.0	3.4
DIGIT[a]	3.2	2.9	PHONE[b]	3.6	3.1
CUBICLES[ab]	3.5	3.0	LOCATION[a]	4.4	3.8
WORDPAIR[c]	4.3	3.7	COUPLES[a]	4.4	3.6
SEST (Range = 0 to 100)					
WORD[b]	54.2	51.3	GROCERY[b]	57.3	51.9
DIGIT[a]	42.3	43.4	PHONE[b]	55.0	48.6
CUBICLES[a]	44.1	40.0	LOCATION[a]	62.9	58.8
WORDPAIR[c]	63.5	56.7	COUPLES[a]	66.7	57.4
CONF1 (Range = 10 to 100)					
WORD[ab]	40.0	54.9	GROCERY[a]	43.1	56.7
DIGIT[ab]	38.2	55.5	PHONE[b]	53.5	63.1
CUBICLES[a]	35.4	51.8	LOCATION[a]	41.5	57.4
WORDPAIR[b]	43.4	56.4	COUPLES[ab]	45.4	60.8
CONF-YES (Range 10 to 100)					
WORD[b]	72.2	76.6	GROCERY	72.8	78.1
DIGIT[a]	62.2	72.7	PHONE	76.0	77.8
CUBICLES[a]	62.8	68.1	LOCATION	71.3	76.1
WORDPAIR[b]	73.7	77.2	COUPLES	74.8	77.8

Note: Means that represent significant task differences have different superscript letters. A complete table, with standard deviations, is available upon request.

21.4, $p < .0001$, $\omega^2 = .06$] on SEST [$F(3,402) = 11.2$, $p < .0001$, $\omega^2 = .03$]; and on CONF1 [$F(3,384) = 6.6$, $p < .0001$, $\omega^2 = .02$]. Efficacy was generally lowest for the phone task and highest for recall of locations and couples' names (see Table 3).

On the everyday measures, age differences were present on SEL [$F(1,134) = 15.3$, $p < .0001$, $\omega^2 = .05$] and on SEST [$F(1,134) = 5.0$, $p < .03$, $\omega^2 = .02$] and approached significance on CONF-YES [$F(1,128) = 3.8$, $p = .053$], with younger adults having higher scores than older adults. Also, CONF1 values were significantly higher for the older adults, as expected [$F(1,128) = 21.5$, $p < .0001$, $\omega^2 = .06$]. These results for the everyday domain were in line with our predictions.

Summary. The results for Sample 2 are consistent with those done earlier, showing virtually no age-by-task interactions, even with more difficult tasks described and a larger N for the analysis. In spite of substantial variation in efficacy as a function of task differences, when age differences occur, they are generally present across all tasks.

Age group differences, with higher self-efficacy for the young, were present in both samples on the traditional measures of SEL and SEST (see Table 4 data summary). The one exception was laboratory SEST in Sample 2. (It is not clear why this result was different.) Age differences, however, were just the opposite on the new measures of confidence, reflecting only "yes" responses. In every case, CONF1 and CONF-YES for the older adults were as high as for the young, and sometimes more so (in Sample 2 only). This supports the view that older adults may not always demonstrate reduced efficacy uniformly across measures, and that researchers should examine multiple measures of efficacy.

In both samples, consistent and significant differences in efficacy responses occurred across tasks; but older and younger adults appeared to react to these task differences in the same manner, because age differences, when they occurred, were significant across all tasks. The results for SEL were similar in both samples. There were, however, some differences in the results from the two samples. Laboratory SEST did not show age differences in Sample 2 even though it had in Sample 1. The expected age variation in CONF1, with higher scores for older adults, occurred only in Sample 2. CONF-YES showed age differences only in Sample 2 and only on the laboratory measures. Finally, task differences in CONF1 and CONF-YES varied in the two samples.

It seems important, then, to explore these sample differences. First of all, the samples varied in educational level, which may have contributed to the outcome, although it is unlikely. Years of education is not highly correlated with memory self-efficacy (West & Bellott, 1990), and the analyses using education as a covariate led to essentially the same pattern of results.

The differences could be attributable to the changes in task difficulty. The twelve-item grocery list and ten-item location recall task described on the MSEQ given to Sample 1 were generally easier than those described on the A-MSEQ (both eighteen-item tasks). The means for most variables on the grocery and

Table 4
Summary of Significant Effects

Sample	Age		Task		Age x Task	
	LAB	EV	LAB	EV	LAB	EV
SAMPLE 1						
Multivariate	*	*	*	*	- -	- -
SEL	*a	*a	*	*	*	- -
SEST	*a	*a	*	*	- -	- -
CONF1	- -	- -	- -	- -	- -	- -
CONF-YES	- -	- -	*	*	- -	- -
SAMPLE 2						
Multivariate	*	*	*	*	- -	- -
SEL	*a	*a	*	*	- -	- -
SEST	- -	*a	*	*	- -	- -
CONF1	*b	*b	*	*	- -	- -
CONF-YES	*b	- -	*	- -	- -	- -

$*p < .05$
Note: The letter "a" reflects higher scores for the younger adults than for the older adults, whereas the letter "b" was used when the older adults scored higher.

location tasks were also somewhat higher for the MSEQ than for the comparable A-MSEQ measures (compare Tables 2 and 3). The changed task descriptions could account for the variations in outcome.

Another possibility is that the samples were different because of their recruitment. The younger adults were volunteers in Sample 1 and introductory psychology students in Sample 2. Some of the Sample 1 older adults had been recruited for memory training and some had been recruited for research, whereas all of the Sample 2 elderly were recruited for a research study. However, previous research suggests that this older adult recruitment difference should not result in significant response variation on memory self-report measures (Berry et al., 1989; Scogin, Storandt & Lott, 1985).

To investigate sample differences, an analysis was done using only the picture task scale. The MSEQ and A-MSEQ items for the picture task were identical, which was the only scale for which the task description was the same on both questionnaires. A MANOVA was conducted using the four dependent measures for the picture task with between-subjects factors of age group and sample (N = 204). Significant multivariate differences were present for age [multivariate $F(4,197)$ = 10.0, p < .0001] and for sample [multivariate $F(4,197)$ = 4.2, p < .005], but not for the interaction. Sample 2 showed higher self-efficacy than Sample 1 in subsequent univariate tests with SEL and SEST, but not the other two measures. At least on this one scale, sample differences did not interact with age. It is not clear what impact these sample differences may have had on the age differences for other scales used in these analyses, because no other scales were identical on the two questionnaires.

The findings can be summarized thus: (1) age differences did not interact with differences between self-efficacy in the laboratory and everyday domains; (2) age differences did not interact with individual task differences; (3) age differences were not present on all measures of self-confidence, but were present on most measures related to "yes-no" responses about ability to perform a specific memory activity; (4) sample differences did not interact with age effects; and (5) sample and task differences were clearly significant and warrant further study.

IMPLICATIONS FOR SELF-EFFICACY IN FUTURE RESEARCH

Using two samples from a data archive, this paper explored the issue of generality of age-related differences in self-efficacy. The findings demonstrated that age differences in self-efficacy generalize across different types of memory tasks, but they do not generalize across different indicators or measures of memory self-efficacy. Generalization across samples was strong for the two traditional measures of self-efficacy—self-efficacy level and strength.

Generalization across Measures

The findings reported here illustrate that age differences in self-efficacy are not pervasive phenomena, extending to all types of measures, but occur on some measures of efficacy and not others. SEL, SEST, CONF1, and CONF-YES did not show the same age patterns. Older adults believe themselves capable of performing fewer tasks than younger people; in most research, including this study and others, the standard variables of self-efficacy level and strength did show age declines. However, confidence is not always lower for older adults than for younger adults. If, in their opinion, a task can be accomplished (they respond "yes"), older adults' confidence can be as high as that of younger people. These results are consistent with the results of some metamemory studies showing that feeling-of-knowing and confidence ratings are often comparable across age groups (e.g., Perlmutter, 1978; Rabinowitz, Ackerman, Craik & Hinchley, 1982). These findings suggest that researchers should be careful about making conclusions about age differences in efficacy that are based only on single indicators of memory self-evaluation. There is considerable measurement variation in the aging pattern. The nature of the question that is asked and the methodology for calculating efficacy may be just as important as the age of the subjects in one's sample. Sophisticated studies of the impact of the item and design features of memory self-evaluation questionnaires are much needed.

The measure differences were particularly apparent for the more-educated older adults in Sample 2, whose confidence was equal to or even higher (CONF-YES on laboratory tasks) than that of the young even though they responded "yes" significantly less often. It could be argued that older adults who are not familiar with laboratory tasks may be overconfident because of lack of experience. If that were the case, we would expect overconfidence to be more likely for the less educated older participants in Sample 1. That was not the case. Alternatively, perhaps the more-educated Sample 2 group had a strong sense of their limitations (lower SEL than the young) but also knew that some skills remained and therefore showed strong confidence in their ability to perform tasks at less-difficult levels. We may speculate then, that this group may be willing to participate in educational programs and to undertake new learning challenges that are self-paced or moderate to low in difficulty. At the very least, this population would not be expected to reject new learning opportunities "out of hand" because of low overall confidence.

Generalization across Tasks

When age differences in efficacy do occur, they are not affected greatly by task variation. The pattern of age effects was comparable across a wide range of tasks, including tasks from everyday and laboratory domains (MSEQ and A-MSEQ) and encompassing tasks of very different types—list recall, spatial memory, digit span, and so on. This suggests that age-related reductions in efficacy probably extend to a wide range of cognitive activities and learning situations.

Two important conclusions follow from this task generality. One is that age-related changes in memory self-efficacy are a general phenomenon. In particular, reduced efficacy level does not apply only to laboratory tests but extends to everyday types of memory activities. Efficacy differences across age would be expected, therefore, to extend to many cognitive activities and could affect adults' perceptions of their opportunities and potential for new learning in structured classroom settings as well as in more unstructured everyday learning situations (e.g., going to hear guest speakers at one's church). Older adults, especially those with lower self-efficacy, would be expected to choose memory-related activities less often and would be expected to show less persistence and effort in memory activities. Such behavioral concomitants of lower memory self-efficacy would be likely to lead to further deterioration of memory skills and a future reduction in participation in learning experiences. This potential downward spiral in memory skill and memory involvement may be prevented with intervention programs (discussed below).

A second conclusion relates to research design issues. These results show that, when examining variations in memory self-efficacy as a function of age, it is not problematic to use a subset of possible memory tasks to study age effects (as long as multiple dependent measures are included). If a researcher is interested in particular task differences, assessment of efficacy for these memory tasks would, of course, be necessary. But any age declines in efficacy observed with a selected group of tasks are likely to apply in a comparable way across a wide range of tasks, as demonstrated here.

Further examination of the relationship between performance and efficacy, and between performance improvement and efficacy change, is needed to understand the practical importance of variations in efficacy that occur as a function of age, task, measure, and sample. It is not clear, for instance, if declines in self-efficacy occur during middle age or only later in life. Sample differences may affect outcome. Also, it is not clear if stereotypes about aging lead to reduced efficacy before changes in skills occur or if changes in skills precede the development of negative self-perceptions. Longitudinal work is needed to explore the latter issue.

Implications for Intervention Programs

Pragmatically, these findings with respect to generality have implications for intervention. If the results had shown lower efficacy for older adults on all measures, it would suggest the value of an intervention focusing solely on efficacy. However, the results did not show this pattern. Instead, older adults endorsed fewer task levels, and fewer difficult task levels, with "yes." This suggests that interventions need to address the development of skills and greater mastery of more difficult tasks.

Self-efficacy theory and related intervention research outline an approach that may be quite useful (Bandura, 1977, 1986). Emphasis is placed on successful performance as a way of boosting efficacy. Beginning with less-difficult levels of a task, individuals are taught how to perform the task, with modeling and/or strategy training. Once success is achieved at the less-difficult task level, the person is presented with a more-difficult task. When that is mastered, higher levels of difficulty are presented (Bandura et al., 1982). This mastery-oriented approach to intervention permits the person to build confidence through successes and to face, eventually, more difficult challenges. This process has been used with some success with phobics (Bandura et al., 1982), children with math problems (see Schunk, 1989), and college students having low memory self-efficacy (Bellott, 1991). A mastery-oriented intervention program can work with older adults as well (see West et al., 1992). By starting with less-difficult forms of a memory task, efficacy and skills can both be improved. An even stronger intervention program would combine mastery-oriented training with discussion of memory beliefs (to reduce negative self-perceptions and encourage positive self-perceptions) so that memory beliefs will change as skill levels change (see

Bellott, 1991; West et al., 1992). Also, it may be beneficial to begin intervention programs before the older years, as a preventive measure.

Theoretical Implications

One important theoretical question in the self-efficacy framework is the relative influence of performance accomplishments, as opposed to societal beliefs, on age changes in efficacy. Although both factors probably work together to reduce self-efficacy and although both are expected, theoretically, to have some influence, one may have more influence than another. Bandura (1977) has suggested that performance accomplishments, social persuasion, arousal, and vicarious experience are the primary determinants of self-efficacy, with performance accomplishment having the strongest overall influence on self-perceptions. Our analyses did not address this issue directly, but we can speculate about the relative influence of these four factors. If changes in efficacy across the adult life span are based largely on stereotyping, or beliefs about the inevitability of age decline in memory, lower memory self-efficacy for older adults ought to generalize across a wide range of tasks. If changes in efficacy with age are based largely on performance or observations of specific memory failures on specific tasks (one's own failures and the failures of peers), there ought to be considerable variation in efficacy evaluations as a function of task and age-by-task variation. In these data, task-related variation in memory self-efficacy was present, but it did not interact with aging, as one might expect it to do if performance on each task is considered independently.

It is possible, then, that the similarity of efficacy responses across tasks for the two age groups might be a reflection of more global processes at work. One such potential global process is stereotyping about aging. Older adults who accept the negative stereotypes may have reduced personal confidence in their abilities regardless of their own personal experience with memory successes or failures (see Camp & Pignatiello, 1988). Or they may observe the failures of their older peers and make an assumption about themselves—"That's me in a few years." If social stereotypes about memory aging affect many people, they would be expected to affect self-perceptions of memory skills as well as one's potential for new learning. The influence of stereotypes would be general, rather than task-specific, which could partially account for the lack of task-by-age interactions in efficacy.

Another potential global process that would affect all types of tasks would be a decline in the functioning/efficiency of a memory process that has an impact on a wide range of memory tasks. One example of such a process is working memory. If working memory deficits are the primary factor accounting for age declines in memory, as some investigators have posited (Salthouse, 1991) and if self-evaluations reflect actual performance change, then the lack of age-by-task interactions could be related to the influence of this process deficit on a wide range of tasks. As we indicated earlier, longitudinal research is needed to establish the relative influence of stereotyping and actual performance decline on older adults' efficacy evaluations over time, to see if actual performance decline precedes or follows changes in attitudes toward one's abilities.

Conclusions

The study of memory self-evaluation and aging has a checkered history, moving from an initial fascination in self-report questionnaires and metamemory measures as proxy measures for memory to a loss of faith in these instruments because (1) metamemory measures of task and strategy knowledge seldom show age changes (e.g., Perlmutter, 1978) and (2) self-report measures were inconsistent predictors of actual performance (e.g., Sunderland, Watts, Baddeley & Harris, 1986). This period of doubt was followed by a recent resurgence in interest, based on the notion that memory self-evaluation, and memory self-efficacy in particular, are intriguing in their own right and worthy of systematic study. This research has explored one of the many issues that have not been examined in this area, namely, the generality of age declines in memory self-efficacy. Our examination with two memory self-efficacy questionnaires suggests that the observed patterns of aging generalize across task domains and specific task types, but not across measures. Further investigation is needed to confirm these findings and to understand more about how memory self-efficacy can affect an older person's potential for lifelong learning.

NOTES

Partial support for this research was provided by grants from the National Institute on Aging (AG00030, AG06014) and a Brookdale National Fellowship from the Brookdale Foundation in New York. Thanks are extended to Forrest Scogin and Kimberly Powlishta for assistance with the preliminary phases of this research. We are indebted to the many experimenters and research participants (too numerous to mention) who made the data archive possible. Requests for reprints should be addressed to Robin Lea West, 114 Department of Psychology, University of Florida, Gainesville, FL 32611–2065.

1. These particular measures were selected because they represent typical measures used in self-efficacy research or because they represent varying types of self-report information to be gleaned from the MSEQ, that is, number of tasks that can be accomplished and confidence on all tasks or a particular subset of tasks. Preliminary examination of other potential measures revealed that the alternative measures were highly correlated with at least one of these four measures. For instance, it is possible to calculate a measure by multiplying one's confidence by the difficulty level of the item. In fact, this measure, and others, were calculated; but they are not included here because the alternative measures correlated over .90 with one or more of the other measures used here and would therefore contribute little to the analysis.

Reliability was calculated across the ten task scales and was acceptable for Sample 1: SEL alpha = .93, SEST alpha = .94, CONF1 alpha = .85, and CONF-YES alpha = .92.

Reliability was acceptable across the ten task scales for Sample 2: SEL alpha = .90, SEST alpha = .89, CONF1 alpha = .88, and CONF-YES alpha = .90.

REFERENCES

Bandura, A. (1977). Self-efficacy: Toward a unifying theory of behavioral change. *Psychological Review*, *84*, 191–215.

Bandura, A. (1981). Self-referent thought: A developmental analysis of self-efficacy. In J. H. Flavell & L. Ross (Eds.). *Social cognitive development: Frontiers and possible futures*. Cambridge, England: Cambridge University Press.

Bandura, A. (1986). *Social foundations of thought and action: A social cognitive theory*. Englewood Cliffs, NJ: Prentice Hall.

Bandura, A., Reese, L. & Adams, N. E. (1982). Microanalysis of action and fear arousal as a function of differential levels of perceived self-efficacy. *Journal of Personality and Social Psychology*, *43*, 5–21.

Bellott, B. D. (1991). *Achievement efficacy and attributions: Effects of memory intervention on college undergraduates with low self-efficacy*. Master's thesis, University of Florida, Gainesville.

Berry, J. M. & West, R. L. (1993). Cognitive self-efficacy in relation to personal mastery and goal setting across the lifespan. *International Journal of Behavioral Development*, *16*, 351–379.

Berry, J. M., West, R. L. & Dennehy, D. (1989). Reliability and validity of the Memory Self-Efficacy Questionnaire (MSEQ). *Developmental Psychology*, *25*, 701–713.

Camp, C. J. & Pignatiello, M. F. (1988). Beliefs about fact retrieval and inferential reasoning across the adult lifespan. *Experimental Aging Research*, *14*, 89–98.

Cavanaugh, J. C. & Green, E. E. (1991). I believe, therefore I can: Self-efficacy beliefs in memory aging. In E. A. Lovelace (Eds.). *Aging and cognition: Mental processes, self-awareness, and intervention*. Amsterdam: Elsevier.

Cavanaugh, J. C. & Poon, L. W. (1989). Metamemorial predictors of memory performance in young and older adults. *Psychology and Aging*, *4*, 365–368.

Devolder, P. A., Brigham, M. C. & Pressley, M. (1990). Memory performance awareness in younger and older adults. *Psychology and Aging*, *5*, 291–303.

Hertzog, C. (1992). Improving memory: The possible roles of metamemory. In D. Herrmann, H. Weingartner, A. Searleman & C. McEvoy (Eds.). *Memory improvement: Implications for memory theory*. New York: Springer-Verlag.

Hertzog, C., Dixon, R. A. & Hultsch, D. F. (1990). Relationships between metamemory, memory predictions, and memory task performance in adults. *Psychology and Aging*, *5*, 215–227.

Hertzog, C., Hultsch, D. F. & Dixon, R. A. (1989). Evidence for the convergent validity of two self-report metamemory questionnaires. *Developmental Psychology*, *25*, 687–700.

Lachman, M. E. & Jelalian, E. (1984). Self-efficacy and attributions for intellectual performance in young and elderly adults. *Journal of Gerontology*, *39*, 577–582.

Lachman, M. E., Steinberg, E. S. & Trotter, S. D. (1987). Effects of control beliefs and attributions on memory self-assessments and performance. *Psychology and Aging*, *2*, 266–271.

Perlmutter, M. (1978). What is memory aging the aging of? *Developmental Psychology*, *14*, 330–345.

Rabinowitz, J. C., Ackerman, B. P., Craik, F.I.M. & Hinchley, J. L. (1982). Aging and metamemory: The roles of relatedness and imagery. *Journal of Gerontology*, *37*, 688–695.

Rebok, G. W. & Balcerak, L. J. (1989). Memory self-efficacy and performance differences in young and old adults: The effect of mnemonic training. *Developmental Psychology*, *25*, 714–721.

Rebok, G. W. & Offermann, L. R. (1983). Behavioral competencies of older college students: A self-efficacy approach. *The Gerontologist*, *23*, 428–432.

Reese, H. W. & Puckett, J. M. (Eds.). (1993). *Mechanisms of everyday cognition*. Hillsdale, NJ: Erlbaum.

Salthouse, T. A. (1991). *Theoretical perspectives on cognitive aging*. Hillsdale, NJ: Erlbaum.

Schunk, D. (1989). Self-efficacy and achievement behaviors. *Educational Psychology Review*, *1*, 173–208.

Scogin, F., Storandt, M. & Lott, L. (1985). Memory-skills training, memory complaint, and depression in older adults. *Journal of Gerontology*, *40*, 562–568.

Sinnott, J. D. (Ed.). (1989). *Everyday problem solving: Theory and application*. New York: Praeger.

Sunderland, A., Watts, K., Baddeley, A. D. & Harris, J. E. (1986). Subjective memory assessment and test performance in elderly adults. *Journal of Gerontology*, *41*, 376–384.

Weaver, S. L. & Lachman, M. E. (1989, August). Enhancing memory self-conceptions and strategies in young and old adults. Paper presented at the meeting of the American Psychological Association, New Orleans.

West, R. L. & Bellott, B. D. (1990, April). A construct validity study of the Memory Self-Efficacy Questionnaire (MSEQ). Paper presented at the Cognitive Aging Conference, Atlanta.

West, R. L., Bramblett, J. P., Welch, D. C. & Bellott, B. D. (1992, April). Memory training for the elderly: An intervention designed to improve memory skills and memory self-evaluation. Paper presented at the Cognitive Aging Conference, Atlanta.

Zelinski, E. M., Gilewski, M. J. & Anthony-Bergstone, C. R. (1990). Memory functioning questionnaire: Concurrent validity with memory performance and self-reported memory failures. *Psychology and Aging*, *5*, 388–399.

IV. THE FUTURE

28

The Future of Adult Lifespan Learning: Learning Institutions Face Change

Jan D. Sinnott

Recent international and national events have demonstrated the rapid pace of change in the modern world even in the short space of one or two years. Learners must adapt to change. When an adolescent asks us what sort of future to prepare for, what career to study for, we pause, failing to envision very clearly the future world our younger friend might inhabit. It is hard to plan for learners to adapt to change as a constant.

What is being learned by adults also is different from what those studying learning usually study. Most learning theories or models have emphasized transfer of non-emotional verbal information (we hoped such a thing existed). Yet nonverbal communication, which has always been a major information resource (Eckman & Friesen, 1975; Izard, 1977), is even more prominent today, especially for the video generations. There is more of all sorts of communication to sort through, and it comes faster, demanding that we learn how to *reject* information. It is daunting to picture communication to adult learners fifty years from now.

Into this shifting reality comes the student of lifespan learning, aware that adults of whatever age must continue to learn in order to adapt. What do we need to do to maximize adult learning in an unknown future? How will the methods of learning-related institutions need to be modified when more and more students are mature adults? The learners and their cognitive processes are changing. The expectation that learning can or will stop after youth has already changed.

We have seen from chapters in this handbook that adult learning is occurring over a lifetime. The overwhelming impression is that adult lifespan learning is not yet well understood, well researched, or well planned, even by the educators and psychologists most involved with this event. The main focus of much organized work reported in this handbook has been on ways that mature adults, learning in younger-adult settings, may not perform like younger adults. The second main focus has been that mature adults usually don't do their major learning in younger-adult settings, but bring their unique experience to unique settings, so that new variables and issues apply. From this incomplete base we are challenged to go on to consider the future of adult learning in a rapidly changing world.

Perhaps we can do better predicting the future of adult lifespan learning if we examine the multiple function of learning-related socially institutionalized experiences for adults in the present, in the past, or in other cultures. What have been the main types of things adults have been asked by their societies to learn, and why? The answer to this question may give us clues as to what is possible for these age groups in a social setting, although it will not answer the question of what is needed in today's changing world.

In this chapter, I will attempt four things. First, I will look at the types of things mature adults historically have been asked to learn to see which of these might be incorporated into the future of adult lifespan learning in our times. Second, I will examine ten problems or limitations currently having an impact on adult lifespan learning. Third, I'll suggest ways to optimize adult lifespan learning. Last, I will suggest what a center of learning for adults, the university, might become in the longterm future.

ADULT LEARNING IN OTHER TIMES AND PLACES

This author does not pretend to be a historian, or an anthropologist, but she is informed by twenty years' reading of interdisciplinary and cross-cultural and historical works in adult development, as well as by personal experience. Several purposes for teaching new bodies of information to mature adults can be described. They suggest the scope of possible adult learning and some factors that make it successful.

One primary type of learning involves conveying new ways to perform a necessary task or role. For example, widowers of traditional-role marriages were taught how to cook for themselves; a generation of workers learned to use computers; pre-World War II women were taught to stay home or work at "women's jobs"; they were taught during that war to do manufacturing jobs; then they were "taught" (post-war) to go home again and have babies. The entire American Indian population was taught with more or less success to adopt a Western industrial philosophy. In each of these cases, adults who were functioning very well at a particular task or role were trained for another task or role that someone decided was necessary for them to know.

A second type of adult learning involves acquiring full membership in a tribe or group by learning the full wisdom of that group. The adult, for example, may learn the stories and rituals that are keys to the culture, becoming the "keepers of the culture." Newly elected representatives to Congress may rise to powerful congressional roles by "learning the ropes" and the "key players." Roman

Catholic priests acquire "fullness of the priesthood and the status of bishop" by acquiring the understanding of the complexities of their church and flock. Practitioners in a field (e.g., social work) learn to be experts, perhaps gaining a credential for their expertise (e.g., LCSW, state license). In each case the beginning level of the skill is replaced by the learning of a body of knowledge that is larger, more synthetic.

A third type of adult learning involves obtaining a "ticket" or entrée to a larger role. In the days of the Chinese Empire, candidates for government positions learned to pass the writing exam (which included poetry and prose) as an entrée to selected government jobs. Academics obtain Ph.D.'s to research or teach or get grants; scientists obtain "postdocs" as tickets to careers. These learning experiences are certificates and permissions in spite of the fact that information learned often is unusable in the actual job.

A fourth type of learning involves updating or retooling a skill that is still very useful. For example, professionals are urged to obtain Continuing Education Credits (Units) to show that they are up to date in their disciplines. Workers in industry attend workshops and classes on their work. The purpose of these activities is to see old things in new ways and to become a better member of the workforce.

A fifth function of learning experiences across cultures and history seems to be one of control: It teaches conformity or discipline. It may serve to strengthen bonds with the group or tribe and weaken those with family or opposition groups. It may effectively limit access to selected resources or privileges. For example, "re-education" of dissidents by Red Guards in China or mandatory harangues and brainwashing of American hostages in Lebanon led to the learning of conformity. Only those holding M.D.'s or plumber's union cards can collect the salaries and make the decisions of "doctors" or "plumbers," whatever level of skill they might actually possess. This is education as social control.

Finally, adult lifespan learning may be used to increase personal development and understanding. The staff of the modern university evolved from the nobility, who pursued knowledge for its own sake, free from economic considerations. Non-credit college courses are often pursued for self-development reasons, as are "peak performance" physical activities. These learning experiences free the individual rather than controlling him or her. They are personal expressions of an individual's desire to learn and grow.

We can conclude that the spectrum of learning experiences for adults seems to be quite broad! Skills, philosophies, interpersonal behaviors, and worldviews are seen as learnable by mature adults. Adults are expected to learn the types of things younger persons learn (for example, languages and basic work skills) as well as the kinds of things young persons are never expected to learn (for example, expertise in managerial skills, mystical skills, and sophisticated interpersonal and organizational relations). This is not to say that all mature adults learn all these things any more than all younger persons learn all skills. But, if any significant number of persons learn a body of information, it is possible for more of us to do so, in spite of documented decline in some learning abilities for some age groups.

Are all these types of mature adult learning occurring today in the United States in this changing global situation? As many of the examples above show, some members of U.S. society take part in these kinds of adult learning. But there seems to be no systematic way to make use of all these learning types for the benefit of our population, or our society, or our world. The kind of systematized adult learning we see most often is for purposes of control, "ticketing," and improving the workforce. Less systematized, but present, are self-improvement efforts selected and supported by individuals.

We might speculate about the pros and cons of expanding our societal repertoire of formalized adult learning possibilities. The rapid changes going on in our world suggest to us that the more we as a society or a species encourage learning by mature members, the greater our flexibility will be to face rapid change. Ironically, this broadening of adult learning is really "going back to the basics." Great variation in learning possibilities, like great variation in the gene pool, allows the hardiest and most flexible variations to exist and to help the group survive. An analogy for our species' need to change and learn rapidly could be that current scourge, the AIDS virus. Mutating at tremendous speed, learning new protein patterns, the virus outruns the body's attack mechanisms, and medicine's as well. The virus is a learner par excellence, adopting other proteins' realities, winning the biological war by seeking to try every possible new way to live, in effect co-opting the opposition.

We have seen some types of adult learning that are possible. In the next section, I will discuss ten specific problems with adult lifespan learning systems as they stand now. We will then try to stretch those systems to see if they can usefully extend learning possibilities in better ways.

TEN CURRENT PROBLEMS IN ADULT LIFESPAN LEARNING SYSTEMS

In the future, we as a culture may want to maximize the potential of mature adults to learn in many ways. To do this, we need to see the learner within a General Systems Theory model as a developing "individual" system, interfacing with biological systems, social systems, a historical system, and other individual systems (Sinnott, 1989ab; 1991a). This adult human is more than a cognitive individual; she or he is an emotional, biological, social, intentional creature, adaptively moving through time, with his or her mind on what seems to be a bigger picture of reality that gives meaning to life. With the General Systems model in mind, here are some problems with current adult lifespan learning situations. They are listed in the first part of Table 1.

1. *Lifespan learning situations have not been structured to make use of the fact that mature learners come with their own motives, goals, developmental tasks, and experiences.* We have discarded the best "pluses" of adult learners, leaving only their deficits to consider before labeling them as different. We have documented adult

Table 1
Ten Current Problems for Adult Lifespan Learning Structures and Potential Solutions

Problems	*Solutions*
1. Lifespan learning situations have not been structured to make use of the fact that mature learners come with their own motives, goals, developmental tasks, and experiences.	1. Capitalize on learners' preexisting motives, developmental tasks, and experience.
2. Competitive, individualistic approaches to learning run directly counter to developmental goals of adult stages of life.	2. Replace competition with cooperative, multiperson learning approaches.
3. Learning institutions have separated the personal-creative aspects of learning from the hierarchical-orderly aspects; this is especially damaging for mature adult learners.	3. Allow the creative-synthetic and the analytic fact-loading aspects of learning to overlap for mature learners.
4. The current emerging generations of adult learners are more oriented to visual forms of presentation of materials, such as video presentations, and less oriented toward linear verbal forms, such as books.	4. Study the processes involved in learning from visual media, such as video. Realize the strengths and weaknesses of each representational mode. Use new visual technologies along with verbal linear materials in learning situations with mature learners.
5. Mature adult learning has mainly been for the purpose of economic survival.	5. Structure learning to serve personal development as well as economic needs.
6. Learning for its own sake has been split from learning for practical purposes.	6. Notice the links between basic and applied, practical and esoteric learning, and foster both.
7. Mature adults are taught as if they are learning alone (as identity-creating adolescents) when they are really learning as selves-in-interpersonal context (as members of families and cultures).	7. Use dialogues among teachers and learners to reap the benefits of postformal thinking and multiple perspectives.
8. "Learning" is too often equivalent to "memory" (in the most rote sense of memory).	8. Think of adult learning as a more complex cognitive event than mere memory.
9. Adult learners too often are told by some authority what they need to learn.	9. Let learners help generate the learning agenda.
10. Current structures of universities do not serve mature adult needs.	10. Restructure the university to meet current needs.

learners' differences using behavior of younger learners as the gold standard. Although this is a valid and important thing to do, it is not enough, as it leaves us seeing from one vantage point as the only one. It deprives us of an understanding of what is possible in mature adult learning processes, which are part of (and clues to) human cognitive possibility. Ignoring the study of adult positive learning differences deprives us of a deeper understanding of human behavior, especially that part of human behavior that is complex and involves multiple biological, emotional, and social systems and motives related to complex lifestage and transpersonal goals (Sinnott, 1989c, 1991b). Learners' motives and intentions are often the strongest forces in their performance; consciousness matters (Sperry, 1987).

2. *Competitive individualistic approaches to learning run directly counter to the developmental goals of adults (Erikson, 1950; Havinghurst, 1953) to be intimate and generative and to work on complex multiperson projects.* Adults often choose learning projects involving expertise, complex interpersonal coordination, and creation of lasting institutions and relationships. But we do not create learning environments that foster these traits. Teaching methods, even at the university level, cater to the child mind, loading basic information given by an authority. Even if adult learners are coming to the learning situation with a childlike knowledge of a field, they are not coming with childlike ways of processing information or a childlike set of social skills or personal incentives.

3. *Learning institutions have separated the personal-creative from the hierarchical-orderly aspects of learning; this split is especially damaging to mature adult learners.* Learning implies imposition of order and structure on an environment. Our scientific experimental paradigm has fostered objectivity. This disregards the other legitimate forms of knowledge based on other paradigms or non-experimental methods, forms such as phenomenology, synthetic (vs. analytic) thinking, case studies, and clinical or group dynamics studies. Fact-laden presentations run counter to the tendency of mature learners to be motivated by solving problems (especially those they have personally encountered) by putting pieces of the puzzling event together. Given the choice of learning discrete, abstract facts and learning problem-related facts, the mature adult selects the problem-related learning. For example, the research scientist who voraciously learns everything possible about some process related to her current study does not take the time to learn the name of the scientist two doors down.

4. *The current generation of adult learners in their 30s and 40s (and younger learners, too) is more oriented to visual presentation of material such as video presentation and less oriented toward linear forms such as books.* A shift is occurring in the dominant representational styles of mature learners. Forms for teaching them have not kept pace. The "TV and computer generation" grew up expecting reality to form patterns with details spelled out, like a picture, and not expecting (as much) to derive concepts from words. The two representational styles, visual and verbal, should be complementary to each other and accessible by all learners, but they are not. Our learning methods are mainly linear and print-related now, while learners are becoming less and less print-oriented.

5. *Mature adult learning has mainly been for the purpose of economic survival*. Harman and Hormann (1990), in their discussion of the meaning of work, suggest that education that simply prepares good workers and sustains their productivity may be misplaced in a time when meaningful work is not possible over a lifetime for everyone. Learning, they suggest, might better be oriented toward developing each person's full human potential. A sense of fragmentation afflicts many midlife adults when their learning is focused on preparation for work-related tasks but has no connection with their other life tasks or their own potential as persons. Most adults are also aware that their work roles will change more than once during their lifetimes.

6. *Learning for its own sake has been split from learning for practical purposes*. Adult learning in our culture and in most others is considered serious only when the outcome pertains to a critical work-related problem at hand. Other learning for its own sake is supposed to be done only by children and retirees who have no other social (work-related) purpose. This polarization deprives mature adult learners of the chance to solve those critical problems they are engaged in in fresh ways. (The children, adolescents, and retirees with the broad exploratory learning are not permitted to apply it to any real, job-related problems. This forces them to remain "impractical.") Overall, investment in learning to meet whatever challenge arises is sacrificed to short-term, crisis-driven investment in learning. This error is analogous to corporations attempting to maximize short-term profits by avoiding costly investments in research and development. Such corporations then have no clear ideas for sustaining performance in changing markets.

7. *Mature adults are taught as if they are learning alone (as identity-creating adolescents) when they are really learning as selves-in-interpersonal context (as generative members of families and cultures)*. The mature learner seeks not only differentiation of concepts (i.e., analytic skills) but synthesis of concepts as well. The mature learner might often do his or her best cognitive work in a cooperative learning enterprise with the stated aim of furthering the good of the group along with furthering his or her own good (Eisler & Loye, 1990; Vygotsky, 1962, 1978). Thinking and everyday problem solving have an interpersonal dimension (Meacham & Emont, 1989; Resnick, Levine & Teasley, 1991).

8. *"Learning" is too often equivalent to "memory" (in the most rote sense of memory)*. The mature adult generally wants learning to go beyond a catalogue of facts to a deeper understanding of matters. The cognitive processes involved in incidental memory and in memory for details may be different from processes involved in learning paths through a problem space when one learns to solve a problem (Sinnott, 1986; West & Sinnott, 1992). For example, many additional processes are involved in map learning (or memory), compared with learning (memory) for strings of numbers (Lipman, 1991).

9. *Adult learners too often are told by some authority what they need to learn*. Sheer imposition of the task makes no use of the slowly developed intrinsic motivations or wisdom of adults. The self-motivated adult will tend to seek out

knowledgeable authorities, allowing for input from both authority and learners (Freire, 1971; Kindervatter, 1983). Projects partly formed by the learners themselves offer the best of both worlds if the authority can tolerate the anxiety of waiting to be asked for his or her expertise.

10. *Current structures of universities do not serve mature adult needs.* No doubt universities will change in the future. They use too many of yesterday's methods to prepare adults for jobs that are disappearing and too often prepare researchers and scholars for scientific careers that will not be supported after training ends. The university seems to have lost its sense of purpose. Its bottom-line function was to be a center of dialogue to prepare students for good jobs. But scholars dialoging together now have a range of options (e.g., networking and dialoging via electronic mail) that allows them to exchange ideas more effectively than if they physically gather at a university (e.g., Mangan, 1991; Wilson, 1991). And university training is no longer the ticket to a secure, good future. The final section of this chapter outlines some ideas on restructuring universities for today's world and for teaching mature adults. But first we will discuss some possible solutions to the ten problems.

POSSIBLE NEW SOLUTIONS TO THE TEN PROBLEMS

We have pointed out ten factors that make current learning experiences less than optimal for mature adults in a rapidly changing world. Table 2 contains a list of some things adults need to learn to do well in the twenty-first century. In the next fifty years, we will need all the human resources we possibly can find to confront the next phase of our species' development on a troubled planet. Optimizing the ability of experienced adults to learn should be a priority investment that will pay off quickly. At first, though, there may be too few instructors or workshop leaders able to use new approaches with mature learners. Several changes are needed in learning-related institutions and methods to make them most useful to mature adult learners. Possible changes—hopefully new trends—are noted on Table 1, each related to one of the problems mentioned before.

Solution #1. Capitalize on the learners' preexisting motives, developmental tasks, and experience. Of course this is easier said than done. To capitalize on these individual differences means that one learning experience cannot be given to all. If it is true that a good teacher of children must first assess what they know and what they need to develop, how much more will this be true for the good teacher of complex mature adults? But some commonalities in experience can be found. We know that most mature learners are involved in work and family roles and have had years of experience to draw from. Drawing on these contributions of group expertise may mean restructuring how material is pre-

Table 2
What Adults Need to Learn to Survive in the Twenty-first Century

- To deal with rapid change
- To heal the mind/body/spirit split
- To understand group dynamics
- To create new myths about the meaning of life
- To revise and expand definitions of truth and reality
- To prepare for several jobs/careers per lifetime
- To learn new metaphors for growth besides expansion
- To understand the dynamics common to all "living" systems including self and society
- To learn from serving others
- To understand their own personal recurring cycles
- To be visual and verbal and kinesthetic learners
- To define all problems in several ways
- To be alone comfortably *and* to be group-minded
- To both belong and be an individual
- To save or generate resources, including human resources
- To feel at home in all cultures
- To develop their own and others' peak performance as a shared resource

sented, but will also mean that learners will come away with a deeper understanding of the material and a greater sense of involvement. For example, a class of mature adult learners was studying research methods. The instructor addressed research paradigms by means of a dialogue on "what do *I* know is true, and why." Research projects were created by each student to take advantage of courses they had taken, their current interests within the discipline, and research opportunities within their current work or family settings. So, although no two learning experiences were exactly alike, they all covered certain basic information. The uniqueness of each student was respected. In the next fifty years, individually structured learning experiences for adults will be the preferred sort.

Solution #2. Replace competition with cooperative, multiperson approaches. In that research class just described, students worked in teams and helped each other construct projects. Team members brought their own interests and skills to any problem-solving scenario. If team members are matched on skill level, a problem-centered community can be created. As problem solving has been demonstrated (Laughlin, 1965; Laughlin, McGlynn, Anderson & Jacobson, 1968) to be more useful and creative when more than one solver is working, the results of such multiperson teams are better products. In the next fifty years, most learning experiences for adults will have a multiperson component.

Solution #3. Allow the creative-synthetic and analytical fact-loaded aspects of learning to overlap in mature learning situations. Data-driven, bottom-up processing involving loading of facts is the computer analogy of the young learner's needs (Sinnott, 1989a). Taking things apart to see how they work, to criticize them, and to plan something better is the adolescent's task. But facts and criticism are not enough; they presume some structure of knowledge already has been built. Yet someone has to build the structure and make the links, to create. The mature adult learner's ultimate goal is to build, with a structure in mind. He or she uses (in computer analogy) top-down processing, using some higher organization to make sense of facts and to build a better theory. To make best use of mature adults' skills, learning experiences must permit both analysis and synthesis, both bottom-up and top-down processing.

For example, a group of displaced, unemployed homemakers was studying possible jobs they could perform. At first, they learned many facts about available jobs and the local economy. Next, they criticized their own resumes and analyzed what they could or could not reasonably apply for. That bottom-up, data-driven learning was useful, but at this point most of the women found they couldn't apply for much of anything among the available jobs. They had not worked, were in their 50s, and couldn't move to another city. Their data-driven learning was successful, but they had failed to address their developmental task: They were still unemployed and roleless women. This was the time for creative, synthetic, top-down learning. The women put together a list of their skills as a group and decided to start their own child-care company. This addition of synthetic top-down thinking to analytic fact-gathering bottom-up thinking solved their developmental problem, too, by getting them jobs as well as factual knowledge. In the next fifty years, learning experiences for mature adults will combine the two types of thought.

Solution #4. Study the processes involved in learning from visual media such as video. Use new visual technologies (e.g., interactive video, networking, virtual realities) along with verbal, linear materials (e.g., books) to present information and experiences to mature learners. We know relatively little about how adults learn complex information from visual materials other than the printed word. We know that memory for designs, route-learning ability, and memory for faces declines in old age (Cavanaugh, 1990; Kausler, 1991). But do mature learners process information received in visual formats such as movies or video differently from verbal information such as the printed word? These studies have not been done. One medium, print, has historically been overvalued as a communication tool (Goodman, 1992). We need to understand the strengths and weaknesses of many communication tools. For example, a medical procedure done by an expert may be much better communicated in pictures than in words. In the next fifty years, we may make much more use of other representational forms.

Solution #5. Structure learning to serve personal development as well as economic needs. There is a legitimate role for learning to get a good job, keep a good job, or retool for another job. But the human organism seems to be a stimulation-seeking, learning animal whatever its economic situation. Also, learning designed to serve existing occupations may not serve occupations needed in the future. After all, there is more to life than work. Harman and Hormann (1990) note that adults seek personal meaning from their jobs, and even bring meaning to jobs. But meaning is key. Although learning might serve to develop peak capabilities, expertise, and new skills, all of which will serve future economic goals, learning most certainly needs to serve the individual's search for meaning and growth. In the next fifty years, learning "for the job" may be replaced by learning for personal development.

Solution #6. Notice the links between basic and applied, practical and esoteric learning, and foster both types. Learning "for its own sake" and learning "to solve applied problems" are not far apart in their real purpose. An analogy can be made to organizations' use of "brainstorming" techniques. Brainstorming, generating all possible solutions to a problem, however useful those solutions may ultimately be, seems like a waste, because all solutions aren't applicable; but ultimately the process proves to be a good source of useful ideas. Adults need both to explore in a wide-ranging way and to narrow down and eventually focus to maximize the utility of their learning. In the next fifty years, adult learning will always involve both applied ("How can we balance trade with Japan?") and basic aspects ("Why do we make the kinds of goods we do if no one wants them?").

Solution #7. Mature adult learning experiences work best as a dialogue. Part of the learning process involves communication. Our cultural experience is that learning occurs when a teacher (who has knowledge) speaks to learners (who lack knowledge). In mature adulthood each "learner" already has some knowledge to share. The learning *situation* also is more complex in that it is best understood (as a situation) by the learners themselves (Sinnott, 1984 and 1993). The learning experience that is most effective is a dialogue between teacher and learners and among learners. A dialogue, as Riegel noted (1976) is influenced by all the participants in it (as opposed to mutual monologues with two speakers who do not influence each other). The dialogue consists of the learners helping to define the problem and critique the solutions they and the teacher propose, with the teacher doing the same. Such a process avoids learning some less useful thing from a teacher who is solving a learning problem students don't have.

A second aspect of the problem involves the nature of real, underlying learning in mature adulthood: the importance of multiple perspectives. The mature adult is developing postformal thought, which is (in part) realizing that truth involves a *chosen* perspective of reality (Commons, Sinnott, Richards & Armon, 1989; Sinnott, 1984, 1989ac, 1991ab). An adult learns postformal processing in part through sharing truth with others and hearing their truths. In the next fifty years, adult learning experience will become mainly dialogic.

Solution #8. Think of adult learning as a more complex cognitive event than memory. "Learning" for mature adults might better be defined as "*finding and retaining complex patterns to solve a problem in a given context.''* This information processing incorporates memory but goes beyond it. For example, ''learning,'' for the displaced homemakers mentioned earlier, did include memory for the jobs on the list and for the skills on the list. But it also meant a synthesis of other elements with those two lists in memory, so that an outcome evaluated as ''useful'' would result. Research is needed on learning of this sort, as distinct from simpler memory. In the next fifty years such research will be performed.

Solution #9. Let learners generate the learning agenda. ''Empowerment'' is a term that is bandied about with too great an ease, and ''responsibility'' is too often taken to mean guilt. What is meant by responsibility is that one *can* respond to a situation. That is the power in empowerment; that is being response-*able*. Adult learners do best when they realize they are response-*able*. For example, adult learners can be the ones to create a grading system in a structured university class. They decide how much to reward various class activities with points toward a grade. In that situation, students work in a more involved way during the class because they have decided their own fates. In the next fifty years, adult students will begin to construct their own learning agendas and grading systems.

Solution #10. Restructure the university to meet current needs. The next section will constitute a description of what the university will become in the next fifty years, if it is to serve the needs of the mature adult learner.

RESTRUCTURING THE UNIVERSITY TO SERVE MATURE ADULT LEARNERS

The university has played many roles in the course of history, not the least of which is that of generator of ideas. The university serves mature adults in lifespan contexts. The university is the ideal mature-adult learning environment to incorporate new approaches to adult learning and adult learners over the next fifty years.

The university has rather consistently been the place where ideas are generated by those prepared to be creative. In a welcoming, sheltering environment such as the university, the implications of new ideas can be played out. The surviving new ''knowledge'' then can be incorporated in public life when the university trains new teachers, researchers, writers, practitioners, or employees who use the ideas and spread them. The university historically has been labeled a success when it can generate sufficient ideas, nurture them, and communicate them to adults who can further develop and communicate them. It has been attacked as ''ivory tower,'' useless, or anachronistic when it either fails to generate ideas, fails to nurture them to the point at which they are useful to others outside the university, or fails to communicate them. At that failure, public or private support for the university dwindles, and others resent academics and those ''privileged adults who can goof off for years as students.''

The university easily descends from the status of ''maker of meanings,'' ''wise adult,'' or ''expert par excellence'' to that of ''ticket puncher'' and ''time filler.''

One way to descend rapidly is to split "wisdom" by disciplines so that all answers seem incomplete to adults. Another way to accelerate descent is to split the functions of the university among many types of universities or campuses. Then each can be attacked for not doing the function that has been given to another part. For example, if one sort of university generates ideas well but doesn't nurture or communicate them well (e.g., the "big-name research university") it can be attacked for irrelevancy or noncommunication to the community; if the "teaching college" or "comprehensive university" focuses on communication, it can be attacked for not offering new ideas to the community or to science. Today universities are appearing to be more and more obsolete, largely because they have split their functions and disciplines.

As the mature adult learner (either as an official "student" or as a scientist or employee/manager seeking expertise) often cannot seek answers and knowledge by going to all disciplines and many sorts of universities, the learner ends up feeling fragmented and confused by his or her partial wisdom obtained at one kind of campus. The learner and the public then ask, "Why support these academic experts with tax dollars and effort, but get so little from them? After all, we can dialogue among ourselves about ideas in boardrooms and on electronic mail networks; we can generate ideas at think tanks; we can communicate ideas related to work in continuing education programs. What can the university give us?" The university may then respond by integrating business into its mix of resources, in order to seem cost effective, involved with the community, and relevant. The university hope is that ideas will lead to products and improved technology. Most ideas do not, however, immediately lead to marketable products, and businesses in the United States are run for short-term profit, not long-term development. The university and the "outside world" of business then suffer further disenchantment with each other.

In the next fifty years, universities need to reorganize their purpose, structure, and methods to serve adult learners at school, home, work, or government in a rapidly changing world. The university has been devoted to furthering "adolescent," data-driven analytic thought; it may now want to devote itself to the synthetic, top-down, big picture, meaning-making thought that is part of mature adult learning. To fail to make this shift is to guarantee that the university will be obsolete soon.

What can the university do to transform? Some changes are summarized in Table 3 and described below. First, it can acknowledge its complex role as the institution that does try to see the "big picture." This acknowledgment may mean that the university is willing to risk doing complex analyses of complex questions (even if many people don't understand complexity or immediately profit from it) by reclaiming its role as philosopher, "lover of the wise." It can refuse to be bullied or bought, knowing that a new source of support can come with the new role. The university may notice that those who bully or buy you never respect you in the morning and constitute a very temporary "fix." In short, the university can begin to be true to itself, the only self that makes it

Table 3
The Transformed University in the Twenty-first Century

1. Focuses on the "big picture": synthesis and summary besides analysis and "taking apart."
2. Focuses on more than the intellectual aspects of problems and learners: includes physical, emotional, biological, interpersonal, cultural, spiritual, and economic.
3. Interprets meanings: an expert interpreter of the many contradictory truths in complex situations; interprets what things mean, overall.
4. Develops human resources: mission is to develop *human* resources, besides developing ideas or technology.
5. Creates problem-focused "campuses": global "campuses" located on various continents and devoted to one problem (e.g., poverty) supported mainly by research/service "parks" selling goods or services related to that problem.

different from other institutions; it can be the seer who looks dispassionately at all sides.

Second, the university can accept its mission as serving what Ornstein (1991) talks of as the many minds within our one mind. If it does so, it will acknowledge and serve the mature human, who is always going forward and developing to new integration, who is emotional and spiritual and physical and social/interpersonal as well as intellectual. It will serve the learner as a world citizen, as a global person.

Third, the university will become what Smith (1991) has called an expert in symbology. In the big picture reality where truth can be seen from many valid perspectives in a postformal mature adult way (Sinnott, 1984, 1991a, 1993; Sinnott & Cavanaugh, 1991), the university will take the role of displaying for the learners and the culture what things can *possibly mean*. It will look at the impact of meaning selection.

Fourth, the university will accept as its main role developing human potential (Hutchins, 1968) rather than developing technologies. The university will not foster the mind/body split, the mind/emotion split, the mind/society split, or the technology/person split. It will, perhaps in light of McLean's triune brain theory (1988) see these splits as outmoded. It will also cast its work of learning in a long-term framework, rather than responding to the demands and needs of the moment. It will be aware that funding sources are fickle and that it is counterproductive to promise to prepare people for jobs when no one is sure where the world or the economy is headed.

In the next fifty years, how will universities restructure physically? If the current fragmented structure and problems are based on limited concepts of learning, how will full awareness of mature adult learning characteristics lead to restructuring of the institution?

The university can solve its problems by organizing itself around problem areas of importance to the nation or to the global community (Sinnott, in preparation). The *problem focus* means that all study and research are cross disciplinary; and every problem is considered in general systems theory terms (Ford, 1987; Miller, 1978; Sinnott, 1989ab) from its intellectual, emotional, interpersonal, cross-cultural physical, spiritual, human developmental, political, and economic perspectives. Course work is oriented around the organizing problem; research, in its applied sense, is focused on the same problem. The "campus" of a university would then be a global one (easy, given current technology). Instances of the problem and experts on the problem exist worldwide. "Research parks" connected to this university may or may not be physically close to its "campus" (which, after all, is quite dispersed) but are affiliated because of their relation to its core-problem focus. These "research parks" or "technology parks" might be industries of the usual research-park sort, using the expertise of the "campus" to serve the business. Alternatively, they may market alternative ideas and services related to the problem focus. They also might be demonstration research sites for service delivery related to the problem focus. They bring in income to the university, whose main support (beyond tuition) then is related to aspects of and expertise about the problem *focus* of the campus.

For example, if the problem focus is "housing," the research parks might test models for housing geriatric families or the disabled in Third World countries and might bring in income from research grants, selling expertise, selling plans for residency, and program grants from NIH and AID and Medicare. Basic research and philosophical treatises and art works and building material research related to the problem focus, housing, would be supported on this worldwide campus, because those are potential future solutions for housing problems.

A university restructured along these lines is no longer obsolete in our rapidly changing world. It retains the core of the university idea. It uses the resources of the mature adult learner and is the expression of a mature, "beyond adolescent" cognition. In the next fifty years we will see such a university and, it is hoped, many of them. They will be the most complex achievement related to changes in our understanding of mature adult lifespan learning.

REFERENCES

Cavanaugh, J. (1990). *Adult development and aging*. Belmont, CA: Wadsworth.

Commons, M., Sinnott, J., Richards, F. & Armon, C. (Eds.). (1989). *Adult development: Comparisons and applications of developmental models*. New York: Praeger.

Eckman, P. & Friesen, W. (1975). *Unmasking the face*. Englewood Cliffs, NJ: Prentice Hall.

Eisler, R. & Loye, D. (1990). *The partnership way*. San Francisco: Harper.

Erikson, E. (1950). *Childhood and society*. New York: Norton.

Ford, D. (1987). *Humans as self-constructing living systems*. Hillsdale, NJ: Erlbaum.

Freire, P. (1971). *The pedagogy of the oppressed*. New York: Herder & Herder.

Goodman, E. (1992). Oliver Stone's hijacking of history. *Washington Post*, January 4, A21.

Harman, W. & Hormann, J. (1990). *Creative work*. Indianapolis, IN: Knowledge Systems Press.

Havighurst, R. (1953). *Human development and education*. New York: Longmans.

Hutchins, R. (1968). *The learning society*. New York: Praeger.

Izard, C. E. (1977). *Human emotions*. New York: Plenum Press.

Kausler, D. (1991). *Experimental psychology, cognition and human aging*, 2nd ed., New York: Springer-Verlag.

Kindervatter, S. (1983). *Women working together for personal, economic, and community development*. Washington, DC: OEF International.

Laughlin, P. (1965). Selection strategies in concept attainment as a function of number of persons and stimulus display. *Journal of Experimental Psychology, 70*, 323–327.

Laughlin, P., McGlynn, R., Anderson, J. & Jacobson, E. (1968). Concept attainment by individuals vs. cooperative pairs as a function of memory, sex, and concept rule. *Journal of Personality and Social Psychology, 8*, 410–417.

Lipman, P. (1991). Age and exposure differences in acquisition of route information. *Psychology and Aging, 6*, 118–127.

Mangan, K. (1991). Colleges use video conferences to trim their travel budgets. *Chronicle of Higher Education, 5*, 23–24.

McLean, P. (1988). Evolutionary biology. Paper presented at the Gerontology Research Center, National Institute on Aging, NIH, Baltimore, MD.

Meacham, J. & Emont, N. C. (1989). The interpersonal basis of everyday problem solving. In J. D. Sinnott (Ed.). *Everyday problem solving*, pp. 7–23. New York: Praeger.

Miller, J. (1978). *Living systems*. New York: McGraw-Hill.

Ornstein, R. (1991). *The origins of consciousness*. New York: Plenum.

Riegel, K. (1976). The dialectics of human development. *American Psychologist, 31*, 679–700.

Resnick, L., Levine, J. & Teasley, S. (Eds.). (1991). *Perspectives on socially shared cognition*. Washington, DC: American Psychological Association.

Sinnott, J. D. (1984). Postformal reasoning: The relativistic stage. In M. Commons, F. Richards, & C. Armon (Eds.). *Beyond formal operations*, pp. 298–325. New York: Praeger.

Sinnott, J. D. (1986). Prospective/intentional and incidental everyday memory: Effects of age and passage of time. *Psychology and Aging, 2*, 110–116.

Sinnott, J. D. (1989a). Adult differences in the use of postformal operations. In M. Commons, J. Sinnott, F. Richards & C. Armon (Eds.). *Adult development: Comparisons and applications of developmental models*, pp. 239–278. New York: Praeger.

Sinnott, J. D. (1989b). Changing the known, knowing the changing: General systems theory paradigms as ways to study complex change and complex thought. In D. Kramer and M. Bopp (Eds.). *Transformation in clinical and developmental psychology*, pp. 51–69. New York: Springer.

Sinnott, J. D. (Ed.) (1989c). *Everyday problem solving: Theory and application*. New York: Praeger.

Sinnott, J. (1989d). General systems theory: A rationale for the study of everyday memory. In L. Poon, D. Rubin & B. Wilson (Eds.). *Everyday cognition in adulthood and old age*, pp. 59–72. New York: Cambridge University Press.

Sinnott, J. D. (1991a). Conscious adult development: Complex thought and solving our intragroup conflicts. Invited presentation, Sixth Adult Development Conference, Suffolk University, Boston.

Sinnott, J. D. (1991b). Limits to problem solving: Emotion, intention, goal clarity, health, and other factors in postformal thought. In J. D. Sinnott & J. Cavanaugh (Eds.). *Bridging paradigms: Positive development in adulthood and cognitive aging*, pp. 169–202. New York: Praeger.

Sinnott, J. (1993). Teaching in a chaotic new physics world: Teaching as a dialogue with reality. In P. Kahaney, J. Janangelo & L. Perry (Eds.). *Theoretical and critical perspectives on teacher change*. Norwood, NJ: Ablex.

Sinnott, J. & Cavanaugh, J. (Eds.). (1991). *Bridging paradigms: Positive changes in adulthood and cognitive aging*. New York: Praeger.

Smith, H. (September, 1991). President's address to faculty. Towson State University, Baltimore, MD.

Sperry, R. (1987). Structure and significance of the consciousness revolution. *Journal of Mind and Behavior, 8*, 37–66.

Vygotsky, L. S. (1962). *Thought and language*. Cambridge, MA: MIT Press.

Vygotsky, L. S. (1978). *Mind in society*. Cambridge, MA: Harvard University Press.

West, R. & Sinnott, J. (Eds.). (1992). *Everyday memory and aging; Current research and methodology*. New York: Springer-Verlag.

Wilson, D. (1991). Students from many countries use computers to simulate international negotiations. *Chronicle of Higher Education, 5*, A25–27.

Index

About the Editor and Contributors

JAN D. SINNOTT is Professor of Psychology at Towson State University in Baltimore. Her research in lifespan cognitive development, bridging many disciplines, has led to several books including *Bridging Paradigms* (with J. Cavanaugh), *Everyday Problem Solving, Everyday Memory and Aging* (with R. West), and *Sex Roles and Aging*.

PATRICIA MALONEY ALT is an Associate Professor of Health Science at Towson State University in Baltimore. Her interests include adult learning, the community-level provision of health services, health policy and administration, and aging.

DAVID ARENBERG was a research psychologist at the National Institutes of Health from 1960 until 1989 where he studied many aspects of cognition and aging. He is currently a free-lance writer and consultant in that area.

WEIZHEN TANG BACELAR is a Ph.D. student in the Intradisciplinary Developmental Psychology Program at Rutgers University. She is currently working on her doctoral dissertation, exploring the role of life experience, personality, and age in the development of postformal reasoning.

MICHAEL BASSECHES is a clinical and developmental psychologist in private practice and at Harvard University's Bureau of Study Counsel, and he is a Fellow of the Clinical-Developmental Institute in Belmont, Massachusetts. His work and published writings focus on higher education, psychotherapy, and the workplace as contexts for adolescent and adult development. He is the author of *Dialectical Thinking and Adult Development* (1984).

CYNTHIA A. BERG is currently an Associate Professor of Psychology at the University of Utah. She has conducted research on the development of practical intelligence across the lifespan.

JANE M. BERRY is an Assistant Professor of Psychology at the University of Richmond. Her research focuses on personality and self-evaluative factors in relation to memory functioning in adulthood.

CYNTHIA BOYD is a doctoral student at the State University of New York in Buffalo. Her interests include feminist theory, research of nontraditional family configurations, and qualitative research methods.

LAURA S. BROSS is a doctoral student in the Clinical Psychology division of Temple University. She is currently working on a study of depression and temporality.

KATERINA S. CALDERONE is a predoctoral fellow in psychology at the University of Utah. Her research interests include contextual and phenomenological issues in everyday problem solving.

JOHN C. CAVANAUGH is Professor and Chairperson of the Department of Individual and Family Studies at the University of Delaware. His main areas of research involve cognitive aging and family caregiving.

PHILIP COTTELL, a Professor in the Accountancy Department, has been a faculty member at the Miami University of Ohio since 1982. He is the co-author of *Accounting Ethics: A Practical Guide for Professionals* and numerous journal articles. His research and teaching interests include accounting for inventories, the CPA profession, accounting ethics, accounting education, classroom assessment, and cooperative learning.

NEIL DAVIDSON is a Professor in the Curriculum and Instruction Department at the University of Maryland. His recent edited books include *Cooperative Learning in Mathematics: a Handbook for Teachers* and *Enhancing Thinking through Cooperative Learning* (with Toni Worsham).

JACK DEMICK is currently an Associate Professor in and the Chair of the Department of Psychology at Suffolk University in Boston. His research interests include cognitive development (e.g., environmental cognition, cognitive style) and social development (e.g., adaption to adoption and other life transitions) across the lifespan.

NANCY W. DENNEY is Professor of Psychology at the University of Wisconsin at Madison. Her research interests include lifespan research on classification, problem solving, intellectual abilities, and memory.

JAY S. EFRAN is a Professor of Psychology and Director of the Psychological Services Center at Temple University. He is author (with Michael D. Lukens and Robert J. Lukens) of *Language, Structure, and Change: Frameworks of Meaning in Psychotherapy*.

LAWRENCE FROMAN, an Associate Professor of Psychology at Towson State University, has done consulting work in the areas of organizational development and applied research, given numerous presentations to both community and academic groups, and published work in the areas of adult learning, organizational psychology, and work motivation.

CAROLYN HARRIGER is currently Director of Conferences and Institutes at the University of Maryland Baltimore County. She was formerly Director of Lifelong Education at Towson State University.

KATHLEEN HEINRICH is an Associate Professor at the University of San Diego. Her doctoral preparation is in higher education with a specialization in the adult learner and she has been teaching adult learners for 15 years.

AARON T. HOGUE is a doctoral candidate in the Clinical Psychology division of Temple University. His primary interests include systemic psychology, adolescent development, and constructive psychotherapy.

LYNN JOHNSON, who received her Interdisciplinary Masters degree in International Communication, has been a television producer/director for fourteen years, six years with instructional video projects in developing countries and two years with NBC TV in Washington, D.C. She is currently Director of the Office of Research Administration at Towson State University in Baltimore.

PHYLLIS KAHANEY is an Assistant Professor of English at the University of San Diego. Her special research interests include rhetorical theory, cognitive development, and legal writing.

PAUL A. KLACZYNSKI is an Assistant Professor at Western Carolina University. His research interests include practical problem solving across the life course, institutional influences on cognitive development, and the transfer of reasoning in everyday and formal contexts.

DEIRDRE A. KRAMER is an Associate Professor of Psychology at Rutgers University. She specializes in life-span development.

DIANE M. LEE is an Associate Professor in the Department of Education at the University of Maryland Baltimore County. Her current research interests include models of adult reasoning and everyday problem solving.

ABIGAIL LIPSON is a clinical and cognitive psychologist and a senior member of Harvard University's Bureau of Study Counsel. She is the author of *Block: The Psychology of Counterintentional Behavior in Everyday Life* (with David Perkins).

LAURA V. MACIUIKA explores adult learning in her work as a psychotherapist at Metrowest Mental Health in Framingham, Massachusetts, and as a part-time professor at Wheelock College in Boston. She has been involved in organizing and teaching summer seminars in psychology to teachers and psychologists in Lithuania through the APPLE (American Professional Partnership for Lithuanian Education) organization.

LISA C. MCGUIRE is an Adjunct Assistant Professor of Psychology at Kenyon College and Denison University. Her recent interests include research on age differences in retention of medical information.

JOHN A. (JACK) MEACHAM is Professor of Psychology at the State University of New York at Buffalo. His interests include life-course developmental psychology, theories of development, and undergraduate education.

SHARAN B. MERRIAM is Professor of Adult Education at the University of Georgia, Athens, where she is coeditor of *Adult Education Quarterly*. Her research and publication interests are in adult learning, adult development, and qualitative research methods.

BARBARA MILLIS is Assistant Dean of Faculty Development at the University of Maryland University College. She has published articles and given workshops throughout the nation on topics such as cooperative learning, peer classroom observations, and the teaching portfolio.

NANCY A. NAZZARO was chosen as one of several undergraduates from across the country to participate in Clark University's 1991 Summer Research Apprenticeship Program in Psychology and plans to pursue graduate study in clinical psychology.

ROMY NOCERA is Project Coordinator of a major investigation of spousal caregiving for Alzheimer's disease patients. Additionally, Dr. Nocera has conducted several studies in the area of human sexuality.

RICK PARENTÉ is Professor of Psychology at Towson State University, an adjunct Associate Professor of Physiology at the University of Maryland Dental School, and a Neuropsychological Consultant at the Maryland Rehabilitation Center.

ARIEL PHILLIPS is a psychotherapist and consultant in private practice in Belmont and Carlisle, Massachusetts. She is the editor of *Education and the Threat of Nuclear War* (with Bell Zars and Beth Wilson) and *Women's Experience and Education* (with Sharon L. Rich).

RENEE ROYAK-SCHALER is Associate Professor, Department of Health Sciences, Towson State University. She is the author of *Challenging the Breast Cancer Legacy: A Program of Emotional Support and Medical Care for Women at Risk*.

MARY STAPLETON is a certified rehabilitation Counselor and a Staff Specialist at the Maryland Rehabilitation Center.

JONELL STROUGH is a predoctoral fellow in psychology at the University of Utah. Her current work examines gender and developmental differences in the goals individuals have for solving their everyday problems.

L. EUGENE THOMAS is Professor of Human Development and Family Relations at the University of Connecticut where he has conducted research with young adults and the middle-aged, as well as with the elderly, examining the effects of beliefs on psychological well-being and behavior. He was a Senior Fulbright Fellow in India, 1989–1990, where he studied religious renunciates.

DENNIS N. THOMPSON is Associate Professor of Educational Psychology at Georgia State University, Atlanta. His major interests include adult development and aging, international psychology, and the history of developmental psychology.

PATRICIA S. WEIBUST is Associate Professor of Education at the University of Connecticut where she is also involved in multicultural aspects of teacher training in urban schools. She is an educational anthropologist, who has done ethnographic studies of sociocultural change and schooling in the Philippines and in Norway.

ROBIN LEA WEST is an Associate Professor of Psychology and Associate Director of the Center for Gerontological Studies at the University of Florida. Her primary research interest is memory aging: everyday memory, memory training, and memory beliefs.